Skilled at All Trades

Men of England, wherefore plough
For the lords who lay ye low?

The seed ye sow another reaps
The wealth ye find another keeps

Shelley

The bronze relief sculpture dedicated to the Tolpuddle Martyrs,
commissioned from the sculptor, Ian Walters, by the TGWU.
The sculpture, for the façade of the Shire Hall in Dorchester
(significant to the Martyrs because it contained the Old Crown Court),
was unveiled on 17 July 1993 (*photo* Katalin Arkell).

SKILLED AT ALL TRADES

The history of the farmworkers' union, 1947–1984

Bob Wynn

TGWU
Frontline

First published 1993

Transport and General Workers' Union
Transport House, Smith Square, London, SW1P 3JB

Frontline States Ltd
5 Spur Road, Tottenham, London N15 4AA

ISBN 1 873639 02 3

The following photographs have been reproduced courtesy of Hulton Deutsch:
4, 9, 21, 22, 30; and Topham Picture Source: 18, 23, 24, 27, 28, 29.
The remaining photographs have been reproduced with the kind permission of
the *Landworker* and the author.

Printed in Great Britain

In loving memory of Toni
who did the initial research for this history

Contents

List of Illustrations

Part One

between pages 104 and 105

1. Local campaigning in Shropshire, 1954.
2. The Skegness annual rally, 1955.
3. Edwin Gooch at a London demonstration, 1954.
4. The wages rally at Marble Arch, 1954.
5. A Northallerton parade, 1956.
6. Tom Williams at Northallerton, 1956.
7. Harold Collison presenting a compensation cheque, 1961.
8. Bert Hazell rewarding long service, 1970.

between pages 136 and 137

9. Demonstrating outside the Ministry of Agriculture, 1970.
10. Reg Bottini leading a London rally, 1971.
11. Reg Bottini addressing a wages rally, 1972.
12. A Dorset area conference, 1980.
13. Joan Maynard at Labour's Annual Conference, 1983.
14. The farmworkers' 'side' leaving an AWB meeting, 1984.
15. Leaders of the Union at the Cromer Biennial, 1982.
16. The inaugural meeting of Region One officers, 1984.

Part Two

between pages 328 and 329

17. A Union branch dinner in Kent, mid-1960s.
18. A sheep market, 1954.
19. An eviction from a tied cottage at Lodford, Lincolnshire.
20. A family's eviction from a tied cottage, 1972.
21. Graham Stride, the first farm apprentice, 1953.
22. Spraying verges in Gloucestershire, 1951.
23. The Women's Land Army, 1950.
24. A labour gang, 1948.

xii
SKILLED AT ALL TRADES

between pages 360 and 361

Foreword by Bill Morris

General Secretary,
Transport and General Workers' Union

I am proud that it has been possible to publish this excellent farmworkers' history during my period as General Secretary of the Transport and General Workers' Union. This union was formed by amalgamation in 1922, and part of our success has been our ability to attract other unions to link their future with ours over the intervening years. None were more important than the National Union of Agricultural and Allied Workers (NUAAW) who, by a seven to one majority in a ballot of the membership, decided to merge with us in 1982.

Agricultural and rural workers, from the time of the Tolpuddle Martyrs, have earned their place in history, and their struggles so graphically described in this book continue today. For so many years, they were a proud and independent Union fighting for decent wages and conditions, against almost impossible odds in the Tory backwaters of rural Britain.

The history of the TGWU and the NUAAW has been linked together by shared experiences and common goals. The goals of social justice, freedom and economic well-being expressed so eloquently by so many of our forebears are just as important today, in the hostile political and economic climate in which we find ourselves.

For many years they were supported by the TGWU, who had joint membership on the Agricultural Wages Board and organised farmworkers in various parts of the country. It was not surprising that when the NUAAW was looking for a new home, they chose the TGWU. This new association, in the form of the Rural, Agricultural and Allied Workers' Trade Group, united all rural workers, who were strengthened by the support of the million-plus members of the TGWU in other industries.

This history of the trade union struggle amongst rural workers is essential reading for those who wish to understand the real nature of rural trade unionism. Packed with details of events and people, it continues the story from *Sharpen the Sickle* to the present day.

Foreword by Barry Leathwood

National Secretary,
Rural, Agricultural and Allied Workers

The struggles of farmworkers to secure a decent life for themselves and their families has captured the imagination of generations of people in industries and places remote from the countryside. Who has not heard of the heroic struggle of the Tolpuddle Martyrs, whose contribution to the Labour movement we celebrate every year in a massive Rally in Dorset?

In this new book, Bob Wynn looks at the history of rural trade unionism from the end of the last war up until now. He carries on where Reg Groves left off in 1948, when he wrote *Sharpen the Sickle*, which told the first part of our story. Bob's sympathetic but nevertheless objective work, is immensely readable and will delight both serious historians and those who simply want to indulge in nostalgia.

He provides an insight into the industrial changes which took place in the post-war years and how the Union responded to them. The struggles of those brave men and women of a century ago are continued today in an industry not known for its generosity to the workers whose commitment to the land knows no bounds. Feudal attitudes towards the workers remain amongst many farmers.

The book tells of the massive subsidies given to the farmers to produce ever more food, which made them rich beyond all their dreams. An expanding industry in terms of its gross product, but quick to start reducing its labour force as technology advanced and the workers became more highly skilled and flexible. Despite their new found wealth, much of it from the public purse, farmers continued to resist the Union's efforts to improve wages and safety on the farm, and fought desperately hard against providing security from eviction for the workers in tied cottages. In later years, as pressure on the industry increased in response to surpluses in many products, farmers intensified their efforts to cut labour costs.

The book charts the improvements won by the Union, including the Rent (Agriculture) Act 1976, which for the first time gave some security of tenure for workers and their families living in tied cottages; the Agricultural Wages Structure, which gave premium rates for skilled workers and those with responsibility for managing the farm or unit; and the Agricultural Training Board which, before it was emasculated by this Tory Government, provided

an excellent apprentice training scheme for the industry. The Union negotiated what is still the only legally-enforceable sick-pay scheme in the country.

Bob also describes the life of workers in this industry, the poverty which
prevails even today, and contrasts that with the pride they have in their
husbandry skills. His book tells of the Union's successes and failures, but more
than anything else it tells of the people who made it all happen. The ordinary
men and women, whose dedication and sacrifice for generations past would
have otherwise gone unrecorded.

He refutes the argument that farmworkers are not at the sharp end of the
class struggle like miners, dockers and car workers. The truth is that they have
always been in the front line in the battle against oppression, not in great
numbers on the picket line in a wave of publicity, or on the factory floor with
hundreds or thousands of other workers, but often in ones and twos, demanding decent wages and working conditions from the bosses who own the very
houses they live in. Farmworkers have had to campaign in the Tory heartlands
for social justice and seek to maintain and extend Union influence in hostile
territory.

The Union owes a great debt of gratitude to branch secretaries and activists
who have often risked their homes and livelihoods for the sake of the Union,
and even today are often subject to excessive demands from their employers.
They collect Union contributions and deliver the *Landworker*, going from
house to house, an out-dated and inefficient system some would say, but it
helps maintain contact with the members. And in these days, when there is a
legal threat to payroll deductions, it may yet come into its own in other
industries.

Bob notes that not only is agricultural and rural trade unionism about the
workplace and the fight for better wages and conditions, it is also about the
community. The need to have decent homes and schools, medical services
and transport have always been a very important part of the Union's campaigns. Health and safety is a concern that doesn't end at the farm gate, but
is extended into the community. An effective campaign against 245–T, a
chemical pesticide which caused birth defects and aborted pregnancies, was
waged on behalf of all rural people against the chemical industry for whom
profit was more important than life. There was no help from the Government,
who needed to count the bodies before they would ban its sale. Fortunately,
forestry and farmworkers refused to use it and won the support of the general
public, who then refused to buy it.

The concept of rural trade unionism and community runs through the
book and culminates with the re-launch of the Trade Group in December
1991 as the 'Rural, Agricultural and Allied Workers'. It tells of the struggle
to stay independent and the differences between the various factions within
the leadership of the NUAAW, and the subsequent Transfer of Engagements
to the Transport and General Workers' Union.

The book profiles many of the leading figures in our recent history and,
amongst the most significant, were Joan Maynard, MP, whose tireless and

uncompromising campaigning on behalf of farmworkers led to the tied cottage legislation in 1976. And my predecessor, Jack Boddy who, as General Secretary of the NUAAW, had the vision to secure the future of rural trade unionism by seeking a merger with the TGWU, and had the tenacity to carry it through.

As one whose life has been wrapped up in the Union since early childhood, reading this book is like a trip down memory lane. The characters, sometimes only dimly remembered, leap out of the page and remind me of the struggles of the past and the people who provided my inspiration.

The TGWU, over the years, since we became a part, has demonstrated its support for the Group on many occasions, not least by the publication of this excellent book, which is by definition part of the history of the TGWU. This is another chapter in the long history of rural trade unionism and provides an incentive for those who continue that work in rural Britain.

Preface

When asked to write the post-war history of the National Union of Agricultural and Allied Workers, I willingly agreed. I grew up in the country. Some of my earliest memories are of men working on the land, hoeing in the rain, sacks strung to their backs to give a little protection, and of women queuing up outside gangmasters' houses early in the morning, hoping to get a day's work potato picking and then returning in the afternoon in horse-drawn carts, weary from a back-breaking job, their peaked bonnets often soaking wet. As a small boy waiting in the doctor's surgery for family medicines, I met men and women with frost-bitten hands after beet singling, or farmworkers with injuries that prevented them from working, desperately seeking a sick note they could send to their clubs, such as the Oddfellows, because they were not entitled to the dole, and would get no money otherwise.

And did not my great grandfather, although not a farmworker, help Joseph Arch form branches of his union in Lincolnshire, before my forebear began his life-long campaign for social justice? So the task of writing this history was congenial and it seemed, in a way, that I would be carrying on in his tradition.

Trade union histories can be dull, even to the specialist. Yet the period covered by this history is packed with social change, hope, incident and excitement. There were great upheavals in the Union, too; unfortunately such upheavals are not good for the archives. Many documents were lost. Consequently, an enormous amount of time was spent searching for missing documents, and the task of writing this history proved greater than I expected.

At times during the period covered, 1947–84, there was no continuous Union record to work from, except the annual reports and EC minutes. The EC minutes can be very brief on matters of great importance, and not very explicit. I have had to piece the story together. Some pieces were never found. This accounts for some of the gaps.

This loss of records has made the historian's perennial struggle to distinguish between reliable and unreliable sources even more difficult: the provision of statistical information, including that from non-Union sources, is at times unsatisfactory and is the reason some subjects are dealt with for only a limited number of years.

I have made much use of the Union's journal, the *Landworker*, which was complete and, it can be safely assumed, reflected the views of the current EC.

I have not wanted to overburden this work with references, but have supplied them where I think the specialist will want to delve further.

One man's minimum of information, has another drowning in a sea of detail. I have tried to steer a middle course. Likewise, figures can make dull reading, but used sparingly they can be a reliable and unemotional guide to varied activities. So, whilst not wishing to wallow in figures, I quote them from time to time to give veracity and substance to the narrative.

It was impossible to convert all the £ s d references into our present decimal currency without sometimes misleading readers as to the exact face value of our former currency, so I have included conversions of principal values on page 441 for those unfamiliar with non-decimal currency.

It is not possible to write an adequate history of a union without setting it in the social and economic background of its times. This I have tried to do within a reasonable space, and does I hope, add to its interest. My remit was the years 1947–84, but to get some things in perspective, I issued my own licence to go back before 1947, and likewise, I have tied up loose ends, and included some developments since 1984.

So this history encompasses the social, economic and political changes in post-war Britain, especially in the countryside, and the great technological revolution in farming practice, for better or worse. At times, I have deliberately set out to give a picture of farming methods seen through the eyes of NUAAW members – methods that have long since vanished.

This is a critical but sympathetic survey of the Union, a warts-and-all job – no cosmetic PR cover up – recording the Union's failures as well as its triumphs, and its mistakes, too. It does, I hope, show that the Union campaigned not only on behalf of its members, but for all ordinary people living in the countryside, which would be a much better place to live in today if more of its aspirations had been achieved.

Farmwork and life in the countryside, generally, cannot be painted in black or white. Neither picture would be wholly correct, and the choice partly depends on the sources used – in this case, mainly those of the Union and the labour movement. This book therefore mirrors the interests of ordinary country dwellers, not those of wealthier sections of the community, whose money mitigates many rural shortcomings.

It might be thought that it reflects unfairly on Britain's farmers, depicting them as mean and money grabbing, extracting every last penny of profit from their employees and the public purse. That other sorts of farmers, kind, caring and struggling, do exist is not denied, but they are overwhelmed by the public utterances and actions of many of those in the forefront of the farming community.

Never has interest in the countryside been greater than it is today. Coupled with concern over the environment, exhaustion of the earth's more finite resources and the safety of some farm products, many people are seeking a greater understanding of rural problems and their solution. But we cannot solve the problems of the present without knowing the past, in which the roots of today's problems lie. I hope that this history contributes in some way to that knowledge and subsequent understanding.

And I hope, too, that readers will be encouraged by the self-sacrificing example of many people who over the years have sought to build a Union that represents farmworkers and country people generally, and in so doing have striven to reconstruct our society in a way that offers each and every one a better life in a more peaceful world.

Bob Wynn, London
May 1990

Acknowledgements

I would like to thank all those who helped in the writing of this history, particularly the officials and staff of the NUAAW, past and present, and rank and file members, too numerous to mention individually, who allowed me to interview them, helped seek out elusive facts not in the records, and arranged interviews with other people.

My especial thanks are due to Robert Moreland, who did much of the later basic research, provided useful ideas for certain chapters, and the graphs on page 6. Similarly, my thanks to Chris Kaufman (Editor of the *T&G Record*), who kindly read the typescript, and spotted several errors. Chris was also invaluable in helping to find additional Union photographs to illustrate this volume.

My thanks to John Creasey, curator of the Museum of English Rural Life at Reading University, for his willingness to dig out NUAAW documents deposited in the Museum's archives and deliver them to me in London; to Dr. Robert Miles, of the Department of Sociology, University of Glasgow, for help with the problem of prisoners-of-war working on the land after the Second World War; to John Boyd for information on the Common Market, and to the staff of the TUC library, the Labour Research Department, the MAFF library in Whitehall, and researchers of the TGWU.

A special word of my indebtedness to the late Dr. C. K. Elliott, the Fenland GP who became an eminent osteopath and homeopathic practitioner. He gave me much valuable advice on the medical aspects of this history. When Dr. Elliott entered private practice, hundreds of farmworkers went to him, and he treated them free of charge. Such was his empathy with people working on the land that he made a special study of their occupational illnesses, and was co-founder of the Institute of Agricultural Medicine and Rehabilitation.

I must make it clear that none of the above-mentioned people is in any way responsible for the conclusions and opinions expressed in this book: like any mistakes, they are my own.

My grateful thanks to a number of friends, Dorothy Davies, Jackie Latham, Nancy Lloyd, Pat and Grace O'Donohoe and Peggy Sharp, who at a difficult time in my life, encouraged me to carry on with this book.

Finally, my thanks to my editor, Peter Sinclair for many helpful suggestions, watchful eye and good humour, as this history was prepared for the printers.

Part One

1

Post-War Britain – A Time of Hope

And he gave it as his opinion . . . that whoever could make two ears of corn or two blades of grass, to grow upon a spot of ground where only one grew before would deserve better of mankind, and do more essential service to his country, than the whole race of politicians put together.

Jonathan Swift, *Gulliver's Travels*

Economic and Political Background

It was Christmas Day in the workhouse for F. Brannigan of Deighton, Yorkshire, with his wife and seven children, in 1947. No, Mr. Brannigan was not some kind of pauper or tramp, but a farmworker. He and his family had been peremptorily evicted from their tied cottage* on Christmas Eve. What heinous crime had he committed to give such inhumanity the full support and majesty of the Law? He had had the nerve to request payment for weekend overtime.

Another farmworker, G. W. Ford, also of Deighton, met with an accident at work. A few days later, while still incapacitated, he was sacked and told to leave his cottage. He and his wife and seven children between five and sixteen were evicted on one of the coldest days of winter – there was snow on the ground – and had to be given shelter by neighbours.

The third victim was F. L. Grainger, a gardener. While no complaint was made about his work, he was suddenly given notice. A possession order was granted for his cottage, but before he could be ejected he moved his wife, seven children and furniture into an old police station.

All were members of the National Union of Agricultural Workers, and in none of these cases, said Jack Brocklebank, the Union's district organiser, was a finger lifted by one of the employers to try to find alternative accommodation. Said Jack, 'If this horrible system is allowed to continue men of spirit will shun agriculture like the plague . . . Is it too much to hope that the Labour Government will realise the iniquity of this social wrong . . . which inflicts

---

* Living accommodation 'tied' to a job.

such unmerited suffering, not only on men who are of vital importance to the nation, but also on unoffending women and children?' But such evictions continued for many years, and were part of the enormous problems facing the Union in the post-war years. It was just one of the factors that caused so many workers to leave the land, together with that of very low wages, poor housing, poor educational facilities, poor social amenities, poor services – in short, a poor life.

The Union fought over the years on all these issues, and many battles were won, but it could not stop the drift from the land – helped along by increasing mechanisation and chemicalisation of farming – so that a once proud and independent Union (it was one of the smallest of the medium-sized unions and represented 1% of the trade union movement as a whole) lost countless members, was reduced to a shadow of its former strength and forced, by the late seventies, to merge with the giant of the trade union world, the Transport and General Workers' Union.

Yet for Union members, the end of the Second World War was a time of hope. A hope they shared with large sections of the British population.

There was no mistaking the mood of the great majority of people at the time. They wanted change. Change for the better. The men and women who had sacrificed so much in the armed services were determined not to go back to the dole queues of the thirties. Their brothers and sisters, fathers and mothers, who had worked in the war factories, and the farmworkers, who had laboured long and arduously to feed the nation and thus make victory over fascism possible, felt likewise.

Farmworkers especially opposed to being put on short time, 'rained' or 'stood off' in winter, and because of poor pay, eked out an existence for their families with savings from harvest pay and help from Public Assistance.

There was no nostalgia for the past. The only looking back was looking back in anger at what had been done to working people before the war, the days of the Hunger Marches, when many were deprived of a worthwhile education, adequate housing and security in old age.

The national outlook wholeheartedly favoured the Labour Party. The NUAW had started life with strong Liberal connections, but it had increasingly allied its fortunes with those of Labour, which it faithfully maintains to this day. When Labour rocketed to power in 1945, the leadership of the Union was overjoyed. For the first time, a Labour Government was formed with an absolute majority; it had 393 seats, an overall majority of 180. It even won formerly safe Conservative rural seats, especially in counties like Norfolk, the old stronghold of the NUAW, whose members deserved much credit for those victories.

Labour had produced a remarkable Election Manifesto called *Let us Face the Future*. It said:

The Labour Party stands for freedom of worship, speech, of the Press . . . The Freedom of Trade Unions, denied by the Trades Disputes Act 1927, must be restored. But Labour will not tolerate freedom to exploit others, to pay poor wages, or push up prices for private profit. The Nation needs a tremendous overhaul, a programme of modernisation, and the re-equipment of homes, factories, machinery, schools, social services. The Labour Party is prepared to achieve it by . . . putting the community first and the sectional interests of private business after.

There was much in this to inspire the millions of war weary-veterans and workers. Rightly, farmworkers expected much to follow this Manifesto. They were, however, terribly forbearing and recognised the many difficulties the new Government faced. As during the war, when the need to produce every ounce of food from British soil was of the utmost importance, they co-operated in every way possible with the Government to help overcome continuing food shortages.

After the farming depression of the 1920s and 1930s, when it suited the capitalist class to rely heavily on cheap food imports, the Second World War had brought tremendous prosperity to larger farmers. This was to continue well into the 1980s, helped largely by Labour's famous 1947 Agriculture Act, which gave the farmers practically everything they asked for (and farmers were never slow in asking) and made Tom Williams, Minister of Agriculture, their idol.*

The Act's aim was to promote stability and efficiency, in place of the pre-war situation when violent fluctuations in prices were common; crops were often not worth harvesting and left to rot. The Act safeguarded the producer. It related prices to cost. Fixed prices were based on the average cost of production and so regulated that they definitely paid the farmer to grow the food the nation needed. There were safeguards to see that public money was not wasted, but the control exercised was very moderate. The county agricultural committees, which supervised much of the working of the Act, were bodies on which farmers predominated; they lacked workers' representatives.

Even with the tremendous efforts of the NUAW, although the conditions of the farmworkers improved, they never did nearly so well as the farmers, and had to wait, despite promises, many long years for the abolition of the tied cottage.

Farmworkers never opposed the farmers' new-found prosperity. The theory was widespread in the Union that only a prosperous industry could pay good wages, but for decades, they still remained at the bottom of the wages ladder. (See the comparison of post-war agricultural and average industrial wages overleaf.) However, the Union was not convinced that the way

---

* Farm revenues rose from £306.5m in 1937–8 to £1,336m in 1954–5. Farm expenditure in 1937–8 amounted to £250m (including £66m on labour) and rose to £1,056m in 1954–5 (including £278.5m on labour). This left a profit of £56.5m in 1937–8 and £280m in 1954–5. *1955 Annual Abstract of Statistics.*

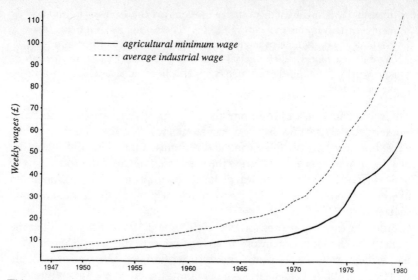

This graph compares the agricultural minimum wage with the average industrial wage in the post-war period. It clearly shows the ever-widening gap between farmworkers' and other industrial workers' wages: the gap in 1950 was £2.50; in 1960, £6.20; in 1970, £14.90; and in 1980, £55.06.

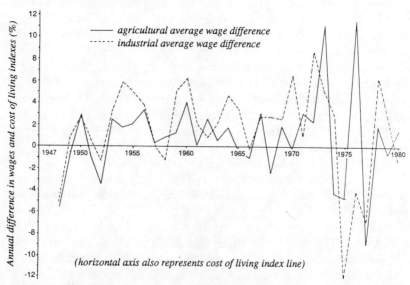

Having indexed agricultural and industrial average wages, using 1947 as the base year, and compared the % wage increases with the % increases in the post-war cost of living index, this graph charts the annual % difference in wage increases for each group and the cost of living index. Two important trends are shown: (1) There were only 9 occasions in this 34-year period when agricultural wage increases (compared to the cost of living) were relatively greater than the average industrial wage increase; and (2) the average industrial wage reflects the slumps and booms of the post-war British economy.

the industry was subsidised by the taxpayer was the best way. The bigger the farmer the more he reaped of the taxpayer's money. The small farmer had only the gleanings for his pains, but little was done to introduce a fairer system.

Rural housing occupied a good deal of the Union's time in 1947. The cessation of new building and repair work since the outbreak of war had left many country cottages in a deplorably bad condition. The Union exerted every effort to get them repaired and make local authorities deal with bad sanitation and impure water supplies.

It continued to press that special harvest rations should be obtainable by the workers and not employers. The Minister of Food refused, despite reports that some members were not getting the additional rations (it was not until 1953 that farmworkers were allowed to draw these rations at the shops). Discontent among workers and employers alike led to the Minister setting up a Working Party which agreed that *where possible* extra rations should be issued on a weekly basis – 2 oz tea, 5 oz sugar, 4½ oz margarine, 2¼ oz cheese and 4½ oz preserves.[1]

Profound economic, social and political changes took place in post-war Britain affecting its cities, big towns and rural areas. Farming and food was, and still is a huge industry in Britain, and without it, we could not have much of the processed and semi-processed food we consume today: bread, meat and poultry, milk, cheese, butter, sugar, confectionery, even chocolate. It also provides basic materials for our clothing and footwear.

Although it no longer employs a large labour force itself, farming is still an important employer in the countryside. Changes in farming techniques – the big increases in the use of petrol-powered vehicles, machinery and other equipment, including computers and the immense input of fertilisers and herbicides – means that it indirectly employs large numbers of people in Britain's factories. Huge concerns like ICI, Fisons, Shell and vehicle manufacturers, owe no small part of their prosperity to farming, but this was not always the case.

Farming is part of the woof and web of changing Britain. It is a vital part of Britain's economy and social structure. In the post-war years, the industry became a powerful lobbying force; Labour and Conservative governments listened, and acted.

Today, British farms produce 60% of our food and 80% of indigenous type products, but partly because of EEC policies, we still import huge amounts of food (at a cost of £9,762 million in 1985): half our lamb comes from the other side of the globe, one third of our bacon, masses of vegetables, and even potatoes. We could, if allowed, produce more ourselves and thus cut our overseas trade deficit handsomely, but instead we are setting aside land, and cutting back production.

None of this was foreseen when America suddenly ended Lease-Lend in 1945, the economic life-line President Roosevelt had extended during the war. This meant that the appalling economic mess the war had left increased immensely, and made life even more difficult for Britain's post-war Labour Government. Many believed that America did not want to see a 'socialist' Britain succeed. The men on the farms, by their huge effort to increase production, helped save the day.

Legislation in Parliament, the introduction of the Welfare State, the NHS, improved pensions, education, holidays with pay, health and safety regulations, had a profound effect on the farming industry, making it a better employer, and improving the lifestyle of its labour force. Many of these huge changes would have been almost impossible without the huge contribution farming made to the national economy. Producing more of our own food was not only a necessity, with most of the Empire winning independence (they needed much of their produce to improve their own living standards), but it made economic sense in a near-bankrupt Britain.

One aspect of the social changes affecting Britain was the huge house-building programme that the 1945 Labour Government launched. This was new political thinking: the State would provide on a large scale where the private sector had failed. Not only were houses built to fill the needs of newly-married ex-Servicemen, but eventually much of our pre-war slum property was replaced. Not all of this was in the great industrial conurbations. It also existed in what might otherwise be thought of as idyllic rural areas. For the first time ever, many rural dwellers got electric light and tap water, to say nothing of inside lavatories.

Another feature of these changes was that farms got bigger and bigger, and decreased in number. Thousands of small farmers were encouraged to retire and their land was taken over by bigger neighbours. Some of the big farms were run by conglomerates, controlled by gentlemen in the City of London. Size helped increase production and cut the labour force, and was considered a good thing by leaders of the industry. Doubts crept in later as to the efficiency of such large units, not only in farming, but in other industries like ICI, which took steps to divide up their operations.

Union Organisation

The Union had never been stronger and was in an excellent position to help the farming industry and the nation, which it continued to do as far as the Government and farmers permitted.

In 1947, Union branches totalled 3,252, the highest number since its formation in 1906. From 1,244 in 1939, they had been steadily increasing in number during the war. Total income in 1947 was £150,915 16s 9d compared with £138,211 6s for 1946. Expenditure was £112, 187 2s 3d, leaving a balance of £38,728 14s 5d. During the year 5,507 payments were made for accident benefit, amounting to £9,444 15s.

The year began with 34 District Organisers (DOs), and ended with 37. During the year, DOs travelled 390,093 miles, held 5,315 meetings and made

10,564 visits to members. Some 30,000 new members were enrolled and 340 branches opened.

The Union sub of 6d per week was among the lowest in British trade unions; with farmworkers so badly paid, resistance to increases was to become a serious problem in later years. By 1970, the Union had become one of ten unions which relied most on members' subs for their incomes, with the highest proportion of expenditure going on working expenses (92.5% in 1947 and 82.9% in 1970).[2] Office staff salaries (excluding the Legal Department) in 1947 took £12,157 6s 6d, and DOs' salaries £14,006 17s 9d. The cost of the Tolpuddle Celebrations and a float at the Lord Mayor's Show in London amounted to £1,112 12s 11d. Contributions came to £142,007 2s and the sale of badges brought in £1,194 14s 6d.

At the time, as had been the case for many years, the structure of the Union was as follows: at the bottom were the branches, with their own officials and committees. Branches were grouped into district committees, each branch electing a delegate. Next there were county committees, whose members were drawn from district committees. These were elected by annual ballot, one or two members from each district.

County conferences were annual gatherings of branch chairmen and secretaries within a county; each conference was attended by national EC members, and the President, Vice-President, General Secretary or other national officers. These conferences enabled local branches to bring before other branches any matter they considered important; this gave the members a feeling of active participation in union affairs.

National biennial conferences were held, delegates being elected from the districts. The biennial was the Union's supreme decision making body which laid down policies to be implemented by the EC. In the post-war years the EC strove to keep the rank and file as passive as possible, and the biennials rarely became a threat to the chosen policies of the right-wing leadership. After discussing various topics, the EC gave its views, which were usually accepted by the delegates. To have its views rejected was a rare occurrence for the EC, although by the early 1970s, the EC was finding it more difficult to control conference decisions and was forced to give way to the feelings of the membership several times. However, biennials were basically democratic, and the main problem for members was to prevent themselves being manipulated by top officials. There was a semi-Marxist grouping opposed to many of the right-wing EC's decisions, but it was a kind of loyal opposition, and fiercely supportive of the Union itself.

The EC in 1947 consisted of 13 members: E. G. Gooch, J. Barsby, T. S. Bavin, W. Blanchard, W. A. J. Case, C. H. Chandler, B. H. Huson, B. Leeder, W. C. H. Luckett, A. E. Pannell, J. Paul, F. Robinson, with A. C. Dann, General Secretary. It was elected by ballot every two years, the county being divided into regions for the purpose. EC members received travel and hotel expenses, and were reimbursed for loss of earnings. The President was Edwin Gooch, son of a Norfolk blacksmith, who first worked at his father's forge. He became a journalist in Norwich, and was active in the early Labour movement in Norfolk. In 1920 he ran the election campaign which resulted in George Edwards, the Union's esteemed founder, being returned to Parliament.

In 1922, Edwin was elected to his parish, rural and county councils, and appointed a JP. His work with Edwards established a firm connection with the NUAW, and after serving on the EC for a few years, became honorary President when Bill Holmes was appointed General Secretary. In 1944, he was awarded the CBE, and a year later elected Labour MP for Norfolk.

He was ceaseless in his work for the Union, travelling all over the country addressing meetings right into his old age, rising to national and international fame; he became President of the International Landworkers' Federation and a member of the agricultural committee of the International Labour Organisation in Geneva.

*   *   *

The Union did not only organise agricultural and horticultural workers, but also a large number of road workers, who played a leading role in it. Ever since the founding of the Union it had had roadmen members, and in some counties, such as Norfolk, the majority of roadmen were members. There was a natural link between land workers and rural roadmen. Farmworkers in the bad old days, victimised for their Union activity, took to working on the roads, and continued their Union activities, often as branch secretary. A man in such a position was safer as a roadman than a farm employee.

Roadmen were the backbone of the Union in Norfolk. There used to be 100 delegates to the NUAW Norfolk Roadmen's Conference and Bert Huson, Norfolk County Secretary for many years, was a roadman. Then Norfolk County Council introduced mechanised road sweepers, grass cutters, hedge trimmers and herbicides, and sacked over 100 lengthmen (so called because they were responsible for a length of road) in one year. Eventually they did away with all lengthmen, who were also lost to the Union. Similar things were happening all over Britain, and the Union's roadmen membership withered away to almost nothing.

The number of full-time workers in agriculture peaked in 1949 at 748,000, higher than at any time since 1929. In March 1949, the agricultural minimum wage was 94s for 48 hours; labourers on the railways got 92s 6d and local authority labourers 98s 6d.

Relations with Labour

Farmworkers and their leaders recognised that the problems which faced the post-war Labour Government were, to a large extent, the endemic problems of twentieth-century Britain. Old and famous industries were now almost clapped out by wartime shortages and the unwillingness of their owners to invest in them. It was very convenient for the owners to have them taken over by the State, which paid lavish compensation – £164,600,000 to the mine owners alone. In the first year of public ownership of the railways, 769 locomotives had to be scrapped.

Despite some criticism of the way the Government was buying out the owners of such industries, the NUAW leaders believed that only by working with the Government could they succeed in building that new and better Britain that their members wanted, and they leaned over backwards to help. That struggle for social justice, greater security for working people, higher living standards and peace, was just the start of a tortuous path that was to take them right up to the authoritarian regime of the arch-Tory Margaret Thatcher, whose great desire was to emasculate the trade unions at all costs.

The NUAW leadership had high hopes of the newly-elected Labour Government. They believed that many of the things that they sought, not only an adequate wage for their members, but the refurbishment of rural England, thus raising the quality of life for all country dwellers, would come about, albeit with some delays because of the battering Britain took during the war.

This made the Union keen to promote the greatest possible co-operation between the Labour Party and itself, recognising that 'it would be extremely foolish to be mindful of temporary discontents' and risk the return of a Tory Government.[3] Edwin Gooch, Alfred Dann and Arthur Holness, editor of the *Landworker*, attended meetings in 1948 of a committee set up by Labour to consider agriculture and rural policy.

One of the Union's main concerns was the tied cottage, and it exerted pressure on Labour to get it abolished. Deputations to the Ministers of Health and Agriculture requested its abolition, making it clear that they expected the Government to carry out the promises made at the previous General Election. (The tied cottage question is dealt with fully in Chapter 12.)

There were other problems too. In 1945, the Union issued 68,000 Thermos flask permits, to enable members to take hot tea to work. That year, delegates to the Biennial at Margate were reminded that 'rationing and other restrictions make it necessary for you to bring along your ration book and also a supply of towels and soap'.

Although the Union was only able to organise about a third of the full-time farmworkers, membership had never been higher, at 137,000 in 1948, three times the 1938 level. Curiously, in its annual reports the Union seldom disclosed actual membership numbers, only increases, often given in percentages. Tactically, this may have been wise, but it makes it hard for historians! The figure of 137,000 is part calculated on the basis of subscription income and part estimated, the best that can be arrived at under the circumstances.*

---

* A difficult exercise, as subscription rates varied, and men and women under 18 paid only half the rate of other categories.

After special membership campaigns in 1948, which led to 416 new branches with 30,000 new members, Alfred Dann announced that the Union had 200,000 members,* but this figure was still well under half the full-time agricultural workers in England and Wales.

*   *   *

By 1947, the Labour Government was in even greater difficulties, largely brought about by the transition to a peace-time economy. Some 150 delegates attended the Union's recalled Biennial in London on 7 October to consider what they could do to help. Tom Williams, Minister of Agriculture, was given a very cordial welcome. He spoke on the shortage of manpower and the work of schoolchildren on the land.

Conference decided: that in no circumstances could it consent to school-children working on the land; that the Government be pressed to introduce early legislation to end the tied cottage; that new houses be built in groups and that farmworkers should get extra rations. In all other respects it resolved to do all it could to help the Government.

Alfred Dann led the Union's delegates to the 1947 TUC Congress at Southport, and F. Robinson successfully moved a resolution calling upon the Government to stimulate recruitment of British workers to the land, by a policy of agricultural wages comparable to those paid to workers in other skilled industries.

It was during this Congress that W. A. J. Case, an EC member and a Wiltshire branch secretary for 26 years, was awarded the TUC's Gold Medal. He had enrolled more than 5,000 members in the Union.

Let us pause awhile to look at some of the other Union activists in those post-war years, and their subsequent careers.

Union Activists

Young Harry Kellow was working in horticulture just outside Portsmouth during the Second World War, growing vegetables. They were bombed a lot, and he felt unprotected, not only from the Nazi planes, but because his working conditions and pay were poor.

'We wanted someone to look after us,' he said. So Harry and his mates, with the help of C. R. Allcorn, DO, formed the Swanmoor NUAW branch in 1944. The Union, and the submarines, helped to put up his wages. 'After the subs had sunk a lot of ships bringing food, we got a rise of 12s, making our wage 48s a week,' he said.

---

*   This figure seems hopelessly optimistic on the basis of subscriptions.

A typical countryman, he grew up in Burcombe, Wilts, where he attended the village CoE school. He left at fourteen to work in nurseries for seven years, and has been on farms ever since.

I called on Harry in 1988 at Barford St. Martin, near Salisbury, where he retired with his wife Sylvia.

Harry went back to Burcombe in 1946 to work on Priory Farm, and stayed there for 30 years. He soon became Burcombe branch chairman, but its secretary got the sack for Union activity, and Harry took over the job, which he continued until 1984. Harry was particularly interested in farm safety, after several 'narrow squeaks' himself, and they won several accident claims. It got people interested in the Union, and membership went up to 60.

At 72, he was hard put to think of any other farmworkers in the village. The changes have been great in this dairying and arable farming part of Wiltshire, and much work was then being done by contractors. 'Fields were much smaller when I started, the biggest was 50 acres, but they started knocking out the hedges and now most fields are 100 acres or more. They went from deep ploughing for root crops for cattle feed, to light ploughing for cereals, now it's direct drilling. They put weedkiller on grassland and kill everything off, and then direct drill; big machines with cultivators deposit seed and cover it.'

Harry, a Labour Party member, was Wiltshire county chairman for 24 years, and despite ill health did much to keep the spark of Unionism going in rural Wiltshire. He was a regular delegate at biennials, and was a governor of Salisbury College of Further Education. When the NUAAW* merged with the TGWU he was the first man in Region 3 to receive the coveted Gold Badge. He had always enjoyed his Union work, but it was never easy. There were difficulties in recruiting non-members because they got the same increases as members. 'We don't need to join,' they told Harry. He told them, 'There's lots of things you don't get,' and would point out all the other benefits membership provided, especially legal protection, which often brought in new members. He also lost existing members 'because the chap next door is not in the Union and he's getting the same increase in wages.'

On the merger with the TGWU, Harry said, 'We were always against it, but we accepted what the membership voted for, although I don't like the closing of small branches and district committees. But the merger has brought higher benefits and an excellent education system; the amount of educational stuff you can get hold of today is unbelievable.'

He thought farmworkers were better off in 1988, with craftsmen Grade I getting £114.38 per week. 'But their ages,' he exclaimed, 'they're all 40 upwards. There's no influx of farmworkers, so what's going to happen in the

---

* The Union added 'Allied' to its name in 1968 and became the National Union of Agricultural and Allied Workers.

future? Already farmers are finding they haven't got the labour, and rely on schoolkids for weekend work.'

Harry found some consolation in the fact that his son Robert worked as a farm contractor. He also had a daughter, Mary.

*   *   *

Another Union member I visited in 1988 was 73-year old Ernest Leake, who lived with his wife Hilda in an old people's bungalow at Skelton-on-Ure in North Yorkshire. Ernest, tall, but crippled by illness, was one of those stalwarts who helped make the Union in the post-war years. A former branch secretary, he worked on the same farm for 51 years, starting straight from school, driving carts. Hilda worked in the house.

There were 70 members in the branch, largely, it seems, thanks to Ernest, who was also a member of the parish council for 30 years. He went out canvassing for members, and no farmworker escaped being asked to join. 'We had 100% membership in this village,' said Ernest. 'We had annual dinners at the Black Lion, £1 for a three-course meal, big helpings as much as anyone could eat.'

'There was no hostility in the village to the Union,' explained Ernest. 'It was the thing to join. Branch met on Sunday mornings in the Black Lion, we had to finish meetings before the bar opened at noon.'

Ernest recalled that Christmas Day was the only holiday of the year apart from Sundays, at a time when wages were 18s a week. It was these conditions that prompted him to join the Union. He regretted the current lack of involvement in farm work. 'There was an interest in the job when we worked with horses,' he said. 'There is not the same pride in farming now, it's just a question of getting the job done.'

He recalled changes in production. 'I never thought I'd live to see the day as we did in the sixties when we got 20 tons of potatoes an acre. When I started it was 10 tons, and you couldn't sell 'em or give 'em away.' There have been other changes, too. His boss was a well-known sheep breeder, but there were never so many sheep about in the fields surrounding Skelton-on-Ure as there were in 1988. There were a lot more cattle. Most of the cattle had gone, due to the EEC milk quota.

When Ernest retired after 36 years as branch secretary the Union pre-sented him with a carriage clock, now standing proud on his mantelpiece. Hilda fished out from the back of a drawer a watch Ernest received from the farmer's son when he retired. After it had been presented, the farmer's little daughter said to Ernest, 'My daddy got that cheap on the 'plane home from Switzerland.' Together Ernest and Hilda did 96 years on that farm.

*   *   *

One man who didn't agree with all the overtime worked by some farmworkers when I interviewed him in 1988, although he had done a lot himself, was Len Day, of Huntingfield, Suffolk. Len, then 67, and retired, was never in his working life employed by a farmer. He always worked as a contractor, it paid better. When he left school he began ploughing for his father, who was a contractor, for 10s a week. He continued to work for his father until he joined the War Agricultural Committee workforce during the Second World War as a tractor driver. Later he went on drainage work, still under contract.

'As a contractor,' he said, 'I was always better off than an agricultural worker. Usually by 30s to £2 a week, but in those days it was a lot of money. I also got so much per acre when I finished, once 15d per acre, and I used to collect it at Christmas; I would get £100 to £150. I used to do 40 hours a week, sometimes we did 40 hours' overtime. We thought we were rich at the end of the week, but we had in fact worked two weeks. I don't really agree with all this overtime, but you had to do it to live. Sometimes in winter in recent years, I was bringing home £80 a week, but with rent of £25, it didn't go far. You needed the summer overtime.'

Len and his wife Marjorie lived in a council house they had occupied for 37 years; they still paid rent. When the Conservatives launched their great going-for-a-song sales campaign, Len refused to buy on principle. He said, 'These houses were built for working people. What are the young ones going to do when they are all sold?'

That was typical of Len. When he left school, he promptly joined the Union. It didn't go down well with his father, chairman of the parish council and a staunch Tory. 'Unions ain't no good boy, you mustn't belong to them,' said father, but Len remained a member, and secretary of Huntingfield branch (now Holton).

As a boy he developed a sense of social justice that was to stay with him all his life. He attended the open air meetings the Union held in the village, and soon imbibed the socialism of some of the speakers. 'I've always been a socialist,' he said, 'and I've always tried to spread the gospel. I didn't, as a boy, like the way the aristocracy treated poor people. They owned every house in the village, and if you didn't touch your cap, you could be out. Today the young 'uns won't be buggered about like their dads, the old 'uns dragged their guts out carrying big sacks of grain and they got damn all for it. Farmers don't treat people as bad today because they know they wouldn't get away with it.'

Although a Tory, his father wouldn't be put upon by the local nobs. He was the first man in the area to own a tractor, and when the hunt came through, they used to pay him £1 to stop so that they could inspect this new-fangled machine. Later the hunt refused to pay the £1, so the tractor stopped stopping.

A newcomer to the village, a solid Labour man, discovered that there were a number of charities that local people never seemed to have heard about. One left money for the poor. Len, a member of the parish council found that the farmers had been drawing out of the fund for their sons, but had kept it secret from ordinary villagers. When Len's son left school, he got £16 from the fund to buy tools, as other villagers subsequently did.

*   *   *

When Jack Halsey married in 1934, he was on parish relief, which meant working in stone pits, digging out gravel and flints four and a half days a week for 23s. Norfolk parish relief rules of those days had much in common with the Thatcherism of the eighties. How Kathleen, his wife managed, is something Jack will never know, although he was not unaccustomed to living on the breadline.

Jack was born in Birmingham in 1913. His father, a Navy NCO, was drowned in the First World War. His mother, a Norfolk girl, took Jack back to East Tuddenham in 1915, and they lived with granny in an almshouse. When gran died they had to move into a house that was nearly falling to bits. Jack was the youngest of three children. To eke out her £1 widow's pension his mother helped in the gardens of the 'big' house, and drove a milk cart. Jack attended the village school, walking two and a half miles to it.

He left school at 13, became a farm boy, working from 7am to 5pm for 10s a week. He later went chopping out sugar beet, and moved into other jobs, including lorry driving, packing in a furniture factory and coal roundsman. Like many Norfolk men, Jack had joined the NUAW as a boy 'because it was the thing to do'. While a coalman, they were supposed to get a 16s a week rise. It wasn't forthcoming, and since no other union seemed to be bothering with so small a number of men Jack took it up, with the aid of the NUAW, and it was paid.

When the Agricultural Wages Board cut the 48-hour working week by one hour off the shortest day, the farmer for whom Jack was working told his men that 'as you have a 10-minute tea break every morning, I reckon by Saturday you've already got your hour off.' About 20 men worked for this farmer, but only Jack spoke up: 'It's no use you coming here with that yarn, we're finishing at 11 on Saturdays. If you want us to go on to 12, you're paying an hour overtime.' Jack smiled, and said to me in broad Norfolk, 'There was no umming and arring after that, we got the hour off.'

Jack, a big, bulky man with large sideburns, was a leading figure in many wage demonstrations in Norwich, and twice walked round the city carrying the county banner. He biked to Norwich when the new Norfolk banner was dedicated in the Cathedral. He was secretary of Mulbarton branch for nearly 20 years and became the first secretary of Hethersett branch when it had 109 members. 'And how many have you got now?' I asked him one day in 1988, wondering if the branch still existed. 'About eighty,' he replied. He remained secretary until 1987, and kept on retired members who numbered about 20. But that wasn't the whole answer to the success of the branch. He had kept the membership up by going round collecting subs, regularly. 'That's the only way you can do it,' said Jack.

Jack was Norfolk chairman for a year and attended every biennial from 1968 until three years after the merger. Despite poor schooling, Jack was Norfolk county treasurer for many years. His books were immaculately kept. He showed me some of them, all written up in bright red ink. This didn't mean that Norfolk was insolvent, just that Jack bought some Biros cheap. They turned out to be red, and Jack being economically brought up kept on using them.

He and Kathleen lived in the same bungalow in Hethersett they rented in the early sixties at 19s a week. In 1988, it was £19. 'It's very nice here,' I said, surveying the open farmland all around. 'Yes,' said Jack, 'it's all right while I can still drive, but when I can't it'll be miles to walk to the Post Office to collect the pension.' It would be like going back to school, but his legs were nimbler then.

*   *   *

There were always magnificent floral displays in the Union's stand at the Great Yorkshire Show at Harrogate, thanks to life-long NUAW member Edgar Clayton, who had been supplying the flowers and plants since the early 1950s, and was still doing it at the age of 83, when I visited him in 1988.

Edgar lived in a former cobbler's cottage in the weathered-stone village of West Tanfield, amid cornfields and grazing sheep. His large garden contained 1,100 chrysanthemums, as regimental as Forestry Commission conifers but a darn sight prettier, 175 dahlias, pink *alstroemeria*, cornflowers, *lavatera*, red *helichrysum*, *gloriosa* daisies, asters, carnations, *achillea* and lots more. Plus fruit and vegetables as a sort of make-weight, with gooseberries by the stone.

'The soil is good here,' explained Edgar modestly. Yes, helped no doubt by the 20 barrowloads of horsemuck Edgar had lovingly spread.

A widower, Edgar had been a keen participant in local affairs. Not that he had a good start. He was orphaned as a small boy, after his mother died following the birth of twins.

Edgar was then cared for by his father, until a waggon side fell on his foot and he died of blood poisoning at the age of 37. Young Edgar then lived with granny, and later an aunt who was a hind on a farm. Leaving school at 13 he helped auntie to milk 13 cows. He never got any wages for it. 'No wonder they called us hinds,' said Edgar, 'we were always behind everyone else.'

Later he went with his uncle on another farm as a double hind, was taken to a Union meeting in a pub and was violently sick. No, he did not sup any beer, but all the members had a half pint each, and each smoked a clay pipe filled with black twist. It was the baccy that upset Edgar. Uncle signed him up in the Union at 3d a week, and he later became branch chairman.

'We had 98 members in Tanfield when Jack Bowen was about,' said Edgar. 'Jack was branch secretary, a character, one of the most faithful Union members that ever lived,' said Edgar. 'He was no speaker on platforms, but a quiet worker, and signed people up right fast. He once cycled 30 miles to start a new branch in Bishops Auckland. We could do with more like him today.'

Edgar worked on various farms, often with horses, shires and Clydesdales, and recalls living on one farm where he learnt to dance. They had a barrel gramophone, but the only records were hymn tunes, so they danced to them.

One farmer's wife was choir mistress at the Methodist Church, and she would gather eight farm lads round the piano on a Sunday night for singing. Edgar enjoyed it, but if they had missed church, they were on the mat next morning. These lads, living in, had to wash each morning in cold water and often had to break the ice on a tank in the yard. 'We had a roller towel which was frozen stiff in the wash-house many a time,' said Edgar.

After his marriage he lived in a cottage at Thornborough, and there he used to hoe 15 acres of turnips twice over; 14s first time and 3s 6d the second. 'Two days running I hoed an acre a day, but have never done it since.'

It was at this time that he won £2 for making his cottage garden produce more food than anyone else. Those were the war years. He served at the Look-Out Post, did Fire Service work and joined the Home Guard. And kept a few chickens and a pig. All this time he kept up his union work, was in the Methodist choir, served on the Post Office Advisory Committee, became vice-president of the cricket club, and was a life member of the parish council, beating all the bacon gobblers (farmers). Edgar was, in fact, just what George Edwards, union founder, thought members should be – in on everything.

At one time he held 16 positions, and his service to the community was so noticeable that he received Maundy Money from the Queen at Ripon Cathedral in 1985. He will proudly show you it, all wrapped in cellophane, should you call at his home.

*   *   *

Jack Bowen, whom Edgar mentioned, died before I began this history, but I can tell you a little about him. Jack was born in Kirby Wiske, North Yorkshire, in 1893. He was christened in the Methodist Church, and remembered as a small child seeing bonfires along the top of the nearby Hambleton Hills, lit to celebrate the relief of Mafeking.

His father was a farmworker on 12s 6d a week. Jack could never recall having any bought toys – just pieces of wood knocked together – but when the groceries came once a month there were usually some boiled sweets which lasted quite a while. He attended Tanfield school, where children were 'brayed unmercifully' for not knowing something, and thinks this turned him into a rebel.

Long before leaving school he was helping a local shepherd, and when he did leave, attended hiring day at Bedale and finished up after hard bargaining with wages of £7 10s a year. He worked on a farm which was a 'good meat house', mostly rabbit, with no fixed hours, which usually meant working all hours of daylight.

He later worked at the Grange, West Tanfield, mostly with cattle. There 'the Wesleyan people got hold of me for a bit' and he joined the Band of Hope. Then came the First World War and Jack literally stepped off a binder while harvesting, and was away to the front.

He survived, returned to farm work in North Yorkshire, and soon had a reputation as a 'red-hot union man'.[4] But he got on well with his employer, for he was a fine craftsman; also their relationship was never soured by the tied cottage problem. Jack was determined never to be caught in that trap, and, after marriage, moved into a council house in North Stainley in 1922, where he lived till he died in 1975.

The National Agricultural Labourers' Union as it was, became active in Yorkshire after the war, and Jack was soon caught up in this activity and became secretary of Tanfield branch, an office he held for 50 years. He cycled everywhere to recruit members and collect subs – membership rose to 88 in 1919 – and Jack often had to call at back doors after dark, for fear of victimisation. (As early as 1920, the *Wages Board Gazette* recorded 20 evictions because of Union membership.) Jack went on cycling round for subs till he was nearly 80.

His canny advice was much valued at conferences. He became chairman of Yorks County Committee in 1929 and served on it for the remainder of his life. During the Second World War Jack became secretary of the newly-formed district committee covering Northallerton, Thirsk and Ripon.

Jack was a man of few words, but they were always worth listening to, especially at the biennials he attended. Throughout his life there was never a march or demonstration but that Jack was there. Little more than a month before he died he was part of the throng lobbying the AWB in London.

Typical of Jack was when he heard there were three days' threshing to be had on a farm at East Tanfield. When the farmer saw Jack coming he said to his foreman, 'Bowen's coming, offer him seven shillings.' The rate was 8s, and Jack refused on principle, although desperately needing the money.

When West Riding Wages Committee was arguing over a 6d increase, the farmers were saying how cheap it was to live on sheep's head broth. 'Mr. Chairman,' said Jack, 'I want to know who's getting the rest of the sheep.'

Jack, Labour activist, was on several local councils, and the 1945 Labour General Election victory seemed to him to mark the end of an era of humiliation and subjection. He never bowed his head in the hardest, leanest years.

*   *   *

These are just a few of the men who contributed so much to the Union's strength in the post-war years. We shall meet more later in this history.

REFERENCES

1. Philip L. Lowe *et. al.*, *Countryside Conflicts* (Gower/Maurice Temple Smith, 1985).
2. G. Latta, 'Trade Union Finance', *British Journal of Industrial Relations*, Vol. 10, No. 3, 1972, p. 406.
3. Annual Report, 1948.
4. Recollections written by Jack Bowen during a WEA/Leeds University tutorial he attended, 1970–4.

2

Feeding the Nation

Agricultural Expansion

Captain Charles Lang, MC, prospective Labour candidate for Exeter in 1947, declared,

> Thanks to Labour's policy, British agriculture faces a future of secured prosperity such as it has never known before in peace time. Those engaged in the industry, farmers and workers alike, have never failed to answer their country's call for service. Given a bold and imaginative lead from a Government which had already helped them so much, they will be both able and willing to win the greatest victory in the battle of the 'gap' [between existing production and production targets] on the outcome of which our future standard of living will so largely depend.[1]

Prime Minister Clement Attlee in 1948 called for 10% increase in production as an 'immediate objective'. 'Ten per cent more coal, iron and steel, manufactures and agricultural produce would put us in a position to pay our way and preserve our standards.' He appealed to all to work together to achieve this, adding, 'We need also that people should be living lives inspired by high ideals . . . we believe intensely in freedom, in democracy and in the acceptance of the validity of moral values.'

Mr. Attlee struck the right note, for Britain was in an idealistic mood, at least as far as the Labour movement was concerned, and contrasted strongly with the greed and grab society that was to evolve many years later under Tory governments.

Yet some strange anomalies existed in 1948. Edwin Gooch told Berkshire County Conference that he had received a request to sign, with Lord Halifax (President, Royal Agricultural Society) and James Turner (NFU President), an exhortation to farmers and farmworkers to make a special effort in the next few months. He said he could not sign it while many farmworkers were unemployed. 'It doesn't make sense to me to ask an unemployed worker to put his back into it.'

Alfred Dann said that the economic crisis was not the fault of Labour, but an inevitable legacy of the war. 'A gigantic effort is needed to repair the ravages of war,' he said.

Another aspect of increasing production came with a plea for 'butter before guns' by J. T. Coe, DO, at Thetford, Norfolk, in 1948, during an inquiry into a War Office proposal to acquire permanently 26,788 acres used for training purposes. He said that families who in 1942 quietly walked out of their homes and farms in Breckland did so with assurances that they could return when the war was over. Service departments held 132½ square miles of Norfolk, a staggering figure for a county whose total arable acreage was estimated at 796,000 (1,244 square miles).

And while farmworkers were doing their utmost to increase production, they had feeding problems of their own. According to an NUAW official in 1948, more resolutions were received from branches against unfair rationing than any other subject. 'I have been looking round a Kent market town and I am beginning to understand why this is so,' wrote a *Reveille* correspondent. 'Every hotel and restaurant was packed, not with farmworkers, but with farmers and their families and the hangers-on of agriculture. One member of a rural council told me that he stayed in town for lunch every day and often had his evening meal there before going home. "It's the only way to make the rations spread." '

This was something a farmworker could not do to stretch his meagre rations. He neither had the time or money. His work could be arduous, and wholesale mechanisation was still some way off. And food was undoubtedly scarce for most people. Yet eggs, kippers, rabbits, chickens and vegetables were said to have been thrown at a dance held at Hungerford by the local Farming Club. B. S. Newman, chairman of Berkshire County Committee, in a letter to *Newbury Weekly News* wrote, 'At a time when the country is short of food . . . the deliberate destruction of food is a crime.'

Members at a branch meeting in Market Harborough in 1948 asked how they could increase production when they had to work on present rations. E. Simkin said he ate his ounce of bacon on a Sunday, and 'for a full day's work on the farm he took with him bread and jam, and then returned home at night to listen to stories of how good the meals were at the works canteen.' Another grievance was clothes rationing. Bro. Simkin said his coupons 'were exhausted in getting clothing which was worn out within a few weeks of hedge-cutting.'

Farmworkers' Importance Recognised

However, in another sphere, the Government found it easier to recognise the farmworkers' importance. J. J. Wilson, Spalding, was awarded the MBE in 1948. The medal was put on the table for members to see at a branch meeting. A. E. Monks, MAFF Labour Liaison Officer and former popular Union DO said that the award of a civil honour to an agricultural worker would not have been dreamt of years ago, but great changes had taken place.

Addressing a huge Union rally at Scarborough, Labour's Herbert Morrison said the Government had watched with admiration the way they had tackled their tasks. No other workers had done more to earn the thanks of the nation for having buckled to and delivered the stuff during the trying post-war years. The Labour Government had been the first peace-time Government for generations to support the full expansion of agriculture not only with words, but with deeds. Edwin Gooch declared, 'We are being treated infinitely better by Labour than any previous Government.' Tom Williams, Minister of Agriculture, said that the delegates were making history. They were meeting in conference for the first time as 'fully recognised and firmly established partners in the industry . . . there was a new sense of security and prosperity in the countryside.'

Some farmworkers would have been excused if they thought that fine words never buttered no parsnips, for they were having a long wait for much needed improvements. Farm wages were still far below those of most other industries and tied cottages still existed.

Among the successful Labour candidates in local elections in 1949, was a young man who was to become prominent in the Union, Jack Boddy, who won a seat on Wymondham UDC in his native Norfolk.

When I interviewed Jack in 1988, he looked back to those post-war years when numerically the Union was at its greatest strength. Jack spoke of its failure to do more for the agricultural worker than it did. 'I believe that in those days, the Union had a dual personality, in that it was concerned with raising standards of farmworkers, but secondly, felt it had a responsibility to the Labour administration not to rock the boat. As a result the EC felt they had to temper their ambitions as far as members were concerned against the objective of the Labour Government which was to initiate and maintain an economic revival following the war. Because of this, the Union missed the boat during the war years and to some extent, again in 1945. If wages had been raised to a decent level, tied cottages abolished and working conditions improved, I don't think this would in any way have inhibited the economic revival, in fact it would have enhanced it. Because of Labour's strong industrial roots, they made the mistake of thinking they couldn't give more to the farmworkers, and also they still confused the farmworkers with the landed gentry and the farmers, despite the fact that Norfolk had gone almost 100% Labour in the 1945 General Election.

'All the activities of Tom Williams appeared to be directed towards assisting the farmers, leaving the farmworkers to pick up what they could from the increasing prosperity of their employers, which left them at the mercy of the Agricultural Wages Board, a situation they had faced ever since its establishment in the twenties. Until John Silkin appointed an iron and steel trade unionist, we never had a workers' representative amongst the independent members, but even he still appeared to support the farmers. Sad to say, I believe Labour felt it could ignore the farmworkers because their ability to influence the results of General Elections was numerically low as they had become a relatively small proportion of the rural workers, and today, as they have become even fewer, that attitude still exists.'

Jack believed the Union's EC was 'largely acquiescent' to this attitude of the Labour Party, because a large number of EC members were not farmworkers. 'One was an insurance agent, Edwin Gooch a journalist, one a self-employed thatcher, another a smallholder, one a haulier, so although acting with the highest possible motives they lacked the drive and urgency to disassociate themselves from the immediate political activity of the Labour Party, and stress the needs and problems of the agricultural worker.'

*   *   *

An article in the *Landworker* in 1949 on Labour's draft election programme, *Labour Believes in Britain*, showed that it was mainly one of consolidation, a logical consequence of earlier reforms. It would not please either the reactionaries or the revolutionaries. Indeed, the *Daily Express* referred to it as 'the mad manifesto,' while the *Daily Worker* declared 'the retreat is sounded'. This surely showed that the programme contained much with which most reasonable people could agree. Generally the writer approved of it, except for one weak point. Labour, he said, was pledged to deal with the tied cottage problem, but to advocate building more houses as a solution was 'shirking the real issue'.

The agricultural returns issued in mid-1949 showed ups and downs in production. There were 6,462,000 acres of cereals and 929,000 of potatoes, compared with 6,727,000 and 1,117,000 respectively the previous year. The reduction in arable acreage was not large – 195,000 acres – but as the agricultural expansion programme announced in 1947 called for a steady increase in home grown cereals, the fall in grain acreage was disturbing. But sugar beet growers exceeded their target by 21,000 acres. There was a general expansion in livestock. Cows and heifers in milk increased by 91,000 and there was an increase in the cattle herd of 340,000. There were nearly one million more sheep and about half a million more pigs.

Yet odd things happened during the general food shortage. Edwin Gooch headed a deputation from the EC to the Minister of Food to discuss the general question of horticultural products, with special reference to ploughing-in of unwanted produce. In 1948, 400,000 tons of vegetables were imported, while home production was about 3 million tons.

The EC in 1949 said that a stronger incentive than largely increased rewards to the farmer was needed if the country was to get the commodities it desperately needed. It urged the Government to consider the reorganisation of agricultural executive committees with the provision for more adequate worker representation; the resumption of directions for cropping (a measure introduced during the war and dropped shortly afterwards); the increased mechanisation of agriculture and the maintenance of county machinery depots; the cultivation of derelict land by the committees; and a serious attempt to raise the degree of efficiency achieved by farmers.*

Call for Council of Action

Edwin Gooch at the Norfolk County Committee urged the formation of a council for action to 'devise plans to overcome the present crisis and clear the way for a full realisation of the Government's production programme'. He 'regretted' that the Minister had not taken the farmworkers into consultation over the industry's failure to reach crop targets. Delegates from the NFU had met Ministry officials to discuss the situation. 'We should have been there too,' he said.

Alfred Dann made the point that workers' representatives could probably have told the Minister something. 'We get about the country and we know the state of the farms,' he said. 'There is no excuse for this failure to reach the target. The responsibility is not ours. Not only are we most unhappy about it, but we feel those who have control of the industry in their hands should be ashamed, after all the Government has done for them . . . If the industry would not do what was expected of it, the only thing was for the State to take control.'

Despite the brushing aside of the Union's request to be consulted, it did not cease to do all it could to help. At the 1949 TUC it submitted a resolution recognising that 'one of the major problems of this country for many years to come' was home food production, and was seriously disturbed that large areas of cultivated land went for more houses, schools, roads, and water supplies, and urged whenever possible that land with no agricultural value should be used for these purposes.

Later in 1949, MAFF revealed that farmers had failed to reach the grain production target that year, after controls were lifted, about which Union leaders had expressed doubt as to the wisdom of the move.

---

* AECs consisted of three NFU nominees, two of NUAW/TGWU, two CLA and five Ministerial appointments. Edwin Gooch tried in Parliament to get three worker nominees, but Tom Williams refused. Earlier, in policy statements, Labour recommended parity with employers. When Gooch mentioned this Williams said, 'When recording our opinions then (neither Gooch nor himself dreamed) that we should be in charge of a Bill of this magnitude and importance.' The Union interpreted this as meaning that policy statements were designed to placate Labour supporters, but that Labour legislation was a different matter. See M. Madden, 'The National Union of Agricultural Workers 1946–56.' Oxford University, B.Lit thesis, 1957, by a former NUAW activist and Ruskin scholar; an analytical history of the Union's first 50 years. Unpublished.

Another aspect of food production, the international one, was referred to by Edwin Gooch later that year. Speaking at Mundesley, Norfolk, he said that every minute of the day and night there were 40 more mouths to feed. The real fear was not one of over production, but of inadequate distribution the world over. He said, 'Let us tackle that before we again start talking about possible food gluts and surpluses.'

Suffolk County Committee agreed that no useful purpose would be served by appeals to members to work harder unless farmers were 'gingered up considerably.'

That farmers were getting enormous public support was revealed by Douglas Jay, Economic Secretary to the Treasury when he gave details of public money involved in subsidies to industry under private ownership. Agriculture easily led with a total of £22,352,000 in 1948–9; next came iron and steel with £7,085,000.

Bad farmers were still around in the post-war years, and undoubtedly contributed to the failure of the food production targets. Under Defence Regulations, possession was taken on grounds of bad husbandry of 374,965 acres from 1940 to 1948.

At the Brighton TUC in 1950 a Union resolution was concerned that targets were 'failing to secure the provision of home-grown food on the scale required to meet the needs of the country, especially bread grains for the nation's loaf . . .' It called for 'vigorous action', for reorganisation, the resumption of cropping directives, and the association of workers, by means of development councils and other bodies, with the 'organisation of the production and distribution of home supplies of food.' The resolution was remitted to the General Council by the unanimous approval of Congress.

Women's Land Army Stands Down

After 11 years of very active service, the Women's Land Army was disbanded in 1950. At one time the 'Army' had a membership exceeding 70,000, but by then it was down to a few thousand. These landgirls were treated with a certain suspicion by farmworkers when the WLA was formed in 1939. J. W. D. Davies, secretary of Bullingdon District Committee, echoed the feelings of many when he wrote in the *Landworker* at the time of their disbandment:

We shall see no more of the familiar green jersey, although some of the girls are staying on the land. The WLA was formed in June 1939, and at first recognition did not come easily. Few farmers wanted them and some of the keenest girls were forced to take other work. What we thought of them when we first saw them, soft and pale-handed, we kept to ourselves, but we soon learnt to respect and admire them. Whether it was slashing the green meadows brown with their ruler-straight ploughing, bottle-feeding a new born calf, haymaking in sultry June, corn carrying in a disappointingly wet August, or picking apples on a windy afternoon, they played an important part at the time of their country's need. They showed rare courage too, in front-line counties of our island during the wartime daylight raids. We in the Union are sorry to see them go. Very many of them were loyal members and some were branch secretaries and did much to create understanding between rural and urban life. Goodbye and good luck, to the familiar figures in corduroy breeches, green pullover and slouch hat.

At the Union's great rally at Skegness in 1951, Tom Williams said that the Government aimed to increase their food supplies by 1952–3 to 50% over the pre-war level. Output in 1950 was 40% in excess of 1938. They were producing 8 million acres of cereals compared with 5.25 million acres before the war. It was a grand contribution towards the nation's economic recovery and it fully justified Labour's agricultural policy since 1945. While at the Ministry he had seen farmworkers' wages rise from 35s to £5 a week, but the really big thing was that their status had improved enormously. 'Farmworkers are no longer the Cinderellas of industry. You have captured the golden slipper and I hope you are going to stick to it for a very long time.'

Golden slipper? Well, if it was, it was of the gold-plated variety, compared to the solid gold most farmers were wearing.

REFERENCE

1. *Landworker*, January 1948.

3

Expanding Activities

Easing of Wartime Restrictions

At a big rally organised at Great Yarmouth in July 1949 by Norfolk County Committee, some 5,000 people heard Edwin Gooch say that the Union's affiliation to the Labour Party bore fruit before the advent of the Labour Government, and during the post-war years there had been abundant evidence of the fact that the Labour Government was easily the farmworkers' best friend. 'Don't kid yourself that 1923* cannot be repeated. With a Tory Government it would be,' he declared.

Among the things Edwin was alluding to were the important agricultural measures promoted by the Labour Government in 1947. The Agricultural Wages (Regulations) Act came into operation at the beginning of that year. The machinery of the AWB was greatly improved by the Act, and embodied some changes long advocated by the Union, but when the Agricultural Bill was being considered in the House of Commons, Edwin sought equal worker representation with the employers on the new County Agricultural Executive Committees. The Minister of Agriculture refused. The Union was dissatisfied with this part of the Bill's provisions, but welcomed the Bill as a whole as one 'which would put agriculture on a firm economic footing and enable it to serve the interests of the community.'

The easing of wartime restrictions, meant it was easier for the Union to organise semi-social functions, and never since the 1934 centenary had there been such a programme of celebrations in memory of the Tolpuddle Martyrs as there was in 1947. For eight days there was an unbroken series of revels and observances which drew large crowds to Tolpuddle in Dorset, and at the weekend thousands travelled by road and rail to attend a giant demonstration. Speakers included Hugh Dalton, Chancellor of the Exchequer, and Bill Holmes, the Union's former general secretary. Edwin Gooch unveiled a memorial plaque on the wall of the Court in Dorchester where the martyrs were sentenced.

---

* The year of the Great Norfolk Strike, following attempts by farmers to drastically cut wages.

In Dorset, where the Union was actively militant, no opportunity was lost to draw its aims to the attention of the public. More than 300 members assembled one June day in 1949 at Blandford, and formed a procession with 13 banners. C. H. Chandler, EC, and Arthur Jordan, DO, were the speakers at the subsequent meeting, and J. Waterman, Spettisbury branch secretary, presided. Paying tribute to the work of Arthur Jordan, Chandler said that Dorset was now one of the best Union districts in the country.

Such strength, it was clear, arose from continuous activity, such as that announced by Jordan when he said that, in future, if members were threatened with eviction, they would demonstrate and expose what was happening.

Not all Union activities were smooth running. When Fred Brown, EC, spent a week in Cornwall with Fred Cole, DO, in 1949, he addressed five branches, and a meeting was to be held in Idless Church Hall by the Vicar's permission. A few hours before it was due, a letter from the Vicar was delivered by hand to Fred: 'It has today been intimated to me that there is some objection felt in Idless to the meeting being held in the Church Hall this evening. As I do not wish to stir up controversy in a small place, like that, especially where people closely connected with the Church are concerned, I must ask you to make arrangements for the meeting to be held somewhere else.' He was sorry to give such short notice.

Who were the people who prevailed upon the Vicar to deny the use of the hall? They were local farmers. These Christian employers not only prevented the meeting, they also so frightened their workers that not one of the twenty men personally invited by Cole to attend, ventured anywhere near the hall. 'It seems that the attitude of the Cornish farmers towards their workers in these modern days is similar to that of the farmers of Dorset in the days of the Tolpuddle Martyrs,' said Brown, '. . . some of these devout farmers are said to be concerned about their workers' spiritual welfare, but . . . if they don't care about their brothers' bodies, which they have seen, how can they care about their souls which they haven't seen.'

Not that it should be inferred from this incident that many members of the Union were anti-church. In 1949, when Somerset got a county banner, a service was held at Temple Methodist Church, Taunton. The banner was offered to the minister by J. Humphrey, DO, with these words: 'Sir, we ask you to dedicate this banner, that it may be to us for all time, a sacred symbol of loyalty to God, our King, and our Country, and our intent to play our part in hastening the day of God's Kingdom among our fellow men, in this our land.'

Not only 'workers' belonged to the Union, it also catered for other rural trades, and in Lincolnshire and parts of East Anglia, many smallholders, usually ex-farmworkers, joined. The question of recruiting smallholders was raised by the EC at a joint meeting with DOs in 1947. The Lincolnshire DO thought they should discourage members from becoming smallholders and smallholders becoming members. He found that part-time smallholders claimed a disproportionate amount of his time and their problems were beyond the scope of the Union's services, and they left the Union on becoming full-time smallholders.[1]

But in 1948, in view of the large number of smallholders in Lincolnshire, its County Committee suggested to the EC that a smallholders' committee should be established to deal with queries and problems of such members. A smallholders' conference was held at Boston and a committee was set up. Its first meeting discussed contracts for sugar beet, extra representation on county council smallholdings' committees, acquisition of land by county councils for smallholdings, and the provision of allotments.

The 1947 Agriculture Act enabled local authorities to acquire smallholdings to enable farmworkers to set out on the path of becoming farmers. Authorities could rent land to be run as holdings, but this part of the Act never worked well, with long waiting lists and too few actual farmworkers being offered tenancies. In 1947, Edwin Gooch and W. A. J. Case, a smallholder joined the Smallholders' Advisory Council set up under the Act.

The Smallholders' Committee functioned for a number of years and the Union continued to recruit smallholders, but their interests were not wholeheartedly with the rest of the membership. Eventually it faded out of existence, and the smallholding membership ceased to be meaningful.

*   *   *

A good example of the Union organisation in the 1950s was Spalding branch with some 1,000 members, the largest in the country. A former branch in the town had gone out of existence but, in July 1933, the energy and enthusiasm of A. E. Monks, DO for South Lincolnshire, gave Spalding a new start with 20 members.

One was Arthur Kirton, who after the shutters went up on the old branch, vowed he had finished with trade unionism. Monks' fighting challenge broke down his resistance, and he and Joe Wilson ran in double harness as chairman and secretary. Within months Arthur had enrolled 280 members; in recognition, he received the TUC's Order of Merit.

He had begun farm work at the age of 12, at £3 a year. In the summer he was on the road every morning at four, attending cows. At the outbreak of the Boer War his wage was 13s 6d a week, with 3s deducted for house rent. He could remember days when there was not a penny in the house, when the larder was almost empty and little fire in the kitchen grate. For months at a time he was 'stood off'. He said, 'I marvel how we lived. There was only parish relief, and you can guess what that meant.' His boyhood experiences made him a bonny fighter. In the 1950s he had 300 members on whom he called personally. He did it all for 'the love of the job.'

Among other South Lincs members who worked hard for the Union was Stan Hall, who became the longest-serving member of the EC on his retirement in December 1976. Stan served on at least 20 committees and bodies over the years on behalf of the Union. He left school in 1921, aged 13, and worked in a Spalding cycle shop before taking a job on the land. For many years he was secretary of Spalding branch, and cycled some 12,000 miles collecting contributions. Another stalwart was Eric Trolley, of Fleet, near Spalding, who followed Stan onto the EC. He was a member of the NUM in Derbyshire for 17 years before joining the NUAW in 1946.

One notable aspect of the way the Union flourished in these post-war years was the large number of social activities organised by branches. They went far beyond darts and skittles, and included many annual dinners and bus outings to the seaside. This kind of activity was very limited in the penny-pinched twenties and thirties.

Labour Fails to Get Rural Seats

In the 1950 General Election, Edwin Gooch, Labour MP for N Norfolk since 1946, was again the candidate. Bert Hazell, who missed election in 1945 by 116 votes was again candidate for Barkston Ash, Yorks, while W. A. J. Case stood at Salisbury. Other Union candidates were Eddy Jones, Leominster, Herefordshire; Sydney Dye, S W Norfolk; F. J. Wise, King's Lynn (Wise won this seat in 1945); Major Chris Mayhew, S Norfolk (he won it in 1945); Stanley Wilson, Saffron Walden, Essex. Archie Crawford (former chair, Leicestershire NFU and an honorary member NUAW), who was convinced that Labour had the best policy for agriculture, contested Melton Mowbray.

Labour won, but hopes of a substantial majority were dashed. In an exceptionally high turn out the Labour vote increased by 1,250,000, the highest vote of any political party in the history of British politics. There was no popular drift towards Toryism, but changed boundaries and new constituencies greatly favoured them.

Labour had hoped to do better in rural areas, but the view that farmers, brimming over with gratitude for what the Labour Government had done for them, would support Labour, proved to be without foundation. By instinct and tradition, the majority of farmers were rock-ribbed in their support of Toryism.

Edwin Gooch was returned for N Norfolk with 2,000 more votes than previously, but with a reduced majority. Dye, whose majority in S W Norfolk in 1945 was 53, won by 260 votes. Wise held King's Lynn. Mayhew, who was later to desert Labour in the 1980s to join the SDP, lost in S Norfolk. Hazell failed to gain the Barkston Ash seat, and in Salisbury, Case, making his first appearance as a parliamentary candidate, did well, polling over 12,000 votes.

At the annual meeting of Norfolk County Committee in 1950, Edwin Gooch reported that Norfolk membership increased the previous year by 1,335 and had reached nearly 30,000. Though some years ago Lincolnshire had outstripped Norfolk membership, the gap between the two counties was getting smaller, and Norfolk could regain its former position as premier county in the Union.

In the contest for the Presidency in 1950, Edwin Gooch was re-elected by 114 votes to 33 for Tom Gasgoyne, a left-winger from Durham.

*   *   *

For years it had been used as a bag for shopping. It was made of linen, but there was something unusual about it, four words were embroidered in green on it: 'Success to the Union.' And Mrs. Cranner, aged 90, of Barford, Warwickshire, knew the secret. Cut open, the bag became a banner, carried by Joseph Arch's followers, nearly 80 years previously. Whether it was originally made as a dual purpose banner-cum-bag to carry documents to Union meetings, or to keep it safe from the eyes of the authorities, is not known. So at Wellesbourne in 1950, at the annual Arch commemoration, there were three banners in the long procession, a new county banner, the national banner, and the Arch's banner, borne proudly aloft by Mrs. Harrison, wife of the Warwickshire DO, F. H. Harrison. The new county banner was dedicated by the Vicar, the Revd. George Evans, during a service.

There was a much more up-to-date innovation at the 1950 'Consolidation Rally', organised by Hampshire County Committee at Southampton in July, in the form of a recorded greeting and message from Alfred Dann.

Early Warning on Costs

Alfred, writing in the *Landworker* in 1950 on the future of the Union, said that members perhaps did not appreciate the extent the cost of running the Union had increased. 'The contributions are the same now as in 1941, but our expenses are nearly five times as much as they were in 1940.' He said that growing membership, the increasing complexity of social and industrial questions and the demand for more comprehensive services to members had made necessary a big increase in both local and head office staff. In 1940, they had a dozen officers and clerks at head office; now they had 50. In the districts in 1940 they had 16 organisers. Now there were 37.

They had perhaps the most scattered membership of any trade union, organised in nearly 4,000 branches, the great majority in villages. This made the work of organisation and administration very expensive. Officials travelled thousands of miles yearly, and the cost of travel was £6,500 more than in 1940. 'We have always prided ourselves on being a thoroughly democratic movement, and in recent years county and district conferences have become a regular feature . . . These gatherings enable branch officers and members to meet their local and national leaders, exchange views . . . and the cost . . . runs into thousands of pounds.'

The Union's marquees at shows were popular with members, but cost a lot of money. Members were keen on Union education and the Union had spent £2,500 on this, the previous year. Accident benefit, funeral benefit and legal aid costs increased substantially every year. In 1940, the Union paid out £2,796 in benefits. In 1949, the sum was £21,837. All other costs had increased tremendously. The printing bill was nine times as much as it was 10 years earlier. 'Our main purpose is to maintain and improve wages, and with a Wages Board such as we have . . . it is unlikely that a large scale dispute will ever arise, but we have to be prepared for a possible, if not probable, emergency. So we, like all other trade unions, must have a substantial financial reserve to enable us to weather any storm.' He said that the Union's income and expenditure would have to be reviewed and given serious consideration by the EC and membership.

* * *

Some branches were a little unusual. When Ron Heap, secretary of Aldrington (Kent) branch, visited N Wales in 1950, he found farming there a very haphazard business, mainly little family farms, and dairy cattle virtually non-existent, there being no pastures fit to maintain them. Sheep were in abundance, and wandered unrestrained among the heather and scrub of the mountain sides. The few farmworkers usually lived in the farm house and took their meals with the employer and his family.

At Capel Curig, he met the secretary of Gwydyr Forest branch, Michael Wormald, who lived in a tent from April to the end of October. 'Sitting in that lonely tent surrounded by gigantic mountain peaks and exchanging Union news with Michael and Gwilym Davies, DO, was an experience I shall not soon forget,' he wrote in the *Landworker*. He found Gwydyr Forest branch 'in its lonely remote mountain fastness, vigorous and progressive . . . an example to many other branches in more populous areas.' The *Denbigh Free Press* wrote:

Little was heard about the Union in Denbigh until recent years, when Mr. E. Lloyd Roberts and four others became pioneers of a movement which led to the establishment of a local branch, and to the enthusiasm and vision of men like Mr. Gwilym Davies and Mr. Roberts, now secretary to the District Committee, can be attributed the rapid progress of Denbigh branch, which has a three figure membership . . . Today we all regard the farmworker with a new respect, for we know his value to the community. But the improvement in the status did not come by accident. As in other industries, his interests are safeguarded by his Union, and . . . the stronger the Union the greater its ability to secure a square deal for its members, and it is surprising that there are still those who are too apathetic to identify themselves with their own organisation, although ready to grasp all the benefits that it has bestowed upon them.

That the position of the farmworker had improved, was illustrated in a radio talk in 1948 by R. T. Paget, Labour MP for Northampton, a farmer and barrister. He said of a farmworker he called George: 'He is a good milker . . . He can help a cow in difficult calving. He has a fair working knowledge of veterinary . . . he can drive a tractor, he can service one too . . . He can build a stack and, at a pinch, he can thatch a stack. He can do a bit of hedging and a dozen other jobs . . . He probably averages about £5 10s a week. Skill for skill against the engineer and factory worker, he is worth his money. His uncle used to work for my father before the 1914 war. His wage was 18s . . .It was probably worth £2 or £2 10s. But George is drawing double that. Last year he took his family to Skegness for their holiday. Next year they are going to Rhyl . . . George's uncle only left the village once, and that was when he went to the war of 1914 . . . George is living quite a different life from his uncle. He is getting a bigger slice of the cake, and a very good thing too . . .'

*   *   *

In Norfolk, the Terrington branch had as guest of honour at a dinner, James T. Coe, of Norfolk, an organiser for 40 years, who retired in 1950. Born at Castle Acre in 1885, James, eldest of a family of five, began farm work at the age of 11. At 21 he became secretary of the newly-formed Castle Acre branch, and three years later was appointed organiser – the only official on its outside staff at the time. His duties took him to many parts of the county and his efforts were rewarded by a rapidly rising membership. He had a long record of public service, being a councillor and magistrate. James died in 1967.

*   *   *

Some EC members were not afraid of taking wider issues to a large public. One such was Fred Brown, who in 1951 was involved in a hard-hitting public debate with the Vicar of Kingston Lacy, Dorset, the Revd. R. A. Bontoft, who deprecated a Red Flag in a Union procession through Wimbourne. Mr. Bontoft said that since the Tolpuddle Martyrs the position of the workers had constantly improved, and present-day workers were not always as hard up as they imagined they were . . . The Red Flag was a symbol of revolution, bloodshed and destruction, and for that reason he challenged its appearance at a Union rally.

Fred replied that he had been a lay preacher in his youth, but had left the church because it had fallen from grace in failing to raise the status of the workers. The Sermon on the Mount had laid down the principles of Christianity, but as centuries rolled by the Church had forgotten its purpose and had failed to put into practice the teachings of Christ. 'The Church has been on the employers' side every time, and the working man has to get his demands for a better living standard only by organising in his trade union.'

If on occasion the Union came into conflict with Christians, its relations with the Labour Government were not always trouble free. In 1950, in the House of Commons, when a Tory asked Labour's Minister of National Insurance (Dr. Edith Summerskill) whether the organisations she consulted before bringing in regulations to prevent seasonal unemployed workers drawing unemployment benefit included the NUAW, she replied that when the National Insurance Advisory Council was considering the question, unions representing agricultural workers made representations to them. Another MP then asked if she was aware that the regulations had had a most unsatisfactory effect so far as women were concerned, and was it not a pity that the advice of the Union was not accepted. She replied that representations were made to her by all the unions concerned. Edwin Gooch asked if she did not agree that the Union had opposed the imposition of these regulations. In true Ministerial style she referred to the answer just given. To another MP she retorted tartly: 'When I am given advice . . . I consider that advice. I do not always take it.' Such snubs by Labour ministers were to increase in the years ahead.

*   *   *

Contingents from as far afield as Durham and Gloucestershire joined Lincolnshire members at the annual rally at Skegness in June 1951. The day's influx included 21 well-filled trains and scores of motor coaches. Headed by three bands and the county banner, the parade through the town numbered about 4,000 members and their wives, and was watched by many thousands of holidaymakers.

Tom Williams said it was a magnificent demonstration which provided the answer to the Tory claim that they represented the workers. He recalled the days when he travelled around Lincolnshire, addressing gatherings of seven to 10 farmworkers in the light of oil lamps so that no farmer could see who was present. There had been a startling change in the strength and influence of the organised workers.

Writing in the *Landworker* in December 1951 on the growth of the Union, Alfred Dann repeated earlier warnings on rising costs and said the EC had considered asking for a contribution of 8d per week. The 6d sub had been fixed in 1941 when the minimum rate was £2 8s a week. Now it was £5 8s. Accident benefit of 7s 6d per week could be increased from four to eight weeks if a new scheme was accepted. Members later voted for an increased sub of 8d a week by a large majority.

Study Labour Policies

Writing in the *Landworker* of the coming General Election in 1951, Alfred Dann again highlighted the Tory policy before the war when in rural areas many farmers went bankrupt, thousands of farmworkers were left on the verge of starvation and thousands unemployed.

> Compare it with the present position under Labour rule, agriculture has never been so prosperous . . . The wages and working conditions are better than ever before in the long history of agriculture. In a few weeks' time wages will be

£5 8s a week for 47 hours and there will be a fortnight's holiday with pay each year, in addition to all Bank Holidays. But a word of warning. In this election the Tories are talking about cutting down expenditure. Nobody will disagree with the aim of economy, but what the Tories mean when they talk about national economy is economy at the expense of the workers. Today we have subsidies on food which at present has a high scarcity value. We have the expenditure on the social services, on housing, on education, and on rearmament. If food subsidies are cut there will be a further rise in the cost of living. Do we want less free houses, and the rents of existing houses to go up. Do we want State expenditure on social services to be reduced, which will inevitably mean lower benefits. Do we want our children to have fewer opportunites for education . . . Your EC have no hesitation in urging you to vote Labour . . . for the benefit and advantage of the whole people and not for a favoured few.

Thanks to the peculiarities of our electoral system, the election was won by Britain's ebullient wartime leader, Winston Churchill, with the Conservatives getting 321 seats with 13,717,538 votes, against Labours 295 seats for 13,948,605 votes.

At the 1952 Biennial at Skegness, E. J. Wilkins, Berks, successfully moved a resolution calling for 'a strong and united effort by the Labour and Trades Union movement for a speedy removal of the Tory Government.' It also called for a 'careful study' of the policies pursued by the Labour Government, and considered that wage freezing and the failure to abolish the tied cottage had contributed to its defeat. It wanted the Union to support a new policy within the Labour Party of higher wages, stable prices, reduction of profits and nationalisation of key industries.

In the *Landworker* of February 1952, Alfred Dann appealed for increased production. Because of the economic crisis it was estimated that the amount by which consumption exceeded our production was £2 million a day (imports were running at 14% higher in the first nine months of 1951 over the same period of 1950, whereas exports were only 6% higher). The Government declared that at all costs this gap had to be bridged, and MAFF made plans to still further expand agriculture.*

Alfred outlined the things that could be done. He wanted the Agricultural Executive Committees reconstituted because they were slack and had lost their wartime driving force. He wanted bad farmers brought up to the average level of efficiency and the Hill Farming Act extended. He again appealed for the greater use of equipment be 'scaled down' so that 80% of British farms

---

* British farmers registered the highest output per head in Western Europe during 1950, a United Nations' Economic Commission reported in 1953. Each worker produced £558 worth of goods. Belgium came second with £465 per head, then Denmark at £430, Switzerland £413, Sweden, Holland and Luxembourg £303 each. Norway, France, Eire and West Germany £198, Greece £145, Finland and Italy £123.

under 100 acres could use it economically and efficiently. He wanted efficiency raised by increasing facilities for training farmworkers and more scientific research into modern farming practice.

Many farmers were not so co-operative. Farmers should not help the Government to increase food production unless their demands for more price incentives were met, was the advice given to Slough and District farmers by the county vice-chairman of the NFU. What an outcry there would have been from Fleet Street if farmworkers said that they would not help to increase food supplies unless their wage demands were met.

At Labour's 51st Annual Conference at Morecambe that year, a successful Union resolution called for 'practical measures designed to achieve a planned production fully related to the needs of the nation . . .' and 'to ensure nutritional value and interest to our national diet that the horticultural side of the industry shall be included in any such future planning.'

*   *   *

The first banner ever possessed by the Union was in July 1952 formally handed over by Edwin Gooch to officials of the Social Centre at Burston, Norfolk, the scene of the famous school strike. The banner was originally presented to the Union by Mrs. B. Adams, of London, a member of the Social Democratic Federation and was accepted by A. Moore on behalf of the Burston officials at a meeting of Norfolk County Committee. J. T. Coe said it would bring back to older members happy memories of the days when they marched from parish to parish during their Sunday demonstrations. The banner, light brown in colour, was hand embroidered with corn in a scroll design, flanked by leaves and flowers. In the centre is a picture of a winged plough. It is inscribed National Agricultural Labourers and Rural Workers' Union and 'We sow the seed that feeds the world'.

Burnham Market (Norfolk) branch set up two records in 1952. Edwin Gooch presented Silver Badges to a record number of 36 members with 30 or more years' unbroken membership. Among them were T. Snell and his four sons, a record of family service.

Labour Pamphlet Criticised

Over 1,200 delegates gathered for Labour's 51st Annual Conference at Morecambe in 1952. The delegates, after six years of constraint while Labour was in power, now felt free to express their views. Harry Earnshaw, chair, 'talked sound sense,' said the *Landworker*, when he reminded delegates that the basic trouble with Britain was that it was consuming more than it was paying for, and that no policy was any good which did not grapple with this fundamental fact. Edwin Gooch was returned to the NEC by 4,823,0000 votes, third in the list of successful trade union candidates.

Criticism of Labour's discussion pamphlet *Our Daily Bread* was voiced by C. H. Chandler for the Union. He said that some of its proposals would arouse considerable dissent among organised workers. For example, the pamphlet did not favour the abolition of the tied cottage. Local leaders of the Union were receiving from Tory MPs copies of the pamphlet, with a letter saying it was clear that the party had shifted its ground on tied cottages and now regarded some such cottages as essential.

*   *   *

No better way of assessing the state of the Union can be had than by looking at a few statistics for 1952, a year of incessant activity. Union DOs travelled 420,343 miles, attended 6,121 Union and public meetings and made 12,662 visits. Their attendance upon agricultural wages committees, county agricultural executives, courts of referees and other bodies totalled 2,288. During the year 17,334 new members were enrolled and 455 more branches established. The EC reported that the great majority of branch secretaries continued to keep members contribution registers in an excellent manner. During the year there were 15,548 quarterly branch audits; of these 15,121 showed complete accuracy.

All this activity resulted in improvements that year in wages for farm and horticultural workers, for roadmen, sugar beet workers, drainage workers, flax workers, and workers in other rural occupations.

*   *   *

In February 1953, a natural disaster occurred that was to profoundly affect many farmworkers. An exceptional wind lashed the sea of our low-lying East Coast to a fury greater than ever experienced in living memory. The wind-whipped waters tore holes in the barriers and rushed in an engulfing wave over thousands of acres of the country's finest farmland. Horses and cattle were drowned or marooned on little islands. Men and women laboured heroically to arrest the floods, to relieve distress, and to seal off the breaches before the next spring tides. Some 30,000 people fled from their homes and nearly 300 lost their lives. Stock, crops, land and property were destroyed or damaged.

Several branches of the Union were affected, reported the *Landworker*. 'In the Foulness area, Essex, where we have a strong branch, none of our members will be able to go to their homes for some time. They are temporarily living at Wakering. Branches at Canewdon, Canvey, Rochford and Wallasea Isle are also affected.'

In the House of Commons, Edwin Gooch said that he had received many reports from his constituency of brave deeds. 'We can never repay the men and women who did such fine and gallant work on that night.' Many of these people were NUAW members. He pleaded for more adequate coast protection schemes.

*   *   *

Writing in the *Landworker* in 1953, Alfred Dann said that the 1947 Agriculture Act was under fire from some industrialists who wanted cheap food
to enable them to pay low wages. The Act was also criticised by the
pseudo-champions of the farmers 'liberty', who talked 'clotted nonsense'
about it making farmers into slaves, stealing their individual freedom and
all the rest of it. The farmers who were now clamouring for freedom from
control and a reversion to a free market for produce 'are sapping the
foundations of the greatest and soundest agricultural policy the country has
ever known.'

Many NUAW branches kept passing resolutions on the necessity of
maintaining a prosperous agriculture. W. E. Cave, prospective Labour candidate for Devizes, told Wiltshire members that he did not think many people
realised how dependent the country was on food imports. 'During the last
year [1952] £1.25 billion worth of food was imported. Exports came to £2.7
billions. So it took approximately half our exports to pay for food imports.'
The way to put Britain's economic situation right was to grow more food.

The drift from the land continued in 1953, with the 20,000 regular male
workers who left the previous year, making an average decrease of skilled men
of 15,000 a year. The call-up of young farmworkers did not account for half
the loss. One disturbing feature of the exodus was the number of skilled
workers between 25 and 40 who changed their occupation. These men
were the backbone of the agricultural labour force. Many agricultural
workers released from the Forces were unwilling to return to their old
occupations.

Despite the lack of response by the Conservative Government, the NUAW
continued to spend time and money on policy documents designed to increase
food production. This practice of issuing policy documents for their respective
industries was continued by most unions till the 1980s, when the Thatcherite
Government abandoned all pretence of working with the unions for the
national good.

Union Policy Statement

Introducing *Health and Wealth Under Our Feet*, an NUAW statement on agriculture in 1953, Edwin Gooch said that the Union was breaking new ground
in preparing a policy document which covered most aspects of farming and
embodied suggestions for maintaining a healthy, sound, efficient and prosperous agriculture. He was disturbed by the undermining of the 1947
Agriculture Act, and thought farming was again at the crossroads with the
absence of anything resembling a long-term policy for the industry. He said
the Union favoured the continuance of subsidies but not a programme of
marketing very cheap food at the expense of the producer.

Harold Collison, of head office, said the cost to the consumer might be reduced if the costs of distribution were lessened. That was a matter which the Government, NFU and the Union would have to tackle. George Brown, Parliamentary Secretary to MAFF in the last Government, said that the policy document had been launched at a time when producers were less certain about what they were going to have to pay for their raw materials or the price they would get.

Later in 1953, the Union was concerned over the Government's decision to terminate control over livestock marketing and meat distribution. The system of guaranteed prices under the 1947 Act had encouraged the development of home-produced meat. The farmers and meat traders had expressed diametrically opposed views as to what should take the place of the present controls. The farmers wanted a producers' controlled marketing board and the traders a return to pre-war auctions with a system of deficiency payments. The Union did not regard either as satisfactory to the industry or the consumer and said that a Public Commission should be established, responsible for livestock marketing, slaughtering, meat importing and distribution. With the TUC they strongly opposed a return to the pre-war system.

One problem facing farmers in the 1950s was competition from some fresh food imports. In 1954, Gooch supported in the House of Commons proposals to raise import duties on certain classes of fresh fruit and vegetables, because 'the horticultural industry was worth preserving.' It was a most important industry with an investment of some £80 million and a workforce of 150,000 people. He did not think the tariffs proposed would increase prices to the housewife, but condemned the Government for reducing food subsidies and thus making it more difficult for many deserving people to live. A bolder policy for marketing and distribution was needed, particularly with regard to middlemen who got too much out of fruit and vegetables. (The problem of marketing is dealt with more thoroughly in Chapter 19).

The fear that the Government's agricultural policy was the beginning of the second betrayal of the industry in a little more than 30 years by the same political party was expressed by G. G. Griffen, presiding at the annual conference of branch officials at Winchester in 1954. The conference declared that this policy was disastrous to British farming.

This familiar pattern of farming under a Tory Government in peace time was reflected in the June 1954 returns of MAFF. A decrease in crop area of 429,000 acres, an increase in the amount of land down to permanent grass, and a drift of a further 24,500 workers from the industry were some of the facts revealed.

Yet again at the Labour Conference at Scarborough that year, Harold Collison moved a successful composite calling for maximum home food production, and Gooch reaffirmed that Labour's NEC stood by the 1947 Agriculture Act.

But the Union was far from happy with the 'workers' stake' in the industry. The *Landworker* in March 1955, referring to wages declared:

> Even if the farmers were able to satisfy the Government that they could not afford the extra 7s a week it was still not necessary to burden the Exchequer with the cost of it (through guaranteed prices). The Government should have taken action to reduce or eliminate the profits of middlemen . . . and thus ensured . . . the farmers could pay the extra wages . . .

After the May 1955 General Election the *Landworker* said, 'A Conservative Government with a comfortable majority – that is the unpleasant fact which we have to face up to.' It spoke of the 'muddle and uncertainty' created in the industry by three and a half years of Tory rule, and made one apprehensive of what was to come, but they 'must never lose sight of the fact that even a Tory Government can be prodded and pushed into action by determined and organised activity.'

And although the new Government seemed largely immune to such prodding, the Union never stopped trying. At the 1955 TUC at Southport, Harry Pearson, Kent DO, put the Union's point of view during a discussion on a successful resolution calling for 'more effective action' against monopolies. He said that 'the cost of machinery, fertilisers and feeding stuffs, if kept artificially high by monopolistic or restrictive practices . . . means that the subsidy which . . . the Government pays to the farmer is in effect going into the pockets of the firms which supplied the industry.'

At that year's Biennial, a resolution calling for a vote of complete no confidence in the Government's agricultural policy and for a long-term plan for the production and marketing of all agricultural produce was carried unanimously.

REFERENCE

1. Minutes of Joint Meeting, July 1947.

4

An Outstanding Leader Dies

Alfred Dann is Succeeded by Harold Collison

The death of Alfred Dann on 19 January 1953, at the age of 59, came as a great shock to Union members. A Londoner born and bred, Alfred had been General Secretary since 1944, but it was an accident of war that brought him into the Union. In the First World War he went from a solicitor's office into the Army and was stationed in Fakenham, where, as one of the soldiers 'lent out' to do ploughing in the food production drive, he had his earliest experience of farming. He learnt at first hand of the long oppression of food producers and soon came into contact with the Union, whose headquarters were then at Fakenham.

Alfred, up until then a Tory, began to help with Union activities, and when the Union moved to London, he took charge of the newly established Legal Department, where his training was invaluable.

In 1941, the General Secretary, Bill Holmes, visited New Zealand, Australia and South Africa for the TUC, and Alfred who had been chief of the headquarters' staff since 1928, became acting General Secretary.

It fell to him as deputy leader of the workers' side of the AWB to conduct the fight which brought, in 1941, the biggest single advance in wages ever received, and raised the national minimum to £3 a week. When, in 1944, Bill retired, Alfred was elected to succeed him by an overwhelming majority.

His outstanding quality was his honesty of purpose. His forthright speeches, devoid of tricks of oratory, found the mark because he obviously believed what he said. With a Cockney accent he could not entirely lose (there is nothing to suppose that he ever wanted to), farmworkers had great confidence in him, and he was very welcome in their homes. He had a few interests outside the Labour movement, his home and his suburban garden.

The funeral was at Golders Green Crematorium. Edwin Gooch, Bill Holmes, members of the EC, head office staff, regional officials and members were present. Lord Wise attend for the Labour Party.

Harold Collison was elected to succeed as General Secretary. He topped a heavy poll in 1953 with 42,785 votes. Other candidates polled: Edgar Pill 31,362; Bert Hazell 24,043; Stan Brumby 21,815; Jack Lambley 8,805; Albert Hilton 8,315 and C. R. Allcorn 3,426.

Harold was 43, and had been educated at Haycurrie LCC School, Poplar, and the Crypt School, Gloucester, until he was 17. He first worked on a farm of a relative, and later as a poultryman and general farmworker. In 1940, he helped form the Stroud & District branch and became secretary. By the end of the year it had 150 members. In 1941, he was appointed secretary of Gloucestershire County Committee, which he occupied until appointed DO for Gloucestershire and Worcestershire in 1944. In 1946, he was appointed head of the Movements Department at head office and in 1948 took charge of the Organising Department as well. For a time he had been secretary of Stroud Labour Party.

An able speaker, he addressed members in all parts of Britain, and by the time he became General Secretary had spoken at hundreds of public meetings. On his appointment he wrote in the *Landworker*:

> I am deeply conscious of the responsibility which now rests on my shoulders . . . with the help of God I shall strive to play a worthy part in assisting to complete the work so ably carried to its present point of achievement by our great organisation . . . and I would endeavour to work with them all [members] as a friend and comrade.

At the 52nd Labour Conference at Margate in 1953, in the election for the NEC, Gooch polled 4,828 votes, again third in the list of successful candidates.

Arthur Holness retired in 1954 as editor of the *Landworker*. A 'man of Kent', Arthur never ceased to extol the glories of his native county. In his younger days he was a Methodist lay preacher and a member of the ILP. As a conscientious objector in the First World War he worked on farms in Kent where there was no rural trade unionism. He was soon enrolling Union members, opening 20 branches. At the end of hostilities he was appointed DO for Northants, and by the end of 1919 had set up 71 branches and enrolled 3,000 members.

Soon after he was appointed national organiser and played an important part in the farmworkers' strike in Northants and was a member of the 1923 Norfolk Strike Committee. He became editor of the *Landworker* in 1940, where his character, wit and literary ability was reflected on every page. An avid reader, with an insatiable thirst for knowledge, he could write authoritatively on subjects ranging from beards to birds.

Dennis Hodsdon, DO, Holland Division, Lincs, took over the editorship, and was succeeded as DO by Jack Boddy.

Co-operation with the NFU

Early in 1954, at the annual dinner of the Downham Market (Norfolk) District Committee, Gooch called for the NUAW and NFU to work together. 'I sometimes think it is unfortunate,' he said, 'that farmers and workers operate in separate compartments when dealing with the welfare of farming. If disaster comes to farming we all go down the drain together. It was so last time. Why cannot we do a bit of collective thinking? Why cannot we envisage working together on policy?'

Co-operation with the NFU had always been the hope of Edwin, and this took various forms. In December 1943, the EC decided by six votes to five to have a lunch meeting with farmers' leaders, 'on condition that the proceedings would be private'.[1] Subsequently it agreed to a fuller conference on the same condition.[2]

Following these talks came an invitation from the NFU to send representatives to examine the possibilities of a joint NFU/NUAW agricultural policy. The NUAW sent Edwin and Alfred Dann.[3] The Labour Party heard of these meetings and became worried, so much so, that in his opening address to the 1944 Biennial Edwin thought it wise to round it off with the assurance that his references to agricultural policy 'did not mean that the Union was abandoning the agricultural policy of the Labour Party.'

That co-operation with the NFU had gone some way, is shown by the fact that the opening of the 1944 conference was preceded by an EC meeting attended by Sir James Turner and Mr. Knowles, President and Secretary of the NFU. Conference was asked to approve further meetings; this was grudgingly given after a long debate remarkable for the number of references to leopards and spots and devils and long spoons.[4]

Edwin told the Conference he hoped that they would be able to tell the Government what the agricultural industry thought it ought to do. 'Agreement on policy was half the battle won.' He later told the Norfolk County Committee that 'the decision to meet the NFU was common sense. All concerned with the future of the industry must sink or swim together.'

It was soon evident that the NFU preferred to do the swimming and preliminary meetings with them led to friction when the NFU wanted to extend an invitation to the TGWU. The NUAW would not agree and the NFU gave in 'for the time being'.

The EC attended with Organisers a Summer School in Oxford to prepare their contribution to a joint policy on agriculture with the NFU. The Organisers were suspicious, having largely been unaware of the project. NFU top brass, like the diplomatic Sir James Turner, were not the same as the backwoodsmen they knew – the farmers on district wages committees, the evicting and the underpaying farmer. They could see no point in the discussions when Edwin explained that wages and hours were excluded from the joint agenda.

A Joint Consultative Committee of the two unions was set up and a draft policy prepared, with the biggest area of agreement being on retaining British agriculture on its wartime scale with guaranteed markets and prices. Joint Consultative Committee meetings were held regularly, without achieving much; it discussed the weight of sacks and a uniform pay-day, but failed to accomplish even these small reforms. The Union later abandoned attempts to reach common policy with the NFU.

But Edwin and a few in the NFU never gave up hopes of such co-operation, as was evidenced at the Downham Market dinner mentioned earlier. Despite agreement from Mr. E. W. Porter, former chairman of Downham NFU, that the two unions working together could achieve more than they could separately, there is little evidence that Edwin's ideas on this were ever taken seriously by the NFU and acted on nationally.

Yet later, in 1954, at a dinner of the Penzance District Committee, similar calls for united action were made. For the first time at a Cornish NUAW function, a representative of the NFU was present and agreed with Bro. Martin that there should be closer co-operation between the two unions.

In 1956, another attempt at NUAW/NFU co-operation was made. A meeting was held between representatives of Worcestershire NFU, NUAW and the CLA which agreed that a county liaison committee should be formed for regular meetings to discuss local problems and to 'instigate joint action where this appears appropriate'. The work of the committee was not to include such matters as the price review and wage claims. It all fizzled out after a short while.

Earlier attempts to work with the NFU had been condemned in the *Landworker* by the then General Secretary, Robert Walker, as 'illusory, for they ignored the real struggle between capitalism and the working class.' Walker's attitude helped give the Union a radical complexion at the time.

*   *   *

There was a tradition of 'family' membership amongst some of the Union's most devoted supporters, and the January 1956 issue of the *Landworker* illustrated this with a photograph of the Mickleburgh family of Norfolk: Mr. and Mrs. H. Mickleburgh, together with their six sons, who had all been members of the Union since leaving school. Bro. Mickleburgh of Hillington, had notched up 48 years' membership; his son Arthur 35, William 32, Sidney 29, Fred 26, Ted 24 and John 12. This gave them a total of 206 years. Also mentioned was C. F. Layton, chairman of Sculthorpe branch. He was 83 and had 38 years' membership. The records of his five sons were: Edmund 40, Fred 40, Richard 36, Arthur 27 and Harold 27, a total of 208 years.

More than one family had every member in the Union, but how many could claim twelve NUAW members? That was the achievement of the Bedford family of Croft, Lincs. Twelve – consisting of mum, dad, nine sons and one daughter. Theirs was the third generation to work on the land; Bro. Bedford, senior, was one of 12 children, his father one of 22.

*   *   *

Changes were made in Organisers' districts in 1954 to reduce areas some had to cover, and a new district comprising Herts, Beds, Middlesex and the Lea Valley was created, with C. R. Allcorn as DO.

The annual Conference of Holland branches at Spalding in 1954 was the first since Jack Boddy took over as DO, and he was able to report that 450 new members had been enrolled in 1953 and the income was £12,050. Total labour force had fallen by 456 compared with June 1952, but he felt sure the new recruiting campaign would pay dividends.

Reflecting on his 25 years as President, Gooch, in the *Landworker* in 1954, wrote that the rise of the farmworker in the social scale was synchronised with and indeed mainly due to the growing strength of the Union. In 1928, there were 998 branches, now there were 3,739. Eleven organisers were then at work in the districts; now there were 36. Head office staff had increased from about 15 to 60. 'The progress of the Union has exceeded the hopes of the most sanguine of the pioneers.'

He went on to outline changes at head office. The Legal Department had in the past dealt with all matters relating to accidents, cottage cases and wages claims, and the Organising and Movements Department dealt with organising matters and work appertaining to wage movements among all members, except agricultural workers, whose interests had always been the special responsibility of the General Secretary. It had been decided to ease pressure on these two departments by forming a Wages Department with Reg Bottini of the Legal Department its head.

Reg, who was 37, married, had been connected with Labour and trade unions from the day he left school, when he applied to join the Labour Party even before he sought a job. As a clerk in 1940, he was directed to land drainage work and joined the Union. In 1945, he was made assistant to E. Hennem, head of the Legal Department. Since then he had been responsible for over 9,000 individual claims which had resulted in £30,000 being recovered for members. Kevin Graves took his place in the Legal Department.

Growing Strength

The 1954 Biennial at Cheltenham revealed the Union stronger than it had ever been in its history. The annual reports for 1952–3 spoke for themselves. No membership figures were given but the Union had achieved an all-time record the previous years, with a national income of over £230,000 and nearly 15,000 new members. Total funds at the end of 1953 stood at nearly half a million pounds.

Commenting on differences between the 1954 TUC and earlier ones, the *Landworker* said:

> There would have been much more talk of 'Brothers' at earlier conferences. Not once from the floor and only once from the platform did we hear delegates referred to as 'Brother So and So'. The only occasion on which the chairman used it was when he wanted to attract the attention of a delegate on the rostrum 'Your time is up, Brother.' 'Mister', 'Sir' and even 'Right Honourable' were bandied about across the floor. It may be a sign of the times, but to our mind it takes away some of the distinctiveness of a TU gathering.

East and North Yorks County Conferences in 1954 condemned the BBC for giving so small a part to farmworkers in the 'Archers'. 'Country life is not complete without the NUAW,' said R. Crackles, Easingwold. 'It seems to me that all it shows is country life centred upon Young Farmers' Clubs, the NFU and Women's Institutes.'

Like most trade unions, the NUAW had to face hostility from the media although, during the early post-war years, many Tory newspapers supported its claims for higher wages. However, by omission and outright lies, newspapers generally could and did rouse public dislike of trade unions to a high level, and often the unions had little chance of redress. At an EC meeting in 1981, concern was expressed at the content of the BBC programme *Farming Today* relating to the merger talks, and 'they would consider approaching the BBC on any inaccuracies.'[5] They had difficulty in obtaining a transcript of the programme and it appears that nothing was done about it. But at the same EC, it was reported that a cheque for an undisclosed sum had been received from the BBC 'in compensation for certain remarks made earlier in the year concerning the Union's negotiators on the AWB, and that an apology had been made.' Such climbdowns by the media are not generally known to the public; if they were, the proverbial man in the street might have a truer conception of some trade union activities.

During the Dorset Conference in 1955, the new Dorset banner was unveiled by Harold Collison. It was referred to as 'a symbol of the Union's determination to march forwards' and showed two men – one in shackles and the other flourishing a spanner – depicting the social and technical progress of the industry.

Reflecting the growth of the Union, the Grand Rally organised by the Lincolnshire County Committee in Skegness in July 1955 proved to be among the most successful ever. Stan Brumby, secretary of the committee, and thousands of members and their wives gathered to hear Harold Collison and Hugh Dalton, MP. Syd King, DO, presided at the meeting, which was preceded by a parade in which three silver bands and hundreds of members with banners took part. The parade was headed by members dressed in old fashioned smocks and carrying posters about wages 'in our grandfather's day'. They were followed by a member driving a tractor and others depicting the farmworker in modern times; they in their turn were followed by members carrying posters demanding that 'wages kept up with the times'. Thousands of holidaymakers watched.

No burning issues were discussed at the Labour Conference at Margate in 1955 and the *Landworker* commented:

> Many of us left the conference . . . thinking that it was a good job the trade unions were in the Labour Party to keep it on the move . . . it would either have remained stationary or dropped into reverse for all the impetus which the politicians provided.

An attitude completely contrary to that of some Labour leaders in the seventies and eighties who sought to reduce trade union influence to a minimum.

*   *   *

Norfolk, home of rural militancy, was largely responsible for the founding of the old George Edwards Union, and in the new union there were a number of Communists. The 1955 North Norfolk Conference adopted a resolution urging that 'no member of the Union who is a Communist or has Communist sympathies should be allowed to hold any office in this Union.' This led to a spate of letters in the *Landworker*. 'How often have I read of the struggle and privations of our comrades in Norfolk in the years gone by,' wrote E. L. Lloyd Roberts, of Denbigh, North Wales, expressing displeasure at the resolution. 'They were men of independent opinions and their struggles against the "landed gentry" – who considered that farmworkers were unable to think for themselves – remain to their eternal credit. How proud they must be of their descendants in North Norfolk!'

'I have . . . been a member of the Labour Party for many years; but from time to time I have found myself supporting demands which Communists have also supported – for example a few years ago it was labelled "Communist" to utter the words "Peace" . . . or even to oppose wage restraint, all of which are quite respectable today. If the Norfolk resolution was acted upon . . . thousands of members who support a more progressive policy for the Union and the Labour Party would be victimised . . .' L. Shears, Winterbourne Kingston, Dorset.

'I feel sure such a motion at our Dorset County Conference would be decisively defeated . . . We have an organiser who is well known to be a member of the Communist Party, and far from wrecking our organisation he has strengthened it considerably. . .' J. J. Waterman, Spettisbury.

It appears little was ever done to formally put the Norfolk resolution into effect, but the Dorset DO mentioned was later dismissed. However, in the years that followed, one Norfolk Communist, Wilf Page, was to be member of the Union's EC, represent it on important bodies and was respected throughout the trade union movement. Times, and the Union, had changed.

*   *   *

The court room which was the scene of the best-known incident in trade union history became the property of the TUC in the mid-fifties. It became a memorial to the Tolpuddle Martyrs who were tried there. The TUC took over the Old Crown Court in Dorchester in 1955 when it ended its 160 years of life as a law court. A TUC statement said it was to be 'preserved as a national memorial to the six men whose stand for the right to organise . . . became a part of our social heritage.'

New Policy for Agriculture

The Conservative Government announced a new long-term policy for agriculture in 1956, and Harold Collison said that, surprisingly, the new proposals were firmly in line with the principles of the Labour Government's Agriculture Act. 'The new proposals have been welcomed by the farmers as a sound and satisfactory basis for the future. And it would appear they have every reason to be satisfied.'6 The Government had undertaken that the total guaranteed income of the industry, then assessed at £1,150 million a year, would not be reduced in any one year by more than 2½%. If production costs rose, the amount of the increase would be offset against the possible 2½% decrease. Harold declared, 'Agriculture appears to have got a large measure of the security to which we have always argued that it is entitled. What we have got to do now is to work to ensure that the industry provides wages and conditions for the workers which will be as satisfactory to them as the new proposals are to the farmers.'

Later, in 1957, the EC issued a statement confirming that a prosperous agricultural industry was essential for the economic well-being of the nation; and strongly opposed any suggestion that agriculture and horticulture products should be brought within the framework of the proposed European Free Trade Area (see Chapter 14 on the Common Market).

It was in 1957 that there were again ominous noises from official quarters on the need for retrenchment in agriculture, particularly in milk and eggs. Production levels were beginning to suggest that they exceeded immediate demands. Britain still imported large quantities of food, and the individual consumption of milk and eggs was less than in other developed countries. The Government's niggardly policies on pensions and welfare milk had checked consumption in those parts of the community needing them most. Overproduction was not that great; if everyone in Britain had eaten one extra egg in the first four months of 1957, the so-called surplus would not have existed.

Labour issued a new policy statement, *Prosper the Plough*. It was based firmly on the 1947 Agriculture Act and proposed to continue the system of price reviews with a return to the system of guaranteed fixed prices, in place of the less satisfactory system of deficiency payments. It pointed out that agriculture was saving the country £400 million a year on imports, and even though only 5% of the population was engaged in agriculture, there was a considerable interdependence of urban and rural prosperity. But it took the view 'that the State cannot itself make agriculture profitable and that it should not be the Government's job to bolster up an inefficient industry indefinitely.'

The *Landworker* was supportive, but noted that unlike the Union's *Health and Wealth Under Our Feet* programme, the new document made no mention of land nationalisation. However, one important proposal would meet with the approval of all sections of the industry, that Labour should establish Treasury loans for farmers. It also proposed permanent machinery to encourage co-operation among farmers, 'a point strongly emphasised in our own policy document'. For farmworkers there were a number of undertakings, probably most important a promise to legislate on the tied cottage, backing for a wages-during-sickness scheme and adequate safety regulations. This document was drawn up by a committee presided over by Edwin Gooch, with Harold Collison and Sydney Dye among its members.

Edwin introduced *Prosper the Plough* at the 1958 Labour Conference, at Scarborough, as a practical policy to be implemented by the next Labour Government. Harold then successfully moved a composite deploring the Tory Government's action in repealing Part II of the 1947 Agriculture Act, welcomed *Prosper the Plough* and called for the restoration of disciplinary powers, provision of short-term credit, re-establishing CAECs, encouragement of co-operation and a satisfactory level of prosperity in the industry.

At the 1960 Biennial, F. Robinson, EC, said that the Government had said that farm incomes should be improved by increased efficiency and not increased gross output. 'This, with the 2½% cut in guarantees, meant that agriculture had been singled out to be penalised for its increased efficiency.' The motion before Conference was moved by F. Waterman, Dorset, stating the Union's *Health and Wealth Under Our Feet* was the best policy for agriculture and instructed the EC to seek its adoption by the Labour Party. J. Dunman, Berks, praising the document, wanted more done by the Union to push the policy in the Labour Party and spoke of the big monopolies dealing with agriculture who 'suck the blood out of the industry'. Other delegates wanted the Union to watch the trend towards larger farming units and T. Hanson, E. Yorks, thought the most economic farming units would be around 400 to 500 acres. The motion was carried.

The agricultural labour force continued to decline. By the end of 1961, the number of full-time workers was down by 18,900. The total labour force in December 1961 was 486,000, against 527,000 the previous December. Yet production continued to rise, with increases in beef and dairy cows, pigs, sheep and fowl. The acreage of wheat increased by over a million acres. 'The only drop shown by the census is in the labour figures,' said the *Farmers' Weekly*, without further comment. Silence on its part was perhaps wise, for even taking into consideration the increased inputs, there must have been a startling rise in output per worker.

REFERENCES

1. EC Minutes, December 1943.
2. EC Minutes, February 1944.
3. EC Minutes, March 1944.
4. M. Madden, *op. cit.*
5. EC Minutes, September 1981.
6. *Landworker*, January 1957.

Loss of Farmland

Remarkable Increase in Productivity

In the sixties, Britain was losing agricultural land at the rate of 50,000 to 75,000 acres a year. And potential farm land was being mis-used or under-used. One gentleman who owned 500 acres of deer forest liked to boast that he employed only three gamekeepers. The 1968 Biennial deplored the acreage which was mis-used, and wanted the Government to stop good farmland being taken for development purposes.

Despite the loss of agricultural land, some of that left was becoming far more productive. Between 1957 and 1967 the total value of cereal crops rose from £230 million to £350 million.

Wheat had always been the principal cereal import – costing £113 million in 1966–7. The main obstacle to cutting these imports was the way bread was made in Britain. Only 20% of the industry's needs were met by home-grown wheat. The main reason is that British bakers demanded a flour that would produce bread which did not go stale quickly. Harder wheats, mostly from North America, were more suitable for this purpose than the soft British wheats.

One hopeful sign was a remarkable increase in productivity in the dairy industry, according to the Economic Development Council. Between 1956 and 1966 average annual labour hours per cow dropped from 124 to 88. But only a small increase in the size of the dairy herd was possible in the next five years, because *brucellosis* eradication was under way and the losses caused by foot-and-mouth disease had to be made up. But an increase of 300,000 dairy cows was forecast by 1972, and together with significant expansion of the beef herd, the total net import savings would be £21.5 million for beef and £14 million on dairy products in 1972.

Labour's new policy statement, *Agenda for a Generation*, was introduced at the Party's 1968 Brighton Conference. The Union was quick to note glaring omissions. Agriculture was one of them. The same neglect of the country's largest single industry was evident in the handling of conference business. A composite calling upon the Government to substitute certain goods, including agricultural products, then being imported, by goods produced at home, was to have been moved by Bert Hazell, but it was removed from the programme. A hastily-organised deputation to the Arrangements Committee succeeded in getting Bert in on the general economic debate. He told delegates that only weeks before, the TUC Conference had adopted a measure seeking a substantial increase in agricultural production. There was an urgent need to save on imports and agriculture could make a substantial contribution.

By the time of the 1972 Biennial at Weymouth, Jack Dunman, Oxon, told delegates, 'The Tory Party is wrecking British agriculture . . . It is taking us into the EEC, contrary to the wishes of the great majority of the industry and it is dismantling the system of guaranteed prices and markets which has done a good job for the farmers certainly, but also for us as well.' He was moving a successful resolution which was 'alarmed' by the possible entry into the EEC, and called upon the EC to 'take the initiative in hammering out a socialist agricultural policy as the basis for a programme for the next General Election.'

That the big farmers were doing well could not be denied. Some fantastic prices were being paid for agricultural land. Up to £1,000 an acre was reported. According to MAFF, the average price during the six months ending 30 September 1972 was £234, which was £45 an acre more than the same time the previous year. And the Ministry returns showed that farm land sales had rocketed by 62% in the six months ending March 1973. A large farm in Essex was sold for £850 and acre, and £1000 an acre was not uncommon. In 1972, a 120-acre farm in Hampshire was sold for £150,000. The vendor made £50,000 on the deal – he bought it less than a week before.

'No one quite knows what has caused the recent surge,' wrote farming correspondent John Cherrington in the *Financial Times*. Nobody? The City, insurance companies and other institutions were increasingly seeing land as a good investment. The *Daily Mirror* reported that in the previous two years some 6,000 investors had put over £11 million into Property Growth Agricultural Bonds, most of which had gone on buying up land at £600 an acre.

Farmers, on the whole, continued to prosper. Prices for their produce were kept high, but at the 1975 Oxford Farming Conference, Professor D. K. Britton found the courage in a hall packed with farmers to deny that cheap food was a thing of the past. He declared, 'If in saying that food will never be cheap again, people mean that we shall never again see the time when the supply and demand situation is such that the price offered is less than the producer considers to be a reasonable return, then I would have to disagree with them. I believe that a maladjustment between supply and effective demand may still be liable to occur in almost any commodity market. Sometimes to the farmers' benefit, but sometimes to his detriment.' He concluded, 'The 1947 Act was right to place equal emphasis on stability and efficiency. But if stability is to be both enduring and profitable this will require the development of a production programme which is not rigid and uncompromising but which makes allowance for regulated adjustment in response to changing external factors.'

Conference theme was 'farming for survival', but judging by some contributions, 'tax-avoidance farming' might have been a better title. Thus Mr. W. R. Young, a Canterbury accountant, described a recent Finance Bill as

'Dracula poised to suck the life-blood of private capital from many productive enterprises.'

Ted Calver, EC, expressed concern at the continued fall in the agricultural labour force, and said more than one authoritative source feared a serious food shortage in the years ahead, 'unless the industry is geared up to meeting production targets at considerably higher levels than now exist.' Wilf Page, EC, said that about 90% of the discussion had been about 'poverty-stricken' farmers trying to avoid the wealth tax.

At the 1975 TUC, Reg Bottini moved a motion on agricultural marketing, seconded by the TGWU and adopted unanimously. It sought an extension of public control of marketing agricultural produce through an Agricultural Marketing Commission with responsibility for both home grown and im-ported foods. 'The next most important thing after the production of food,' said Reg, 'is its distribution through the wholesale and retail chains to the housewife.' He also said that the Union was 'solidly behind the Government in their declared farm expansion target of 2½% a year for the next five years.' But it had got off to a bad start, and what was needed was a vast co-operative effort, aided by decisive and far-reaching Government action.'

One answer to the agricultural crisis was the development of long-term contracts. Arrangements of this kind could only be effectively carried out by a statutory buying and selling agency with powers that went far beyond the present hotch-potch of free and controlled marketing.

At Labour's Conference at Blackpool in 1975 Reg spoke in a debate on world food sources. A motion called on Labour to reconsider its proposals in the White Paper, *Food from Our Own Resources*, on the grounds that Government policy sought an extension of the number of British livestock, which would involve increasing grain imports as a major source of food. The motion asserted that the feeding of massive amounts of grain was wasteful and abhorrent and that an increase in grain imports economically undesirable. Foreign Minister James Callaghan accepted the motion on behalf of the NEC, saying it was not the intention of the Government to abandon the proposals for agricultural expansion in the White Paper.

Changing Methods of Production

On the occasion of the Union's 70th anniversary in 1976, Bert Hazell, reviewing the past 25 years, said that the changes in methods of production had been phenomenal, and output from our ever-decreasing acreage had risen to levels never before thought possible. 'We have seen as great a revolution in production methods as was witnessed in the years of Coke of Norfolk when he introduced the four-course system of farming – and we have not yet reached the optimum. With the combined forces of the engineer, chemist and research worker, I am confident further progress will be made, although I am conscious of the fact that some will question whether in fact it is progress.'

His remarks came at a time when increasing farm mechanisation and the overall efficiency of intensive methods of production were beginning to be questioned within the Union. Widespread concern was expressed that there were now more tractors than workers on UK farms. It was suggested that whilst UK agriculture might be thriving in 20 years' time, if the drift from the land continued at its present rate into the 1990s the NUAAW was unlikely to exist. There just wouldn't be any agricultural workers left. The MAFF figures showed a drop in the farm labour force of nearly 18,000 in a single year. At that rate it would be less than 20 years before all farmworkers had disappeared from the land.

These changes in the pattern of UK farming were reflected in an increase in the total area under cereals during 1976, with increases in wheat and oats more than offsetting decreases in barley and mixed crops corn. There was a decrease in the area of fodder crops; the dairy herd was almost unchanged during the year, but the beef herd decreased. The figures showed total workers at March 1976 as 288,500, as against 298,300 in March 1975.

Productivity Rises to New Levels

Labour productivity in agriculture rose to new levels towards the end of the seventies. The *Annual Review of Agriculture, 1979* showed that figures for the previous four years for net output and labour productivity (defined as gross product per person engaged in agriculture) were as follows:

	Net product at constant prices	Labour productivity
1975	100	100
1976	91	91
1977	115	115
1978 (forecast)	122	117

Source:*Annual Review of Agriculture, 1979*

Minister of Agriculture, John Silkin, said that this confirmed 'that the farming industry has substantially increased its contribution to the nation's wealth'.

When the White Paper, *Farming and the Nation*, was published in 1979, this updated version of *Food from Our Own Resources* received favourable comment from Jack Boddy, now General Secretary, in that it continued to look at the future on an optimistic basis and indicated that increasing productivity must remain the objective, and that acknowledgement was made of the contribution of the workforce to agriculture's notable record of improved efficiency and productivity. He recalled that the problem of serious shortcomings in the marketing and processing of agricultural produce was constantly debated, and noted this was now the subject of a committee of inquiry with terms of reference to enable it to carry out a review of existing marketing arrangements. 'An examination of this issue is long overdue as the pressures on an unstable market have tremendous influence on the profitability of British agriculture.' He promised continued Union support to reach the productivity targets, but this meant 'a recognition in real terms of the skilled agricultural worker.'

Unfortunately, before the year was out, a new Thatcherite Government came to power, and all such hopes were dashed, although the Union still expressed the hope that it could 'work with them'.

Farming continued to thrive financially into the eighties, and total net farm incomes more than trebled. They rose from £504 million in 1968 to £1,737 million in 1978, while the area under cultivation dropped from 2,377 to 2,069 thousand hectares over the same period. With increased mechanisation and decreased labour requirements labour productivity rose 3.5% on average within this time scale. Financial success was achieved partly by huge subsidies that came from the same public purse, which according to the Government, could not afford to invest in education, health and welfare, housing and transport. At the same time, social benefits and pensions were being slashed in real buying power.

Not that this prosperity prevented many farmers pleading poverty when it came to wage negotiations. In August 1982, a *Landworker* editorial said that the 'real eye-opener at this year's Royal Show was the price farmers pay for machinery – without blinking. A marvellous new combine harvester, priced at £55,000, caught our reporter's eye. And it wasn't for the lucky few. Its makers were not short of potential customers.' Joan Maynard, the Union's sponsored MP in the House of Commons, unearthed a further fact about farmers' finances. The bankruptcy rate among farmers was 0.17% compared with 2% among industry as a whole.

That farmers had hit the jackpot was underlined when the Government's *Annual Review of Agriculture* was published in 1983. It showed that their incomes had nearly doubled in the previous two years. The *Review* spelt out just how big was the farmers' crock of gold. Net farm incomes went up from £1,027 million in 1980 by 24% to £1,275 million in 1981, and by a massive 45% in 1982. This meant there was an estimated £574 million jingling in farmers' pockets in 1982. Support from CAP (Common Agriculture Policy) shot up from £612 million to £972 million for the year 1982–3, a 55% hike. Labour productivity continued to rise and money paid to hire workers in the previous five years had risen by some 50% as against roughly 70% to farmers, family members and partners.

Much of this prosperity was bound up in the seventies with Britain joining the Common Market, however high a price paid for it by the consumers and taxpayers. The story cannot be fully told without examining the EEC, which is done later.

6

Progress in Living Conditions

Golden Jubilee, 1956

The Union celebrated its Golden Jubilee in 1956 – fifty years after George Edwards had another try at getting the farmworkers of Norfolk to form a Union. The Union of 1956 grew out of his efforts, and farmworkers throughout England and Wales owed much to his pioneering spirit and to the fortitude of the Norfolk men in those early days. The May issue of the *Landworker* in 1956 contained the reminiscences of old timers, together with those of leading figures, looking both backwards and forwards. Edwin Gooch recalled that when George Edwards set out to found the Union, the sceptics said it couldn't be done because the farmworkers wouldn't stick together. But it was. 'What a long way we've come, and how wonderful our advance!' Reflecting upon the great and powerful organisation the Union had become, he recalled the time when all the delegates to a biennial could have fitted into the boardroom of Headland House.

In a similar article, Harold Collison pondered on the outstanding contribution the Union had made during its 50 years. 'Some no doubt would point to the progress made in terms of living conditions, developments of transport and other rural services. Some would point to the vastly improved educational facilities made available to our children, others would draw attention to the changed nature of the industry and the part the Union has played in changing it. All of these are of importance, but underlying them all, particularly the effort the Union is making on behalf of all agricultural workers in the wages field, is the strength of our organisation.'

At the Jubilee Biennial at Yarmouth, branches sent in over 400 motions and amendments. Wages and conditions figured largely among them, and the shadow of the rejection of a recent wage claim hung heavily over discussions. But there was one bright spot. For years at biennials they had had motions on accident legislation. That year all the agitation carried out by the Union in this respect could be seen to be bearing fruit. The Agriculture [Safety, Health & Welfare] Provisions Bill, was before Parliament, and whilst not all the Union desired, was a great step forward.

At a giant Jubilee demonstration on the Sunday before the conference, Hugh Gaitskell, the new Parliamentary Labour leader who had taken over

from Clement Attlee said: 'No one would deny that over the years farmworkers have achieved a much higher degree of independence, but to complete
this task it needs more than anything, the abolition of evictions from tied
cottages. This Labour will do when we win the next General Election.'

Earlier he had marched with 3,000 members and their wives in a parade
through one of Yarmouth's main shopping streets. Among the guests at a
banquet were Sir James Turner, NFU president, Wilfred Beard, TUC
chairman, and Sydney Dye, MP.

'This is the highest honour this Union can bestow and never was it more
deserved,' said Edwin Gooch when presenting the Union's Gold Badge to Bill
Case, EC, at Wiltshire's Golden Jubilee supper. Bill was secretary of Bower-
chalke branch for over 35 years, county secretary for nearly as long and
vice-chairman of the EC for many years. D. Simpson, secretary Fiskerton
(Notts) branch and F. Collishaw, secretary East Bridgeford (Notts) branch,
also received the Gold Badge in 1957.

Aswarby Park, near Sleaford, was the setting for the Lincolnshire Show in
1956, when a great number of members visited the Union's marquee and
bought copies of *The Revolt of the Fields in Lincolnshire*, a history of the farmworkers' struggle to improve conditions. Rex Russell, the author, attended the first
day when over 350 copies were sold.

Throughout the fifties the Union sought new members, often with considerable success, but was far from achieving its aim of getting every agricultural
worker into the Union. New ideas for recruiting were constantly tried out,
and Arthur Jordan, DO, Dorset, a very successful recruiter, declared that
'only by ensuring that the area work of the Union is run as democratically as
possible . . . can the fullest co-operation of all members be expected. This is
the basis we have taken for our work in Dorset.'[1] They had a monthly *Dorset
Bulletin* to keep members informed of key events; this stimulated activity, and
was no doubt reflected in the 48 motions and amendments from Dorset to
the last Biennial. Attendance at the annual county conference was raised from
70 to 80 delegates to 120, and an important aspect of their activity was to
enable members to enjoy themselves. The annual outing numbered between
600 to 700 members and 1,200 went to the Festival of Britain (a national
exhibition in London). They ran an outing savings club and their annual
dinner attracted 250. They had their own film projector and a good film at a
meeting made it an evening for the family. They got their news to all local
papers and the BBC. They had raised sales of the *Landworker* from 829 to 1,110
in a year. There had been a fall in membership, so a number of canvassing
teams were formed, and in the first half of 1956 they enrolled 300 new
members against 200 in the same period of 1955.

Door-to-door canvassing, more publicity, more organisers and extension
of Union benefits, paid collectors and greater educational facilities, were just
a few of the suggestions put forward by district committees in reply to a head
office questionnaire on organisation in 1957. A report compiled from these
replies was considered by the Organisation Sub-Committee in order to

formulate proposals to put before the membership in accordance with a resolution at the previous year's Biennial. Replies indicated that about half the branches attended district meetings. The average attendance was highest where the committees met on weekdays and least when they met on Sundays. The majority met on Saturdays and two-thirds believed that transport difficulties prevented some branches from attending.

Many replies stressed the need for greater publicity; two-thirds of the committees said they reported their activities to the local press. The biggest reason for loss of members was transfers to other industries. Other important factors were the call-up and difficulties in collecting subs. The work of the Legal and Wages Departments was considered by more than two-thirds of the committees to provide the most successful appeal in making new members. About half considered that the next two most important factors were the Union's efforts to raise wages and the service the Union gave members. Of 123 committees, 80 said that they held organised canvasses, and all but four reported that they were successful in making new members. Forty committees did not canvass at all.

The suggestions coming up most frequently were for more organisers and smaller organising districts, paid help for organisers or paid collectors. Also some form of financial help for voluntary workers, particularly for canvassing. Canvassing, supported by letters from head office, was considered to be the best way of extending the Union's influence. Some committees felt the *Landworker* should be free and an extension of the Union's educational facilities was a fairly consistent demand.

* * *

Owing to the 1957 bus strike, the usual Tolpuddle Rally was cancelled, but members took part in other demonstrations. At Weymouth there was a parade of Dorset members, and traffic was held up in Ripon where a similar parade took place; the Cambridge County banner was carried at a rally organised by the Cambridge and Essex county committees at Felixstowe, while at Skegness, members from many counties paraded with banners flying.

A note in the *Landworker* stated that the TUC approved the new arrangement of granting a licence to Odhams Press for publishing Labour's *Daily Herald*, believing that it would preserve its existence. There was much criticism of the *Herald* among members, and Frank Robinson, EC, said in a letter that in one issue three pages were given to sport, half a page to the TUC conference, and two inches to the wages award. But the *Manchester Guardian* gave 80 lines to the wage award, had adequate coverage of the TUC, and he thought the *Herald* should do a lot better for its loyal supporters.

Douglas Machray, *Herald* editor, replied saying, 'It is better that 5 million people should willingly read, in an attractive report, what its conferences are doing, than that 4,900,000 of them should turn away from an unduly long report and therefore not be influenced by a single line of it.'

Later, the *Herald* was renamed the *Sun*, became famous for its page-three female nudes, was strongly pro-Tory and anti-trade union. The vexed question of a national newspaper for the Labour movement continued over the years, and in the eighties, a new paper, *News on Sunday* was published with backing from the unions, including the TGWU. Unfortunately it treated readers as if they had a low IQ, trivialised events, and closed down after a few months. It was disliked by many agricultural workers.

Battle to Consolidate Earlier Gains

The Union was stronger by 600 members in 1957, despite the continued drift from the land. Yet this drift resulted in many thousands of members going into other industries and was coupled with a reduction in the potential membership of the Union. 1957 was described as a year of 'consolidation, examination and experiment'; and 'Our members, branch officials and organisers have been successful in finding from the smaller labour force sufficient new members to more than replace losses to other industries and through retirement and death.'[2]

This was achieved in part by the 'growing realisation of the value of organised canvassing. Teams of members and organisers got the Union message to non-members on their doorsteps. Head office posted thousands of letters to potential recruits, and this helped canvassers to get a favourable response from non-members.' These tactics resulted from the earlier study of the Union's recruiting problems.

The 1957 report of the Chief Registrar of Friendly Societies said that the funds of the largest unions ranged from £11.3 million for the AEU, £586,000 for agricultural workers, down to £227,000 for public employees. It was a different story looked at in the light of how much per member. On that basis the amounts ranged from £23 6s 11d for iron and steel workers, £3 16s 9d for agricultural workers and £1 4s 8d for public employees.

*   *   *

With extraordinary prescience, in view of the atomic energy disaster that was to come many years later at Chernobyl, Sister G. M. Warren and E. Atkinson, Essex delegates, moved and seconded a successful motion at the 1958 Biennial relating to a serious accident at the atomic plant at Windscale, which was played down by the authorities. It read: 'This conference is perturbed at the happenings at Windscale. It feels that greater care should be taken in the future, so that a repetition should not take place.' It was supported by the EC, which recommended that local consultative committees be set up in order to establish 'public confidence.'

This was just what the authorities wanted, as part of their cover-up, but the trade unions were not to know this at the time.*

A curious sidelight on the Union's earlier desires to help the nation was revealed when Gordon Dales, Lincs, successfully moved the £5,000 interest-free loan to the Treasury be withdrawn, and used by the Union.

Delegates discussed the need for a Vice-President, but this entailed an alteration to rules and a motion in favour was defeated by 92 votes to 55.

This Biennial decided that problems of Union organisation could only be dealt with on a county basis, and the report of the EC of the replies to the questionnaire mentioned earlier was adopted. Wilf Page, Norfolk, called for a real effort by the organising staff to attract youth, and Jack Dunman, Oxon, said the report was very good but they needed more and better branch meetings. 'We believe that if we have no branch meetings we have not got a Union at all; we could have a friendly society, but that is not enough.' R. L. Jones, Wales, wanted help from the EC for canvassing, and John Hose, Notts, sought more consideration for branch secretaries by head office.

The importance of publicity was stressed by several speakers. J. Langford, Salop, said that people joined after reading in their local paper what the Union was doing on their behalf. R. Bellechamber, Bucks, noted an improvement in the Union's public relations at a national level, but their weakness was locally.

A strident letter in the *Landworker* criticised the journal. J. Bolton, Over Stratton, Somerset, said it was not easy to sell. 'A glance at the issues of the past few months explains this, for it reads like a school magazine (minor public) and for the most part is completely devoid of any sign of socialism . . . There is a sort of milk-and-water atmosphere on every page. . . ' and ended by calling upon the editor to resign.

In another letter, P. M. Gillians, Bletchington, Oxon, was 'flabbergasted' at the Union's attitude to the agricultural debate at the Labour conference. 'Nationalisation is not a panacea for all our agricultural ills, but if any farmworker thinks that the economic status of Union members can be substantially improved under capitalism, then he is living in a fool's paradise.'

---

*   The fire at the Windscale (later renamed Sellafield) reactor led to pastureland in Cumberland being highly contaminated with radioactivity. Milk from 150 farms was poured down the drains because it contained high concentrations of Strontium 90. Then it was discovered that much of the contamination had occurred from radioactive particles escaping from the reactor chimney, long before the fire. Scientists warned of the dangers, but the Tory Government decided to deceive the public as to what was happening in the interests of making plutonium at the plant for atomic bombs – never a watt of electricity was being produced there. At the time of the fire, workers at the plant were warned to stay indoors, but the public were allowed to walk the streets, and farmworkers remained in the fields. A plume of radioactivity from the fire travelled across England to Holland, and its full effects, such as causing leukemia in children, were only being publicly evaluated by the late 1980s.

But A. C. Stock, Chelmsford, perhaps unwittingly, provoked an early debate on the 'consumer society' that goes on to this day. He wanted politics left to constituency organisations and said, 'keep the *Landworker* about farm-workers and for farmworkers. As an inhabitant of a "fool's paradise" I sincerely believe that the economic status of Union members . . . is being improved under capitalism . . . and I have a TV aerial to prove it.' A remark which provoked an indignant response.* George Thirkle, Penzance, replied: 'Perhaps if we had a little more socialism Bro. Stock would also have a television set and not . . . just the aerial! However, we must not sack the editor, like all papers his journal merely reflects its readership. Until the whole country, and not just a few odd spots like Norfolk, begins to return socialist members to local and national government, we shall have to put up with lower earnings, a long working week and a painful lack of amenities.'

Jess Waterman, Blandford, Dorset, did not share Bro. Stock's opinion on the economic status of Union members under capitalism. 'The logical con-clusion of his line of reasoning is that socialism is not worth striving for whilst we can own a TV aerial'. He referred to the 600,000 unemployed saying, 'This obviously represents a considerable measure of misery and despair,' and of Stock's suggestion that the *Landworker* should be primarily concerned with farmworkers said, 'I think it is, but heaven forbid that it be an almost negative concern, with socialist views and political issues excluded.'

The controversy continued into 1959, with David Naginton, Ercall Heath, Salop, saying that, 'the political philosophy of Bro. Stock seemed to be based on two incorrect ideas: (1) That the Labour Party is socialist; and (2) that the way the basic industries are nationalised and how they are run is socialism in action. Neither was correct. Only industries not making profits were nation-alised . . . and . . . were then run by retired military men and aged trade union officials which led to a great deal of inefficiency and discontent.'

Back came Bro. Stock, revealing that he was a member of his local sailing club. He bought his boat for £75 in 1948 and he had 'several thousand hours of pleasure out of her . . . and the sun and the wind are ultimate socialists and equalisers, they shine and blow on rich and poor alike.'

G. McQueen, Morpeth, replied that some people's political education had been neglected. 'The post-war Labour Government gave us the welfare state, the present Tory Government sabotaged this by prescription charges and increased health stamp payments . . .' B. Wilson, of Writtle, Essex, thought Stock's attack on socialism fell flat because his self-defined object of attack was state capitalism, not socialism.

*   *   *

---

* When Bro. Stock was accepted for the Winter School in 1960 it was noted that he was 'an active Conservative'.

Josiah Sage, who was at the famous meeting at the Angel Hotel, North Walsham, which got the Union under way, and was on the committee that drew up a constitution, died in 1958. Joe was always very proud of his record, and was originally a member of Arch's Union. Mrs. Sage was George Edwards' secretary for many years.

Joe was a great friend of the Higdons, of Burston Strike School fame, and after their deaths, moved into their cottage. He became respected in the village, and regularly attended parish council meetings. Always interested in politics, in 1946 Joe cycled 40 miles to register his vote. At the time he was 74.

It was in December 1958 that another prominent Union figure died, Sydney Dye, the 58-year-old Labour MP for South West Norfolk. Son of a smallholder, he started work on the land at 13 and joined the Union at 16. Three years later he became secretary of Wells branch, and a year later secretary of the local Labour Party and won a scholarship to Ruskin College. Labour Agent, Methodist Lay Preacher, Norfolk County Councillor, MP – these were just some of the jobs he did. At the time of his death (he was killed in a car accident) he was on his way to the House of Commons to attend a committee on the Small Farmers Bill.

In the resulting by-election, another Union member, Albert Hilton, held the seat for Labour with 15,314 votes, against a Tory vote of 13,960.

Alf Pannell did not seek re-election to the EC that year. He first represented Essex members on it in 1928, and held many Union posts. His place on the EC was taken by C. E. Morris, secretary Epping branch. Also ending a period on the EC was Jim Bradshaw of Lancashire, whose place was taken by P. Schofield of Cheshire.

Let us take a closer look at Bro. Morris, who was to become well known in the Union.

Early Work Experience for EC Man

When Chris Morris left school just before he was 12, his first job was hoeing sugar beet at 30s an acre, which usually took about a week to do. He was put on a nine-acre field. To young Chris, it looked like a big nine acres. 'I'm going to bring a chain and measure it,' he told a workmate, who was taken aback by his cheeky boldness. Next day Chris began measuring. 'You can't do it,' pleaded his alarmed mate, 'he's watching you.' But Chris continued measuring; it was a full 10 acres. And without further ado, he went and told the farmer. 'Well lad, I bought that field as nine acres, I must have made a bargain,' said the farmer. And he paid Chris for hoeing 10 acres.

This daring confidence was to mould the pattern of Chris's life and was no doubt one of the reasons he served on the EC for 20 years, that, and a tough beginning. Chris was born in London's Marylebone – where those with extraordinary hearing claim they can hear Bow Bells – of a family of East End

Cockneys. His father was killed in the First World War when Chris was little more than a baby; his mother remarried and they moved to Thornwood Common, near Epping, where Chris attended Epping Town School. Chris was not fit, he had consumption, his mother and stepfather were both invalids, and there was a sizeable family to bring up. Chris had two sisters and a brother. His stepfather died. 'I left school to earn money to keep the family,' said Chris aged 74, when I visited him in 1988 at Epping, where he still lived.

'I knew what parish relief was all about as a child. We used to go to the Relieving Officer and he gave us a chit for 7s to 8s to take to a store to get groceries. We used to be asked if there was anything we could sell. Sell! We hadn't got any proper furniture, just bits and pieces.' For clothes, Chris and his siblings were fixed up at the workhouse. 'The lady there just handed out anything she had, whether it fitted or not. We looked a sight.' And long before his first full-time job, Chris had gone pea and potato picking.

So Chris learnt the hard way, and by the time he was 13, the men on the farm where he worked, having noted his prowess with a chain measure, were soon taking advice from him. 'We used to do a lot of piece work,' said Chris. 'The farmer would come along and suggest we do such a job at so and so. I used to work out the possibilities and was soon advising my mates on whether we should do it on piece or day rates. They usually accepted my advice.'

It was, however, some years before Chris joined the Union. His first tenuous contact was when a man who had had a row with a farmer said, 'He doesn't know I'm in the Union.' The man never told Chris what the Union was, and he remained none the wiser for several years until he joined in 1943. He had married in 1939, and he and his wife Ruby were to have two sons and two daughters. In 1943, he was working at the Copthall Estate as a sawyer and, as he was apt to, always arguing about the men's rights, and his own. One man said, 'You'd best go to the Union meeting in Epping.' He did; about half a dozen attended, and he was made chairman right away. 'I wasn't even a member,' said Chris. He soon became secretary, a district committee member and then county committee member. He stayed on the EC until 1978, when after being dogged by illness for years he had a stroke.

While on the EC he was evicted from his tied cottage. Looking back he was quite philosophical about it. 'I had a lot of time off work for political and trade union reasons, and they were fed up with it,' he said. 'They didn't rush the eviction.' Rush or not, it still meant hardship. An elderly neighbour let them live with him for 18 months, but there wasn't room for the two girls and they had to live with relatives.

Three dwellings, known as Creeds Cottages, stood empty on the outskirts of Epping. Chris asked the farmer who owned them – a fellow member of Epping Upland Parish Council – if he could have one. The farmer said 'choose one'. Chris and Ruby had been there ever since, and wouldn't want to live anywhere else, with views of the rolling countryside at the rear and the Forest just across the road.

In addition to Union work Chris was a founder member of Epping Labour Party, its secretary for many years, and its Parliamentary Agent in 1945. Union members like Chris worked hard for Labour during the 1945 General Election, but it is often said, that Norfolk apart, no rural seats resulted. This was not the complete picture. A number of semi-rural seats, like Epping on the edge of London were won.

'I'm proud of my part in getting the first Labour Government with an absolute majority,' said Chris. 'The Union played a big part in Labour's victory. We had tractors ploughing with posters saying "Vote Labour".' He recalled those days with pleasure. 'I used to go round on my bike flyposting with a bucket of paste and brush, we put up posters everywhere, on trees and barns, even on tied cottage gates.'

But it took a long time to win Labour seats on local councils. 'Farmers still had the whip hand because of the tied cottage,' said Chris. One farmer standing for the council told villagers, 'No free dung for you if I lose.' He won.

Chris never lost his boldness. Once when he was off ill for three weeks, he signed up 100 new members and got a Union shield for it. Despite all his Union and Labour Party work, Chris found time to be a governor of St. John's Comprehensive School for 40 years, and master of St. John's Church Tower for 20 years, where he taught Ruby and lots of youngsters the art of campanology.

He believed, with reservations, that the Union's biggest victory since the war had been the Rent Agricultural Act. 'It hasn't worked as well as it ought,' he said. 'It was a big improvement, more in favour of farmers than workers; it never abolished the tied cottage. It meant we were accepting the tied cottage for ever, the farmers still operate them. The Act went part of the way by stopping farmers turning anyone out, that's all.' He referred to recent appeals he had been involved in against possession, and said, 'The council agreed they had the job of supplying a house, but said they hadn't got one. The fight is still on to abolish the tied cottage. We never got wages up to where we should have done because of the tied cottage. And people are still scared to do anything because they are in a tied cottage. That's why some people are doing all this overtime today, and I know of at least one case of underpayment of wages, and again, those concerned daren't have anything done about it.'

Chris was bitterly opposed to the merger, and claimed it need not have happened if other steps had been taken. He believed the old Union should have been more economical, and recalled moving a resolution against automatic increases in EC allowances when he was on the EC. It didn't get a seconder. He also blamed the staff for seeking higher wages, and said the Union contributed too much to the staff superannuation fund. He believed the Union's decline began when it was squeezed out of organising the Norfolk roadmen. Chris was chairman of the Organising Committee when the Union was forced to sell off some of its assets. 'We should have sold Headland House, instead of merging,' he said. 'It was worth a lot of money'.

Chris, grey haired, and moving slowly, said he'd enjoyed life, 'It was just one big campaign.'

*   *   *

Maintaining its interest in broader Labour movement issues, in 1959 the *Landworker* carried a two-page spread setting out Labour's policy in the General Election and called upon members to vote Labour, as the Labour Party's aims are clear 'and they have a special appeal to the rural voter.' Labour was pledged to preserve the independent decisions of the Wages Boards and institute a payment-during-sickness scheme. 'And a cross against Labour on the ballot paper can cross out the evil of tied-house evictions for ever.'

But there were not enough crosses against Labour, which dashed hopes of a Labour Government. Some would claim that earlier readers' criticism of the lack of real socialist policy was a contributory factor in Labour's defeat. Len Pike and John Stewart were not able to pull off the Union's aim of doubling its representatives in Parliament. Edwin Gooch and Albert Hilton held well against the tide and were returned. But Stewart failed to take N Suffolk and Pike failed at Taunton.

The elections for the trade union section of the Labour NEC produced a personal triumph for Edwin Gooch. He topped the poll with 5,321,000 votes, the highest recorded in these elections.

Jack Boddy, DO for Holland, Lincs, for six years, became the new organiser for part of Norfolk in succession to Albert Hilton, who resigned on becoming an MP. His successor was Alf Witherington, of Cowbit, a former chairman of Lincolnshire County Committee and a farmworker all his life.

*   *   *

One sign of the times, and the changing countryside, was that by the late fifties many DOs ran cars, usually bought on loans from the Union. In the 1960s these loans were at 3%. They had to sign an agreement that the car was the 'absolute property of the NUAW' until all loans had been repaid.

The Union was tight when it came to loans. When Jack Boddy was buying an Austin 260 Deluxe Saloon in 1968, the total cost was £882 16s 8d, and after an allowance of £60 16s 8d for his 1960 A60, the final cost £822. After negotiating a loan with head office, he received a letter from Harold Collison with a cheque for £30 'to enable you to purchase your new car.' Jack replied, saying, 'your optimism intrigues me but then I assume you are joking! Alternatively, if you honestly believe that it is possible to purchase a new car with the exchange of my old one and £30 I am willing to pay your fare to Norfolk to undertake the negotiations on my behalf. I think I shall still be in pocket.' He got the right amount by return of post.

This loan arrangement continued until the Union's merger with the TGWU, when staff cars were provided, and as most DOs clocked up 20,000 or more miles annually, they changed each year. Earlier the Union had examined what it would cost to hire cars for organisers. This would have saved 0.24p per mile, but as neither the Union or DOs would have ever owned a car under this arrangement, the Union decided against.

*   *   *

In 1960, for the first time the Biennial was held in the North West, at Chester Town Hall. Its opening was the culmination of many years of work on the part of members in Cheshire and Flint, which were, in terms of Union history, comparatively 'new' counties. There had always been a nucleus of members in this dairying area; two branches, Audlem and Hampton, had existed since 1917, and by 1943, the number had increased to 19. When John Hockenhall became organiser in 1948, it had increased to 72. By the time of the Chester Biennial, Cheshire and Flint could boast 41 branches.

Edwin Gooch, who had recovered from an illness which prevented him attending the Isle of Wight Biennial, was given a warm welcome by delegates. He was re-elected President, thus entering his 33rd year of office. He reported improvements in membership, organisation and finances, and said that in the past two years the Union had recovered £362,313 in accident and wage claims, making a total of over £2,620,000.*

With the defeat of Labour at the General Election in the minds of delegates, some of the longest speeches were on a motion dealing with Labour policy. Proposing, Joan Maynard said that many felt the party had been moving away from socialism over the years, and the further it moved the more votes it lost. She referred to Clause 4 as the clause which asks for public ownership, and said the new Clause 10 gave the leaders 'a blank cheque to interpret it to suit themselves.' The motion called for a reaffirmation of the socialist basis of the Labour Party, public ownership of the means of production, distribution and exchange. E. A. Sales, Dorset, seconding, said, 'You do not trim your fundamental principles, which were right for Keir Hardie and just as right for us today.'

An emergency addendum moved by Jack Dunman, Oxon, considered that the proposed new Clause 10, by recognising the continuance of private enterprise and the State, buying shares in private profit-making concerns 'weakens and contradicts Clause 4 and should be rejected.' After further discussion, Harold Collison said that there was more in the Labour statement than just Clause 10. 'The people who say we should retain the old formula

---

* The Annual Report states that 11,800 new members had been enrolled, leaving a net increase at the end of the year of 1,300 over 1959. In July, subscriptions had been raised from 3s 3d to 3s 6d per week.

and not seek to expand it more fully are putting the means before the end. You do not want to make the word "socialism" a thing to be put on an altar of worship for its own sake.' He denied that to accept Clause 10 was to cease to be a socialist, and asked conference to defeat the addendum, which it did by 114 to 20 votes, and the motion was carried.

The Biennial made Union history with a decision to have a Vice-President, on a motion moved by D. Hall, Lincs, seconded by L. Miles, Norfolk. There were five nominations, but three withdrew, leaving A. V. Hilton, Norfolk, and J. Waterman, Dorset. Hilton received 88 votes, Waterman 73.

Edwin Gooch, then 73, announced in 1962 that he would not seek re-election to the House of Commons at the next Election.

The 1962 Tolpuddle Rally became a huge wage demonstration. At it, R. H. Crossman, MP, said there were three simple morals relevant in 1962, '1. Don't rely on politicians. 2. Don't think that by attending a demonstration on a Sunday afternoon, you have done your political or trade union duties. 3. When the Tolpuddle Martyrs were condemned to deportation, respectable public opinion was, overwhelmingly against them. Every good idea was opposed by respectable public opinion to start with. This is something we have to remember in the Labour movement.'

At the 1962 Biennial at Bournemouth, three stood for the vice-presidency. The votes were A. V. Hilton 61, J. Waterman 56 and W. A. J. Case 18. Hilton was therefore elected for a second term.

*   *   *

A strangely-worded item appeared in the April 1963 *Landworker* under the bland heading, 'Organising changes'. It ran: 'Bro. Cole, who since March 1949 has been the Organiser for Cornwall, will be taking over full responsibility for the County of Dorset just as soon as the EC have appointed someone to replace him in Cornwall. In the brief intervening period Bro. Cole is to be officer responsible for both counties.' It went on leisurely to give details of Bro. Cole's past work for the Union, the fact that he had 'two bonny children', and continued: 'The vacancy in Dorset was occasioned by the fact that at the end of last year, the Executive found it necessary to terminate the services of Bro. Arthur Jordan because in their view he had failed, in his capacity as a full-time officer of the Union, to conform to Union policy.' It went on to say it was a difficult decision because of his 'extremely hard work' during his 17 years on the staff, and 'the high regard with which he was held' in Dorset.

This was the first mention in the *Landworker* of the sacking, and this attempt by the EC to hide away what they had done, points to their dilemma. Jordan was one of the most successful organisers the Union ever had but, unfortunately for the EC, he was also a member of the Communist Party. Only a year earlier, the *Landworker*[3] had reported that a branch census reliably showed that 80% of farmworkers, 99% of forestry workers and 40% of roadmen in

Dorset belonged to the NUAAW. His sacking brought protests from Union members all over the country.

Edwin Gooch had been too ill to attend the EC meeting in December 1962[4] which sacked Jordan. Albert Hilton presided. Harold Collison said that Jordan had written an article in the World Federation of Trade Unions' journal and it did not conform to Union policy.* Jordan appeared before the EC and said the WFTU was not a Communist organisation and the journal's contents were 'only the expressions of trade unionists'. After Jordan had retired from the meeting, J. Waterman said the situation was regrettable as there was no complaint against Jordan's work. An amendment to the motion that Jordan be sacked was moved; it wanted him to give an undertaking to follow Union policy, but it was lost by three votes to eight, and the dismissal carried by eight votes to one, with two abstentions. There were no names in the minutes as to how people voted, so there was none of the proverbial pack drill.

At the February EC,[5] two representatives of the organisers (Syd King and Jack Brocklebank), attempted to get Jordan reinstated. A petition signed by 375 people in Dorset was presented, and a deputation from Dorset County Committee received, whose Vice-Chairman Alf Fookes felt Jordan had been dismissed for 'trivial and irrelevant reasons'. It was all to no avail, and the dismissal stood.

The minutes of the EC for the previous years reveal the extent of its 'Jordan problem'. Although he frequently appeared before them charged with promoting Communism in the Union (which he denied), they were aware of his good work, and earlier resolutions to sack him received little support. However, there were many difficulties with the Labour Party, which objected to Jordan speaking on NUAAW platforms with Labour speakers. In 1952, the Rt. Hon. Herbert Morrison was due to speak at Tolpuddle, but the Labour NEC objected to Jordan's name appearing on rally bills.

F. Brown, who disapproved of any change in 'printing arrangements', resigned from the EC and the Union in protest. The EC then decided not to organise the rally on a national basis and left it to the Dorset County Committee (which always backed Jordan) to 'get on with it',[6] and a later EC noted it was 'successful on the whole'.[7]

The *Dorset Bulletin*, that Jordan edited, frequently got up the nose of the EC. He was called before it in 1961[8] and told by Edwin Gooch that although 'it was an excellent document' it did not 'always embody Union policy'. They objected to a reference to unilateral disarmament, but J. Waterman pointed out that unilateral disarmament was accepted by the Dorset County Committee.

---

* The 1956 Biennial decided that no one should be allowed to hold office in the Union 'who is known to be acting contrary to the objectives of the Union', but rejected any political discrimination. *Landworker*, July 1956.

At the 1949 Tolpuddle rally, when a number of 'Communist' banners appeared in the procession, Alfred Dann and Edwin Gooch refused to take part in it, and Edwin also refused to speak at the subsequent rally.

Jordan not only got the backs up of some EC members, he also upset Dorset NFU – which at one time refused to work with him – and also the Forestry Commission, which banned him from their land. Later, both relented.

And it was not only peace issues which upset some members of the EC. Dorset County Committee, undoubtedly under Jordan's influence, tried to set the pace on wages and the tied cottage; it wanted the EC to take a much more militant stand. They didn't like the 'tone' of some Dorset resolutions.[9]

Jordan appears to have had widespread backing in the county, but there was some opposition to him in the Wimbourne branch. W. Martin, a member of the County Committee, frequently criticised Jordan's activities at EC meetings, and 'undertook to supply the office with further information'.[10]

So the EC finally got rid of Jordan, who asked his fellow organisers to do no more on his behalf, and went off to other work. His sacking became something of a *cause célèbre* in the Union, and it made many district organisers more circumspect. Their position had never been easy in relation to the EC. The number of DOs allowed to attend biennials was severely limited. Constant contact made them aware of members' needs and desires, and many of them became powerful centres of influence, which the post-war ECs always attempted to restrain and control. A number of DOs had been sacked in the past – none for such blatantly political reasons – hence the rise of their own Organisers' Association to negotiate pay and conditions, and doubtless to protect them from the EC where possible.*

*   *   *

At a conference of organisers at Harrogate in July 1963, Bert Hazell, surveying the membership, said, 'One day we might wake up to find ourselves parties to a takeover bid.' He felt the General Secretary (Collison) might be getting a bit away from the Union at times. He knew of his heavy commitments with the TUC, and absence of the figurehead had its effect all down the line. In reply, Harold Collison enumerated his services to the workers on the TUC, in the international field and on the Gas Board.[11]

A possible repercussion to this criticism of Collison, came two years later. Bert, by then an MP, was not invited to the next conference of organisers at Weston-Super-Mare in May 1965. Stan Brumby asked why Bert had not

---

* Several top Union officials told me of EC 'secret' minutes being kept in relation to the Jordan sacking. I could find no trace of any in the Union's depleted archives; there was reference in one EC minute to other 'private' minutes, but that referred to an entirely different matter.

been invited, 'bearing in mind that Bro. Hilton had been invited to the first conference held after he had been elected MP.' Collison explained that the EC had decided that, 'as Bro. Hazell was no longer a member of the staff he should not be invited.' Albert Hilton said a 'good deal of consideration' had been given, but the EC had decided against. Stan felt that everyone heard these remarks with 'dismay', and they 'could only draw their own conclusions.'[12]

The front page of the October 1964 *Landworker* was headlined: 'October 15th is polling day. Vote early and VOTE LABOUR.' Inside, once again many pages were devoted to why members should vote Labour. Not least because Labour promised to make eviction from tied cottages illegal unless suitable alternative accommodation were available. A trio of Union officials were standing for Labour – two in Norfolk and one in Somerset. Albert Hilton again stood for S W Norfolk, and Bert Hazell, Norfolk born and bred, seemed a good choice to follow Gooch in North Norfolk, and Len Pike was again contesting Taunton.

Labour won the General Election with a tiny overall majority. Hazell held North Norfolk by a narrow majority of 58 and Hilton lost S W Norfolk by 123 votes. Pike failed at Taunton. The new Minister of Agriculture, T. F. Peart, said they would 'implement the undertakings which were made in our election programme for agriculture . . .'

At the 1964 Biennial at Felixstowe, Edwin Gooch was unanimously re-elected President, and said that the EC would never let up in its declared aim to achieve for farmworkers a standard of living equal to that enjoyed by other workers. On the current debate on trade union structure, he made the Union's position plain. 'We accept there is room for improvement, in some cases amalgamation; and we would not evade our proper responsibilities on these issues, but we are very definite on one thing – there will always be a need for a separate union for agriculture and allied workers.' Albert Hilton was re-elected as Vice-President with a comfortable majority over Joan Maynard. In 1964, Harold Collison was elected chairman of the TUC for 1964–5.

From time to time, over the years, there was rank-and-file criticism of Union officials for taking on too many outside jobs beyond the confines of trade unionism. In 1965, King's Lynn District Committee wanted Harold Collison to 'resign from some of his appointments outside the Union in order that he can properly fulfill his duties for the membership'. This plea was rejected by the EC which said Harold had their 'full confidence'.

*   *   *

Fred Bond, the Union's Finance Officer, who retired in August 1964, never sought the limelight. He came from a strong Labour and trade union family, and joined the staff in 1921, becoming Finance Officer in 1922. He was soon to become a participant in a bitter and historic struggle. Although Edwin

Gooch was treasurer for the Norfolk Strike Committee Fund, its distribution was in the hands of Fred; a formidable task, as £11,337 was collected from outside sources. Before it had finished, the strike had cost the Union over £30,000. Fred died in 1968.

The new Finance Officer was Bill Neate, a familiar figure at conferences – as the payer of expenses. In the RAF in the First World War, he joined the Union's staff in 1919, at the age of 18. He became deputy to Fred in 1947.

Death of Respected Leader

Edwin Gooch, president of the Union for 34 years, died on 2 August 1964, at the age of 75. He was born, lived and died in Wymondham, where 400 years earlier there was the Kett Rebellion against the injustices of the times. The Kett Rebellion was a bloody affair, but Edwin was a peaceable man, and when he espoused the farmworkers' cause he did so peacefully, and perhaps in the long run, more effectively than Kett, but the farmworkers were still short-changed in many ways. Said the *Landworker*:

> In the history of our Union the name of Edwin Gooch will always be writ large and bold, and to many it might seem that his death marks the end of a chapter. In fact it marks the end of an era. For Edwin was the last of a few public spirited men who, although never farmworkers themselves, came to the assistance of those who in the early days struggled to get the Union on its feet. They gave of their spare time, knowledge and their ability, and took advantage of their relative independence, to build up the Union into an effective organisation.

Edwin gave more than his spare time. All his time became the Union's time as the years rolled by, from the days of the 1923 Norfolk Strike, to the days when he became one of the best known names in agricultural trade unionism, not only in Britain, but in many parts of the world.

Under his leadership, the NUAW did grow in size, and effectiveness, influence and prestige. And with it the status of rural workers. Tributes to him were diverse. The *Daily Express* said, 'He gained for his members the respect which their work merits. May his successor carry on the struggle until the men on the land earn as much as those in the factories.' And *The Times*, 'He lived to see his organisation become influential in trade union policies to an extent far beyond what might have been inferred from its status and membership when he first became involved.' The *Eastern Daily Press*, 'It was his forthright honesty in what he stood for which won him honour nationally and in the trade union movement, and recognition internationally in agricultural affairs.'

Tributes flowed into the NUAW from many sources including George Woodcock, TUC; Len Williams, General Secretary of the Labour Party; Christopher Soames, Minister of Agriculture and Sir Harold Woolley, NFU president.

The sun shone kindly on Wymondham as the funeral cortège wound through the streets of this small town, and walking in front of the eight-car procession, bearing 40 family mourners and some 200 wreaths, was Fred Mayhew carrying the banner of Wymondham and Silfield branch, of which Edwin had been a member since July 1919. Pall bearers were Norfolk County Committee men, R. Clarke, W. Dixon, F. Howell, B. Huson (secretary), B. Leeder, EC, and C. Winter.

Among the congregation packing the small Methodist Church were leaders of the Union, Members of Parliament and prominent trade unionists from home and abroad. The service was conducted by the Revd. M. O. Mann, and a tribute to Edwin was paid by Lord Wise who said he was a quiet man, with 'nothing flamboyant or self-seeking about him'. The service ended with the benediction from Dr. L. Flemming, Bishop of Norwich.

His death did, as the *Landworker* said, mark the end of an era, but not quite in the way the editor intended. Edwin firmly believed that only a prosperous agricultural industry could pay the workers well, and was ever ready to spring to the defence of the industry and welcomed the growing prosperity of the farmers. Little enough of this prosperity rubbed off on the workers as was his wish, and although he often expressed disappointment at what the farmers offered in the way of wages, he never changed his idea of co-operating with them.

It was Edwin who gradually altered the Union's position, who turned it from its radicalism of the twenties to that of 'moderation'. This move began with the departure of Robert Barrie Walker, the left-wing general secretary, who went off to Australia, thus giving scope to Edwin's theories of moderation.

During his years as president, he and the general secretaries, backed by the 12-strong EC and a team of officials at head office, were able year after year, to get successive biennials to back their 'moderate' thinking and actions. Often their relationship with organisers out in the field (who were frequently more militant and allowed little real say in Union policy) was tense and lacking in harmony, which led to acrimony and feuding.

After Edwin's death there was a high turnover in leading positions in the Union, and long-established moderate policies were strongly fought by left-wingers. A fundamental shift in Union policies was to take many years to emerge, and the question of where the farmworkers' loyalty should lie – with the farmers or with those of workers in other industries – was never completely resolved, only debated more heatedly.

Bert Hazell, a Norfolk man of a similar political mould to Edwin (he was later to succeed Edwin as president) played his part in resisting policies of the left-wingers, and had a great admiration for Edwin. He told me, 'Edwin and Ethel [Edwin's first wife] were both hard workers. He was a very good president, but he had his limitations. I don't think he really understood the farmworker, he trained as a journalist and found it difficult to get down to their level. He made tremendous sacrifices for the Union. I often think of him when an old man, waiting on some lonely railway platform on a cold night after addressing a meeting. He was sometimes taken in by the farmers into believing that they couldn't afford any more than they offered. He was never aggressive enough from the farmworkers' point of view. He was too kindly.'

*　　*　　*

At their meeting in August 1964, the EC unanimously elected Albert Hilton acting president until the position could be filled according to rule.

In 1965, the *Landworker* announced that Harold Collison 'sets another milestone in the history of organised farmworkers by joining the Labour benches in the House of Lords.' He had been asked by Premier Harold Wilson to assist Labour in the 'Upper' House, and had agreed, 'provided it did not involve giving up his NUAW, TUC or ILO work.' He became a Life Baron, Lord Collison of Cheshunt, CBE.

A stalwart of the 1923 Norfolk Strike, Bert Huson, was presented with the Union's Gold Badge by Mrs. Mollie Gooch, widow of the late president, at the N and S Norfolk Conference in 1964.

Row Over District Organiser

It was the practice of the Union to hold annual staff conferences, and one at Weston-Super-Mare in 1965 proved momentous for Jack Brocklebank, the energetic Yorks DO.

It met at the Grand Atlantic Hotel on 14 and 15 May, and the organisers were to meet the night before the formal conference. Jack, as chairman of the organisers, was just going to this meeting when he was met by Harold Collison. 'He was shaking,' said Jack in 1988, 'and he asked, "Can you appear before the EC". I played for time, I said, "Look Harold, I've only just arrived after a long drive from Yorkshire, can it wait?" Harold agreed.'

Jack had some inkling of what it was all about. At a Yorkshire County Committee meeting he had read a letter he had sent to Harold, and according to the EC minutes, Frank Robinson, an EC member, 'had had to remind Bro. Brocklebank that he was a paid officer of the Union.' Jack put some clothes on this bald fact. 'I must have criticised the EC and Collison's attitude to the Housing Bill in which Crossman [Housing Minister] had promised to deal with the tied cottage, but hadn't. It was a great crime to be loyal to members, you were supposed to be loyal to the EC.'

The carpeting should have taken place at 10pm on 13 May, with Jack accompanied by another organiser, Jack Boddy, but they did not turn up till 11pm. John Hose, EC, considered Jack's keeping them waiting deplorable and 'felt that the EC should not await Brocklebank's pleasure.'[13] Jack apologised, and explained there had been a misunderstanding as to the time. Harold then read the letter addressed to him concerning the Rent Bill and the tied cottage, in which he deplored the fact that Bro. Hazell had not been invited to take part in their deputations on the tied cottage, urged visiting the Prime Minister and recalling the Biennial. The EC considered Brocklebank's action a 'dereliction of duty', in that he did not follow EC policy.

Replying, Jack said that at the district committees he had attended, the EC's view was explained. He had some very vociferous members in Yorkshire. They had already been steamed up when the Protection from Eviction Bill came out, and in their view Crossman gave way to the NFU. There had been an explosive situation in the area when the Rent Bill came out and his object in reading the letter to the County Committee had been with the very best of intentions.

'For fifty to sixty years we had wanted this thing ended and it did seem to many that this was the opportunity we had all been waiting for. We saw this opportunity gradually slipping from our grasp – an opportunity that our members all over the country had been hoping, longing and waiting for. If sometimes an officer of the Union got carried away with emotion on a very serious issue of this kind he would plead it was only because he had the best interests of his members at heart.'

Harold conceded that Jack had a perfect right to write to him and express the view he did, but to read the letter to the County Committee was in conflict with the EC's decision.

After Brocklebank and Boddy had left the meeting, the EC concluded that Brocklebank had said nothing to indicate that he had followed the wishes of the EC and could not accept that he was unable to control events in his county if he wished to do so. There was a discussion as to whether he should be warned that this should not occur again or he would be dismissed; or whether he should be suspended forthwith. It was agreed that he should be required to sign an assurance that in future he would loyally support EC policy, 'failure to do which would mean instant dismissal'. If he refused to sign, he would be instantly dismissed.

Brocklebank signed. The meeting ended at 12.55am. Recalling the event, Jack commented, 'There was a suggestion that if I had been sacked, a list of those present on the EC would be put up at every Union conference, but it was the last thing I wanted. The EC was so pig-headed, it wouldn't give way, but for the sake of the unity of the Union I felt I had to sign.'

Said one organiser, 'We would have withdrawn everything on the agenda of the conference if Jack had been sacked.'

At the organisers' conference which followed, it was noted by Stan Brumby that a 'colleague had been asked to sign a document under duress' and he sought an assurance that they were 'free to express the truth as they saw it'. Collison said there was no objection to anyone at conference expressing any point of view, but as paid officials they were expected to abide by EC decisions. Albert Hilton refuted suggestions that a document had been signed under duress.

After lunch, Stan Brumby said the Organisers' Association had decided to ask the EC 'if they would kindly consider withdrawing the document which Bro. Brocklebank had been asked to sign.' The EC refused, unanimously.

A rather desultory discussion then took place on other matters and Albert Hilton closed the conference earlier than expected on the Friday. Any organiser who wished to return home was free to do so. The EC would deal with hotel bills but no daily allowance would be paid for the Saturday. It was felt that the organisers 'had committed an undeclared act of defiance'.[14]

On a suggestion of John Hose, a letter was sent to the Organisers' Association deploring the conduct of its members 'in ruining the business of the conference', adding that the EC at some future date would seriously consider terminating staff conferences.

*   *   *

For the second time in 1965, another Union leader was elevated to a life peerage. Albert Hilton, as Baron Hilton of Upton, could speak for the Union in the House of Lords.

On the election of Harold Collison to the chairmanship of the TUC for the year commencing September 1964, the EC gave him leave of absence; Dennis Hodsdon was appointed Assistant General Secretary *pro tem.*, and later confirmed Dennis's appointment as AGS, officially creating a new Union post.

On leaving Alleynes Grammar School, Stevenage, at 19, Dennis opted for agriculture, and was soon holding managerial posts in Surrey and Wilts. At 28 he was appointed organiser for Holland, Lincolnshire in 1949. Earlier he had been secretary of the large Stratford-upon-Avon branch. He was also vice-chairman of his local constituency Labour Party. When his appointment as AGC was confirmed, he relinquished the editorship of the *Landworker* to Stan Hayward, who had become a correspondence clerk in the Wages Department 12 years earlier. Previously Stan had been a farmworker in Gloucestershire where he was a branch and county secretary. He was a member of the Labour Party and on Tetbury RDC. The son of a miller, he was apprenticed to the drapery trade until he helped in his father's business. Later he became a social worker in London. A man of strong principles, he was a conscientious objector during the First World War.

Bill Neate, Finance Officer since 1964, retired two years later after a long period of service to the Union. No other officer had been employed by the Union for so long. Trams rattled along Gray's Inn Road, and trace horses had to be used to help pull loaded waggons past the head office up the incline from King's Cross when Bill started work for the Union in 1919. Bill's first job was to join three other men in dealing with wage arrears cases, which came in at a fantastic rate in those early days. One of his most significant memories was that all letters to branch secretaries had to be sealed and sent first class.* Recipients feared that otherwise their employers might find out they were Union members and sack them.

REFERENCES

1. *Landworker*, November 1956.
2. Annual Report, 1957.
3. June 1962.
4. EC Minutes, December 1962.
5. EC Minutes, February 1963.
6. EC Minutes, April 1952.
7. EC Minutes, July 1952.
8. EC Minutes, November 1961.
9. EC Minutes, August 1953.
10. EC Minutes, July 1948.
11. Report of Organisers' Conference, August 1963.
12. ibid., June 1965.
13. Minutes of EC interview with J. Brocklebank, May 1965.
14. op. cit.

---

* In those days second-class mail had to be sent unsealed.

7

Prospects for Farming Bright

Diamond Jubilee, 1966

The NUAW Diamond Jubilee Celebrations in 1966 opened with a May Day Rally in Weston-Super-Mare, where for the following five days the Union held its Biennial. Reminiscing, the *Landworker* said that agriculture was entering a period when the prospects for the industry were brighter than they had been for some years.

> Not only because there was a Labour Government . . . not only because our Union had a direct say in framing Labour's policy – which is basically a good policy; but because events of recent years compelled even the last Conservative Government to exercise some wisdom and initiate certain measures which are more appropriate to a planned than a *laissez-faire* 'let it rip' economy.

There had been another General Election and Bert Hazell retained the N Norfolk seat with a majority of nearly 700 more than he obtained in 1964; there was a national swing to Labour which increased its working majority by 92 seats. Albert Hilton was made Lord in Waiting by Premier Harold Wilson. What did the job entail, wondered many NUAW members, not too familiar with every-day Lords in Waiting. It meant that Albert, still acting President, became one of three government whips in the House of Lords, and would be Government spokesman on agriculture. Wilson said Hilton was the first farmworker 'to reach such an exalted position'. He had certainly gone a long way had Albert, from the day when as a boy he was evicted with the rest of his family from a tied cottage. At Weston-Super-Mare, Albert told delegates he would not be standing again for the presidency.

Delegates voted in Bert Hazell as the new President; the other nominee, Ted Calver, was defeated by a large majority. Bert, now 59, was the son of a farmworker in Attleborough. Like the Union's founder, George Edwards, one of Bert's first jobs when a boy was to scare crows off barley with clappers. His family moved to Wymondham, where he started work at the age of 14. At 26 he became election agent for East Norfolk Labour Party. Three years later he became NUAW organiser for the Lea Valley, but shortly after moved to East Yorkshire where he stayed as organiser for 25 years. He was appointed to the AWB in 1946, awarded the MBE the same year, followed by the CBE in 1962.

There were four candidates for the vice-presidency, and in the voting Joan Maynard, a rising star in the Labour Party, came out well on top in beating Ted Calver, R. H. Clarke, Tom Hanson and Andrew Baynham.

Conference raised contributions from 4s 10d to 5s 6d, clearly recognising that something had to be done to improve Union revenue. The fact remained that in the EC's view nothing less than 1¼ times the hourly rate was required to provide the cash to convert the disturbingly large deficit in 1965 into a credit balance in the years to come. The total income in 1965 was £316,412 and expenditure £331,245, leaving a deficit of £14,833.

An attack on trade unionism had been mounted in recent months, but if trade unions had never been invented, the technological revolution would have given birth to them, said Tony Benn at a Diamond Jubilee Rally at Weston-Super-Mare. The Postmaster General highlighted an important aspect of the Union when he said, 'The thing that really makes your Union impressive is that it doesn't take a narrow short-term view. But it has always had the courage and imagination to look ahead on the industry itself, knowing that the future of those who work in it depends upon the health and stability of the industry.'

In private session, J. Robinson, Yorks, moved, 'That this conference, in view of the economic circumstances of the Union, the appointment of the Assistant General Secretary be annulled.' Gordon Dales, Lincs, seconded. After the resolution was defeated by a large majority, Ted Sales, Dorset, then successfully moved an amendment to rules that the AGS should be elected by ballot of the membership. The question was raised as to when the election was to take place. The chairman ruled that as the appointment of the AGS had been confirmed with the acceptance of the EC report, the new rule could only apply when the post became vacant. This position was accepted.

During the private session, Ted Sales, Dorset, successfully moved that any full-time official dismissed or suspended had the right to an appeal to an Appeals Committee elected by the biennial. The five then elected were: E. Sales; E. Collinson, Hunts; W. Page, Norfolk; A. Etherington, Yorks and F. Peachey, Hants. This move was undoubtedly an outcome of the sacking of Dorset DO, Arthur Jordan.

'For God and the Union' ran a *Landworker* heading reporting Diamond Jubilee rallies. One at Thirsk, Yorks, was addressed by Jeremy Bray, MP for Middlesbrough West, who said there were now only 10,000 in agriculture in the North Riding. Sixty years earlier, people had the idea that anyone who lived a rural life should have their conditions and opportunities limited. Such ideas were out of date: 'We shall attract people to agriculture only if pay and conditions are good.' Canon S. Linsley, archdeacon of Cleveland, conducted a service on Thirsk racecourse.

An Epworth, Lincs, rally also had a religious flavour. Frank Robinson, EC, preached at a service which concluded the event, lessons being read by Harold

Snell, Laughton secretary, and George Walsham, Market Rasen secretary. Prior to the rally a service was held in Epworth Parish Church, the preacher being Canon N. Rathbone, chancellor at Lincoln Cathedral. George Curtis, DO, and Ralph M. Kitson, NFU secretary, Isle of Axholme, read the lessons.

Special speaker at the 1966 Tolpuddle Rally was Michael Foot, MP for Ebbw Vale, who stressed the importance of maintaining a strong link binding the Labour movement's industrial and political wings.

*   *   *

The front cover of the *Landworker* had a picture of the Union's new office, Headland House, opened by George Woodcock, TUC General Secretary, on 26 August 1966. In tribute to the Union's proud record during its 60 years, Woodcock said the NUAW was unique, because it was the only Union that had a group to itself on the General Council of the TUC; this ensured that there were discussions on agriculture within the TUC movement.

Attending the ceremony in addition to the EC, officials from head office, and three organisers were some 40 representatives from the counties and two Union trustees, Jack Lambley and Andrew Baynham. One special guest was Herbert Harvey from Norfolk – the only surviving member of the Union's foundation meeting at North Walsham.

It was the 1962 Biennial that voted for a new headquarters. The new accommodation and equipment were expected to cost £145,000, and be found by realising investments and not from current income; this did, however, lead to a drop in investment income. The building totalled 8,000 square feet. A lift went to the top floor, which was let to tenants. The building was of reinforced concrete with mosaic cladding on the front. Windows were double-glazed and there was gas-fired central heating. Michael Gooch, the architect, was the son of the late President. The new building was valued at £200,000, and largely because of this the balance sheet showed an increase in total assets from £692,400 in 1965 to £729,400 in 1966.

Introducing the Union's new policy statement *Farming for the Future* in the *Landworker* in July 1965, Harold Collison said it brought up to date the old policy document, *Health and Wealth Under Our Feet*. The Union believed it contained the answers to the problems facing agriculture, but *Farming for the Future* had not met with universal approval. None of the proposals were put forward for doctrinaire reasons. They arose because the Union was openly prepared to face the basic problem that confronted the industry, and they had tried to work out the best long-term solutions. 'This is particularly the case with our proposals for the public ownership of farm land – because we see no other way in which the necessary rationalisation of farming units is going to be effectively carried out.'

Writing in the *Landworker* in 1966 on the Labour Government's National Plan, Fred Peart, Minister of Agriculture, said one of its aims was to correct our balance of payments situation, which was in the red. 'Agriculture has been given a key role in the Plan.' Firstly, by increasing production it was being asked to meet a major part of the expected increase in the demand for food. Secondly, by increasing output per man more rapidly than the increase in production. He recognised a shortage of manpower, but in successfully meeting the even greater demands made on them by increasing mechanisa-tion and the need for specialisation, agricultural workers had already helped to raise the industry's productivity from 4% per annum in 1954–60 to 6% in 1960–4. 'This is more than double the rate of improvement in the economy as a whole and it is a very fine achievement.'

Such glowing tributes to agricultural workers, were not uncommon in the sixties, but there was still much to be done if some of the problems were to be overcome. Mr. Ian Reid, of Wye College, Kent, told the Oxford Farming Conference in 1966 that milk production, for example, was expected to show an increase of nearly 20% by 1970, although the increase in dairy cows was estimated to be only 13%, and they would have far fewer acres to graze upon. By 1970, it was expected that three million acres of forage crops would be ploughed up for cereals. And urban development would swallow up 300,000 acres in the next five years. Mr. Reid had compiled a partial budget in which he estimated that the selective expansion programme would provide farmers with an additional income totalling £243 million by 1970. He had allowed higher costs for all items except labour, for which he assessed a decrease of £80 million. This figure was disputed from the floor by the Union repre-sentatives (Ted Calver, Stan Hall and Stan Hayward), on the grounds that by 1970 there would be a statutory wages structure likely to give an excep-tional boost to farmworkers' earnings.

Labour again faced a General Election in 1966, and in the April *Landworker* Collison urged full support on the grounds of their achievements in power since October 1964, and there was a special message from Harold Wilson. He said that when Labour had come to power the list of reforms in agriculture crying out to be brought in was endless. Fred Peart had shown that he was ready to get things done, and the Government had built on the foundations laid by the 1947 Agriculture Act. Their selected expansion programme should meet a major part of the expected growth in the demand for food resulting from higher living standards and a rising population. The agricultural worker would not be the forgotten man of British agriculture. The 1956 Agriculture Bill provided, for the first time, for minimum rates of sick pay, and they had raised sickness and unemployment benefits. They had plans to set up a training board for agriculture under the 1964 Industrial Training Act to improve their skills. Labour won the Election with a much increased majority of 96, with 363 MPs. In 1968, after a cabinet reshuffle, Peart was appointed Leader of the House of Commons, and Cledwyn Hughes took his place as Minister of Agriculture.

After two years of near stagnation, agriculture had staged a good recovery during the previous six months, with an increase in output of 6%, the *Landworker* noted in 1968. 'Continued at this rate the output should this year easily outstrip the £2,000 million mark which is far and away in excess of any other industry. It also amounts to roughly two-thirds of the foodstuffs that we consume of the type that we can grow in this country. With the active collaboration of all concerned we could go a long way towards producing the other third,' it commented. It went on to point out that the worker was doing his share, but the farmers were blaming Government policies for their difficulties and lack of incentives.

*   *   *

At the Labour Party conference in 1966, Albert Hilton stood down as the Union nominee on the 12-member union section of the NEC in favour of Bert Hazell, but Bert was narrowly beaten.

In its evidence in 1967 to the Royal Commission on trade unions and employers' associations, the TUC dealt with itself as a body engaged in daily consultation with Government departments on all aspects of working life, national and international affairs. The TUC Social Insurance and Industrial Welfare Committee, with Lord Collison as chairman, formulated policy on national insurance, with NHS and occupational health and safety. The TUC claimed an enormous impact by workers through their representatives where top decisions were made. The TUC said the ten main objectives of trade unionism were improved terms of employment; improved physical environ-ment at work; full employment and national prosperity; security of employ-ment and income; improved social security; fair shares in national income and wealth; industrial democracy; a voice in government; improved public and social services; public control and planning of land.

*   *   *

Early in 1968, to save money, the printing of the *Landworker* was moved from the Co-op Printing Society to a private firm in Carlisle. The Union subsidy on the paper in 1968 was £2,505 less than it was in 1967 (£10,730).

Following an historic decision at the Aberystwyth Biennial, the NUAW became the National Union of Agricultural and Allied Workers in 1968. The new title recognised what had been a virtual fact for many years. With a declining labour force, the number of members who were farmworkers as a proportion of those in allied industries had been reduced, although perhaps not as much as might have been expected. In 1968, there was an intake of 8,400 new members. Total membership was 4.3% lower than that of 1967, but this was regarded as a 'considerable achievement', for the Union was 'operating in a situation which could be expected to result in a substantially reduced membership figure.'[1] The *Landworker* told readers, '. . . the new name will be welcomed . . . by our forestry, land drainage, roadmen and British Sugar members, besides our growing membership in industries like poultry packing and processing.'

The controversial Recruiting Officer scheme which the Union had operated for a number of years was wound up, as the result of a decision taken in private at the 1968 Biennial. A. Johnson, Warwicks, moved, 'That this Conference calls for the Recruiting Officer scheme to be expanded to cover the whole country owing to the low percentage of full-time agricultural and horticultural workers in the Union.' E. Sales, Dorset, moved an amendment to wind it up and to absorb the Recruiting Officers into the organising staff. The EC supported the motion and opposed the amendment, but this was carried by 67 votes to 56. Conference then adopted the substantive motion.

A report to the Organising Sub-Committee in 1963 on the membership made by Recruiting Officers said, 'contribution income now covered the cost of salaries and milage.' It considered their appointment 'justified'.[2]

By December 1965 the Union had 115,000 members divided into 89,500 full members and 25,500 half-rate members. Six Recruiting Officers were then operating in the 24 organising districts. Although the number leaving the land was greater in Recruiting Officers' areas, the number of new members made per 1,000 members in Recruiting Officer counties in 1965 was 128, against 80 in all other counties; the recruitment rate in 1965 as compared with 1959 showed an increase of 8.8% in Recruiting Officer counties, as against a drop of 13.9% in all other counties.[3]

New members enrolled by Recruiting Officers would have had to be retained two years to cover the actual £5 cost of recruiting each one. Some Recruiting Officers were averaging one or two new recruits a day, although one, Eddie Collinson, made 107 new members in April and 208 in November.[4] The Organising Department under Frank Coffin made a careful monthly analysis of members lost and gained, and income, and a summary of Recruiting Officers' expenses showed that they sometimes reached £50 a month. A rather costly exercise for a small return, but presumably the EC wished to retain Recruiting Officers because it was desperate for new members.

By the following year the reports of branches with falling members had become dismal. Croxteth branch: This area completely built up by Liverpool overspill. Colchester: No scope for expanding . . . two remaining members transferred to Ardleigh. Waltham Cross: CWS Nursery has closed, members, mostly Italian, have left the area. Woodhall Spa: Only four members left. Barnack (Northants): All members have left the industry. West Isley (Berks): Impossible to get secretary . . . best incorporate members into Central Register. Moore (Cheshire): One remaining member transferred to Central Register. Leeds (Kent): Secretary resigned due to advancing years, members transferred to Sutton Valence. Dunraven (Glamorgan): Only one member left due to run down of Forestry Commission. Garden Produce (Hunts): Consisted solely of Pakistani members, 'opened hopefully' but unable to maintain. And so the sad catalogue could go on, and on.

*   *   *

In the bright sunshine of a July Sunday, James Callaghan, Home Secretary, outlined to a thousand-strong Tolpuddle Rally four requirements to invigorate the links between the Labour Government and the trade unions. First, the unity between the Party and the organised workers must be strengthened. Second, the Party must stimulate the enthusiasm of its members who are drawn from and represent a wide cross-section of the country's workers. Third, the enthusiasm and idealism of our youth must be channelled into the Labour movement. 'Fourth, we must convince the regions that the Party recognise their essential role . . . in the political and economic developments of the country.'

*   *   *

The introduction of the National Giro system in 1968 was the result of 40 years' campaigning by the TUC for a cheap banking system for the man in the street, and it gave the Union and branch secretaries an easy means of sending contributions to head office. The Post Office made no charge and the money paid in was automatically credited to the head office account. The need for money orders, postal orders, cheques and registered envelopes ended.

The EC election results were announced in December 1968, and three men who had between them served 85 years on it had not sought re-election. They were Bill Case, representing Wilts, Hampshire and part of Somerset (38 years); Bert Leeder, Norfolk (22 years); and Jim Paul, Glos, Herefordshire, Shropshire, Worcs and Wales (25 years). R. Clarke took Leeder's place, Tony Hemming succeeded Paul, and Ted Parry took over from Case.

General Secretary Resigns

'Resignation of General Secretary' exclaimed the *Landworker* in September 1969.

> We painfully report that on the day we went to press the EC sent this message to all branch secretaries: 'The EC . . . have today [August 21] with great regret, accepted the resignation of Lord Collison from the post of General Secretary in order that he may take up the chairmanship of the Supplementary Benefits Commission.'

Lord Collison said his new work was 'of great social significance and importance to those in greatest need . . . But I leave the Union with regret . . . and . . . I shall always be with you in heart and mind.[5]

Lord Collison's departure may have been something of a shock to members, and although left-wingers may have been glad to see him go, his leaving does not seem to have raised any strong emotions in the Union. Jack Boddy told me in 1988, 'No one felt strongly about the matter, many believed it was the right sort of thing to do to accept the appointment he was given.'

Left-wingers in the Union, although fed up with the right-wing policies of the EC, made no attempt to capture the general secretaryship, possibly recognising that they were too weak to mount any effective challenge to the two right-wingers who were fighting for the office. They were Reg Bottini and Dennis Hodsdon, and a third candidate, Edgar Pill, an amiable character who was at times to move rapidly round Labour's left–right political compass. Bottini polled 19,964; Hodsdon 17,092; Pill 7,783.

Bert Hazell introduced the new General Secretary at a celebratory dinner in December, and Reg Bottini said that it was urgent to bring to a conclusion the 'eight years' haggle over wages structure.' It was about time the NFU were willing to accept a wages-during-sickness scheme for farmworkers; and the Government must have another look at the position of the tied cottage. If the present methods were not gaining results, other methods of wages bargaining must be looked at.

Reg Bottini was born during the First World War in which his father was killed. Not without a struggle his mother managed to send Reg to a grammar school. He had been a member of the Labour Party since 1933 and served five years as chairman of the East Reigate (Surrey) Constituency Party. During the Second World War he worked on the land and, then as a land drainage worker for the River Nene Catchment Board. He joined the Union's Folkesworth branch, and later became secretary of Yaxley branch. In February 1945 he became assistant in the Legal Department at head office, and later was appointed head of the newly-formed Wages and Movements Department, a position he held till his election as General Secretary. He was involved in a wide range of responsibilities, including membership of the AWB, the Central Council for Agricultural and Horticultural Co-operation, and the Economic Development Committee for the Food Manufacturing Industry; secretary of the trade union side of the Forestry Commission Industry and Trades Council and the National Negotiating Committee for British Sugar (Beet) Industry, and chairman of the trade union side of the Rivers Committee of the National Joint Council of Local Authorities Services (Manual Workers). He was awarded the CBE in 1974.

*   *   *

Bert Huson, secretary of North Pickenham Branch for 43 years, died in 1969 at the age of 73. Bert was Norfolk County Secretary for 25 years and an EC member for 12. This is the bare bones of the fine Union record of Bert, who was the son of a trawler cook and started work as an odd-job boy earning 2s 6d a week. He fought on the Somme in the First World War, returned home and took part in the Norfolk Strike in 1923. He held the Union's Silver and Gold badges.

*   *   *

An early warning of financial difficulties ahead for the Union, came from Jack Ding, deputy Finance Officer, in the *Landworker* of March 1970. He wrote about the low contribution rate and pointed out that if contributions were in the same proportion to earnings in 1939, they would soon be well over 10s a week. He had written earlier on the need for a substantial increase 'to put our house in order', but it was rejected at the 1968 Biennial. He went on '. . . and in the past two years our financial position has further deteriorated.' He said that in 1967 the Union showed a small credit balance of £4,000, but in 1968 this was reversed to a deficit of £26,000. During 1965–8 the Union had overspent by nearly £50,000. 'Last year [1969] we had a deficit of £49,000, as much as the total for the previous four years and this was during a year when we had no biennial . . . They must take a careful and honest look at 1969 and then plan their future.'

At first sight total income did not look too disturbing. Individual contributions were down by £142, investment income down by £1,261. But if readers took into account the increased value of contributions in July 1968, then the 1969 contribution income was by 'no means satisfactory'. Expenditure had risen sharply. Salaries increased by over £8,000 and printing and stationery costs had risen by £3,749 but this was mainly due to a new computer system which it was hoped would be a considerable benefit when in full operation.

Jack said, 'We are not broke – far from it. But we have a serious financial problem, and I would be failing in my duty if I did not draw your attention to it.' He ended, 'The EC will be asking delegates at the 1970 Biennial to agree an increase of 2s a month . . . a contribution increase of less than 6d a week is surely not excessive.'

Perhaps a little to Jack's surprise, the Biennial did raise the contribution by 2s to 8s a month. The EC's proposal on this was greeted by a flood of arms raised in support, with no sign of a single hand against. Later the Union tried to cut the cost of biennials, and among other measures ended expensive, formal final night dinners.

Lord Hilton was again elected to the EC in 1970 for W and part of S Norfolk by a comfortable majority, beating T. Paget, G. Sandle, A. Howes and A. Blott.

In his presidential address to 110 delegates to the Conference at Whitley Bay in 1970, Bert Hazell had indicated that the activities of the Union, of necessity, required close collaboration with other trade unions, so it was not surprising that the newly-elected General Secretary, Reg Bottini, was on 7 January 1970, invited by the TGWU General Secretary Jack Jones, to a discussion on 'mutual problems'. Reg, accompanied by Dennis Hodsdon, met Jones. In response to a hint from Jones that the TGWU would be interested in a merger, both NUAAW officials made it clear that the Union was not interested in submerging its identity in any other Union but on the contrary was convinced that there was a continued need for an independent rural trade union. This point was fully accepted by Jones.

At Whitley Bay, Bert Hazell was re-elected President. He received 89 votes, Wilf Page 21. Joan Maynard was re-elected Vice-President, defeating Ted Calver and Bill Dawes by a substantial majority.

Delegates had scarcely returned from the heady debates at Whitley Bay when it was announced that the General Election was to take place on 18 June.

Two candidates were sponsored by the Union: Bert Hazell once again in N Norfolk, and a newcomer, David Naginton for Ludlow, Salop. David was a farmworker until a spinal injury caused him to find other employment in 1964. He joined the Union in 1951, was a branch and district committee chairman, and for 12 years chairman of Shropshire County Committee. He was fighting a Tory majority of 3,480 and campaigned on tied cottages and improvement to rural housing.

Labour lost the Election and Bert Hazell was defeated, breaking a 25-year run in which the Norfolk seat had been held by a Union man. David Naginton failed at Ludlow.

*   *   *

After 28 years on the EC, Frank Robinson retired for health reasons in 1970. He was easily its longest serving member and had put in over 50 years' service to the Union; he held the Union's Gold Badge and the TUC Silver Badge. Despite poor health, he was still doing his bit for the Union when I was in contact with him in 1984.

Frank enrolled as a lad in 1918. It seems a sad waste of talent that Frank, a boy bright enough to reach Standard X7 at 13, then had to leave school to work on a farm six days a week, 6am to 6pm, with no overtime or holidays. He later joined the East Yorkshire Regiment, serving in Egypt, India and China; he was badly wounded and discharged. He rejoined the Union in 1930 and took over as branch secretary of Patrington, Hull, which had dwindled from 300 members, in the early 1920s, to 19. He rebuilt the membership to 300, and during the Second World War it rose to 400.

He was secretary of Patrington for over 40 years and a district secretary for 30 years. A member of the AWB for 20 years, he served on many other agricultural committees, both nationally and locally. He managed to do all this and run his coal business too! In 1967 he received the OBE. Frank was a Methodist lay preacher and active in the Labour Party. He was keen on sport, holding the chairmanship of both Patrington football and cricket clubs.

Looking back, he believed that one of the Union's great achievements was in 1936 when commercial gardeners were brought under the 1924 Agricultural Wages Act. In the same year, after intense pressure from the Union, farmworkers were brought into the National Unemployment Scheme. At first, this only gave them inferior status, but Frank recalls with pride how equal rights were eventually won.

Frank often clashed with left-wingers in the Union, especially on such issues as the abolition of the AWB. He said, 'Some workers have talked about disbanding the AWB, but I cannot support this. Over many years it has been responsible for greatly improved conditions, including wages when sick, holidays with pay, overtime payments, etc, which I doubt would ever have been achieved by wages councils. I have known times when wage awards have been won on the AWB by the vote of the appointed members and the workers' side only, the farmers voting against.'

Recalling the Control of Engagements Order, which brought many people into agriculture instead of doing National Service, Frank said it meant new recruits to the Union, who soon became active. 'Many were able speakers, having perhaps been blessed with better opportunities for education.'

He believed the Union still had plenty of problems to solve, in matters such as safety, health and environment, housing with modern amenities, and in addition, good wages, equal to the best. He thought all wages should be raised to that of the Craftsman Grade, 'for all workers today, regularly employed, are skilled at their job.' He added, 'I fought hard for the Wages Structure within the framework of the AWB. It's a tremendous boost, but the "other worker" category should be eliminated, leaving Grade I and II as the minimum.'

Frank had many happy memories of Union stalwarts. 'My old faithful EC colleague, Hubert Luckett of Kent; we served 21 years together on the EC. He died in my arms at the Oulton Hotel during a winter school at Clacton on Sea. He was a great lad; we shared rooms during the war at a lodging house in London, and, one night, something told me that we were going to have an air raid, so I just popped under the sheets without undressing. Hubert went to bed in his pyjamas. Ten minutes later the siren sounded. Hubert got up and dressed, but the "all clear" went, so he again undressed and got back into bed. The warning went again; a bomb shook the building. "Come on, Hubert," I cried, "we're on the third floor. Let's get down on solid earth." So we rushed downstairs, Hubert putting his coat over his pyjamas. There was a blaze lighting up the sky. "It's our head office, Hubert. Let's go." "Take the key," said the landlady. "Let yourselves in when you get back".'

So, with searchlights scanning the sky, they rushed off towards a blazing building. It wasn't the Union's headquarters, but the huge Mount Pleasant postal sorting office. A vast crowd watched the firemen at work, and when the call came for volunteers, Frank worked inside the building in a chain of 30 men pulling out mail bags. At 3.30am the volunteers were ordered to stand clear as part of the building was collapsing. 'So we stood outside, almost roasted with the heat.' But they still shivered with cold, and although told to hang on for 'tea and cake', Frank set out for his lodgings. 'Half way down Gray's Inn Road I met poor Hubert, no hat, his hair looking almost white.' 'Good heavens, what are you doing here?' exclaimed Frank. 'You've got a key.'

'I thought you were dead,' said Hubert, his pyjamas flapping about his ankles. Frank took him to a tea stall near King's Cross station and got him a hot drink. 'He was a loyal trade unionist, and Kent, I know, were rightly proud of him.'

Continuing his reminiscences, Frank said, 'In Northumberland, Jack Short, one of our county committee men, lived up at Nesbit, and at a meeting one night, a packed room of some sixty were discussing the possibilities of a Wages Structure. The debate went on till after 11, when a wee laddie of about 16 years got up and said, "I think the most important man on the farm is the loose man," meaning, as we called him, Tommy Cut – the young starter. "Quite right son," I said, and we closed the meeting, but not before signing up the wee lad, and many more.'

They were great lads up North, the shepherds on the hills close to the Scottish border. 'I once stopped at a shepherd's cottage three miles from Otterburn, up in the Cheviots, among his sheep. A ladder led up to the attic in the roof. I was surprised to see daylight through the tiles. The shepherd said, "Why that's nowt man, you want to see it when it blows; I put a rope round the bed." '

'Why don't you go and live down in Otterburn,' Frank asked. 'Why man, I canna leave my sheep.'

Frank regarded it an education to see them driving the sheep with their dogs. 'I once went with a shepherd and his dog into the Cheviots. It was a beautiful sight, the falcons flying, the babbling brooks splashing over large boulders of stone.'

'Are you not ever lonely living out here?' Frank asked. 'Why no man,' came the reply. 'Me and Shep [his dog] often have a sit down on this stone here and have a chat with Jesus – he's with us always.'

'What a tribute to his faith, the old Methodist spirit,' declared Frank, 'the spirit of George Loveless, Joseph Arch, and George Edwards, our founder. Scores of Methodists were among our organisers.'

Frank paid a heartfelt tribute to his wife, herself a Union member. Without her, he said, 'I could never have carried out the work as the EC member covering the whole of Yorkshire, Durham and Northumberland, requiring long days, sometimes weeks, away from home.' His wife must have taken a lot of Union subs at their door.

*　　*　　*

In 1970, the retirement of S Lindsay DO, Stan Brumby, meant that there was no officer left in the field appointed before the Second World War. Stan's earliest Union charge covered the counties of Somerset, Devon and Cornwall. The eldest of a family of seven, he was hired as a farmworker for a year at Scunthorpe May Fair. He 'lived in'. Well, almost. He was only allowed in the farmhouse for meals and at bedtime. But he was allowed in to write a weekly essay for a correspondence course. He kept his text books in a corn bin. He later studied at Ruskin College, and before Stan was appointed organiser in 1936, Somerset was looked after by Fred James from Dorset. There had been no organiser for Devon (total membership 18), and Cornwall was 100% unorganised. The war speeded things up and by 1943 over 1,000 members were enrolled in Somerset. Stan held many Union and local authority appointments in Lincolnshire, and was succeeded there by Alec Russell, a former tractor driver, and previously Recruiting Officer for Cheshire, Lancs and W Yorks.

The bold statement that 'Cornwall was 100% unorganised' will surprise no one who knew it between the two World Wars. But changes were to come. Let us have a look at some of them through a leading member of the Union.

Big Changes in Cornwall

Bodmin Moor, that 20-mile stretch of often blasted heathland between the ancient Cornish capital of Launceston and the granite-built town of Bodmin, has had its meagre agricultural economy completely transformed over the last 50 years, and Arthur Fanson, aged 67, of Croanford, has lived through all these changes, which have mostly been for the better.

Curlews and buzzards still soar across the lichened stone hedges and the sparse soil is often thick with creeping dodder beneath layers of cloud that suddenly part to reveal clean pools of pale blue, then close up, a sullen leaden mass; that aspect of the moor has not changed much since Arthur left the CoE school at Alturnun in 1935 and started on a 150-acre farm employing two people; he was horseman, at 5s a week and his midday meal.

He had his horses fed, cleaned and harnessed ready to start in the fields by 8am. He was expected to plough one acre a day, with a single furrow plough which had to be lifted round at each headland. Later a turnover plough made it a little easier, but after the day's work, the horses still had to be fed and cleaned, and once a week the harness cleaned and brasses polished. It was a six-day week and on Sundays the horses had to be attended to. The other man looked after the cattle and did all the other farm work, for 28s a week.

Arthur stayed for five years, was paid every 13 weeks, helped with the cattle rearing, mainly Aberdeen Angus and Galloways. They used to break in the special breed of Bodmin Moor pony for the Durham coalfields.

Hay harvesting then was a two-man operation, one working the grass machine, the other sharpening knives which had to be renewed every four or five times round the field. At 10am the horses would be taken to the stables to be fed and rested until 4pm, when they would start again and continue until dark. There was no rest for the men. While the horses were bedded down, the men would be in another field, turning with pikes hay that had been drying.

Corn harvesting was also a busy time with long hours. The main crops were oats and barley, and a binder drawn by three horses would go round the field, while two men would stack the sheaves in stooks of eight or 10. Ten days later the corn would be taken by wagon to a small yard called a 'mewhay' or put in ricks. The oats were fed to the horses, the sheaves being cut to chaff by a machine with two knives on a big wheel which was turned by hand.

Harvesting had its compensations. The farmer's wife would come to the field with a basket of pasties, scones and saffron cake, and there would be supper in the farm house, usually cold ham, beef and pickles. This was the highlight of the day.

When the Second World War began, Arthur took up steam threshing, and drove round farms threshing corn for eleven years, a slow job too. Arthur explained, 'My boss had 11 threshing sets, each one consisting of a steam engine, thresher, chaff cutter and a wire baler, all pulled by the engine weighing 9½–10 tons; the thresher was 4½ tons, chaff cutter 1–1½ tons, and the baler loaded with wire was 4½ tons. We did about seven miles an hour. We were allowed by law to block the road for 20 minutes and sometimes it took us that to get into a field, we often had to widen the entrances. We rose at six to light the fire and get steam up and we would work until dark, and after dark we would shift from one farm to another with two blokes going ahead with hurricane lanterns.'

Most of the threshing was done October to April and they sometimes got snowed up. Bodmin in winter is when Cornwall recklessly reveals its true nature – it is not friendly to man. Shrivelled cart tracks disappear into nothing amidst snow-ridden gorse. Threshing teams consisted of two men, plus 14 supplied by the farmers. 'It's all done now by one man on a combine,' said Arthur. 'The two men with the machines used to sleep on the farms from Monday to Friday night and go home Saturday night, to be ready to start on Monday.'

It was at this time that Arthur married Beatrice, a girl off the moor, and they went on to have seven children. During the war Arthur was inadvertently called up. He reported to Glasgow, and while on the train a telegram arrived saying 'not to report', as steam threshing was a reserved occupation.

Eager to better himself and his growing family, he tried to escape the arduous farm life of Bodmin Moor by renting a smallholding of 36 acres from the Forestry Commission on Dartmoor. He kept it for nine years, then the Commission wanted to sell it and he hadn't the money. 'My bank begged me to buy it, and offered £1,000 for extra stock, plus £5,500, but I couldn't see where I was going to find £500 a year to pay the mortgage, so I went to work on a sheep farm of 1,250 acres.' He stayed seven years, then moved to another farm and joined the Union. 'I was always for the Union; I wasn't in any trouble, I just thought it a good thing to be in, and I've been involved ever since.' He joined the Wadebridge branch, became secretary, and was elected to district and county committees. Later he was on the National Horticultural Committee, served on several others, became delegate to the regional trade group committee and a member of the Meat and Livestock Commission for the South West.

Arthur has some unusual memories of Bodmin Moor. When he was 15, a man died 2½ miles out on the moor when snow was up to the hedge tops and the occasional clump of misshapen little trees were being thrashed by strong winds. Arthur joined a party of men who took a coffin out to the dead man's house, where he was kept in it for two weeks, until they dragged it off the moor on a door-like sledge, known as a 'dray'. By tradition, if a body in a coffin passes over the moor, its path becomes a public footpath. 'People immediately made use of this footpath,' said Arthur, 'because the coffin party had shortened a route to an outlying farm. The owners of the land objected, and it came to court, but it's been a public right of way ever since.'

In the old days most of the farmworkers lived in tied cottages, usually with no mod cons; the lavatories were earth closets, sometimes sited over a running stream. In 1948 Arthur lived in such a cottage with no bathroom or tap water, but they had electricity. One of the farmworkers' perks, if on a dairy farm, was a quart of milk a day. If a farmer planted potatoes he would allow his man to plant two or three rows for himself, providing his own seed. And he could have firewood by cutting it in his own time with an axe and crosscut saw.

But all that has changed, partly thanks to the NUAAW which helped prod social progress into a quicker pace. And when I interviewed Arthur in 1988, a tall, bronzed man, he had been working for Sir Arscott Molesworth St. Aubyn at Pencarrow as gardener-cum-chauffeur for 15 years.

Arthur recalled other changes on the moor. During the Second World War the first tractors began to be used, by 1944 wages were £4 a week, and during the sixties, technology really began to take over. Stone hedges were bulldozed, fields made bigger, weeds controlled by sprays, and tractors with three or four farrows could plough a large field in a day. As elsewhere, this meant layoffs.

'But the major change was living there,' said Arthur. 'One farmer I worked for could never have made a living if he hadn't a sideline as a blacksmith. So these grants have kept people on the moor. Today the best part of the moor is dressed with lime and basic slag, something unthought of years ago. There are still common rights for sheep and cattle running over the moor, and some cottages have the right to graze 10 geese. And of course, there's been that other diversification, tourists, and lots of cottages do B & B today. Now there's pony trekking and one farmer is doing vacuum-packed hay purely for horses.'

Arthur regrets there are very few Union members on the moor today – its labour force has declined by nearly 70% – most of its remaining workers are farmers' sons. 'Conditions on the moor are much better, there's been more changes in the last 50 years than in the previous 300. In my young days, nobody burnt coal, you used to cut turf. You cooked with it, and a fellow with a horse and trap came round selling paraffin for lamps. No turf is cut now, it's either coal or electric.'

Most people either attended the Church of England or Methodist chapels, which played a big part in the social life of the moor. 'I was on quite a few committees that started in chapels,' said Arthur. 'There would have been no social life if it were not for the chapels, many now sold off as homes. Most parishes had a clubroom where billiards and skittles were played. It cost a shilling a year to be a member and this was where most workers spent their long winter evenings.'

*   *   *

The printing of the *Landworker* was moved to the Co-operative Press, Manchester in 1970, where it was printed on web offset presses with advanced photo processing and computer typesetting.

At their May 1970 meeting, the EC accepted the resignation of AGS Dennis Hodsdon, who was to become assistant to Tom Bavin,* General Secretary of the 4-million strong International Federation of Plantation, Agricultural and Allied Workers. In voting for a successor, Edgar Pill, education officer, polled 15,489; Eddie Collinson, recruiting officer, 6,910; Jim Watts, head of Legal Department, 6,735. So Edgar, aged 62, had won by a big majority. An eloquent speaker, forthright and provocative, he was always popular in the districts, and those who attended the Winter Schools during the previous 20 years, would probably have been influenced by Edgar for the rest of their lives.

He had been closely associated with the Union for over 25 years. When working in his native Wiltshire he was elected secretary of Chiseldon branch, and in the late 1940s was organiser for Lancashire. His abilities were quickly recognised and he later became head of the General Office at headquarters. His deep interest in education as reflected in the governorship he held of Ruskin College and his membership of the Agricultural, Horticultural and Forestry Industrial Training Board.

Following Edgar's election, the EC disbanded the General Office and created a new department – General Services. Frank Coffin, after nearly 18 years as head of the Organising Department, was appointed head of the new department. Eddie Collinson replaced Frank as head of the Organising Department.

Jack Brocklebank was elected to the EC in 1970 to succeed Frank Robinson as representative for Northumberland, Durham and Yorkshire.

The differences between the right and left were beginning to show. Said Jack, 'The atmosphere when I joined the EC could be cut with a knife. Bert Hazell was President, Joan Maynard, Vice-President. When it came to voting, you didn't have to look to see what other people were doing, it was automatic where people stood on any particular issue. There were only three of us for a progressive policy, all the rest followed the lead of John Hose, whose policies we thought disastrous for the Union, as in fact it turned out to be.§ Hose followed Hodsdon and Collinson in advocating Recruiting Officers, we regarded them as an expensive luxury, bleeding the Union to death, we thought recruiting should be done by DOs. The computerisation of branch membership accounts at head office was a complete disaster: head office had to write to branch secretaries saying "tell us how much you owe." Three thousand branches. Some secretaries had in their cottages computer printouts of membership which would stretch from kitchen table to the back door.

---

* A former NUAW official and EC member.
§ John Hose, naturally, thought otherwise. See Chapter 21.

Gordon Dales arrived at one biennial holding up two bags full of branch money, but nobody would take them from him. All this was reflected in the tense atmosphere at EC meetings.'

*   *   *

There was a record turn out of 5,000 people with banners and placards at the 1971 Tolpuddle Rally in July. The weather was perfect and a huge crowd gathered on the lawn outside the Martyrs' Cottages, including people from Australia, Canada, France and South Africa. Harold Wilson, Bert Hazell and Mrs. Hazell, Jess Waterman, EC, and Fred Cole, DO, led the march through the winding streets of Tolpuddle. In a reference to the Martyrs, Wilson made comparisons between the Government then in power and the present-day Government. He said, 'Exactly 125 years after a Conservative Prime Minister, Sir Robert Peel, repealed the Corn Laws another Conservative Prime Minister has wilfully and obsessively introduced a system of agricultural levies on imported food which will do nothing for the British agricultural worker or indeed the average farmer . . . the Government is now trying to push Britain into a restrictive European market on terms which will have to be paid for by every British taxpayer, family and housewife. No one has the right to ask our still relatively lowly-paid farmworkers to contribute to the system of inefficiency that governs Europe.'

Disposing of a Vice-President

The Union's financial position failed to improve in the early 1970s, and this was reflected in several contentious cost-cutting resolutions at the 1972 Biennial at Weymouth. One resolution had political as well as economic implications.

In a statement on the deepening financial crisis, Reg Bottini spoke of the increasing yearly deficit over expenditure. In 1970, despite reorganisation and reducing field staff by five officers and an increase in subscriptions by 2s per month, the deficit was £50,859. Further economies and cuts in staff were made in 1971 and 1972, and the deficit for 1971 had been reduced to £23,000, but it was still a deficit. Over this period, there had been a serious erosion of the Union's reserves, more than £150,000 had been withdrawn to meet deficits. 'However . . . the ship is turning round in financial terms, every item of expenditure is being scrutinised, but a rise in some costs is inevitable . . .'

There was some criticism by delegates of staff at head office. L. Wilshire, Wilts, said he was not criticising heads of departments, but he was appalled to see 'people lolling about all over the place . . . not attempting to work.' He thought they were not paying enough to get the right person. He was speaking on a motion instructing the EC to make 'a close scrutiny of numbers and quality of staff' and calling for higher efficiency at lower cost.

Reg Bottini said, 'They may loll about, but I have trade unions to deal with as well you know. You try and get rid of somebody these days . . .' He promised to do their best to improve efficiency and successfully asked for the motion to be remitted to the EC.*

One 'save money' resolution called for the suspension of Winter Schools until the Biennial of 1974. The schools cost £3,000 a year. After searching discussion the motion was lost.

Another motion, for the same reason, sought to end organisers' conferences. Bottini said the EC would not like to be committed by a positive instruction never to consult with their organisers other than through their Chief Executive Office, at any time, and that would be the effect of the motion if carried. He thought, however, that the number of conferences might be reduced and asked for the motion to be remitted to the EC. Conference agreed. A motion to stop sending people to Ruskin College (costing nearly £1,000 yearly) was lost.

In private session came the most contentious and acrimonious debate of the entire conference. Andrew Baynham, Worcs, moved 'That in order to economise in overhead expenses this conference herewith decides that a Vice-President is not necessary and that the office shall cease to exist as from the passing of this resolution'. He said it was not a personal issue, his appreciation of the yeoman work done by the Vice-President made 'it extremely hard' for him to move the motion. He was aware that the economy would be small, but they were making every effort to save money where possible. Joan Maynard's efforts would be better directed at obtaining a seat in Parliament where her advice on the tied cottage would not be lost 'in the wilderness as it is at the moment'. Referring to the current Joseph Arch centenary and making an imaginative evocation of Joan of Arc saving France, he said, 'Who knows, in years to come this Union may say "Thank God for Joan and Arch." '

Seconding, H. Kellow, Wilts, said there was no longer need for a Vice-President to chair meetings while the President was absent in the House of Commons (Bert Hazell having been defeated as an MP since the office of Vice-President was instituted) and R. Haines, Rutland and Leics, supported this contention.

L. Shears, Dorset, did not want to drag out any dirty washing, but recalled the last two or three years before there was a Vice-President, when it was Bro. Gooch as President who decided who should take the chair in his absence, and it was not a senior member of the EC. 'This brought out something that nearly caused disruption of our EC before the conference ended.' He did not want to have the same kind of episode crop up again.

---

* By the 1960s, staff salaries at head office had fallen way behind those of comparable organisations; London staff also had to pay heavy fare increases to get to work. Their pay rises never caught up with those similarly employed elsewhere.

E. Sales, Dorset, recalled the 1958 Sandown Conference when 'Bro. Gooch had our Conference torn apart,' with factions all over the place as to who would take the chair. 'All sorts of fancy statements are being made about expenses, that Joan Maynard gets £1,500 or £3,000 a year, but look at the accounts.' The EC expenses were £6,002 in 1971 – for 14 members that came to £470 a head. 'Is this a fortune . . . and those people have to travel all over the place.' They all wanted national speakers at county conferences and the Vice-President had taken on no end of these activities and only been paid her fares and expenses. He thought they were getting good value for money from their Vice-President. W. Dawes, W Norfolk, said, 'We know this is a "Save Expense Week", but you can make too much use of a pruning knife and kill the bush altogether.'

John Hose, EC, emphasising that he was speaking as an individual, said the circumstances surrounding the election of a Vice-President 'no longer apply' and supported the motion.

Gordon Dales, Lincs, said, 'I know what has got into your heads . . . wanting to save a few bob on a person who can draw in more pounds than anybody else on the top table.' Joan brought in more pounds from women members than anyone before in the history of the Union. G. Brown, Bucks, thought a Vice-President essential. Noting that they had a lady Vice-President, he declared 'a lot of you are against because you feel a lady's place is in the house washing the dishes.' G. Sandle, Norfolk W, wanted to know how you could run without a second-in-command and appealed for the resolution to be thrown out.

Bert Hazell ending the discussion said, 'I think this is essentially a matter for the floor and the EC have no observations.' Strange, obviously they had views, one had already spoken in a 'personal capacity.'

When a card vote was requested there were cries of 'No' and 'Show of hands'. Hazell said, 'The answers seems to be no card vote.' He then rejected a request for a vote on whether they should have a card vote. The tellers, W. G. Coe (chairman), E. Amey, F. Hansford, and W. Wellman moved into position and the motion was carried, 50 for, 37 against.

Sandle then asked where Joan Maynard was to go; she was not a member of the EC and not even a delegate. He told one delegate who had suggested that she stay where she was, 'You cannot do that, you have adopted the motion that has thrown her out.' He moved that she 'stay as an honoured guest'.

Hose declared, 'We have no power to allow anyone in this room apart from the people who are allowed into private sessions,' and said they could not start bending rules. Hazell said it was an exceptional situation, and there was a proposition that Joan remain for the rest of the Conference.

At this stage Wilf Page, EC, said he was 'convinced . . . the tellers made a mistake in their calculations. I am not suggesting the votes were wrongly taken, but I think there ought to be another vote.'

Hazell, who had earlier pointed out that a number of delegates had not voted, said it was not possible to challenge the arithmetic of the tellers.

Jack Dunman, Oxon, tried to move a suspension of Standing Orders so that a card vote could be taken. There were cries of 'No' and Hazell said 'I have no authority to accept that.' A motion to allow Joan to stay for the rest of the Conference was passed.

The Conference went on to other business, but the scrapping of the vice-presidency would not lie down. In the afternoon E. Sales said, 'a very serious mistake has been made this morning. We have had a quick check round some of the delegates and have already found that there were 41 who voted against the motion abolishing the vice-presidency. I think it would be a grave disaster if we . . . allow a post like this to be abolished in error.' He moved a ballot be held and this was seconded. Hazell said delegates had said 'No' to a ballot vote, and he had to stand by the figures given by the tellers. He moved to other business. Sales then moved suspension of Standing Orders and was supported by Dunman, who said Conference had decided not to ballot 'before it had been proved that a gross error has taken place.'

Hazell: 'Whatever high feelings there might be as to the decision, the fact remains that a decision has been taken . . . there is nothing in Standing Orders that gives me authority to change a vote that has been taken.' Dunman pleaded with him that as the vote was wrongly recorded to 'do something to enable this to be corrected.'

Hazell: 'I have no information that the vote is wrong.'

H. Hinds, Notts: 'I oppose all this rubbish, these people have lost and they should face it.'

G. Brown, Bucks: 'No we didn't lose.'

Hinds: 'Shut up, George . . . I would ask you [Conference] to move onto next business.' Hazell formally moved 'next business', and this was done.

But the fight was still not quite over. On the last morning of Conference, when T. Hanson, chairman of Standing Orders Committee moved that, 'Conference continues where it left off last night', Dunman moved reference back to give Conference an opportunity of upholding rules of the Union. He said Rule 14 reads:

> The system of voting shall be by a show of hands. Tellers being appointed by Conference and the decision of the majority shall rule. In cases of dispute the President shall – not may or might, but shall, order a further vote, which may be by roll call of the delegates, if he so decides, or if so demanded by one third of delegates present . . .

A. Neatherway, Sussex, on a point of order moved they carried on with next business. Dunman persisted: 'This conference cannot vote for the rules of this Union to be broken, and the rules of this Union have not been carried out. If there is a dispute . . .'

Hazell: 'There is a point of order. I must accept.' A delegate seconded, and it was carried.

Dunman: 'We have a right to take you to court for a refusal to carry out the rules of the Union.'

Hazell: 'The decision of the chairman is final . . . We now proceed with the agenda.' And so ended the battle to rid the Union of one of its most charismatic campaigners of recent years, all for the sake of a few hundred pounds. Many felt that if Joan Maynard had been a right-winger, others might not have been so keen to save such a small sum by abolishing the vice-presidency. In the weeks following the Conference, Joan received legal advice that she had a good case in law over the doubts about the voting figures and the Union Rule 14, but decided not to pursue the matter in the interests of Union unity. It had clearly been a battle between left and right, but most of the participants were members of the Labour Party, including Joan Maynard. Wilf Page and Jack Dunman were Communists.

Jack was an Oxford graduate, who after working on a farm to help his health, was immediately taken by the farmworkers' cause. He joined the Union in 1941 and built up a branch at Charlbury which became the largest in Oxfordshire. Later he became county secretary, and the county committee met in a photographic studio owned by his wife Helen. He put in a lot of work for the Union, always being willing to mount his push-bike during the war years to travel to wherever help was needed. He later became county chairman, and his energy seemed inexhaustible, which is perhaps fortunate, as he was also to become a full-time Communist Party official, a fact that probably got up the nose of the right-wingers in the Union. Jack, an amiable man, died before the Union's attitude to such left-wingers changed, so he never had the chance to rise to the same heights in its esteem as did his comrade, Wilf Page.

Joan, of course, despite smooth words, was paying the price for her militancy, which contrasted strongly with the 'moderation' of men like Hazell and Bottini. Many believed she had brought a breath of fresh air to the EC, but it was too fresh for the more right-wing members. Her removal from the vice-presidency saved about £400 a year, so few in the know believed that the saving was the paramount motive for getting rid of her.

The move did not lessen Joan's influence in the Union, nor in the Labour Party, as subsequent events were to prove. At that year's Labour Conference Joan was elected to the NEC. She secured 2,974,000 votes, almost 400,000 more than the previous year. Although he failed to secure election to the NEC, Bert Hazell also did well to improve his 1971 vote of 537,000 to 1,410,000. Joan Maynard continued to denounce the right-wing policies with which Bert was associated, and in 1975 challenged him for the presidency, but only got 26 votes against his 69. On this occasion, the left-wing vote was split, as Wilf Page also stood; he got four votes.

Another major office abolished by the Weymouth Biennial was that of Assistant General Secretary but, so as not to upset the feelings of the holder, Edgar Pill, not until after his 'normal retirement'. Edgar was due to retire in 1973. The successful mover and seconder of a composite abolishing the AGS were respectively Cyril Tabiner, Holland, Lincs, and H. Dellar, Cambs.

After the abolition of the vice-presidency, when nominations for President were called for, there were several for Bert Hazell and Joan Maynard. In a moving speech Joan declined in the interests of maintaining unity. Bert was acclaimed President with enthusiasm.

The EC's bid to raise contributions by 20p to 60p failed, but, through a successful amendment by Ted Sales, Dorset, they were raised to 50p per month from 1 July 1972.

*   *   *

Arthur Leary became head of the Organisation Department in 1972 to succeed Eddie Collinson who died in a car crash. Born in Manchester in 1917, Arthur witnessed the wretchedness arising from the slump that hit the industrial areas in the twenties and thirties. He married and settled in Newport Pagnell, Bucks, and was later East Midlands organiser for the National Union of Vehicle Builders. He was chair of Buckinghamshire Labour Party and later won a scholarship to the USA, where he was able to make a comparison between British and American trade unions.

*   *   *

In the 1970s, it was estimated that allowing for members who were not farmworkers, about 40% of regular farmworkers were in the Union, and that Norfolk, Lincolnshire and Yorkshire accounted for two-fifths of the membership. In the sixties the proportion of NUAW members in other occupations – forestry, roadmen, drainage men – was nearly 35%, and continued to increase as the Union stepped up recruiting in poultry and mushroom plants.

In 1973, the Union launched a campaign to increase membership by 10% over the 1972 figure; no figures are available as to its success or otherwise. The Annual Report judiciously claimed 'varying levels of success', and that 'where organisers stimulated interest and activity, recruitment figures are well above 10%'. Many who took part believe that the campaign was largely a failure.

A General Election was called for 28 February by the Tory Government and the *Landworker* as usual exhorted readers to vote Labour. The Tories had created chaos, and only Labour could bring the country back to sanity.

Labour did win the Election, and one of the first letters that the new Secretary of State for the Environment (Tony Crosland) received was from the Union reminding him of the Party's last assurance on the tied cottage. He was written to immediately after the Queen's speech opening the new Parliament made no mention of tied cottages. A reply was awaited by the EC 'aware of Labour's vulnerable position as a minority Government. Even so the system must go.'

A number of important decisions were made at the Biennial at Clacton in 1974, with inflation biting into the purchasing power of the pound. The EC modestly asked for an extra 10p a month in contributions from July 1974 and a further 10p from July 1975. Conference, by a small majority, virtually halved these amounts and authorised contribution increases respectively of 1p and 2p a week from July 1974 and 1975.

Later in 1974, Labour announced that it proposed to abolish the National Industrial Relations Court and repeal the Industrial Relations Act. The affairs of unions and employers' associations would once again be dealt with by the Registry of Friendly Societies, pending the establishment of the Conciliation and Arbitration Service as a statutory body.

The broad effects of the provisions in the new Trade Union and Labour Relations Act on legal immunities was to return to the position as it existed before 1971. The provisions substantially unchanged were: the protection against action for civil conspiracy; the protection of peaceful picketing; immunity which existed before 1971 for persons inducing breaches of contracts of employment in furtherance of a trade dispute was restored. The Act represented a considerable victory for trade unions. Their outright opposition had made the Industrial Relations Act unworkable.

REFERENCES

1. Annual Report, 1968.
2. Minutes of the General Purposes Committee, October 1963.
3. Organising Sub-Committee minutes, December 1966.
4. Organisers' Reports for 1969.
5. *Landworker*, November 1969.

8

Strife Over 'Social Contract'

End of Free Negotiations

When the minority Labour Government decided in 1974 to go to the country again, the *Landworker* carried a statement by the Party's General Secretary, Ron Hayward, that the Tories' attitude towards trade unions was 'a threat to democracy', and the present Government had ended an era of confrontation with the unions. The National Industrial Relations Court had been abolished. The responsibility for good industrial relations had been returned to the employers and unions – where it belonged.

The Election fight was going to be tough. The forces ranged against Labour were immense. According to *Labour Research*, more than 370 companies donated £922,329 to the Tory Party and anti-socialist organisations in 1973–4. In addition, retired Army officers were in the news seeking to raise 'civilian forces' to run the country should trade unionists 'step out of line'.

That year's TUC Conference was the quietest on record. The central point of interest was the Social Contract.* A composite gave full support to the efforts being made by the TUC and Government towards solving the economic problems facing Britain, registered belief in free collective bargaining, and rejected a statutory or compulsory incomes policy.

The General Council backed the Social Contract, which General Secretary Len Murray said was not just about wages, but about sensible ways of dealing with industrial relations, about social justice, and about relations between the TUC and the Government whose policies would make it possible for the unions to achieve their objectives.

Ken Gill, Secretary of the AEU's technical sector, argued that a 'social contract' could only be accepted when substantial progress had been made on the re-distribution of income and wealth, measures to improve housing for lower income groups, a substantial increase in public ownership, and substantial cuts in defence expenditure. After a forceful plea by Murray, the engineers withdrew their motion, and an overwhelming vote, including that of the

---

* A 'contract' between the Government and TUC which dealt with industrial relations.

NUAAW, then passed the composite. The TUC thus played its part in clearing the decks for the hoped-for Labour victory at the polls, which for most delegates was the main object of the exercise.

Labour did win, albeit with a smaller majority than hoped. There was one bright spot for the NUAAW: Joan Maynard won Sheffield, Brightside. It had long been a Labour seat, but the previous occupant, E. Griffiths, had proved too right-wing for the local party and they sacked him. He stood as Independent Labour. Result: Maynard, 18,108; Griffiths, 10,182; R. Walker, Cons, 4,905; W. T. W. Blades, Lib, 3,271. Majority 7,926.

However, the outlook for the NUAAW itself was not all that bright: one sign of the ominous future came when Frank Frolish, Finance Officer, wrote on the Union's 'Vanishing Returns'.[1] He said that despite tremendous efforts by everyone, income over the previous ten years, 1964–1973, had failed miserably to cover gross expenditure to the extent of an average loss of £42,963 per year. The Union's investment income had reduced the shortfall to £17,055 per year. In 1964 the total investment was £433,000, in 1973 this had fallen to £222,159. Basic reasons for this decline were the fall in contributions, the drop in membership, and the sale of investments to cover deficits.

He reviewed the reluctance of biennials to go for a substantial increase in subs, saying, 'The full rate of contributions is 15p per week at present, the price of a loaf . . . Surely members can afford to pay a little more in order to help their Union to survive!' He said that because of the financial situation, the EC had decided to recall biennial conference delegates in May 1975.

The recalled Biennial was asked to increase subs to 20p per week, to ensure that Union funds were not again eroded by rising costs. And to cut costs, district organisers had been reduced by 13 and head office staff by 10. But 1974 had shown an explosion in running costs. Expenditure increased by £57,554. Contributions rose by £50,000. Reg Bottini told the Conference that a recent increase in subs totalling 2p a week 'stands out starkly as quite inadequate' and the EC wanted them to go up by 4p per week.

The EC failed to secure the 20p, but the final outcome made the 94 delegates' journey to London worthwhile. Not because the effective result of a decision for an 80p monthly contribution from August was almost up to the EC's figure, but mainly because the principle of gearing contributions to the hourly rate, abandoned at the 1966 Biennial, was re-established. The resolution for the new rate, moved by D. Taylor, Kent, seconded by L. Wilshire, Wilts, and adopted, was, 'That contributions shall be the equivalent of one hour's pay per calendar month based on the basic ordinary adult male rate as per AWB Order rounded up to the nearest 5p as from 1 August 1975, and thereafter the first full month after any rise in the basic minimum adult male rate.' It was passed by 44 votes to 32.

On the eve of the 1976 Biennial at Malvern, Reg Bottini analysed progress made since the 1974 Biennial. He said that the repeal of the Industrial Relations Act and the introduction of the Employment Protection Act were two outstanding features of the Government's legislation, which among other things extended 'unfair dismissal' provisions to firms employing fewer than four people and required the provision of itemised pay statements, something farmworkers had long sought. And on the Union's 70th anniversary that year, Bert Hazell, reviewing the past 25 years, said that in 1951 when two weeks' annual holiday was secured, this was hailed as a tremendous victory. At first farmers were anxious to keep people at work, even though it did cost an extra week's pay. Times changed, however, and it was rare that a worker failed to take up his holiday entitlement, now three weeks.

The importance of the Union securing paid holidays cannot be stressed too much. Since 1936 it had campaigned for a week's paid holiday and did benefit from the Holidays with Pay Act of 1938, but as with unemployment insurance, farmworkers were singled out as the poor relations; when wage committees ordered holidays, employees were not allowed to take more than three consecutive days off. By 1944, Agricultural Wages committees had almost fixed uniform holidays at 10 days per annum, consisting of four public holidays and six days with pay. But many farmworkers still worked through their holidays for extra money, so by 1976, the changes were truly revolutionary.

Less than two years after his retirement as AGS, Edgar Pill was on the national scene again, this time as EC member for District 11. On leaving the staff, Edgar had moved to Swindon, and continued to make his presence felt throughout Wiltshire and beyond. With the delightful abandon members had come to expect, Edgar let fly at the Labour Government at the 1976 Hampshire County Conference. 'Mrs. Thatcher might be an improvement on the present bunch of incompetents,' he said, after declaring that 'We have lost the opportunity to enter into "free negotiations" with our employers over wages. That right has been taken away by the Labour Party with the connivance of the TUC.' He condemned the TUC for giving away the right of free bargaining in return for 'specious promises' from a Government that clearly had no control over inflation. He described the Social Contract as a 'fraudulent prospectus' that would put directors of a private company in the dock for making false returns.

The EC did not quite see it that way when the incident was discussed at the November meeting. EC members and Union officials, it was agreed, should be 'guided' by Union policy.

Bedfordshire and Buckinghamshire County Conference asked the EC to discontinue the sponsorship of Joan Maynard as MP. The resolution generously conceded that she was entitled to express her views, but her 'views have too often been at variance with NUAAW/TUC policy.' This request caused a furore inside and outside the Union. Joan replied in the *Landworker* saying that Conference had 'a perfect right to do this', but she should have been given a chance to state her case, as right-wing MPs, Reg Prentice and Neville Sandelson, had been. She was proud of what she had done for organised workers. 'They need someone to speak strongly on their behalf and with great support from my Sheffield constituency I shall go on doing it.'

George Scales, Epping, wrote, the Bucks and Beds Conference delegates' 'rounding on Sister Maynard was an act, so contemptible, it makes me feel ashamed of my class, my Union and the name farmworker. Have they no sense of history? Do they honestly believe we would have progressed so far as we have if our destiny had been left to the reforming aspirations of the right-wingers or the middle-of-the-roaders? Their act was a slave's turning on Wilberforce – and a shame on them for that.'

The *Landworker* weighed in saying that differences of opinion on major aspects of Union policy were being brought to the surface, and 'In Freudian terms the effect on the Union may not necessarily be unhealthy, but is not without danger.' On the complaint that Joan had not followed NUAAW/TUC policy it pointed out that these 'are far from being identical. Unlike the TUC and "the cheap food" consumer lobby, the NUAAW want to see UK farming adequately funded, even if this requires a modest devaluation of the Green Pound – which Sister Maynard, along with the Labour Party and the Minister, oppose.' She had attacked the Social Contract despite the fact that the Union went along with it providing that lower-paid workers were given adequate protection. They hadn't been, and the call for free collective bargaining was demanded by Joan and many others within the Union and outside it . . . It could be that Joan was right on these issues and official Union policy wrong.

Mrs. E. Peden, Moreton, Essex, wrote to say Joan was doing a very good job for members. 'Far more than anyone else has done,' while Marian Neville,* Redhill, Surrey, thought ' Previous Union-sponsored MPs sat in the House for longer and with much less to their credit than she had' and wanted Beds and Bucks to rescind its resolution.

The Social Contract came up at the Norfolk County Conference where Wilf Page said, 'We are told we are all in the same boat under it. Then we hear Jim Slater [a City financier] on TV saying cheerfully that he owes a million pounds. Five per cent of the population still owns 49.6% of the nation's wealth. We are still two nations. Workers should not be taken in by propaganda saying that they were threatening the existence of a Labour Government. Local and by-election results showed that it was the Tory policies of the Labour Government which threatened its existence.' All the same, Ross Pierson from head office, told delegates, 'We are bound by the Social Contract for this year at any rate, though what Norfolk thinks today the country will often think tomorrow.'

*   *   *

With the May 1977 issue of the *Landworker*, Stan Hayward retired. Despite his firm views on many subjects, he was determined always that all points of

---

*   Mrs. Neville later became Joan Maynard's secretary in the House of Commons.

view should be reflected in the journal's columns, as essential to democratic debate. He no doubt believed his trenchant editorials would put people right.

His successor was 31-year-old Francis Beckett, an example of the new breed of Union officials, usually graduates. At the University of Keele he took a degree in history and philosophy, and later worked for the housing charity Shelter and the NUS, editing its newspaper, *National Student*. Francis was soon to give the *Landworker* a modernised and more lively appearance, making it more militant too.

Two prominent members left the EC in 1976. Edgar Pill retired, but was to remain active in the Union until his death in 1988. Jess Waterman, aged 68, defeated in the EC election, was for 40 years secretary of Spettisbury (Dorset) branch, and was succeeded by P. C. Woodland.

Another General Secretary Resigns

A few minutes after 11am on 22 September 1977, at the meeting of the EC, Bert Hazell took the unusual step of summoning all five departmental heads to join the meeting. Then he uncharacteristically stood to make an announcement, which a stunned executive had heard only a few minutes earlier. The General Secretary, he said, had received a warning that his health was not up to continuing with a job as arduous as the one he had shouldered for the past eight years. He would have to retire at the relatively early age of 61. Reg Bottini would stay in office till 7 February 1978 to give the Union time to elect a new General Secretary. He would also become, from 1 October 1977, a member of the Meat and Livestock Commission and chairman of its Consumers Committee.

The *Landworker*[2] carried tributes to Reg's work, in which Bert said he had been a loyal and hardworking officer for 33 years, and 'no one could ever doubt the enthusiasm for the Union which Reg exudes whenever he appears on a platform.' He said that Reg was a formidable opponent as any employer would concede, and it was in this field he had achieved his greatest victories. Among other tributes was that of Stan Brumby, EC, at the North Lincolnshire dinner at Market Rasen, who said that under Reg's leadership the Union had achieved a five-day 40-hour week, a sick-pay scheme, a wages structure and the end of the tied cottage system. The Gold Badge of the TUC was presented to Reg at the 1978 Congress, on retiring from the General Council.

There were five candidates for the general secretaryship, and in the January 1978 Landworker, each spoke his mind, and each reflected on the increasing difficulties facing the Union as an independent national body. Jack Boddy was 'pleased to receive 73 nominations for the post'. He was in no doubt that the Union was facing a critical situation arising out of financial problems caused by inflation and the failure to attract new members. He wanted a sustained campaign to improve wages and conditions.

1. Campaigning work locally and nationally was important if the Union's objectives were to be achieved. This was recognised by the Shropshire members, seen here in their home territory in July 1954.

2. Skegness was a favourite resort for the Union's annual rallies. The turn-outs were usually impressive, as at this one in June 1955.

3. Edwin Gooch, President (*second from left*), greets some of the Union's 700 members who formed up in Brunswick Square, London, before marching to Hyde Park, on a demonstration for higher wages in October 1954.

4. After marching down Oxford Street the farmworkers were addressed by the Union's President at a rally at Speakers' Corner,

5. North Yorkshire members parade in Northallerton in 1956, for the dedication at the parish church of a new Union banner. The turn-out demonstrates the strength and the support the Union had in rural areas.

6. Tom Williams, Labour's post-war Minister of Agriculture, addressing members at the dedication of the new banner in Northallerton. With him on the trailer are: (*left to right*) Edwin Gooch, President; George Dodds; Tom Gasgoyne; and Dr. Ramsey, Archbishop of York, later to become the Archbishop of Canterbury. Williams was said to be the best Minister of Agriculture the farmers ever had; he gave them almost everything they wanted. He was less ready to satisfy the claims of the farmworkers. Gooch does not appear to be impressed by his speech – he seems to have gone to sleep.

7. The Union's Legal Department did splendid work on behalf of members injured at work or during their non-working activities. In May 1961, Harold Collison, General Secretary, presented W. Day, a member of Over Wallop branch, with a cheque for £12,500 in respect of his claim for injuries received in a car crash. With them is Mr. Day's mother.

8. Bert Hazell, President, presents to Frank Robinson a seven-day clock from his colleagues in recognition of his 28½ years' service on the EC in 1970. By their sides are their wives.

Arthur Leary wrote of his experiences of the 'tough business of negotiating will all kinds of employers from one-man organisations to multi-million pound companies.' He had been a trade unionist since the age of 11, a shop steward, branch secretary, a collector and thought the Union desperately needed better understanding and co-operation between head office, branches, districts and counties.

Ross Pierson said that the priorities for the new General Secretary must be significant improvements in pay and conditions, and to bring into membership the 50% of farmworkers who had never been organised. He believed the Union could survive as an independent Union. Leonard Pike believed that 'Our Union, even with its scarce resources has a great tradition in the countryside, a tradition with which the NUAAW must remain identified. Its services must be strengthened in terms of efficiency, speed and understanding by which the advice and help is given to each individual member when in need.' Jim Watts declared 'that my 19 years of service with the Union, 12 years of which have been as head of the Legal Department has given me a deep understanding of the problems affecting the membership, and the insight into the Union's affairs that the position demands.'

Jack Boddy who was elected with over 1,000 votes more than his nearest rival, was further to the left than any General Secretary since before the Second World War. In his initial statement he said, 'My first priority will be to get our members' wages improved until they reach those in other industries.'* The loyalty and admiration of his own members in Norfolk must have accounted for some of his 11,065 votes, but over the years his reputation had spread outside his own county. His nearest rival, Watts, received 9,810 votes. He was followed by Pierson, with 5,940; Leary with 5,915; and Pike 2,436. 46.6% of the members voted out of a total membership of 75,463, and Jack received 31% of the votes cast. His election meant that for the first time since the Union was founded, both the President and General Secretary were Norfolk men.

Jack was the first district officer to go straight from the 'counties' to the general secretaryship. After defeating three head office candidates, some members of the head office staff felt he didn't have an easy time when he first arrived there. But with his cheerful disposition, despite the many problems he faced, this gradually changed, and he managed to streamline many head office procedures, and save money.

---

* Between 1949 and 1972, average weekly earnings increased by 291% in agriculture and 376% in other industries, and this situation was made worse by the longer hours farmworkers worked. The ratio of gross weekly earnings in agriculture relative to all industries rose from 75 (average 1970–3) to 82 (average 1974–80). See Lund, Morris Temple and Watson, *Wages and Employment in Agriculture: England and Wales, 1960–80*, Government Economic Service Working Paper No 52, MAFF, 1982.

From Farm Boy to President

At the June 1978 Biennial, after 57 years' service to the Union, Bert Hazell bowed out as President. Wilf Page said Bert had most admirably filled the huge gap following the death of Edwin Gooch. Let us get more closely acquainted with Bert.

Bert, President from 1966 to 1976, was doing the ironing when I called on him in 1988, in his semi in a better-off suburb of York. It was not long since Dora, his wife, had died.

Bert, then 81, was greyer than during his presidential years, but still with that healthy glow to his face, and as nimble as ever. He had a big garden which he looked after, in addition to caring for his daughter's garden and that of a blind lady next door.

There was still a trace of a Norfolk accent, despite his many years in Yorkshire. He was born in Attleborough, opposite the cider works, the son of a farmworker. Later they moved to Wymondham, where his father was a horseman at 14s a week. He attended the village school, and like so many of the less privileged of his age, left to become a farm boy, doing everything for 7s 6d a week. By 16 he had a team of horses, all the crocks, because he was still the 'boy'. By 21, he was on 15s, but in 1923, he was back on 7s 6d, after the scrapping of the Corn Production Act which caused prices to fall and led to the famous Norfolk Strike.

Bert explained: 'Dad's wages had dropped from 50s to 25s in December 1922, and the Farmers' Federation [forerunner of the NFU] gave notice of a further reduction. Dad's wages were to go down to 18s and mine to 6s. I was then 17. So farmworkers had had enough. The strike began.'

Forty-five men worked on the farm with Bert, all in the Union, including Bert, who had been enrolled immediately he began work. Bert soon became active in the Wymondham branch and organised the Silfield Horticultural Show, splitting the profit between the Union's benevolent fund and the Labour Party. He was on the EC of South Norfolk Labour Party, which had George Edwards as President and Edwin Gooch as Chairman.

He recalled 1931 when Edwin was prospective Labour candidate, but didn't want to commit himself. ' "My bosses [he was a sub editor in Norwich] won't like it and I won't win after this Ramsey Macdonald business!" Gooch said. George thumped the table saying, "Edwin my boy, you don't back down now, you've been too long associated with this Union, you'll stand." Stand he did, but it was some years before he became an MP.'

Bert was fully involved in Labour Party work as well as that of the Union, and in 1933 became full-time Labour agent for E Norfolk, where Labour always lost its deposit. At the next election Labour increased its vote by 6,000 and saved its deposit.

It was in 1936 that Bill Holmes, General Secretary, asked Bert to join the staff as district organiser, and he left Norfolk and took over the whole of Yorkshire, a move he never regretted. He coped with this enormous area until

1942, when on his recommendation Jack Brocklebank took over North Yorkshire and another DO was appointed for the West Riding. In 1937, there were about 250 members in the whole of Yorkshire; by the mid-war years, the numbers rose to nearly 9,000.

In 1945, Bert fought Barkston Ash (so named after a little village with an ash tree) for Labour, never previously anything but Tory, with big majorities. Bert cut the Tory majority to 116. As is so often when a Tory seat is in danger, when he contested it again in 1950, a number of 'Labour' areas had been removed from the constituency, and he lost by about 5,000 votes.

He held many important regional posts, including membership of the Production Board for Yorkshire, and the East and West Riding Regional Board for Industry; he became chairman of the latter in 1954. He had been a member of Leeds Regional Hospital Board since 1947; after reorganisation he became chairman of North Yorkshire Area Health Authority, and in 1982 was made chairman of York Health Authority.

But he was not to sever his ties with Norfolk. In 1962 Edwin Gooch told him he was considering retiring from Parliament and asked Bert to stand instead. Bert did, and retained the seat by 53 votes in the 1964 election, and in 1966 by 732 and held it until 1970. Despite all his regional activities, Bert had remained a DO until he became an MP; there were no vacancies for DOs when he lost his seat, but he was busy as Union President.

Looking back over the years, Bert believed the Union could have done more to retain members. 'I didn't believe joining up with a big union would help, and I got the impression we were appointing officers in the Union who were prepared to accept it as it was, and not do the donkey work necessary to build the Union. The organiser was the Union, and some were very weak; they regarded it as an administrative job. DOs were father figures, they looked after the members and saw to the social side, but they didn't see it as the evangelistic job, like George Edwards did. We didn't attract the best people, we had some good people, but not enough with real zeal. Other unions were paying higher rates, they got the better people.'

Bert believed that the greatest achievements of the Union in the post-war years had been, firstly the setting up of the AWB for fixing wages at national level, and secondly, preventing evictions from tied cottages. And he felt that the Union's social work was important, especially that of the Legal Department. 'Wages were a major achievement, you have a tradition in the countryside of getting away with as low a pay as possible, and in spite of all the criticism, farmworkers have been brought nearer to the wages of industrial workers with shorter hours.'

Bert said he always opposed Britain's membership of the EEC. 'I don't believe our membership has brought us any blessings. I can't think of any major improvements that have stemmed from it for farmworkers.'

Of Alfred Dann, Bert said, 'He was a character, a true Cockney, put a tremendous amount of enthusiasm into the legal side. He became extremely popular throughout the Union. He felt very strongly about the tied cottage.'

Of Harold Collison: 'We saw a different breed in the Union. I liked Harold. More philosophical sort of chap, a deep thinker, constructive in his speeches. Could be very emotional. Once when a Biennial turned down a 6d increase in subs, he went back of stage and said "I'll throw it all up." ' Bert persuaded him not to. And of Reg Bottini: 'Again a different personality, he got the top job he wanted, and felt important. Very good negotiator. I liked Reg, but I wasn't happy about the way he finished. I think he felt he had had enough and saw what was coming and didn't want the responsibility.'

Bert believed that the Union was badly let down by the Labour Party on the tied cottage over the years. 'I led the Union delegation to Jim Callaghan when he was chairman of Labour's home policy committee. He said, "We will take the abolition on board," but he didn't. Similar pledges before came to nothing. I think Labour's parliamentary party thought they were opening too many doors, to the police and others living in tied cottages. It was disheartening, it lost them votes in rural areas, but not enough to lose seats, because they hadn't got any except in Norfolk. A lot of farmworkers were happy in tied cottages – for some it was the only way they would ever get a house – but when they were about to be thrown out it was a different story.'

In the sixties and seventies, Bert felt there was over-organisation at head office and too much 'empire building'. 'The Union was part of our life, it was not a job, it was a way of life, there was a comradeship about the villages. You'd go to a school or hall, you were among friends, they might disagree with you, but they were still friends.'

A Man with Evangelical Zeal

One man who possessed to the full that evangelical zeal Bert spoke about, was Jack Brocklebank, CBE, life-long Union and Labour activist, but his passion and enthusiasm often got him into trouble with the Union.

Jack was in fact, a protégé of Bert's, but their political paths were often far apart. Jack was on the left, Bert on the right, or as he might have claimed, a 'moderate'. I visited Jack in 1988; then 76, he lived in retirement in a bungalow at Dishforth, near York. He was still busy collecting Union subs, and still paying the full rate as a member. 'I wouldn't want anyone telling me I'm a half member,' said the always jovial Jack. There I met his wife Ada, and experienced something of her warm hospitality. She served a lovely meal, and her melt-in-the-mouth home-made biscuits will long be remembered.

Jack was born in Holderness in the East Riding, and attended the village CoE school. It had a very good headmaster, and pupils were encouraged to take an interest in civics, which is perhaps reflected in Jack's later life.

On leaving school Jack helped a farmer with the harvest, and then lived-in on a farm for £7, from August to Martinmass (11 November). His next full year's wage was £17, for which he handled horses, ploughed, harrowed, and 'knocked about' some fallow land by taking the wheels of the plough off and did 'swing ploughing'. He looked after the horses Saturday afternoons and Sunday mornings. 'We heaved a sigh of relief when the horses were turned out of the stable at the end of April, and we were freed of that weekend work.'

Jack had always been a voracious reader, and the chairman of the Leven NUAW branch always made sure there was a *Landworker* in the stables. Jack read it avidly, and at 17, joined the Union, paying 4d a week. Another eye-opener for Jack was a cowman, Charlie Grey, who introduced Jack to the Stock Exchange. 'He understood how it worked, and I've been anti-Stock Exchange ever since.' He has fond memories too, of Tommy Gasgoyne, 'who taught us all we knew about how to get things through and beat the platform.' Another great influence was Harry Maulson, an EC member. 'Harry was a Methodist lay preacher, and right through the Depression years he was so powerful, he held the Union together.' Frank Robinson, another Methodist lay preacher made a 'remarkable contribution'.

Some years later Jack saw an advert in the *Landworker* for a District Organiser and applied. He didn't get the job, but the branch secretary said, 'I understand you've bin writing to London, we'd better make you a branch officer.' He became chairman, a post he held for four years, until he became North Yorkshire DO in 1942. Jack didn't apply for the job, Bert Hazell, who had spotted his talents, recommended him. He kept the job, sometimes by the skin of his teeth, until 1970.

He found it easy to build the Union during the Second World War. 'They were joining almost like apples falling off trees. I was helped by the number of hostels set up for farmworkers, some were land girls, some conscientious objectors directed to farm work, some drifters, who came because there was a home for them in the hostels.' When he took over, there were only 12 established branches, some of them '1918' branches, the magical year when the Union first got going in Yorkshire. Within five years Jack had nearly 100 branches, membership went up from 600 to 2,000. Some were in unpromising territory such as in Carperby in Wensleydale, which was mainly grassland without much hired labour. Jack found two recruits there, Joe and Bill. It was the latter, Bill Sutill, a very good Dalesman, who started the branch there which was built up to 30 members. Then some farmworker at Hawes, 'capital' of Wensleydale, got a branch going there. 'I was pleased at raising the Union flag at the top of one of our famous Dales. They were lovely people.'

Working conditions were still bad in many parts, and Jack was shocked to find, in the late forties, people still working until 4pm on Saturdays. 'I decided the only way to beat it was to get a branch in almost every village.' He did, and started clouting farmers with claims for overtime for Saturday, which they wouldn't pay. Some farmers offered Jack money to stop his campaigning, but he told them to pay it to the men they owed overtime. Soon all overtime finished.

There was no Union banner for the North Riding, and Jack set his heart on getting one. He had banner ticket books printed, which sold at 1s each or 20 for £1. Some buyers were disappointed there were no prizes. 'What are you complaining about,' said Jack, 'you're now part owner of a lovely banner.' And it was a splendid banner, which depicted horses, trees, glasshouses, a combine, a shorthorn cow, a large white pig, sheep and collies, representing all aspects of rural Yorkshire. Archbishop Ramsey dedicated the banner in Northallerton Parish Church, which was packed with 800 people, and 2,000 outside.

After the war, Jack noticed that the NFU was constantly having slap-up dinners, and thought, what's good enough for them, is good enough for us. So he started NUAW dinners in his district, which were a great success, often with attendances of nearly 200. 'These were very important, they got farm-workers together and made them realise their strength. I always made them into political events with Labour speakers.'

In addition to his Union duties, Jack was chairman of Thirsk and Malton Labour Party, and a county and district councillor for many years, but most of his energy was devoted to the Union. Jack somehow found time for a vast amount of local government work and was on the National Rural District Councils' Association, and only missed being its first chairman by one vote. Instead, he became vice-chairman, and was involved in discussions with the Government on local authority matters. Later, Harold Macmillan invited him to be a member of the Central Housing Advisory Committee, which gave scope to Jack's keen advocacy of better rural housing, and fitted in well with the Union's policy. 'I had the good luck to get into the mainstream of post-war building. But we made the mistake of thinking old farmworkers would want to live in the hamlets where they'd worked, and we built there, but they didn't. They wanted the larger villages with shops and public transport.'

Jack was critical of much local government reorganisation. 'Bigger authori-ties have led to bigger bureaucracies, and their policies become controlled by officials; the language these officials use floors many lay members, and the bigger the authority the less efficient they become. It can only be put right by going back to smaller authorities.' He was appointed liaison officer to Fred Peart, Minister of Agriculture in 1964, and went on to serve under seven Ministers, and was a Government director of the British Sugar Corporation for four years, until it was taken over by Berrisfords.

Another important job Jack did was on the Northern Pennines Rural Development Board, as vice-chairman. This was a splendid attempt to bring farming, forestry, tourism and transport together to serve the best needs of isolated areas, and it was succeeding when there was a change of Government in 1971, and Edward Heath became Premier. 'We had interfered with the free transfer and sale of land, we were more interested in giving economic security to the people already there. There was a great deal of fragmentation in land ownership, with people crossing other people's land to get to their own, and we had powers to buy that land and hold it until such time as we could redraw boundaries and make it into a more economic holding and then sell it back. We had enormous support in the area and people liked what we doing.' But the new Government didn't, and wiped out the Board.

Jack felt it was important that Labour people should hold onto as many posts as possible in local and regional authorities, and in 1970 had resigned as DO to do just this. He knew that the post of DO would go to one of them, but other posts might not. The Development Board had been paying him £1,500 a year, and the North East Electricity Consultative Council, as chairman, paid £1,000. 'It was more than I was getting as an organiser, so I knew I could manage financially.'

Jack was a strong advocate of Union stands at county shows. 'Members are proud to have a stake in the big shows and come over to the Union tents with pride; we always made new members at shows, often at the Great Yorkshire Show we would make 20 members a day. It showed us as an important part of industry and that's what I wanted all the time.'

He believed that the Union played a substantial part in Labour's 1945 victory, when rural seats were won. 'While we were strong in 1945, the NFU was also strong and was building up the most powerful lobby ever seen in Parliament, and I think that prevented us making the progress that we should have done.' For Jack the Union's greatest achievement since 1945 was the restrictions on eviction from tied cottages; the greatest failure, wages and conditions. He also believed the Union failed to recruit all it could in the post-war years. 'Isolation of the farmworker was the greatest problem.'

A staunch opponent of Britain's entry into the EEC, Jack did, nonetheless, feel that we were not using EEC regulations on conditions of employment that we could and should. However, he believed that a serious attempt should have been made to overcome the difficulties of getting out of the EEC. 'My idea of a European Common Market would unite the whole of Europe, including Eastern Europe.'

Jack had a number of brushes with the Union's executive, the most important has been told earlier, but in 1976 another came when Yorkshire County Committee decided to break with tradition and not invite the General Secretary to be chief speaker at their county conference, and invited Joan Maynard instead. This decision followed a report by Jack on the Biennial at Malvern, which he said censured the standard of service provided by the Union's head office. Reg Bottini claimed that he had been libelled in a report of Jack's speech in a Yorkshire evening paper, and the case was to have gone to the High Court of Justice, Queen's Bench Division. As both were Union officers, the Union was paying the legal costs of both parties! Recalling the event Jack said, 'I was quite upset. I had always regarded Reg as a friend. I had been to his home, and knew his wife, it was not the sort of thing I wanted.' Jack denied libel, and one day his solicitors got a telephone call from Reg's solicitors, saying that 'Mr. Bottini, in a spirit of sweet reason, wished to bring the litigation to an end and withdraw the action.' Reg did just that, and sensibly, it was the end of the matter.

*   *   *

After the retirement of Bert Hazell, the Union's new President was 51-year-old Nottingham forestry worker John Hose, who set himself four priorities. First, he wanted to stop the Union looking like a friendly society and start being a union. Second, he wanted a massive recruitment drive; third, re-deployment of officers in the field; and fourth, concentration on the real activities of the Union instead of outside activities such as chairmanships of boards. John had won 59 votes to Joan Maynard's 29 and Edgar Pill's 4. Unlike most top Union men, John was not a member of any political party.

*   *   *

Two new organisers were appointed in 1978: James Boddy, 28, took over West Norfolk, and Peter Medhurst, 34, started in Suffolk. James, who had worked on farms most of his life, took over the Norfolk job from his father, when he became General Secretary. Peter had lived in Suffolk, but had for the previous 15 years been a cabinet maker in Yorkshire where he was active in the NUAAW.

A new Finance Officer, John Tye, was appointed in 1978 to succeed Frank Frolish, and was something of a rare breed: an accountant with a lifetime's commitment to Labour. He was 52, treasurer of Herts & Stevenage Labour Party, and in every job he had held, he had where possible been active in the relevant trade union.

*   *   *

'Labour or Dark Ages' asked the *Landworker* in May 1979, as the nation prepared for a crucial General Election. It was clear that if the Tories won, they intended to dismantle state-owned industry, welfare rights and the council housing system.

> Gone are the days of conservatism-with-a-human-face – the comparatively gentle approach of Mr. Heath. Mrs. Thatcher and her group of Neanderthal advisers intend to beat the workers back to the stone age . . . whatever the Labour Government's faults, Labour is still the only party for the workers and the alternative is too appalling to contemplate.

Labour lost the Election, Mrs. Thatcher was installed as head of the new right-wing authoritarian Government, and the *Landworker*'s dire predictions proved only too true in the years ahead.

Writing in the *Landworker*, Jack Boddy said that they didn't want a Conservative government, but now they had got it they had to work with it and try to strike a proper working relationship. Which was why within a week of the Election he had had a meeting with the Minister of Agriculture, Peter Walker, who understandably at that early stage was not ready to commit himself, but he was at least ready to listen. They had to work with them, but that did not mean they would get 'our unqualified support'. If they mount the sort of attack on trade unions or on the legislation which protects workers 'we, along with the whole of the rest of the trade union movement will do our best to oppose them.'

That year's Tolpuddle Rally was the biggest ever, with 6,000 NUAAW members and other trade unionists descending on the small village. It was an impressive display of strength. Practically everyone was wearing a wages campaign sticker calling for £100 a week for farmworkers.

Jack Ding, deputy Finance Officer, retired after a lifetime of service to the NUAAW. He joined the Union as an office junior in 1930, making a record just short of 50 years' service.

Tory Promise of Hard Times

Soon after its election in 1979, the new Tory Government outlined its plans to weaken the trade union movement and take away the individual rights of employees. 'The effect will undoubtedly be to worsen industrial relations,' said the *Landworker*. The Tories proposed further restrictions on picketing, and pickets could be held to have 'conspired' with someone who was not allowed to picket but had joined the picket line out of sympathy. The employer could then sue for damages and a picket could be imprisoned if he or she refused to pay. Any form of sympathetic picketing would be illegal, and picketing could be made almost impossible by going to the brink of outlawing it. There were proposals for postal ballots on strikes and changes in union rules which would weaken shop floor, branch and conference structure, and increase the influence of press comment on members who never bothered to go to any meetings when they had to decide how to vote. The Tories proposed scrapping legislation which the NUAAW had successfully used to hoist members' wages to a reasonable level. The NUAAW believed that the 'Government seems to intend first to tie the hands of the workers and then blindfold them.'

Dorset Area Conference[3] unanimously condemned the financial restrictions imposed by the Government on social services, the NHS, education and increases in VAT. In an effort to weaken such Union opposition, the Government was introducing the misnamed 'Employment Bill', which went further than the Industrial Relations Act 1971 in restricting communication to other trade unionists at different work places during strikes. The Union believed it contrary to Article 10 of the European Convention on Human Rights which provides that 'Everyone has the right to freedom of expression.'

*   *   *

As befitted a Union with close links with the land, the NUAAW in 1981 held a big celebration of the 600th anniversary of the Peasants' Revolt. It was commemorated on the same day as the 1981 jobs 'revolt' reached London.

On 31 May, 500 out-of-work men and women reached London after a month-long trek from Liverpool. In the capital, 150,000 supporters joined them in a march from Hyde Park to Trafalgar Square.

GLC leader Ken Livingstone gave them a civic reception and Opposition leader Michael Foot cheered them on their way at Hyde Park and then drove to St. Albans where 1,000 farmworkers were celebrating the Peasants' Revolt. By the end of the day the link between the two groups was as clear as Nelson's Column.

TUC General Secretary, Len Murray, spoke in Trafalgar Square and his deputy, Norman Willis, was in St. Albans, telling farmworkers that the battle started in 1381 was far from over. Speakers in London and St. Albans made the connection. The peasants revolted because of appalling conditions and serfdom, and in 1981, farmworkers were still badly paid, with Mrs. Thatcher making job security a thing of the past for many industries.

There was a march through St. Albans, and the thousand marchers crowded into the ancient cathedral to hear a service which included a musical re-enactment, composed by Alan Bush, of the murder of the peasant leader Wat Tyler, performed by the Workers' Music Association.

*   *   *

Determination to reverse the policies of the Tory Government, which by common consent was the most vicious anti-working class administration for decades, was a recurring theme at Union conferences in 1981. Many resolutions condemning Government actions were passed. No less than three motions about Government spending cuts were passed at the S & E Devon Conference. Yorkshire Conference condemned the 'slashing of rural bus services', while North Devon deplored cuts in local authority spending which had a 'considerable impact on people in rural areas'. Three resolutions against public spending cuts were carried at the North Lindsey Conference, and the South Wales Area Conference opposed the sale of smallholdings by some county councils.

REFERENCES

1. *Landworker*, January 1975.
2. *Landworker*, December 1977.
3. *Landworker*, January 1980.

9

Move for Merger Rejected

Emotional Discussions

In May 1980, the Union's Biennial returned to the birth-place of the modern Union, Norfolk. The small seaside town of Cromer played host to 100 delegates who met in the Pavilion Theatre at the end of the pier, with the sea as a dramatic back-cloth to emotional discussions on the Union's independence. The Union's financial difficulties had led many members and officials to believe that the only way to fight off bankruptcy was to merge with a larger union.

However, such a merger was to be delayed. By 69 votes to 39, after a two-hour debate, delegates backed a bid to remain independent. They asked the EC to put more muscle behind the move by giving a positive lead in recruiting. Jack Boddy said, 'Now the decision has been taken, it's up to every member to help to build our Union. The EC will give a lead, but the best recruiters are the rank and file members . . . The case for Union membership has seldom been stronger with the attacks on all workers coming from the Government.'

The debate was serious and agonising. 'There's no room for sentiment in the battle to keep rural trade unionism alive,' said Ted Sales, Dorset, 'for many older members, the Union represents a huge slice of our lives. But we cannot live on sentiment. We have to think of younger members, and look to the future.'

'We are in Norfolk where we were born and old members would turn in their graves at the thought of a merger,' said Andrew Baynham, Worcs, proposing an independence motion. 'Our present position is due to financial starvation and we must find a cure or die.' In 1978 there were 2,500 branches of which 50 paid nothing to head office; and 1,246 made no new members. The previous year there were 2,471 branches of which 86 failed to remit any contribution, and 1,295 did not make one new member. 'If we pull together we can remain independent,' he went on. 'If this Union is taken over, many members will resign, and be left with no protection whatsoever.'

Bert Slack, Derbys, seconding, said only the NUAAW would look after the interests of agricultural workers. 'It would be criminal to throw away years of sweat and toil which have been put into building up the Union.'

Charles Brown, Berks & Oxon, said that the Union did not want to find itself in the hands of 'another asset-stripping' trade union. The NUAAW was, he said, the finest rural union in the world.

Putting the case for amalgamation, Joan Maynard said, 'I am sure every one of us would prefer to keep an independent Union, but some of us believe that is no longer possible.' The Union's deficit at the end of 1979 was £49,689 and she understood that a deficit of £80,000 was predicted for the current year. The Union had not lived on its contributions income for many years. 'We have really lived on the seed corn of the past for a very long time, while we have had fewer and fewer members because of the dramatic reduction in the labour force.'

Barry Salmon, Suffolk, said it gave him no pleasure to support a merger but they had to face hard financial facts. If the Union remained independent, its weaker areas might be lost and it could find itself an eastern-based union, where there was a large membership. 'We are here to try and keep the Union organisation with as many members as possible.' Tom Carlile, Somerset, said, 'We have a completely divided EC on the principle of amalgamation. The alternative to amalgamation will mean reorganisation and reduction in staff. Some people would rather cut the Union's throat than amalgamate with another Union.' D. Chapman, S Devon: 'The TGWU would transfer 12,000 of their members into our trade group if we amalgamated.' Dorothy Mills, Kent: 'There has always been this problem that everything has had to be penny pinched.' Frank Lewis, Staffs: 'At the present rate of withdrawals, this time next year you won't have a penny except Headland House.' Herbert Sutton, Notts: 'Many branch secretaries have stated they do not wish to carry on if we amalgamate. We have had our backs to the wall many times before and come out fighting.'

Edgar Pill, Wilts: 'We are very definitely in favour of remaining independent. We feel that with better management, economies can be made without inflicting hardship on the staff or membership. One suggestion – sell Headland House and move into the countryside if that is necessary.' Mike Bisset, Herts: 'Unions are made of men, not money. If the men are there to do the work, money will come.' Hugh Harnwell, Wisbech: 'This is the place where the Union was born. Don't let it die here. If the founder could start without finance in 1906, surely we can continue now.' Bill Francis, Hereford: 'The only thing Transport House would be interested in would be your contributions. Service would go to the wall.' Marjorie Ward, Hunts: 'We are not talking about amalgamation but annihilation.' A. Minett, Cambs: 'I have orders from my branch that if we amalgamate we will be 160 members short.' Maurice Housden, Hants: 'If we don't merge we shall have to part with the service of organisers, which is worse.' George Sandle, Norfolk: 'Don't slay the lamb on its own ground.'

Jack Boddy said the EC recommended support for the independence motion. 'In the two years since I have been General Secretary, my task has been to try to ensure this organisation remains independent to continue to represent rural workers.'

Anyone who listened to the debate could not fail to be impressed by the undoubted pride of speakers on both sides of the argument, at the history, traditions and achievements of the Union. But there was a disquieting lack of strategies for salvation. One thing was sure, a policy of cutting back, without a complementary positive approach, would have been a recipe for suicide.

At Cromer, John Hose received a vote of confidence to carry on as President, defeating a considerable challenge from Joan Maynard, with EC member Stan Aston, coming third.

Edgar Pill renewed his suggestion that Headland House be sold when he stood for election to the EC later that year. He re-asserted his strong belief in independence and declared, 'In order to strengthen the Union it is essential to make economies at all levels and release money now tied up in premises that are admittedly too large and no longer necessary for the administration of the Union.' He wanted the money raised to be used to establish headquarters outside London and the surplus to be invested and used to supplement contributions income to provide a satisfactory service to members.

'Jack Boddy asks: "Have you recruited a new member this year?" ' was the question on a new leaflet issued by the Union later in 1980. On the cover was a picture of a stern-faced Jack, finger pointing in a Lord Kitchener pose. The intensive recruiting campaign of recent years was being stepped up, but it was largely a failure.

Before the year was out the price of the *Landworker* was doubled to 10p. The heavy subsidy the Union was paying on its journal had become too big a drain on a very limited budget. And the paper announced that the 97 delegates to the May Biennial would be recalled on 29 November to decide whether to put up the subs. The move followed a demand from 13 area committees to hold a recall Biennial. The EC was to propose: 'This conference accepts that as an alternative to amalgamation and to ensure the continued independence of a rural trade union, the monthly rate of contributions to be 140% of the AWB hourly rate.'

That was in the October *Landworker*, but on the front page of the November issue was the news that at the Special Conference, there would be a second motion proposed by the EC. It had decided to take this action in the light of the many amendments received from branches to the first motion it submitted on subs, and which the Standing Orders Committee felt unacceptable. Motion 2 said: 'This Conference instructs the EC to re-open the discussions, held early in the year with three major unions, with a view to a merger with one or other. Following these talks the recommendations to the membership by the EC shall be made in the best interests of the current membership to ensure the maintenance of Rural Trade Unionism at the highest level.' Each branch, district and area committee could submit one amendment.

Ken Tullett, Malton, S Yorks, said, 'No one will be particularly surprised that the Biennial is having to be recalled . . . branch secretaries must be gloomily aware that their best efforts in enrolling new members in ones and twos are of little avail if hundreds are being shed in poultry processing and forestry. If, at Cromer, those on the EC in favour of continued independence had spelled out more clearly the inevitable price, it is possible that the vote on amalgamation might have gone the other way. There seems little alternative now to amalgamation on the best terms we can get . . . who knows what the verdict of history on the last years of the NUAAW will be? Plenty of bad luck, yes, but some failures in imagination and will.'[1]

Merger Plan Gets Go-Ahead

The special Conference, held at the NUT's Mander Hall in Mabledon Place, London, on 29 November 1980, was chaired by John Hose. After heated debate, and some recrimination, delegates gave the thumbs up to a merger with a bigger union.

The end of the independent Union came mainly because the massive cut down in the agricultural workforce had decimated membership. Whether the Union might have husbanded some of its earlier strength by a more militant policy in the fifties and sixties, and secured a greater share of the wealth its members played such a large part in creating, will doubtless be argued for many years to come. But the fact that farmworkers had been treated so badly by their employers, at times backed by both Conservative and Labour Governments, did not encourage many potential recruits to join the Union. And this forced many good men and women, who could have played an active role in the Union, into other industries.

This was partly reflected in the discussions at the special Conference, particularly in the belief of some delegates, that a merger with a larger union would give them greater strength in wage negotiations, with the possibility of militant action to back up their demands. In the event, no such militancy as regards strike action on a large scale ever emerged after the merger. That it might have done, had it not been for the Thatcher government's legal strangle-hold on the unions, is open to discussion.

The idea of a merger was not new. Jack Boddy told me that approaches to merge 'took place upon the election of every NUAW General Secretary, including myself, since the TGWU's inception in 1922. Such a merger came nearest in 1939, when an agreement was complete enough to be considered by both ECs. Members who remember this period, believe that only the outbreak of war, with the subsequent large rise in NUAW membership, stopped it going ahead.' At the 1972 Biennial, Tom Potter, a left-winger from Burston, Norfolk, had moved a composite that in view of the continuing decline in the fortunes of the Union, the EC 'immediately take measures to enter into exploratory talks with the leaders of other unions catering for agricultural and allied workers with a view to amalgamation.' It was seconded by W. Boulton, Lancs, in 'the full belief that we are not competent enough to get the farmworkers a reasonable standard of living.' Another left-winger, Ted Sales, Dorset, opposed on the grounds that they had a programme for reorganisation and it was up to them in the field to get the additional members to make the whole thing worthwhile. 'So, for God's sake, let us make the effort to make this Union work.' The EC's view that there was no other Union which 'could organise and negotiate on behalf of agricultural workers in the manner of this Union' was accepted, and the motion was lost.

At the 1980 Special Conference it was Ted Sales who proposed an amendment to the EC resolution calling for merger talks. He said it 'beefed up the original EC resolution' and the amended motion went through by 47 votes to 39. It said: 'This conference instructs the EC to re-open discussions, held earlier in the year with three major unions, with a view to a merger with one or the other. Conference now accepts that there is no alternative to a merger . . . Conference therefore further instructs the EC to seek immediately the best possible terms for a merger with the union of their choice on the understanding that they will establish an agricultural and allied workers' division within their organisation. The final proposals to be put to the membership at the earliest possible opportunity.'

Time and money had indeed run out on the NUAAW and more muscle was needed to back the farmworkers' fight for wage demands. This was again one line of argument used by delegates pushing for a merger. Not all possible means of remaining independent had been explored, said those against, and farmworkers risked losing autonomy and identity if tied up in a bigger union.

'It doesn't give me any pleasure to come to the rostrum,' said Ted Sales, when proposing the successful amendment, 'but when I came into the Union many years ago it was growing and giving the finest service in the land. Now we look set to make district organisations even thinner on the ground and this means reduced services to members. We cannot carry on as we were. The AWB has treated us with contempt. Let's go straight into a bigger union with our own independent section for the muscle we need to give the farmers a fight.'

Edgar Pill, Wilts, condemned the merger move as 'arrant defeatism' and still wanted Headland House sold. He claimed that there was a potential investment income of £100,000, which if married with increased contributions, would enable the Union to remain viable (a point to be denied by Jack Boddy). He criticised the staff saying, that they 'run the bloody show,' adding, 'I know that to be the case, as an ex-member of the staff.' He also wanted staff to pay 15% on their mortgages from the Union, not 3%, a perk that was 'out of this world'.* He also questioned the £40,000 being put into the political funds which would go 'willy-nilly' to the Labour Party§ (this was in accord with biennial decisions). He also questioned the £12,000 being spent on Union education, but Ted Sales as trustee, said 'that this figure represented a considerable reduction in costs from the time Edgar was Education Officer.'

Joan Maynard, seconding the amendment, said, 'However beautiful small

---

* Whenever the low cost of these mortgages was raised, DOs quickly pointed out that similar facilities were granted by other unions.

§ The political levy was at the time based on 71,500 members, 732 having contracted out.

is, we just can't go on as we are . . . If we go under now and don't merge, there will be nobody looking after the interests of rural workers.'

Barry Salmon, Suffolk: 'We exist to get better wages and conditions. The AWB hasn't done it. We may need to take action . . . We need a merger. If you want a national union rather than an eastern counties' organisation you are going the wrong way about it to remain independent.'

Tom Girling, Suffolk: 'United we stand – with another union.' Bill Morrison, Kent: 'We must get higher wages and safety representatives. For the sake of the young workers we must merge.' Andrew Baynham, Worcs, a fierce opponent of merging, said: 'People could go into the TGWU now if they want. We want their members transferred to us. If the NUAAW merges, I and my members will resign.'* Alan Minett, Cambs: 'All unions are losing members. Unite to save the NUAAW.' Tom Barker, Notts: 'There are as many low-paid members in the TGWU. They negotiate with us on the AWB and what good has that done? They are just looking for our £800,000. If we merge we'll lose our independent voice.' Doug Oswick, Norfolk: 'I'm a descendant of a founder member. But it's time we stopped this sentimental clap-trap. We need a life-line.' He said the Union started to go into financial decline 20 years ago. 'Twenty years ago inflation was 1½% and we were losing money. Now people are stupid enough to think we can make a go of it when it is 25%.' Peter Becks, Beds: 'The NUAAW has done more for forestry workers than any other Union.' Paul Holdsworth, Yorks: 'This Union has grown out of amalgamation.'

When formally moving an emergency motion increasing the contribution rate to 140% of the standard ordinary minimum adult rate from 1 February 1981, Jack Boddy replied to the debate on the merger, pointing out that the Union had to survive in the meantime, hence the need for increased contributions. Jack said the Union had been losing money for many years, and in the past 12 to 15 years there was never sufficient income to meet current expenditure. He had not been able to reverse that trend, despite every effort by the EC to reduce expenditure. Inflation had caught up with them, and was one of their basic problems. And the AWB minimum was making the agricultural worker worse off year after year. With current inflation it was estimated that by the end of the year they would have overspent by £80,000. 'Whether we amalgamate or whether we remain independent we cannot continue as we are.' They had only survived for so long because of income from investments. And each year they had less and less to invest. They had cut staff and were doing their best to maintain services. Their auditors had said an increase in subs of 150% of the minimum was needed, but as they were letting more of the office in London they believed the 140% would suffice.

The resolution on subs was amended, and Conference decided by 50 votes to 19 to substitute 125% instead of 140% of the adult hourly rate.

---

* Andrew later resigned as a trustee and relinquished his membership.

Following the merger vote, Jack Boddy announced that merger talks would take place with the GMWU, TGWU and USDAW, and their main aim was to preserve 'a real, recognisable identity for our Union within the overall structure.' Jack went on to say that there was a trend towards trade union mergers and this had now caught up with the NUAAW. The jobs in farming had been falling steadily for more than 30 years. They had strengths within the allied industries, but that alone was not enough to secure their future. He was looking ahead rather than back, and he hoped members would too. 'We are not going into this as beggars or on our knees. If we do decide to merge then we shall walk in with our heads high.'

Ted Sales, Dorset secretary and trustee, wrote in the April 1981 *Landworker*, that there was no alternative. The Union's financial position had deteriorated to such a degree that it would only be possible to remain independent by making drastic cuts in outside staff, with loss of service to members, who could so dwindle away that, in effect, 'we would only be adequately servicing the membership in the eastern counties. Elsewhere it could become merely nominal; we would in fact cease to be a national organisation.'

The Union had not paid its way from contributions since the early sixties; after a substantial contribution increase in 1972, plus cuts in outside staff, there had been a tremendous upheaval and opposition from areas affected. One county committee endeavoured to form a break-away union.

At the end of 1979, the Union had at least got back into surplus, but when delegates assembled at Southport for the 1978 Conference, unbeknown to them a time bomb was ticking away. Finance deputy Jack Ding said from the platform, that under Schedule 11 of the Employment Protection Acts, any group of workers who could prove that they were being underpaid as compared with most other workers in similar employment could lodge a claim with their employers for parity. If not granted they could take their case to the industrial courts. Head office staff had lodged such a claim because they were grossly underpaid compared with staff of other unions and this could involve the Union in a deficit of anything from £50,000 to £100,000 by the end of the year. The head office staff received their increases. And the outside staff immediately claimed similar amounts, went on strike, and got them.

'During 1978 and 1979,' Ted continued, 'our losses were £120,000 and the market value of our resources, apart from head office, were below £160,000; a desperate situation, I think all must agree. The EC pursued two lines of action; one, discussions on reorganisation of areas, with the aim of reducing staff, both at head office and in the field; two, the 1978 Conference had empowered them to make approaches to other unions to see what terms would be available in the event of a merger.

'It appeared that a merger could be arranged which guaranteed our staff continued employment so reductions in staff were held back until the 1978 Conference had made its decisions. The decision to stay independent was made, discussions with staff re-opened and dragged on. By the end of August our deficit for the year had risen to £88,000 and by the end of September £99,347.

'Is it surprising that a number of area committees said "Enough is enough" and requested a special conference. You know the result, and terms for a merger are being sought. But the final decision will be by the first ever ballot vote of all members. The provisional deficit for 1980 at 31 December was £119,475; at January 1981, it was £21,501, as January is always a bad month for returns. But this year was well below last. The Government are proposing to cut back on forestry; poultry packing stations are closing; food processing plants are closing and now reductions are coming in the British Sugar Corporation. All these proposals represent a potential loss of members. Reports are coming in of resistance to increased contributions, with some loss of membership. The staff in all departments are seeking wage increases and 10% has been offered at an annual cost in excess of £49,000. District organisers have refused to accept. I have been a trustee for many years so the financial figures have always been available to me.' He believed that a merger with a stronger organisation was the only way to ensure adequate protection for rural workers. 'Brothers and sisters, the decision will be yours. I pray you will make the right one.'

Ted's reference to Jack Ding's powder keg revelation, was thus reported in the *Landworker* for the first time. At the end of Jack's speech, one top leader* of the Union declared that he would not have let him make such revelations if he had known of Jack's intentions. (Presumably, it was censored from the *Landworker*'s reports of the 1978 Conference.)

On the opposite page of the *Landworker*, Andrew Baynham, S Worcs secretary and also a trustee wrote: 'Thousands of agricultural and allied workers can't all be wrong by selecting the NUAAW as the organisation they wish to be in. If these people had thought their interests could be better served by another organisation they would no doubt have joined it. Why then, are some of these members asking for a merger with another Union? Maybe they think the members would get better wages, but when we already have co-negotiators from the largest union assisting in this project and none of their banners or members in evidence at the national lobby, it shows their interest is purely academic. Perhaps they believe we shall get more industrial muscle. I cannot see the dockers, lorry drivers, shop assistants or municipal workers coming out on strike in support of the agricultural workers when they don't support their own members to the full.' He knew the Union was in financial difficulties, but the slide had been arrested, and if a merger took place, their assets which were in the region of £1½ million would be taken over, lock stock and barrel. 'I am not being emotional when I say these were mainly from the investment of the early members and were cashed in to buy Headland House and to assist with loans, at a low rate of interest, to organisers to buy their

---

* He retired before the merger.

homes. At Cromer last year, I moved the resolution that this Union stay independent and it was passed by a slender majority. As soon as the vote was declared, I was told by a delegate that a special conference would be called within six months to get the decision reversed.' This Conference was recalled and the result changed. He thought that if Headland House had been sold, and head office moved to the provinces, after the costs had been met, they would have had enough money to invest that would have yielded about £80,000 a year in interest. With contribution increases and staff reductions, that income could be increased by about £60,000 this year and if, in the near future, fixed assets were realised, they could next year look forward to it being increased to £100,000. He failed to see why panic stations had been called. What else could the Union do? Its lifeblood was membership and it needed a large intake which was not possible, as in 1980 over 2,000 branches never made a new member. 'When trying to recruit country folk, who are a breed unto themselves, politics should be in a low key. They should enrol people of all political colours and religious creeds and learn to live with and accept them.' He failed to see any other organisation catering for country folk as well as the NUAAW and pleaded for members to vote for independence.

Ted Sales' reference to outside workers 'going on strike' needs further explanation. They did indeed threaten to withdraw their labour, but worked to rule instead. And this wasn't very effective. If a member sought a DO's help, he did something about it.

At the time of the 1978 financial crisis, the EC considered further staff cuts, and closing regional offices. No overtime was allowed at head office and it was proposed that certain staff might redecorate their own offices to save money, but it did not happen. The EC also considered dismissing DOs on a 'last in, first out' basis, and then filling vacancies by older officers from other areas, but the idea was abandoned because the older DOs were on contracts appointing them to a specific area.

Members wrote to the *Landworker* for and against the merger: some wanted to carry on independently, some thought extra subs the answer, others, that only a quick merger would save the Union from bankruptcy.

Many members believed that the only Union they were likely to merge with was the TGWU, the only serious rival with a farmworker membership, and that mainly in Scotland. But that rivalry had at times hurt. As far back as July 1963, the possibility of asking the TGWU to withdraw from agriculture was discussed by the NUAAW's General Purposes Committee, but as the TUC was discussing trade union structure, it was decided to 'await events', and there is no record of this proposal ever being carried out.

REFERENCE

1. *Landworker*, November 1980.

10

Merger with the TGWU

Argument and Heavy Hearts

In its June 1981 issue, the *Landworker* announced that the NUAAW was likely to merge with the TGWU. The EC was to recommend such a step. The decision had been taken at a special meeting in May, and ballot papers were being sent to members. Jack Boddy said, 'I believe, and so does the EC, that the terms of the merger will ensure the best possible arrangements to preserve the identity and integrity of our Union.' A legal document setting out the merger terms was being drawn up for submission to the Government's trade union Certification Officer, which he had to approve.

The Union team negotiating with the TGWU was led by Jack Boddy and John Hose, with EC members, Jack Brocklebank, Ted Calver, Wilf Page and Pip Snell. TGWU General Secretary, Moss Evans, was in hospital, so the TGWU team was led by Executive Officer, Larry Smith. With him was National Officer, Ron Todd, and Administrative Officer, Sid Forty. There was general agreement on the principle of a separate Agricultural and Allied Trade Group.

In the *Landworker*, Jack Boddy tried to answer readers' questions, and asserted they could not solve the Union's financial problems by selling Headland House and moving to Peterborough as had been suggested. Not all the staff might be willing to move and as good employers the Union would have to make a decent redundancy settlement which would cost a great deal of money. A few people were concerned about the militant reputation of the TGWU, but a decision to strike could only be taken by a trade group to which members belonged. He did not think there was much extra muscle for farmworkers in the merger, but other TGWU members would not cross picket lines if they set them up.

Jack did not believe there was much in the merger for the TGWU. 'They are concerned at the prospect of rural trade unionism disappearing if the power of the NUAAW deteriorates any further.' In return for its 75,000 members, the NUAAW was getting financial stability and extending its area of influence: now they had only one MP to speak for them in parliament – the TGWU had dozens. 'We stand to gain more from this than the TGWU.' He also reassured members that the *Landworker* would remain independent, responsible solely to the Trade Group EC.

The EC of the NUAAW was near to agreement on merger terms with the TGWU, Jack told branch secretaries in a circular sent out in October 1981. It listed key points agreed: the NUAAW would become the Agricultural and Allied Workers' National Trade Group; it would remain at Headland House; current TGWU members in agricultural or allied industries would be transferred to it; the NUAAW's 13-strong EC would be joined by four from the TGWU's current agricultural set-up; the NUAAW's Legal Aid Benefit would be maintained and the *Landworker* would be the new group's voice; the subs would go up slightly, but benefits would be better.

In the November *Landworker*, Jack said, 'They need have no fears of disappearing without a trace within a larger union. The TGWU had twelve trade groups, each fiercely independent, who were not dictated to, any more than farmworkers would be.'

Under the heading 'Can we afford not to merge?', Finance Officer John Tye gave the Union's financial position over the previous two decades. A 21-year profit-and-loss breakdown showed that the Union's investments had tumbled from £470,000 in 1960 to £98,979 in 1980. He forecast a small loss for 1981, which was the year the subs had risen from £1.45 to £2. Despite this increase, accounts did not look like getting into the black in 1981. Investments standing at less than £100,000 could be wiped out in 1982 by the cost of the biennial and the merger ballot.

In December, the *Landworker* announced that the EC had agreed merger terms and ballot papers would be sent out on 14 December.

On the centre pages, Jack Boddy reiterated the facts concerning the Union's weak position and declared, '. . . I am heartily sick of going to the AWB representing only half the men and women who work on farms. Farmworkers should be able to demand, not plead as they did in the days of Joseph Arch's union . . . Can the NUAAW make that happen if it does not amalgamate with a bigger Union. Our membership has decreased steadily since 1948, and every effort to halt the decline has met with failure.' He could see no future in 'limping along' and to move head office to Peterborough would 'virtually cut off' members in the West Country, Wales and the North West, and would not even help members in the Eastern Counties, 'for who, nationally, in government, in the NFU or anywhere else, is going to take notice of a trade union which only organises in one corner of the country.' Any saving would soon be eaten away by travelling expenses and bigger telephone bills in meeting government ministers, farmers' leaders and others in London.

In a message to readers, Moss Evans, General Secretary TGWU said,

I am excited by the chance a merger will provide to strengthen our rural base and our links with farming, which we have had for many years. The proved history and tradition of the NUAAW can only benefit the TGWU . . . Our first joint venture will be a massive recruitment campaign in agriculture. Increased membership is the key to improved wages and conditions.

In its statement on the financial position sent out with the ballot papers, the Union said that although the 'grim deficit of 1980 which amounted to £134,458 has not been repeated – the financial position has continued to get worse.' Although the 1981 contribution went up to £2 per month, and they had no exceptionally large items of expenditure, by the end of November 1981, expenditure still exceeded income by £5,500. The deficit for the year was expected to be £66,639.

The draft of the accounts for 1981 showed at the time of the merger the Union was getting about £24,000 per year in rent for part of Headland House, and subsidising the *Landworker* by £23,500. The cost of the ballot was expected to be £29,955, with legal fees of £10,965. The bank overdraft was £23,292 and sundry creditors were owed £90,998. Income from 1981 subs was expected to be £1,183,400 as against £1,015,010 in 1980; total income was £1,226,946 as against £1,052,314 in 1980. Head office expenses, including £240,911 for salaries (previously £212,591) amounted to £369,740 against £318,369 in 1980.

Ballot forms had to be returned by 25 January 1982 to the Electoral Reform Society. They were accompanied by an EC recommendation to vote 'Yes', a copy of the merger terms, and a letter from Jack Boddy confirming the NUAAW's dire financial straits.

By January, the merger 'score' at area conferences was four in favour, two against. Notts and Derby had voted against. Devon and Yorkshire in favour. Notts and Derby thereby joined Wilts in the anti-lobby, while Devon and Yorks joined South Wales and the North East among the 'pros'.

Complaints at the long delay in balloting (caused by longer-than-expected consultation with the Government's Certification Officer) were echoed at the Surrey & Sussex Area Conference, while Staffordshire, Cheshire and Flintshire Conference deplored the way in which talks had been handled. Neither came out, for or against.

A decisive six to one unity vote was announced on 25 January: for 29,787; against 4,709. Majority, 25,078. There were 42 blank papers, 9 spoilt. 52% of those eligible voted.

Immediately after the historic vote was announced, Jack Boddy declared, 'I am absolutely delighted at the decisive vote in favour of rural trade unionism ... there is sadness at the end of an era, but I am excited by the challenge of a fresh chapter in our history. We will now have the stability from which we can redouble our efforts to attack the problems which face agriculture and allied workers – low pay, poor and unsafe working conditions and the catastrophic decline in rural amenities . . . We still have much unfinished business to get on with. We are happy to do so in company with our urban trade union brothers and sisters. It is a move which will strengthen us all.'

Threats to form a break-away union came to nothing, and the overwhelming 'Yes' vote was welcomed by NUAAW representatives up and down the country, who feared that the widely-forecast narrow majority would leave deep divisions amongst the membership.

The EC had considered merging with two other unions, the United Road Transport, a small union with membership mainly in the Midlands and Lincs, affiliated to the TUC. Jack Boddy had got to know its officers while DO in Lincs. This Union, and the Bakers' Union, were both contacted as prospective partners, but both advised that they had conference decisions opposed to amalgamation.

Negotiations to merge with USDAW never got into any depth. 'They were keener on amalgamation with us than we were with them,' Jack Boddy told me. 'Somehow USDAW didn't seem, on the face of it, to be appropriate for agricultural workers.' Jack felt that as the TGWU was already represented on the AWB and on county wages committees, it would be better to link up with it. The EC had finally agreed with him.

Historically the TGWU had been a rival union, and some EC members still bitterly opposed the merger with the TGWU, among them John Hose, who refused to sign the merger agreement.

The run up to the merger was a traumatic time for the NUAAW leadership. In response to a query about the Union's solvency, on 24 March 1982, the trustees and the EC authorised the lodging of the Union's remaining investment certificates valued at £85,596 with the Co-op Bank, in order to secure the Union's cash requirements. While a strike at Bernard Matthews (the Norfolk poultry concern) continued, this was likely to be £15,000 a week, and John Tye, Finance Officer, told the Bank that the Union was likely to need £40,000 for the Biennial in May. 'Apart from these considerations I would hope that the income will be sufficient to meet our expenditure.' He added, 'There is a ballot at Bernard Matthews today and of course the financial stringencies of our situation would suggest an urgent need for settlement of the strike, but only the membership can determine if the terms are acceptable.'

This was an aspect of the Matthews strike that greatly worried Jack Boddy and the EC, and there was some criticism that they put pressure on the strikers to settle on the best terms available, but the dire financial position of the Union was played down publicly, so as not to weaken the strikers' position. The Union was close to financial collapse, and only Jack Boddy and his closest colleagues knew the mental anguish and torn loyalties the situation imposed upon them.

Jack told the April EC that the Matthews strike had cost the Union approximately £75,000; the Union had a net deficit of £80,291 in the first three months of 1982 and the TGWU had loaned them £40,000 to help them out. The Finance Department had been told not to make any payments unless absolutely necessary. Jack also told them the Biennial was only three weeks away, costing £50,000, and that 'the Union was committed to expenditure it could not meet'.

Representatives of the TGWU, Larry Smith and H. Timpson, then joined the meeting, and Smith stated that the TGWU would not allow a situation to develop where the NUAAW was so short of funds that it did not have the means to back up its activities. He then offered an interest-free loan of £150,000, with Headland House as collateral. It was accepted with relief and gratitude by the EC. It was only after the merger with the TGWU that the Union's overdraft was cleared at the bank.

The Union had started to go into decline in the late fifties, a decline that accelerated in the sixties and seventies. There was one main reason, a rapid reduction in the labour force, from a peak just after the war of some 500,000 full-timers to less than 200,000. The number of full-time workers declined by 400,000 (72%) between 1950 and 1980, and was still falling by over 10,000 per annum in the late eighties.

Leaders of the Union, Bill Holmes, Alfred Dann, Harold Collison, Reg Bottini and Jack Boddy, tried hard to stem the tide, with little success, especially during the post-war boom years, when there were alternative, better-paid jobs available to many farmworkers. A similar situation existed after the First World War, when membership fell, and Union staff were reduced to a minimum. But despite the much reduced labour force of the 1920s, there was still a vast potential for recruitment. In the seventies that potential disappeared, and by the eighties, when the merger decision was taken, the labour force was set to decline even further. The merger decision was an agonising one for both those for and against. Only time will tell how effective the new trade group will become, but that there was no alternative but to merge, few now have any doubts, even if the regrets remain.

Delegates at the N & S Norfolk Conference which followed the merger were keen to grasp the challenge it presented. Mushroom worker Donna Holman, 'chuffed' to be the area's first woman chair, set the tone telling the Conference, 'I hope that we shall be able to see we were forward thinking in that we did merge. It could be a triumphant year of new life.' John Hose told them, 'Some people seem to think that because we have joined the TGWU, the biggest trade union in the country, everything is going to be rosy and done for us, but you are going to have to fight for yourselves. It is no good sitting back and thinking somebody else will do it for you.'

There was less enthusiasm at the Gloucestershire, Warwickshire and Worcestershire Conference, whose chairman asked delegates to stand for a minute's silence 'in memory of the NUAAW'. Jack Boddy tried to create a more buoyant mood. 'Joining forces with the TGWU meant a step forward and not a swallowing up,' he told them.

Reaction to the merger was generally enthusiastic. Bury St. Edmunds District Committee chair, Don Pollard, wrote in the *Bury Free Press*, 'I urge all agricultural and allied workers to join the new trade group.' The merger was welcomed by many DOs. Devon's Albert Warren and North East's Terry Hammond told their local papers that they were 'delighted'. The *Leicester Mercury* ran a poll of local NUAAW members and found no fears about the merger. Dorset DO Peter Venn promised members, who might be worried, that 'I'm not likely to grow horns overnight.' Threats of resignation were not generally carried out, though S Derbyshire District Secretary Hilda Draper told the *Derby Evening Telegraph*, 'If I conclude that farmworkers are less well represented . . . I shall resign.' The *Eastern Daily Press* commented, 'the Union, corporately, can move on now in the certain knowledge that its finances are secure.'

Meanwhile, plans were made to maintain and improve services to members; additional facilities were the TGWU education services, which included courses for shop stewards, safety representatives and women. The TGWU ran convalescent and holiday centres, and members were entitled to two weeks' free accommodation with return fares paid. Commission to branches on contributions would rise from 10% to 15%.

Merger Postponed

But vesting day for the merger, planned for 5 April, had to be postponed. The delay was caused by complaints of eight members to the Certification Officer over the way the ballot was run. Jack Boddy had already dealt with five similar complaints, but not until he asked for the Certificate was he told that the further complaints had been registered and would be heard on 28 April. The Certification Officer intended to hear three, the rest were insubstantial. One complainant told a newspaper that he hoped to delay the merger until the Biennial and 'start a fresh lobby'. However, under the law, the Biennial could not overturn the ballot. One complainant withdrew, so two members were holding up the merger which almost 30,000 members voted for.

The complainant who withdrew was Andrew Baynham, the trustee who opposed the merger. In letters to the Certification Officer he claimed members were still 'in the dark' about the Union's finances. He complained that with the ballot paper was a statement setting out the financial position which was misleading in that the 'loss' of £372,000 between 1960 and 1981 made no reference to the fact that out of this money a considerable sum had been used to build Headland House, which he believed was now worth £1.2 million, and could be sold.

Andrew also questioned the accuracy of membership records and complained that there was no second envelope to place the ballot paper for sealing in the official envelope; without it there could be ballot rigging. No such claim was ever subsequently made. He withdrew because he was a pensioner, and 'I am in no way able to bear the cost of legal action.'

The two objectors who went ahead attended a hearing at Birmingham on 28 and 29 April 1982. One was A. D. Millar, chairman N Cumberland District Committee and chair N W Area Committee. He complained that there had been 'interference and constraint' on members because the General Secretary had sent with the ballot papers a financial statement which was not inaccurate but was 'not explanatory enough'. It gave no reason for the total drop in investments from 1960 to 1982, gave no figure to show current assets, and no forecast of the expected effects of the rise in contributions due in

February 1982. He objected to the figure of £5,500 as the amount by which expenditure exceeded income by the end of November 1981, saying it was an unaudited mid-quarter 'convenient' estimate which would be a 'compelling influence' for a 'yes' vote.

Dismissing the complaint, the Certification Officer said that while every member must be allowed to vote without interference or constraint, this did not prevent a union from recommending that members vote one way or another, nor prevent it supporting that recommendation by providing 'such information as it thinks appropriate'. He was satisfied that none of the evidence produced at the hearing showed that the financial passage in the letter to members was in fact misleading.

The other complainant was David Young, secretary of Pershore branch, who was assisted by the Revd. B. L. Druce. Mr. Young complained that ballot papers were not sent to some members entitled to vote, and sent to some not entitled to vote. He said the ballot was based on outdated members' lists and that the voting procedure was inefficient and unsatisfactory.

In evidence, Jack Boddy said the Union had about 63,500 members at the end of 1981, some 15,000 to 20,000 were in factories, the rest in 2,300 branches, mainly small, scattered over a wide area. It was the branch secretary's duties to give head office details of membership and contributions paid. A two-yearly branch register and a six-monthly contribution return form constituted the Union's record of membership. A member six months in arrears was removed from the books. They went to great lengths to ensure all those entitled to ballot forms got them, but there were occasional slip-ups, which he regretted.

The Certification Officer commented, 'I have no hesitation in finding that the system was such that, so far as was reasonably possible, every member was given a fair opportunity of voting.' He noted that over 56% of its members voted, which for a merger ballot was not a low turnout. And that 86% of those voting voted in favour, and it was not conceivable the result could have been affected by the votes of those six months in arrears. He dismissed the complaint. He formally registered the Transfer of Engagements to the TGWU as from 1 May 1982. The objections had cost the Union £6,189 in legal bills.[1]

There were some strong feelings in the Union against the objectors, and W. Francis, County Secretary of Herefordshire County Committee wrote to the Certification Officer stating that the objectors were from a minority 'defeated at our Special Conference'. The objectors are those who 'fear the loss of their own personal trade union status within the new alliance'.

These fears were genuine enough, and in view of the cut backs in the agricultural trade groups in the late eighties, might be claimed to be justified, but they were mainly the result of a big fall in the membership of the TGWU as a whole, which followed huge job losses as Britain's industrial decline accelerated, and affected all trade groups within the TGWU.

A significant minority of TGWU national and regional officials were opposed to the merger, as they considered the NUAAW bankrupt, and believed it would become a millstone round the TGWU's neck. And some TGWU officials did not like the idea of an agricultural trade group having separate delegations to the TUC and the Labour Party, believing a situation could occur with agricultural delegates voting against the main TGWU delegation. This opposition was not general, and many TGWU officials and members welcomed the NUAAW into their ranks, especially those in the TGWU's small agricultural group.[2]

The TGWU, although loath to admit it, had been losing members from its small foothold among agricultural workers, and feared it could lose its long-term entitlement of three members on the AWB. The last year any figures are available for the TGWU agricultural group is 1968, and they were 11,232 members, a decline of 30% from 16,500 for 1962.[3] Over the years, the TGWU agricultural group had lost members to the NUAAW, mainly because of the superior services it gave members as a purely agricultural union for farmworkers; a service that was so costly as to play a considerable part in its downfall.

*   *   *

The first meeting of the old EC as the trade group executive included four nominees of the new parent body, the TGWU. It was recorded 'that the members of the EC of the ex-NUAAW viewed the past achievements of the Union with justifiable pride and satisfaction, and looked forward hopefully to a bright future within the parent organisation.' John Hose was confirmed as chairman of the new trade group.

It is to be noted that some of the right-wing opponents of the merger who remained in the new trade group, were amongst the fiercest fighters for the promised 'rights' of its members.

Opening the Agricultural Trade Group Conference at Skegness in May 1983, John Hose said that the previous 12 months had not been easy with the merger. The change from a centralised administration to regional organisation had been the cause of upsets and confusion, and much misunderstanding, and although 'the attempts to reconcile the rule book with the Transfer Agreement has been achieved amicably, in some Regions much remains to be done.' The retirement of so many of the NUAAW staff was likely to emphasise the trend towards a more active participation by the lay membership, and this was not a bad thing. He attacked the Government's hypocritical Victorian morality – laying down minimum levels of wages in the private sector and refusing to implement those minimums with its own employees. 'We stand ever close to 1984 and the date cannot but conjure up the nightmare vision of George Orwell. We must all be aware that such a vision could become reality, but from the right of politics rather than the left. If there is a failure to recognise such a possibility at the ballot box, then our only defence will be the trade unions.'

John's allusion to 1984 was not wildly fanciful. In 1982, criticism of the Thatcher Government became a crime meriting instant dismissal. That was the harsh lesson the Union's recently-retired Lincolnshire DO, Sir Sidney King, learned when he criticised the Government's pay policy. He was instantly dismissed as chair of his regional health authority. He had had the temerity to suggest that nurses were not being paid enough. Three other regional health chairmen were similarly dismissed. All four had trade union or Labour backgrounds. They were replaced with what the Government hoped would be 'yes men'.

One of the important merger assurances was of continued separate affili-ation to the TUC and Labour Party, and the new trade group was able to air its views at the 1982 TUC Conference on vital topics of agricultural policy. However, the *Landworker* warned in 1983 that the TUC 'could be about to drop an awful clanger'. A change in arrangements for representation on the General Council had been agreed by 20 votes to 19 at the last General Council meeting, threatening to disenfranchise important sections of organised la-bour. The seat reserved for agriculture was earmarked to go in the re-shaping operation. It said that Jack Boddy on the General Council 'spoke for the rural worker, and it would be a terrible irony if at a time when the Labour Party is awakening to the importance of rural issues . . . the TUC for lack of sensitivity and thought, set its face in the opposite direction . . .'

But at the 1983 TUC Congress the trade group lost its rights to affiliate separately. Like the dyers and bleachers and medical practitioners in ASTMS, it would have to affiliate in future under the banner of its parent body. It was argued that these sections did not have sufficient independence to qualify for separate affiliation under TUC rules. A fiery speech from Jack Boddy calling for the retention of separate affiliation nearly succeeded in winning the vote. But after backing from Eddie Haigh of the dyers and bleachers, and Douglas Poirier of the Medical Practitioners' Union, the hands went up in a three to two ratio against.

This was a setback, but not a disaster. It meant that without Jack on the TUC General Council, any action for farmworkers would be proposed by the TGWU General Secretary at future TUC congresses, and they would have to ask the TGWU to place on the agenda any matter specifically affecting farmworkers. It was inconvenient, but it would not silence the farmworkers' voice. Those who opposed the merger saw this decision as confirming their fears. But when the TGWU made the old NUAAW the offer of separate affiliation they meant it. They could not predict that Congress would change the rules.

Fears of NUAAW members that they would be 'swallowed up' by the TGWU, and that the big Union's policy of cheap food would mean that it would never support higher wages for farmworkers, have proved neither wholly true nor false. The Agricultural Trade Group has retained an individ-ual identity; funding at a national level is more generous than that of any other trade group, and the TGWU national leadership under Ron Todd has fully supported the agricultural group in its national wage campaigns. In the TGWU Regions, there are now some agricultural regional trade groups, much favoured by activists who prefer them to a multi-trade group district committee. Others have district committees. In most cases, a reasonable working relationship has been established, with former TGWU officials trying to understand and meet the needs of their new agricultural members, while some former NUAAW DOs have taken on other trade group tasks, with commendable efficiency.[4]

Strenuous efforts were made in many Regions to get to know the new agricultural trade group members, through meetings and social events, and a sense of common purpose grew. Since the Trade Group has moved to Transport House, the understanding between it and TGWU officials at a national level has improved considerably.

During the merger negotiations, the NUAAW said it would be taking in 85,000 members, but the TGWU found it only had 67,000. Jack Boddy denied that they had bumped up the membership to get better terms. He said, 'The higher figures were absolutely correct, we had them independently checked. The TGWU "lost" members on transfers, either because members left the Union, or failed to have their subs collected.' This was denied by some TGWU regional secretaries. Undoubtedly some NUAAW members were not enamoured of the new set up and failed to continue their membership.

Tories Attack Unions

Under the heading 'Destroying the Spirit of Tolpuddle', the *Landworker* said in 1983 that the Government's latest Green Paper on 'Democracy in Trade Unions' continued the Tory attack on union democracy. It said that a government elected by the vote of well below half the electorate pretended to be concerned about insufficient participation in union affairs by members, but was really intent on 'tying the unions and their members in a web of laws to prevent them campaigning effectively for a better standard of living'. The Tolpuddle Martyrs were transported just for that. It said that the Green Paper threatened to impose laws which would allow disgruntled members to take a union to court if they thought it was not meeting the standards set by the Tory Government. It also wanted to make union affiliation to the Labour Party more complicated and expensive (a move later overwhelmingly defeated in union after union in voting on political funds). It declared that all unions already had rules allowing members to change their constitution and 'there is clearly no democratic need for State intervention'.

'I will neuter Unions – Norman Tebbit' was the headline the *Landworker* had run earlier in January 1982. Beneath it was the story of the TUC's warning to Employment Secretary Norman Tebbit that it could not and would not accept the Government's proposals for further industrial relations legislation. This legislation was to herald the Thatcher government's most vicious action against the trade unions to date.

Norman Tebbit was a working-class lad, fortunate enough to attend Edmonton County Grammar School; he went on to be a journalist, pilot and assistant director of information for the National Federation of Building Trades Employers, an industry with a long record of bad work practices and a high accident rate. On his progress upwards he acquired a deep hatred of trade unionism.

A delegation from the TUC had met Tebbit in December and told him that the TUC would campaign against his proposals. In a statement, Tebbit had said his aim was to 'neuter' the effects of the closed shop. He said, 'I used the word "neuter" because I've been told I must not use the vernacular when describing what I'm doing to the unions.' He was told that the 'workers need as much protection as possible against the deep scars being inflicted by the return of mass unemployment and the lowering of living standards'.

The new proposals would further worsen the labour laws, already badly flawed by the 1980 Employment Act. The TUC believed they would provoke conflict between workers and employers, complicate and worsen disputes, and lead large groups of law-abiding citizens to regard the law as being perverse and prejudiced. The TUC did not relish the prospect, preferring to work with Government and employers to create an improved climate and framework for industrial relations. The aim of the proposals was to encourage non-unionism by offering monetary incentives to individuals, and extend the grounds on which industrial action would be held 'unlawful' and expose union funds to massive damages. Also, they aimed to undermine 'closed' shops, but the TUC said that cases of controversy and difficulty involving the closed shop were rare, never more than a handful each year, whereas employers lost about 9,000 cases of unfair dismissal a year before industrial tribunals. Said the *Landworker*:

Mr. Norman Tebbit must be one of the oddest and nastiest specimens ever to be given a key job at a crucial time. He was given the job of Employment Minister by Mrs. Thatcher just at the time when the Tories needed a conciliator, who could demonstrate that he cared about unemployment and wanted to do something for the workers. Of course, he'd have to throw a sop to the Neanderthals in the Tory ranks. There would have to have been some vindictive little piece of legislation that showed Mrs. Thatcher's wilder adherents that his heart was in the right place – against the workers and especially against those in unions. She had such a man in Mr. James Prior, and threw him out. In his place she put someone with that obsessive hatred of the working class that you only find in a man who has clawed his way out of it and doesn't wish to look back on his origins. And Mr. Tebbit is busy working out his neuroses on the rest of the country, to the applause of Tory Neanderthals from ancient families, who no doubt despise him for his proletarian antecedents but are quite happy to let him do their dirty work for them. The fruits of Tebbit's labours are shortly to come before Parliament in the shape of the ironically named Employment Bill.

The Tory 1982 Employment Bill would turn the clock back to Tolpuddle. The *Landworker* recalled the words of George Loveless as he was sentenced to transportation, 'We meant nothing more, Sir, than uniting together to keep up the price of labour, and to support each other in time of need.'

It said that the trade unions were still the working man and woman's only defence, and the Government had signalled its intention to destroy them, to bankrupt them by fining them up to £250,000; drag unions through the courts for defending their members; outlaw union solidarity and encourage the sacking of workers who refused to return to work until a dispute was settled.

Jack Boddy declared, 'Farmworkers were in at the birth of British trade unions. They will not stand idly by and watch that great movement be throttled by the true descendants of the landed interests who had the Six Men of Dorset transported for the crime of forming a trade union.'

The history of trade unionism is that of a long battle by organised labour fighting unjust laws made in the interests of the ruling class, laws that protected property and the power of the employing class. But since the 1920s, until Thatcher took office (with the important exception of the 1927 Trade Disputes and the 1971 Industrial Relations Acts), Parliament had been something of a progressive force. The old Combination Acts which prevented workers combining to alter wages or work conditions had been repealed, and trade unions were partially released from these restrictions.

The last Act to define trade union immunities from acts done in furtherance of a trade dispute was the Trade Union and Labour Relations Act in 1974, still in force at the time of Tebbit's new Bill. The Tories claimed that the unions were too powerful, and with a baying press on their side, did a lot to convince the public that this was the case, and that the 'power' of the trade unions must be 'curbed'.

The unions' efforts to fight the Bill failed, despite some imaginative campaigning. Len Murray, TUC General Secretary, said, 'The Government is using its own well-oiled and well-financed propaganda machine to spread the illusion that this wolf of a Bill is really a sheep, not likely to harm anyone ... a moderate and modest Bill ... a more apt description would be malicious and mad. It is malicious because it is inspired by a desire to cripple trade unions ... it is mad because it can only result in tensions at the workplace, disorder in industry, and friction between management and worker.'

Malicious and mad maybe, but it went through Parliament. Unions were fined hundreds of thousands of pounds for trying to defy its measures, their assets sequestrated, and the unemployed were pushed back to Poor Law conditions for getting the dole – especially the young, who were denied it altogether, and reduced to sleeping on the streets in London. And as a side effect of this weakening of the unions, the Tory Government was able to push through its attacks on the social services and the National Health Service. The Act made it very difficult for the unions to resist the lowering of wages, working conditions, dropping of safety standards, poor hygiene, and scores of other bad work practices that were thought to be things of the past.

The Union's changing political attitudes were illustrated by a review in the *Landworker* in 1981 of a book that it would once never have mentioned, or if it did, have fiercely attacked. It was *The Secret Constitution* by Brian Sedgemore, MP, which it believed to be 'one of the most important books written about the British political establishment'. Sedgemore argued that real power did not reside in Parliament and that there was little democratic about the use of that power which had to be perpetrated by secrecy. Power lay in the hands of an elite few, mainly civil servants, industrialists, financiers, senior politicians, trade union leaders and media owners. He argued strongly for open government, and the public right to know certain facts then denied, and thus strengthen the democratic process. His views were very much those of activists in the Union.

In March 1983 Francis Beckett resigned as editor of *Landworker* and Chris Kaufman was appointed acting editor. Chris, aged 36, had been acting editor in 1980 while Francis was President of the NUJ, and won for the paper the TUC Trade Union Journal competition.

Beckett's resignation was among that of a number of key officers, and Stuart Neale told the N Wales Conferences that he was anxious to see them replaced or the agricultural workers were in danger of losing their identity inside the TGWU. By July the vacancies were being filled. Reg Green took up the vacancy in the Legal Department, Sue Longley and Yvonne Quinn were installed in the Publications Department, and arrangements were being made in the regions to give district officers special responsibility for rural membership.*

Incomes Policy Rejected

The Isle of Man was an historic trade union occasion in 1983, when the 13th Biennial Delegate Conference of the TGWU met there, the first attended by delegates from the agricultural group. These delegates were moved by the warmth of their reception by the rest of the thousand delegates, and many friendships formed across industrial boundaries. Agricultural delegates were prominent speakers. The first was Don Pollard, Suffolk, and amongst those who followed were Margaret Holmes, Kent; Mike Weiler, Surrey and Sussex; Tom Barker, Lincs; Bill McBeath, Norfolk; Roger Shutt and Bill Ferris,

---

* A generous 'package' was negotiated for any NUAAW employee who wanted to leave after the merger. This deal is estimated to have cost the TGWU over £750,000. They were entitled to severance pay as follows: those having less than five years' service, a sum equal to a statutory redundancy payment plus 20% of annual salary for each year of service; those with five years' service or more, two years' annual salary. NUAAW officials were said to be surprised at these high levels of payment.

15. Leaders of the Union at the Biennial at Cromer in 1982. Fifth from the left is John Hose, President, and to his left is Ted Calver, EC. On the far right are Jack Brocklebank, former N Yorks DO and later EC member, and Wilf Page, EC.

16. The inaugural meeting in January 1984 of the officers of Region One, after the merger with the TGWU. Wilf Page (*centre front*) is presiding. Chris Kaufman, *Landworker* editor, is on the far right.

13. Joan Maynard, a leading campaigner in the Union, was voted back on the Labour Party's NEC at their Annual Conference in October 1983. Here she is being congratulated by TGWU delegates: (*left to right*) Ron Todd, National Organiser; Walter Greendale, Chair; and Moss Evans, General Secretary. Todd and Evans were to play important roles in the merger of the Union with the TGWU.

14. The farm workers' 'side' leaving an AWB meeting in 1984 to settle the Union's wages claim. Judging by the expressions on their faces it must have been a grim session. At the front (*left to right*) are Jack Boddy and Arthur Mills; at the rear, Br. Bolton, Peter Woodland, Barry Leathwood, Ted Marsh, Sid Cooke and Ted Calver.

11. Reg Bottini, General Secretary, addresses a wages rally in 1972.

12. Delegates and Union officials at a Dorset area conference in 1980. Amongst them are leading Union figures. In the front row (*left to right*) are Ted Sales, Herbie Pitman, Peter Vean, Peter Woodland and Franci. Becke   n the   ond row (*third from the right*) is E nie A   ey, the indefatigable Union recru   r and   senter   mpensation' cheques to members   no have been injured.

9. Farmworkers demonstrating outside the Ministry of Agriculture in January 1970, when they came to London from all over England to back up their claim for higher wages.

10. Reg Bottini, General Secretary (*second from the left in front of the Lincolnshire banner*), accompanied (*to his left*) by Vic Feather, General Secretary of the TUC, leads a Union rally in London in October 1971.

Herefordshire; Howard Wright, Wilts; Ted Marsh, Somerset; Mark Johnson, Glos; Ken Tullet, Yorks; and Tom Baptie, Northumberland.

Conference rejected any form of incomes policy as being against the interests of working people in a capitalist economy, and called for a national minimum wage of two-thirds of the industrial average and a 35-hour week.

*   *   *

Following Chris Kaufman's departure to head the TGWU's Publications Department and edit its journal, the *Record*, at the end of 1983, Jim Innes, aged 36, took over the editorship of the *Landworker*. Jim, a graduate, had been working in the Labour Party's press office. The first *Landworker* of 1984 announced that it was to be free to all members. The move was part of the TGWU's desire to strengthen the separate trade group.

Some evidence of the 'muscle' resulting from the merger came at the end of 1983, at the Wiltshire Area Conference. Les Collet, DO, told delegates how he prevented a member with less than six months' service from being sacked from a farm without references by threatening to stop milk and grain deliveries. It was to be the last Wilts 'area' conference, for local branches had already established their new divisional committee with John Cater as chair and Howard Wright as secretary.

In February 1984, the first ever National Committee* of the Agricultural and Allied Workers' Trade Group was elected. The representatives from 11 regions met at Headland House, marking the trade group's real beginning as an integrated part of the TGWU. Nine members were survivors from the old EC, which had negotiated and agreed the merger.

Major Changes in Organisation

Following the decision of the Trade Group Committee in Region 3 to send Ted Marsh to represent them on the TGWU Regional Committee, Ted was elected vice-chairman, a position normally reserved for long-serving committee members. Trade Group Secretary for the region, Barry Leathwood, said, 'What more positive proof of the success of the merger could be required than to have one of our own elected to share in the leadership of 130,000 members in the South West.'

Wilf Page, the outgoing trade group representative on the TGWU EC since the merger, received a glowing tribute from the Union's chairman,

---

* Members: J. Hose (chair), J. Baptie, W. Brack, J. Brown, D. Chiappa, R. S. Cooke, V. Cross, K. Feeley, R. Gamwell, M. Hancock, D. Halstead, J. Maltby, I. Monckton, W. Page, B. J. Salmon, P. Shearman, D. Sheppard, P. Stockton, P. Webster, P. Woodland, M. Wright, Jack Boddy (secretary).

Walter Greendale, in 1984. He said that Wilf had done 'a magnificent job for farm and allied workers as their first representative on the TGWU EC'. He was followed on the EC by Scottish forestry worker, Bill Brack. Wilf took over as chairman of Region 1 (S & E England) trade group committee.

One man who saw the changes the merger wrought from the inside, was John Lilley, caretaker/printer at Headland House. A member of SOGAT, John was capable of turning his hands to anything from fixing the electricity, general repairs – including locks, broken desks, in fact, anything – and over the years must have saved the Union a mint of money. He also knew where everything was in the office, which was invaluable. A judo expert, he held the job for 30 years, and was still doing it after the trade group left the premises for Transport House.

One part of the country where the merger brought great changes was Scotland. Poultry workers, forestry workers and other allied workers had long been represented in Scotland by the NUAAW, but ever since their absorption of the Scottish Farmworkers Union, the TGWU had represented farmworkers north of the border. With the merger, the new trade group acquired a whole new area for recruits, and the man given the job of organising them was Hugh Wilson, a Scot with firm socialist principles and a ready sense of humour. Hugh, based in Dumfries, was a 53-year-old former dairyman, and as the new Scottish Secretary of the trade group had no illusions about the enormity of his task – to get the 26,000 Scottish farmworkers 100% organised. A former Royal Marine and factory union organiser, he knew that the fact that only 20% of the Scottish farmworkers had been organised had diminished the impact of their wage claims over the years. Plans were drawn up for the annual wage round in close harmony with the Union in England.

Meanwhile major changes were taking place in England. 'The last two years haven't been easy,' Peter Allenson, DO, told 60 delegates at the Cambridge and Bedford Conference. 'It has been a story of dramatic change,' he said, 'from 63 branches to 23.' But the rationalisation had to happen. It was an attempt to get rid of the situation whereby everything depended on the energy of one person. He said that the changes happening all over the country were beginning to work. Adrian Hobdale, new regional trade group delegate, echoed his words and said, 'We now have a better basis for working within rural communities.'

Not far away, 50 delegates and 24 resolutions made the 1984 Suffolk Conference one of the best for a long time. Ken Weetch, the only Labour MP in East Anglia, brought fraternal greetings and warned of further attacks on working people by the current government. 'There is work to be done,' he declared. 'We must build up the trade union movement and the Labour Party.'

*   *   *

One Union official who saw the merger as offering new opportunities to the rural worker was Peter Medhurst, DO for Suffolk. When Peter, a Barnardo boy, was fostered out at the age of five to Bill and Betty Thompson in Woodbridge, Suffolk, he was sent to the village school. He mixed with farmworkers' sons and, as young as he was, found their poverty unbelievable. One boy lived in a tied cottage; it had no taps, they got their water from a well, and their earth closet in the front porch had no door to it – you could just sit there and stare across the road. The family's staple diet was bread and cheese.

This early experience gave Peter a feeling of affinity with farmworkers, but a lot happened along the way before he became Suffolk DO.

Peter, aged 44 when I met him, lived with his wife Pat, a schoolteacher, in Ipswich (they later moved to Norwich when Peter became Norfolk DO). He soon discovered the reason his adoptive parents lived in a council house was that nobody else could afford the rent, 'dad' being a skilled worker could manage it. They moved to Norton on Teesside when Peter was 11 and on leaving school, having artistic inclinations, he wanted to do something creative. He became an apprentice at Robert Thompson's (no relation) handmade oak furniture workshop in the tiny village of Kilburn, on the edge of the North Yorkshire moors. Like all apprentices, Peter was put to work carving the firm's famous trade mark, a mouse. Later he made chairs, tables and church furniture.

Being brought up by Mr. and Mrs. Thompson, who were active in the Labour Party, Peter naturally joined the furniture makers' trade union, based in Leeds. 'Although they could have had Thompson's 40 skilled men in the Union, they never sent anyone out to the place,' said Peter. 'I decided I wanted to be in a Union active in the area, so I joined the NUAAW.'

Kilburn NUAAW had about 20 members, and another 10 were recruited from the furniture factory. 'They had legal cover for accidents at work, and had any disciplinary issues arisen, they would have had cover on that too,' said Peter. 'They were quite happy in the NUAAW, it seemed the natural Union to join. If the NUAAW had been geared up for non-agricultural workers, we could have done a lot more.' Peter became branch secretary and later chairman of Thirsk branch, which had Joe Maltby as secretary.

The 1966 General Election was an important event for Peter. 'The area was true blue all over,' he told me in 1988. 'I said to a bloke at work, "We can't put up with this, is there no Labour Party round here?" He said, "Go see Joan Maynard, she's the Labour Party in this area." ' He went to Joan's house in Sowerby, with the intention of collecting stickers and posters. Joan opened the door to Peter's knock, beamed at him, ushered him in, and firmly closed it. 'Joan looked upon me as corn from Egypt,' said Peter. 'Kilburn was a wealthy Tory village.' Several party members in her house were busy filling election envelopes and Peter joined in, and finished up a member of the Labour Party. Eventually he became chairman of Thirsk and Malton CLP, and was appointed a JP.

Peter started going to Union biennials, joined Yorkshire County and Northallerton District committees. 'I was spending a lot of time on Union work. I had a good job, but couldn't fit it in, so when I heard of the Suffolk DO's position being vacant, and Jack Boddy had become General Secretary, I felt I would like to be a full-time DO, having been encouraged by attending the Union's weekend schools.' Also, he liked the idea of going back to Suffolk. 'It was still a rural area, semi-feudal, and the challenge of that appealed to me.' He moved to Suffolk in 1978, taking over from John Stewart.

Peter had a strong, resolute voice, and said characteristically, 'Some in the county didn't want me with my left-wing views. They associated me with Joan Maynard, but there were others, both left and right, who did want me – to sort of prove myself.'

And he did just that. With the same forthright approach to both industrial and political matters, he tried to encourage links between the Labour Party and the Union, and managed to get one or two Union branches to affiliate; not one had been affiliated in the past. Peter stressed 'that the Union always did better when it worked hand-in-hand with the Labour Party in rural areas. The Union in Norfolk was built on the two working together.' People in Suffolk began to appreciate someone who would speak out on issues, even if sometimes they didn't agree with him. Suffolk had always been opposed to the abolition of the AWB. Peter was in favour, and encouraged Suffolk members to reject the AWB and seek a statutory Joint Industrial Council for wage negotiations and escape from being in the hands of the independents on the AWB. Suffolk switched on this issue. The Suffolk delegations to conferences became more outspoken on major issues, and developed determined views of their own.

With Peter's background as a non-agricultural worker, it is not surprising that he favoured a broad approach to rural issues and rural membership, and would have liked the trade group to take up environmental issues. 'I feel that having not worked in agriculture, but having lived in rural areas most of my life, I have a number of advantages. I don't look at the countryside as a farmer would, but as a dweller. The environment that farmworkers and rural workers are subjected to is as important to protect as negotiations for higher wages. I encourage people who work for environmental concerns such as the Suffolk Wildlife Trust, the National Trust and community programmes based on improving the environment, to join the Union, because the Union is another force that could be used to change policies in agriculture and rural development. We also have a branch structure in rural areas which no other union has. If we were involved in wider issues, we could gain support and respect, not only from the point of view of membership, but also in political awareness of what socialism could do for rural dwellers, who at the moment are at the mercy of market forces and the philosophy of greed and me first.'

Peter was keen on education. 'The WEA was a great asset to me when I was in Yorkshire,' he said. 'Weekend schools in economics and history raised members' ability to understand issues, express themselves and gave people the confidence to make a case. The most important task facing the trade group today is to give people the confidence to do things for themselves. It's not that people don't know what's going on, it's that they don't know how to react to it. We've got to give them the tools educationally to do this.'

One man firmly opposed to Peter becoming DO for Suffolk, was Fred Brett, a former county chairman. 'I was among a lot on the county committee who didn't want him because of his left-wing views,' he said, 'but now I'm glad we've got him. He's been a very good officer, is hard working and he's kept the county committee going despite a big fall in membership. If we had known what he was like, we wouldn't have opposed him. I'm more than happy with him. We don't always see eye to eye on everything, just like with Joan Maynard, but she did a great job for agricultural workers; she was very keen on getting resolutions right, down to the last word, and that is how it should be done.'

Fred also opposed the merger, but now believes it to have been for the best. 'I think that if the old EC had been a bit more careful about whom they employed, and how we spent money, we might have carried on independently. But we must have a union to hold up to the agricultural worker. I have an idea the farmers wouldn't pay what they are supposed to today if the wage awards were not statutory; my old boss was fair, but most farmers are still a lot of buggers!' Fred was among the growing number who believed the trade group must go after the general rural worker. 'Some are covered by NUPE and COHSE, but a lot are not in any union, and we should recruit them,' he said.

Like many active Union workers, Fred, chair of Kesgrave (Ipswich) branch in the fifties, found that the Union's legal aid system did wonders for recruiting members. 'We had a chap knocked off his motor bike one Sunday afternoon,' said Fred, 'and the Union got him three or four thousand pounds. Recruiting leapt up.' Fred himself was not so lucky. A year before he was due to retire, a forage feeder stripped the skin and flesh off his hand when, without thinking, he tried to unblock it without switching off. He was on the sick list a year before retiring, and couldn't claim compensation because of his own negligence, but as an OAP he got an additional 30% disability allowance.

Fred, who joined the Union in 1948 after 5½ years in the RAF, left school at 14 and became a shepherd boy, earning 8s a week. 'We used to start at 7am and left off at about 4.30pm,' he said. Fred worked at Grange Farm, Kesgrave, from 1948. There didn't used to be a branch in Kesgrave. 'We went out knocking on doors on Sunday morning recruiting drives,' he recalled, when I interviewed him in 1988, 'with Fred Brown, county chairman, and John Stewart, DO. A lot of chaps joined because of the legal aid offered, and the tied cottage of course.'

When he first went to work at Grange Farm and its nursery, there was a staff of 40. Everything was done by hand; they had horses and one tractor. 'Now,' said Fred, 'they've got about seven staff on the farm, and three on horticulture and the nursery, plus casual labour. Potatoes and beetroot are now all done by machinery.' He was proud that the Union had nearly 100% membership at the farm, and was then secretary of the Kesgrave branch.

When Fred married in 1950, Kesgrave had about 3,000 inhabitants, and was already very much a dormitory for Ipswich. 'Today most of the inhabitants work in Ipswich. They reckon the farm will go before long and we'll be part of Ipswich,' he said, a prospect that Fred is not too keen about.

In 1989, a strange little item appeared in the *Landworker*. It began:

> An out-of-court settlement of £200 has been won by hair-stylist Lynda Gillingham from her former employer. The Union was taking Benito Salvia to an industrial tribunal on the grounds of sexual harassment. Lynda (24), who lives at Dean Farm, Witchampton, had been senior stylist at 'A Cut Above' in Vernwood for three years, but she felt forced to leave four months after Benito took over.

Readers who knew their geography, and that Witchampton is in Dorset, would not have thought that this news item had defected from some hairdressing journal. They would naturally have assumed that Dorset district secretary, Ernie Amey, was behind it all.

Ernie, a stalwart recruiter to the Union, had signed up hundreds of new members in his time, and believed, like Peter Medhurst, that the Union should truly be for 'rural' workers, and not just farm or forestry men, and would sign up anyone who needed a shoulder to lean upon, be they poet or peasant.

And Ernie, despite ill-health, had been instrumental in winning what must be hundreds of financial settlements for anyone in trouble, as the constant pictures in the *Landworker* of Ernie presenting a cheque to somebody testify. One might be excused in thinking that cheque presentations were the chief job of the Union!

Ernie, who joined the Union in 1943 and became a branch secretary, was once employed as a part-time agent for the Labour Party, for whom he enrolled 200 members. For a time, he worked for the Forestry Commission. As an indefatigable recruiter to the Union, he quickly received the Union plaque for recruiting 100 members, and continued in the same way from that time forward.

*   *   *

Back on the national scene, in 1984 came the retirement of Moss Evans. He was succeeded by Ron Todd, who as the National Officer was well known to agricultural trade group members, and had attended their first annual conference at the TGWU's modern conference and holiday centre at Eastbourne, where in future all trade group conferences were to be held.

Tolpuddle Commemorated

There was a special issue of the *Landworker* in July 1984, to commemorate the 150th anniversary of the Tolpuddle Martyrs, and in it Jack Boddy called on all members to recruit a new member in their memory. He wrote that the Tolpuddle story was 'especially relevant today' because of the Government's current attack on trade unionists. The rights our predecessors fought so hard for are being attacked, and the Government's 'policy of high unemployment . . . has no concern for working people or those less able to fight for themselves in the free-market economy that Mrs. Thatcher holds so dear.' As rural workers they should draw inspiration from the Martyrs and 'for the battles to come'.

There were messages of support from other national leaders, and Eric Heffer, MP, chair of the Labour party said, 'as in 1834, membership of unions is being made illegal [a reference to the Government's ban on unions at GCHQ] . . . This Government . . . wants to drag workers' conditions down and return to the days of Queen Victoria, when workers knew their place, at the bottom of the heap.'

Union branches sent big donations to the miners in their dispute, and on the anniversary of Tolpuddle, Jack Boddy welcomed Kent National Union of Miners to Headland House, to share the office space while the dispute lasted.

A mural to commemorate the great Copenhagen Fields demonstration in support of the Martyrs was painted by artist David Bangs; TUC President Ray Buckton and TUC Deputy General Secretary Norman Willis planted a sycamore in Caledonian Park, Islington, the starting point of the great London rally.

A commemorative badge and an oval platter for the anniversary were sold by the Union, and the TUC produced a wide range of items, including mugs and plates, a pamphlet entitled *The Story of the Dorchester Labourers*, two badges, a number of postcards with historical and contemporary illustrations, and posters of the magistrates' court.

In March, the Post Office arranged a first-day cover of six agricultural stamps from Tolpuddle, and the 7.84 Theatre Company toured with a new production of the play, *Six Men of Dorset*.

As the sun rose over the rolling Dorset countryside on the day itself, 1 July, trade unionists and Labour supporters started to arrive in Tolpuddle, and by mid-morning there was a two-mile tailback of vehicles. They came by the thousand from all over Britain, and held what was to be the biggest trade union rally ever staged in a rural setting. By 11.30am an enormous crowd had gathered for a tree-planting ceremony on the green. It was grown from a seed from the original martyrs' tree by a National Trust warden, and was planted by Oliver Trevett, Dorset area chairman, and blessed by the Revd. W. Gowland from Luton Industrial College. Wreaths were laid at the grave of James Hammett by Neil Kinnock, Len Murray and international trade union representatives.

By the time the march began, the crowd was massive, probably 20,000. At the head was the Tolpuddle branch banner, the POEU banner, Dorset County banner, and a new national AAWTG banner, showing the traditional furrows and modern equipment, with an inset of the old NUAAW emblem and the words 'Agricultural and Allied Workers' National Trade Group TGWU'. There were nearly 300 other union and Labour banners in the procession. Marching five or six abreast they went down the hill towards the village, a spectacular sight as the banners came on and on, waving in the gentle breeze. By the time the head of the march had returned to its starting point the tail was just leaving.

All six speakers were given an enthusiastic reception, including Jack Boddy, and a taped message from Bob Hawke, the Australian Labour Premier went out over the public address system. A collection of £1,300 was taken for the relief of distress among families of striking miners. (That year, workers at Bernard Matthews paid a debt of honour and raised £700 for the miners, who had sent them £1,025 during their strike.)

Another anniversary was commemorated in 1984, the 70th anniversary of the Burston School Strike. Trade Group banners from Norfolk, Suffolk and Essex, TGWU: Region 1 banner, Labour Party banners from Norwich and Eye were to be seen in this Norfolk village on the occasion; CND, USDAW, NGA and the striking miners were also represented.

About a thousand people heard speeches by TGWU General Secretary elect, Ron Todd, Jack Boddy and former pupils of the school. Todd drew a modern parallel when he said that Tom and Annie Higdon were accused by local landowners of causing disruption – 'any modern-day teacher who happens to think nuclear weapons are a bad idea faces exactly the same tactics . . . this time the accusers are . . . the Conservative Government.'

*   *   *

The race to set up the first regional trade group for farm and allied workers in the TGWU had been won by the West early in 1983. Ron Nethercott, TGWU regional secretary, announced in January that this region had set up their trade group, and its secretary would be Somerset DO, Barry Leathwood. Newly-elected chair was Howard Wright of Wilts.

*   *   *

Another trade group secretary was Tony Gould, secretary South East England and East Anglia Region, a committed socialist from personal experience and conviction, not because he was brought up to be one. Tony was born in Wimbourne, Dorset, where his father was a journalist on the local paper and his grandfather a bus cleaner in Bournemouth. Tony's father gave him to believe that if he worked hard and kept his nose clean he would automatically prosper, as would anyone. He passed the 11-plus and went to grammar school; a number of careers were open to him, but he liked working with animals, so chose to go on a farm. He began as general farm boy, became a pigman, eventually a pig herd manager. At one time, he worked at the Liscombe Experimental Husbandry Farm on Exmoor.

As he told me in 1989, he didn't join the Union until he was 28, when working on a large estate in Cornwall. 'I was impressed by the inequality of wealth and income. The estate owner was getting very rich, and nobody seemed to object to the endless drive for production and hard work for the many and wealth for the few. The only voice of dissent seemed to be the NUAW. I was a member of the Labour Party. My parents were yuppies – it annoys me today to hear yuppies described as a new phenomenon, they've been around for a long time. I couldn't accept their outlook on life. My experience on the farm showed me their belief, that by hard work you would prosper was manifestly untrue. I saw farmworkers who lived blameless lives, yet they were very poor. 'I knew a farmer who had five point-to-point horses. their fodder was the same as that given to the cows, it was tax evasion. This farmer was getting richer and going round talking about being honest. People should not take a swede home, if you did, you'd be clobbered. I joined the Union out of sheer commitment, not because dad said join. He hated trade unions.'

One day, while working in Cornwall, the pig herd manager, his boss, said, 'I think your job and your trade union activities are incompatible.' He was sacked three months later. He had earlier unsuccessfully applied for a Union job as organiser, but Edgar Pill told him the interviewing committee had been impressed by him and he should stay in touch. So when he was sacked he again applied for a Union job, but there wasn't one. However, Edgar told him there was a vacancy at Ruskin College, Oxford, and Tony finished up doing the Oxford Diploma in Social Studies. He had moved to Oxford with his wife and their three daughters, Kate, Charlotte and Amelia, all born in tied cottages, and like their father, committed socialists.

The Union had a separate scholarship to Ruskin, and because of the children, Tony received a higher grant. 'They paid; it was the equivalent of a local authority grant. The Union was brilliant,' said Tony. After getting his diploma, Tony went to Corpus Christi College where he gained an honours degree in Politics, Philosophy and Economics. 'It reinforced my socialist convictions; my Economics tutor, Andrew Glynn, gave me a philosophical basis for believing that socialism was both just and possible.' Two miners' strikes occurred while he was there and he joined their picket line at Didcot Power Station. 'There I learnt lessons about the industrial struggle that you never learn on a farm; there are no pickets on farms.'

Shortly before Tony obtained his degree, Charlie Leathwood retired as Kent DO and Tony took over in June 1975, remaining in Kent until 1984, when he was appointed Regional Group Secretary. He was also the last lay secretary of the S E Regional Council of the TUC from 1983 to 1985, when he resigned to enable a full-timer to be appointed.

Tony saw no point in pretending that there was a bright future for British agriculture. 'With CAP there is so much productive potential in Europe, the future for British agriculture is dim,' he said. He believed there was, however, a future for the agricultural trade group, providing it identified itself with the rurally-based worker. 'Farmers in future are going to hammer the core of the agricultural labour force, placing even greater reliance on part-timers, particularly in the South East, so we need to expand even more our activities in the preparation and packing of food prior to transportation to supermarkets. Also we need to expand into rural amenity occupations; this rural leisure thing isn't going to go away, and there will be a lot of maintenance work to be done.'

REFERENCES

1. Annual Report, 1982.
2. 'Merging with the T&G.' A dissertation by Edward Blissett, 1989.
3. Blissett, ibid.
4. Blissett, ibid.

Part Two

11

The Quality of Life in the Countryside

I have no relish for the country:
it is a kind of healthy grave

Sydney Smith

Union Fought on a Broad Front

The Union has always been concerned with the quality of life in rural Britain, not only for its own members, but for the population generally. This has meant concern about housing, schools, transport, and the infrastructure as a whole – rural depopulation, the lack of alternative jobs to agriculture and many of the social amenities commonplace in towns.

Since its foundation the Union had always fought on a broad front, taking up many social issues vital to the country dweller. It continued to do so after the Second World War, when lack of housing was the great problem facing the rural working class. County committees reflected this concern and, typically, Jack Brocklebank, DO, on behalf of the Yorkshire County Committee, wrote in 1948 to local councils:

> Our committee has for many years been very greatly concerned about the drift from the countryside, averaging 14,000 workers each year. Slowly the tide is being turned, and new entrants are coming in. To attract still more, and to hold them, our committee is convinced that the new houses to be built should be in or near existing villages where the opportunity for village community life and modern amenities, such as water and electricity, will be more likely to be available. Shopping facilities and a school for the children are also very important.

Some councils had more progressive housing policies than others, and were closer to the Union's aspirations. One was Wimborne and Cranborne RDC, Dorset, which in 1949 completed 120 houses and had 60 under construction. Of 156 houses already allocated, over 55% were to agricultural workers. This percentage was good, as the majority of applications were from non-agricultural workers. For the time, the standards were good, too, brick with tiled roofs and admirably planned. Each had a kitchen, dining and sitting room, electric light and piped water. Upstairs were three bedrooms and a bathroom with a flush W.C. The rents were 10s a week plus rates. Several Union members became tenants and were full of praise for them. Bro. W. Martin was a member of this RDC which, said the *Landworker*, 'is to be congratulated on a fine housing programme.'

The Union had always encouraged members to stand for local councils, and where they did so with success, councils often had better policies for the housing of workers. Writing in the June 1949 *Landworker*, Frank Knowles, a Union and Labour Party activist, gave details of the Isle of Axholme (Lincs) RDC of which he was a member. Since the war they had erected 154 houses and eight bungalows. All the new dwellings were well equipped. Bungalows let at 3s 1d per week; houses with three bedrooms let to agricultural workers at 8s per week.

Not all such developments were approved by some farmers. During a debate by Haverford West RDC in 1953, the clerk said farmers objected to council houses being in groups near villages. They wanted isolated cottages built as near the farms as possible. 'I felt it was the desire of the NFU to treat this council as a sub-committee of the NFU for housing purposes,' said the clerk, who added that the NUAW was in favour of the council's policy of building in groups.

The Union let nothing escape its notice where the well-being of the country dweller was concerned. In 1948, Edwin Gooch, in Parliament, asked the Minister of Agriculture if he would inquire into the number of footpaths diverted during the war with a view to their early reinstatement. The reply was that about 2,500 footpaths were diverted under defence regulations, then revoked, and farmers told that the paths should be restored. The *Landworker* suggested that Union branches check if all footpaths had been restored.

In 1968, the EC decided not to object to the Government's plan for introducing British Standard Time (Summer Time would be in operation throughout the year). They felt that it would be beneficial to the community as a whole, including Union members, and might help bring about a statutory 5-day week. But, at the 1968 Biennial, the introduction of BST was not viewed with favour by five delegates. They were concerned that attempts would be made by employers to bring about a later starting time, especially in Winter. Conference wanted commencing and finishing times to remain as they were.

That improvements had been made in rural life was illustrated when I visited the little Norfolk village of Trunch – a pleasant place, the older houses mostly of the usual flint, with a warm red brick and pantiles, all made at the local brickworks. A hesitant sun broke through a cloud-patched sky, and took the chill of the autumnal winds that blew in from the North Sea as Arthur Amis, aged 81, Union and Labour stalwart, took me to see the village pump. We approached a neatly-trimmed greensward that used to be the village pit where the horses were watered, and there at one end was the Trunch Town Pump, erected 1922, according to the notice. It consisted of three 25-foot tree trunks, which had been laboriously bored through with a giant auger, and then forced down into a 60-foot well and sealed with a mixture of resin and mutton fat; an iron rod once went up and down as the villagers pumped up the water. 'The majority of villagers got all their water here,' said Arthur.

That pump had long since been out of use, but it epitomised the hard life that was once the norm of Norfolk villages. There was a piped-water supply in 1988, and much more besides. Not that some of the good things of the 'bad old days' had not gone too.

Arthur was in a reminiscent mood when we returned to his little cottage alongside the flint and stone church, and sat against the parlour window. A strong sun was streaming through, encouraging a lovely smell from a vase of roses. Arthur, son of a cowman, was one of 11 children, and attended the village school until he was eight, when he went to a school in Mundesley, a three-mile walk. He left at 14 and became a cowman, seven days a week, 5am to 5pm, making 84 hours in all, for 10s a week. He gave his father 9s to help keep the family, then there was 2d a week union sub, 2d a week to the men's institute in the village. 'I might buy a bag of monkey nuts on a Friday night with what was left over,' he said. 'Our main food was bread and margarine, sometimes with jam or cheese. Perhaps we would get a little meat at weekends, otherwise it was potatoes or toasted onions.

'I don't know how we managed. We went without, but struggled through. I couldn't afford a bike, so I had to walk three miles a day to work.'

Many old Union stalwarts joined on starting work at an early age, some barely had time to get into long trousers before they were signed up, often by their fathers.

Arthur joined in 1922, the year he started work. 'It was a thing to do. Father said, "you have to join," and I've never regretted being a member.'

At the time of the 1923 Norfolk Strike, Arthur was second cowman at Mundesley. Seven men worked on the farm and, strangely for Norfolk, only Arthur was in the Union. One Friday the farmer told the men, 'I'm cutting your wages from 25s to £1.' The other men never said a word, but Arthur said, 'I'm in the Union. I shall be on strike if you cut me down.' The farmer replied, 'You've no right to be in the Union, but I can't cut your pay. I must keep you milking.' Arthur remained at work, and when he finished in the evenings, would go to the men in the village and urge them to remain in the Union. He worked closely with Herbert Harvey, the area strike leader.

Arthur married Gladys in 1933, whom he met at a Methodist Synod. He never held an official post in the Union – being a cowman took up all his time – but he was active in the Labour Party, and in 1958 became Labour Agent for North Norfolk. When Labour lost North Norfolk, Arthur believed it was largely because of the influx of 'furriners' into the villages, mostly Tories.

He was parish councillor, district councillor and county councillor, and helped the Union whenever he could. He believes one of the Union's greatest achievements was obtaining unemployment benefit for farmworkers, and thought the Union's legal advice service a great blessing. 'We were, I suppose, illiterate in legal matters. Where we would have been without the Union, I don't know. Our education wasn't much – the last two years I spent at school we used to play noughts and crosses most of the day.' Arthur regrets that sparse education, and once on a visit to the University of East Anglia, could hardly believe his eyes, when he saw what was offered to students. Even so, he didn't like the way children were taken from village schools to town schools. 'The village way of life is being destroyed by present-day education,' he said.

A Methodist lay preacher, he still helped the Union when he could, kept a trim lawn and flower beds, and had a vegetable patch with a greenhouse. The latter was full of tomatoes. 'I've had 386lb out of it this year,' he said.

Integrate Agriculture and Industry

A resolution seeking the integration of agriculture and industry, submitted by the Union, appeared on the agenda of the 1949 TUC. With the object of achieving a better balance between urban and rural life, it suggested that suitable industries operating in small units be assisted to establish themselves in the countryside. 'The dispersal of industry would do away with the segregation of the mode of life of the two sets of workers, facilitate the provision of public services and amenities, and the maintenance of community life, make for great equality in wages, provide employment for seasonal workers in both agriculture and industry.' The Union continued to urge the need for more light industry in rural areas right into the 1980s, for vast areas still needed such developments, but no such industry, on the scale needed, was ever provided.

It was in 1949 that the National Parks and Access to the Countryside Act, one of the most important pieces of far-sighted legislation introduced by the Labour Government, became law. After more than 60 years of agitation to make the loveliest stretches of the countryside accessible to the public, a Commission was put to work to make these areas into national parks.

Many branches were ever alert to rural needs generally, and in January 1952 Waltham Cross (Herts) discussed the Conservative Government's proposal to reduce educational facilities for workers' children by closing smaller schools, cutting travelling allowances and scholarship grants, and withdrawing the subsidy on meals. It passed a resolution saying, 'that neither the interests of the children nor those of the nation can be served by these measures.'

The Union's concern over schools came to the fore in the post-war years, when much educational reorganisation was planned. Suggestions that education in rural areas be orientated to keep young people on the land were condemned by the Union in a memo to the Rural Development Panel of the Council for Wales and Monmouthshire, who were conducting a pilot survey in mid-Wales. It suggested that urban bias in curricula could be avoided by having secondary schools in rural areas fed by surrounding villages.

When seven-year-old Carole Clarke, of Willesborough, Ashford, Kent, in the 1950s, brought home specimens of her school work on toilet paper, she told her surprised parents that the class worked 'on lavatory paper'. A protest was made, and Carole's grandmother, a daughter of Freddie Bones, NUAW county president, fought for higher standards.

A private inquiry into conditions of 134 rural schools in widely separated areas by the Head Teachers' Association, confirmed that much needed to be done.[1] Many had changed little since they were built, and one in every three had inferior sanitary arrangements, still relying on buckets or earth closets. Seven out of eight were reasonably served for water, but the remainder relied on wells or springs which dried up in Summer. Only two in seven had hot water. One school in ten was lit with oil lamps, some schools had central heating, but one in three relied on coke or oil stoves, or open fires. The *Landworker* congratulated the Association on its report and declared, 'It serves to underline the fact that rural schools are still the Cinderella of our education system.'

The 1958 Biennial wanted abolition of the 11-plus exam to ensure fairer treatment of the late developer and the rural child, who far too often suffered from a poor primary education. Some children had an advantage simply because they lived where more grammar school places were available.

Although critical of their lack of facilities, most NUAW members strongly supported the retention of village schools as centres of primary education. In 1977, a country-wide movement sprang up to fight the imminent closure of 50 village schools.

Francis Beckett reported to *Landworker* readers from two of these villages with a proud tradition of fighting for their schools. Gissing (Norfolk) village school had 23 pupils, one full-time teacher and one part-timer, and practically every villager wanted it to remain open. So did neighbouring Burston, whose overcrowded school would have to accommodate the Gissing children if the closure plan went through. Burston, home of the famous School Strike, produced a key man in the fight to save Gissing's school: Tom Potter, youngest of the six Potter children involved in the strike. Tom, local branch secretary, sat on South Norfolk RDC, the only socialist there; district councils were normally expected to know their place and not interfere in educational matters. Tom persuaded his district council to take the unheard-of step and oppose the closures.

These closures roused a lot of passion because it was feared that the villages would become 'ghost towns'. Young parents did not want to live in villages without educational facilities, so the fight was not just to save a school, it was to save a community. Gissing's battle was mirrored in villages throughout Norfolk, and holidaymakers were often startled to see strident 'Save our School' banners strung across other village streets. Alas, many of these schools, including Gissing's, were later closed.

'Goodbye' to No Amenities

In February 1953, the *Landworker* noted that when a questionnaire was sent to 200 land workers and a similar number of young men who had left the land for urban jobs, to find out what they disliked most in their working conditions, wages came first, with houses second and lack of leisure facilities third. There was also the wider question of rural regeneration. People left the countryside not only for economic reasons, but for human reasons. The *Landworker* also noted that 'the women are a factor no longer to be ignored'. Not only were farm wages not good enough, they were not content to live in a village where all the services and amenities were absent. It advocated better housing and amenities.

At the 1953 TUC, an NUAW resolution urging the development of a cheap and plentiful supply of electricity to the countryside was remitted to the General Council. Five years after nationalisation the number of farms supplied with electricity had risen by 50,000, but the need to expand agricultural production and improve rural amenities provided strong justification for further attention to the rate of development.

Debates on housing were frequent at district and area conferences, and the 1958 Biennial instructed the EC 'to bring pressure on the Government, landowners and farmers to improve rural cottages, and ensure that they were supplied with mains water, electricity and waterborne sanitation as soon as possible.'

At the 1959 TUC, an NUAW motion on the deterioration in rural transport was composited into one from the NUR, which urged the need for transport improvements and sought to ensure that rail passenger services were not withdrawn purely on financial grounds. It was referred to the General Council.

That year the Government set up the Jack Committee* to look into the inadequacy of rural bus services. The Union gave evidence that the real answer would be the integration of all public transport under the control of the British Transport Commission. With all services under one roof, there would be a better chance for non-paying ones to continue. Its main point, perhaps, was that the question of subsidising essential transport services should be faced. No new principle was involved; bus operators already subsidised rural transport from urban profits, rural housing received extra subsidies, as did rural water and electricity.

'In a few years' time, man may be able to get to the moon. But will he be able to use 20th century public transport to get from Puddlecombe-on-Slosh to the nearest market town,' asked the *Landworker* in January 1963. 'As things are going it seems unlikely.' It was referring to a deputation to Government ministers, on which the Union, along with the NFU, CLA, WI and local authority representatives, met the Prime Minister and Minister of Transport,

---

*   Committee on Rural Transport, set up in September 1959 under Professor David Jack.

and impressed upon them the steadily worsening rural bus and rail facilities. The hardship that lack of public transport caused the young, the aged, the infirm and those unable to afford a car was made plain. The Ministers agreed that something had to be done. The main recommendation of the Jack Committee was that there should be a subsidy for rural bus services.

In 1964, the Government issued *Rural Transport Survey Reports* on six rural areas which admitted that rural transport was not good enough. It found that between about half and three-quarters of persons in households without private transport were 'hindered in some way by an inadequate bus or train service'. Well over a quarter of the people without cars had difficulty in getting medical or dental treatment, and visiting people in hospital. This survey told NUAW members nothing new.

The 1964 Biennial reaffirmed Union opposition to the Beeching rail closures. Chris Morris, EC, reminded Conference that the Government had taken no action on the Jack Committee recommendations: 'We must oust the Tory Government and ensure that public transport is publicly owned and run in the interests of the community.'

A new TUC pamphlet, *Transport Policy*, published in 1965, recommended the establishment of a British Transport Commission to run a national door-to-door transport service and co-ordinate train and bus services. In order to halt the decline in services, it wanted the obligation to make profits on public passenger transport abolished.

The *Landworker* backed much of the TUC's thinking, stressing the need for subsidies for rural bus services. It said, 'new thinking is required about the types, integration and financing of public transport,' quoting the White Paper, *Transport Policy*, presented to Parliament in 1965. It welcomed the fact that 'Rural transport is not ignored in the White Paper. Neither is it given the detailed attention we should like.' The Government was to encourage local authorities to draw up and finance their own schemes for improving passenger road transport in rural areas. The declared intention to help towards these costs could add a bonus crucial to the success of plans the local authorities may be drawing up. But it was to be at the authorities' 'discretion' and this was bound to raise doubts in the minds of those who wanted to see a quick improvement in rural transport.

Unfortunately, the writer's fears were well-founded. Little was ever done to implement the proposals, and public transport continued to decline under both Labour and Tory administrations.

At the 1966 Labour Conference the Union got a reference to 'rural areas' included in a composite calling for priority in improving 'poor communications' in the under-developed parts of the country. Chris Morris reminded Conference that the White Paper said that the declining demands and steeply rising costs 'cannot be allowed to lead to a wide-scale withdrawal of rural bus services'. The resolution also called on the Government to initiate legislation to establish an integrated transport system, including road, rail, canal, air, coastal services and ports.

Rural bus services continued to decline, and in 1971 the Union EC issued a statement that it had been to the fore in the battle to maintain or improve them. It had been a largely rear-guard action, and not highly successful, but the evidence was that the then bad situation would have been far worse, but for the pressure by the Union. It recalled that the Union recommended to the Jack Committee that rural services should be subsidised. The Committee had made this one of its main recommendations, but the Tory Government did not implement this proposal. It wanted remedial action.

At the Labour Conference at Blackpool in 1975, Chris Morris, now the Union's chief spokesman on public transport, wanted the Government to hand out concessions on the buses and railways, and also suggested petrol concessions to tradesmen delivering in 'outlandish' areas, as petrol costs tended to push up prices in country districts. The measure to which Chris was speaking was adopted. It called for more investment in the railways and other publicly-owned transport to enable modernisation to take place. The 1976 TUC Congress similarly adopted an NUAAW measure prompted by growing concern at the deterioration of public transport in rural areas.

During the Thatcher regime in the 1980s, privatisation of many bus services led to a further decline in some rural services. The Union's forecast of what would happen under privatisation became an unhappy reality.

Rural Health Problems

In 1961, from all parts of the country, members protested at Tory proposals to increase NHS charges and contributions. They saw them as a direct attack on the principles of the service itself and as a deliberate move to pass on costs to those least able to afford them. The EC protested to the Minister of Health.

The Union welcomed the setting up by Labour in 1966 of the new Ministry of Social Security, to replace the National Assistance Board. The new ministry aimed to offer service at all its 1,200 offices, covering the whole range of social security benefits. A new earnings-related benefit scheme, for those earning a minimum of £450 a year, would ensure additional benefits to the flat sickness and unemployment payments, which would help the low paid in rural areas.

At the TUC Women's Conference in 1968, one of the Union's delegates, Mrs. M. Bareham, Kent, successfully moved a measure supporting the TUC's efforts to secure increased family allowances for low-income families.

*   *   *

When the school leaving age was raised to 16, the *Landworker* called for the scrapping of the 11-plus exam. It questioned the theory behind this method of selection which had been worked out in the 1930s by 'experts' in children's intellectual capacity: 'The theory that a child's intelligence is virtually unchangeable has since become suspect and . . . never applied to rich children anyway. The alternative was comprehensive secondary education.'

Rural comprehensives were developed, which involved much bussing from villages, and the old-fashioned village school continued to disappear. There was continued controversy in the Union on the merits of village schools, and one man not sorry to see them disappear was George Scales, of Epping.

George was born on Good Friday, a day after All Fools' Day in 1920, in the middle of one of the wettest nights on record. He lived in a tied cottage right from the start, and got most of his education at a CoE village school. He wasn't certain which was the greater drawback, which probably accounted for his life-long demand: 'Rent books, not hymn books'. At school said George, the teaching was very poor, and virtually the only thing he learnt was singing – psalms and sea shanties.

This all happened at Hatfield Hyde, now part of Welwyn Garden City, where he later went to a school which had a socially conscious headmaster, who told pupils that they should play their part in society. That headmaster made up for the deficiencies of the village school. 'He gave us the feeling that things weren't as they were because they were willed from above, but because the bosses organised things as they were and a lot of people felt it easier leaving things to the boss, and it's still like that today,' George told me in 1988, when I called upon him at his retirement bungalow in Sheering, Essex.

Despite his bad start at the village school, George finished up as a farm manager. Not that George had any extended formal education – sons of low-paid agricultural workers didn't go on to higher education in those days. On leaving school his first job was as delivery boy at W. H. Smith's. 'I read every paper and book I could get hold if,' said George. 'I was a very well-read boy.' Another influence was Welwyn itself, in those days a very socialistic town, trying to conform to the ideas of its founder Ebenezer Howard. And young George saw be-medalled First World War soldiers busking to supplement their meagre pensions. 'I was angry that these heroes were reduced to begging,' said George.

His next job was working with his dad in an engineering factory. There George was annoyed that a lot of workers went crawling to the bosses, to anyone in authority over them. 'A lot of the men were from the Lea Valley where horticulture flourished. Each Monday, they would bring into the factory, flowers, tomatoes and other out-of-season greenhouse produce. The foreman's office used to look like a church in the middle of a ruddy harvest festival.'

George joined the Constructional Engineers' Union one Thursday evening. Next morning he was pulled up sharp by his father in the work's yard, yelling, 'Put that horrible card out of sight you stupid little bugger, waving it about like the ace of trumps, you'll get us both the bloody sack.'

His dad was only half right. Only George was sacked, that evening. So George joined the Army and served in the Royal Engineers during the war, and when it ended, went on a farm under an ex-Serviceman's Rehabilitation Scheme. These trainees were paid by the Government £3 a week; the only thing the boss paid was overtime. 'He didn't pay much of that,' said George, 'he used to be on the farm at five o'clock to see me off. I didn't learn much. I started in March, potato riddling, and stayed on it 'till May. It was just cheap labour, like the YTS today.'

When he was foreman on a dairy farm, a workmate was severely injured by a cow and unable to work. George asked the manager what they were going to do about 'poor old Bert'. The manager said simply, 'We want his house.' George said, 'You can't do that, he's got five kids at school.' The manager replied, 'We can, you must tell him.' George refused, but the manager had no difficulty in doing this and Bert lost his job and house.

George promptly applied to join the Union, but nothing happened until three years later when he shifted to a farm at Epping. 'I moved in on a Saturday and Chris Morris was round on Sunday morning to sign me up,' said George, who finished up as chairman of Epping branch, chairman of Brentwood District, then on Essex County Committee, and Essex press officer. It was perhaps the latter job which led George to his true *métier*, writing. He soon had letters in the local press and *Farmers' Weekly*. At first the local paper didn't always publish what he sent, so he went to the newspaper office and said, 'You can't treat me like that, I represent the biggest industry in the country and the most important industry.' His letters soon began to appear, and sometimes when he hadn't sent a letter for some weeks, they used to ask him for one.

He used to write about everything, including ploughing matches and farm competitions. He objected, strongly. 'I didn't like the idea of a farmworker's mantelpiece being loaded with cups showing what a good and skilled work-man he was, when he hadn't got any coins to jingle in his pockets. It got me into trouble with most Union members, but it gave me a curiosity value.' He also objected to long service medals. He called them 'docility medals'. He preferred farmworkers got a good retirement pension. The ceremonial dish-ing out of such medals at county shows was something George found it best to avoid. 'The thought of those old timers obediently waiting in line, like English sheepdogs, not knowing whether they're going to get a Bob Martins on the tongue, or a Dr. Martens up the rear, fills me with boundless fury and does nothing for my blood pressure.'

He must have stayed away from many such presentations, because his blood pressure didn't seem bad when I chatted to him in his sitting room, over a lovely meal prepared by his wife Doris. George was grey-haired, spectacles dangled from a chain over a check shirt, his weathered face never far from a smile, and it was the smiles in George's life that have probably kept that blood pressure down.

Among targets for his letters was the *Landworker*, usually taking the opposite view – strongly – but his sense of humour must have showed, for the Editor, Francis Beckett, asked George to write a regular column, and he became one of its most popular contributors. Not that everyone agreed with him. 'You never write a single word worth reading,' complained one correspondent. George smiled. 'Strange, he couldn't have been able to put me down, poor chap.'*

He never found being a farm manager for 23 years conflicted with his Union membership. It helped in some ways, and enabled him to spend a lot of time writing. He didn't drink, didn't play darts or cards, he mostly read for recreation and mental stimulation. He liked to read the sports pages of newspapers, especially about soccer. 'Soccer is capitalism in the raw, when you're up, you're up, when you're down, nobody wants to know,' he explained.

George believed the Union would have fared better if it had dropped its 'agricultural' tag. 'He's got a stigma attached to him, has an agricultural worker, a sort of dim wit. Much better to have called themselves a rural workers' union; then the village postman, the blacksmith, could have joined. When a boy said he was going to work on a farm he would be told: "Bugger me boy, surely you can find something better." If we had opened the gates wide, we might even have got a few schoolteachers in the Union, and we wouldn't have frightened away the farmworkers if such people had joined. When anyone joins a union he wants to feel it's got depth and good motives, and I think members would have welcomed a certificate on those lines, rather than just a membership card; it would have helped them to feel they belonged to something important, something bigger than themselves.'

One Hundred Houses 'On the Bucket'

During the 1964 Biennial, delegates were determined not to let up on the over-riding need to improve rural housing. They decided that all dwellings let to tenants or service occupants 'should conform to statutory minimum standards which should include the provision of flush lavatories and bath-rooms'. A. Baynham, Worcs, said that he knew of one council that still had over 100 houses 'on the bucket'. Commenting on a Commons' statement that there were 1½ million houses without inside lavatories, A. Maybourne, Kent, said, 'You can bet most of them are in the country'.

At the same Biennial, Ted Sales, Dorset, welcomed Mr. Callaghan's pledge that Labour would reform the whole system of taxation which was weighted against the lower paid. He moved a composite against the income tax rate that was levied on the lowest paid, in order to obtain greater relief for farmworkers, forestry and land drainage workers, without at the same time giving even greater relief to those on higher incomes. 'On tax allowances, you

---

* The best of George Scales' columns are published in *Weighing Up* (Journeyman Press/TGWU), available from T&G Publications, Transport House, Smith Square, London SW1P 3JB, price £3.95.

are allowed £120 for your wife,' said Ted. 'You try to keep your wife on that,' he added, amidst laughter. There had got to be taxation for education and social services, said A. Maybourne, but he regarded spending money on missiles as unnecessary.

At the 1966 Biennial, the problem was discussed of housing farmworkers reaching retiring age. Living in tied cottages would be used as a lever to make them work longer after they would have liked to retire. J. Mason, Worcs, told of a 69-year-old colleague cutting cabbages in the pouring rain. 'You know how it is,' he said. 'I am living in his house. If I do not do it, he will want it for somebody else.' A resolution urging that more suitable accommodation should be built for retired farmworkers was passed.

At a rally before the Biennial at Aberystwyth in 1968, great strides were reported in the provision of rural houses. Premier Harold Wilson said that almost 23,000 dwellings were completed by rural district councils in 1967 – a staggering increase of 60% over 1963. As to amenities, in the previous year grants of £4 million and £21 million respectively had been promised for the provision of piped water and new sewerage work.

An outsider listening to the debates must have been struck with the delegates' deep-rooted desire to advance policies designed to ensure the long-term prosperity of agriculture and ancillary industries. Obviously the wages and conditions they sought were likely to be provided only by a thriving rural industry, but delegates also knew this could be highly beneficial to the nation's economy and essential, if the rural community's social and economic health was to be maintained and improved.

The Union never ceased to campaign for higher educational standards in rural areas, and its delegates to Labour's Brighton Conference in 1969 submitted a motion deploring current proposals to cut spending on education, particularly with regard to school meals and milk, staff and buildings. It wanted the Government to reverse this policy. Chris Morris forcibly put the Union's case. Alice Bacon for the NEC, however, persuaded delegates to vote solidly against the resolution by the simple device of drawing attention to the Government's commendable overall record for education since 1964.

At the 1970 Labour Conference, Bert Hazell seconded a composite on regional development calling for an effective regional policy to reduce the high levels of unemployment in development, intermediate and rural areas. It sought the promotion of new publicly-owned industries, and extension of existing ones. The resolution was adopted and could have been of material benefit to many NUAAW members when Labour again attained power, especially as Conference deplored 'the Parliamentary Labour Party's refusal to act on Conference decisions.'

On the second day of the Labour Conference in 1971, Reg Bottini moved a composite embracing no less than 11 resolutions expressing disgust at the Government's abolition of free school milk for seven-year-old and over children. It also called upon the next Labour Government to restore free milk and the subsidy for school meals.

At the Weymouth Biennial in 1972, Bert Hazell referred to the traumatic changes in local government boundaries, which would do away with many cherished traditions and transfer a great deal of power from authorities to large administrative centres, with professional administrators taking firm control. He thought these larger authorities would make for better planning of services, prevent overlapping and, maybe, ginger up areas where progress had been less marked. 'A lot will be expected of the new authorities but their success will largely depend upon those we chose to elect to serve our interests.' A regional health authority and an area health authority would replace the existing regional hospital boards, hospital management committees, health executive councils and so on, but membership of these authorities would be by selection and not election, and 'the amount of public involvement would be substantially reduced, which is unfortunate'.

Much of what Bert foresaw came true, but whether the changes were always for the better, is debatable. Many NUAAW members found local government becoming remote and out of touch with the people. While many rural hospitals were closed, giant complexes replaced them, which medically might have been more efficient, but were hard to get to, making it extremely difficult for the patients and would-be visitors.

In 1973 it was revealed that since June 1970, when the Tories came into power, food prices had risen by 40%. A resolution calling for the control of food prices, rents and rates, was adopted by the TUC by a large majority. NUAAW delegates abstained because it was felt that cheap food helped keep farm wages down.

That rising prices were causing hardship to the lower paid was acknowledged, and the 1974 Biennial at Clacton protested at the massive rate increases in rural areas where wages were low. E. Hudson, N Norfolk, said rate demands were having a 'devastating effect on our members'.

The Labour Conference at Blackpool in 1975 made a decision pleasing to NUAAW members, something they had sought for years. It called for requisitioning powers to take over empty houses, and make statutory the obligation on councils to house the homeless.

Rural medical services were discussed at the 1976 Biennial at Malvern. Yorkshire delegate Roger Fieldhouse successfully moved a resolution asking for adequate Government funds 'to maintain all the medical services required by new doctors coming into rural practices with the ultimate objective of a salaried service'. It was government policy not to approve an application to set up a practice or replace an outgoing doctor if the area had less than 1,800 patients. This hit rural areas. Seconding, R. Carey described the problem in his village of 3,000 inhabitants. Their doctor emigrated to foreign parts because the village was not a paying proposition. Now they shared a doctor with a small town four miles away, with a surgery in the village. The waiting room was a one-time barber's shop.

The determination of members to secure rural amenities matching those of the towns was highlighted when Somerset delegate, Ted Marsh, said that he had represented the Union at three different centres in Somerset in a series of discussions on the rural community. Three main issues had emerged. First, that people now demanded the same standard of living as those in the towns. Second, that communication between different levels of decision-making bodies was a major problem. And finally, 'there is a growing need to balance the control between local and central decision-making'.

*   *   *

Ted, with gentle West Country overtones in his voice, was not all he seemed to be. He was Cockney born, if not quite bred. One of a family of eight children who began life in West Ham in the East End of London, Ted, at the age of nine, and a brother, were evacuated by train to Bruton when the Second World War broke out. He didn't return until 1945, by which time he was well and truly a country lad. 'We had been told we were going on holiday,' said Ted, 'but when Chamberlain made his war-is-declared announcement on the wireless, I think we realised we were staying. It was the longest holiday I ever had.'

They were allocated foster parents in Sparkford, and, significantly, in a farmworker's home. At school, a local boy who used to milk cows challenged Ted to do likewise. 'You be a cissy if you can't,' he declared. Ted took to milking like one born to it. 'It was a bucket-and-stool job then,' he said when I met him in 1988 at Sparkford, where he then lived in a bungalow with his wife. 'I loved every minute I milked, as a boy.'

So much so, that when it was time to return to London when hostilities ceased, Ted didn't want to go. He was 15 then. His father wanted him to take up electrical engineering at Tate & Lyle's in Silvertown. 'I couldn't stick factory life,' said Ted, 'so I wrote to a farmer I knew in North Barrow and he offered me a job.' That was in 1946, and Ted had lived in the country ever since.

Ted did four years as a general farmworker, and at 20 wanted to get married to a village girl called Ellen, whose father was secretary of North Barrow NUAW. 'Well,' said dad, 'if you want to marry my daughter, you'll have to join the Union first.' Ted did, married, and never regretted doing either. Ted got a job on a farm on the outskirts of Castle Carey, remained 24 years, then went milking at North Cadbury.

Ted used to help Ellen's dad with the Union books, found himself collecting dues, and eventually became branch secretary. He was elected to various Union posts and eventually became county secretary. After the merger he became divisional secretary. He was a member of the EC from 1979 to 1982, and became Trade Group delegate to Region 3 committee and vice-chairman in 1985. He was a member of the Labour Party.

It was contract milking he took on at North Cadbury, but he had to give it up because the job made him ill; he developed back trouble and other complaints, and worked on a large country house estate in 1988. Ted explained, 'The EEC milk quotas have had a drastic effect on the West Country. Within my branch, four men were made redundant. The smaller man is pushed out and the large units are getting bigger and bigger, putting more stress on the cowmen, and the animals. All an operator does now is to work a machine to do the milking. When I went to North Cadbury in 1974, I had 80 cows, but by the time I left in 1986, I had 175. I gave up because the stress of looking after 175 cows was too much for me; milking that number of cows on your own, having to make sure you get the same amount of milk from the same feed, the health of the cows deteriorates. In addition, the cowman today has to get used to fertility records, milk production records, feed costs, and it all goes through a computer. Not only has he to get acclimatized to computerisation, but on top of that, you have to be a vet, electrician, in fact, a jack of all trades. The cows become ill, go lame and develop diseases that they once seldom had. Cows once had 10 or 12 lactations, living for 12 years, now they have about five calves and then go for beef-burgers. They're worn out by the high milk productivity rates they are supposed to keep up because of the high protein we kept pushing into them. A cow once gave 900 gallons a year, now they're expected to produce 1,300 gallons. The system wears them out, and the cowman. We milkers were exploited left right and centre, and we were the biggest fools to do it.'

Ted recalled other changes. 'When I started there was one cow per acre, today it's 3½–4 per acre. Organic manure wasn't a problem, but as they increased the size of the herds, it became a problem and they had to bring in these slurry systems. Where there was mixed farming, the arable was used for cattle feed; most feed now is imported, and it's becoming very expensive. So they're trying to make their own silage again in larger quantities. Today labour is only 16% of total costs, feed concentrates about 25%. Top of the bill is fertilisers about 34%. They got rid of a lot of labour as a result, but they're no better off in the end.'

He had been up to his boss's farm that day, and they were using a combine costing £72,000, with one man driving it. 'If they had kept some of the smaller machines, they could have done it much more cheaply,' said Ted.

Like other farmworkers, Ted was worried about the latest development in dairy farming in 1987, especially the use of bovine growth hormone, known as 'Somatropin'. Three farms had been given the go-ahead by MAFF for trials, and Ted and his fellow Trade Group members kicked up a fuss when they found that the milk was being sold to the public. 'We don't think the public should be put at risk until it's proven that there is no risk.'

Reflecting on the fact that nationally today only 22% of farms employ labour, Ted said, 'The merging of the smaller farms into the bigger units did not benefit farmworkers. Big farms do employ workers, but they don't pay them any better.'

Ted recognised that the lot of the remaining farmworkers has been improved by mechanisation and as the result of gains by the Union. There is not so much drudgery as there was 30 years ago, something, he believed the new generation of farmworkers did not appreciate. Health and safety had improved, although there was still a lot to be desired. Ted believed the farmworker's biggest setback was that he hadn't been adequately reimbursed for the progress and productivity made since the Second World War. And a lot of farmworkers were still working long hours of overtime because farms haven't got enough staff. 'Even today,' said Ted, 'the farmworkers couldn't survive without overtime and the farmers know it, and take advantage of it.'

Like many others, Ted thought the greatest Union achievement since the war was that the tied cottager was no longer at the mercy of bailiffs. 'But the Rent Agriculture Act leaves a lot to be desired,' he said. 'The majority of ADHAC [Agricultural Dwelling House Advisory Committee] cases go in favour of the employer, often because the chairman, nine out of 10 times, agrees with the employer.'

Ted believed the Union's biggest failure was not being able to stay independent. 'That was due to lack of recruitment. We never had enough active lay members who were willing to go out and sign up non-members. They made a lot of effort at the top to organise recruiting, but once you started to ask people to recruit, many just didn't want to know.'

'I felt the state the Union was in, in 1981, that there was no other way but to merge. I had the facts and figures and knew it was inevitable, but if we had increased our membership by each member recruiting one more, we could have saved the day and remained solvent. It was a very sad day. At the 1976 Malvern conference I seconded the motion seeking talks with other Unions. I could see the writing on the wall.'

On being in the EEC, he said, laconically, 'I didn't go a lot on it – and it's been getting worse ever since. As far as the agricultural worker was concerned it was a catastrophe – flooding Britain with imports which people were kidded into thinking were cheap, and now they haven't got much choice and they're not cheap.'

Fighting the 'Cuts'

Cuts in public expenditure in 1976 meant drastic changes in health and social services during Labour's term of office; this was raised at the 1976 TUC Congress, and much concerned the NUAAW delegates. The Government said that high-priority large hospital schemes would continue, but the Union believed that many of the small hospitals should be kept open, and sought an expansion of the health centre programme in rural areas.

Following the 1976 Malvern Biennial resolution that the men's pension age should be lowered to 60, the EC and the Labour Government exchanged letters on the subject. 'There is no logical justification for the different pension ages, but there are many difficulties in reducing men's pension age, the most important being the very high cost,' replied Stanley Orme, Minister of State for Social Security. The Union's main argument was that the reduction would enable many unemployed to find jobs. A further resolution adopted sought a substantial increase in pensions. The Minister again rejected it on the grounds of cost. These wholly negative answers were received by the EC with extreme disappointment.

The Minister would not accept that there had been a decline in rural medical services, declaring that the areas now 'least well-supplied with doctors are industrial rather than rural.' On the cuts, he claimed that in real terms the expenditure on health and social services would be 11% higher than in 1973–4.

The EC considered a long letter from the Under Secretary of State for the Environment, Ernest Armstrong, in reply to Biennial resolutions covering housing and amenities, including rural transport and cuts in public expenditure. On housing, the Union wanted authorities to give priority to local residents, but Armstrong said that houses should be allocated to those with greatest need. He denied there had been a cut in house building. The EC were bitterly disappointed at this negative attitude.

Public expenditure cuts were 'dictated by a determination to create the conditions under which unemployment will be brought down.' This was the 'Whitehallese' claim made in a letter from Employment Minister Albert Booth, in reply to one from Reg Bottini, drawing his attention to the Biennial resolution opposing the cuts. The EC found Booth's logic, or lack of it, unacceptable.

Letters on similar lines were sent to the Parliamentary Secretary of the DHSS, Richard Moyle, and to the Minister of State for Education, Gordon Oakes. Two typical extracts from their replies:

> The Government have accepted that public expenditure must be curtailed in 1977–8 so that our industry can have the necessary resources to take advantage of the expected up-turn in world trade in order to reduce our very large public sector borrowing requirements. *Richard Moyle*

> . . . if economic recovery is to be achieved . . . a greater share of our national resources must be made available to support industrial development and exports, and these resources will not readily be forthcoming unless expenditure on the public services can be kept under strict control. *Gordon Oakes*

Were these Labour ministers so completely in the hands of the mandarins of Whitehall? 'Their' replies might have been those of any Tory Minister excusing cuts in social services they regularly made when given the chance. Alas, the Establishment had little difficulty subverting Labour people, sent to Parliament for supposedly different purposes.

Cuts in public spending began hitting rural areas hard in 1977, and opposition to them, often spearheaded by NUAAW branches, would not be easy for the Labour Government to overcome. That was the unmistakable message coming from county conferences. Farmworkers, Cornwall delegates believed, were bearing an ever greater share of the tax burden, like other low-paid workers, and getting ever decreasing services for it. They opposed all cuts in the NHS.

The answer to the income tax problems was slightly different in the North West, in Northants, and in Hunts, Peterborough and Rutland, but the philosophy was the same. Their conferences all took the line that part of the tax burden should be lifted from low-paid rural workers by raising the personal allowance. Boots and clothes farmworkers needed for their work were getting more expensive and the tax system had never allowed for it. Cornwall's concern about hospitals was followed up in Kent, with the novel suggestion of a national lottery for hospitals. In the North West, concern focused primarily on cuts in school transport, which drew strong protests.

An NUAAW motion tabled at the 1977 Labour Conference at Brighton condemned cutbacks in social services, schools, hospitals and transport. The motion could only be seen as a rebuke to the Labour Government and, after an hour-long debate, there was an overwhelming vote in favour of a composite proposed by Bert Hazell, condemning Government cuts.

Joan Maynard became chair of a Labour Party working party on rural areas when it was set up, and three Union men were members: the new General Secretary, Jack Boddy, and EC members Jack Brocklebank and Jack Paget. It set to work consulting with Labour MPs from rural areas, union members and organisations associated with rural affairs. Reporting in 1979 on its work,[2] Joan said that they had decided against a ministry for rural affairs, because they did not want rural areas to be separate and different. Farmworkers had always been isolated and lost out. To make sure that they were not overlooked by a future Labour Government, they suggested a co-ordinating ministry which, whatever service or proposal was being discussed, would have special responsibility for rural areas.

They regarded employment needs a first priority, with transport closely linked. Car ownership placed a very heavy financial burden on low-income groups. They did not oppose less conventional solutions to the transport problems, such as community buses, but felt the real answer lay in publicly-owned transport. Light industry, craft industry and tourism could be sources of work in rural areas, and in health and social services they favoured bringing the services back to the people by way of mobile units. One day such a unit would go round the villages collecting electricity accounts, the next it would be a DHSS services shop, the third, Department of Employment, the fourth, Citizens' Advice Bureau, and so on. On hospitals, the Committee thought that bigness and efficiency dehumanised people's lives.

The Ever Lonelier Country

More criticism of Labour came at the 1978 Biennial, when Shropshire and Somerset demanded a reversal of 'the Government's policy of starving rural areas of the money to pay for the necessary social services – schools, hospitals, health centres, etc. This policy, which has already caused many people to cease to live and work in the rural areas, will in the end kill off the countryside.'

Later that year, the *Landworker* reported on the decline of village life in a four-page feature entitled 'The Ever Lonelier Country'. Barbara Wilcox dealt with the swallowing up of rural housing for second homes, holiday homes and retirement. She reported an experiment in the Lake District where planning permission for new homes was only given if it was to be occupied by a local worker. She found that the amount of rented accommodation was steadily decreasing and in 20 villages in North Norfolk no less than 256 homes still had pail toilets.

Chris Kaufman visited Luxborough, Somerset, and Francis Beckett, Ashmanhough, Norfolk, two dying villages. Luxborough, originally a thriving community based on iron ore mining, farming and forestry, once had a population of several hundred. Of the 145 people remaining there, only two were hired farmworkers, a few more were farmers and less than a dozen in forestry. Jobs had gone and so had the people. Nearly every cottage was tenanted by the retired or second-homers. In the 1940s, ninety children attended the village school, but by then it had closed. Once it had two buses into Minehead; when Chris visited it there was no public transport.

Ashmanhough, with its 170 inhabitants, wasn't just dying, it was almost dead. No school, no shop, no pub, no transport. Unless you owned a car or bicycle, you would have had to set aside a day to go to the nearest shops, three miles away in Wroxham. A few new houses had been built, almost entirely for the elderly and retired. There was not much work about, either, and most people worked in Norwich or Wroxham.

The feature also surveyed the fight for school transport and the need for capital investment. In all, it was a good example of the Union's continuing fight to preserve and make the best of the countryside. It added flesh and bones to the resolutions at every biennial fighting rural decline.

'The devastation of rural community life should serve as a terrible warning to the rest of society about the danger of allowing technological advance in industry to undermine the needs of the rest of the population,' Jack Boddy told a London conference on the future of the rural community in 1979. He believed that employment was the key to the future of rural communities. He told them that agriculture was still the major influence, yet farmworkers were still appallingly badly paid. 'It is no wonder then, that there has always been a steady stream of the countryside's more enterprising sons leaving the land to find better paid jobs with a proper career structure in the towns.'

Jack surveyed the decline in rural life, the loss of amenities, presided over by district and parish councils, which, 'to put it euphemistically, had not fallen over themselves to provide answers.' What was the Union looking for to revive the quality of rural life? They did not want a return to the squirearchy, and any changes had to be sensitive to the need to protect the countryside. They wanted a fair share of Government resources. Employment was crucial. They welcomed technological advance and wanted to see it used to enrich all their lives. To breathe new life into the countryside they did not require massive job-creation programmes nor great resource costs, but small-scale projects creating perhaps 2,500–3,000 jobs annually. He wanted the National Enterprise Board to support rural industrial projects on a scale appropriate to the particular area. To get these schemes off the ground they had to overcome the resistance of the countryside's *nouveau riche*, the weekenders and commuters who sought to protect their rural idyll from any change.

*   *   *

It's a lonely landscape that surrounds the busy market town of Spalding in the Lincolnshire fens – flat fields stretch to distant horizons. In Spring, some are carpeted with daffodils and tulips, in Summer, cereals sway in fresh winds from the Wash. Some days heat hazes can blur the vision, on others it can be the smoke of burning corn stubble. Above all, one has the sense of an amazing amount of space, with large fields and open skies. Often there is not a single figure to be seen, just an occasional combine harvester at work, or a car speeding up a narrow lane. The peace is unbelievable. An almost primeval stillness – only the primeval creatures are absent. Suddenly the tranquillity is shattered by a US jet streaking across the sky on a practice bombing run over the Wash. It was not always like this, as I learnt from Union stalwart, 73-year-old Gordon Dales, of Cuckoo Lane, down the road from the NFU's garden showpiece, Springfields.

I interviewed Gordon in 1983. He was a big, quick-witted man, who spoke with the directness of a sharp spade breaking new ground: 'When I was a boy, there were hundreds going to work on their bikes. Today, I can look out of my bedroom window and there's no one to be seen, just the odd car going to Peterborough. It's shocking to see so few people working round here. There ain't no hedges, no verges left, they've filled in most of the dykes. There's no birds chirping, no pigeons to coo, no pigs in sties, it's wicked. Once there was 200 ducks in a pond, now there ain't a blinking quack.'

As Margaret, his second wife, made tea, Gordon told of the changes during a lifetime on the land. 'They pulled all the old waggoners' houses down, today there's 1,000-acre farms without a house on them. At the end of the Second World War, I worked on a 1,000-acre farm. It had 47 regular workers and used two gangs for regular work. Today there's only five people on the farm, one's the boss and he don't work. They don't need anyone, they only grow wheat and barley. They might occasionally have a crop of taties. Lots of farms like that once had 50 men on them, now you can't see anyone working on them. I know a farmer with 1,000 acres and he don't employ one man, it's all done by contract. People who used to work on the land went to work at Perkins at Peterborough 18 miles away, some at Stamford.

'They don't do no hoeing in the Spring now, they just spray it. They band sew and there's no weeds come.' He recalled gapping and singling sugar beet, and back hoeing at £2 4s an acre. 'You had to stick it night and day to try to do two acres a week.' During the war he mowed dykes out for 6d a chain (22 yards). He sometimes mowed 40 chains a day. In Winter, he worked at the sugar beet factory. 'That was a saviour, you got wages up to Christmas.' We were called "catch hands" then. I've been to farmers' houses at 8pm and got a day's threshing, if I'd been in regular work, for 32s or 33s a week, it would have been regular poverty.' He set potatoes at 7s an acre, and once he was offered a regular job at 1s a week less than he was getting on the dole, and the dole was very meagre in those days.

Gordon elaborated on the changing workscene and citing the case of one man combining a big field in a day, added indignantly, 'I've seen them do it on a Sunday. Why work on a Sunday? They just want all that overtime, that's no life.'

'All my life round here they've been trying to do away with labour. They started planting tulips in ridges and then did it with daffs. Then the agriculturalists got hold of the idea and had huge fields planted with bulbs mechanically.' He recalled in the thirties pulling flowers for 5d a thousand and 3d an hour. 'I sometimes pulled 20,000 a day, others did 24,000. Now they don't bother to pull the flowers unless they can get a good price on Mothering Sunday, they just go for the bulbs.' Most of the pullers in the old days were women. Gordon didn't have any trouble getting them into the Union.

Gordon was two when he was brought from Haugh to Spalding by his father, who had been getting 15s a week and 20 faggots. He had been offered 18s in Spalding. 'Don't you go, Will,' said his old foreman, 'if they're going to give you 18s, there's a catch in it somewhere.'

However, Will risked it, and it was in Spalding that Gordon grew up. He started tending calves on the roadside with his sister, aged nine. 'Dad may have got a shilling for us, but we never saw it. His hours were 6am to 8pm. He never earned more than 48s a week, and he was never better off than when he got his pension. He lived to 90.'

While courting Ida (his first wife), Gordon worked in the beet factory's lime kilns for 1s an hour, including Sundays. It was so hot his skin blistered. 'Are we going to be blistered alive,' he asked a workmate. 'You should join the Union,' he was told. He joined right away and was 'spellbound' by Arthur Monks, DO in Spalding. He was soon on the Sugar Beet Negotiating Committee, and that meant going to London, where he had never been before.

'I'll be lost,' he told Arthur. 'You get a taxi to the place in Piccadilly,' was the reply. He got there and found himself facing a big lift. 'Chap says, "Come this way, sir." Don't you call me sir, mate, I'm no sir.' At his first negotiations, they got 6d an hour extra for one section of the workers.

By then Gordon was fully involved in Union work. Spalding branch was the biggest in the country with 1,000 members and eight collectors, with Joe Wilson as secretary. It was unwieldy, so they formed the Fulney branch, with 300 members, and Gordon became its secretary and held the post for 18 years. 'They were happy days, we were struggling, but people welcomed you,' he said. 'We got 3d in the pound for collecting dues, and it meant you could go home and give the missus a couple of bob.'

Gordon, like other branch secretaries, was especially busy during the war. WLA girls, picking bulbs, went into a glasshouse for dinner, where Gordon found one crying. 'What's wrong, luv,' he asked. 'We've been given mutton dripping sandwiches to eat, nothing more.' Gordon told them to bring dry bread the next day, and he would bring a 2lb pot of jam. The girls, who were only 18 or so, said they would join the Union as soon as they had any money. Meanwhile, Gordon showed the dripping sandwiches to Arthur Monks, who had become liaison officer between MAFF and the Ministry of Labour. Arthur took the sandwiches to the hostel where the girls lived, and found that the mutton that should have been in them had been sold on the black market. The matron was sacked. Union membership among the girls soared.

Gordon recalled the early years of marriage when he never had a full working week from Christmas to May. 'I had two kids and sometimes only got 18s a week. Later my wages were 32s, the rent 8s. When we lost one little boy, we hadn't got a shilling.' Arthur Monks came and said, 'I hope you don't mind,' and gave him 10s.

The last 15 years of Gordon's working life were off farms – 'they drove us off, they didn't want us,' and he worked for the East Midlands Electricity Board. He did all sorts of jobs, from cleaning showrooms to working as a line inspector. 'I earnt more then than I ever did on a farm.' All the time he was still collecting for the Union. 'It was my life,' he said, 'I couldn't give up after working with men like Arthur Monks and Jack Boddy [when DO in Spalding].'

While with the Electricity Board, new tasks befell him. He found customers only getting a spark of light when machinery was working nearby, and when TV arrived, one householder's set went 'phut' when a neighbour used an electric shaver. 'What was he using,' said Gordon, 'a lawn mower?' Another farmworker's wife had to bake at 6am before too many were using electricity. There was only a 6,000-volt line and 11,000 was needed. It was soon installed. Gordon was a member of the local electricity advisory committee, and once refused to sign the minutes, 'when things weren't right.'

Gordon never regretted a moment of his lifetime's work for the Union. 'The old boys had to struggle, George Edwards and the like, I saw no reason why I shouldn't, but since then, there were too many who wanted to build castles for themselves. There were some good people in the Union in my day, people like Ted Sales and Arthur Jordan. People ganged up against them. That's what's wrong with the Labour Party today. We built the Union on pennies, but it was worth it.'

Foreboding at Tory Victory

When the Tories won the 1979 General Election, the Union was full of foreboding of the adverse effect the Tories would have on rural amenities. Village schools continued to close, and at the North West Conference in 1979 Nigel Ward, Carlisle, made a passionate plea to end these closures.

The same complaint went from Dorset County Conference to the County Council. Ernie Amey, that indefatigable recruiter to the Union, said that the village school at Tarrant Gunville had closed, 'and the village now seems quite dead without the chatter of the children in the playground.' This theme was taken up by John Hose later that year when he said that the sharp decline in the last few years in transport, hospital and school services in rural areas meant that the quality of life was plummeting. He told the Tolpuddle rally that he reserved special contempt for the Conservative idea that cottage hospitals could cease to be supported by the State, but kept open by voluntary contributions by the low-paid rural community.

Jack Boddy declared[3] that Tory public spending cuts would hit farmworkers hard. A family with two schoolchildren would be £9 a week worse off. This figure was made up of the increased cost of school meals, travel to school, and the absence of school milk. The £9 was a big bite out of the statutory minimum wage of £48.50 paid by many farmers.

At the Dorset Area Conference, Ted Sales said that if the County Council proposal for charging for school transport came into operation, somebody with three children could be paying £4.50 a week. People in towns didn't pay. This was blatant discrimination. At Dorset's County Conference, Peter Venn, DO, wanted to know what would happen if his members could not pay. 'Are the County Council going to start prosecuting them?' Delegates unanimously condemned school closures and cuts in meals-on-wheels to old people.

In nearby Hampshire, the two sides of the farming industry combined to protest to the County Council over their proposal to cut school buses or charge for them. A joint letter from Hampshire NFU and the NUAAW said: '. . . we have joined forces to emphasise to you the very unfair burden which will be placed on rural dwellers if the County Council decides to cut school bus services or to charge the economic cost. Many Hampshire schools have been closed. Therefore, the proper transport facilities must be made available for rural children to travel into the towns.'

District Organiser Tony Gould wrote to all members of Kent County Council urging them to subsidise school transport and give rural children equality of opportunity with those in the towns. North Lindsey annual Conference condemned the running down of rural transport. Then it turned to school meals, and noting that there was a £4 subsidy on every meal provided to MPs in the Commons dining room, declared that before there were cuts in schools meals subsidies, MPs should first pay the full price for their grub.

The increased cost of school meals and transport figured at many county conferences in 1980. Surrey carried a Puttenham motion expressing concern. North Devon believed 'that the widespread cuts in education should be opposed.' Yorkshire's successful Market Weighton motion said, starkly, 'Cuts in school meals, cuts in teachers, cuts in everything. Fight these at every level.' The joint conference for Cheshire, Flintshire and Staffordshire expressed concern over the growing cost of sending children to school. General protest against the cuts came from Sussex, whose Conference called on all branches

172   SKILLED AT ALL TRADES

to co-operate with local trades councils in campaigns against them. Nottinghamshire and Derbyshire Conference called 'on all members to take any possible action against the cuts ...'

These cuts were being made by local councils, but it was the Government's deliberate chopping of grants to councils which forced them on these authorities. So, in February 1980, a petition with well over 162,000 signatures was presented to Prime Minister Thatcher by members of the NUAAW and NUPE. Jack Boddy told Norfolk County Committee, 'The proposals are a disaster for rural families'. He said that the transport proposals were 'pernicious'. They would mean thousands of 5 to 11-year-olds walking alone along dangerous roads.

In March 1980, the TUC organised a great march in London against the spending cuts. Over 100,000 people marched from Hyde Park Corner to Trafalgar Square, including more than 100 NUAAW members under four county banners.

The Union's Biennial at Cromer clashed with the TUC's later Day of Action against the cuts, but was suspended to enable delegates to swell the ranks of people attending the local Trades Council's march and rally. Cromer never saw a day like it. Nearly 40 NUAAW banners were proudly carried through the Norfolk resort, and the rally was addressed by Boddy, Hose, Umberto Lamagni (EFA) and local trade unionists.

Because of the Tory Government's large majority in the Commons, the fight against the cuts might have seemed hopeless, but battles were won in some spheres. In 1979 Boddy fired off broadsides at everyone in Government over the proposed withdrawal of rural telephone boxes. Jack made the point that the Government had already taken away village hospitals, what would happen if people became suddenly ill or had an accident? In 1980, the Post Office agreed to allocate money to support 'unremunerative but socially-valuable call boxes'.

At the 1980 Biennial, public-spending cuts brought protests from 20 branches, which were telescoped into one composite. The Government was told to stop the cuts.

Mrs. Thatcher's Government continued to be criticised at Union conferences throughout 1981. Yorkshire deplored the 'ever increasing plight of the unemployed', and at Suffolk, Theresa Mackay, Tuddenham, got a big hand when moving a successful resolution which said, 'The prospect for the future is equally grim as capitalism falls further and further into decline and the working class continue to pay for a crisis not of its making, but made by those who exploit it for greed and profit. In another two years, unless we do something about it, there will be four million on the dole.' Unemployment did rise to that figure, although the Government 'massaged' the official figures to a lower level.

It was the same story at Hertfordshire Conference, where motions from Brickendon and Huntingford attracted strong support. The first expressed disgust 'at the vicious policies . . . which are a direct attack on the working classes'. The second called on the NUAAW to continue to apply pressure 'to make this Government realise its mistakes and hopefully aid a future Labour Government to make this country work again'. Delegates at the Hampshire Conference heard a fighting speech from Arthur Leary, who said, 'We are living in a capitalist society and we have to apply a capitalist philosophy. And that is a determination to fight for what we want.' Fred Peachy chimed in, 'We consistently get a raw deal from any government in power. Governments look to voters and they are not primarily in rural areas. The sale of council houses is wrong and in many cases immoral, because it is destroying the structure of rural areas.' The Cambridgeshire Conference strongly condemned the cuts, and Wiltshire Area Conference came out against the sale of council houses.

That year discontent among hospital staffs at the run-down of the NHS rose to a new pitch when the nurses rejected a miserly 7½% pay offer, and an appeal went out to agricultural workers to support them. 'The low pay of nurses and other hospital workers has been a national scandal for years,' said Jack Boddy, who asked all NUAAW branches to join local demonstrations on their behalf. He told them that agriculture and health workers were very similar, with a strong sense of responsibility that made them reluctant to strike. 'The Government that was holding down farmworkers' pay was the Government that was imposing a 5% cut in regional health authority budgets, and rural services suffered first from these cuts, which was only one more attack on the quality of life in rural areas.'

A Sort of Active Life

One man much concerned with health matters, who did support the nurses, was Tom Girling, of Bradwell, near Great Yarmouth, Norfolk, one of the more active members of the Trade Group. Although retired, he cycled 25 miles a month collecting dues, was a member of the Suffolk Farm Safety Committee, represented the Trade Group on the Meat and Livestock Commission Eastern Region, went fishing, had a quarter-of-an-acre garden, and five allotments. He used to go hang gliding. He gave it up a year or two earlier, but although 81, he still had the equipment lying on the stairs when I interviewed him in 1988, and it was obvious that he hadn't quite given up the idea of participating in the sport.

Not that Tom was the sort to give up anything. A thin, wiry man, all five feet six inches of him, with short grey hair, as plentiful as the produce on his allotments. When I spoke to him he had recently been on a march in support of the nurses. He had felt a bit groggy on the march, so back home the doctor was called. The doctor readily came, saying he hadn't seen Tom for 30 years. 'He told me my heart was missing a beat or two,' said Tom, 'and I wasn't to think I was still 31,' So Tom didn't, not that it seemed to make any difference to his way of life. He still went round houses selling chrysanthemums from his allotments at 50p a bunch, was still vice-chairman of Suffolk County Com-mittee, and was active in the Norfolk Pensioners' Association ('We're in Norfolk here now, because the authorities have "turned us over" to that county'). Recently he had attended a pensioners' school on ways to save the health service. 'If only the young 'uns were as active as we old 'uns,' he lamented.

He and his wife Rachel had lived at Bradwell most of their lives, where they brought up two sons and two daughters. I settled into their parlour and noticed the absence of a television. 'We bunged it at the bottom of the garden,' said Tom, 'never got nothing done with it.'

Tom was very keen on farm safety. 'We had a resolution in 1952 asking that all children in their last year at school should be taught first aid. There's always someone who survives an accident, and half as many wouldn't die if survivors knew what to do.' Amongst Tom's many activities, was membership of the St. John Ambulance Brigade.

One aspect of farm safety Tom campaigned for, was to curb aerial spraying. 'We've had spray run down the windows of this house,' he said, 'and just up the road, the same spray killed goldfish in a pond.' Aerial spraying was too much hit and miss. Once when the kids were coming out of school, spraying was taking place, and a lady on a bike was drenched. The spray dissolved her nylons. 'I told her to go to hospital and get them to wash her down and see if there was any antidote. If she'd been all in nylon, she'd have been the first streaker on a bicycle.'

When he related that story to one biennial, there were roars of laughter. Tom had never seen any reason why you shouldn't have a laugh, even when dealing with serious subjects. There was never a smile far from his weather-beaten face. He received a cup from Suffolk Farm Safety Committee for his work against sprays; ROSPA also gave him a certificate.

Tom was born at Bradwell and went to the village school at Belton, where the actor John Mills' father was headmaster, and John a fellow pupil. John went on to higher education, but Tom was not so lucky. When he left school Tom worked for a nurseryman, then as a gardener, and the last 12 years of his working life were spent at the Birds Eye factory in Yarmouth.

One thing Tom didn't like about current working methods was the long hours. 'Instead of 12-hour shifts, they ought to work 8 hours and give somebody else a chance of a job. You see them working with floodlights at midnight. Some of them work all night. On a big arable farm near here, there's only two working on it, from 7am to 8pm right through the Winter. All this scrabbing, they don't plough properly, it's only slubbed over; it's no way to farm, or to live. This is what gets me, they say they can't afford to pay wage increases, but they willingly pay 1½ times for Saturdays and Sundays.' He bemoaned modern farming methods which kill off wildlife.

Tom still went to all the Trade Group demonstrations. 'Thing is to keep going when you retire,' he said. 'I see old folk sitting around in libraries reading papers, hardly moving. You can see them deteriorate, month by month.' He was then a life member. 'I done wrong in that,' he said, 'if you are not a fully paid-up member, you can't go to conferences.' I'm sure Tom found something else to do.

*   *   *

Like Tom, members of the NUAAW are generally concerned about the wanton destruction of wildlife. This often came up at branches and conferences, and in 1983, the Hampshire Conference noted the escalating destruction of wildlife habitats. The main cause was the capital over-intensification of farming and forestry, 'spurred on by the narrow-based, short-term grant aid policies of MAFF and the CAP'. Conference urged members to refuse to work on such sites and to press the Minister to give grants to promote conservation and benefit the rural economy. Conservation was debated at the Eastbourne Conference in 1983, which urged all members to press for MAFF to provide grants for farming activities that promote conservation.

When Labour in 1983 issued the statement *New Hope for Britain*, it recognised the harm Tory policies were doing to rural areas, and said it would encourage light industry, improve public transport, and wherever possible, village schools would be retained and mobile health clinics and community services run. Extensive measures were promised to expand all types of housing. Hare coursing, fox hunting and all forms of hunting with dogs would be made illegal, but not shooting or fishing. The use of snares would be illegal. Over a phased period, all extreme livestock systems would be banned and legislation introduced to ensure that animals were slaughtered as near as possible to the point of production. At the heart of the proposals was an emergency programme to create jobs through a massive programme of investment in industry, transport, housing and energy conservation. Social services would be rebuilt.

This programme was generally welcomed by the Union, although in the hunting counties, some members had reservations about bans on this sport.

At the Eastbourne Conference in 1983 delegates again deplored the run down of rural services and amenities, and calling upon the support of all trade groups, demanded a 'concerted and vigorous attack' to pressurise the Government to stop the cuts, and pledged 'to fight for the return of a Government who cares, a Labour Government'.

Although there was little response from the Tory Government, the Trade Group did not let up on its campaign to save all that was best in the Health Service. The *Landworker* said, 'the 1,000-plus kidney patients who die each year might not appreciate her [Thatcher's] application of the "market principle" to health.'

Delegates from the Trade Group joined others from health councils, local authorities and the medical professions in Warwickshire's National Agriculture Centre, in June 1984, for a conference on rural health. Frank Dobson,

Labour's Shadow Health Minister told them that all over the country there was a growing concern about health care in rural areas. Unfortunately, too many people in authority had ignored the groundswell of public opinion. He attacked the policy of concentrating resources in district general hospitals, a policy the Union had been critical of for some time. Mr. Dobson said that Labour was committed to restore and improve rural health services.

Long Fight for Piped Water

An adequate supply of wholesome water is the foundation of health for any community, and in Britain the demand for water for personal needs is about 25 gallons per day, and if commercial and industrial purposes are taken into account, the daily demand rises to 40 to 50 gallons per head. Much of it is drawn from rivers and stored in reservoirs.

A good water supply was always of special interest to NUAAW members, for rural areas were the last to get a piped supply, and even where there was one, in the days of the old private water companies the taps sometimes went dry and had to be supplemented by water carts. The Union consistently pressed for better supplies, and its resolutions on the national water supply, at the TUC in 1954 and 1961, argued that there was no technical reason why certain parts of the country should suffer the periodic disasters of drought or flood. The 1951 Census revealed that over 20% of rural households were without piped water; 17% had no kitchen sink; 35% no W.C. and nearly 50% – well over one million – were without a bath. By 1956, the number of rural households with piped water had risen to 88%.

Before 1902, when the Metropolitan Water Board was formed, Londoners were supplied with water by eight companies, and the service was often unsatisfactory. The amalgamation produced one of the largest water undertakings in the world and a considerable improvement in London's supply.

The extraordinary difference in public services in town and country that still existed after the Second World War was emphasised by an inquiry into water supplies within Halstead (Essex) Rural District Council in 1950 at which the Union was represented. The Council had prepared a scheme for piped water for 33 of its 39 parishes, and in these 33 parishes there were 22 schools, 74 shops, 351 farms, 4,328 houses and 12,174 people. The two main sources of water were bores and shallow wells. The bores went deep into chalk and supplied villages with water that contained so much iron that it turned galvanised pails rusty.

About 35% of the people got bore water, the rest got their water from wells, springs, streams and ponds. There were 768 wells, but rain water that had seeped through farmyard manure and the contents of earth-closet pails found its way into the wells at the bottom of gardens. Over 3,000 people drank this water. Some people preserved rain water in butts, but there was difficulty in providing school meals where there was no piped water.

The Union representative at the Inquiry, Frank Coffin, submitted a paper detailing the difficulties for the farming industry and the rural worker, and said that they could not hold workers in agriculture while their working hours and home life were made so difficult through lack of water. It pleaded for an imaginative scheme to end the water shortage, a step which would raise living standards over a large area, and lead to cleaner milk for the towns. In *Reynolds News*, Tom Driberg, MP, commented: 'Apart from the good case put by the Clerk to the RDC, only the spokesman of the NUAW stated a really thorough and urgent claim for people living in these appalling conditions.'

The Union's work at the Inquiry was yet one more example of the way it fought to improve conditions for all rural dwellers, and indirectly town dwellers, through cleaner food, both in its handling and wrapping. At the 1952 Biennial at Skegness, F. G. Noble, Shropshire, moved a successful resolution regretting 'that there has been no progress in the hygienic washing, handling and wrapping of food in this country for many years and demands that the Government takes legislative action to force all goods sold for human consumption to be adequately wrapped . . .'

The 1960 Biennial at Chester called for 'immediate Government action to improve water supplies to rural areas and to bring modern sanitation to the villages'. G. H. Shute, Dorset, told of a village where sewage was laid on, and all the houses were connected except that of a farmworker. His property belonged to a college with the motto 'Manners Maketh Man'.

Not surprisingly, the Union's 1961 TUC resolution sought to bring the control of natural water supplies on to a uniform, socialised basis, providing good water for all. The Government gave vague undertakings that it would bear in mind the 1961 resolution, and the subsequent Water Resources Act 1963 was a modest step in this direction.

This Act replaced the River Boards Act of 1946, and the numerous existing River Boards gave way to 26 River Authorities together with the Thames Conservancy and the Lea Conservancy Catchment Boards. In addition, a central Water Resources Board was set up, a move criticised by the Union because it was only advisory and not executive.

Some people in rural areas were living in worse conditions than the stock they tended, said J. Sadler, Thornham, at the Conference of West Norfolk branch officials in 1962. Even cowsheds had hot and cold water nowadays. Conference demanded that local authorities should do more to speed up sanitary facilities in rural areas.

River and Drainage Workers

The Union was not only interested in water as a vital commodity, for among the workers for river boards and land drainage authorities it had many members. In 1948, the rural land drainage worker got £4 10s for a 45-hour week; the AWB rate at the time was £4 10s. Urban land drainage men got

£4 11s 10½d. And in Greater London it was £5 0s 3¾d. The working week of 45 hours had only been won after it had been referred to the Industrial Court. Previously it was 47 hours. The Union also had to go back to the Industrial Court to defend a sick/accident pay scheme, when the employers attempted to vary payments according to workers' marital/parenthood status. The Union argued that all employees should receive wages less statutory insurances, as before. The Industrial Court agreed. By 1955, the Greater London rates had risen to £7 4s 4½d; in all other areas it was £6 16s 10½d, still for 45 hours. It was not until 1959 that the first general reduction in hours was won; they were cut to 44, and by 1981 a 39-hour basic week was being worked.

In the mid-fifties, the Union representatives in the NJIC for River Authorities were Reg Bottini, who was vice-chairman, and Stan Brumby, Lincs DO. In 1960 the Union, in addition to a wage claim, sought an extra week's holiday. The employers offered 5s 4d a week increase, but refused point blank the holiday claim. The Union threatened to go to the Industrial Court, and the employers then offered 7s 2d increase, which was accepted. Later that year the holiday claim was renewed, and three extra days were won for employees with 10 years' service.

As a consequence of the Water Resources Act 1963, the NJIC for River Authorities was dissolved and a River Committee formed, to be linked with NJIC for local authority manual workers. Reg Bottini and Stan Brumby were appointed to the new committee. An outstanding event was the decision at its first meeting to introduce the 40-hour week.

In 1968, following the local authorities employees' wages settlement, an increase of 11s 8d per week was won for workers employed by river authorities, making a basic rate of £13 5s for a 40-hour week. A year later this rate was increased by 17s. In 1970 Reg Bottini and Stan Brumby were replaced on the River Committee by Ross Pierson and Ernie Hackney.

This reorganisation of river and drainage authorities continued in 1973 when a new Water Act shifted responsibility for water from the local authorities to new water authorities. In March 1974, the National Rivers Committee was wound up, and its responsibilities were transferred to the new NJIC for the Water Service.

Three other Unions also organised in this sphere, NUPE, TGWU and GMWU, and objected to the NUAAW organising these workers. There was a long battle over this, and the matter was referred to the TUC which recommended that the NUAAW should not recruit outside its existing membership. The NUAAW reluctantly agreed. Within a few years, NUAAW membership in the bigger river authorities ceased to exist. There were still a few within the small authorities, who abided by what the bigger Unions negotiated.

The year of the big drought, 1976, saw the issue of water conservation raised again at the TUC Congress at Brighton. The Labour Government had appointed Denis Howell, Drought Co-ordination Minister, and he spoke on an NUAAW resolution urging 'the formulation and implementation of an overall policy for water conservation and procurement, requiring a comprehensive study on water demand'. Reg Bottini said that these were questions of long-term policy. 'You cannot put matters right by a few emergency measures.' Howell backed the NUAAW proposals, which were passed.

Rural water supplies have much improved since the Second World War, but in the seventies a new problem arose, the leaching of nitrates into rivers which end up in drinking water. This came about because of the increased use of fertilisers. Again the Union addressed the problem, but at the time of writing it was far from resolved.

In 1976, a closed shop agreement was reached with the four unions covering the water services, and the NUAAW was recognised for the river division workers. A period of difficult pay negotiations followed because of the Government's Social Contract but, after it ended, a complex package was agreed early in 1979, which included a new grading structure, consolidation of a £6 pay supplement, standby and productivity payments, together with a £5 per week special efficiency supplement. It was expected to increase earnings by £12 a week.

Industrial action was threatened after difficult pay talks in 1979, but a 10.2% increase was won without any withdrawal of labour. However, the Annual Report for 1983 notes, 'Trade Group members played their full part in the successful strike action relating to the 1982 pay claim. They are to be applauded for their courage and endurance.'

This was the first ever all-out national water strike and Trade Group members around the country backed a 15% pay claim. 'Rock solid,' said Colin Down, Devon DO, whose members refused to clear filters in Torbay, Newton Abbott and Teignmouth. The strike was finally settled for greatly improved basic rates.

In 1983, Jack Boddy took Ross Pierson's place on the NJIC after Ross left the Union's service. Many of the previous national tasks were transferred to the regions, but the Union's major work amongst water workers was virtually at an end.

*   *   *

To find out more about the Union's earlier role in organising water and drainage workers, I went to see Ted Calver, former EC member. There could be no better person than Ted to tell me because he was a drainage worker for most of his life. Ted, by then retired, lived at Gorefield, Cambs, in the heart of rich farmland largely created from marshy fen by drainage work on a gigantic scale by the Dutchman, Vermuyden, in the 17th century. It had needed people like Ted to keep the waters at bay ever since. If the predictions about rising sea levels are correct, such workers will be needed more than ever in the next century.

I drove to Gorefield, past ancient banks which kept out the waters of the Wash in pre-Roman times, along flat fen roads beneath a cloud-curdled sky. I passed field upon field of young roses, which would have appeared strange to older fenmen, more used to corn, taties and sugar beet.

Ted, 74 in 1988, and fitted with a pacemaker, was busy in the large garden of the council house he had lived in since 1951. He had a healthy face, and moved with a fenman's slow dignity. 'I never wanted to leave this house, I must have put my roots down,' he said, as he showed me into the spacious interior, its sills crowded with African violets, all carefully nurtured by his wife, Ellen. Across the road a 20-foot high hedge of hawthorn, staked out with sycamores and beeches, protected the house from some of the fierce fen winds.

Ted was one of a family of seven children, living just outside Gorefield. He attended the village school, which he left in 1928, and started fruit picking on piecework. 'I could earn as much as a man, 5s 6d a day,' he said. He felt right proud, those earnings helped his hard-pressed family. He did farm jobs for several years, and then joined the Leverington Internal Drainage Board as a labourer in 1942. He had married on Christmas Day 1934, joined the Union in 1940, and became secretary of Leverington branch in 1942.

After marrying, he rented a cottage for 4s 6d a week. It took some finding, with wages at 30s 6d and 9d off for stamps.* 'That's what made me join the Union. My wife used to write out grocery lists, and then one by one cross off essentials because we couldn't afford them.'

He recalled his early days as a drainage worker, maintaining banks, clearing reeds and weeds, and keeping the water courses open. Mostly it was done by hand. They cut hawthorn to fill broken or water-worn banks, which then had earth rammed over them. Similarly, the big river boards used willow to make mats for constructing new banks. They used to float the mats down rivers to where they were needed. The Fens are full of dykes which used to be cleared out with shovels. 'Then the draglines came,' said Ted, 'and you could get out as much in a dragline's bucket as a man with a shovel would get out in half a day. And in rivers, the draglines could reach the middle where you couldn't dig.' Fenland rivers and watercourses are continually silting up, and where this happened in the days before draglines, they used to dam off a section and dig it out. They used to wheel the mud out in barrows, with the aid of horses.

Chemicals now control the weeds and reeds; there is still some cutting to be done, but it is now mostly done with machines. 'But they still do awkward places with scythes,' said Ted, who was using one up to the day he retired in 1979.

Typical of many Fenland drainage boards, the Leverington Internal Drainage Board was a small one. 'We shared a dragline with another small board,' said Ted. Only Government schemes for clearing out drains made

---

* All health and pension contributions were paid by these 'stamps'.

some of the work financially possible, when four men would work with a dragline. Sometimes the AEC would do some of this work, and would supply a dragline and one man with it to help smaller boards.

River authorities were responsible for keeping rivers clear, and the drainage authorities were mainly concerned with man-made drains. All the land-drainage workers were men, but during the war a few WLA girls took on this tough work. Ted recalled that drainage workers' wages got in advance of the AWB rates with the bigger boards, and the small boards usually paid more because it was difficult to get the right men. They got a shorter working week, from 8am to 4pm, and did piece work.

Ted was a member of the old NJIC, and said that the changes in 1974 led to better conditions for their workers, and made pay negotiations easier. But mechanisation and the use of chemicals cut the number of workers needed. All Nene and Welland River Board workers belonged to the NUAAW except for a half dozen; they were signed up by Ernie Hackney, when Recruiting Officer.

Despite the demanding nature of his drainage work, Ted was very active in the Union, and at one time served on no fewer than 43 different committees. He attended every biennial from 1946 to 1983, except in 1954. He served on district committees and was a member of the EC from 1963 to 1984. He was a pioneering member of the Agricultural Training Board, and during his last few years, was vice-chair. He was on the National Proficiency Test Council from 1964 to 1987, and was chairman and vice-chairman over a number of years. A member of the AWB for 15 years, he also found time to be active in the Labour Party.

In the Fens, the CWS had a huge farm at Coldham – it was said that you could walk eight miles on public roads without losing sight of Co-op land – but the NUAAW never got much of a look in there. The TGWU had an agreement with the CWS, and was organised strongly at Coldham, subs being deducted from the men's pay packets. There was an agreement between the TGWU and the NUAAW that the latter would not form a branch where the TGWU existed, but joint meetings were held with the TGWU at Coldham. Ted said, 'Some farmworkers wouldn't join the TGWU and used to send us subs by post.'

Known in the Union as a 'moderate', Ted said disarmingly, 'All my life I've been one of those running around with a smoothing iron,' and recalled going to Coldham 'when we had a bit of trouble there,' to help in the negotiations.

Ted opposed the merger and said, 'If only the subs had been put up it wouldn't have been necessary.' But looking to the future added, 'There's still scope for recruitment today. It's up to members to recruit on the large farms and in horticulture where there's lots of labour.'

At the time I met Ted, the privatisation of water supplies was being pressed by the Conservative Government. 'I'm dead against it,' said Ted. 'I can remember when it was in private hands in this area. The Wisbech Water Works was supposed to supply Wisbech and district with pure water. It supplied Wisbech and part of the district, but the unprofitable outlying areas just didn't get any piped supply. We had to rely mainly on rain water off the roof, and in the whole of this area there were what was known as "tea water pits" – and that was the supply – water drained off the land, no springs. This water was pretty grotty, with frog spawn in Spring and decomposing matter in the Autumn. I can remember, when I was a boy, a man coming round with petitions for a water supply, but we never got it until it was municipalised. In the pit where the water came from that I drank, there was a huge barrel in the bottom, and we often had to wait for that to fill up and then bail it out with a saucepan. Then we had to carry it home 250 yards. We don't want to go back to that.'

REFERENCES

1. *Landworker*, February 1959.
2. *Landworker*, May 1979.
3. *Landworker*, January 1980.

12

Fighting the Greatest Evil of the Countryside

The system under which you hire your cottages makes you complete serfs.

George Edwards

Democracy Mocked

The tied cottage, as the Duke of Marlborough, with typical aristocratic arrogance once openly said, was a weapon forged 'to keep the labourers in check'. It worked, effectively, for nearly a hundred years.

It not only kept farmworkers in check, but mocked at democracy itself. The tied cottage* helped to keep farmworkers' wages low, and conditioned many farmworkers' attitudes to the community surrounding them. It was a system that held the farmworker and his family in feudal-like thrall to the farmer and owners of big estates, and was complementary to the authority farmers occupied in the local social system. Coupled with the positions they held as magistrates, councillors and school governors, the farmers as a group wielded considerable power, against which agricultural workers were virtually powerless. They not only controlled the tied cottages, but through the local councils the entire housing stock likely to be within reach of the low-paid farmworker.

Tied cottages were not prevalent until attempts were made to form agricultural trade unions in the 1870s, although they were beginning to increase in number from the time of the Enclosures. Both Joseph Arch and George Edwards roundly condemned them. In those pioneering days, farmers were not content with tied cottages already in existence on their farms, but often bought cottages wholesale in the villages; in many cases the occupants were evicted with no regard to their ages, condition or circumstances.

---

* The occupant forfeits the right to the house one month from the date on which notice of termination of employment is given.

No wonder social change for the better in rural areas was often much slower than in the towns. Tied cottages fostered a forelock-touching deference among rural workers (whatever their private thoughts) during the 19th century and the first half of the 20th. Woe betide any farmworker who had the temerity to put up a Liberal or, later, a Labour poster, in his window at election time.

Farmworkers' daughters would be found 'suitable positions' in rich households through the good offices of landlords and big farmers, while their sons were likewise placed on farms through the landlord–farmer grapevine. Should any farmworker or member of his family step out of line, it was no job, and very often, in the long run, no home.

This situation did not improve with the coming of the 20th century. By buying up cottages, farmers increased their stock of tied dwellings by about 1,000 a year, and even late in the 20th century, the proportion of farmworkers in tied cottages rose from 34.3% in 1948 to 52.8% in 1970. By 1975 that figure had risen to 55% in England and Wales.

It was an obvious evil that employers should have such a grip on a man's home as well as his job, and the NUAW and its predecessors fought a long, hard and tireless battle against it, with much bravery and stoicism shown by many farmworkers and their families in the face of eviction and homelessness.

For years, many farmworkers lived in fear of eviction, and hundreds were to experience its horror. Kay Cailliau, a farmworker's wife, broke down and wept when she got home from hospital with her new baby; she found her cottage had been stripped of all the family's possessions, the furniture, the children's toys, pram and cot had all vanished. They had been loaded onto a removal van on the orders of her husband's employer. Their trouble began when Kay was taken ill towards the end of her pregnancy. Michael, her husband, took a Saturday morning off to look after her. Hours later he was dismissed from his herdsman's job and given notice to quit. Three days later he joined her in London, where she had gone to have the baby near the rest of her family. It was only when they returned to Yorkshire that they discovered what had happened. The farmer even refused to say where their possessions had been taken. This eviction did not take place during the harsh values of the Victorian age, nor even at the beginning of this century, but in 1974.

Many a woman, and man, has wept over a tied cottage eviction. And the tears do not end even when a new home is found. Patricia White and her husband, of Farringdon, Berks, were evicted on 31 May 1968. 'We are still recovering from the terrible humiliation,' she wrote in the *Landworker* in 1970. 'We were I suppose "lucky" being given temporary council accommodation in a "not so nice part" just 24 hours before eviction. The removal firm required £21 in advance . . . We lived temporarily in the house given, being warned that whether or not we remained in that area depended on whether we paid our rent. The stigma of eviction had started. In six weeks we moved into our present house . . . When our three children, all under ten, started school, they were classed as "perhaps troublesome". I had to battle to explain to the teachers that the children needed very careful care until they had settled down quietly again after so much upset . . . People are now just beginning to see that we are normal, honest-living folk. Had we been given a house in the village where we were evicted we wouldn't have had such a stigma . . . Being evicted . . . makes the worker feel worse than a criminal . . . having committed the crime of being classed medically unfit for farm work.'

In 1953, at Thaxted, Essex, prayers were offered in the parish church for a farmworker and his wife and three children who were threatened with eviction. After praying for the Queen, the Revd. Jack Putterill, who was well known as the local 'Red', said, 'It is a terrible thing for a family to be without a home, and we must all pray that somehow a new home will be found for them.' Mr. Putterill said, 'The tied cottage system is the greatest curse of the countryside, and the Church ought to make a stand against such evils.'

Alas, vicars of Mr. Putterill's calibre were few, and the Church of England did little. It was left to the Union to fight this evil; probably the most difficult long-running fight ever undertaken by the Union.

Union leaders such as Bert Hazell, Harold Collison and Reg Bottini were regarded as 'moderates', and fierce opponents of left-wing 'extremists', who perhaps in turn regarded the trio as 'right-wing extremists'. In opposition to the tied cottage they were united, yet their 'moderate' leadership did little to persuade the Labour Party leadership that removal of the tied cottage system was urgent. That was left to the militant Joan Maynard who '. . . when projected into Parliament at short notice . . .' used it as a platform to harry her own Party into abolishing tied cottages. This was staple Union policy, which had received lip service only from the Labour Party for some time. It was her personal triumph to abolish the tied aspect of workers' accommodation.[1]

Before that happened, countless resolutions from Union branches, district committees and the EC had over the years called for its abolition. In the mid-thirties, in response to Union initiative, the Government set up an inter-departmental committee to consider whether it was necessary to retain the tied cottage system. A majority of the committee concluded that it could not be justified. A minority advocated retention, an attitude echoed down the decades by both employers and successive governments.

Farmers persisted in adding cottages to the system to the benefit of their pockets. At Cambridge NFU AGM in 1947, J. F. Phillips, assistant general secretary, pointed out that the farmer could provide new cottages for his workers – a very lucrative proposition. A licence* up to £1,300 would be granted. Of that sum, £600 could be got back at £15 a year for 40 years, and income tax relief on the full £1,300 would be returned to the farmer. 'If there are any plutocrats here who pay super-tax I could show you how to make a profit,' said Mr. Phillips.

---

* Licences to build were then needed.

At the Labour Conference at Margate in 1947, a resolution called upon the Government to abolish the system immediately. It was moved by Union delegates Harold Weate and E. Hennem. Aneurin Bevan, Minister of Health, while admitting that the idea of the tied cottage was repugnant to Labour and not to be tolerated any longer than could be helped, advised delegates to vote against. It was carried by 1,558,000 votes to 1,550. Another resolution against the tied cottage was moved by Alfred Dann at the 1948 Labour Conference at Scarborough, again opposed by the platform, but carried.

From 1947 up to 1979, when they virtually died out because of the 1976 Rent (Agriculture) Act, the Union contested 12,482 tied cottage eviction cases. In 1947, the number of ejectment cases the Union contested in court totalled 401. It fell to 320 the following year and stayed at the 200 to 300 mark for a number of years, until it rose to 342 in 1965, and then remained around the 400 mark until 1976.

The number fell dramatically to 12 in 1978, which was 'clear evidence that the 1976 Rent (Agriculture) Act achieved its purpose of giving security of tenure to tied cottage occupants'.[2] The number rose to 25 in 1979, since when no figures were kept by the Union, but the numbers are believed to have been very low.

But we must return to 1947, when the Union circulated petitions against the tied cottage, and thousands of signatures were obtained. Then, in view of the need to give wholehearted support[3] to the Government fighting an economic crisis, the EC suspended the collection of further signatures.

Militancy Increases

Evictions continued unabated for years. Union militancy increased, public protests occurred, marches in quiet villages took place and much publicity was gained, especially in the local press, which at one time often played down evictions, no doubt not wishing to incur the anger of local farmers.

> Evicted from a cottage at Gt. Hayes Farm, Stow Maries, on Tuesday morning, a family of nine! Father, mother, four sons, two daughters and a three-year-old grandchild have since been homeless. Several members of the family have been spending their waking and sleeping hours besides their piled up furniture on the greensward, wondering where to go and what to do.

Thus ran a story in the *Essex Weekly* of 12 March 1948. It said that the only shelter for the family was a car in which sat the mother, who was suffering from varicose ulcers, and was in bed with 'flu when the bailiffs, accompanied by the village constable, carried out the eviction. Dad, aged 61, stood disconsolately, while his children grouped around him. Until recently he had never been out of work for a day.

*   *   *

At the 1948 TUC Conference at Margate, Alfred Dann asked for an assurance that the TUC would deal with the problem of tied cottages with greater urgency. Sir George Chester, for the General Council, assured him that the matter would not be allowed to rest until satisfaction had been obtained.

On 1 October 1948, Braughing (Herts) District Committee, alarmed at the increase in evictions, declared, 'if the Government did not take steps to curtail this, the Party [Labour] could not expect the support of the farmworkers in the next election.'

Despite the failure of the Labour Government to deal with the problem, there was no official let up in the Union's campaign, strangely tempered with praise for Labour. At a meeting at Walsingham, Norfolk, in 1948, Edwin Gooch said that the workers were grateful to the Labour Government for the improved social conditions after the Second World War. 'But they are not happy about . . . the tied cottage. The time is long past for further debate on this subject, it is time for action.'

If the Government would take no action, many Union members were in the mood for it. There was a certain liveliness in Woodhouse Eaves, once described as 'the quietest and most beautiful village in Leicestershire', one Sunday morning in 1949. Many Union members bearing banners with slogans condemning the tied cottage, marched to a protest meeting near the church.

They were demonstrating against the threatened eviction of James Jacks, a young ex-Serviceman who had fallen off a farm waggon and injured his knee. A torn cartilage necessitated an operation. His employer gave him notice and, a week later, notice to quit the cottage. While James was in hospital, the employer threatened his wife that if the cottage was not vacated in three days the furniture would be put out.

E. W. Pollard, DO, told the farmer that other accommodation would be available, but the employer refused to allow a few weeks' extension. Leicester District Committee decided to hold a protest meeting. The village constable said, in effect, 'You can't do that 'ere'. Pollard was not to be bluffed into believing that the meeting was not possible.

Tentative permission was received for the use of the village hall. On Saturday morning Pollard rang to tell a local newspaper and a reporter said, 'Oh, you can't do that, Sir Somebody or Other will not allow it.'

'But,' replied Pollard, 'I have provisionally booked the village hall and was to be informed by this morning if it was not available.' Half an hour later a telegram arrived. It read, 'Village hall not available'.

Not to be foiled, Pollard, to prevent further intervention, kept a new venue secret. The march through the village the next morning was orderly, and the meeting decided to march to the farm to see the employer. The village constable who had been watching in his Sunday best, called Pollard aside and said that the employer would not take any action immediately. But members still insisted on visiting the farm. The constable hurried home to change into uniform and met them at the farm gate saying the farmer did not wish to see them. From a distance of three yards, Pollard told the employer of their feelings. 'I think we have won a moral victory by our action,' he told Union members.

Moral victories did not, however, stop more evictions. Later the same year, delegates representing 2,000 members in North Lincolnshire, meeting at Brigg, strongly protested against an ejectment order against H. B. Johnson, whose cottage was required for three casual workers. The eviction was carried out on Friday, 11 November. While a gale was blowing and in pouring rain, a policeman and a worker carried out Johnson's furniture and stacked it on the side of the road.

The evicted family consisted of Johnson, a single man, his aged mother (a cripple), and a sister with two children. The children were taken to a home, the mother to another home, and the brother and sister were taken in for a day or two by villagers and then moved into an aerodrome hut. The eviction aroused strong feeling locally.

At about the same time, a Kent newspaper reported that a stockman of 55, who won the DCM in the First World War, tied a 56lb weight round his neck and drowned himself in a tank. A short time previously he had returned to work after illness and was very depressed by notice to leave his job and cottage. He did this while 'the balance of his mind was disturbed' was the inquest verdict. Is there anything more calculated to disturb the balance of a man's mind than the fear of his family being without a home?

All too often, many farmers seemed completely indifferent to the welfare of their employees. Writing in the *Landworker*, a farmer's wife declared, 'What a godsend it would be to all farmworkers' wives if this curse could be lifted. My husband has been off work for three weeks through illness. His employer would not allow him anything while he was ill. Why? We live in a tied cottage. My husband, I am glad to say, is thoughtful and kindly. His employer is not. He expects his workers to put in long hours and shows them little consideration. Why? We live in his tied cottages . . . I am not condemning the farmers as a class. I have met some very kind ones, although I fear the majority are rather grasping.'

E. T. Jones was a highly-qualified cowman who changed his job. Having previously been on a farm where scrupulous cleanliness was observed, he was not favourably impressed with his new farm. He remarked about the dirty milking sheds and general lack of cleanliness. For this he was summarily dismissed, and ordered to leave his cottage immediately, and within a few weeks the employer removed the door and all the windows. His wife hung up a carpet at the door and filled the windows with newspapers.

A. Peasegood, DO, got in touch with the Totnes housing authorities who telephoned the employer and ordered him to replace the door and windows. This led to the employer's wife going to the cottage and shouting threats against Jones' wife. He had done 'the silliest thing out' in getting in touch with the Union, and her husband would see that he was never able to get work on a farm again. Later the Joneses were given a council house.

During the debate in the House of Commons on the King's Speech in 1950, Julian Snow, Labour, Lichfield, said, 'There is a feeling of unrest, of unsettlement, of resentment amongst agricultural workers over the tied cottage. It is not a bit of use for people to say that in these days of enlightenment, farmworkers are not being evicted in inhuman circumstances. It is just not true. They are evicted, and frequently in circumstances one can describe only as deplorable. I do hope, therefore, that the Government will grasp this nettle . . .'

Still the Government did not act. Excuse after excuse came for not introducing legislation to deal with the situation, evictions continued unabated, and Union members felt more angry than ever. (Also, see the next chapter dealing with the work of the Legal Department.)

Gooch Disappointed

At the Biennial at Margate in 1950, Edwin Gooch confessed to a sense of disappointment that more was not done by the Labour Government to meet their requests. 'The Minister of Agriculture has leaned too much towards the farmers. Let him lean our way for a while and he will be surprised at the response he and the Labour Party will get.'

Tom Williams, Minister of Agriculture, addressed the Conference, and on the tied cottage referred to the Government's small majority in the Commons which gave them 'all the responsibility and very little power'. He declared, 'I hope delegates will appreciate that within my limited power I have tried to do what I could to alleviate hardships inflicted on agricultural workers from time to time.' He had met the NFU which had agreed to try to dissuade members from resorting to eviction proceedings.

This remark was greeted with ironical laughter, and the Minister retorted that the NFU had intervened in a number of cases. The tied cottage was a delicate and difficult problem which would require not only a government with a reasonable majority, but heart-to-heart talks between the NFU, the NUAW and the Ministry of Health.

Jack Dunman, Berks, moved a resolution calling 'upon the Government to bring before Parliament a Bill making such alterations in the Rent Act as are required to give agricultural workers the measure of protection enjoyed under the Act by the majority of householders . . . and that no worker should be evicted from his home unless it can be shown that suitable alternative accommodation is available for him and his family.' Jack said that by passing the resolution delegates would 'utterly and completely turn down the miserable case' which Tom Williams had made.

G. Thomas, Cornwall, seconding, said that around his small village of Gulval, population 600, evictions were taking place every week. Miss M. Quick, Worcs, moved an addendum calling upon Union members to support fellow members threatened with eviction, 'by organised resistance on the doorstep'. The resolution and addendum were carried.

The increasing pressure the Union leadership was being forced by members to exert over the tied cottage had some farmers worried. This was shown by Hampshire NFU, which urged their headquarters 'To take stronger action in an attempt to counter the persistent propaganda of the NUAAW for the abolition of the tied cottage.' Replying, the NFU head office said that their policy towards the 'service' cottage had been made very clear to the Government and it 'could be fairly claimed that the attitude of the Union has been responsible for the retention of the system . . . in spite of repeated resolutions passed at successive conferences of the Labour Party and TUC.' This was in effect a claim by the NFU to have more influence with the Labour Government than had the whole working-class movement.

Try as it might, the Union could not always stop evictions, often with tragic consequences. In Staffordshire, a farmworker was told to leave the cottage he had lived in for 31 years. Shortly afterwards, the 62-year-old man was found by his wife hanging from an apple tree. At the inquest she said that after an accident during haysel her husband was off work for five weeks; the farmer wanted the cottage for a younger man to replace him. His doctor agreed to let him return to work, but he strained an arm pulling beet and developed a swollen hand. He had to stay in bed. His wife said he had been a very happy man. 'Nothing troubled him until he knew about the house.'

In Norfolk, Union activist Wilf Page had a different approach. 'My tied cottage cases,' he told me in 1988, 'were all victories.' The Union used to fight cases through legal channels. 'In Norfolk we "du different".' He recalled once addressing a diocesan seminar of about 20 clergymen and telling them that although they were much in sympathy with the poor, they didn't do much about it. Afterwards he felt he had perhaps been a little unfair to them.

A few days later a man in hospital received notice to quit his cottage. Wilf promptly rang the Bishop of Norwich, spoke to his secretary, and asked for help. The Bishop sent his industrial chaplain to see Wilf, who promptly took him to the about-to-be-evicted family. It was a wet and raw night, pitch dark. As was his way, Wilf knocked and opened the door saying, 'Wilf Page here'. There kneeling before the hearth was the man's wife, praying they would not be thrown onto the street that filthy night. Said Wilf, 'The chaplain opened his eyes wide, this was obviously no Communist plot.' It was a moving experience for him, and Wilf. The chaplain promised to do what he could. Wilf believed the Bishop's office got in touch with the squirearchy, for a few days later the family was given a council house.

On another occasion when a family was to be evicted, Wilf persuaded them to squat in an empty army hut on some big estate. 'They won't want you there long,' he assured them, 'you'll soon get a council house.' He then telephoned the police and 'hoped' the family would not be disturbed. 'They'll be all right for the weekend,' came the reply. Within a week the family was given a council house.

Once, when no house was available for an evicted family (the mother of which was expecting a baby within days), Wilf persuaded the local council to give them a house that was still being built. They settled into an empty shell, while the builders finished the house. They were still there 20 years later.

At the 1950 Labour Conference at Margate, Hubert Luckett, an NUAW EC member, told delegates that farmworkers were losing confidence because the policy to abolish the tied cottage was not being carried out. Aneurin Bevan said a review of the Rent Restrictions Acts would involve eight million houses. The NEC was considering what modification could be made in the tied cottage system, but if they thought the Government was going to present a controversial measure to the Commons where they had a majority of six, they could think again.

Later that year Kent County Committee unanimously called for action and said that unless Labour redeemed its pledge before the next election, 'it may adversely affect the chances of the socialist candidates in every rural constituency in Kent.'

Plan to Restrict Certificates

In July 1951, James Dalton, Minister of Local Government and Planning, announced that the Government proposed to abolish the cottage certificate system, under which large numbers of free houses were turned into tied cottages. This was in response to the request of the NUAW and his announcement was welcomed by Edwin Gooch who said, 'It will not mean the end of the tied cottage system but it will certainly remove part of the grievances.' In August, the Minister of Agriculture said that during 1947–50 the number of applications dealt with was 7,224, certificates issued 3,770 and the number withdrawn 1,581.

Not all tied cottage cases in Court left the farmer completely unscathed. A Kent farmer sued for possession, and evidence was given that after a previous eviction order, granted because the cottage was required by another worker, the cottage had been left empty for two years. Judge John Neal, said at Maidstone County Court 'the farmers have a dreadful power over those who occupy tied houses and the Court has little power to end misuse of this power by the farmers.' The Judge said he was not going to have the Court used as an object of oppression, but did nonetheless, make an Order for possession in nine weeks.

In Shropshire, at the County Conference, a party of 10 members was formed to go into action whenever a farmworker was threatened with eviction. This 'vigilance squad' included two former regimental sergeant-majors, an ex-pilot and an Army ex-officer.

Up in County Durham in 1952, when a farmworker broke his leg, and he and his family were being turned out of their cottage, feelings ran so high that when the news reached other members, they immediately downed tools and brought five farms to a standstill. After the eviction such had been the publicity that the family was offered the first house completed by the district council.

Yet legislation to end such practices seemed as far away as ever, if not further. The Labour Party issued a discussion pamphlet, *Our Daily Bread*, by

Harry Walston, a millionaire Labour life peer with an Eton schooling, which did not seem to commit Labour to anything, and certainly did not favour the abolition of tied cottages. Instead Walston, who farmed 1,200 hectares around his ancestral home, Newton Hall, Cambs, said, 'We must see that the interests of tenants are far more securely protected than they are at present,' but did not make any specific proposals. Nothing was said about whether the Union was ever consulted on the pamphlet, but it seems unlikely.

The Labour Government was defeated in 1951 and the Conservatives returned to power. Evictions continued unabated. It was still dangerous to break a leg, or be in any way incapable of working in the middle of the 20th century – it could lead to homelessness.

In 1954, the Union succeeded in getting Labour to amend its *Challenge to Britain* policy statement so that when Labour was returned to power, a definite assurance was given that 'no farmworker will be evicted . . . unless alternative accommodation is proved to be available.' Harold Collison said, 'We must make it quite clear that this time we shall expect the Party to carry out its promise.' Labour MPs put down in the House of Commons a new clause to the Housing Repairs and Rents Bill which would abolish the system of issuing 'cottage certificates' for houses farmers bought. It was included in the Bill and became law that year.

Feeling on tied cottages continued to run high in the Union. At the giant Jubilee demonstration at Great Yarmouth before the Biennial in 1956, Hugh Gaitskell, Labour leader promised that Labour would 'abolish' evictions from tied cottages when they won the next General Election.

At the Conference, the tied cottage led to some straight talking between the floor and platform. E. Parry, Hunts, moved a motion calling upon the EC 'immediately to embark upon a more vigorous policy to bring about its abolition'. He believed the EC to be out of line with the membership and that it was 'not active and virile enough'. L. Shears, Dorset, seconding, said that the motion had 'more meat' in it than any previous motion on tied cottages before biennials, while T. Gasgoyne, Yorks, urged militant action on the doorstep at evictions. M. Crofts, Sussex, was critical of lack of action on the part of the Union, TUC and Labour Party, while A. Abbey, Somerset, said that the tied cottage was one of the biggest difficulties faced in the struggle for higher wages. Edwin Gooch assured them that any instructions they gave the EC were 'faithfully carried out to the letter'. The matter would only be dealt with by amending the law, and that could only be done in Parliament.

On the question of local action, Harold Collison said that in the previous year they had an average of five cases a week in the courts, quite apart from the many others that never reached that stage. The EC had always taken the line that they would not advise members to break the law because it would be the members and not the EC who had to pay the penalties. 'If ever the position arises that we feel we have to take stronger action, believe me I will not ask members to go and break the law, I will do it myself.' The resolution was carried unanimously.

Not letting up, H. Hogg and Joan Maynard, Yorks, moved a successful resolution calling on the next Labour Government to introduce legislation to put all tied cottages immediately under the Rent Restrictions Act.

In 1956, Labour put before its Annual Conference a comprehensive housing policy, which recognised the abuses of the agricultural tied cottage, but went on to say, 'We must face the fact that it is not possible to abolish the tied house completely.' The *Landworker* commented, 'Many would vigorously oppose that statement. But there is really no need to argue this point, because it is perfectly clear that the proposals which follow will abolish the system which enables a landlord to have an occupant evicted without alternative accommodation being available.'

The proposals included a system of registering cottages in any industry as essential or not essential to a man's job, and in the case of those that were, the local authority would be expected to provide housing for the worker on retirement or if he had to leave the cottage through no fault of his own. A farmer could then only obtain possession through an application to the Courts if the local authority could offer suitable alternative accommodation.

The *Landworker* thought the proposals met the Union's requirements. Although tied cottages were never divided into these two suggested categories, the proposals had similarities with the Rent (Agriculture) Act which ended most evictions from tied cottages, some 20 years later.

One problem for tied cottage occupants were the demands made upon them that were seldom made elsewhere. A factory owner does not usually ask an employee's wife to act as a domestic servant, or for the worker's family to help with the job. He makes no demands that another employee should be given lodgings, does not debar a worker because he has children, and probably does not care whether his employee is CoE or a Buddhist. Farmworkers seeking work may face one or more of these conditions. A study of 'sits vac' in a weekly farming paper over seven weeks showed 627 advertisements, of which 120 (19.1%) were concerned with more than just the applicant's ability.

No less than 40 advertisements (6.3%) required the applicant's wife to work in the farmer's home, and another 14 (2.2%) said that such work was 'optional'. Calls for full- or part-time assistance from wife, son or daughter to look after stock, milking or poultry accounted for another 60 (9.5%). Two (0.3%) required the worker to house a lodger, two specified no children and two made conditions regarding the worker's religion.

The 1961 Biennial in the Isle of Wight called on the Labour Government to honour its pledge to deal satisfactorily with the tied cottage. But Labour failed to win the General Election, and there was further disappointment when the Tory Minister of Housing said that the problem facing the occupant of a tied cottage, whose contract of service ended, was best met by increasing the stock of housing available.

*   *   *

'The Labour Party . . . will ensure that no occupant of a tied cottage is evicted until alternative accommodation has been provided,' declared George Brown, deputy leader, in a speech outlining Labour's agricultural policy in 1963. This policy had been hammered out by a sub-committee on which the Union was represented. The following year, at the Biennial at Felixstowe, a composite welcomed Labour's new pledge on tied cottages.

Labour won the General Election in 1964 and Harold Wilson became Premier. Within a week Harold Collison had an interview with Fred Peart, Minister of Agriculture, and reminded him of the steps that farmworkers would be expecting on tied cottages. Harold also saw other Ministers and was assured that work was going ahead preparing legislation.

Protection from Eviction Bill

In the House of Commons the Government set about implementing its promise. The passage of its Protection from Eviction Bill was making speedy progress. On 8 December the Bill went through the Report Stage and had an unopposed Third Reading. It was expected to be on the Statute Book by Christmas. The Bill was intended as a temporary provision to give tenants some security until the end of 1965, when the Government intended to replace the notorious Rent Act of 1957.

'The fact that under Clause 1 (Section 5) of the Bill, tied farm cottages are expressly included, must afford our members considerable satisfaction,' wrote the *Landworker*. Specifically, the Bill required that landlords of property with a net annual value of £400 or less could not obtain possession without obtaining a county court order. Proceedings through magistrates' or High Court would be barred. The Bill's most useful provision was that which empowered the county court to delay the execution of any possession order for up to 12 months.

But it was not all plain sailing. The Tory Opposition was strongly critical of the provisions affecting tied farm cottages. The NFU circularised all MPs before the Second Reading. For the Committee Stage the NUAW did likewise. In the event, Richard Crossman, Minister of Housing, no doubt to facilitate the passage of the Bill, made some concessions to the Opposition. An amendment by the Opposition to delete all reference in the Bill to tied cottages was defeated. Crossman rejected another amendment in favour of the farmer. To assist them, however, he stated his intention to substitute an amendment himself at the Report Stage. Perturbed at this news, feeling it would weaken the Bill and prejudice the ultimate major legislation, the EC took quick action. George Hook, head of the Legal Department, saw the Parliamentary Secretary that morning, and the same evening, Harold Collison, Bert Hazell and Hook visited the Minister and told him of the EC's fears. They recognised the tactical reasons behind the proposed amendment, and Crossman promised to have early consultations with the Union on the subsequent Bill. Crossman was also encouraging with his statement in the House later that night: 'We are going to give security to the agricultural worker in our permanent legislation . . . we shall work out a permanent system of security for him as we were pledged to do.'

Under the Minister's amendment the court would have to have regard to whether the efficient management of agricultural land would be seriously prejudiced unless the premises were available for occupation by another workman. Speaking on this amendment, Hazell said the Minister had 'bent over backwards in trying to meet the wishes of the farmer'.

Less than 40 days after the Protection from Eviction Bill was first presented to the House, the Bill received the Royal Assent on 17 December 1964. Although limited in scope, the Union believed it gave occupants a greater degree of security of tenure than they had ever previously enjoyed. Later, Fred Peart told the *Landworker*, 'Of course we stand by the pledge on the tied cottage . . . a start has already been made.'

A start, yes, but it continued to be a serious problem, with an estimated 120,000 tied cottages still in existence in England and Wales, with nearly 50% of the adult farm labour forced to live in them. In May 1965, Collison wrote in the *Landworker* on the next move, and on the Government's 'long awaited' new Rent Bill, then before Parliament. He said the Union could not support the proposals as they did not honour the election pledge, that they would make it impossible for a farmworker to be evicted unless suitable alternative accommodation was available. The Minister of Housing recognised that the Bill 'did not fulfil the Party's pledge in its original terms; but that if, after a trial period, evictions still take place without suitable alternative accommodation, the Government would be prepared to consider further action to secure the terms of the Party's undertaking.' The EC told the Minister that they still found his proposals unacceptable. They recognised, however, that the Bill's provisions, if they became law, 'constituted a considerable advance on the position which has appertained for many years . . . therefore . . . they would not seek to oppose . . .'

'We shall be watching the operation of the new legislation with a very wary eye,' declared Harold.

During the debate on the Third Reading of the Rent Bill, Richard Crossman said that the new Act which dealt with the special provision of agricultural employees was just to farmer and worker alike, 'and will finally eliminate what was already a dying form of victimisation.'

The new Rent Act 1965 came into operation on 8 December 1965, and its immediate effect was to consolidate and make permanent the protection given by the Protection from Eviction Bill 1964, which was repealed.

The 1965 Labour Conference, being the first for more than a decade when Labour was in office, meant that delegates were dealing with problems that were now Labour's responsibility to deal with, and not just talk about. Joan Maynard, Thirsk, moved her constituency party's resolution that Labour 'abolish the tied cottage immediately'.

The motion was seconded by the Bakers' Union, and Harold Collison reaffirmed the Union's belief that the new legislation did not honour the Labour Party's pledge to make eviction impossible unless suitable alternative accommodation was available, but would support the motion if pressed. 'We were not happy about the wording – we have never sought the abolition of the tied cottage but a change in the law to prevent eviction unless suitable alternative accommodation were available.'

Richard Crossman repeated his undertaking to look at the matter again if it proved necessary, but also felt it would be better if the resolution was remitted to the EC. To this, Joan and Conference agreed.

There was another General Election in 1966, and urging support for Labour in the April *Landworker*, Harold Collison wrote of their achievements while in power, including the tackling of the tied cottage problem. 'At last,' he declared, 'there is some security of tenure for the farmworker.' Labour won the Election, and their 97 overall majority gave them the power to carry out their mandate.

One month later, at the Union's Jubilee Biennial at Weston-Super-Mare, many delegates condemned the Labour Government for failing to properly honour the Party's pledge not to allow evictions unless suitable alternative accommodation was available. The EC also came in for criticism for what Vice-President Joan Maynard, when moving a resolution, called 'this sordid sell-out of our membership on this issue'. On Richard Crossman, Joan said, 'He tried to be fair to both sides. God knows why he wanted to be fair to both sides; for generations, comrades, we have suffered from the unfairness of the tied cottage system. The main point had been overlooked: this was to remove the power which the farmer has over the worker, irrespective of whether he uses it or not.' She referred to the debate at the Labour Conference when Harold Collison had said that the Union had never been for the abolition of the tied cottage. 'Well, if that does not stun you comrades, nothing will.'

During the debate, H. Beck, Lincs, said that the Labour Government had previously a majority of only two or three, 'now they have got a hundred, surely something can be done about the tied cottage today.' L. Shears, Dorset, was bitter in his condemnation of the Labour Government's broken promise. He believed the Union leadership had been blackmailed into accepting this situation. He thought they should have 'come away with nothing rather than give up their principles.'

Replying, Collison said the EC also deplored the Government's action, but they did not accept the contention that the EC had not campaigned vigorously enough. On his statement to the Labour Party, he pointed out that the words 'abolition of the tied cottage system . . . are open to misinterpretation'. He repeated that abolition had never been Union policy. 'Our policy has always been . . . no eviction . . . unless there was suitable alternative accommodation.' He referred to the numerous talks with Crossman, who had asserted that if an 'alternative accommodation' clause were inserted in the Bill, some Labour MPs would vote against and the Government would be defeated. Eventually the EC agreed not to oppose the clause because it was in the members' interest to keep the gains that had been made. Crossman had threatened to remove the clause completely if the EC opposed it.

Nonetheless, the Jubilee Conference carried unanimously the resolution which deplored the action of the Labour Government in not carrying out its pledge and regretted the attitude of the Union EC in not fighting more vigorously for the removal of this pernicious evil.

Not Satisfactory

An unsigned article in the *Landworker* in 1968 said that the provisions in the Rent Act 1965 had not proved satisfactory and had failed to stop evictions. There had been 12 since the 1965 Act. This compared with about 30 a year before the temporary Protection from Eviction Act 1964 came into force. 'So there has been some improvement. But a single eviction is still one too many.'

These points were forcibly put on 2 February when an eight-member deputation from the Union met Anthony Greenwood, the new Minister of Housing. The Minister said that he felt one answer was to build a sufficient number of houses in the countryside. Some progress had already been made in this direction by virtue of the 1¼ million houses built since the Labour Government came to power in October 1964. As to the 1965 Act, he pointed out that under this, there had been over 600 cases in which a suspension of execution had been granted, including 346 cases of 28 days and over. He stressed the reduction in the number of eviction cases, but was quickly informed that there would have been at least 25 more in the previous two years had there not been prompt action by the Union.

Harold Wilson spoke at a rally which preceded the Biennial at Aberystwyth in 1968, and was listened to with rapt attention by the 800 or so present when he referred to the tied cottage. He claimed that the 1965 Rent Act had given farmworkers greater protection than any previous legislation. During 1966 and 1967 there had been only a dozen evictions. 'The officers of your Union . . . have done much to help ensure that your members get justice.' He went on to say that there was not sufficient experience to take stock of how the new legislation had been working, and promised consultations with the Union.

When replying to a debate, Harold Collison said, recent evictions 'are only the tip of the iceberg and below the water there is a conglomeration of worry, fear and anxiety in the minds of farmworkers and their wives when they are under threat of eviction, whether eviction takes place or not.' He reminded them that Richard Crossman had told him that the Union could go back to him if evictions continued and the Prime Minister had now undertaken to review the workings of the law. A composite, whilst appreciating the efforts to control evictions by the Rent Act, deplored the failure of the Labour Government to implement their pledge in this respect, was passed with the backing of the EC.

NUAW delegates, Mrs. P. March and Mrs. Bareham, Kent, secured unanimous support at that year's TUC Women's Conference for the Union's policy on the tied cottage.

And strictly from the Union's point of view, the Centenary TUC Conference at Blackpool was a highly successful event. Three resolutions in which the Union was involved were all adopted without noticeable dissent. SOGAT submitted a motion, calling for, 'The earliest possible legislation abolishing the tied cottage system.' The Union moved an amendment, accepted by SOGAT, incorporating the 'suitable alternative accommodation' principle. The SOGAT delegate said that *Labour Research* estimated that there were some 850,000 houses in Britain tied to a job. Some of his paper-making members were in such houses.

Joan Maynard, seconding, said she believed the system was spreading; local authorities were letting council houses to employees of particular firms. She reminded them that the Minister of Housing told a local government conference the previous year that 'No man is free if his choice of employment is restricted by considerations of accommodation.' Joan declared, 'Talk is cheap. We want him to act . . .' She called for Congress's unqualified support. Congress gave it.

A strong appeal to the Government to take account of the plight of the agricultural worker occupying a tied cottage was made at the Labour Conference by Harold Collison, speaking in support of a resolution calling on the Government to implement their promise in the 1964 General Election Manifesto. He said that Crossman's belief that the 1965 Rent Act would prevent evictions had been proved wrong, although there had been a reduction in number. Seconding, Joan Maynard said, 'It may seem a hard thing for me to say, but land is more important than people,' and went on to instance a judge using his discretion under the 1965 Act in favour of the farmer, and giving a married couple just three weeks to get out of their cottage. 'As socialists we should surely stand exactly opposite to the principle of property being more important than people.' The resolution was, like that at the TUC, endorsed unanimously.

Anthony Greenwood, replying, said that while evictions had dropped in number the 'real point . . . is that there is constantly a threat hanging over the heads of farmworkers . . . in tied houses.' He expected to start discussions with all interested parties to see 'how the remaining weaknesses can be removed.' Union discussions with Ministers did start, but never got near resolving the problems.

Despite such procrastination, the Union leadership still strove to be loyal to the Labour Party. In an internal letter to Harold Collison on 19 August 1969, Jim Watts, head of the Legal Department, referred to a Devon member killed when a tractor overturned, and the employer the following day told the widow that she must leave the cottage. It was a case about which they would normally inform the media, but 'in view of the present negotiations with the Government I advised Warren [local DO] not to bring the local or national press into the picture for obvious reasons.' He then went on to say that so far the DOs had been 'manageable' but it 'occurs to me that if one or two bad cases were to crop up in certain other areas . . . the Organiser may well make the violent criticism of the Government we have undertaken not to do.' He suggested circularising DOs 'without giving details' that negotiations were in progress with the Government and instruct them to 'refrain from making violent criticisms until the outcome of the negotiations is known.'

I could not trace whether such a circular was sent. Certainly many DOs would have been difficult to restrain, not least Albert Warren, who fought many an eviction case.

When winding up the debate on the tied cottage at the Whitley Bay Biennial in 1970, the new General Secretary, Reg Bottini, said that the President had asked the Prime Minister to receive a deputation from the EC. Two days later a letter from the Premier was read to the Conference. Harold Wilson wrote saying the Government had decided to strengthen safeguards for agricultural workers in the Agricultural Bill now before Parliament. 'You will know that an amendment to this part of the Bill was carried at Committee Stage in the House of Lords on 5 May against the advice of Government spokesmen. I can tell you that the Government are intending to restore the Bill to its original form when it returns to the Commons.'

This news was received with considerable approval, but delegates had scarcely returned from the heady atmosphere of Whitley Bay when a General Election was announced for 18 June. The Tories won, and the evictions continued.

Later that year, Ronald Childs, his wife and three children aged 10, eight and seven, were evicted from their tied cottage after a row over working conditions. In June 1971, his employer, Gerald Capes, of Hatherdene, Andover, had issued the following edict to staff:

> Regarding overtime: if you are asked to work either weekdays or weekends, I shall expect you to do so unless a satisfactory reason is given either to myself or my foreman. Time off, in order to go shopping, is not considered a valid reason. Please carry tea with you when you are working overtime as farm transport is not provided for you to return home. To run my business profitably, it is becoming more and more important to be 100% efficient. Therefore you must abide by the rules which I consider essential to achieve this efficiency.

Ronald complained to the Union that his employer's attitude appeared to be dictatorial. Discussions took place between the NFU and the NUAAW, but the NFU were not prepared to intervene. In August 1971, Ronald was dismissed because he failed to return to work on a Sunday evening when relatives called and he spent the evening with them. The Union fought for Ronald in the courts, but failed to stop eviction, and he and his family had to live in a van and a tent.

One aspect of tied cottages was that, because of spiralling house prices, farmers had an added incentive to empty their tied cottages and sell them at high prices.

'Redundant farmworkers are being forced out of their tied cottages to make way for the affluent "townies" looking for a dream home in the country with roses round the door,' declared the *Sunday Mercury*, a Birmingham paper. Len Pike, DO, told the *Mercury*, 'We take exception to the precipitate action being taken by some landowners to get workers out of cottages when often the same cottages remain empty for months afterwards.' Keeping them empty, was often a dodge leading to their eventual sale, to say nothing of the need for time to doll them up and plant roses round the door.

Similar problems were arising in the West Country. Two members, who had been injured while working, had eviction orders obtained against them. Albert Warren, DO, pleaded without success for a stay of eviction for one member whose house was said to be desperately needed by another worker. But it was a long time before the other man moved. The other evicted member made numerous attempts to rent an empty property, only to be told it was 'not to let'. However, during the summer months it was always let to holidaymakers at a high profit. He had to spend his savings on a caravan.

There was a new surge of evictions. Four during June and July, in Kent alone – an unprecedented rise in such a short time. Vacated, these cottages were a potential goldmine, which was proof how bad the problem was becoming, particularly in the South East, where cottages were fetching enormous prices for use as holiday or weekend homes.

Labour's 1974 General Election Manifesto clearly stated: 'The Labour Government in its first period of office will abolish the agricultural tied cottage.' Labour won and with Harold Wilson back in Downing Street, many NUAAW members expected instant action. They had, however, to wait a further three years before 'abolition' became a fact. The Government made a slender majority the excuse for doing nothing, when 'more important' tasks had to be tackled.

Parliament Lobbied

Angry at the Labour Government's silence on their pre-election pledge, some 80 delegates from the Clacton Biennial in 1974 travelled to Westminster on 9 May to lobby MPs. Liberally decorated with tied cottage posters, two coachloads arrived at Labour's headquarters in Smith Square. They were met by Tony Marshall from head office who handed out 30 placards, and then marched in procession to the House of Commons where they asked to see their MPs. The turnout of MPs was not impressive. However, in a committee room, under the chairmanship of Harlow Labour MP, Stan Newens, a lively audience was addressed by a number of Union people, including Ted Calver, Colin Down, Jack Langford, Barry Leathwood, Joan Maynard, Chris Morris,

Arthur Neatherway, Wilf Page and Douglas Oswick. 'If we give a pledge we should do our damnedest to carry it out,' declared miners' MP, Alec Woodhall, setting the tone of the small Labour group which attended the meeting.

Coachloads of NUAAW members again converged on Parliament on 3 December 1975 to lobby their MPs on the tied cottage. The turn-out was bigger than expected, about 1,000, and they heard Gavin Strang, Parliamentary Secretary to the Minister of Agriculture, announce that legislation would be introduced before Easter to assure farmworkers the same security of tenure as workers in other industries.

Bert Hazell said, 'This will be the greatest social advance of the past century for our people, and it cannot come too soon.' Members were greeted as they arrived by Joan Maynard, who said that the size of the lobby killed the lie put around by farmers that the workers did not want tied cottages abolished. Reg Bottini warned that there was still a long way to go before the Bill was law.

That year the NFU annual meeting seems to have developed group hysteria when delegates discussed the tied cottage. NUAAW policy, it was alleged, was inspired by 'Reds under the bed' and 'neo-Communist activists'. Joan Maynard came under particular attack. Describing her as the '*femme fatale* of the NUAAW', the *British Farmer and Stockbreeder* (an NFU mouthpiece) reported as a 'general feeling' among delegates that she alone had organised the tied cottage plot.

Reg Bottini wrote[4] about the Government's Consultative Document *Abolition of Tied Cottage System in Agriculture* and noted that the preface stated that the Government intended to honour its commitment to abolish tied cottages. The document examined the necessary legislation, proposals and options, and said the Government's overriding aim was to disengage farmworkers' conditions of employment from the circumstances in which they were housed. 'The focus should be on how to shape legislation on the lines that will enable farmers, farmworkers, local authorities and other interests concerned effectively to adapt themselves to the changing requirements of modern society while maintaining the key contribution which this great industry can make to the national economy. That is the purpose of this document.'

During a press conference Government spokesmen said that the document was concerned with 'how' and not 'whether'. It was committed to legislation, but wanted views as to how it should be framed. It was made clear that only about half the labour force at present lived in tied cottages and that barely half of all tied cottages were occupied as such. Nevertheless, about 70,000 workers were working under the shadow of eviction.

'Not surprisingly,' said Reg Bottini, 'the NFU and the CLA immediately reacted, and predictably, with outright opposition to the abolition of tied homes. It is crystal clear that whatever legislation the Government bring before the House of Commons . . . will be opposed tooth and nail by the farmers' and landowners' organisations and by the Tory Opposition.'

He welcomed the Government's reiteration of its commitment to extend farmworkers' 'ordinary security of tenure' and said they 'must mobilise the strength of our Union' to ensure that the legislation is brought forward speedily and to ensure that it will secure 'the majority vote in the House of Commons'.

In the April before the 1976 Biennial at Malvern, Reg reviewed the progress made since 1974. For the whole of the previous two years they had had a Labour Government, though from February 1974 until October of that year it was a minority Government. With the securing of a slim majority in the October 1974 General Election, a great deal of beneficial legislation had been forced through, often against vigorous opposition. On the tied cottage he said, 'We have been assured that legislation will be introduced before the forthcoming Easter recess to extend the Rent Act security of tenure to agricultural tied cottage occupants . . . We shall not rest until that legislation is secured.'

He declared a month later, 'At long last a Bill for security of farm and woodland workers. On Monday 12 April, the Government published a Bill to extend Rent Act security of tenure to tied cottages. The proposed legislation was a watershed in the long struggle, down generations, to secure the same kind of security as other workers who are protected by the Rent Acts.'

Reg said that ever since the Government published their Consultative Document there had been a spate of reports that there should be a scheme of registration of tied cottages. The Union opposed such a scheme and the Government finally decided not to introduce one. The main proposals of the Bill were:

> That unless and until suitable alternative accommodation is proved to be available an agricultural worker whose employment has ended will have security of tenure like any other Rent Act protected tenant. Also, there will be a statutory obligation imposed on local housing authorities to give priority for council housing to farmworkers living in tied cottages in respect of which there is an agricultural need for the farmer to secure possession.
>
> Where a farmer claims agricultural need . . . he will make application to the local housing authority. Unlike in the ordinary Rent Act case, the mere production of a housing authority's certificate that alternative accommodation has been offered will not automatically require the Court to make an order for possession.

Security of tenure would apply where little or no rent was being paid and there would be protection for the worker's widow or other surviving members of the family, retired or part-time and semi-retired workers. The Government decided not to take away the power of the AWB to fix the normal permitted value of a cottage – then £1.50 per week. Reg stated that the Union believed 'quite clearly' the Bill fully met the demands of successive biennials that before a farmworker left his cottage there should be suitable alternative accommodation.

Rent (Agriculture) Bill

The subsequent Rent (Agriculture) Bill, whose Second Reading was passed in the House of Commons during the 1976 Biennial at Malvern undoubtedly affected the tone of the debate on the tied cottage. Anger at previous conferences gave way to a mood of qualified expectation that the Union's 70-year-old policy target was at last in sight.

That the Bill would be a tremendous value to farmworkers if it reached the Statute Book in its current form was made crystal clear. 'Of course the key point of the Bill,' said Agriculture Minister Fred Peart, 'is that no one who qualifies under the Bill will have to leave a tied cottage unless suitable alternative accommodation is available and has been offered.' The effectiveness of the Bill would depend largely on the extent to which local authorities re-housed outgoing workers. A number of resolutions on the tied cottage were still formally passed and it was wholly appropriate that Joan Maynard, staunch campaigner on the issue, should successfully move the main motion, which fully supported the abolition, rejected any kind of registration and sought full protection under suitably amended Rent Acts.

Harry Cocksedge, Hants, said, 'Throughout the years I have stood on this platform at biennials and a storm has raged over the tied cottage system. We knew then and we know now that it is a family problem, a heart-breaking problem, a destroyer. But now we have seen the Minister on the platform this morning and seen the storm breaking. We see the sun beginning to shine in the distance.'

In Parliament, although the Government did not have an overall majority, it secured a majority by two votes during the Second Reading of the Bill. Majorities of 33 and 32 in two successive divisions resulted partly from the support of the Liberals and other minority parties, and partly from low-key Tory opposition. The Secretary of State for the Environment, Peter Shore, said that the Bill would abolish a long-standing injustice.

Francis Pym, Tory spokesman on agriculture, claimed that agriculture had a good record and reputation for looking after its workers' families no less than its workers.

Joan Maynard declared, 'Farmers have security of tenure. I support that, and I support the new clauses in the Agriculture (Miscellaneous Provisions) Bill to extend that security to the nearest relative, with certain conditions. But why should farmworkers not enjoy the same security?'

The House of Lords removed from the Rent (Agriculture) Bill the security of tenure for those employed in dairy farming, grazing and meadowlands, livestock, orchards and forestry. At their October meeting the EC bitterly condemned the Lords' action, and called for the Bill's restoration to its original form.

On 8 November, the Government was successful in winning its guillotine on five Bills amended by the Lords. This included the Rent (Agriculture) Bill, which on its return to the Lords was accepted as recommended. It became an Act on 1 January 1977. However, the Lords had made some changes to the draft. It was not a perfect law in the first place, gamekeepers were excluded, and above all there were not nearly enough chairmen of ADHACs with trade union backgrounds who understood the workers' problems and were sympathetic to them.

'Red Letter Day in Union history,' proclaimed the *Landworker* above an article by Reg Bottini. He wrote, '. . . from 1 January 1977, the tied cottage system as we have known it for so long, will cease to exist. From that date workers occupying "tied" cottages . . . will assume the status of "protected occupants". January 1, 1977 . . . will mark a new era in our industry . . . The agricultural worker will at last be able to "stand up and be counted", and this can, in the long term, be only beneficial in the industry as a whole. The Union has many more battles to fight, but I am convinced that this particular achievement is the most significant development in the Union's history.'

Joan Maynard, who in and out of Parliament had played a major role in this 'significant development', was not invited to the press conference the Union held to mark the occasion. This snub angered many Union members.

The NFU now had to face up to the fact that the law had been changed and announced that it would co-operate in trying to make the tied cottage legislation work. John Quicke, CLA President, said that they would co-operate with the NUAAW to ensure that the legislation operated as effectively as possible and with maximum harmony among the parties involved.

Commenting in the *Landworker*, Joan Maynard said, 'What a struggle our members conducted to get the Act. Resolutions, demonstrations, lobbies over more years than we all like to count. The injustices which our people suffered because of the tied cottage always ate into my heart and, from joining the Union in 1947, I was determined to do whatever I could to help members get rid of it. How fortunate that because of my work for the Union and in the wider Labour movement, I was elected to the NEC of the Labour Party in October 1972. I did not realise then that this would give me the opportunity to influence the two Election manifestos of 1974. In fact I did just that. I made sure that the tied cottage pledge was in both manifestos, at the same time being aware that this was only part of the way along the road to an Act of Parliament.

'Then, in 1974, I was elected to Parliament . . . This gave me the opportunity to try to get the promise in the Manifesto into the Queen's Speech.' Joan failed the first time, but succeeded the second time with the help of the Union, '. . . only just in time, for by the time we reached the Committee Stage of the Bill we were already in a minority position as a Party in the House.' The Act, she declared, 'does not give us abolition of the tied cottage system, but it does give our people security of tenure within the system, which is important.'

How did the Act work in its early days? In the latter half of 1976 there was a marked upsurge in the number of possession summonses against tied cottage occupants, clearly an attempt to obtain possession before the new Act came into operation. Jim Watts, on the first anniversary of the Act, revealed that in

1977, somewhat surprisingly, possession summonses continued to be issued, although on a much-reduced scale, and the Union had no difficulty in obtaining dismissals or withdrawals of the proceedings.

'It would seem that in those cases referred to ADHACs,' stated Watts, 'a certificate of agricultural need was issued in the majority of cases. But to think this is "rubber stamping" can be misleading. The number of ADHAC hearings during the six months under review is something like half the number of possession summonses issued the previous year, and it would seem from this that farmers who do not have genuine grounds for repossession are not referring their cases to the committees . . . in the majority of those cases referred to ADHACs, the worker concerned supports his employer's application (obviously in an attempt to get "freed" accommodation). To that extent, the system seems to be working satisfactorily . . .'

While the Act did not apply to Crown estates, including the Forestry Commission, the latter agreed to operate as if it did, from October 1977.

'To summarise, the first six months' working of the Act indicates that the situation is reasonably satisfactory, in that farmworkers are no longer being automatically dragged through the courts for possession of their cottages the moment their employment ends. It is too early to form any final conclusions and we are carefully watching the standard of alternative accommodation being offered to ensure that the Act's definition of "reasonable" is properly interpreted,' Jim concluded.

In answer to Joan Maynard, the Minister of Agriculture said in Parliament that in the first six months of the Act there had been 389 applications to ADHACs. In 366 the ADHACs found genuine agricultural need; 84% of the applications concerned people looking after livestock.

Farmers Still Get Possession

Doubts about the efficacy of the Act rumbled on among Union members, and surfaced at the 1982 Biennial at Skegness when a composite was passed calling for a tightening up of the Act in a number of areas.

Ian Crawford, West Midlands DO, explained in the *Landworker* that the Act gave no security of tenure once employment ended. 'At best the Act gives our members a stay of execution of up to six months where the employer has proved his agricultural requirement of the cottage for another worker . . . if no suitable alternative accommodation has been found by the local authority at the end of this period, then our member and his family can be put in temporary accommodation.' He pointed out that when ADHAC sits, the farmer is supported by a report from MAFF. There was no provision for the Union to submit documentation on behalf of members. Instead members had to depend on their own and representatives' verbal arguments. He wanted facilities for the Union to submit documents to redress the balance of information. 'These ADHACs when they meet are not functioning on behalf of our members. They are, in most cases, nothing but a cosy tea party or a wine-and-dine in some quaint country pub,' he declared.

In 1983, it was revealed that tied cottage dwellers had decreased to 45.1% of the agricultural labour force.

'Seven years on, it's time to take a long, hard look at the last Labour Government's tied cottage law,' Essex's George Scales told the Trade Group's annual conference at Eastbourne in 1983. He wanted all workers' representatives on ADHACs to get together to see whether they were making the best use of the law.

It was later seen that farmers still went on getting possession of cottages with the help of ADHACs. Commenting in 1988 on the working of the Act, by which time the Union had had a lot of experience of its deficiencies, Joan Maynard said, 'I think it's been wonderful for the farmers, they still own the cottages; without the odium of going through the courts they can still get possession, and they do. I can't think of any occasion when an ADHAC has not agreed to possession. ADHACs have too much say in these cases and they are on the side of the farmer. The thing the Act does is to give security of tenure while the farmworker is re-housed, but that is becoming more difficult because of the sale of council houses. The Act has stopped people being put on the streets, but it pinpoints our failure to get total abolition and break the tie between the man's job and home.'

Also commenting in 1988, Jack Boddy, the last General Secretary of the old Union before it merged with the TGWU, said, 'I think the Labour leaders after the war, with the Government's huge majority, could have abolished the tied cottage completely, but they didn't and they let us down without a doubt.' The 1976 Act brought an improvement in the situation, and they had to be grateful to the Labour Government which brought it in. The fact that they didn't achieve as much as some hoped should in no way denigrate the advances which were made. Referring to Joan Maynard's constant campaign against the tied cottage he said, 'The eventual success in getting this Act must to a substantial degree be laid at Joan's door. That she was not invited to the Union's press conference about the Act was an absolute disgrace.' He also recalled the splendid work of Jim Watts during the months prior to the Parliamentary debate, and the many hours of campaigning Jim spent with MPs and other influential individuals to ensure the Act was as good as possible.

Looking to the future, he said that the final solution for tied cottages was that no employer should own property occupied as a condition of employment. The fact that occupants could not be evicted so easily coincided with a further fall in the Union's membership, and Jack believed it possible that this had made some people feel they no longer needed the Union.

One Union leader much aware of the shortcomings of the Act is Tony Gould, secretary for the Trade Group's South East England and East Anglia Region. He told me in 1989 that farmers in the South and East of England in the early eighties were winning vacant possession in nine out of 10 ADHAC appeals, with an increasing number of farmers conning the committees to let them sell off valuable farmworkers' homes. 'A survey of ADHAC rulings in the two MAFF regions I deal with, the S Eastern Region based in Reading and the Eastern Region based in Cambridge, shows this to be true.' The table below sets out the results, but the basic facts are that in 1984 farmers were getting repossession in 86% of cases. This figure rose to nearly 88% in 1985, and following Union pressure fell to 82% in 1986, but the latest figures showed that the 1987 figures rose to 90%.

Agricultural Dwelling House Advisory Committee results 1984–7

COUNTY	Total hearings in 4 yrs	NEEDS				NO NEED				Farmer obtained repossession	% Success rate for farmers
		'87	'86	'85	'84	'87	'86	'85	'84		
Berkshire	32	5	7	4	8	—	4	—	4	24	75%
Bucks	27	3	6	7	9	1	1	—	—	25	92.6%
Oxfordshire	72	14	14	13	13	3	5	5	5	54	75%
Surrey/Middx	57	16	6	12	18	1	3	—	1	52	91.2%
Hampshire	136	40	30	27	28	1	3	4	3	125	91.9%
West Sussex	115	25	17	38	20	2	8	2	3	100	87%
Isle of Wight	8	—	5	1	1	—	1	—	—	7	87.5%
East Sussex	72	10	11	19	15	4	5	6	2	55	76.4%
Kent	139	17	25	46	33	5	2	8	3	121	87.1%
Norfolk	42	12	8	6	12	—	—	2	2	38	90.5%
Suffolk	50	13	11	7	14	1	2	1	1	45	90%
Lincolnshire	75	23	17	19	10	—	2	1	3	69	92%
Essex/Herts/ Gt. London	113	22	21	31	25	4	4	1	5	99	87.6%
Cambs/Beds/ Northants	63	23	12	10	9	2	2	3	2	54	85.7%
Total	1001	223	190	240	215	24	42	33	34	868	

Percentage in farmers' favour   90.3 81.9 87.9 86.3

Source: *MAFF (South Eastern and Eastern Divisions)*

Tony referred to two cases. A herdsman was made redundant and the farmer applied for possession, which was refused. A second application also failed, but on the third attempt the farmer claimed he needed the cottage for a young farmworker. The ADHAC granted a 'three months' need' order. The herdsman was offered a council house, but turned it down because it was outside his village. Later he moved into a house owned by his son. No farmworker moved into the empty cottage, and it was eventually sold for over £120,000. A member from Maidstone was made redundant and the farmer applied for possession, claiming that his son was getting married and going to work on the farm. The Union member told ADHAC that as far as he knew the son was not even courting, but ADHAC gave possession. The son did not marry and never occupied the cottage, which was sold.

'Our representatives on ADHACs must be specially alert to the "fibs" that are told by farmers, as the opportunity for profit and unbridled greed shown by some employers illustrates why these tied cottages should be taken out of the hands of individual farmers and placed under the control of local authorities,' declared Tony. 'ADHAC chairmen usually have the outrageously middle-class view that the farmer is entitled to make his business pay over every consideration of humanity. Lots of former tied cottages in Essex are being sold to the Yuppies. One went for £145,000, none go for less than £80,000. It is scandalous, because a lot of them were put up with Government grants.'

REFERENCES

1. Peter Worrall, *Anatomy of Agriculture*, Harrap, 1978.
2. Annual Report, 1978.
3. Annual Report, 1947.
4. *Landworker*, September 1975.

13

Age-Old Fight for Decent Pay

The cultivators of the soil are the least inclined to sedition and to violent causes.

Aristotle

Little Muscle to Back Claims

In most industries, the laws of supply and demand affect wages claims and general wage levels. This does not seem to apply in agriculture, even during great labour shortages. Why? There are several possible reasons, not the least being that there was seldom any ready muscle to back wage claims, due partly to an under-unionised labour force, and consequently no major strikes or bans on overtime. Even in the few instances where there was any urge to strike, the Union leadership in the post-war years did its best to thwart such moves. The idea of strike action was unsuccessfully raised at the 1946 Biennial for the first time for 20 years, but was strongly opposed by Edwin Gooch.

In 1947, agricultural workers were still putting in a basic 48-hour week, with six days' paid holidays per year, plus Bank Holidays, for a national minimum of £4 10s for men, and £3 8s for women. This compared with an average industrial working week of 46 hours 36 minutes for £6 3s 4d. Women got £3 3s 11d for 41 hours 24 minutes.[1] Some petrol pump attendants in rural areas were getting £6 10s a week. The rent value of a tied cottage was 6s when taking into account the minimum farm rate.

The total number of agricultural workers in 1947 was 844,000, against 850,800 for 1946. These included casuals as well as prisoners-of-war. The total number of unemployed farmworkers on 13 October 1947 was 5,200, as compared with 4,344 a year earlier.[2]

Rates for other Union members negotiated in 1947 were: county council roadmen, 90s a week in many areas, 92s in a few areas, 100s in the South Eastern Metropolitan area. In the provinces, the rate for glasshouse workers was 100s and for market garden and fruit-farm workers 95s. Catchment Board workers got 90s a week in rural areas, 92s in urban areas, 100s in London.

Wages for Forestry Commission workers: 'Reliable men of outstanding skill who required a minimum amount of supervision,' 5s a week above the AWB minimum; 'Reliable men whose skill is about average but who require a reasonable amount of supervision,' 2s 6d extra. Ordinary 'labourers' got the AWB minimum.

County Agricultural Executive Committee wages were: lead foreman 140s to 160s a week; foreman 115s to 125s; gangers 95s to 105s; tractor drivers 97s to 105s. Women got lower pay, ranging from 105s to 115s for 'head foremen', to 70s to 102s for tractor drivers.

Piece-work rates in Holland, Lincs, were: thatching per running yard (i.e. once round the eave divided by two) 2s 9d per yard, 3d up or down, with 4s extra for gable-ended stacks. Potato picking: King Edwards, 5s up or down (154s 9d per acre); Majestics, 5s up or down (137s 9d per acre). Graving and strawing, one-seventh of the picking price; 3s extra where gang fetched straw from stack. Beet: lifting in heaps, 5s up or down (146s 3d per acre); lifting into rows, 5s up or down (124s 9d to 151s 9d per acre). These prices were meticulously worked out (and they didn't have pocket calculators then) and stipulated 'knocking off soil and topping'.

The Union failed to maintain the real wage of the farmworker in 1947. The prime cause for a decline was a rise of over 50% in the Index of Retail Prices between 1947 and 1956. AWB wage awards did not match wage rises in other industries.

A special conference of trade union executives in London in March 1948, accepted the responsibility for restraining wage increases until the country had recovered from serious economic difficulties. Vincent Tewson, TUC General Secretary, denied that the General Council was conspiring to reduce the standards of living of the people.

At a meeting of the TUC Economic Committee after the Budget, it was clear that a number of trade union leaders were concerned because the Chancellor's proposals included no control of prices and profits. They believed that if trade unions 'are to forego wage claims a corresponding sacrifice must be made by the employers.' Although the *Landworker*[3] reported these criticisms it gave no indication of the Union's policy on these matters. It would appear that the Union leadership had difficulty in fitting a cap to its wages campaign, whilst acquiescing to general restraint on wages.

When opening the Biennial at Scarborough in May, Edwin Gooch, seeking to pacify the more militant members, said the Labour Government had been contending with tremendous problems but despite the difficulties, Acts of Parliament to implement Election promises had poured on to the Statute Book. Two measures of great importance to all land workers were the Agricultural Wages (Regulation) Act, which gave agricultural workers the best wage-fixing machinery they had ever had, and the Agriculture Act, which gave new life and hope to those in agriculture.

The Agricultural Wages Board for England and Wales was set up in 1948 under the Agricultural Wages (Regulation) Act. Its great advantage for workers was that once it had set a basic minimum, the wage was statutory. Also County Wages Committees could no longer make awards below the central board's figure, only above it. The AWB consisted of eight employers' representatives, eight workers' representatives, plus five 'independent' members appointed by the Minister of Agriculture. Decisions were taken by majority vote; in practice the independents normally voted with one side or the other to produce a majority. Each year, farmers rigidly stuck to making low offers, and final settlements were usually near to what farmers offered.

Edwin Gooch revealed to the 200 delegates at the Biennial that the EC had 'approved the general principles of the Government's policy'. The workers had to exercise a 'sense of responsibility in wage demands'.

F. Robinson, EC, moved a resolution accepting the broad principle of the White Paper on Personal Incomes on the assurance that wage negotiations 'may still be justified in order to remove present injustices and anomalies'. J. Dunman, Berks, opposed because there was no serious move to limit prices and cut profits, but it was passed by 116 votes to 39.

At the 1948 TUC Conference at Margate, Bert Hazell moved a successful resolution calling for measures to attract labour to farms, with wages equal to those in the towns.

Despite their low wages, the National Savings Committee did not fail to exhort *Landworker* readers to invest in National Savings. Its adverts carried illustrations of 'someone worth saving for', usually small boys dressed in prep school rigouts. Not exactly the prevailing fashion for farmworkers' children.

More in touch were adverts for reconditioned clothing. One in May 1949 offered ex-Army trousers at 10s a pair, raincoats at £1, and pants at 3s 6d. Another advert, perhaps indicative of the land workers' penurious state, offered socks that wouldn't need darning, claiming they wore up to seven years without holes.

Following the Union's application for a 'substantial increase' in November 1948, the AWB recommended an increase of 4s a week for adult males, with proportionate increases for women and juniors, a reduction in hours from 48 to 47, and seven days' holiday with pay instead of six. This brought the adult males up to £4 14s a week.

For many years farmworkers in Cumberland, that county of hills and valleys, had remained impervious to trade unionism. Low wages were rife; many farmworkers there became alive to the need for organisation, and in April 1949, at special meetings in the Carlisle district they came in large numbers to hear the Union's message. A packed audience kept D. J. Diston, DO, and F. Robinson, EC, answering questions to past 11pm. Diston later told the first-ever conference of branch officials held in Cumberland that 50% of local farmworkers were not getting the minimum. In Cumberland he found a lot of things which he thought had died with his grandfather: the hiring system, the 60-hour week, people not knowing if they were due for a holiday or not, men carting manure on Boxing Day – a state of affairs that was much envied by the farmers of Rutland.

A resolution was carried unanimously by Rutland and Stamford NFU declaring that all industries, including agriculture, must return to the working hours of pre-war years with no increase in wages, in order to increase production. There was no suggestion that the farmers should return to pre-war profits.

The earnings gap between agricultural and manual workers widened throughout the 1950s and 1960s. And for the period 1949–55 there was an actual decline in real wages. Possibly, if the NUAW leadership had been bolder, and refused to accept miserly AWB awards, their members might have done better. Another factor was that conditions in the farm labour market were changing so fast that they may well have believed that strike action was becoming less and less feasible. And there was Edwin Gooch's overriding belief that co-operation with the farmers would produce a decent wage for employees.

That the AWB failed to do justice to farmworkers over this period was tacitly admitted by Simon Gourlay, chief negotiator of the NFU on the AWB. Interviewed in the *Farmers Weekly*, he suggested that the NFU and AWB were to blame for the earnings gap because they did not raise farmworkers' wages in the 1950s and 1960s, when significant improvements were possible. 'The NFU should have been more enlightened and should have worked harder to give workers parity.'[4]

The proportion of farmworkers receiving the AWB minimum declined from 34% in 1950 to 5% in 1970, suggesting that a growing number were doing better in their own wage bargaining with their bosses, than their representatives on the AWB.[5] The EC was caught in a trap. There was dissatisfaction with AWB awards, but they had no other policy than commitment to the AWB.

Higher Living Costs

But to return to 1949, when wages were not the only worry of farmworkers. The Labour Chancellor produced a bleak Budget, which the *Landworker* said was a 'shock'. Expected cuts in purchase tax on commodities 'that cannot by any stretch of the imagination be regarded as luxuries' were not forthcoming, and while the increase in food prices would only amount to 1s 8d per week for a family of five, 'there are low paid wage-earners who cannot afford even this slight advance in the cost of living.'

At the Suffolk County Conference it was claimed that the last increase in wages would largely be swallowed up by the rise in prices resulting from the Budget, and a resolution condemning the 4s increase as 'grossly inadequate to meet the rising cost of living' and demanding that the EC immediately go for a further and substantial increase was carried unanimously. Conference also wanted the adult wage at 18 and a flat rate of 2s 6d an hour for all harvest work. The 140 delegates at the West Norfolk Conference called for a minimum wage of £5 10s. The Essex Conference sought another way to improve take-home pay; it wanted all overtime to be free of income tax.

Pay increases were won for other workers in the Union. A claim to the National Council for County Council Roadmen had been refused and the

Union took its case to the National Arbitration Tribunal whose awards were: London, 104s; Zone A, 97s; Zone B, 94s.

At the 1950 TUC at Brighton, despite appeals from the platform for 'patience and moderation' delegates decided by a narrow majority to 'abandon any further policy of wage restraint'. And the agenda for that year's Biennial left no doubt what loomed largest in members' thoughts. No fewer than 154 branches demanded a minimum wage ranging from £5 to £6 with a 44-hour week. The Biennial decided to claim a substantial increase.

That agriculture was prosperous could not reasonably be disputed. A White Paper showed that income from farming rose by £25 million during 1949, output from £553 million to £591 million; wages took £217 million, salaries £13 million, while profits, rents and depreciation netted £361 million.

No wonder, with wages being kept down, that the NFU Accounts Scheme for 1948–9 showed the profitability of all types of farms to be a striking feature. On an identical sample of 2,693 farms with an average 198 acres, average profit rose by 82.1%, from £482 per farm in 1947–8 to £878 per farm in 1948–9. On 373 farms in East Anglia, with an average of 240 acres, profits went up 190.7%. The average profit per farm rose from £441 in 1947–8 to £1,282 in 1948–9. The Economist[6] recognised that 'income from farming' had increased five-fold since before the war, while farmworkers' wages had trebled. The Times admitted that farmers had done well out of the February Price Review,* and said, 'There is no doubt that the industry is capable of absorbing the cost of any increase in agricultural wages.'

In March 1950 the Government discontinued the direction of labour. Men from 18 to 50 and women from 18 to 40 had been covered since 1947 by a law which prevented employers engaging them, otherwise than through the Ministry of Labour or approved employment agency. This made it difficult to move freely from job to job.

Many meetings and demonstrations were held in support of the Union's claim for a substantial increase. But the Union only managed to squeeze out of the AWB an increase of 6s for men and 5s for women.

Scottish farmworkers were even worse off: they got no increase. Edwin Gooch sought to remedy this when he asked Tom Williams, in the House of Commons, if he did not think the Scottish AWB should follow the 'example of their more enlightened colleagues across the border' by granting an increase. Williams simply replied that the Scottish Board had rejected a wage increase. Mrs. Jean Mann, Labour, said, 'If they have no increased wages to meet, can you explain why brussels sprouts are 9d in Glasgow and only 5d in London?' Williams replied, 'It is one of the peculiarities of Scotland.'

'There was a steady advance towards our goal, and the lot of the land and rural workers has been bettered to an extent never before experienced in this country, or in most other countries of the world,' was the somewhat

---

* Government review of prices to be paid by way of subsidies for farm products.

complacent claim in the Annual Report of 1951. But the rising cost of living had negated the previous year's increase, and the Union again claimed a substantial rise, a 44-hour week with two weeks' holiday. This time the Union won the backing of the appointed members who supported a wage increase and 12 days' annual holidays. The employers remained intransigent. These proposals were submitted to 47 regional agricultural wages committees for observation, where the employers either objected outright or pushed for a 10s increase instead of 8s, and no extra holidays. When the proposals went to the AWB for ratification, the appointed members voted with the Union and won the day. The campaign for two weeks' holiday with pay was far too important a victory to be conceded for an extra 2s. This gave adult men £5 8s a week, the highest minimum wage they had ever reached.

However, the farmers' revenge was swift on workers who 'lived in'. They moved that board and lodging rates be increased to £2 a week. Rates were raised to 38s for men, up 8s, thus cancelling out that year's increase; women's rates went up to 34s, a rise of 7s, more than their 6s rise. The farmers based their claims on the rising cost of living, something they denied happened when the workers based pay claims on rising living costs.

With a frankness missing when employers opposed pay claims in other industries, the *Farmers Weekly* of 20 April 1951 said (in anticipation of another pay claim) that while the Union's arguments for an increase could be readily understood, rearmament must be paid for and our standard of living must inevitably suffer.

Alfred Robens, Minister of Labour, stated that it was inevitable that wages would rise to meet the increased cost of living, and he did not believe that the defence programme should involve a reduction in the farmworkers' standard of living, but it could mean a reduction for the community as a whole.

Many younger farmworkers continued to leave for better wages elsewhere. In the industry, the prospects were not always tempting, especially the adverts in the *Landworker* for work in one of the last of Britain's colonies. Shepherds were required for the Falklands. Five-year agreements were offered, free passage, living quarters and other perks. Minimum wage £15 per month.

Farmers again in 1952 attempted to destroy the two weeks' holiday. During wage negotiations they 'offered' a 7s increase (2s up on their original offer) if the workers would forego the extra week's holiday. This was the first time in the history of the AWB that employers had offered an increase. These moves were defeated by the Union and appointed members. However, the appointed members would not support wage increases higher than those proposed by the farmers of 5s, and the Union campaigned for more without avail.

After this miserly offer, the EC was embarrassed by a large number of branch resolutions demanding rejection and a recall conference. This surge of support for better wages was not entirely welcome to the EC, for in a circular they had sent out voicing their 'grave concern' at the outcome of the wage negotiations, they had failed to disclose that they had instructed their negotiators 'to take the necessary steps to ensure that the 5s increase was not lost'. This was really a grudging acceptance of the award, but there was confusion among the rank and file, as many of them interpreted the circular as an invitation by the EC to continue opposition to the award. The EC were liable to have their bluff called. A walk-out at the AWB threatened the continued existence of statutory wage negotiations, while a recalled conference could have led to a strike which a majority of the EC believed would be a disastrous failure.[7] They immediately disowned the idea of a one-day strike, and the offending county committee which had informed the press of their call, was told that the General Secretary's consent in writing must be obtained before any local decisions could be circulated and made public.[8] It also decided not to recall conference.

The EC had undoubtedly moved a long way from Joseph Arch's strong belief that members had a vital and active role to play in union activities, especially wage bargaining. After some hesitation, it did not mind members being exhorted to attend wage rallies and protest meetings, and write letters to the AWB, but it never wanted them to seriously consider industrial action.

As Colin Hands, the retired DO for part of Yorkshire, said, in a letter to the *Landworker* in June 1980, 'During the late 30s and 40s, an essentially defeatist attitude developed in the minds of the leadership of the NUAW. These men had lived through the disastrous years for trade unionism between 1926 and 1939 and, not surprisingly, they acted with great caution on the question of involving the membership in any industrial action. The introduction of a national Wages Board shortly after the war, whilst restricting the NFU's mean-minded ways to a certain extent, also provided the NUAW leadership with a second "Aunt Sally", for now they could blame farmers and "the Board" for their inability to mount a successful wages campaign.'

A report of the AWB negotiations to the August EC referred to a request to adjourn the proceedings. This would have delayed the operation of the new wages order, but the negotiators, as instructed, took steps to ensure that the 5s rise was not lost. The cause of an initial hesitation was that 11 districts and 600 branch protests were received by the AWB. The negotiators took the view that this was a poor demonstration of dissatisfaction and the EC endorsed their views.[9] Admittedly the number of resolutions did not match the 1,454 received by the first Wages Board on 20 February 1920, but they could hardly be seen as a 'poor response'. More likely the EC ignored them because its acceptance of the AWB machinery, and therefore its decisions, was the only policy open to the Union.[10]

The unsatisfactory outcome of the wage claim was doubly hard because farmworkers were again living under Tory rule, and the slashing of food subsidies cut into their living standard. The Isle of Ely and Cambridgeshire annual Conference wanted a minimum of £7 for a 44-hour week, and the *Daily Express*, owned by the maverick Tory peer, Lord Beaverbrook, who had farming interests, attacked the NFU saying that the farmworkers' problem was how to keep a family on £5 8s a week. 'The nation's sympathy is with him in his demand for a higher wage. With him also should be the sympathy of the EC of the NFU. That body spends much time and money in trying to get publicity for itself. It would fare better in public esteem if it spent an equal amount of time trying to secure a decent living wage for the men who work on Britain's farms.' Advice that was completely ignored.

Warwickshire Conference was among those asking for an increase and the Biennial at Skegness was unanimous that the minimum should not be less than the average for industrial workers. Some wanted £8, but it was agreed that the target should be £7 for 44 hours.

In the House of Commons on 11 June 1951, Stanley Evans, Labour, gave farmworkers a blow in the face. He said, 'The agricultural workers asked for £7 a week. My platelayers [he was sponsored by the NUR] paying 23s 6d a week for a house, with no garden, no fowl, no pig at the bottom, no free milk and no perquisites, have a basic wage of £5 10s, living in an urban area.' This attack was totally out of keeping with the traditional support the NUR had given farmworkers in their earlier struggles.

Alfred Dann wrote to Evans telling him his statements were not correct. The minimum wage of platelayers in the provinces was £5 10s for the first year, £5 12s 6d the second and £5 14s 6d the third, for a 44-hour week. The farmworkers' minimum was £5 8s for a 47-hour week. And most did not receive the perks as alleged.

It is doubtful if the post-war railwayman ever had to put up with conditions inflicted on farmworkers. A letter in the *Sunday Pictorial* read, 'Recently, I picked peas in a heat wave for a farmer. He sent along a lorry and sold water to his pickers at a penny a cup.' In West Hartlepool, a farmer charged with exceeding the speed limit explained to the magistrates that he was hurrying to his farm, where he was employing a squad of potato pickers at £1 a day. When the boss was away, he said, they could not be trusted to work. He was fined £3, a sum, no doubt, easily made off his picking squad.

A £7 minimum and double time on the short day, Sundays and Bank Holidays was the demand of 200 delegates at the Nottinghamshire and Derbyshire Conference. 'Let us get up off our bended knees,' said Jim Fletcher from the mining town of Blidworth, where nearly every house had TV. 'I feel like the colliers' poor relation. If I want to see TV I have to walk 1½ miles to my pal who works down the pit.' Walter Crafts, a cowman said, 'When I come to meetings like this, I have to pay a man to do my job, and pay him twice as much as I draw to do it.' Essex also called for a £7 minimum, as did many Kent branches.

That feelings were running high in 1953, plus good organisation, was evident when Harold Collison addressed a wage rally in Dorchester. The Corn Exchange, seating 350, was packed; about 200 more accommodated in the Town Hall, also packed. 'One of the best Union gatherings I have ever attended,' said Harold. Arthur Jordan, DO, said the meetings proved that the wages claim had the backing of the workers and was not 'inspired by Union agitators'. Harold took back to head office a resolution urging an increase in wages, and a petition bearing 2,000 signatures seeking a minimum of £7. These were presented to the AWB which proposed that the minimum should be £6 – a rise of 7s for men and proportional increases for women. Harold considered it a step in the right direction and was, as so often, 'gratified'.

That farmers could have afforded more was shown by an NFU analysis of farming profits for 1951–2, based on returns of 5,000 farms in England and Wales – profits rose by 17%.

Foreign Workers Help Keep Pay Low

In the aftermath of the Second World War, the Labour Government attempted to resolve severe labour shortages by using prisoners-of-war, displaced persons from Eastern Europe and short-term contract labourers from Europe, known as European Volunteer Workers (EVWs). Their presence reduced pressure for wage increases in sectors experiencing a labour shortage. Whilst the TUC accepted foreign labour, it was never enthusiastic.

Their work here led to dissension in the trade union movement, not least in the NUAW; as part of its campaign against the depressing effect they had on pay rates, the NUAW opposed the prisoners' own low rate, and this was raised to the agricultural minimum.

The first use of foreign labour had begun much earlier, when in July 1941, 2,400 prisoners were set to work in gangs employed by the War Agricultural Executive Committees (WAECs). When in 1942 large numbers of Italians were captured in Libya, some 20,000 were allocated to farms here. By June 1944, their numbers had risen to over 50,000.

In 1946, the Cabinet Manpower Committee put the labour deficit at about 600,000, which would be increased by the raising of the school-leaving age in 1947. There was a drop of 11,000 school leavers entering agriculture in 1947–8 compared with 1946–7 because of the higher leaving age.

When in 1946 many Union protest meetings were held against the AWB's refusal to order a £4 10s minimum, the use of prisoners frequently came up, and at York, Alfred Dann said the Union would support any members victimised because of refusing to billet prisoners. At Worcester, Harold Collison said that 'cases had arisen where British workers had been dismissed in favour of prisoners.'

In several areas WAECs were allowing prisoners to do farm work while skilled farmworkers were unemployed. 'In some areas this vast slave army is making it extremely difficult to negotiate reasonable piece-work rates, and the feeling is growing that this reservoir of foreign labour is being utilised by the employers against any move for better conditions.'[11]

The EC was facing a situation it had not foreseen; it had expected a labour shortage, but owing to the prisoners, the WLA and the voluntary efforts of schoolchildren, students and holiday makers, this had not happened. If these workers were removed (they represented about 25% of the labour force) the resulting labour shortage would force farmers to pay better wages.

In Holland, Lincs, employers refused to negotiate piece-rate increases and it was felt their attitude was largely because of prisoner labour. A Union conference at Spalding decided that 'the employment of German prisoners is not conducive to the maximum production of agricultural produce.' It asked for their withdrawal, and got EC support.

When, in 1946, the Ministry of Food suggested using Poles to supplement German prisoners in sugar beet factories, it was opposed by the EC because there was sufficient British labour available. The Union dealt with more than 100 cases of farmworkers, dismissed from jobs to make room for prisoners.

Once more, the loyalty of the NUAW leadership to the Labour Government was to give rise to problems within the Union. For the first time in 41 years, the Union held a recalled Biennial in London in October 1947, mainly to discuss ways of helping to deal with the post-war economic crisis facing the Labour Government.

The Union had been mandated by the 1946 Conference to remove all foreign workers, and decided to have the recalled Biennial addressed by Tom Williams, Minister of Agriculture, 'since his demands were contrary to Conference decision.'[12] The EC complained that the Minister was more interested in supporting farmers' earnings than the workers. They were hoping the Conference would cause the Minister discomfort.

It didn't. Williams adroitly side-stepped the tied cottage issue by referring critics to the Minister of Health. He hardly touched upon wages, and Conference agreed to halt the campaign for a 44-hour week and higher wages 'until after the crisis'. Williams' success left the EC temporarily without a wages policy.[13] With wage restraint over the next few years, it was some time before it could put together a convincing policy, convincing that is, to those outside the industry.

At the recalled Biennial, Edwin Gooch had to admit that the prisoners issue was 'another thorny subject'. He said the Union had been trying to build up the British labour force and were concerned with protecting the interests of their own people. C. H. Chandler hoped that a resolution demanding that every German prisoner would go home by the end of 1948, would have some effect.

L. Lewis, Hants, said that farmworkers were being stood off, and 'it was a very funny thing that an amazing number of secretaries of our branches are being stood off...' Tom Gasgoyne, Yorks, said that the bulwark of capitalism had been a reserve of labour. 'That is what is being provided... by the Labour Government... they are very susceptible to petty bribes to do the job under the rate. We know it has happened as far as prisoner labour is concerned, a few cigarettes and a lighter here and there.'

Edwin then successfully proposed, 'Whilst being opposed to foreign labour, this Conference instructs the EC, while foreign labour remains, to continue to take steps to protect in every way the interests of the British worker.'

During 1947 there were more than 100,000 prisoners working in agriculture in England and Wales, a seventh of the total number of British workers. Unemployment was increasing in rural districts, and late in 1947, the Suffolk secretary of the NFU was credited with saying that many of the men sacked from farms were 'rural drones who refuse to do an honest day's work.' Edwin Gooch was quick to warn, 'If they think they can sack British workers because they have foreign workers they are making a mistake.'

In November 1947, after discussions with the NFU, the Minister of Labour estimated that 85,000 more regular workers would be needed in England and Wales by mid-Summer 1948. It was expected that 43,000 would be provided by EVWs, men from the Polish Resettlement Corps and German prisoners who had elected to remain as civilians. An extra 42,000 British workers would be required.

The prisoner controversy continued, but the problem finally resolved itself as the German and Italian prisoners were repatriated; it was mainly the Poles who remained, many of whom soon went into more remunerative jobs. Some 23,000 German prisoners remained here at their own request, and the few that stayed on the land joined the Union.

The main concern of the Union then became the EVW scheme from 1946 to 1951, which at the end of one recruitment drive brought 83,000 workers here, mostly from Eastern Europe: 65,409 men and 17,422 women. Over 70% of the men went into agriculture and coal-mining, and 95% of women into textiles and domestic work. Under the scheme these workers were compelled to 'sell' their labour to certain employers, which considerably limited their power to improve their own wages and consequently helped to keep the wages of others low. 'The EVW scheme illustrates the way in which the State can restructure the scope of the labour market in the interests of employers experiencing labour shortages,' declared Dianna Kay and Robert Miles of the Department of Sociology, University of Glasgow.[14]

EVWs were, in the early fifties, released from employment restrictions. Most left the land, and that particular problem for the Union was resolved.

Partners, Or Just Low-Paid Workers

At the Christmas Dinner at King's Lynn in 1954, Harold Collison said, 'We do consider ourselves partners in this great industry and are concerned just as much as the farmer to see that agriculture in this country is efficient.' Harold didn't seem to realise that the farmer did not consider the farmworker a partner at all, but an employee, and was only interested in agriculture being profitable; if this meant making it efficient too, that was fine, but efficiency was not the only way to profit.

It is somewhat surprising that Harold still advanced the 'partnership' theory, because in 1955, John Hughes, a tutor at Sheffield University made a revealing study of farmworkers' wages. He found that virtually every other occupation offered better wages than an industry in which the State 'lavishes so much money on the farmer that it nearly compensates him for his entire wages bill.'

In 1955, agricultural subsidies were estimated at £240 million. Total wages paid were £280–90 million. This meant that farmers were only having to provide out of their own pockets less than a fifth of current wages. Declared Hughes, 'The farmworker does not need telling that Government support is necessary to maintain a flourishing agriculture, but he ought to have no illusion as to how little he shares in agricultural prosperity. Agriculture is not depressed, but the conditions of farmworkers are.'[15]

Purchasing Power of Farmworkers' Minimum Wage Rates, 1947–1955
(September 1947 = 100) Male Adult Farmworkers, England and Wales

Date of increases	Money wage rate after increase	Cost of living	Purchasing power of wage rate	
			Before increase	After increase
September, 1947	100	100	90	100
March, 1949	104	108	93	97
November, 1950	111	115	91	97
October, 1951	120	128	87	94
August, 1952	126	136	88	92.5
August, 1953	133	139	90	96
January, 1955	141	144	92	98
In June, 1955	—	150	94	—

Note: In March, 1949, the standard working week was reduced to 47 hours from 48. The figures have not been adjusted for this, which is equivalent to a 2% increase in wage rates.

Measuring wages by what they would buy, Hughes produced this table of the purchasing power of farmworkers' minimum rates from 1947 to 1955 which showed that after increases, taking 1 September 1947 as 100, declined to 98 in 1955, having fallen to 92.5 in August 1952. The cost of living had risen from 100 in September 1947 to 144 in January 1955. This meant that farmworkers had never recovered the purchasing power of their rate in September 1947, and were by 1955 some 6% below it. Some partners!

An interesting lesson was that this decline in real wages was during 'wage restraint', which was set out to be advantageous to the farmworker. When it came to comparing figures for productivity, the contrast was startling. Until 1953 there was a stagnation in real earnings, while output per man rose very rapidly – an increase of one-third in six years. By comparison, industrial production rose by only 24% in the period 1947–53.

So while many industrial and political leaders were suggesting that increased productivity was the only way to increased wages, it certainly did not happen for the farmworker. Hughes also produced tables showing that the wage cost to the farmer per unit of output had fallen considerably. By 1953–4 it was only about four-fifths of 1947.

Hughes noted that it was sometimes argued that high incomes were necessary for farmers so that they could improve their capital equipment. But *The Economist* revealed that the net investment (increase in capital after allowing for depreciation) in British agriculture had declined; using 1948 prices, from £26 million in 1948 to only £8 million by 1951. Increased incomes had not been ploughed back into equipment.

Mr. Hughes did a thorough job by comparing the hourly earnings of farmworkers with people in other industries.

Agricultural Workers' Earnings Compared with Other Workers

All figures refer to male adults. (Farmworkers' earnings as 100)

Industry	Period to which data refers[1]	1953			1954		
		Average weekly earnings	Average hours worked	Average hourly earnings	Average weekly earnings	Average hours worked	Average hourly earnings
Agriculture[2]	Apr. to Mar.	100	51.4	100	100	52.1	100
ALL MANUFACTURING INDUSTRY of which:	Apr./Oct./Apr.	139	47.9	149	142	48.4	153
Metal Manufacturing	—	149	47.6	160	153	48.4	165
Engineering	—	149	47.6	160	145	49.1	154
Vehicles	—	148	47.3	160	152	47.8	166
Building and Contracting	—	132	48.7	139	134	49.3	142
Transport and Communication (excluding Railways)	—	124	49.7	128	128	50.7	132
British Railways	Mar./Mar.	127			Not available		
Coal Mining[2]	May/Oct./Apr.	176	37.4[3]	242	183	37.73	250
Dock Labour	Oct. to Dec.	151			155		

1. The dates chosen in each case have been adopted to fit as closely as possible the annual period over which farmworkers' wages are calculated, e.g. for 'all manufacturing' an average of the earnings reported in April 1954, October 1954 and April 1955, is compared with the average earnings of the period April 1954 to March 1955 for farmworkers.
2. Including allowances in kind in earnings figures.
3. Hours of work in mining are estimated from the 1954 NCB Report by taking eight hours as the time of the average shift.

Source: *Ministry of Labour Gazette*, and Ministry of Agriculture Reports on the Economic Situation in Agriculture

This table shows without any doubt how far the earnings lagged behind. Farmworkers' hourly earnings would have to increase by nearly a third to catch up with transport workers, by over 40% to match building workers, and by just over half as much again to catch up with the average worker in factories.

Between 1947 and 1954, the average weekly earnings in all industries covered by Ministry of Labour surveys rose by 60%, while those of farmworkers by only 49%. All the allegedly good intent of improving the wages of the lower paid was definitely not working. There was a distinct widening of the gap between the earnings of farmworkers and people in other industries. The purchasing power of the farmworkers' £6 7s a week in November 1955 was less than his wage of £4 10s in 1947.

Mr. Hughes concluded that it was no use farmers arguing that if forced to pay higher wages it would lead them to mechanise and reduce their labour needs, they were already doing that as a consequence of very low wages and the shortage of farmworkers.

Early in 1954, local Union conferences had been passing resolutions on wages, and they all had the same tone – that despite the increase to £6 the previous August, the minimum did not provide a decent standard of living. At that year's Biennial at Cheltenham, time and again speakers emphasised that low wages were forcing men to leave the land and seek better living elsewhere.

The 1954 Biennial rejected any idea of strike action. J. J. Waterman, Dorset, moved a composite for a substantial increase, and affirming that nothing less than £5 would be 'satisfactory'. Seconding, Gordon Dales, Lincs, said he knew men in his area getting up to 8d an hour more than farmworkers. An amended composite, making it clear that £7 was wanted, was carried.

On 14 June the AWB turned down the claim. Union members immediately reacted with annoyance and disgust, as letters pouring into the head office made clear. Reports showed that many believed action spoke louder than words. Six men left one farm to work in a factory ten miles distant when the Board's decision was announced, with considerably fatter wage packets.

Following reports that farmers were thinking of applying for troops to get in the harvest, the EC decided this quite unwarranted. The NUAW in no way wished to hinder harvesting and suggested the temporary release of national servicemen: this was done, and the harvest gathered.

To emphasise the injustice of low wages, county committees organised demonstrations; Dorset distributed 5,000 leaflets advertising protest meetings; Lincolnshire had a petition; while Worcestershire and Shropshire lobbied their MPs. Protest meetings were held up and down the country and Yorkshire had a big meeting at Scarborough on the eve of the Labour Conference.

All these activities culminated in a national demonstration in London. Over 700 members went to the capital to support the £7 claim, many lobbied their MPs and attended a meeting in Hyde Park, addressed by Edwin Gooch. They went by coach, car and train, a few by taxi. Women headed the parade through the streets carrying placards declaring: 'Our members grow the nation a square meal – help them to get a square deal'. The parade was well received by onlookers. One office worker presented EC veteran Herbert Luckett with a bouquet – and a kiss.

After lobbying MPs, the protestors held a meeting and Charles Smith, General Secretary of the Post Office Engineering Union, told them, 'If I were a farmworker I should have got a little sick of fine tributes when they are substitutes for a decent standard of living. Pats on the back are very nice. Pence in the pocket are very necessary.'

Harold Collison reported to the EC that the task of the Union's AWB negotiators had not been made easier by a speech by Arthur Deakin, TGWU General Secretary, stressing the need for wage restraint. The TGWU had seconded the NUAW's wage increase motion at the AWB, and suggested that the workers' side should bypass the AWB by demanding that their claim should go before the national arbitration machinery. Harold advised against this as it would undermine the authority of the AWB and also 'because a danger existed that the wage initiative in agriculture would pass from the NUAW to the TGWU who were experienced in this type of negotiations.'16 A fresh claim for £7 was made to the AWB, and the independent members supported an increase of 7s, taking the minimum for men to £6 7s. The Union's great campaign played a big part in this change of heart.

Some farmers proved adept at getting the last penny's worth out of employees. Having worked on the same farm for 20 years, at the age of 72, Bro. H. Martin finally retired. Calling on his employer to bid him farewell, he was told to pay 1s for two pints of milk supplied on two days he was not working. The farewell was not, presumably, a fond one.

In April 1955 the Union sought a shorter working week of 44 hours (instead of 47), improved overtime rates and the adult wage at 20. They knew that the basic working week was a fundamental element in determining earning capacity. Official figures showed that for a week of 48½ hours, industrial workers earned an average of £10 4s 5d; farmworkers, for 51½ hours earned £7 6s 9d.

Meanwhile, the annual area Conference at Worcester called for £7 10s for a 44-hour week, and Warwickshire area Conference also endorsed a motion seeking £7 10s. Delegates called for 'guerrilla' strike action to support the claim.

Time and a half for all overtime and the male adult rate at 20 was the final outcome of the Union's latest claim (it was not until 1962 that women got the adult rate at 20). The claim for a 44-hour week and double time at weekends was rejected. In October the Union presented to the AWB a claim for £7 – and won an increase of 8s, making the minimum £6 15s for 47 hours.

Commenting, the *Daily Herald* declared, 'Never was a reasonable request more unreasonably refused . . .' The *Daily Express*: 'It is welcome news that farmworkers are to get a rise. But nobody could claim that it is a generous one . . . farming must be made to pay. But for its own prosperity it must be made to pay not only for the masters but for the men as well.' Even the right-wing *Daily Telegraph* noted that the full claim was 'well within the reach of what the farmers can afford . . .'

Harold Collison declared, 'The 8s will not even keep the agricultural workers' wage in step with the increase in the cost of living since we made our last claim in October 1954.'

Thus it ever was, any gain in wages had to be accompanied by a fight not to lose it through increased living costs, which had little relation to the pay increase itself.

Following this miserly increase, the Union made a further claim and launched another campaign to bring the position of farmworkers to the notice of the public. This didn't stop the vice-chairman of Monmouthshire NFU saying there was no justification for the claim, and that successful claims in the past may have gone to their heads. The Union, after claiming a 'substantial increase', finally squeezed out a rise of 6s for men, making the new minimum £7 1s.

Steps Towards a Wages Structure

At the Biennial at Great Yarmouth in May, one of the most hard-hitting debates was on a wages structure. At the previous Biennial the EC had been instructed to set up a committee to investigate the possibility of such a scheme. Their report said that 'a wages structure was both practicable and desirable.'

The idea of a wages structure had a long history, and as early as 1946, when the Union pressed its wages claim based on skilled urban workers' rates, the farmers claimed they did not mind paying for a particular merit, but the NFU was not then optimistic about creating a satisfactory wages structure. Edwin Gooch was able to tell the 1946 Biennial that 'we have always contended that a system of grading is unworkable in the present organisation of agriculture and finally the employers endorsed our views.'

In 1949, the Union attended the first meeting of the Apprenticeship Council for Agriculture, sponsored by the AWB and supported by the NFU and TGWU. In preliminary discussions the EC had refused to agree to a proposal that apprentices would receive less than the AWB rate. Nor did it agree to the suggestion of setting up the Council on the agreed principle of an apprenticeship scheme and shelving differences on details until later.

The Union's refusal held up the work of the Council until October 1949 when the NFU informed the EC that since the majority on the AWB was in favour, the Council intended to introduce apprenticeships without delay. It appealed to them to join in, and the EC wrote to the AWB saying that the scheme would fail if it was inaugurated without the willing participation of the NUAW.[17] The EC then consulted the counties and found that 33 rejected the idea outright and 28 supported it, providing there was no reduction in wages for apprentices. In view of this unanimity, the General Secretary met the TGWU, and pointed out that since there was no provision for a craftsman wage there should be no cut in earnings during training. He got agreement that the scheme be delayed until the two unions could report back. The EC decided to bring the matter before the 1950 Biennial.

After discussions on wages with two leading organisers, who felt that some form of wages structure was required if agriculture was to keep its skilled workers, the EC was asked to add to the Biennial resolutions one that would instruct the EC 'to explore a wages structure in the industry in the light of changed conditions.'[18]

How much the General Secretary had leaned on them is not known, but this was very much his point of view, and his enthusiasm for the apprenticeship scheme came from the possibility of a wages structure arising from it. He was confident that wage increases for an elite could be wrested from the AWB at a time when claims for the whole body of workers would be rejected.

The organisers' suggestion was brought before a pre-Conference meeting of the EC which decided by 10 to 1 to bring both a wages structure and apprenticeship before a private session of the Biennial. Both were thrown out by large majorities.

When the issue came before the 1952 Biennial, it received savage treatment from several delegates, and the General Secretary only rescued it from probable defeat by suggesting that it be remitted without a vote, on his promise that such a solution would in no way commit the membership. This pleased the EC for it gave them a mandate, however shaky, to explore the question further.

But the leadership's support for such a structure continued, and a meeting took place in February 1955 of a wages structure sub-committee to 'thrash out the details of a wages structure rather than to discuss the principle involved.' The EC observed that a mandate from membership would be necessary before recommendations of the sub-committee could be accepted.[19] it was attended by A. E. Monks for MAFF and T. J. Healy, national secretary of the TGWU's agricultural section. Harold Collison said that the NUAW membership were opposed to all suggestions of grading the individual workers, which left only the possibility of grading specific jobs. The meeting agreed, and resolved that plus rates should be assigned to jobs connected with beef, milk, mutton and poultry, thatching, drainage, machinery maintenance and threshing. The committee met a month later, and considered a draft scale of premiums, but rejected them because they were too low. A joint meeting of Organisers and the EC in July was told that the NFU did not favour a wages structure.

In face of this opposition, and that of their own members, the EC continued to support the principle of a wages structure. In March 1956, in readiness for the Biennial, they sent a memorandum to county committees asking for rank and file approval, claiming that rural/urban wage parity depended on acceptance of a wages structure.

At the Biennial, H. Hogg, Yorks, moved that specific proposals be placed before the AWB to provide additional payments for specified skilled jobs. Joan Maynard, Yorks, moved an amendment opposing plus rates until the basic rate was equivalent to that of industrial workers. Harold Collison said the EC urged Conference to support a wages structure, but the amendment was carried by 80 to 69.

For the tenth year, the Union in 1957 claimed a 44-hour week and once again was unsuccessful, but wages were increased by 9s. This meant the adult male minimum had gone up by a total of £3 since 1947, an average of 6s a year; for women by £2 6s, up by 4s 6d per year.

Against these miserly improvements the farmers were doing well. There was an annual increase of £46 million in farmers' net income to a record of £360 million.[20] Farmers' spendable income increased by £65.5 million to 73% above their 1947–8 level.

Sixteen 'planes, all piloted by farmers, landed in a Bedfordshire field. The pilots then went shooting and bagged 237 rooks. This report in the *Daily Express* might have convinced its readers that there was more money in farming than farmers would have them believe. Perhaps they were only small 'planes.

In 1958, the Union again claimed for the 44-hour week, which again was rejected, but wages went up by 6s. At the Biennial, delegates carried a motion moved by C. A. Wilson, Lancs, urging the EC to fight the proposed wage-freeze policy of the Government.

Again the subject of a wages structure produced the longest debate of the week. G. R. Forth, Lincs, moved that the EC get a wages structure to present to the AWB as soon as possible, while A. Baynham, Worcs, moved an amendment, that the EC draw up a draft scheme and ballot members on it. He was supported by F. Brown, E Suffolk, and F. Langford, Salop. W. Clough, Cheshire, opposed, because it would cause difficulties between members. When put to the vote 67 delegates voted for the amendment, 86 against. The resolution got a large majority.

At least some progress was made in December 1959, when the AWB reduced the working week to 46 hours. However, the wage increase was only 4s, taking the minimum to £8 for males and £6 1s 6d for women.

Progress was also made in establishing a single uniform AWB Order. Until 1959 there were 47 County Wages Orders, then they were reduced to three, one of which covered all counties in England and Wales, except Cambs, Yorks and Holland, Lincs, where special orders still applied.

There were still some differences in wages from county to county. Years of agitation had led to the 1924 Agricultural Wages Act, but even then the initiative for fixing wages was left to County Wages Committees. Not until 1940 was a national uniform minimum rate obtained, and in 1948 a uniform standard week of 48 hours fixed. The Wages Acts of 1947 and 1948 transferred to the central AWB the power to fix the national minimum.

The 1960 Biennial sought a substantial increase and a 40-hour week. There was, despite strong opposition, support for the principle of a wages structure and the EC was urged to go ahead with their proposals in this matter as 'it was the only way forward'. At last the EC had won over the majority on this issue.

The AWB finally increased the minimum by 9s a week, as from 2 January 1961, making the minimum for men over 20 £8 9s for 46 hours.

Later in 1961, new problems faced the Union on the wages front. As the EC noted, '. . . there has been the special problem of the Chancellor's Pay Pause. The farmworkers' negotiators were able to pierce the Pause, a feat for which due credit should be given; yet we fully note and join in our members' dissatisfaction at the smallness of the wage award and the total rejection of the hours claim.' The 'piercing' amounted to an increase of 6s per week.

Proposals were also submitted to the AWB for a wages structure, which listed the conventional categories, such as cowmen, tractor drivers, stockmen, poultry men, etc, together with special categories such as glasshouse workers and combine harvest drivers. Against each category there was set a percentage rate which the Union felt would be the appropriate minimum to receive above the basic rate. By making these proposals, the Union was starting something entirely new in agricultural wage negotiations.

At the Biennial in Bournemouth in 1962, Edwin Gooch told delegates, 'it is ridiculous for the industry to think that it can continue indefinitely with a working week at least four hours longer than is average in industry, and on an hourly rate more than three-quarters of the way down the list of 200 rates paid in industry as a whole.' There was a significant change in the measure finally adopted on wages. This time the claim would be for £10 a week. The formula 'substantial increase' of earlier conferences was discarded by 79 votes to 43. Big wages demonstrations occurred that Summer, and an increase of 8s was finally won, making a total weekly wage of £9 3s.

The Union's proposed wages structure was rejected by the AWB, but it was agreed to draft a questionnaire to NFU branches and farmers, to ascertain the existing voluntary structure arrangements, and to see if there were any common factors in the payment of premiums. On some 7,500 farms it was 'discovered' that the reason for paying premiums was 'skill and ability of the worker'.

In February 1963 the AWB rejected the claim for a 40-hour week, but in May it was reduced by one hour to 45 hours, for a wage of £9 10s.

At the Biennial at Felixstowe in 1964, motions for a £12 claim and a 40-hour week were carried. A motion for a wages structure was unanimously adopted. In the Autumn the AWB granted a 12s increase, bringing the minimum up to £10 2s. It was the biggest single improvement since the war.

In 1965 farm wages were increased by 8s a week, and the working week reduced from 45 to 44 hours. Whilst falling short of the Union's attempt to secure parity with industrial workers, 'it was the best dual hours and wages agreement ever.'[21]

Yet workers were leaving the land in ever increasing numbers. Between June 1964 and June 1965 over 25,000 left, a bigger annual scuttle than any since 1961, when 27,000 left.

Dissension Over Pay

One issue dominated the TUC Conference at Brighton in 1965; the Labour Government's new proposals for legislation to underpin the Prices and Incomes policy. They were to cause widespread dissension in the labour and trade union movement in the years ahead.

Among the proposals was that manufacturers should notify intended price increases and the unions notify wage claims and, where necessary, these increases and claims should be referred to the Prices and Incomes Board (PIB) for investigation and comments. Any increases should be deferred until the Board had made its comments. There was no suggestion of statutory interference in price fixing or wage bargaining, once the Board had commented.

The General Council, anxious that this voluntary system should work, wanted unions to notify the TUC of impending claims. During the debate there were those who insisted that the only job of a union was to get the maximum it could for its members and who rejected the Government's incomes and prices policy; others supported the General Council's recommendation to back the proposals.

Finally, a motion rejecting an incomes policy was defeated. A motion of support, asking for special measures to identify increased prices, rent and charges, was carried. The NUAAW delegates voted for the motion supporting Government policy.

At the Union's Diamond Biennial at Weston-Super-Mare in 1966, there was a strongly-backed call from W. Dawes, Norfolk, for an immediate increase in wages, together with a national demonstration in London to secure a 'just claim' for £14 per week. The EC thought the time ripe for a campaign and told delegates that £14 was 'reasonable'.

On the need for the early introduction of a statutory wages structure, Conference was emphatic, and carried a motion calling for the EC to intensify their efforts to secure such a scheme without further delay.

'Grade the job not the worker,' urged W. Linwood, Yorks. J. Rayner, W Suffolk, said he came from a county where members had previously turned down the idea. They did not understand it. 'Today we do,' he said, urging delegates to pass it 'with all their strength'. Harold Collison said the NFU also believed in it, but they would require time to persuade their members of its necessity.

It should be said here that perhaps many farmers had a genuine suspicion of the paper qualifications that such a structure would imply, coupled with their reluctance to pay more. Farmers, as a body, had up to the early post-war years not been conspicuous by their education, many leaving school at 15 or 16. Also the majority acquired their farms by accident of birth, and had little formal training for the job. Their task was that of management, which did not necessarily mean knowing how to do an actual job.

At their meeting in July 1966, the EC expressed 'grave concern' about the likely effects of a proposed Government wage freeze on lower-paid workers and decided to notify the AWB of the intention to claim a 'substantial increase'. But a motion declaring 'its opposition to the Government's panic measures in relation to a wage freeze announced in the House on 20 July' and which 'does not believe that the legislation proposed in the Prime Minister's statement is anything but the destruction of collective bargaining' was lost by the Chairman's (Bert Hazell) casting vote, i.e. 6 votes to 7. This was surely against Union policy as agreed at the 1964 Biennial to oppose a wage freeze, as long as farmworkers remained below the average industrial wage. The EC was trying to have it both ways, and decided to go ahead with its pay claim, as they were among the lower-paid workers. The Union went to the AWB for a substantial increase.

There was a batch of letters in the *Landworker* critical of the Government. In October, B. Waind, Northallerton, Yorks, wondered, 'how long we are going to sit down and allow the so-called Labour Government to interfere with Union privileges,' while P. Norman, Hurstpierpoint, Sussex, was struck by the 'flowery' messages of support for agricultural workers from top Labour ministers and the realities of the treatment they received, and wondered whether the time had come for the NUAW to discontinue support for the Labour Party.

At that year's Labour Conference resolutions opposing the standstill were not supported by NUAW delegates and were lost. Meanwhile, negotiations with the AWB proceeded at their leisurely pace, and on 30 November the Board proposed an increase of 6s, bringing the rate up to £10 16s from 6 February 1967. Harold Collison said, 'we feel sure this very modest proposal comes within the criteria set out in the White Paper on wages during the period of severe restraint.'[22]

Harold's beliefs were due to be shattered. The Government referred the increase to the PIB and an angry EC issued a statement saying that they were appalled, and in view of the fact that farm earnings were lower than those of other workers, there could be 'no justification for the Government taking this step'.

When the AWB met on 11 January, it unanimously confirmed the 6s increase – no doubt the farmers thought they were getting away with it exceedingly lightly.

The Union gave oral evidence to the PIB, whose Report in February turned out to be a favourable endorsement of their claim, but that there was an urgent need for a farm wages structure and other improvements.[23]

That latest increase meant that over 10 years the male basic rate had gone up by a total of £3, and women's by £2 3s 6d, while the working week had come down from 47 hours to 44 hours. It left a large part of the membership dissatisfied at such slow progress in obtaining equality with industrial workers, who averaged over £20 a week.

Early in 1967 the workers' side of the AWB gave notice that they would be submitting a claim for £14; the EC had earlier advised the TUC of its intentions. The TUC Wages Policy Committee decided that it was 'not incompatible with the incomes policy'.

The Union launched another big campaign in support of the claim, with meetings throughout the country culminating in a well-publicised rally in London.

At that year's TUC there was more criticism of Government policy; a motion was adopted that a voluntary incomes policy should be conducted against a background of vigorous Government price control, and that there should be a £15 national minimum wage. The NUAW, surprisingly in view of its earlier experience, opposed a composite stating that 'the Prices and Incomes Acts had been detrimental to the best interests of trade unionists and call for their repeal.' A wage increase of 15s was finally won in 1967, postponed until February 1968.

Prime Minister Harold Wilson spoke at an eve-of-Conference rally at Aberystwyth Biennial in 1968, and said that it was more important than ever that there should be an effective prices and incomes policy. He fully understood that farmworkers did not think that the last 15s increase was enough, but 'it was a useful' improvement. Bert Hazell said it would be possible to raise earnings to a satisfactory level when a properly negotiated farm wage structure came into being.

The Conference called for a new target of £16 for a 40-hour week. The claim was passed by the TUC's wage vetting committee and submitted to the AWB. The employers proposed an increase of 17s, and this was adopted by the AWB in November.

As in 1966, the Labour Government intervened – the 17s increase represented a 7.3% increase, more than double that desired by the Government. It proposed that 7s of the 17s should be frozen and referred the increase to the PIB; annoyance was widespread in the Union. But there was relief when the PIB's Report in January 1969 confirming all the Union had said on wages, stated that the 17s was outside the terms of the White Paper on incomes, and suggested that the award should be a special exception. No further Government intervention was made.

At the Biennial, Wilf Page, Norfolk, moved that the EC withdraw its support for the 'Prices and Incomes Policy' as it had meant a cut in real wages for members. Harold Collison, opposing for the EC, said that in a wages free-for-all the more powerful unions had 'substantial advantages not available to workers' organisations without that power'. The motion was carried by 64 votes to 54.

A letter in the June 1968 *Landworker* began, 'We the undersigned members of the Hurstpierpoint branch were disgusted to hear that the Prime Minister had been invited to address the Biennial . . . As to why this arch enemy of the trade union movement should have been invited is beyond our comprehension. As an alternative to hobnobbing with discredited and devious politicians the leaders of the NUAW would be serving the interests of the members to better advantage in condemning the present Government's intended unjust and malicious legislation against British trade unionism.' It was signed: F. Head, G. Blake, B. Norman, A. Weatherhead. Tagged on was the Editor's comment: 'With all due respect to the writers, this letter seems to me to be largely abusive and entirely negative. Worse, it is downright rude to a recent distinguished guest of the Union.'

The writers were attacking the Government's Prices and Incomes policy, and the August *Landworker* letters included one from J. Gunston, King's Lynn, who denied that they were rude or abusive. He continued, 'Harold Wilson is undoubtedly the worst Prime Minister Britain has ever had. The workers have never been so wrongly treated. They are worse off now than when Wilson took over No 10 . . . rewards go to those who can grab them . . .'

Alan Piper, Staplehurst, Kent, recalled that Wilson told delegates that the farmworker had doubled his output. 'We were rewarded with a miserable 15s.' Paddy Smithe, Foxton, Herts, failed to see the justice of the Editor's comments, adding, 'A man definitely should not be classed as rude or abusive via offensive remarks in your periodical,' and declared that Wilson and his Government were champions at sitting on the working class and breaking promises. Frank Goodright, St. Leonards, Sussex, considered the Editor's comments 'fair and justified . . . I am not starry-eyed about the present Government, but . . . they are doing their best in a difficult situation.' Bill Moore, Worthing, Sussex, recalled that at a recent meeting of Brighton District Committee, Hurstpierpoint moved that the Union disaffiliated from the Labour Party. Only two voted for this resolution. R. Beddoe, Bramfield, Herts, thought the Labour Party 'has clearly forfeited the right to the support of the lower-paid workers.' Bob Tullett, St. Albans, thought the Union had been let down by the Government but Henry Toch, Stamford, claimed real advances in the welfare of farmworkers since the Government took office.

These letters no doubt expressed the bewilderment, contempt, mixed with long standing loyalty to Labour, that the Government's policies were causing amongst Union members. And at the Labour Conference there was a massive defeat for the Government when a composite moved by the TGWU seeking an end to incomes restraint was carried by 3,974,000 votes – those of the NUAAW being among them.

NFU Accepts Wages Structure

At the end of May 1968, the NFU publicly announced their proposals for a statutory wages structure. Harold Collison pointed out that negotiations were still going on, and that outright agreement so far was mainly confined to the acceptance of the principle of a wages structure.

There was a wide divergence between the farmers' approach and that of the workers' side: the workers favouring the rate for the job whilst the farmers canvassed the rate for the man idea. The NFU proposal was that all regular full-time workers not qualifying for one of the premium rates would not get a premium. For craftsmen they proposed: (i) regular full-time workers aged 23 and over who had completed three years in the industry and who were qualified by passing various tests should get a 10% premium; (ii) regulars who had completed a 3-year apprenticeship, 10%; Grade II regulars who had responsibility for a herd or for arable or horticultural operations, 20%; Grade I regulars with complete responsibility for a herd or for arable or horticultural operations or a farm enterprise, 30%.

Harold Collison said that at first sight the NFU's emphasis on age limit and proved qualifications appeared to differ widely from the Union's approach. But the Union would be unrealistic if some form of qualification was not accepted.

In 1970 Labour lost the General Election, but one thing not affected was the agreement announced on 21 May by the AWB on a statutory wages structure. This historic decision came after nine years of intense and often bitter discussions. It came into effect on 29 May 1972.

'This agreement while falling short of our real aspirations does, however, represent real progress in that for the first time in the long history of agricultural wage fixing, skill and responsibility are to be recognised and the appropriate plus-rates enforceable under WB Orders,' declared the Union.[24]

After Union pressure it was agreed that the County Wages Committees should act as conciliators between workers and employers who refused to issue a 'Declaration of Competency'. Proposed rates for 'plus' workers on a national minimum of £16 were:

	Men	Women
Craftsmen	£17.82	£14.26
Grade I	£19.44	£15.55
Grade II	£21.06	£16.85

Some Union members thought that the wages structure did in fact grade the man and not the job. 'By attaching the new grades to the simultaneously introduced New Entrance/Training Scheme or, for existing workers, an employer's declaration of competence . . . it was clear that the man rather than the job was being graded.'[25] However, the Union had succeeded in broadening the scope of the craftsman's grade sufficiently to include the majority of workers, thus obtaining in effect a rise in the statutory minimum.

After some years' experience of the workings of the wages structure, Barry Leathwood, Trade Group Secretary, said in 1990, 'Most members think it has generally worked satisfactorily. But not so well in the appointment grades. The craft grades have been the most advantageous to members.'

*   *   *

That the wages structure did not operate smoothly at first was plain to many people involved at the time. Ken Tullett recalled his attempts to get a Craft Certificate by taking a 'test'. On the appointed day he was sent hand-weeding alone into a field. 'The idea being, I suppose, to convey the impression that I was not even competent to use a hoe. They asked me what I did when I wasn't hand-weeding and spoke separately to the acting manager, the late employer's son. He took the line "he is not a craftsmen, none of my men are craftsmen. If I give it to him they will all want it".' After a battle Ken got his Craft Certificate.

Some might not have been so persistent as Ken, a persuasive speaker at biennials and a student of philosophy, who joined the Union for the most unusual of reasons. In 1972 Ken was doing A-Level Economics at an evening institute, and a question was asked about Joseph Arch. 'I didn't know a thing about Arch,' Ken told me in 1984, 'so I answered another question about the steel industry. But I was an agricultural worker, and I felt so bad about it that I read up Arch after the exam, got interested in the Union and joined.' Later he became secretary of Swanland branch, then chairman of Hull Divisional Committee.

Ken, who is a good example of one 'willing to have a go', didn't find it easy to join. 'It was a job discovering who was in the Union and who was secretary, but I eventually did and I was reluctantly signed up, provided I paid three months in advance.' This he did, but found there were no branch meetings 'because nobody would attend'. However, Ken booked a hall and 20 to 30 came. 'We signed a lot of them up and within a few months we had nearly 40 members.'

When I met him the membership was down to 25, reduced by the nation-wide fall in membership which, Ken said, the Union had struggled bravely and tenaciously against, although he believed some of the top figures in the Union had earlier resigned from office because they saw its collapse coming.

'In Place of Strife' Causes Turmoil

The Royal Commission on Trade Unions' and Employers' Associations set up by the Labour Government in 1965 under Lord Donovan* (Harold Collision was a member) reported in June 1968. It said that agriculture was a relatively well-organised industry with exceptional circumstances, with wage fixing bodies, including 57 wages councils, covering nearly four million workers.

Wages boards were necessary, was its verdict, because employment in agriculture was spread over a large number of scattered units. Statutory regulation was needed to secure adequate enforcement. Although the Commission recommended that wages councils could be abolished if a union wished, it pointedly refrained from making any such recommendation so far as AWBs were concerned. However, it wanted wages boards to be equipped to handle grievances not covered by wage regulations. The report rejected legal sanctions for stopping strikes, a recommendation which gave no joy to the Tories, or for that matter to Barbara Castle and Harold Wilson, who thought Donovan's remedies inadequate. Mrs. Castle wanted penal sanctions to curb unofficial strikes.

At that year's TUC Congress the debate on the prices and incomes policy was very lively, and by a massive majority of 6,724,000 votes, that included the Union's 115,000, Congress sought repeal of the incomes legislation. A

---

* Donovan, an Appeal Court Judge, formerly a Labour MP.

measure supporting that part of the policy which aimed to provide all employees with a share of the savings from increased productivity was supported by the Union and carried.

Hard on the heels of the Government's attempt to stop farmworkers getting the 17s pay award, Barbara Castle, Minister of Employment, unveiled *In Place of Strife*, a White Paper on industrial relations. Its proposals included tighter legislation on trade unions, including a 27-day conciliation period in certain cases with financial penalties for contraventions, and a ballot of members imposed when a strike was threatened.

Whatever its intention, the document certainly produced a great deal of strife in the Labour movement. At a special TUC conference a resolution affirming that the movement was completely opposed to the proposal for statutory financial penalties on workers or trade unions in industrial dispute was passed by 8,252,000 votes to 359,000.

The left of the Labour and trade union movement opposed *In Place of Strife*, and Wilson and Castle had to capitulate, with the TUC in June 1969 providing a face-saving formula of their own guidelines for strikes – but these were not legally binding. *In Place of Strife* became the forerunner of Edward Heath's Industrial Relations Act of 1971.

At their June meeting, the EC authorised a claim for £16 for a 40-hour week, and that year's TUC at Portsmouth passed a GMWU/NUAAW composite seeking a national minimum of £15 for a 40-hour week.

More than 2,000 members went to London to take part in the biggest demonstration by farmworkers in the capital since the war. There was a splendid array of Union banners and posters making the main points of the wage claim. Heading the procession, as it left the Embankment for Westminster, was the Manchester Post Office Engineering Workers' Union band, playing a lively tune. Earlier, some 50 coaches filled with enthusiastic members from all parts of the country had reached London; they came from more than 20 counties, Norfolk sending the largest number – eight.

Leading the singing, cheering procession were NUAAW members on the AWB, and Bert Hazell, Harold Collison, Frank Robinson and Reg Bottini. Most of the EC were in the procession, which stretched a quarter of a mile and took 15 minutes to pass the Houses of Parliament, then to Trafalgar Square, where the rally took place. Cyril Plant (Inland Revenue Staff) paid tribute to the high technological development of British agriculture, which had no need to pay such poor wages. Harold Collison said that the annual earnings of the adult male industrial worker were £22 8s 3d, against the farmworkers' £15 16s.

The motion, unanimously adopted, was moved by Herbie Pitman, Dorset, seconded by Ron Jones, Essex. The procession reformed and went to the Ministry of Agriculture where the resolution was handed in by the mover and seconder, together with D. Chapman, Devon, A. Broughton, Lincs, A. Butler, Yorks and M. Stubbs, Norfolk. Parliamentary Secretary John Mackie received them, and as the *Landworker* put it, 'so ended a glorious episode in

Union history. The demonstration was mainly organised by Frank Coffin, the energetic national officer.'

Tough negotiations won an increase of 15s, bringing the minimum to £13 3s, with a cut of one hour, making the working week 43. The hour's reduction was by means of five days of eight hours and a short day of three hours, and the Union thought it 'should bring materially nearer' a five-day week.

When the AWB met on 9 January 1970 to confirm the award, about 50 Union demonstrators arrived with the intention of speaking to the appointed members about the farmworkers' plight. They became angry when they discovered that these people had slipped in by the back entrance. There were scuffles on the stairs with security men and calm was restored when an official let a group into a room to consider further action. They asked to see Mr. A. L. Armitage, Board Chairman, but he refused to meet them. Bert Hazell arrived, and left armed with a resolution signed by the group which deplored the 'cowardice' of the independent members. This was read out by Mr. Armitage to the Board, together with another one adopted by the demonstrators deploring the inadequacy of the award.

At the 1970 Labour Conference, a threatened Tory Industrial Relations Bill cast a dark shadow, resulting in the unanimous acceptance of a composite declaring full support for trade union efforts to secure better wages and total opposition to restrictions on collective bargaining.

From 1 November 1971, farmworkers secured an annual holiday of three weeks for full-time and regular part-timers, thus breaking through the hitherto necessary qualification of needing to have worked on the same farm or for the same employer for 20 years.

On 17 June Robert Carr, Secretary of State for Employment, issued the long-awaited Code of Industrial Relations Practice. It was called a consultative document, which to say the least, was rather presumptuous. The Government firmly refused to consult with the unions on this divisive measure and could not complain if the unions spurned the document, which they did.

It bore the imprint of the clinical approach of the back corridors of Whitehall and in consequence was remote from the realities of life on the coal-face or the farmyard. It said that management had the primary responsibility for good industrial relations and should take the initiative in creating and maintaining them. It suggested sanctions against trade unionists who may default, but not against defaulting employers.

The Industrial Relations Bill which followed had the devilish effect of dividing the Labour movement on how it should be opposed. This division was much in evidence at a TUC rally against the Bill. There was undoubtedly a genuine difference of opinion as to whether the Bill should be fought along the relatively undramatic lines as advanced by the TUC, or by more short-term stoppages, or even a General Strike, as canvassed by the more militant minority at a rally at the Albert Hall.

About 6,000 trade unionists, including 12 representatives from the NUAAW, attended the rally. The first speaker, Opposition Leader Harold

Wilson, had a rough ride. He was greeted with slow hand claps, jeers and cries of 'sit down'. The noisy minority did not like it when he said, 'The Labour Government set out to tackle the main problems, inter-union disputes, which none here would seek to justify, and those unofficial, unconstitutional strikes where a small number of men producing, for example, components for the motor industry, can throw thousands of their fellow trade unionists out of work . . . If between us we tore ourselves apart on the so-called penal clauses, this was because your Labour Government felt that action must be taken to deal with inter-union and unconstitutional stoppages.'

Professor K. W. Wedderburn, London University, dealt with legal aspects of the Bill. He said it 'sets out to replace totally our existing legal framework with a new system, largely based upon ill-chosen snippets of American laws unsuitable to British conditions.' It 'is a charter for blacklegs and non-union-ists.' He received a standing ovation – unlike the final speaker, Vic Feather, TUC General Secretary, who at one point was driven to shout 'This is a demonstration of irresponsibility.'

The *Landworker* warned against direct industrial action against the Bill, and called on members to sign a TUC petition asking Parliament to drop the Bill.

The TUC General Council secured backing by a Special Conference at Croydon in March 1971 for all their seven recommendations on the Bill. A card vote was necessary on only two – numbers 1 and 7 – among the list set out below. The votes on these were respectively 5,005,000 to 4,284,000 and 5,366,000 to 3,952,000.

The seven recommendations were: (1) Affiliated unions were advised not to register; (2) The General Council would seek explicit assurance from the Parliamentary Labour Party on repeal of the Act; (3) This urged unions not to sign legally-binding contracts and not to co-operate with the Commission on Industrial Relations; (4) This concerned inter-union disputes and instructed unions to continue to observe the Bridlington Agreement; (5) Trade unionists should refuse to serve on the National Industrial Relations Court, the CIR, or Industrial Tribunals; (6) This authorised the General Council to meet a union's costs in legal actions under the Act; (7) Congress would concentrate its support behind the TUC's positive recommendations and 'preserve its unity of purpose that had hitherto characterised the campaign of opposition.'

On registration, Vic Feather said that under the Bill a union could find itself on the full register without knowing how it happened, and whether it wanted to register or not. Unregistered unions would be subject to a harsher tax treatment of provident benefits for their members; on the other hand, in certain circumstances registered unions would be subject to lesser liabilities than unregistered ones. 'If every union looked at this purely as a business proposition each one might well opt to register. But the General Council are saying that unions should not approach this one by one as a business proposition. If they do so they will be picked off, one by one.' The seventh recommendation meant, among other things, that unions should not initiate or support industrial action against the Bill.

Both Jack Jones, TGWU, and Hugh Scanlon, engineers, spoke against the first recommendation on the grounds that the TUC should issue a clear instruction to their affiliates not to register in order to secure a solid front among all the unions. Dan McGarvey, boilermakers, said the Government was bringing in a law that was creating a state of fascism.

The seven-member NUAAW delegation voted for the TUC policy in its entirety. They were Bert Hazell, Joan Maynard, Reg Bottini, Stan Hall, Tony Hemming, John Hose and Wilf Page.

At its August 1971 meeting, the NUAAW EC 'decided not to de-register, which means that we will eventually take steps to secure full registration for the Union.' This was done mainly for financial reasons.

Reg Bottini told that year's TUC, 'My Union has been fully associated with the trade union movement in total and complete opposition to the Government's legislation . . . On the day of the Royal Assent we immediately instructed our members on industrial tribunals to resign . . . But it is well-known that a number of unions, because of their special difficulties . . . feel that their best interests – or survival – depend on registration . . .'

A composite to instruct affiliated unions not to register was carried by 1,125,000 votes, and the General Council's Report advising unions not to register was adopted by 281,000 votes.

At the 1972 Biennial at Weymouth, the EC showed some change of front since the TUC Conference and supported a successful composite 'to de-register forthwith'. It was moved by Jack Dunman, Oxon, seconded by Peter Medhurst, Yorks. Reg Bottini said the Industrial Relations Act cut across TUC and union practices. It removed all important forms of protection in trade disputes from de-registered unions but retained some forms of very limited protection to registered trade unions. It provided a long list of unfair industrial actions and created a situation in which unions could no longer authorise members to take strike action. If unions would not agree to sign binding procedural agreements acceptable to the employers, the employers could seek the imposition, unilaterally, of a legally-binding agreement. Free-entry closed shops were null and void. All forms of sympathetic action in support of workmates in other industries were outside the law.

'This is the shortest resolution on the agenda, but not the least important. I hope Conference will think it is the sweetest,' said Jack Dunman moving the resolution to de-register. The Tories were out to destroy the trade unions. 'If we register, they will under certain circumstances remit us a little bit of tax money, perhaps £5,000. Fines for unfair industrial action will only be £25,000. If we de-register they will be unlimited.' It was seconded by Fred Rendall, N Riding.

'We cannot afford to be de-registered* because of the income tax saving to this small union,' said Andrew Baynham, Worcs, opposing the motion. 'To

---

* By February, 95 unions with 8.5 million members had decided to de-register or remain unregistered.

take advantage of the wrongful dismissal clause we have to be registered. The clause, with its right to claim compensation, was of particular merit in an industry like ours with tied cottages.'

Les Shears, Dorset, declared that the Act was intended to smash trade unions. Alan Pullen, Surrey, thought 'The Union had no more right to ignore the law than an employer.' He opposed the motion, unlike Alan Johnson, Worcs, who believed 'that this Conference must confirm its loyalty to the TUC.'

On behalf of the EC, Reg Bottini said that there had been unanimity in opposition to one of the most vicious pieces of class legislation of recent years. 'We are therefore considering the question of tactics and not principles. The Act was deliberately designed to divide unions . . . Following the Croydon conference, when the EC committed itself unreservedly to opposing the Act, under the provisions of registration the EC decided . . . that because of the financial implications . . . de-registration in our case meant the loss of just over £5,000 a year.'

'Courageous decision by the EC,' said Jack Dunman in reply. The motion was carried without the need for a card vote.*

The Biennial's demand for a £20 minimum also called for 'positive and direct action' if the claim was not fully met. Although the motion did not mention strikes, it was interpreted as such by all concerned, and the EC tried to persuade the mover to withdraw, but he refused. Support for it came mainly from North Norfolk, North Yorkshire and Essex, where members were said to be 'ready for action'. The motion was carried by 47 votes to 46.

After countrywide demonstrations, an increase of 20% (£3.30), bringing the minimum up to £19.50, was awarded by the AWB on 30 October 1972. But the farmworkers were not to get it, because on 6 November, Premier Edward Heath announced a wage freeze.

Bert Hazell and Reg Bottini met the Tory Minister of Agriculture, Joseph Godber, who claimed he regretted that farmworkers had been caught by the freeze and said that the AWB proposals would be implemented 'in full' at the end of the freeze period. The EC sought to meet Edward Heath, but he evaded them.

The 'positive and direct action' taken by the EC was to instruct County Committees to consider the proposals and make comments. Several suggestions were made for selective stoppages in sugar beet lifting, fruit picking and pea vining, but nothing came of them, and in the end 'positive and direct action' was reduced to the usual lobbying exercise. The £3.30 was not paid until 1 April, when the Government lifted the standstill on farm pay.

---

* There is no mention in the Union's documents I have seen to show that the Union formally de-registered, but it must have done so, for the 1972 Report of the Chief Registrar of Trade Unions' and Employers' Associations shows that the NUAAW's name had been removed from its permanent register.

40-hour Week At Last

It was in 1973 that farmworkers at long last achieved the 40-hour week. The workers' side of the AWB had claimed a 40-hour five-day week in March. The employers opposed, but at a Board meeting on 5 June, on the proposal of the independent members, the decision to introduce a 40-hour five-day week was reached unanimously.

Another step forward in 1973 was towards equal pay for women. Women in Grades I and II achieved equal pay from 1 April. But it was not until 29 December 1975 that complete victory was won and women's rates brought up to those of men in all grades.

In September, the Union put in for a minimum of £25, and an increase of £2.30 was won, making a minimum of £21.80. A novel feature of this award was the introduction of a 'Threshold Agreement' providing a flat pay increase of 40p per week to be paid for 7% in the Retail Price Index. It was to last for a year (the year that Sir John Stratton, chair of the Fatstock Marketing Corporation, received a £16,416 rise). These threshold payments by late October reached £3.20 per week.

At the TUC Conference a Union resolution wanted the Government to annul statutory orders which made the AWB subservient to the PIB. Reg Bottini told delegates that when he saw the Secretary of State, Maurice MacMillan, about the frozen farm pay, MacMillan thought it was a shame but he couldn't do anything about it. 'After all,' he said, 'the Government's trying to be unfair as fairly as possible.'

A. Baynham, Worcs, moved a composite calling for £35 by January 1975 and £40 by January 1976, at the 1974 Biennial. Supporting, Joan Maynard, Yorks, moved an addendum seeking 'selected strike action in support of this claim'. It had been said that when talking about industrial action she scared the pants off members. 'If this is the case then we have got a job of education to do. I am quite convinced that I scare the pants off Head Office and the majority of the EC, but the important thing is that we also scare the pants off the farmers.' T. Young, Warwickshire, supporting, said it had proved effective in other industries. Jack Langford, Salop, said such action would divide the Union. Jim Rayner, Suffolk, denied it was possible to muster the strength to take action other unions had. Reg Bottini did not think that Joan scared the pants off the EC. The EC did not rule out industrial action and he asked the addendum be remitted. Conference agreed.

Despite these appeals for 'moderation' at the Biennial there was a rising tide of militancy in many branches, and members' hopes were heightened, no doubt, when Labour won the General Election in 1974, albeit with a small majority.

Inflation was running at 20% and the Union claimed £35 at AWB negotiations. The Board finally agreed to a two-stage increase to £28.50 from 20 January and £30.50 from 21 July. Taking into account the 'threshold payments', the settlement meant that the minimum had been increased by £7 over the year.

In July 1975 the Union claimed £40. £2,000 a year for farmworkers sounded good, but meant little more than keeping pace with the rise in the cost of living. An increase of £6 from 20 January 1976 was finally won, far short of £2,000 a year. It was the maximum obtainable under the TUC-Government 'Social Contract'* then in force.

In 1976, attempts to improve wages were held up by this Social Contract. Although the Biennial expressed support for the principle of this policy, it did not stop delegates unanimously calling for £60.

Between the two biennials of 1974 and 1976 the minimum had been forced up by £14.70. This was more than the rise in the Index of Retail Prices, yet the onward rush of rising prices robbed members of a great deal of the gains. The Social Contract was to take the robbery even further. By the end of the year, the AWB had proposed an increase of £2.50 and the EC lodged an objection because the proposal did not even reach the maximum allowable under the Government's counter-inflationary policy. But the Board refused to concede and the £2.50 increase remained.

Smarting under this refusal, the EC saw Labour Chancellor Denis Healey's £2,500 million cuts in public expenditure 'as the most savage attack on living standards of low-paid workers ever mounted by a Chancellor, Labour or Tory.'

The General Secretary and President called for the relaxation of the Social Contract after Phase Two.§ Writing in the *Landworker* in 1977, Joan Maynard said that she had asked the Secretary of State for Employment what he was going to do about the miserable £2.50 award (nothing apparently). She noted a further 'scandal' that under the Social Contract the overtime rate was then little more per hour than the flat rate (this was later raised to £1.50 per hour), but still not restored to time and a half.

In July 1977, Phase Two of the Social Contract ran out. Denis Healey and TUC General Secretary Len Murray were trying to arrive at a formula for another year of pay restraint that the unions would buy. Phase One allowed increases up to £6; Phase Two, increases of £2.50 or 5% (whichever was greater). With inflation running at 17.5% agreement was going to be difficult.

It looked like a knife-edge decision for the TUC due to meet in September, and as the NUAAW's policy-making conference was not until 1978, its policy was due to be decided by the EC. S Yorkshire DO, Colin Hands, sent a letter to all his branch secretaries seeking either a special conference or a national ballot of members on the subject. 'It will not be good enough,' wrote Colin, for the EC to make up its mind without some form of membership consultation.' A county action committee was set up by Yorkshire members opposing a further round of pay restraint. Clear opposition, too, came from the county committees of Oxfordshire, Cornwall, Norfolk and Staffordshire.

---

* An agreement between the TUC and the Government to limit pay increases which ended 'free collective bargaining'.

§ The Social Contract was divided into three phases.

It was left to the TGWU to 'solve' the NUAAW's dilemma. Its annual conference voted against the Social Contract, and its 1.9 million votes were expected to be more than enough to swing the TUC Conference, which finally agreed to the Government's request for a '12-month rule not to go in for more than one pay rise until 12 months after their last one.' This was accepted on the understanding that it would be the end of pay restraint.

The decision came after Prime Minister Jim Callaghan, who since becoming a Labour MP in 1945 had with his other financial interests become a wealthy farmer, told them that, 'The benefits of the Social Contract have been delayed,' and noted that many groups, including the NUAAW, had received increases under the guidelines laid down by Phase Two, and said the NUAAW's £60 claim did not breach the new 12-month rule.

The TGWU had opposed the 12-month rule, so too did the NUAAW, after a careful debate inside its delegation. On a card vote, supporters of the 12-month rule mustered over 7 million votes, with over 4 million against.

Making its claim for £60 to the AWB, the Union sought consolidation of pay supplements for overtime; the restoration of craft differentials; abolition of lower hourly rates for part-time/casual workers and a 35-hour week. The AWB proposed £4 bringing the minimum to £43, with increases for craftsmen and other grades.

A lively year on the wages front ended with an unprecedented move, when Labour's Minister of Agriculture, John Silkin, objected to the £4 because it exceeded the government's pay guidelines by 10%, or 10p on the basic wages. There was vehement objection from the Union, and the AWB stood by its decision.

At the Biennial in 1978, delegates sought an £80 minimum from January 1979, and prolonged negotiations took place with the AWB, against a background of severe pay restraint; they were galvanised by a powerful Union lobby of the AWB on 7 December. But there was no settlement. There were one-day strikes at horticultural experimental stations at Luddington, near Straford-on-Avon, and Rosewarne, Cornwall. Luddington strike leader, Dave Wright, said, 'We may be sons of the soil, but we are no longer silly sods.'

The AWB December meeting had seen a change in Union thinking. For the first time, the EC formally called for a lobby at a specific time, 12 midday, and simply said 'Be there'. Members responded magnificently. About 500 turned up, and Jack Boddy came out to tell them that the farmers were still insisting that £1.65 was the limit. The police tried to prevent slogans being shouted and banners displayed, and when one demonstrator sat on the Ministry steps he was arrested. But the good humour of the demonstrators overcame most of the problems; many followed a determined Joan Maynard to the House of Commons, where she assisted in the setting up of another lobby.

What effect did this very militant lobby have? Most members had no doubt that it influenced both farmers and independent members, and felt that the decision for £5.50 for a 40-hour week when the AWB met again was partly due to the impressive lobby.

The 1978 Biennial rejected a call to set up a special strike fund, not, it was made clear, because delegates opposed the idea of strikes. The motion called for 2% of all contributions to be put in a strike fund, and Arthur Leary, head of the Organising Department, said that this would only produce £16,000. This could be used up in two or three strikes; a better way was to set up a general fund and then, if needed, make a special levy. The motion had been proposed by Paul Holdsworth, North Yorks, who thought they had to show they were able to finance industrial action.

*   *   *

The name Paul Holdsworth seldom crops up at biennials, yet he is one of those hard-slogging members, without whom the Union would find it difficult to keep going. Paul, a tall, bronzed, angular man of 45 with a ready smile, joined the Union in 1962. One day the district officer knocked on his door and asked, 'Will you be branch secretary?' Paul replied, 'Yes.' The DO responded, 'Well, here's the books, any problems, just give me a ring.' That was Paul's start as a Union activist.

Few could have been better. Paul, who lived in Askham Bryan, North Yorkshire, was secretary of Askham Richard branch, and held numerous other regional positions when I interviewed him in 1988.

Born in Bradford, he left at eight and grew up in Ripon, the son of publicans, both Conservatives. Paul left school at 15 and worked in a nursery at Harrogate. 'I always fancied working outside,' he explained, and that first job put him on the way to becoming a full blown countryman. He later worked in a garden shop, next to the gardens of Lord Bolton's estate in Wensleydale, and then went to Askham Bryan Agricultural and Horticultural College as a student, and after various other gardening jobs, was then a college groundsman.

Before the merger, to which he believed there was no alternative, he always worried about communications as the branches contracted and the organisation got further apart. 'It is important to me,' he said, 'if you have a branch secretary with only three members, he is there to service those members.' He regretted the further loss of close contact since the merger. 'We've got to recruit and service members on a small scale. That is something a big union has got to learn. We must learn to keep in contact with people.'

His branch was then 45 strong. He once got it up to 60 but that vital contact was lost. Many of the losses occurred when there was a lot of anti-union propaganda in the media. 'I don't know where agricultural workers are now, there are four farms round here and there's no workers on them, they're run by families and the same applies to the next village and the next.'

He didn't have much contact with the students, most of whom were bosses' sons, but occasionally found one already in the Union. Not that he didn't attempt to get the others into the Union. 'It's no good trying to approach them when they first come here on the YTS – there's an anti-union attitude. After they've been here six months, you recruit more easily.'

Paul believed the main task of the Agricultural Trade Group was to improve wages and conditions. 'This is the best recruitment leaflet I've ever had,' he said, handing me a poster-sized TGWU Compensation Settlement Sheet for the March Quarter, 1988: all the legal settlements for dismissals and accident cases, ranging from £17,500, to two at £25,000, and one at £50,000.

Somewhere along the way, Paul joined the Labour Party, lived with his wife Dianne, daughter Ruth aged 18, who worked in a shop, and a son Ben, 15, in a College house. When I asked Paul what he did in his spare time, Ruth, who was in the kitchen, put her head through the sitting room door and said cheerfully, 'I'll tell you what he does, union work.' She added, to make sure I knew she approved, 'I've just joined the Union.'

*   *   *

During 1978, the Union made a major wages breakthrough on standby payments. From January 1979, farmworkers became entitled to payments during harvest time when asked to standby without being called upon to work. The agreement provided for pay for 24-hour periods during which a worker was on standby on Sundays, public holidays, annual holidays or the weekly day off.*

The TUC announced that it would have nothing to do with the Labour Government's newly announced 5% pay 'norm', and the Union proposed to the AWB an £80 minimum for a 35-hour week. That year, with the prospect of an imminent General Election, the TUC Congress tried to ensure that not too many obvious divisions opened up in the Labour movement. Nevertheless, the 5% pay deal was roundly condemned.

No one was surprised that the NFU had used Callaghan's 5% guideline as an excuse for rejecting the NUAAW claim. Jack Boddy appealed to members to write letters to the AWB on the justice of it. Increases from £5.50 to £7.26 were won.

The £100 Pay Claim

The launch in 1979 of the Union's £100-a-week pay claim took place on May Day. Jack Boddy announced the claim at a rally at Ipswich, in one of the most strongly-worded statements ever delivered by an NUAAW leader. He said that politicians were for ever exhorting workers to increase productivity, but farmworkers who had done just that found themselves in the poverty trap. Thousands of NUAAW members' wages were below the official Government poverty line and they claimed Family Income Supplement. 'They have to

---

* Water Authority workers had won standby payments of £4.90 in 1972 and county council roadmen received 2 hours' pay on standby.

suffer the indignity of having to ask the State to make up to a living wage which their employers won't pay. The taxpayer forks out what the farmer owes his workers.'

Farmers rejected the claim, and the NFU suggested it would put £1,000 million on the industry's wage bill and send up farm gate prices by 15%. This was nonsense; even if all the extra costs were passed on to the consumer, prices would go up by less than 1%.

This £100 claim was made during a General Election which saw the return of a Conservative Government headed by Margaret Thatcher. The outlook for farmworkers was not good as the years of Thatcher rule began, with her Spongers' Government, with big handouts for the rich, and kicks in the teeth for the poor and lowly paid.

Finally, after tough negotiations, the AWB conceded a basic minimum of £58 from 21 January 1980. Farmers' leader Simon Gourlay declared, 'It's a black day for agriculture.' Black or not, that Christmas, Britain's farmers got an extra £150 million bonanza as a result of a devaluation of the 'green' pound, giving them a 19% increase in their selling prices in the coming year.

After 75 years of negotiations the Union was still some distance from achieving its ultimate objective – obtaining for rural workers equivalent standards to those of their industrial colleagues – and the 1980 Biennial wanted the AWB to go. Conference wanted wages to be set by a statutory joint industrial council, something that left-wingers had been campaigning for over the years. This was an almost unanimous decision of principle by the Conference; just two years earlier a similar resolution had been rejected by the Southport Biennial. Joan Maynard said she was not suggesting that a statutory joint industrial council would be the millennium, but it would help get better wages.

To back up their wage claim, Jack Boddy asked members to collect evidence that it cost more to live in villages than towns. He made it clear he was not attacking village shopkeepers, who provided a valuable service and could not buy as cheaply as their big supermarket competitors. An analysis of replies revealed that 12 basic items cost more in villages.

The most acrimonious wages talks in living memory broke up with the workers' side walking out in protest at the miserable level of the farmers' offer on 26 November 1980. They objected to an imposed settlement of 10.3%, an increase equivalent to a £64 minimum, which was less than a 11.2% package on offer three weeks earlier, which the farmers went back on.

As had become the custom in recent years, the AWB had been vigorously lobbied by NUAAW members, and they attended a rally, where John Silkin, former Labour Minister of Agriculture, John Hose and Joan Maynard swelled the chorus of condemnation of farmers refusing to pay the bill for skilled workers. The farmers claimed that the earlier offer was made not by the NFU, but by the independent members. Jack Boddy told the *Landworker*, 'I understand that Simon Gourlay, leader of the farmers' side, had the barefaced nerve to tell the press, "The workers would have got 11.2% if they had not called for an adjournment at the last meeting". In all my years of negotiating experience this has been the one and only instance where the employers have shifted their ground from the point of adjournment.'

Delegates to the special NUAAW Conference on a merger with the TGWU instructed the EC to set up a sub-committee to work out, with the membership, strike action in support of the next wage claim. Not a single vote was cast against. In January 1981, the AWB rubber stamped the 10.3% (£6) rise.

After the Tory Budget of 1981, which made savage inroads into workers' living standards, the Union claimed an interim rise, saying that January's 10.3% had already been absorbed by higher rents and rates, and extra for gas and electricity. The AWB turned down the claim. Professor Charles Miles, its retiring chairman, said the independent members felt if there was to be an interim rise it would have to be agreed by 'the Board as a whole' and they could not impose an award on which the Board was not unanimous. A strange new formula this – it gave farmers an effective veto over any rise.

The new chairman was appointed by the Tory Government: Gordon Dickson, Professor of Agriculture at Newcastle upon Tyne University. The Union found that 'the board's deliberations were conducted in a changed manner, with the discussions being held between both sides in one another's presence.' By the end of 1981, the Union had secured a basic rise of £6.40.

Since the Tories took power, the average cost of food for each person had gone up by £1.40 a week, it was revealed in 1982 – a fact which added impetus to the calls at the Skegness Conference that year for a claim of £120 for a 35-hour week. Delegates also voted by a large majority to scrap the AWB and replace it with direct farmer–worker negotiations, backed by a statutory joint industrial council.

That year the farmworkers' pay demonstration went to the NFU headquarters, a massive, ornate building in the heart of London's fashionable Knightsbridge. NFU Deputy Director General, Phillip Butcher, agreed to see a small delegation, consisting of Francis Beckett, Joan Maynard, Trade Group Committee member Dennis Chiappa and Wiltshire area chairman Howard Wright. Butcher listened politely, but unyieldingly, to pleas on behalf of the low-paid farmworkers.

If they were unyielding at NFU headquarters, they were positively destructive at the Ministry of Agriculture, where the talks were taking place. Some 400 farmworkers went from the NFU to MAFF where negotiations dragged on until 8.30pm, when a shameful decision was announced: the minimum was to go up from January 1983 by £5 to £75.40, with increases in craftsmen and appointed grades. No other changes were won, in what had been the best year* in farming for many years.

---

*   Figures in the Annual Review of Agriculture showed that in 1983 farmers' incomes had nearly doubled on the previous two years. Their net incomes rose by 24% in 1981, and 45% in 1982.

Farmworkers did however win a second rise in 1983 of 5% only months later, once the full extent of farmers' 1982 profits were known, and was achieved in face of bitter opposition by farmers. The minimum was increased by £3.80 to £79.20 for a 40-hour week.

There is one law for the farmer and another for the farmworker. In 1981, according to the Department of Employment *Gazette*, the average value of milk and potatoes received by farmworkers was 10p per week. For farmers, there was no such short commons. The 1982 Annual Review allowed £13 million for 'farm' cars. Under the headings of 'machinery' and 'depreciation' car expenses were set off as business expenses. The farmworker trying to run a car could look with envy at an average figure of £154 for insurance, £262 repairs and £410 depreciation for the farmers' cars.

'No wonder,' declared the Union, 'farmworkers see their net pay as very different from net farm income.' And adding, 'Quite apart from those itemised expenses, we do not believe it can be argued that farmers actually pay for petrol out of their net income. Whether from the farm pump on large farms, or at the account garage, petrol for private motoring comes out of the £118.7 million allowed in the Annual Review.' The same was true of the cost of telephones, electricity and fuel, house repairs and decorating, water charges and so on.

Many farmworkers, the Union decided, 'would be surprised to learn that among the items farmers were allowed to deduct as farm expenses was any expenditure incurred for the welfare of employees, including Christmas parties and staff outings. While their Union sub could not be claimed as a PAYE deduction, their boss could claim seven-eighths of his NFU sub as necessary expenditure.'

At the 1983 Trade Group Conference, by 33 votes to 27, the narrowest majority on the issue ever, a demand for strike action during harvest time was rejected.

In 1984 the NFU campaigned to improve their public image, which had taken a knock, partly due to their mean treatment of farmworkers. However, they made a somewhat inauspicious start by stating on 23 March that their financial situation was such that the workers could not have any pay increase. Their negotiators on the AWB, however, decided to be 'generous' and offered an increase of 1½%, finally settled for £3.60, which represented 4.6%.

A month later, the Tory Government dismissed the AWB chairman, Gordon Dickson, who told the AWB members that he had been called to see Agriculture Minister Michael Jopling. 'I felt like a small schoolboy in the headmaster's study.' He said that Jopling told him he 'did not have the confidence of the employers'. The reaction of the workers' side was one of sheer disbelief. Jack Boddy protested to Jopling at the manner of Dickson's sacking, making it clear that his main concern was what it augured for the future. 'Do you,' he asked, 'intend to appoint a puppet of the NFU as a new chairman?'

The harsh truth of Professor Dickson's sacking was not revealed until 1991. Speaking on the BBC's *Country Life* television programme in February,

Professor Dickson said he had been sacked because of a 'directive down from the cabinet office.' He had been asked to make sure Board decisions conformed with Government advisory guidelines on pay. In response to the question, 'So you were told it was your job to hold wages down?', Professor Dickson replied, 'That's right.'

Reporting this disclosure in March 1991, the *Landworker* declared, 'The Union [at the time] believed Dickson had upset the farmers by accepting that agricultural workers had a case for claiming pay parity with industrial workers.'

Professor David Walker, head of economics at Exeter University, was appointed the new chair. He did not agree with equality of pay with other industries and told the *Landworker*, '. . . if I was to say I agreed with parity I would be sacked rather rapidly too.' He just 'hoped' to see wages moving ahead a bit.

For the first time since the 1920s, members of a general section of the industry took industrial action. Region 1 banned harvest overtime, in response to the 4.6% settlement, between 27 August – Bank Holiday Monday – and Saturday 1 September. Members were not asked to neglect livestock.

NFU circulars suggested that an internal battle took place over whether farmers should sack workers who refused overtime. One said dismissal 'would hardly be appropriate' but, presumably thinking some farmers would consider dismissal, it then spelt out the way it could be done whilst preventing workers winning a case for unfair dismissal. A later circular advised farmers to avoid confrontation, stressing the need for 'harmonious working relationships'.

Some controversy followed as to whether the overtime ban was successful; the NFU claimed it was not. 'Nonsense, complete nonsense, and they know it,' was Jack Boddy's response. 'There was no open revolt in the fields – in many parts of the country there was no need. Good weather, and an early harvest, combined with the good sense of many farmers and workers in avoiding confrontation. But contrary to NFU claims, there was a distinct lack of movement in their fields on August Bank Holiday Monday.'

Reports to head office show that the greatest response to the ban came in the big establishments, experimental and research farms, and big farms with a large organised staff. It was clear, however, that any future industrial action would require more educational activity prior to implementation to ensure an all-round response.

At the Trades Group Conference at Eastbourne in 1984, delegates came out squarely for £130 for a 35-hour week. That year the Scottish AWB voted for a 5% increase, which took the basic wage from £79.20 to £83.20.

So NUAAW members again set their sights on a reasonable 'liveable' wage. They had a long way to go as a survey[26] showed that the gap between them and those in other industries was growing ever wider. For the year up to April, £159.30 a week was the average top line of the average male worker. Men in non-manual jobs averaged £209, manual workers £152.70. MAFF figures up to June 1984 showed average earnings of all hired men in agriculture and horticulture to be £120.59. For this they worked 6.6 hours overtime. The gap between general farmworkers and the average industrial worker was £47.98.

Agriculture in 1945 was still closer to the farming of the 1880s than the 1980s. Since 1945 the whole thrust of technological development has been to replace labour with machinery and chemicals, although few people, including the Union, at first anticipated this rapid transformation of agricultural practice. The proportion of the UK workforce in agriculture has become one of the smallest in the world. By 1977 it had dropped to 2.2%, compared with 2.4% in the USA, 9.5% in France and 11.4% in Western Europe as a whole. Between 1960 and 1971 the number of agricultural workers fell by half, and farmers by a third. By the 1980s, nearly three-quarters of UK farms had no hired labour at all, being run by the family with occasional hired help.

However, farming is still Britain's biggest single industry and farmers receive more State aid than any other industry. Why then could Britain's prosperous farmers still get away with not paying their rapidly diminishing workforce a decent living wage? This declining workforce, often only one or two men per farm, was increasingly difficult to organise, and the NFU had another immense political advantage – its symbiotic relationship with MAFF, which had a single-minded devotion to the farmers' cause.

This fall in the labour force had a devastating effect in many areas where there was no alternative industry. In the Countryside Commission's *Uplands Landscape Study* (1983), the number of farms fell by 40% between 1950 and 1976 (their average size increased by 56%), and the number of farmworkers was reduced to almost vanishing point in some areas: in Snowdonia 79% of full-time and 70% of part-time jobs went in the eight years 1965–73; two-thirds of full-time jobs on Exmoor and Dartmoor disappeared between 1952 and 1972. Full-time agricultural workers declined by 400,000 (70%) between 1950 and 1980, and was still falling at the time of writing by over 10,000 per annum.

One Somerset doctor told me that many of these displaced farmworkers would, through no fault of their own, never get a regular job again. 'They exhaust their unemployment entitlement, their often low standards of living are further reduced, which leads to all kinds of illnesses, so I sign them on the sick, that's the least I can do. They've been badly treated by society. I know other GPs do the same.'*

In this situation, the farmers hold the whip-hand on what they pay their remaining workers. The post-war expansion of agriculture ended in 1984, so the big farmers were once more to be heard pleading poverty when wage claims were made; their coffers might no longer be brimming over, but they were still doing nicely, thank you.

---

* Interviewed in 1983. A Devon doctor made a similar statement.

Taking the Farmers to Court

The Union's most successful sphere of work was the legal action it took to defend members' interests and those of their families. This was done by the Union's Legal Department and solicitors, Robin Thompson and Partners, and the Wages Department, who over the years won millions of pounds in payment of underpaid wages, in compensation for injuries and in redundancy payments.

Expansion of the Union into the more backward parts of the country brought a crop of minimum wages claims in 1947. For comparison, in 1944 the Legal Department took up 4,677 new wages cases, in 1947 the number was 7,123. Workmen's compensation settlements in 1944 totalled £37,520, in 1947 they reached £56,231. Total money recovered in 1944 was £65,506, in 1947 it was £95,363. It was in 1949 that the Union first passed the £1 million mark recovered for all claims; it reached £2 million by 1957; £3 million in 1963, and only four years later had passed £4 million. The £5 million mark was passed in 1971, and £10 million in 1981.

A shepherd, aged 63, in West Wales was underpaid by £15,000 during the 26 years he worked at a farm in Dyfed, Cardiff Crown Court was told in 1978. David Jones, of Tregaron branch, lived in a tied cottage at Llanddewi Brefi with his wife and invalid son. He could not legally claim the whole of his back pay. But his lawyer said he was entitled to £10,300 from his former employer. The parties reached an agreement for Jones to get £9,000. David went to work at the farm in 1952 for £3 10s a week. By 1975 his wages were £7 a week – as against the AWB minimum of £28.50. At the time of the court hearing, the AWB minimum was £43, but since June 1975 when the court action started, David said he had received nothing, although he carried on doing his work, from dawn to dusk, looking after nearly 2,000 sheep, hedging and ditching.

Although it was suggested on many occasions, the Union refused to operate a black list of 'bad' employers. The EC was reluctant to get into the business of recommending some employers, which would have been in effect a black list, in case such recommendations went sour.

With the coming into force of the Industrial Injuries Act in 1948 two developments affected the Legal Department. Firstly, it set up machinery to advise members and see that they received what they were entitled to under the Act; secondly, to act for them, including making claims for damages against employers when they were injured at work.

After being in charge of the Union's Approved Society for nearly 30 years, Arthur Holmes became a civil servant when the Society was taken over by the Ministry of National Insurance in 1948 as part of the Labour Government's welfare changes. E. E. Hennem, who joined head office staff in 1919, and succeeded Alfred Dann as head of the Legal Department on the latter's election as General Secretary, left the Union to join the Ministry of National Insurance. A. L. Marriott, who read law at Glasgow University, succeeded him. George Hook was appointed chief assistant to Marriott, and was later to take over from him.

Just how much farmworkers needed the backing of the Union and its legal come-uppance, is shown by a letter in January 1948 from the Lizard, one of the most southerly points in Britain. T. Beckerley, secretary of the newly opened Grode Ruon branch, said local farmworkers had worked from 7am to 6pm, on all six weekdays, and put in four to five hours on Sundays without being paid for the hours worked in excess of the scheduled number. 'Now there is no work in excess of 48 hours, or on Saturday or Sunday, which is not paid for at the proper overtime rates. The workers no longer go in fear of their employers, but boldly express their views in public and stand together against victimisation.'

Workers in fear of the boss was all too often the lot of the agriculture worker, and only the constant work of the Legal Department secured some semblance of justice for many of them. By the 1960s, the Union was handling over 5,000 legal cases a year, most of them accident cases.

There was a very special meeting of the Downside (Surrey) branch in 1950, at Cobham, when Geoffrey Smith, a young member, was presented with a cheque for £4,500 in compensation for an injury to his eye. Making the presentation, George Hook explained why the settlement was so significant. It concerned a claim which would have had no foundation in law prior to 5 July 1948, when changes in accident law introduced by the Labour Government became operative. Geoffrey was struck on the side of his face by a chopper which had slipped from the grasp of a fellow worker. Throughout the negotiations the Union's claim had been strongly resisted, but it had secured a compromise offer of £2,500 which Geoffrey and his widowed mother had been inclined to accept. The other side was finally induced to offer £4,500.

Arrears of wages amounting to £490 were awarded at Nottingham Police Court in 1950 to a farmworker, aged 60, who had worked for an employer for 15 years, and had never had a holiday or a day off. He had worked an 11½-hour day, six days a week, with an additional 6½ hours on Sundays. He was said to have milked 40 cows a day. All he had received was his board and £1 a week, from which 14s was deducted for tobacco. The prosecuting solicitor thought that the story was 'so fantastic that it was almost like a page from Dickens', and said that the worker should have received, in addition to his keep, £3 4s a week, plus overtime payments. For the defence, it was said that 'if the case were Dickensian it was not so in a wicked way. Rather did it concern the type of farm community of olden days where the worker lived with the family and was treated as one of them.' The employer was fined £20, and ordered to pay £10 10s costs in addition to the £490 arrears.

In 1966, Jim Watts, now Legal Department head, reported a grand total of £231,000 in damages recovered in common law and miscellaneous settlements during the year. It was the largest amount ever recovered in a single year, and brought the total won by the Union in accident settlements to £3,805,910.

Thanks to the Union's action, and that of the MAFF Wages Enforcement branch, farmers were becoming more careful and fewer of their workers were being underpaid by the late sixties. A Report on Safety, Health and Welfare and Wages in Agriculture[27] showed that more farmers were adhering to the provisions of the Agricultural Wages Act 1948. During 1967, some £5,131 was recovered in wage arrears, £2,051 less than in 1966.

One of the biggest settlements of all came when another Union member, a passenger in a car, received terrible injuries after it hit a tree in 1971. A young farmworker, Barry Smallacombe, of South Devon Central branch, received £58,000 compensation after action by the Legal Department.

'See Me Under The Old Birch Tree'

Other problems faced the Legal Department, such as when George Wright returned home to his tied cottage one day and found a note saying, 'See me tomorrow under the old birch tree.' No, it was not from Fairy Tinkerbelle; the note had been left by George's employer. It continued, 'I have been looking for you and could not find you.' This incident was recounted at a Manchester Industrial Tribunal in the seventies. It was alleged to be one of the reasons why George had been given the sack. Another was that dog droppings, unswept from kennels, had angered the employer, Sir Harold Bibby. It was also alleged that George had failed to maintain fencing and was responsible for an untidy garden.

Things came to a head, said Lady Marjorie Bibby, when George took a day off without seeking Sir Harold's permission. This was what had led to the meeting under the old birch tree. George claimed that the dismissal had been unfair, and won his case with the Union's help. The Tribunal assessed compensation of £350. George said he always swept up droppings and put them in a paper bag. Lady Bibby had also cleaned them up on occasions. 'The only time I refused to do it was a Sunday. I said I was not going to clean up after a dog on Sunday. It is my day of rest'. George Neish, DO, who represented George, said, 'Mr. Wright had one day off in 15 years and seven weeks' holiday in seven years. He earned £25 a week.'

One Summer's day in 1957 changed the life of Lincolnshire farmworker, Leslie Snow. He was on the roof of a corn-drier helping to replace some cyclones,* which had been taken down for overhaul, and tripped, crashing through the asbestos roof. Leslie survived, but was completely paralysed below the waist. The Legal Department sought damages, and almost three years later, George Hook presented Leslie with a cheque for £12,000 in the village hall at Wootton. Leslie was also given the tenancy of a council house, together with a motorised invalid carriage.

On Christmas Eve 1981, Harry Goodwin, of Aylsham, Norfolk, was cleaning out a bull's enclosure at Flash Pit Farm. The bull attacked and gored

---

* Cyclones, by rotating the airstream, cause particles to separate out by centrifugal force and are widely used in many industries for dust collection.

Harry who was paralysed and never able to walk again. The Union rejected an initial offer of £5,000 and an out of court settlement for £80,000 was finally agreed in 1989 – Harry had died in November 1988, but his widow received the money.

Another example of the Union's persistence on behalf of an accident victim finally paying off came in 1989, when another lengthy case was settled. £50,000 was obtained for a member suffering from mushroom grower's lung. George Bailey worked on a mushroom farm in Horley, Surrey, from 1972 to 1986, and suffered wheezing and shortness of breath, and realised it was related to his job. Mushroom grower's lung is caused by spores released by the fungus, and is a recognised industrial disease. He had to leave mushroom growing, and at 52, went back to his old trade of carpentry.

These are but a handful of the cases taken up by the Union over the years, and the outcome of many of them helped to alleviate hardship throughout rural Britain. But it was a costly business – especially as the Union often sought Counsel's opinion in difficult cases – and as the Union's membership declined, it became more and more difficult to sustain financially.

An increasing part of the Legal Department's work, especially as employment legislation improved, was its success in claiming compensation for unfair dismissal. These sums ranged in 1980–81 from £2,500 for a Norfolk member, to £8,000 for a Devon man. Over this two-year period the Union won £92,751.79 in respect of unfair dismissals.

In 1980, in an attempt to rein in the cost of such services, the Union set up a new department called Members' Services, which combined the work of the Legal Department and the case work of the Wages Department. To head it, the EC chose Kevin O'Reilly, who studied at London's College of Law. Following a policy of not refilling certain posts when staff left, the new department ended up being smaller than its predecessors.

These cutbacks led to criticism by some members, and at the 1984 Eastbourne Trade Group Conference an emergency resolution was passed expressing concern over the further reduction in staff of the again renamed (in 1983) Legal/Health and Safety Department at Headland House, which had been cut from pre-merger days from eight to five. It wanted assurances that the department would 'continue to service members in the manner envisaged under the merger agreement.' The work of this department was later transferred to the head office of the TGWU in Smith Square.

Three men, Alfred Dann, George Hook and Jim Watts, contributed in a big way to the success of the Legal Department during and after the Second World War. Alfred was succeeded by George Hook in 1950. A Londoner, George had previously worked in the legal section of the GMWU. He devoted long hours to secure the introduction of the safety, health and welfare legislation, and with a conscientious devotion that was second to none, made remarkable efforts over the years to help the victims of the tied cottage system. In February 1965, he left the office one evening, collapsed from a heart attack outside a hotel and was rushed to hospital, where he died a few hours later.

George was succeeded by another Union official tireless in his work for members, Jim Watts, who was 39. Jim had joined the staff of the Legal Department in 1958, and had been deputy head since 1963. Also a Londoner, he had joined the Navy at the age of 17 in 1943; his ship was torpedoed and he was seriously injured. He had a deep interest in the Labour movement, with a special concern for education. He was an amateur musician and once played in a dance band.

Like George, he gave a great deal of his time to the tied cottage question, and just before the Rent (Agriculture) Act 1976 spent several months trying to see that the proposed legislation gave tied occupants the best protection that the then Labour Government would allow. He retired in 1980. Kevin O'Reilly, who took over from him the legal work, later accepted 'severance pay' after the merger.

Long Struggle for Training

The Union never accepted that the agricultural and horticultural worker was anything other than a skilled man, or woman. And the changing tempo of the industry in the post-war years, with increasing mechanisation and chemical-isation, meant that farmworkers needed greater basic and technical education than did their forefathers in order to make their full contribution to the success of the industry.

It had always encouraged members to extend their technical knowledge, and helped them to take advantage of whatever farm courses were run by local authorities and other institutions. When the De La Warr Committee on Further Education in Agriculture was set up in 1957, S. Brumby, DO for Lindsey, Lincs, was a member. In evidence to the Committee, the Union drew attention to the poor showing of the industry in releasing young workers for part-time education, and the need for a basically sound general education prior to leaving school. It also pointed out that the industry did nothing to encourage workers to seek further educational or technical qualifications.

Against early opposition by farmers, the Union looked upon higher qualifi-cations as a means of obtaining better wages, and the Committee claimed that one of the factors discouraging the wider development of agricultural education was the lack of a wages structure related to definite educational standards. Informal arrangements for pay above the minimum provided little positive incentive to a young employee to pursue a course of study.

The Committee believed there were no insuperable difficulties in the way of expansion of agricultural education, and proposed that all young workers between 15 and 18 should engage in part-time courses over a three-year period, ending with an examination. The release courses could take the form of either day release or block release, leading to a general technical education for all entering the industry. The Union's EC welcomed the proposals and felt that a recommendation to transfer the responsibility for agricultural education to the Minister of Education would be likely to ensure that the facilities for agriculture would be on a par with those provided for other industries.

In a memorandum to MAFF, the Union wanted the De La Warr recommendations put into effect as soon as possible and pointed out that successful implementation depended on the 'active support of employers, since the co-operation of workers is useless unless the employers will make a real effort to release people for part-time education.'28

During 1959, the Lampard–Vachell Committee (LVC) was set up to advise the Minister on the Report's implementation. W. C. H. Luckett, EC, was the Union's representative on it. But, as with so many Parliamentary Committees' recommendations, nothing happened for a long time.

Meanwhile, a limited number of people had trained under the old Agricultural Apprenticeship Council, but in 1960, only 500-odd apprentices had completed training in the previous five years. In 1960, the Council decided to reorganise its scheme and put proposals to the AWB that would mean new wage rates for apprentices and a payment over and above the national minimum when they qualified.

In 1960, the LVC agreed with almost all points of the De La Warr Report, which the Minister of Education accepted. They included a three-stage scheme of courses, planned by the City & Guilds Institute.

That year the NFU organised a conference on industrial training, attended by NUAW representatives W. C. H. Luckett and Edgar Pill. The Union was optimistic that at national level the NFU was doing all it could to encourage both the apprenticeship scheme and general participation in agricultural further education. They were encouraged by the way local education authorities were setting about implementing the recommendations.

Over the years, the Union had done much to encourage technical education and many of its most experienced leaders and officials sat on governing bodies of local authority farm institutes. There was some feeling in the Union that it spent too much time and money from its limited resources on this work, and that technical education should have been readily supplied by the State and the industry itself. This belief grew in the seventies and eighties, with too little to show in real wage advancement for all the efforts the Union had made to see that such education was available and taken up.

In 1962, the City & Guilds Institute formally set out a scheme for part-time education in horticulture. Local initiatives were taken up by some NUAW branches, which arranged lectures on subjects ranging from tractor maintenance to dairy farming.

A note of caution to the euphoria over training was sounded. The Union felt that neither farmers or the workers gave enough attention to formal technical training needed to ensure the industry's future, but said that 'an increasing number of members are taking some form of training – some with conspicuous success.'29

When, in 1964, the Government set up the Advisory Council on Agricultural Education, Harold Collison became a member. That was the year the

Industrial Training Act came into force, and empowered individual industries to set up training boards; the Union regarded the Act as, potentially, most beneficial and called for the establishment of a board for agriculture.

The Agricultural, Horticultural and Forestry Training Board (later shortened to ATB) was set up in August 1966, and the Union members were Ted Calver, Bill Case, John Hose, Harold Midgelow, EC, and Dennis Hodsdon and Edgar Pill. It was a key event for the Union,[30] which regarded its equal employer and employee representation as a big step forward. The Board explored ways of levying employers and of making grants to employers who provided training for employees.

A system of grants for 1968 was announced: employers of approved apprentices, £100 per year; £6 monthly for employers of sandwich course students; and for employers of workers attending approved courses, full cost of wages and up to 75% of course fees. A levy on farmers was set at £6 for each regular full-time employee and £3 for part-timers. The latter was rescinded after protests from employers. The levy system generally came in for considerable criticism from farmers, but the Union gave its full support.

At the start of 1968, the NFU and NUAAW made joint representations that extra Government cash be given beyond the first 12 months normally financed by the State. The Government provided £450,000, on condition that the Board levied farmers for the remainder of its budget; this happened when an anti-ATB group in the NFU was whipping up opposition to its spending. At the end of 1968, demands were made by the NFU to scrap the Board and set up training machinery in a totally different way. The NFU was obviously reluctant to press farmers to continue to contribute towards the cost of training.[31]

Employer opposition to the administration of training by the ATB continued throughout 1969, and the Government suggested deducting the cost of running the Board from the annual Price Review. The NUAAW was not convinced this was a good thing, but did not object if it were the only way for the ATB to continue. Finally, the NFU agreed.

In 1971 the ATB launched a New Entrants Scheme, but due to limited funds could not train as many as it wished. The following year the Government proposed that all training boards should come under a Central Training Agency, and all parties on the ATB objected and wanted to keep 'oversight' of training in the Minister of Agriculture's hands. In 1972, the National Proficiency Test Council sought to improve the standard of its tests and to reduce the cost to students. Forestry was withdrawn from the scope of the ATB after trouble with employers over the levy system, and responsibility given to a new body, the Forestry Training Council.

By 1974, the Union was able to report that the ATB 'is now well and truly established, having the approval of all sides of industry and there is considerable satisfaction with the work it is doing.'[32] That year saw the official winding up of the AAC, its work over.

The number of people taking apprenticeship training courses had by 1975 risen to 4,069 from 1,141 in 1967 under the AAC (the ATB took over in 1971).

The number qualifying for craftsmen certificates rose steadily from 410 in 1972 to 1,464 in 1980. The total number of apprentices between 1967 and 1983 was 69,381 of which 11,344 were recorded as gaining craftsmen certificates. This amounted to 19% and seems low, but one reason was the many drop-outs, indicating the strong pull of better-paid jobs elsewhere. In 1976, the NPTC confirmed that the number of people taking tests to qualify as craftsmen had increased, no doubt due to the enhanced pay rates available under the Wages Structure.

There were Union fears in 1979 that the work of the ATB would be curtailed following a budget cut after the election of the Conservative Government, but training levels remained stable in the early eighties; the fall was to come later. The Government reduced the number of Board members. After 1981 only S. Neale, S Wales, and Ann Hock continued as NUAAW representatives.

During 1984, growth in training was maintained in all programmes except for Entry Training. The Union was disappointed by this fall in the numbers taking up apprenticeships, with 'the situation particularly serious in the East of England.'[33] This was when grants for apprenticeships stopped, and the ATB told that the industry would have to continue to bear a greater share in training costs.

The ATB did good work, but it never had sufficient funding to adequately do the job for which it was established, and the cash benefits the higher technical education should have given its students were not always readily forthcoming.

Chris Morris, for many years chair of its Horticultural Advisory Committee, told me, 'It led to better farming and better-trained workers, and the farmers were pleased to have their men taught at college, but some farmers didn't half muck about. They pretended they had not received the proficiency test certificates and wouldn't pay the rate, but we forced them.'

The ATB training courses remain in force to this day (1989), but the Apprenticeship Scheme was shut down, and the number of workers going through the part-time craft courses was reduced very substantially during the period of Thatcher Government cuts. The ATB did increase the number and variety of short courses. These could be on shearing of sheep, dehorning calves, castrating pigs, or budding roses. Commenting on these short courses, Tony Gould, Regional Officer No 1 Region, who was on the Cornwall ATC in the late 1960s, said, 'Our objection to this sort of regime is that a worker can take a great number of courses and become quite skilled without ever being entitled to more money. Once the idea was that if a worker was trained to a skill, he got more money, now the trend is towards giving them training, but no extra money.'

Another trend was the Tory Government's controversial Youth Opportunities Programme (YOP), which affected agriculture. John Hose told the 1980 TUC Congress that YOP was 'wide open to abuse'. John was following up complaints that some farmers were using the scheme simply as a source of cheap labour. Monitoring the use farmers made of YOP workers, the Union carefully checked up on the way the scheme worked. At the Berks Area Conference in 1982, Geoff Beer, DO, confirmed that farmers were taking advantage of young unemployed people by using them as cheap labour. He knew of regular workers dismissed in trumped-up cases of redundancy, and 'the next week that farmer had a youth employment man in there.'

To cover up the YOP failures, 1983 saw the coming of the Government's so-called Youth Training Scheme. It became the most significant event in agricultural training for years, for it not only provided work experience on the farm, but 13 weeks of job training and education for 16- to 17-year-old school leavers. It was unacceptable to the Union, which was not satisfied that 'the blatant abuse of job substitution which took place under YOP would be eliminated in the proposed YTS.'34

Paul Redgate, Regional Organiser, Region 10, recalling the earlier YOP scheme told me, 'It was a complete farce. Farmers just wanted cheap labour. One farmer even insisted that he would only take YOP workers who could drive a tractor, completely contrary to the alleged purpose of YOP – to train workers.'

The Union was also concerned about general education in rural areas. In its 1965 policy document, *Farming for the Future*, the Union declared, 'A poor basic education, hindered further education for the young adult, both technical and general. The Union believed that the higher entrance qualifications, set by some farm institutes in the sixties, tended to reduce the proportion of entrants from farmworkers' homes, because their children did not have the same opportunity of acquiring GCE qualifications as did children of the boss.'

The Union sent a student each year to Ruskin College, Oxford, and in addition to having fees paid, the student was allowed £2 per week.

Another arrow to the Union's bow was the Workers' Education Association, which it had always supported. The WEA organised evening classes in various subjects with the help of local education authorities, and the Union tried to get as many of its members as possible to attend. At the WEA annual general meeting in London in 1949, the Union had two resolutions, one calling for village community centres, and the second, for the preparation of children for their civic and social responsibilities by senior schools. The first was referred to the EC of the WEA, the second carried.

Writing of the 50th anniversary of the WEA in the *Landworker* in 1953, Edwin Gooch said that many farmworkers in his younger days started without any schooling of any kind. An increasing number of men from the land not only went to school in their youth, but returned to it after they had been at work for some years. It had all been made possible through the good offices of the WEA, which 'provided an organisation in which working people and educationalists could carry on a ceaseless fight for education equality.'

The Union also ran its own weekend and week-long winter schools, mainly on social and trade union issues, and had its own education officer who organised them; one outstanding officer in the post-war years was Edgar Pill.

The merger gave new strength to the Union in the field of education, other than strictly technical training for the industry. The educational facilities offered by the TGWU are first rate, and far exceed anything the old independent Union was able to provide.

REFERENCES

For general information, see A. Sked and C. Cook, *Post War Britain: A Political History*, Pelican Books, 1984.

1. B. R. Mitchell, *British Historical Statistics*, Cambridge University Press, 1988.
2. MAFF figures.
3. *Landworker*, May 1948.
4. *Farmers Weekly*, 1981, p73.
5. Howard Newby, *The Deferential Worker: A study of farmworkers in East Anglia*, Allen Lane, 1977.
6. 12 May 1950.
7. M. Madden, 'The National Union of Agricultural Workers 1906–56', Oxford University B.Lit thesis, 1957. Unpublished.
8. EC Minutes, July 1952.
9. EC Minutes, August 1952.
10. M. Madden, op.cit.
11. *Landworker*, July 1946.
12. EC Minutes, August 1947.
13. M. Madden, op.cit.
14. *Journal of Refugee Studies*, Vol. 1, No 3/4, Paper 3.
15. *Landworker*, September 1955.
16. M. Madden, op.cit.
17. EC Minutes, October 1949.
18. EC Minutes, April 1950.
19. EC Minutes, December 1955.
20. White Paper on Price Review, 1957.
21. Annual Report, 1965.
22. *Landworker*, January 1967.
23. Annual Report, 1967.
24. Annual Report, 1971.
25. Newby, op.cit.
26. New Earnings Survey, October 1984.
27. HMSO, 1969.
28. Annual Report, 1958.
29. Annual Report, 1963.
30. 'Outlook for Agriculture and its Environment, 1976', NUAAW.
31. Annual Report, 1968.
32. Annual Report, 1974.
33. Annual Report, 1984.
34. Annual Report, 1983.

14

Common Market: 'Disaster Day' Looms for Britain

A fool sees not the same tree that a wise man sees
William Blake

Widespread Opposition

Britain's joining the Common Market had a considerable effect on our agriculture, and consequently, farm and horticultural workers. There was widespread opposition in the Union to joining, and many battles were fought within it before Britain signed up.

During 1954–6 there had been much discussion in the Union on the European Free Trade Association.* Right from the start the EC had adopted the attitude that agriculture should be excluded from EFTA. But the matter came before the 1958 Biennial in a motion opposing EC policy. E. Atkinson, Essex, moved a resolution that it was essential for Britain to join EFTA. British farms could never supply all the needs of the home market, but if maintained in a healthy condition need not fear competition within the European partnership. J. Dunman, Berks, opposed, supporting the EC and the motion was lost.

What the Tory Government's intentions were with regard to the favoured alternative to EFTA, the Common Market, especially in regard to agriculture, had become a burning question by the early sixties. A debate took place in the House of Commons in June 1961, but it did not offer much enlightenment as to the Government's position. All that emerged was that both the Tories and Labour were divided on the issue.

Edwin Gooch said, 'The Government has not yet made up their minds about it. Nor have the Opposition. I made up my mind a long time ago. I am

---

* An economic free trade area created in 1960 composed of Austria, Denmark, Norway, Portugal, Sweden, Switzerland, the UK and Finland. Unlike the Common Market, there was no common external tariff on imports from the rest of the world, and members retained their own agricultural policies.

utterly opposed to it from the point of view of agriculture, and I shall continue to tell the farmworkers that it will be a disastrous day for them if Great Britain enters the Common Market.'

Later in 1961 Prime Minister Harold Macmillan announced that the Government would be applying for the opening of negotiations for Britain to join. In the intervening months, opinion had been growing that the interests of Britain would best be served by joining the Common Market, or the EEC, as it was known. But to have done so on the existing terms of the Treaty of Rome would have been to agree to the ending of the existing methods of supporting agriculture in Britain. It would also mean the ending of preferential trading arrangements for the Commonwealth.

The detailed agricultural policy of the EEC had not then been formulated. Only the broad outline was contained in the Rome Treaty. The basis of it was that no country should have individual subsidies for farm or horticultural produce, that there should be free trade in these products between member countries, and that imports of food from outside the Six* should be subject to tariffs. The level of prices at the farm gate would be determined by what were called target prices, but there would be no guarantee that these prices would be reached. Because of tariffs, prices would be higher than world prices and the cost of food to the consumer would be higher.

This was in direct opposition to our system under which prices to farmers were guaranteed and imports allowed into the country with very few restrictive tariffs or quotas. To accept the Rome Treaty as it stood was virtually to abandon the Agriculture Acts of 1947, 1957, 1964 and 1967, which set up a system of State support based on an annual review of farm incomes, costs and profits. The guaranteed prices meant that produce went as cheaply as possible to the consumer, and it was virtually all consumed, not stockpiled or deliberately destroyed as was later to be the case under EEC dictates.

The Union recognised that not to join the EEC could lead to the dumping of its farm surpluses here and make it very difficult to maintain support for British agriculture. It was for these reasons that the Union's EC confirmed their earlier position that they could not agree to Britain's entry on the terms of the Rome Treaty. The Prime Minister said that satisfactory solutions would be sought to each of these problems.

Defending the Union's 'uncommitted' attitude, Harold Collison said that both the TUC and Labour Party had adopted 'a wait and see policy'.[1] Until negotiations revealed exactly how the Rome Treaty would be interpreted in relation to Britain, it would be impossible for anyone to make a final judgement. There was an understandable concern because of the conditions which existed in agriculture in the old free trading days of this country. 'If Britain were to join the EEC, our markets would be free for trade from other member countries, but they would be protected against competition from the

---

* France, West Germany, Italy, Belgium, Holland and Luxembourg.

rest of the world. Nevertheless it is clear that we could not sustain our present system of agricultural support if we signed the Rome Treaty as it stands, and it would be stupid if we were to agree to throw away the very foundation which, for the first time in living memory, has enabled the industry, and those in it to enjoy a moderate degree of security.'

The NFU originally opposed entry, but supported it under the Conservative Prime Minister Edward Heath, and Labour's former Minister of Agriculture, Fred Peart, also an anti-Marketeer, changed to passive acceptance saying that while the Common Agricultural Policy was not perfect, it was negotiable. Attempts to reform CAP were still going on 20 years later, without much success. Leader of the NFU, Sir Henry Plumb, saw to it that the farmers did well when Britain finally entered, and ended up as President of the European Parliament.

Decks Cleared to Join

After weeks of argument, the Six countries of the EEC in January 1962 reached agreement on the next stages of their agricultural policy, which had a twofold significance for Britain. It meant that the decks had been cleared for the negotiations arising out of Britain's application to join. The basic principle on which the agricultural policy of the Six would rest was the fixing of common price levels for all products except fruit, vegetables and wine. These would be maintained above the world price level by import levies on goods from countries outside the Six. If farm gate prices fell below 'target' prices, governments would either buy up the surplus or impose special import restrictions. There would be no target prices for eggs, pork or poultry, but they proposed import levies based on the target prices of feed grains. The idea was that these levies would measure the differences between feeding costs inside and outside the EEC.

At the 1962 Bournemouth Biennial, the Union formally registered its adherence to official Labour policy on the EEC when – by 70 votes to 51 – Conference carried an amendment to a composite moved by Joan Maynard, Yorks: 'This Conference welcomes and supports the lead given by our President in opposing Britain's entry. We cannot agree to decisions concerning the policies of our country being taken other than by our elected Government.' Emphasising the political aspects of Britain entering, Joan quoted Professor Hallstein, EEC president, 'We are in politics, not in business'. Joan said it was a proposal not to unite Europe, but to keep it divided. Seconding, Alf Fooks, Dorset, said entry would make Britain merely an off-shore island of the Continent whose people would come to look upon us as 'relics' of a once great world power.

Ted Calver and H. Dellar, Cambs, moved and seconded the amendment which deleted all words after Conference and inserted: 'is opposed to Britain entering the Common Market until a satisfactory solution can be found to safeguard the interests of British agriculture and the interests of the Common-wealth.' John Hose, Nottingham, an 'unrepentant free trader' supported the amendment.

Reminding delegates that our wages were the highest in Europe, A. Baynham, Worcester, believed that entry would level these down. The notion that the EEC would extend free trade was disputed by Ted Sales, Dorset. W. Dolan, Notts, said that foreigners would be no threat to British farmworkers who had the best record in the world.

Harold Collison, replying, said entry meant that food prices would go up. 'Because people do not pay a proper price for food, our chaps do not get paid enough.' The amendment carried, it became the substantive motion; only a few voted against.

In 1966, just before the General Election, Harold Collison made a definitive statement of the Union's policy on entry in light of a changing situation. Declaring that the NUAW was on all fours with Labour on the question, he said, 'Our Union would not oppose Britain joining providing adequate means can be found to safeguard the interests of agriculture, the Commonwealth and EFTA.

'It seems that they [the Conservatives] would be prepared to throw overboard the principles of the 1947 and 1957 Acts which have provided the agricultural community with a longer period of sustained prosperity than the industry has ever known. It has been estimated that the abolition of deficiency payments in favour of a variable levy system proposed by the Conservatives would add about seven per cent to British food prices . . . prior to entry we should require minimum assurances calculated to enhance rather than depress our agricultural economy, and help rather than hindrance to our Union's declared aim of improving farmworkers' wages . . . I also believe that in due time Britain and other EFTA countries will join the Common Market . . . But our many related interests must be first considered with great care. Otherwise, if we rush prematurely into the EEC we may meet disaster and fall flat on our economic face.'

Application to Join

Labour won the General Election in 1966 and Harold Wilson's cabinet decided by 13 to 8 on unconditional application for membership. It was vetoed by General De Gaulle.

Times had changed, and both the main political parties were now in favour of Britain entering the EEC, said Ted Sales, Dorset, at the 1968 Biennial when moving that 'Conference reaffirms its previous decision to oppose entry . . . unless satisfactory conditions are negotiated . . .' E. Peachey, Hants, and A. Hemming, Worcester, supported entry on the grounds that our agriculture required a large economic area for expansion.

Harold Collison said that the industry was split through the middle on the question. Cereal farmers were in favour. It was not a question of voting for or against entry, but reaffirming the Union's earlier decision that they were opposed to entry unless the interests of the Commonwealth, EFTA countries, and above all, agriculture were safeguarded. Ted Sales agreed that the motion did not flatly oppose entry, and it was carried.

This stance was echoed at the Labour conference a year later when Jack Jones, TGWU, called upon the Government, in any negotiations, 'to insist on adequate safeguards for Britain's balance of payments, cost of living, National Health and Social Security systems, and power of independent decision in economic planning and foreign policy.'

Ted Sales kept up his opposition when he moved, 'That this Conference opposes Britain's entry' at the 1970 Biennial. Seconding, G. Easton, N Yorks, said, 'I cannot see us getting better wages with being in the EEC.' Peter Medhurst, Yorks, said that CAP maintained an inefficient agriculture artificially through high prices and would be a growing burden to both taxpayers and consumers.

Cyril Tabiner, Lincs, thought the balance of payments surplus achieved by the Labour Government would be thrown away if we joined. How right he was; in the years that followed, Britain achieved all-time record balance of payments deficits.

There was some support for joining. F. Peachey, Hants, thought European workers did better for social security, holidays and sickness aid, while G. Beer, Berks, said wages and the growth rates were higher in the EEC.

The motion was carried by two votes. This decision was reaffirmed with much larger margins at later biennials at Weymouth and Clacton, and meant a change of position, for previously the Union had not opposed entry providing the interests of EFTA countries, the Commonwealth and UK agriculture were fully protected.

A similar composite opposing entry came up at the 1970 TUC. It firmly opposed entry, believing that the Treaty of Rome would 'impose injurious social, economic and political effects on present and future generations of British citizens.' Earlier, Vic Feather, TUC General Secretary, had asked delegates to reject both pro- and anti-Market resolutions and to accept one report which urged Congress to reserve its position.

The composite in which the NUAAW was associated was moved by Dan McGarvey, boilermakers' leader, seconded by Clive Jenkins, ASTMS. Reg Bottini said entry would drastically increase the cost of living. He criticised one report for making no mention whatever of the loss of national sovereignty. 'If this trade union movement is opposed to any attack on trade union rights should we not be similarly opposed to whole chunks of the laws of our land being subordinate to the Commission in Brussels?'

In the event, the NUAAW-supported resolution was lost. The report of the General Council was opposed by the NUAAW but carried by Congress, which meant that the TUC policy as formulated and agreed in 1967 awaited the outcome of the current negotiations.

Anti-EEC Position Maintained

At the 1970 Labour Conference, Reg Bottini conscientiously put the Union's anti-entry position. He failed to see the need for entry when it was evident that the best possible terms would not improve our standard of living. The NEC secured a 95,000 vote defeat of a composite moved by the TGWU to keep Britain out.

In 1970 the Union issued a 16-point document outlining its objections to Britain's entry. The relative stability and prosperity of British agriculture, already put at risk by Conservative policies, would be further eroded if we joined the Six, said the Union. On farm wages, factors like differing social service arrangements made meaningful comparisons difficult, but during 1968 the wages of farmworkers in Germany, France and Belgium, were inferior to those paid in the UK. Also, that forbidding living-costs booster, VAT, would be imposed on Britain. The document concluded that the EEC was a 'rich man's club'.

On television, Opposition leader Harold Wilson hinted that he hoped to pressure Mr. Heath into an early General Election, with Britain's entry as the overriding issue. He said, 'As to the general proposition that it would be a good thing to get into Europe if the terms were right, I have no disagreement.'

And the great EEC debate continued; it was a constant topic at county rallies and opponents included both right and left wingers. Bert Hazell told members at Mulbarton, Norfolk, that 'Britain built her industrial wealth and prosperity by dealing with the whole world. Once you create a block you set up prejudices and suspicions which is the very opposite to real trade union principles and understanding.'

Peter Shore, Labour's most effective anti-Common Market spokesman, told the Skegness Rally, that he foresaw the UK, should we join, being part of an economic and monetary union in Western Europe. The total annual cost of entry could be over £700 million. 'It isn't a bargain, it's a surrender. It doesn't make sense.'[2]

Later in 1971 the *Landworker* criticised the White Paper, *The UK and the European Communities*. It was not so much a White Paper as 'a party political tract' and a 'study in evasion of real intent' and declared, 'The majority of the electorate . . . recognise full well that they were "had" by Heath's promises in 1970 and the nation must, therefore, guard against being taken for a similar ride on this most crucial issue.' It reiterated the view that Britain had much to lose by joining.

A special Labour conference, in London in 1971, accepted a statement that the NEC would agree on a definitive resolution on Britain's entry on the terms contained in the White Paper, taking into account the proceedings of the special conference. The NUAAW delegates, Bert Hazell, Reg Bottini, Jess Waterman, Chris Morris, Ted Calver and Ted Chamberlain, supported the NEC, but were clearly mandated by the Biennial to vote against entry when the matter went to the vote at the Labour conference later that year.

Conference listened to no fewer than 50 speeches equally divided between pro- and anti-Marketeers, confirming, that like the Tory and Liberal parties,

Labour was split on this crucial issue. Peter Shore won loud applause, as did dedicated pro-Marketeer John Mackintosh, MP for Berwickshire and East Lothian, the bulk of whose constituents made their living by agriculture and fisheries. Clive Jenkins mischievously asked the Labour Committee on Europe to declare the source of their finances which enabled them to mount an expensive propaganda campaign, second only to that conducted by the Government with taxpayer's money. 'Until they do so, suspicion will grow,' he said. Roy Grantham, CAWU, aspired to an academic approach and was wildly pro-Market.

As part of the move towards entry, it was announced in 1971 that from April 1973 both SET* and purchase tax were to be replaced by VAT. The NFU wanted farm products free of VAT, and the Union wished the NFU every success in this overture. Unlike the EEC countries where food was taxed, the British Government made it clear that food here would not be taxed. It was some years before this pledge was broken and VAT added to restaurant and hotel bills, and take-away food, such as fish and chips.

At the 1971 Tolpuddle Rally, Harold Wilson said that while advocating a free competitive market, the Government was now trying to push Britain into a restrictive European market, on terms that would have to be paid for by every British taxpayer, family and housewife.

The EEC was again one of the major issues at the 1971 TUC Conference. By a strong vote, including the Union's delegation, Congress carried a composite opposing the current proposal to join, and demanded a General Election before any decision was taken.

The Labour Conference that year rejected the EEC terms arrived at by the Government. The Union delegation abstained on this vote since its policy was still one of outright opposition, whatever the terms negotiated by whatever Government.

Arguments continued over membership, and a Labour White Paper published in 1970 was followed by the Government's promise to enter into negotiations with the Six. Formal negotiations were planned for July, but on 19 June, Labour lost a General Election. Conservative Ministers had only been in office eight days, when instead of asking for a postponement, picked up Civil Service briefs and went into the negotiations. The basis of Wilson's intended negotiating speech was delivered by the Tory, Anthony Barber, in Luxembourg.

Britain Joins

It was on 26 October 1971 that 69 Labour MPs voted with the Tories, and 20 abstained, giving the Tory Government a majority in favour of EEC membership. The leader in the Labour revolt was Roy Jenkins, and his lieutenant, William Rodgers, who later, with David Owen and Shirley Williams formed

---

*   Selective Employment Tax.

the breakaway Social Democrats, which helped keep Labour out of office for many years.

At the 1972 Biennial at Weymouth, Bert Hazell said that two years previously it voted against Britain joining the EEC. This decision reflected the opinion of the majority of people in this country, yet the Government had gone ahead in its plans to secure membership, failing in the process to obtain the views of the electorate. He made it clear that the Union was still against the concept of the EEC, and 'until Conference changes that policy it must remain'.

Largely due to entry, the seventies saw a change to the pattern of life in Britain unequalled in any previous decade. Huge changes came about in agriculture, and in social and industrial policies; VAT bore heavily on poorer sections of the community, and enabled taxation on the rich to be reduced.

To all this the Union had to adjust, often painfully, at a time when membership was falling. At the 1972 TUC, the Union continued to fight EEC membership, and to withdraw. Reg Bottini noted at that year's Shropshire County Conference that entry had brought into public focus the whole question of food prices, and 'The recent dramatic rise in the prices of the main farm products had focused public attention on this sharp contradiction.' The Government sought to blame 'world prices', but as *Labour Weekly* pointed out, '. . . figures that are available show that Britain's food prices were rising faster than those of any country for which figures are known.'

It was in 1973 that Labour published *Programme for Britain*, setting out policies a next Labour Government was likely to introduce. The buying-in of excess supplies under CAP created an artificial shortage to keep the prices up in the shops. This buying up and dumping of 'surplus' products meant heavy taxes to finance these payments. Labour believed that measures could be introduced to deal with the excess food and change CAP into a more sensible policy.

The document contained a reminder that Labour's Annual Conference in 1972 opposed British membership on the terms negotiated by the Tory Government. Whilst the consent of the British people had never been obtained, many of the key facts about the negotiations, including the crippling cost to Britain had been suppressed. The British people must still be given an opportunity to express their view before the question could be regarded as settled.

Referendum on Membership

Labour won the General Election in 1974, but it was a minority Government, uncertain about the support it was going to get for its policies from other groups, such as the Liberals. Its declared aim for UK agriculture was to return to the old days of cheaper food, combined with a support system for the farmers based on guaranteed prices. They wanted to re-negotiate the terms under which Britain joined the EEC, with the right to subsidise key foods.

There was a lively debate at that year's Union Biennial at Clacton which reaffirmed opposition to the EEC, and at a special four-day Labour Conference in November 1975 delegates violently opposed EEC policy. Bert Hazell pointed out the absurdities of CAP, and in a resolution backed by the NEC and carried by an overwhelming show of hands, the Government was told that the much heralded referendum on membership should take place no later than October.

In an editorial running up to the referendum, the *Landworker* quoted Labour's respected elder statesman and anti-Marketeer, Douglas Jay, saying, 'The crucial question is not whether any individual foodstuff is cheaper in the EEC or outside, but whether we have the power in the future to buy where that commodity is cheaper . . . If that power is limited, we are bound to be worse off . . .'

A TUC statement explained why it had turned its back on EEC institutions. 'Congress is concerned about British sovereignty, about British power to decide what is right for Britain.' Congress suspected that free movement of capital would drain away British resources (which is precisely what did happen and helped towards the de-industrialisation of Britain in the eighties).

In a *Landworker* article, Tony Marshall asked, 'Where are all the benefits we were told we'd receive from membership? Remember the prosperity we were promised by Mr. Heath before he dragged us in? Look at the unemployment figures – how they've got much worse since we came under Brussels' domination. With nearly three quarters of the EEC's Budget going towards financing CAP, you'd think that agriculture in this country might have seen some benefit even if other industries did not. And yet we've just seen the first cutback in overall home food production for years. Beef, poultry, eggs and the horticultural side of the industry have all been hit in recent months – workers are being laid off left, right and centre . . .'

In a special article Bert Hazell advised members to vote 'No' on June 5 in the referendum held as promised under a new Labour Government. But the 'antis' had an unequal fight on their hands.

Labour Research pointed out that the pro-Marketeers spent ten times the amount the antis did in the months leading up to the referendum. Britain in Europe spent £1,481,583 against only £133,630 by the National Referendum Campaign. Of the 43 contributors who gave over £10,000 or more to Britain in Europe, 27 were also important backers of the Tory Party, Aims of Industry, the Economic League and other anti-working class organisations. The number of companies who contributed was 291, including ICI, Shell, Ford, Unilever, plus insurance companies and banks. In the referendum, 67.2% said 'Yes', and 32.8% 'No' to continued membership.

The folly of CAP was highlighted in *Tribune* in 1975 by Ron Thomas, MP, Bristol N West, who revealed that thousands of pounds were being made by British and continental grain importers, shipping French barley into Avonmouth docks, unloading it and shipping it to some other EEC port. A ship unloaded 900 tons of barley; next day it was reloaded for Italy. EEC regulations allowed advantage to be taken of a subsidy to deal with price differentials. The profit was over £3,000.

Financial resources of CAP were made up of variable import levies, taxes on food entering EEC countries and a proportion of VAT. This system tried to give farmers a pre-determined level of prices for their products by end-price support. Variable import levies made the consumer, not the exchequer, pay a high price for food. Hundreds of millions of pounds went on buying up the surplus 1.1 million tons of skimmed milk powder, and a further £339 million was set aside as 'aid for skimmed milk intended for animal feeding stuffs'. *The Economist* said: 'This means that EEC money is issued to subsidise buying milk from farmers, converting it into skimmed milk powder, and adding water to it so that it can be fed back to calves of the cows that supplied it in the first place. This in turn will enable the calves to grow up so that they can produce more subsidised milk! What could be more absurd?'

Brussels Lays Down the Law

Although the pro-Marketeers said it would never happen, in 1976 it became apparent that the EEC bureaucracy began to lay down the law on British farm policy. The Government admitted that an EEC move to force the use of skimmed milk powder in animal feed would remain the law in Britain. Already price rises since joining the EEC had led to a reduction in the demand for home-produced beef. British beef was starting to build up in intervention stores, and reached an incredible 7,000 tons after only a few weeks.

Its objections to CAP were repeated in 1976 in the Union's major policy document, *Outlook for Agriculture*, the third produced since the Second World War. It recognised that the agricultural situation was vastly different from that at the time of publication of its *Farming for the Future* in 1965. The most crucial change was the UK joining the EEC. Despite the fact that CAP is, stated the new document, 'in some disorder and needs urgent re-shaping, due account must obviously be taken of its future impact on most of the main identifiable elements of UK agriculture; those for example of production targets, marketing and use and ownership of agricultural land . . .' It said, 'CAP must somehow be made sufficiently flexible to adapt itself continually both to the Community and world conditions which are changing all the time. Basically, we want to see it more outward looking than it has been over the years, with emphasis on encouraging rather than restructuring trade through the world.' The Union reiterated that it was not happy with the EEC pricing system, preferring something like the old UK price-deficiency payment system.

Early in 1977, the *Landworker* asked why there was an estimated 10% surplus of milk and milk products in the EEC, 'when in this country we not only consume all we produce but are a net importer? A good deal of the credit for the UK situation must lie with the Milk Marketing Board, for the effective manner in which they have promoted the sale of liquid milk.' It all 'reinforced the logic of the NUAAW's policy on marketing'. If there had been similar bodies in Europe we would not have a 'surplus' milk problem.

Reg Bottini, in 1977, came to the defence of Britain's embattled dairy industry suffering from 'surpluses' that threatened the jobs of nearly 10,000 dairy workers. He called for free school milk, and said, 'one of the most destructive acts of petty meanness of the last Tory Government was cutting off free school milk.'

However, the Union had to face the fact that Britain was now in the EEC, the press largely hid the appalling cost to the consumer, and criticism of the membership was becoming more muted; the Union felt it could best help agriculture and the consumer by seeking to mitigate the worst effects of the EEC on Britain by seeking changes to CAP. At the 1977 Labour Conference at Brighton, Reg Bottini defended the Union's position on the EEC. He said CAP needed reforming, but the Union opposed a move by the Newcastle upon Tyne Labour Party which sought a possible withdrawal from CAP, and cheap food for Britain from other countries.

'Capitalism is responsible for our troubles – not the EEC,' Jack Boddy told the 1978 Biennial when he opposed Kent's call for the UK to get out. Kent's Mike Johnson, and Roger Fieldhouse, N Yorks, mounted a strong attack on the EEC and especially on CAP. Fieldhouse said CAP was a mechanism for keeping farm prices up and 'there is no evidence that high food prices are passed on to farmworkers in the form of higher wages.' The motion to leave the EEC had already been lost, and he was proposing a resolution which opposed any increase in food prices, and sought fundamental reform in CAP so as to remove taxes on food and permit cheaper imports. He sought to bring the Union's policy on CAP into line with that of the TUC and the rest of the Labour movement, a change from the policy decided two years earlier at Malvern.

Cyril Tabiner, Lincs, supported a fundamental reform of CAP, yet opposed the motion as it stood. 'How the hell can we keep food prices down and put wages up?' he asked. For the leadership, Jack Boddy said that cheap food had meant a disastrously low income for agricultural workers. 'I agree we don't get any more if food prices are higher,' he said. 'The only way we get more is by fighting for it. But you cannot extract money from an industry which has not got it.' The motion was lost.

CAP is harming the British economy and its working people – and if our present high contribution to the Community budget is not drastically cut we should reconsider our membership. This was the main drift of Wilf Page's speech to the 1979 TUC on a composite proposed by the NUAAW. The resolution, unanimously backed by Congress, noted that Britain made the highest contribution to the EEC Budget, a large proportion of which was 'absurdly spent on dumping or storing surpluses', and called upon the Government 'to negotiate an end to the present imbalances in levies, intervention payments and stockpiling; further the Government should refuse to pay more than its fair share of the EEC budget failing which, membership of the EEC should be reconsidered.'

Setbacks for Farmworkers

By the end of 1979, job losses were beginning for British sugar beet processors, and the farmworkers who grew the beet, following EEC cuts in sugar production.

British fruit growers were threatened by imports of large quantities of French 'Golden Delicious' apples, while many traditional English apples were spurned by the retailers. The 1980 Biennial called for a review of CAP and all its illogicalities and demanded an import ban on the French apples.

Despite the Tory Government crowing loudly in 1980 about its 'success' in cutting Britain's membership fee for the EEC by around £750 million, it was in fact a hollow victory, for the money was not handed back to Britain to spend. It could only be spent on projects in Britain approved by the EEC.

As part of its 'rationalisation' of milk production, the EEC insisted on cutting back production in Britain. Some dairy farmers did not find this unacceptable. They got an EEC 'golden handshake' – £700 to £750 for each cow slaughtered. For a herd of 60 that was £45,000, but for the herdsman who lost his job, he got only about a week's pay for every year of service. The Union demanded compensation to match that of the farmers, but they never got it.

By 1980 almost 7,000 dairy farmers got out of milk. More than 250,000 cows were involved, with an average herd size of 37, higher than in any other EEC country.

The wife of one herdsman told the *Landworker* what the slaughter of their herd meant to them. His redundancy money came to £700. At the age of 33, he wrote and telephoned about new jobs, and placed adverts under 'situations wanted' in four publications at a cost of £25, without success. His wife said, 'We are prepared to move to another part of the country, the £700 would just about cover removal costs, but this is not a step which can be taken quite as lightly as Mrs. Thatcher seems to think – it will create problems with my husband's parents, both of whom suffer ill-health but are presently close by.'

Another factor to be taken into account with a herdsman, not common to most other workers, is his personal involvement with his cows, which by the nature of the work is inevitable in the interests of good husbandry. This herdsman's wife added: 'The fact that the herd which my husband has worked so hard to produce and which represents several years of his life's work is soon to be slaughtered has absolutely shattered him and I know, as only a wife can, the genuine anguish and distress this is causing him.' Such anguish was very real. One herdsman killed himself after being made redundant.

To hell with the Brussels mandarins – let's expand our dairy industry. That was the firm message from the 1980 TUC Congress after it heard NUAAW Lincs organiser, Alec Russell, say, 'We must stop the slaughter of our cows ... Farmers could carry on with other sorts of farming, but workers who lost their jobs joined the dole queues.'

In the early eighties, when the total cost of State support for British farming within CAP was estimated at between £3 billion to £5 billion annually, the Union continued to press for compensation for redundant cowmen, but the EEC made it clear that workers would get nothing. In a letter to Jack Boddy, the EEC's Deputy Director General for agriculture told him: '. . . should, however, the case of redundancy arise for dairy workers, we do not expect that they would have particular difficulties in normal circumstances to find alternative employment . . . if, however, special circumstances occur where dairy workers cannot find alternative employment in a particular field, they can have recourse to the European Social Fund which provides finance . . . for the retraining of workers for other occupations.'

Jack reacted angrily to this flat 'No'. 'It's all very well . . . to talk about retraining him. He's got a rare and vital skill – why should he throw it away, why should he do so for nothing.'

The *Landworker* declared in March 1981 that the EEC had stolen well over 4,000 jobs in agriculture in the previous few months. 'And these are only the redundancies directly resulting from EEC interference in UK agriculture.'

The Union turned its attention to the UK glasshouse industry, threatened with destruction by Dutch competition, which was clearly unfair under EEC rules. Subsidised Dutch tomatoes, cucumbers and pot plants represented a real threat to jobs in the UK. It was at this time that the NUAAW launched its 'Buy British, Save Jobs' campaign. Coverage in national and local papers, radio and TV was high, with Union members much in demand to appear before cameras and microphones. With pickets at the docks and high street stores, the campaign caught the public imagination, more of which is discussed in Chapter 20 covering the poultry industry.

The Trade Group Conference at Skegness in 1982 voted for Britain to get out of the EEC. Closing the debate on the call for withdrawal, 'in the best interests of British working people which would move the Trade Group into line with Labour Party and TUC policy,' Jack Boddy said. 'We are not asking to get out because we are against Europe, and don't think all our problems will be solved by this move. We will have new ones – but the TUC and the Labour Party are currently working out new plans for the future.'

Moving the motion, Joan Maynard said, 'going into the EEC was one of the greatest disasters that has ever happened to this country. We have lost our sovereignty – the right to take action over our own affairs. We've only gone into part of Europe. It is nothing to do with socialism. It is there for the multi-nationals . . .' Most delegates spoke against membership, although Stuart Neale, S Wales, accepted the loss of sovereignty, saying, 'That is the whole idea of Europe'.

The TUC policy for withdrawal was confirmed at the 1982 Congress; there were still good reasons for getting out. In 1982 the price Britain paid for EEC beef was 65% above the world price. For butter and cheese 45% more, for cereals 25% more. We were paying 70p tax on a pound of beef, 50p on a pound of cheese, 42p on butter, 8p on sugar, and 2.7p on wheat.

Thanks to CAP, British consumers were paying over £2,000 million more than they should be for their food. These figures were given by Chris Jones, who worked for Labour's EEC spokesman in the House of Commons. Mr. Jones also revealed how we paid as taxpayers, too. That year's CAP Budget was £7,000 million. Administration and storage costs came to £1,000 million. Destroying food,* feeding human-quality food to animals, selling it cheap to charities (Eton College, that well known 'charity', got cheap butter), cost another £1,400 million.

A new Labour Government would negotiate Britain's withdrawal from the EEC within five years (this policy was dropped in 1989 under Neil Kinnock's leadership), that was one major pledge given by the Party in 1983 as the basis of its manifesto for the next General Election, called *New Hope for Britain*. It said, 'Britain needs a good agricultural policy much more in line with our needs and this is one of the prime reasons for leaving the EEC. Instead of the inflated prices of the EEC's CAP, we will support our agriculture through deficiency payments, coupled, where necessary, with limited intervention buying and direct income support.' But no Labour Government was to emerge, the Tories again won the next Election.

Under the headline 'Slim the Farmer', Stephen Milligan wrote in the *Sunday Times* in 1984 an article that aptly summed up the position of the British farmer within the EEC. 'You have to admire their cheek, British farmers are more subsidised than the miner, more protected than the BL workers and more cosseted than civil servants. But when their privileges might be reduced there was a farmyard chorus of squeals and bleats.' Farm Minister Michael Jopling had agreed to a series of reforms to CAP, and the 'excessive prices' that they were guaranteed would fall by 0.6%. But 'much of the Tory Party is rallying to the defence of the fattest lame duck in the national pond.' He pointed out that in 1983 Britain's 201,000 farmers got a handout of £1,688 billion, worth £8,440 to the average farmer, paid partly by the national exchequer and partly by the EEC. 'But this was merely the marzipan on a fruity cake. British farmers also received far higher prices for their products than prevailing world prices.'

Labour's John Silkin was the only British Agriculture Minister who made a real attempt to reform CAP, but he was to be placated by special arrangements, such as subsidising butter for British consumers. Finally, in the 1980s, European Ministers had to face up to the fact that CAP, with all its absurdities and extravagances, was a monstrous castle of bureaucracy and waste, and agreed to reform CAP, then grabbing over 70% of the entire budget. That reform took place with the alacrity of a spavined carthorse, and the British consumer still had to pay the full manipulated market price for food.

---

* The EEC destroyed 2.6 million tons of food in 1987, according to Labour Euro MP Stan Newens (*Daily Telegraph, 20 December 1988*).

The EEC never boosted investment in Britain, but between 1973 and 1987, the total of British capital invested in other EEC countries totalled £36,401 million, money badly needed by our native industries. The EEC had lived up to expectations as the big businessman's club, as many NUAAW leaders had predicted. In 1987, UK citizens were taxed an extra £3,600 million for CAP and also paid an extra £4,000 million to £5,000 million in higher food prices. The National Consumer Council estimated in 1988 a family of four in Britain paid an additional £13.50 each week because of CAP.

Entering the EEC cost Britain heavily, and still does. The cover up continues in most of the pliant British press, some of it linked to transnational companies which have done well out of the EEC.

REFERENCES

1. *Landworker*, November 1961.
2. Total average annual EEC Budget payment by the UK 1976–86 turned out to be £987 million.

15

Women in the Union

Would men but follow what the sex advise,
All things would prosper, all the world grow wise.

Pope

Changing Attitudes

Women have for centuries played an important part in agriculture, especially at harvest times, and as casual labour during sowing, when many extra hands were needed. And more than a few women over the years preceding the Second World War became full-time workers in the industry.

Yet, until recent times, they were allowed only a very subordinate role in Union affairs; they were the tea makers and loyal supporters of their activist husbands in 101 ways. One suspects that much of the office work of many a branch secretary was done by his hard-working wife.

A post-war year book of Shrewsbury Trades Council, to which NUAW branches were affiliated, had a graceful foreword giving thanks to the women, 'who spend lonely evenings at home whilst we are attending meetings; who share our agitation and triumphs when we return home; who never complain when we dash in and dash out without bothering to sample the nicely cooked meal; who keep our papers orderly and suits neatly pressed ready for "unexpected" meetings; whose evening out is so frequently upset when we advise them that we have got an "emergency meeting". ' To which the *Landworker*, without a trace of irony, added, 'We hope this expresses what our local branch officers feel about their womenfolk'.

Women in the Union not only had to fight the prejudice of men, but the prejudice of some women as well, women who were apathetic about their role in the affairs of 'mankind'.

Some were content to be the 'decorative' element when they accompanied their husbands to Union conferences, but this didn't mean that there were not many women in the Union and outside it who were keen to further the cause of the NUAW and the farmworker – how could they be otherwise? Often they had to bring up families on the industry's traditionally low pay, and they and their loved ones suffered the deprivations of living in rural areas;

the poor education and poor housing, which included the frightening possibility of being made homeless if they lived in a tied cottage.

Those women who defied the tradition of generations as second-class citizens started the fight for an equal role in society, and the Union. Some, like Joan Maynard, rose to a great height in the Union, and today it is difficult to accept what a lowly position they were once allocated.

When an Organisers' Social was held in the Pindar of Wakefield in Gray's Inn Road in January 1948, the *Landworker* reported, 'A dance band was engaged and the younger members of the softer sex present displayed considerable suppleness and grace.' Today, we would consider that sexist, but they hadn't even heard of the word.

Not surprisingly then, only two women were delegates to the 1948 Biennial at Scarborough: they were Mrs. M. Workman, Gloucester, and Mrs. G. Butterfield, Essex. But in the ballot for delegates, Mrs. Workman headed all candidates, with 1,826 votes.

At the first annual dinner of Walsingham (Norfolk) branch in 1954, Edwin Gooch presented a cheque to Mrs. Sarah Norman, of Wells branch, who although 80 years of age, still acted, as the *Landworker* phrased it, as unofficial collector to the Union, a job she had done for over 30 years. Sterling work, yet 'unofficial'.

In 1947 the *Landworker* had noted that 'women are playing an increasingly important part in our movement', and was 'confident' that there was not a younger woman secretary than Audrey Manners, of Houghton (Hants) branch, 'or one who is doing better work on behalf of the Union'. Audrey, aged 17, had completed a course at Sparsholt Farm Institute and worked on her father's smallholding.

Undoubtedly women were playing an increasing part in the Union. In 1949 the *Landworker* published a picture on its front page of 18-year-old Joan Anderson, with another girl, stooking corn. Joan, for two years, had been chairman (there were no non-sexist 'chairs' in those days) of Marske-by-the-Sea branch in Yorkshire, of which her father was secretary. Joan worked on a poultry farm, and as the membership of the branch was very scattered, found her pushbike very handy.

Ongar branch in 1949 was the largest in Essex, and was started 26 years earlier by Harry Butterfield, a roadman. After a year or so the membership rose to 18, but dropped to eight, and Harry was thinking of giving it up. Then his wife Alice took over as secretary and under her leadership the membership speedily increased until at one time she had over 400 members. Mrs. Butterfield died in 1948 and Grace M. Warren, wife of a farmworker, took over the job. Another sign of the times was when Mrs. L. E. Oakden became the first women secretary in Derbyshire when she took over Brailsford branch in 1953.

There had always been, of course, the 'good work' done at women's conferences, as by the Union's delegates at the Conference of Labour Women in Edinburgh in April 1953. The Union proposed: 'This Conference emphatically protests against the clause in the Housing Bill providing subsidies and grants for cottages held on a service occupation, thus extending and encouraging the worst type of tied cottages . . .' Mrs. F. E. Hunnyball, Cambs, and Mrs. S. H. Lambley, Norfolk, put the Union's case, and the resolution, which pledged to abolish the tied cottage, was passed.

When the Conference of Labour Women met in London in 1956, Mrs. Lambley was again a delegate, with Mrs. K. Gouch of Lancashire. The Union submitted a successful motion calling for better rural transport.

The Union was increasingly keen on education for its women members. In December 1955, the *Landworker* carried an article about Hillcroft College, Surbiton, for women trade unionists. A former student outlined the courses there: literature, political theory, economics, history, comparative religions, history of art and psychology. It was a non-vocational college, which meant that women could go there for the pure love of studying, although some did consider going on to teachers' training colleges.

At the 1968 Biennial, Tom Potter, Norfolk, called for increased efforts to get the growing number of unorganised women in agriculture into the Union. By the early 1970s the Union was having a considerable success in this, especially in the expanding poultry and mushroom sectors.

One woman activist, Donna Holman, branch chairman, shop steward, secretary district committee, delegate to the county committee, spoke out on the role of women in the Union in 1977.[1] Mrs. Holman, a mushroom picker, had been in the Union seven years. She had always taken a great interest in human rights and the bettering of working conditions for the working classes. However, as 'a woman activist I often feel that our brothers are being patronising and not taking us seriously. We are often downrated and sometimes just a decorative addition to the group, especially in our Union, as few women have ever crossed the path to the plough. It's high time we realised we are equal.'

At the time Mrs. Holman was expressing her views, Ellen Peacock, five years a member, married with three children, was shop steward at Geest Industries, Lincoln. Most members Ellen represented were women. It gave her great satisfaction that 'the ladies have enough faith in me to come to me with their problems, knowing I will do my best to help.'

Phyllis Dennis, secretary of Bodmin (Cornwall) District Committee, was married with one daughter and three grandchildren. She said, 'I believe in the Union's aims and feel considerable personal satisfaction when an obvious wrong is put right because I took the trouble to investigate.' Lynda Fuller, branch secretary and shop steward at Brake Bros., Lenham Heath, Kent, found being a woman helped, as 'the management tend to sit back and listen instead of shouting about.' And no doubt, it helped to cut down the swearing.

Another woman who took on Herculean tasks was Phyllis Saban, secretary of five branches, vice-chairman of Saffron Walden District Committee, secretary of Essex County Committee, and president of Saffron Walden Trades Council; she was proud of her 24 years' Union membership.

Long Fight for Equal Pay

There was the long fight for equal pay. It was helped by the increasing number of women trade unionists generally. The proportion of women in all trade unions had grown in the years 1968–74 from 23.2 to 27.0%, which was perhaps reflected in the Equal Pay Act of 1970.

Although the achievement of equal pay was obligatory on the AWB under the 1970 Equal Pay Act, 'In respect of both sick pay and equal pay, anomalies and malpractices are happening, or could happen, so the Union will continue to press for improvements wherever possible,' said the Annual Report in 1976. It was possibly referring to one anomaly, a formula introduced on the AWB giving equal pay, but introducing a lower rate for casual workers and part-time workers employed for 30 hours or less a week.

Then in 1975 came the Sex Discrimination Act, which compelled employers to offer most jobs to both men and women on equal terms, but it failed to remove some of the main reasons for differences in earnings between men and women, such as the large amount of overtime worked by men, and the fact that many women were part-timers in agriculture.

Three NUAAW women members won a claim for equal pay at an Industrial Tribunal at Ashford, Kent, on 3 May 1976. It ruled that a fruit grower had discriminated against the women when new pay rates were introduced. The women said that they were singled out for a lower rate, a claim upheld by the Tribunal. Ann Harris, Kathleen Kidd and Iris Morris were packers and paid a basic £36.50 for two weeks in January, but in February their hours were cut and their pay reduced to £24. The three were told that their hours should be restored to 40 a week, and they should be put on the full weekly rate. They were each awarded £100 compensation. Paul Rossi of the Union's Wages Department represented the women, and the case was an important milestone indicating that sex discrimination did take place on farms. The case had implications for thousands of women in other parts of the country who were badly paid.

It was the only successful case of sex discrimination brought in agriculture, and led to improvements for women workers. The NFU was alerted to such breaches of the Sex Discrimination Act, but some wily farmers laid off their regular women workers, and then re-employed them at lower casual rates. After much campaigning, rules were introduced for equal pay for equal value, as against equal work, which was more easily circumvented.

A North Country Lass

One woman, above all, played a big part in Union affairs and rose to national prominence, not only as a trade unionist, but as an outspoken left-wing Labour MP, and that was Joan Maynard. Her success, due partly to grit and stoic North Country determination, aptly illustrates the growing role of women in the Union, and society as a whole. 'Anyone less like the traditional firebrand of the militant left the media so loves to depict, Joan is a homely, but smartly dressed figure with a touch of modesty in her attire, and has dedicated her life to the farmworker and the Labour Party.'[2] Let me tell her story.

In a small Georgian terrace house opposite St. Oswald's Church, Sowerby, Thirsk, Yorkshire, there were a lot of cats. All manner of the feline species were represented: small cats, big cats, furry cats, long-haired cats, mostly with opaline eyes. None were real, there were china cats, plaques of cats, a cat tea cosy, cat table mats, and one porcelain cat sitting on the backroom hearth was so authentic in appearance, that a visitor would not have been surprised if it suddenly miaowed. But not a living cat in sight.

Their owner liked cats, but could never keep a real, live cat. 'It would have tied me down too much,' said Joan Maynard when I interviewed her in 1988, aged 67, one of the Union's leading activists in the post-war years. Joan, the *bête noire* of the capitalist press, and sometimes that of the Union leadership too, ardent opponent of the Tories and champion of the workers' rights, had lived in this pleasant house most of her life, and its furnishings told something of its owner.

It was full of good, heavy, wood period furniture, as dependable as Joan herself, the only modern items being a fitted kitchen, the telly, a record and cassette player; for Joan was a keen watcher of cricket at Lords (Thomas Lord was a Thirsk man) and tennis, and was devoted to music, from Bach to James Galway and the Chieftains.

In the front parlour, with its Georgian mantelpiece and pastel green walls, I admired four splendid watercolours. 'I like those,' I said, 'but I don't recognise the artist.'

Joan gave another of her infectious grins and said, 'Don't laugh, they're by Nicholas Ridley! [The Tory Environment Minister.] He's a better painter than a politician – if only he had stuck to painting.' She first saw them at a members' exhibition in the House of Commons. 'I told him I liked them, and asked "How much?".' £50 was the reply. She didn't buy at first, but was much taken by one of Westminster Bridge. The Tory Minister later told her he had some more paintings and said, 'Come up to my flat and see them.'

'Talk about "come up and see my etchings",' laughed Joan. She went. 'How much is the Westminster Bridge one,' she said. £200 was the reply. 'I thought your lot was keeping inflation down; that's gone up fourfold.' Joan settled for four at £50, the pre-inflation price. 'Another little indulgence,' she said, 'and I'm trying to protect the environment by keeping the artist painting.'

Her hall was hung with photos of her campaigning in the Labour movement, and cartoons from newspapers, not always very flattering. There were, in addition to many vases of flowers, many other mementoes of her life's work. Gifts presented to her after this and that campaign, from miners, factory workers and, of course, farmworkers.

The little market town of Thirsk was only five minutes' walk away from Joan's home, and a stroll round its streets with Joan also told you something of her. Set amid profitable agricultural land, it was as Toryish as any rural area, and it seemed natural that the Conservative Club backed directly on to the rear of the Town Hall, as some kind of an appendage. Everywhere we went it was, 'Good morning Miss Maynard,' or 'Hello Joan,' or just 'Hello Luv.'

And yet it was not all that many years ago that Joan first began fighting local elections for Labour, when even the well-disposed thought it was a hopeless task. First she defeated a local chemist, then the vicar, and finally, the squire. There couldn't have been that many Labour voters around. She garnered many Tory voters on the way, and kept them. Those solid Yorkshire folk knew a fighter when they saw one, liked what they saw and finally put her at the top of the polls. Not bad going for a left-winger who made no bones about her desire to see a real socialist Britain.

This was James Herriot country, and his veterinary surgery was in Thirsk, but Joan was born in Easingwold in 1922, where Joan's father worked for a corn merchant. When she was four, the family left to go to granny's small-holding of nearly 17 acres near Ampleforth. There she went to the village school until she was 14; they left for Thornton-le-Street in 1936, where her parents took over a 28-acre smallholding known as Post Office Farm. She grew to love farming, harrowed with horses, hoed turnips, ricked hay and stooked corn, and brought in the cattle.

She had a sister and two brothers, one – Roy – who later lived with her. She read a lot of Dickens and Hardy, and listened to her father and other brother discussing politics. Both were socialists. 'I thought they were talking nonsense,' she said, 'but my own experience convinced me. People were very nice to you providing they didn't feel you were challenging their social position. We were very poor. In Winter we could only afford two bags of coal and would drag logs in from the woods for fires; in Summer we picked brambles to take to the market to make a few bob.'

Joan also acted as postwoman – her first experience of sexual inequality. She was paid less than a man for exactly the same work. In 1946 Joan saw an advert in the local paper inviting anyone interested in forming a Labour Party in Thirsk to a meeting. She went, along with nine or 10 other people. Union DO Jack Brocklebank was in the chair. Joan became secretary, a job she kept for 25 years. A year later, Jack enrolled her in the Union.

From then on she represented the Union branch at district committees and at county conferences in York. Next she was elected to the county committee and soon became county secretary, a position she still held when she entered Parliament in 1974. She started going to biennials in 1958, and began standing for the EC. She got very close to unseating the local member, F. Robinson, but finally got on as Vice-President in 1966.

Meanwhile, she was very active in the Labour Party, and was elected to its NEC in October 1972. In October 1974 she was elected MP for Sheffield, Brightside. She was greeted by a Labour Minister who said, 'Nice to see you Joan, but what a damn nuisance you are going to be to us here.' Joan responded, 'If you get rid of the tied cottage system I won't be a moment's bother.'

Joan was engaged in continuous battles in the Union, and she made many attempts at biennials to persuade delegates not to go for nebulous things like 'substantial' pay increases, but for fixed figures instead.

Another battle was over the AWB. 'The AWB was good when it came in,' she said, 'but it became detrimental to the Union; you got the pay increase whether or not you were in the Union, and the appointed members made the decision anyway. I did persuade them that they should move from AWB to a statutory joint industrial council, which would mean direct negotiation between the NFU and NUAAW. If they didn't agree, it would then go to independent arbitration which I thought would be slightly better than with the so-called independents on the AWB.'

While in Parliament, although she represented an industrial constituency, she fought vigorously for the farmworkers' cause. 'The pledge on the tied cottage would never have been in the October 1975 Labour Party Manifesto if I had not been a member of the NEC,' she said. 'Not because the majority of the NEC were opposed [only one person opposed – James Callaghan], it was just that the argument was they were not going to do it anyway, so why put it in.'

The day after Labour won the General Election, with Joan as a new MP, she wrote to 10 people in the Labour cabinet and said, 'Please get the tied cottage pledge into the Queen's Speech.' She told me, 'Maybe they did try, but we failed. So we tried again and got it in the following year.'

'When the Agriculture Rent Bill was published I was very alarmed to see it did not contain abolition. I tried to alter that, and discussed it with the Union, who announced the day the Bill was published at a Press Conference with Hazell and Bottini that the Bill gave the Union everything they had asked for.'

The Bill was published just before the Union's Biennial, where Joan was still arguing that the Union ought to try to amend it in order to get complete abolition. This was countered with the usual plea, 'Don't rock the boat, we might lose everything.' To which Joan replied, 'Nonsense, if we try to amend it the only thing you can do is succeed or fail, and if we fail the Bill still stands.' She didn't succeed in this argument, and is convinced that 'certain people' at the top in the Union, didn't want her to get any credit for abolishing tied cottages.

Joan spoke of her constant clashes with some of the Union's leaders. 'They hated me so much, luv, because I stood for everything they abhorred. They didn't really want to run a trade union, but a friendly society. I know the difficulty of running a rural union, but I believe they used these difficulties for not doing things. It was wonderful to talk about the iniquities of the tied cottage, and while they could talk about that, they couldn't keep on about what they should be doing about wages.'

A fierce opponent of Britain's entry into the Common Market, Joan said, 'I think it's been disastrous from an environmental point of view; it's worked against small farmers and for big farmers. It's been extremely bad for the land in the sense that it has encouraged chemical farming, the type of farming based on high capital investment and high energy input and low labour input. It's been bad for people who live in rural areas and certainly bad for people who did work on the land and no longer do so, and it's been enormously costly to the consumer.'

Joan would have liked to see Britain move to lower input farming with a smaller, but less costly output, and towards organic farming, which would conserve the land for future generations, and in addition to employing more workers, would lead to safer food for the consumer.

Reflecting on changes in Union membership in the sixties and seventies, Joan welcomed the poultry workers, mostly women, who joined the Union, and said their membership helped make up for the loss of farmworkers, but regretted that the women's militancy was never effectively linked with the man on the farm.

On the merger she said, 'Closing small branches has been disastrous, it lengthened the lines of communication. And I don't think we were ever told during the merger negotiations of the power of the TGWU regions; some seem virtually autonomous, and bad things can happen.'

Joan believed in the class struggle, which she saw as an extension of her Christian faith, helping the poor. 'It's not popular to talk about class warfare today,' she said. 'The Tories never mention it, they're too busy fighting it, the most vicious war on the British working class for half a century.'

*   *   *

The NUAAW appointed its first full-time, and youngest ever head of a department at head office in 1975. She was Anne Hock, aged 24, Education and Administration Officer. She came from Newbury, Berks, where her father was a charcoal burner and sawmill worker. Like so many new Union officials, she was a graduate and had gained a BA degree in Government and an MSc in Industrial Relations. She had worked for another trade union, had been a shop steward, and turned out to be an ideal officer, winning admiration for the way she ran the Union schools. She left the Union at the time of the merger. Prior to her appointment the only other full-time woman official was Mrs. A. Tracey, who worked with Italians on farms here and is mentioned elsewhere in this volume.

Other women soon followed Anne's appointment, notably Sue Longley, a lively young history graduate, who later edited the *Landworker*, and was to replace the cosy 'Family Page' with features of an 'out of the kitchen' type, such as 'Women, Your Place is in the Union!' Sue also helped organise some of the Union's most effective national campaigns. Margaret Holmes, a former branch secretary, was appointed DO for Suffolk in 1989.

When the Union took to organising grooms and others in the racing and equestrian world, it was left to a woman to take on this mammoth task. Giving such responsibility to a woman, would never have been contemplated a few years earlier.

A Woman Takes on a Horsey World

In 1982, a brave little organisation, the National Association of Grooms, founded by one of them, 30-year-old Christine Stafford, balloted its members, who voted by a large majority to throw in their lot with the Agricultural Trade Group.

The decision was enough to make the hackles of the horsey world rise, but it had by then got used to Christine, a tall, quiet-spoken brunette, and knew that it was facing a formidable opponent of the ruthless exploitation of its workforce.

It all began in 1966, when young Christine left her comprehensive school, madly in love with horses, determined to work in the industry, and completely ignorant of trade unions, with no thought of joining, let alone founding one.

Her parents insisted that she get some formal training. There was little available, so she went to work at a stables as a live-in groom. For a few pounds a week and a promise of riding lessons, she cared for five horses single-handed. She often worked from 6.30am until late in the evening, rarely had time for those lessons, and frequently went to bed hungry. When she complained she was told to like it or lump it, there were plenty of girls eager to work with horses. She went on to jobs in other stables and became groom to some of the top names in the business, later working in Switzerland, Canada and Italy. She was one of the lucky ones, life was comparatively good, but she couldn't forget all those girls back home who were not so lucky, the girls who were expected to do all sorts of tasks; from herding cattle, general domestic work, babysitting, cooking, walking the dog, driving the car on shopping expeditions, all for very low pay and bad accommodation their employers wouldn't dream of allowing their horses to live in.

Back in England, married, her husband a farm manager, she decided to do something about those working conditions, but the idea of forming a union was still far from her mind. She got together a handful of other grooms and formed the nice little body called the National Association of Grooms and nothing much happened until they tried to place an advert in the bible of the horsey fraternity, the *Horse and Hound*. It refused their advert. 'They said we were not registered,' said Christine. 'Rubbish. You don't have to be registered to advertise. They just hoped we would fade away, and what little publicity they did give us was unfavourable.'

However, NAG discovered that the only place an organisation directly involved in protecting employees could register was the Certification Office of Unions and Employers' Associations. Overnight their nice little association had become a nice little trade union, with the *Horse and Hound*, the unwitting midwife. They got a lot of publicity. For once the press loved a trade union, Britain's youngest. The exploitation of these girls was so bad that there were plenty of good stories in it.

Christine's telephone was jammed with callers and membership enquiries flooded in. Christine ran NAG from a PO Box address near her Gloucestershire home because 'people around here would not understand. They would probably think I am some kind of an agitator,' she told the press at the time.

NAG was off to a flying start, and Christine soon had 100 to 150 members enrolled, each paying £4 a year subscription, although she found before long she had to subsidise NAG out of her own pocket.

The horsey establishment gave the Union a very cool reception. The idea that NAG should press for a minimum wage was preposterous to them. That it wanted a minimum of £40 for a 40-hour week instead of the £6 to £20 for 50 hours that members were getting seemed like the end of their world. NAG was told it was far too much and would force people out of business. Christine said, 'If people only kept their horses by underpaying staff, then perhaps they should keep fewer horses. We did recognise the difference between a hard-pressed employer who genuinely tried to give an employee a reasonable deal, and one who set out to exploit a vulnerable and, up to then, unprotected source of cheap labour.'

There were plenty of that sort about. Among the letters Christine received was one from three girls who worked in a pony breeding establishment with a swanky riding school attached. The girls worked for their keep and riding lessons, but were not averaging even one lesson a fortnight; they worked a 12-hour day, six days a week with one weekend off in four, and received no pay at all.

Christine knew of school leavers working even longer hours. With NAG's help, the parents of one 16-year-old girl took her case to an industrial tribunal which found her employer had broken the law on several counts. He had worked the girl so hard that she collapsed from exhaustion after only one month in the stables. All this was far removed from the glamorous image of show jumping presented on television.

An NUAAW DO, Peter Venn, had already been involved with grooms. Two girls working at a stud in Dorset had actually got an agreement that they would be paid extra if they had to stay up overnight, but the money was never paid. One girl was called a 'lazy bitch' and dismissed. Peter obtained a £100 settlement for the two, not much, but better than nothing.

The fight for better conditions proved hard. The section of the horse industry Christine was trying to organise had close connections with the racing industry, and its philosophy of exploitation was much the same. Attempts to organise the lads in the racing stables by the TGWU go back to 1937, and pay concessions were made, with the lads being allowed one Sunday off in three.

The TGWU managed to establish a basic wage of £23.43 a week in 1974, and a strike erupted in 1975 at Newmarket – home of gigantic tax evasion by top figures in the industry – and on 1,000 Guineas Day, the lads sat down across the course. Willie Carson, Lester Piggott and two other jockeys, assisted by angry racegoers, forced their way through the line of lads. Even *The Times*[3] rebuked the racegoers: '. . . the sport of kings is in danger of developing into a blood sport . . . racegoers in the members' stand, determined that their afternoon's enjoyment should not be spoilt, took the law into their own hands and set about clearing the course. The result was a mêlée involving stable lads, jockeys, highly-strung thoroughbreds, normally sedate ladies, retired military gentlemen, whirling binoculars, stabbing hat pins, thrashing shooting-sticks, flailing whips, boots and fists and torn jackets. It was a performance which, had it occurred in the Fourth Division football stadium of some fifth-rate town, would have besmirched even the mucky face of professional soccer.'

NAG never encountered such violent tactics, but they faced the same mentality on the part of many stable owners, whose gorges rose in 1982 when the Low Pay Unit produced a report on the pay of grooms. 'Cut-rate stable girls "taken for a ride" ' was the headline in the Tory *Daily Telegraph* over a story which began 'Wealthy stable owners are taking their grooms, who are mostly dedicated teenage girls for a "ride" by paying them less than subsistence earnings.' Some were paid only £10 a week for 50 hours, and one girl from Gwent earned £5 for a 60-hour week. The Low Pay Unit's study showed that half the 20,000 grooms earned less than £30 a week and one in 10 less than £10.

None of this was news to Christine, but it did give her campaign for grooms powerful backing. In June 1982 Christine was to have met the British Horse Society to discuss the future of the industry, but at the last minute the BHS backed out, saying later that they had no mandate to negotiate conditions of employment for grooms. In preparation for that meeting, she and Caroline Burt, another NAG member, went to London to have talks with the NUAAW, who gave full support for their aims. The NUAAW donated £100 to NAG, who were extremely grateful for this encouragement. Knowing they needed the backing of a larger organisation, NAG decided to ballot members on a merger with the NUAAW. They voted by an overwhelming majority to throw in their lot with the Agricultural Group as it had by then become. Jack Boddy declared, 'We will now try to recruit as many of this disgracefully badly-paid labour force as we can. The exploitation and sweated labour is even worse than among farmworkers, and the wages even lower.'

From then on Christine fought on for her fellow grooms as a staff member of the TGWU. I met Christine in 1988 in her office in Transport House. It seemed far removed from rural riding schools, but her office walls were more in keeping with her commitment. A *Horse and Hound* calendar of Major Show Trials, pictures of splendid horses going through their paces, and copies of the *Racing Post* on her desk; a desk neat with well-ordered files, typical of a well-organised person able to take on one of the toughest jobs in trade unionism.

Christine told me how the Youth Training Scheme had, surprisingly – possibly because of the incredibly bad conditions – proved a blessing for young entrants to the industry. 'We support the YTS. It has a total of 130 schemes at stables, riding schools, studs and racing establishments covering every branch of equestrian sports. Thousands of youngsters are involved and it is now the recognised route of entry into the industry.'

There has been a growing membership of the Racing and Equestrian Section since Christine's involvement with YTS on the racing side, and since YTS began, wages have increased. The YTS has crowded out the much abused 'working pupil system' and they are getting closer to AWB rates for agricultural workers, which is their aim. 'Conditions have not improved as much as I would have liked,' explained Christine, 'but while on YTS there is a more effective monitoring system. We have access to these trainees and can effect a measure of control. They are still subject to long hours once off the scheme, but while in it we can educate them to what they should get as employees and they are far more aware now of their rights.'

Once the major horse organisations refused to recognise unions, now they have to. Christine is a member of the National Joint Horse Education and Training Council, the Horse Racing Advisory Council, the National Joint Council for Stable Staff and other bodies. Because of her great knowledge and talent as a horsewoman, Christine is accepted everywhere in the horse world. 'I feel our greatest achievement is recognition for employees in the horse industry, gaining them respect and a more professional status,' she said.

We had to draw the interview to a close. Christine was off to Windsor Racecourse to inspect hostel and catering facilities for the staff. Together with Brian Cox, National Officer of the TGWU, they were to inspect eight courses that season. 'We hope to get the Jockey Club to do something about it, where we find conditions are wanting,' said Christine.

The leading roles women like Christine, Joan Maynard and many others now play in the Union, would have surprised many old timers, but their activities have given it new strengths. Many in the Union believe that the best is yet to come, as women everywhere assume their rightful place in society.

Gang Labour

One Union campaign that was especially important to women came in 1983 when it launched a drive against the gangmaster system of hiring farm labour. Women had for a century or more made up the majority in these gangs, although the widespread unemployment of the eighties and increasing casualisation had led to a growing number of men in the gangs.

Gang labour was condemned as 'a very pernicious system' by Poor Law Commissioners as far back as 1843.[4] A dossier of the activities of modern-day gangmasters was drawn up by Paul Redgate, DO for Lincs, where, with the Cambridgeshire fens, the system was prevalent. It gave details of under-payment of wages, victimisation for Union membership, non-deduction of tax and insurance, and poor conditions. In the Commons, Joan Maynard demanded the re-introduction of the licensing of gangmasters. She said the problem was growing in South Lincs, Norfolk and the Cambridgeshire fens, where farms had been casualised, and the casual or seasonal rate was the lowest. Full-time workers got £1.89 an hour, part-timers £1.74, and seasonal workers £1.60.

Seasonal workers under gangmasters were covered by AWB Orders, but because of unemployment, gangmasters were able to exploit workers, who had no right to holidays and sick pay. Joan said that 'Geest always had 12-week contract workers. Now they are called seasonal workers and paid £1.60 an hour instead of £1.74.' The gangmaster scheme was similar to the old casual dock labour scheme where dockers would line up in the hope of a job. 'The women wait outside their doors in the hope they will be given a job and some pay by one of the gangmasters.' Joan summed up, 'I would describe these conditions as 19th century. As there is no licensing, any unscrupulous person can set up as a gangmaster.' A licensing system* should cover their activities, with a substantial fee to deter fly-by-night boys becoming gangmasters.

Tory MP Selwyn Gummer, Under-Secretary of State for Employment, said he 'did not believe it was true that there are large numbers of unscrupulous people who go in for intimidation of their workforces and that there is widespread abuse.' He would investigate any complaints. Four years later the Union was still trying to get the Government to recognise that there was a problem.

Paul Redgate recalled in 1989 being appointed DO for S Lincs and how appalled he was when he discovered how the gangmaster system worked. Paul, a Cornishman accustomed to many 'backward' practices on farms in the West Country, said, 'I was shocked to find that the arcane agricultural practice known as gangmasters that Karl Marx had referred to in *Das Kapital* still continued.' He said, 'The local Conservative MP Sir Richard Body, a Quaker who was sympathetic to farmworkers, called for the re-introduction of the gangmaster licensing system, but being a *laissez-faire* politician deemed it also appropriate to set up a Gangmasters Association to self-regulate their workings. One was being set up, but it later fell apart.

'Although Sir Richard accepted the Union's view that gangmasters should be licensed, this position was never accepted by the Government and the Bill that Sir Richard presented to the House of Commons for registration of gangmasters, which had been compiled in consultation with myself, unfortunately fell after the first reading, due to Mrs. Thatcher calling a General Election.

'Since the early eighties, despite the Union's campaign, MAFF has resolutely refused to carry out any form of investigation and has insisted that its Wages Inspectors would deal with any complaints presented to them by gangworkers, conveniently failing to recognise the fact that the gangmasters' operation ensures that any employee who did complain would find future employment as a temporary gang worker non-existent.

'Through monitoring where the gangworkers came from, the Union found that workers were commuting from South Humberside, South Yorks and the

---

* An old system of licensing by magistrates had ceased to operate with the new Local Government Act in 1960.

Black Country, so the Union extended its publicity campaign to the whole of the East Coast, stretching from Yorkshire and the Midlands down to East Anglia. Subsequently the media carried hostile stories about the gangmasters.

'As a result of this the Inland Revenue and the Police have taken action against gangmasters and successfully prosecuted them. The only relevant agency that has not fulfilled its statutory duties is MAFF Wages Inspectorate, despite the fact that I, as an advisor to MAFF, have raised this issue on a number of occasions with Government Ministers.

'Private conversations with Agricultural Wages Inspectors had revealed that there is a policy, or something akin to a policy, which prevents them from carrying out a full investigation in a way other Government departments do. The reason appears quite clearly to be that whilst the Government is concerned where gangmasters are defrauding the Inland Revenue and the National Insurance, the fact that agricultural workers are being illegally paid is of no consequence to them, because the State has an underlying philosophy of encouraging a low-wage market.'

A philosophy that sees women as a natural part of that cheap labour, to which the Union is firmly opposed.

REFERENCES

1. *Landworker*, July 1977.
2. Peter Worrell, *Anatomy of Agriculture*, Harrap, 1978.
3. 3 May 1975.
4. 'Employment of Women and Children in Agriculture', Reports of Special Assistant Poor Law Commissioners, 1843.

16

Land and Politics

It will become a matter of wonder that there should ever have existed those who thought it admirable to enjoy without working, at the expense of others who worked without enjoying.

Herbert Spencer

An Age-Old Objective

Nationalisation of farmland has long been the cry of socialists in Britain, and the subject of fierce debate in the NUAAW and the Labour movement. The 1945–50 Labour Government tinkered with some aspects of land ownership through the Agricultural Holdings Act 1948 which gave tenant farmers protection from unscrupulous landlords, but it was the 1947 Agricultural Act that was to become the cornerstone of farming for a quarter of a century. In no way did it nationalise the land, but it virtually 'nationalised' farm finance by providing handsome State subsidies for farmers. With 60 million acres for the UK's 56 million people – or one acre per person – few enjoy owning much of it, and the prospect of doing so are limited. As Mark Twain said, 'Nobody's making it any more.'

The 1932 Labour Conference accepted a report recommending nationalisation of land. But in 1950, at a meeting in Norfolk, Edwin Gooch said that, 'Nationalisation of the land or of farming would not itself produce more food.' The *Landworker* declared, 'But Bro. Gooch was quite right. Nationalisation represents at most a change of administration. Nationalisation of the land would not mean that any of the fundamental problems of food production and distribution had been surmounted. On the contrary it would create a lot of new problems. Nobody in his senses would seek to embark on this adventure at a time when maximum food production is a vital necessity and is possible only with the co-operation of all the people engaged in the agriculture industry.' It went on to say that Labour was not abandoning its doctrines. Mr. Shinwell* made this clear at the previous year's Labour

---

* Emanuel Shinwell, Labour Minister and MP for Easington until 1970. Later Lord Shinwell.

Conference at Blackpool. He said, 'The principle of nationalisation was accepted by the Labour Party many years ago. We have not abandoned that principle, but we believe that we are vested with adequate powers within existing legislation to enable us to acquire land if and when we require it.'

In keeping with this line of thinking, an EC amendment at the 1948 Biennial removed the word 'agriculture' from a resolution calling for the nationalisation of all land. But at the Biennial in 1950, P. Makepeace, Northumberland, moved, 'That the EC presses the Government with more vigour than hitherto to have steps taken to nationalise the land, at an early date, in order that agriculture can be brought up to full efficiency, which is impossible under the present landlord and tenant system.' Wogan Phillips,* Glos, seconded. Some villages in Gloucestershire were completely owned by one man, he said. 'Just because his great-grandfather pinched the land a man had complete power over the villagers.' M. Madden, Oxon, thought we have 'practically enough power over the land at the present time.' A. E. Calver, Cambs, agreed with nationalisation of land, but not of agriculture, while C. H. Chandler, EC, said it was not immediately practicable. The resolution was defeated by two votes.

Joan Maynard put the case for nationalisation in the *Landworker* in 1953. Entitled 'Why Nationalise the Land', her article began, 'Let me say at once that I do mean land, and not farming, for there is an important difference. I consider the present tenant farmers are the most capable people to farm our land.' She said that it was important to grow more food here. We could do it, but agriculture needed capital. 'At the moment the NFU is crying out afresh about the shortage of capital and no wonder, with interest rates at 6%. Many farmers were unable to, provide the capital needed. Even so, more public money is being put into this private industry than into any one nationalised industry, and too much of this money finds its way into landowners' and farmers' pockets without building up our capital resources, or increasing production. Without ownership there can be no real control of land usage, for the present system is just a hotch-potch of inefficiency . . .'

Replying, the Editor denied the system was a 'hotch-potch of inefficiency' and questioned whether the State could afford to purchase land or administer it. Nationalisation could cause grave disruption, 'and in present circumstances we would prefer that the powers of the Agricultural Act should be more fully utilised.'

Sir Hartley Shawcross QC, MP,§ President of the Board of Trade in the previous Labour Government, was next to enter the fray. At the 1953 Tolpuddle demonstration, he said that nationalisation would be immensely

---

*   A Communist, who later sat in the Upper House as Lord Milford, inheriting the
    title from his father.
§   To become Lord Shawcross, director of many big companies. He later left the
    Labour Party.

difficult to accomplish and involve the country in crippling expense. He went on, '. . . nationalisation of land would create an enormous army of bureaucrats which would disrupt agriculture and cause a great deal of social and economic chaos.'

Jack Dunman then wrote in the *Landworker*, 'It is a hard thing when Labour leaders devote themselves to putting over the Tory case. That is exactly what Sir Hartley did . . . His arguments against land nationalisation might have been taken out of the Tory Speakers' Handbook.'

Joan Maynard also replied to the Editor's criticism: 'I think you misunderstood my statement that the present system is an "hotch-potch of inefficiency". The present system of grants, subsidies and controls is clumsy and inefficient; so I am assured by someone who helps to administer it, and so it appears from the way in which farm profits have outstripped production . . . If you saw, as some of us do, the inefficiency of some of our farmers and the condition of their farms you would realise that in certain respects the 1947 Act is not being put into operation. This does not destroy my argument that, by and large, the present tenant farmers are the best people to farm our land. They are not perfect, but can anyone tell me who could do the job better at the present time.'

The Editor returned to the attack: '. . . those who read the report of the speech will know that Sir Hartley advocated the taxation of land values as an alternative to land nationalisation . . . to say that Sir Hartley was putting forward the Tory case . . . is arrant nonsense.' Turning to Joan Maynard, he asserted that the present system of agriculture had 'produced results which are not negligible. Farming inefficiency is grossly exaggerated . . . Output per acre is greater than that of most other countries . . . There is no case for taking land away from the present owners without compensation.'

The 52nd Labour Conference at Margate followed this discussion; it went down as a 'moderate' conference, for amendments which proposed further nationalisation were decisively beaten. John Mackie,* Lanark, moved an amendment asking the Party to reaffirm the principle of land nationalisation, and to place a plan for carrying this out before the electorate at the next election. George Brown said the problem of the next Labour Government would be to raise food output very considerably and land nationalisation would be of less help than the plans for assisting agriculture which the NEC had put in *Challenge to Britain*. The 1947 Act gave the Government powers to take over any food-producing land which was being badly farmed.

A. Harman, Bucks, supporting the amendment, said that the important thing was to get the right people into vacant farms. Harold Collison opposing, reiterated that the Union was not against land nationalisation, but felt it unwise to commit the next Labour Government to such a step. Tom Williams said the amendment would involve the repeal of a large part of the 1947 Act. He hoped they would not be led away by 'snappy slogans' that had no application in modern politics. He called for the rejection of the amendment.

---

*   A Labour MP and former minister.

Edwin Gooch, for the NEC, said that in examining the 1947 Act they had had advice of practical men, and their restatement of policy was in sound and practical terms. The NEC had no quarrel with the amendment's reaffirmation of the principle of land nationalisation, but he asked conference not to insist that the Party make this an issue at the next election. It would antagonise rural voters. The amendment was rejected by 4,367,000 votes to 1,794,000.

When the Union's policy document, *Health and Wealth Under Our Feet* was discussed at the 1956 Biennial, Ted Sales, Dorset, moved a motion in the form of an amendment to that section dealing with land nationalisation, stating that nationalisation was essential for any really substantial increase in production. It called upon the next Labour Government to begin with 'some selected large estates to be developed as models for the future public ownership.' W. Graham seconded, and those supporting included A. Calver, Cambs, who believed that when land was reclaimed from the sea it should be taken over by the State and not left in private hands. Bill Case, EC, pointed out that the reference to nationalisation in the document was as had been decided at the previous Biennial, and asked for rejection of the motion. It was carried by 89 votes to 56.

In Labour's new policy document, *Prosper the Plough*, which came before the 1958 Labour Conference at Scarborough, there was no mention of land nationalisation. It was the highlight of the conference when Edwin Gooch introduced the document, and Joan Maynard moved a resolution instructing the NEC to explicitly accept nationalisation of land as Labour policy. She said the Union's policy was in favour of nationalisation, but Dennis Hodsdon, *Landworker* Editor, claimed that to say the Union was in favour of nationalisation and leave it at that was to misrepresent the position. The Union believed in the ultimate nationalisation of farmland, but recognised that it would probably be unwise to tackle wholesale nationalisation and that therefore the 1947 Act should be so strengthened as to bring increasingly greater areas of land under public ownership.

Tom Williams urged support for the policy document; Joan Maynard refused to withdraw her resolution, and when put to the vote it was heavily defeated. *Prosper the Plough* was accepted with only a few hands against.

But the question of land nationalisation would not lie down. At the TUC at Brighton in 1972, an NUAAW resolution on it was composited and moved by the AUEW (Engineering Section) and seconded by Wilf Page, EC. He made it quite clear that, 'The State would become the farmers' landlord, and farmers would thus be guaranteed security of tenure . . . From history we know that men – hungry men who stole a sheep from the common, found themselves on the scaffold, while the men who stole the commons from the sheep found themselves sitting in the House of Lords.' The contemporary scene would be just as unjust if they tried to implement policies for the 1970s on a pattern of land ownership basically unchanged since the 1800s. The motion was passed unanimously.

New Campaign Launched

In September 1973, a Campaign for Nationalising Land was launched. It wanted Labour to adopt and implement a land nationalisation policy. This included farmland in a broad sense, with the object of catching the get-rich-quick developers and speculators. Among its five originators were two prominent NUAAW members, Jack Brocklebank and Joan Maynard.

Their manifesto stated: 'We propose that . . . all freeholds should be nationalised, and everyone who owned a freehold would be deemed to be a leaseholder . . . from the Crown. We think there should be no exceptions whatever . . .' It suggested that all land should be transferred to a 99-year lease and after that had elapsed it would be in the freehold of the State. These leaseholders would not pay rent, and any new buildings could be financed either by themselves or by a new body which would charge interest on the capital involved.

The policy was adopted by the Labour Party, and had merits that the current generation of landowners could hardly object to, as it would not even affect their immediate heirs. Yet it was not taken seriously by the Labour Government when it assumed power in 1974, and not without reason the Country Landowners' Assocation (CLA) stated, 'We don't see the scheme as a serious threat, as the Labour Party has already refused similar such systems in the past.'

As the 1973 TUC Conference, Wilf Page supported an AEU/NALGO composite calling for the nationalisation of *all* land. Wilf drew attention to rocketing farmland prices, and said, to deter this, 'public ownership of land was essential'. The motion was unanimously adopted.

Meanwhile, the 1970s land boom was almost as dramatic as the Yukon Gold Rush of the 1880s, and certainly more profitable for most of the money-crazed speculators. That deeply entrenched part of the British class system had already concentrated vast acreages in very few hands. The landed gentry, unless besotted gamblers or the victims of crass mismanagement, did not normally sell their land. They added to it by craftily planned marriages, and kept adding by all means, fair and foul. This began to change in the twentieth century. The shooting was let to syndicates and city gents, and many a big house pulled down as uneconomic. Yet only a minuscule amount of their land was sold off. During the 1950s and 1960s, 2% of the 16 million hectares of farmland in England and Wales was sold annually, and by the 1970s this fell to 1.5%.

Farmland was to become a better investment than the Stock Exchange. Until 1965, the capital appreciation of farmland was untaxed and, by 1972, the land boom was on, with headline-hitting farmland sales of almost £2,500 per hectare. Some farmers resented the way 'outside money' had magnified their death duty problems, and some tenant farmers feared the land boom would push up rents. But some owner-occupier farmers saw it as the passport to unbelievable wealth. The boom died down in the mid-1980s, but most big farmers were still doing very nicely.

John Cherrington, the southern farmer who wrote very knowledgeably for the *Financial Times* declared, 'The present high cost of land, coupled with the incidence of Death Duties and Capital Gains tax, will I am certain, wipe out most family farming within a generation or two. Opinions differ as to whether that would be a good or bad thing for the countryside as a whole. For myself, I would sooner farm a nationalised leasehold farm than none at all.'

'Some of us went to church yesterday and we heard that the good Lord made the land and the fields for everyone. He didn't say nothing about them lords and ladies owning it.' That was Doug Oswick, Norfolk, making an effective contribution at the 1978 Biennial, when speaking in favour of land nationalisation. A Somerset motion, 'This conference demands that the Labour Government honours its election pledge to nationalise agricultural land in the next session of Parliament,' was passed.

The Union and the Labour Party had, in recent years, become more militant in their advocacy of land nationalisation. There was much less equivocation than there had been a few years earlier, and this policy brought the CLA out in a sweat in 1978. It commissioned a public opinion poll on a 'State takeover of farmland', and fired the first warning shots in a strongly-worded attack on land nationalisation in its journal, *The Country Landowner*. The Union went into action, and quickly planned a booklet explaining the benefits of nationalisation.

The CLA (motto: 'to promote and safeguard the interests of owners of rural land') seemed to want to chill the blood at the prospects of ruthless State land grab. A dramatic piece in its journal, headed 'The Threat of Nationalisation', highlighted the benefits of private ownership against what it called 'the political and constitutional threat of public ownership.' It went on to challenge the main points of the Labour NEC's proposals, arguing against the 'apparently moderate' gradual approach to State acquisition, and spelt out the unpleasant consequences to consumers, farmers and farmworkers. Labour had suggested that nationalisation would bring to the farmworker greater job security and industrial democracy. And who could dispute the CLA reply that current 'labour relations in agriculture are without equal'? Few industries could even approach agriculture's embarrassingly low wages, poor safety provisions and disregard of proper labour relation practices.

The CLA poll result claimed that more than 70% of the public opposed plans for nationalising agricultural land: 65% thought that such moves would mar the beauty of the countryside; 73% were against the State acquisition of agricultural land, and 72% thought it important for a 'free' society that agricultural land should be privately owned.

The NUAAW replied: 'The questions are so loaded; the timing of the survey and its publication so obviously politically manipulated, and the results so dubiously interpreted, that it is quite valueless. We say this because (1) Only 10% of the people sampled knew there were any proposals for land nationalisation in the wind. So those interviewed had only the CLA's account of the proposals. (2) The questions are all framed with loaded phrases like "acquired by the State" and "free society". Obviously if we wished to counter it we would talk of "acquired by the people" and "democratic society". (3) Despite all this, the CLA has still only managed to get the barest majority for keeping land in the hands of the small proportion of the population entitled to be CLA members. Thus only 56% strongly agree that "it is important for a free society that agricultural land should be privately owned." The CLA inflates this to 72% by including those who "agree a little". (4) Most important, the CLA timed its survey after it has already run a campaign against, and before the argument has been heard.'

Planning or Privilege

As the 1978 Labour Conference drew near, the NUAAW demanded public ownership of agricultural land in the next session of Parliament. The Union issued a booklet entitled *Planning or Privilege*, designed to answer the hysterical propaganda put about by the landowners. It was in question and answer form: 'Wouldn't nationalisation remove all incentive and pride in one's own piece of land?' Answer: 'The NUAAW finds this an insulting and offensive argument. It assumes that the only people who have pride in agriculture and the land are the people who own it. Our members own no land – but they take pride in their work . . . anyway, a great deal of the land is already farmed by tenant farmers or farm managers – just as it would be under national-isation . . . The only difference land nationalisation would make to tenant farmers and farm managers is that ultimately their responsibility would lie with the public, not to large financial corporations or rich individuals.' Nationalisation would make it easier, not harder for people to break into farming; the small farmer, the tenant farmer, the worker and consumer all stood to benefit. The booklet was exhibited at the Labour Conference in October, when Jack Boddy successfully put a motion for land national-isation. 'The task is now,' said Jack, 'to persuade the Government to act on Conference policy.'

But the Union failed completely to get any Government action. By the late 1980s, the Labour Party, under Neil Kinnock, seemed resolutely opposed to any further nationalisation whatever.

It was claimed by opponents that the Union's policy on agricultural land nationalisation did not have the support of members. But the critics were proved wrong at every county conference where the issue was raised. News-papers and landowners spent some time before the Nottinghamshire and Derbyshire Conference gloating over a motion on the agenda opposing nationalisation. *The Times'* Agricultural Correspondent, Hugh Clayton, wrote that this was another nail in the coffin of the Union's policy, and an embar-rassment for President John Hose, since it came in his own county. Never were high hopes so cruelly dashed. The Conference overwhelmingly defeated the motion and went on, unanimously, to adopt a resolution favouring land nationalisation. Oddly, *The Times* never got round to reporting the downfall of Mr. Clayton's prediction.

The question of foreign buyers of land was taken up by some county conferences, with much opposition to it. It was in 1979 that the Northfield Committee recommended that the buying of English farmland by financial institutions and overseas buyers should be restricted; that MAFF should have the power to veto the sale of smallholdings; that the way to help tenant farmers was to relieve the tax pressures on their landlords; and that land should not be nationalised. The Committee, set up under a Labour Government, took a long time and reported to a Conservative Government. In the words of Francis Beckett, 'intentionally or not, the Committee delayed its Report until the heat surrounding the issues had died down and there was a Government in power which could confidently be relied on not to take any drastic steps, even if the Committee had recommended them. In the event the Committee did not recommend them.'

The Committee said that financial institutions owned about 214,500 hectares, about 1.2% of all farmland. Land owned by merchant banks and farming companies was not included in this figure. It included only land owned by insurance companies, pension funds, property unit trusts and property bonds. As for foreign buyers, Northfield's best estimate was that they owned over 1% of agricultural land.

Northfield recommended that the activities of foreign buyers and financial institutions should be 'monitored', a time-honoured official device for doing nothing. Nationalisation, with the State renting out land to tenant farmers, as proposed by the NUAAW, was not the answer, said the Report. The solution proposed was one a million miles away from the minds of those who pressed for the inquiry, and was a tribute to the unremitting lobbying of the NFU. The way to solve tenant's problems was to ease the tax burdens on the landlord!

Because of its negative conclusions, the Northfield Report was not marked out to become a landmark in farming history. Its general message was that things were not too bad, and should be disturbed as little as possible.

Jack Boddy reviewed the Report with mixed feelings. 'It comes up with some useful recommendations but does not go far enough. I welcome the majority recommendations for a register of land. However, it speaks of this as a long-term plan. How long term? We want it as soon as possible.' He approved its recommendations for alternative housing for retiring smallholders, and noted the limited suggestion of the State acquiring land in lieu of tax. 'In our view the questions investigated can only find their answer in public ownership of agricultural land.'

The case for land nationalisation was ably put in 1985 by W. H. Pedley, in a paper for the British Socialist Agricultural Society, of which Jack was President. It argued not that farming itself should be nationalised, but that land should be taken over by the State and then rented out to farmers, farming co-operatives and other community enterprises. In acquiring the land the community would obtain an asset which would immediately produce a return in the form of rent, and a more efficient rural economy, more rationally organised and continuously stimulated by the inflow of highly qualified management.

Campaigners for land nationalisation like Jack Boddy, Jack Brocklebank, Wilf Page and Joan Maynard, in retirement, still believe it vital for the future of British agriculture. Joan said in 1988, 'Whoever owns the land, controls it in a positive way, and the changes that are taking place make me extremely worried as to how we are going to protect our beautiful rural areas; planning controls are being further weakened, county structure plans are going to the wall. With only top-grade land still going to be protected, the rest could be grabbed by developers . . . public ownership could prevent some of the worst abuses.'

Land nationalisation could become an explosive issue by the beginning of the year 2000. With Green politics to the fore in an age of increased leisure, land, especially in scenic areas, will increasingly be sought for public access, conflicting with the post-war concentration of private ownership: the old aristocracy, agro-businessmen and city institutions, are not likely to use it entirely in the best interests of the general public. As Labour said in a draft policy statement in 1982, 'Only through public ownership and control of the land, will we be able to eliminate that power and influence.' All the Union's old ideas on land nationalisation, and renting out to farmers, will be more relevant than ever.

*   *   *

Doug Oswick, of Norfolk, well known at biennials, was given a standing ovation when moving the final vote of thanks at a trade group conference in the eighties. Standing ovation for a vote of thanks? A bit unusual. Not at all if you knew Doug. He liked a joke, was good at them was renowned for his effective one-line contributions to debates, yet was a deadly serious man. His seriousness stemmed from his anger at the poverty of the farmworker, poverty in pay, in education and life style.

In that vote of thanks, intermingled with jokes and anecdotes which had delegates in stitches, he banged home how underpaid was the skilled farmworker. 'The farmworker is a lorry driver, a tractor driver, machine operator, machine repairer, carpenter, electrician, bricklayer and welder. And if he couldn't do all these things a kilo of spuds would cost £3.'

Doug said to me: 'You know what we are? We're the victims of the education system of the capitalist state, that's what we are. I was taught just enough to become a ploughman, a soldier for the bloody State, and then afterwards back to the land again. I couldn't do any more, because that was all they taught me to do.'

Mind you, Doug loved the land, as I discovered when I met him in 1984. He started on a farm at thirteen and joined the Union the same week, the fee being 4½d in 1932. He became a member of Fulmodestone branch, joining on a Saturday evening at the local pub. All members lined up in front of the chairman and secretary, paying their dues.

His first job was with a horse and tumbler cart, taking kale to cattle. He went on to do just about everything on the farm, until just before the Second World War he got fed up with it and joined the Army. By the end of the war he had married, and when he left the Army was determined not to go back to the land. He tried to find work and a home in London, but couldn't get anywhere for his family to live. 'Then someone said to me, "Well boy, if I was you I'd go back home." So I did, just to get somewhere to live. And you know what, I was trapped in a tied house for years.'

He went to work for Mr. Richard Winch (later High Sheriff of Norfolk) of Swannington Farm, and lived in a tied house with his wife Sybil and seven children; three boys and four girls, the eldest marrying George Barnard, DO.

Doug worked for Mr. Winch as a lorry driver, and after 23 years with him was suddenly sacked for truculent behaviour. That was in 1975. 'The day I was made redundant, I got my pay before noon and was told to keep off the farm. After 23 years it really affects you. I had worked for him 90 hours a week sometimes when we were pushed. It took them 23 years to find out I was truculent. Of course, the real reason was my trade union activity. I had appeared on the telly discussing wages and conditions with the NFU. Mr. Winch said I did well, but some other farmers didn't like it and said he should get rid of that bugger.'

The Union took the matter to Court and Doug was given three months' stay of eviction from his tied cottage, and he 'just about got a council house in time.' The Union took the dismissal to an industrial tribunal where Mr. Winch said he was a good workman, honest and trustworthy, and the chairman said he had never come across a case like it. The tribunal found he had been dismissed unfairly, but it was 'justified'. Warnings about his truculent behaviour were not properly given and he was not given an opportunity to explain to Mr. Winch. He had received £870 in redundancy money and final pay; no further compensation was awarded as he was adjudged partly responsible for his dismissal.

Doug commented, 'I still think to this day that Winch was a good employer, but he had one weakness, that was listening to other people.'

Later he went to work for Bernard Matthews. 'I hated every moment of it, being shut up in the turkey houses. I felt I had reached rock bottom after being outside.' Doug must have been good at hiding his real feelings. He showed me the reference he got from the manager of Matthews' Haveringland Farm: he was conscientious and co-operative with other employees and had 'settled down well to indoor work.' He later drove a lorry for a horticultural hardware firm, until he retired.

At the time of his eviction, Doug was secretary of Sparham branch, and still had five children at home. 'My two young daughters were hurried into marriage. There was a lot of us; they married to enable the rest of us to get into the council house, which was much smaller.'

Recalling the days when he ploughed with horses as a boy, Doug said 'I've seen horses worked to death. They'd go down on their knees when they were about twelve, exhausted, and I've seen a farmer sole 'em with a stick to get 'em up, and when they couldn't make it, while they were still alive, they'd drag them by the head to the gate to get them on the knacker's cart.'

'When I was a young man, they'd work men and horses to death, now in these modern times, we're poisoned by pesticides and herbicides.'

Doug, an affable, tall, ruddy-faced man, always had a smile, and dry wit, and always got to the point. Once, when a biennial delegate from the Home Counties was complaining that recruiting was an uphill task for him, Doug said, 'It's an uphill task in Norfolk too, and we've got a head wind.' His outspokenness could be mistaken for truculence, depending on where you think you stand in the social order. Once an employer said to him that he was his 'Guv'nor'. Doug said, 'Oh no, I've only got one Guv'nor, and she's at home. You're the employer.'

Doug's wife, Sybil, like most farmworker's wives, had managed marvellously on poverty wages. 'I don't know how she did it,' said Doug proudly, 'We never had anything to spare, but we didn't owe a penny to anyone. You could just live on farm pay. But you couldn't do anything. You couldn't take holidays. A lot of workers went off to work for someone else during holiday week. I remember a time when I was ditching. I had a hole in one of my rubber boots. I needed a new pair and my son needed a pair of shoes to go to school. He got the shoes and I got back into the wet ditch with the hole in my boot.'

When, in 1970, Mr. and Mrs. Oswick were invited to a reception at Downing Street, Reg Bottini, in a letter to Doug confirming the arrangements said, 'a dinner jacket will need to be worn . . . if you haven't got one of your own, the Union will hire one.' Doug recalled his meeting with Prime Minister Harold Wilson. 'I failed to tie Harold down to anything serious like wages or farmworkers being held in bondage by the tied cottage. He put me off by explaining that Mary, his wife came from Diss, Norfolk. Then when I had another go, he started on about football, pulling my leg about Norwich City, and saying that Huddersfield was his team.'

At least Doug had a go, something he will go on doing till the end, truculent or not.

International Duties

As an important part of the Labour movement, the Union took its international duties seriously, and never failed to voice its views on world affairs, especially where these directly affected the interests of Britain and its people. It also tried to influence the growth and development of world agriculture, especially in third-world countries.

It sought to advance the cause of working people everywhere, and whilst, in the post-war period and at the time of the Cold War, some of its stands could be viewed differently today, they often reflected the position of the Labour Party and certain Labour leaders.

In turn, the *Landworker* provided Labour leaders with a platform on which to influence Union members, and in the May 1949 issue, Morgan Phillips, secretary of the Labour Party wrote on the great challenge of our time, ' . . . World Communism and its temporal fortress, the Soviet Union.' Mr. Phillips said that:

> The success of democracy even in a country so vast as the USA is worth little if collapse in the area from Europe through the Middle East to China puts the measureless resources of the Eurasian continent at the disposal of aggressive Communism . . . By putting under public enterprise the key industries which private industry left derelict we have assured a sound basis for economic recovery and obtained a powerful weapon against world depression . . . The great task which now faces us all alike is to organise peace and plenty throughout the democratic world.

That peace and plenty was to be heavily influenced by the USA which, both by open and devious means, sought to influence the trade unions of the 'free world'. Genuine contacts were established between American unions and their counterparts in Western Europe, but at the same time, large funds were available through the agencies of the CIA to get the American Government's viewpoint accepted.

Prominent in the Union's international influence was Edwin Gooch who, in 1948, was among the 500 delegates from 57 countries assembled in Washington for the fourth annual conference of the Food and Agricultural Organisation (FAO) of the United Nations. He listened as President Truman said, 'One of the ways to restore stability to the world is to produce plenty of food and see that it is distributed fairly. Hunger has no nationality. Abundance should have no nationality either.' Sentiments which conflicted strongly with the USA's later policies. Edwin pointed out in the *Landworker* that the FAO was not only concerned with actual food production. It was equally concerned with rural welfare, something dear to his heart. This part of the FAO's work was closely associated with the Permanent Agricultural Committee of the ILO, of which he was also a member.

On his visit to America Edwin met the president of the National Farm Labour Union, and noted that they were putting up a big fight to organise the 3 million men and women in agriculture, and bring these workers to a basis of equality with other workers, not dissimilar to the struggle for British agricultural workers.

The international scene was bedevilled by the split between the trade unions of the East and those of America and Western Europe. In 1950, the NUAW supported the newly-established Free Trade Union International. A resolution proposing this was moved at the 1950 Biennial by H. J. Guest, Devon, who said it was in line with TUC policy. W. J. Morgan, Devon, seconded. It was opposed by a leading Communist in the Union, Jack

Dunman, Berks, who said the Union should use its influence to get the British trade union movement back into the World Federation of Trade Unions, which he said, was one of the greatest obstacles against the onset of war, and therefore did not suit American millionaires or the American trade union leaders who worked so closely with them. He was supported by G. Thomas, Cornwall, and J. J. Waterman, Dorset. Mrs. L. M. Thring, speaking for the resolution, was not prepared to be dominated by a bureaucracy that had betrayed all the principles of the Russian Revolution. The resolution was carried.

During the 1950s, much time was devoted by the leadership to what they conceived as the Communist menace at home and abroad. At the 1950 TUC at Brighton, Harold Collison, head office, moving a Union resolution to increase food production in Britain, said 'Communist propaganda has to have prepared soil to fall upon, and if you have semi-starvation, and the misery and suffering caused by semi-starvation, you will have the danger that Communist propaganda will take root, and make our task as a free country more difficult.' The resolution was remitted to the General Council.

At the 1951 TUC, anti-Communism was the main theme, and the *Landworker* noted:

> At the heart of the Trade Union movement there is a sincere belief that a Labour Government is the only guarantee of continued social and economic security. These convictions were made abundantly clear at the 83rd TUC at Blackpool . . . The Bevanites and the muddle-headed dupes of the Communists were decisively routed and the policies of the Labour Government in both foreign and domestic fields received overwhelming support from over 900 delegates representing 200 unions.

At the Hampshire Conference at Winchester in 1951, a motion calling on the EC to take a more active interest in the international crisis and stating that they were 'not impressed by the continued propaganda against Communism' was defeated. But G. G. Griffen, chair, expressed concern at the 'witch hunting' which he thought might start being directed against Communists, and develop into a hunt against other political parties. Edwin Gooch denied there was any witch hunting in the Union.

One issue of the fifties, in which Edwin was often at variance with some Labour leaders, was German rearmament.

At the Cheltenham Biennial in 1954, Edwin Gooch voted against German rearmament and applause greeted him when he announced that he had signed a House of Commons order paper which read:

> This House believes that democracy has now to meet a prolonged period of challenge in which success will depend at least as much upon moral, social, political and economic as upon military policy, and particularly upon an effective international plan for world mutual aid . . . and a new allocation of national resources between defence expenditure and the economic cost of helping the peoples of the under-developed countries.

C. G. Boyt, Dorset, successfully moved a resolution deploring that 10s 4d in every £1 of Government expenditure was on arms and the national debt, while at the same time insufficient was spent on health and social services.

G. R. Andrews, Dorset, moved a motion opposing Britain's longer period of military service than any other NATO country, and called for a cut to one year. L. P. Jones, Kent, moved an amendment opposing German rearmament, and the amended motion was carried unanimously.

At the TUC in Brighton in 1954, Jim Campbell, General Secretary of the NUR, moved a composite opposing the rearmament of either Eastern or Western Germany, and Jock Shanley of the furniture trades union said that the industrialists who backed Hitler were still there, and the German militarists were their tools. Vincent Tewson for the General Council said that the vacuum in Western defence must be filled. When the resolution was put to the vote the Union's card went up in favour, but it was defeated by 4,090,000 votes to 3,622,000.

At the Labour Conference at Scarborough in October 1954, German rearmament again came up. The Union delegates were mandated to vote against, and a motion to this effect was carried by a small majority.

When Frank Cousins became secretary of the TGWU in 1956, the right-wing power base in that Union began to weaken, as in 1955 both the TGWU and the GMWU annual conferences had voted to support unilateral disarmament. Tom Williams of the GMWU recalled his conference to get the vote reversed.

At the 1960 Labour Conference, it was a shock for their leader, Hugh Gaitskell, when delegates voted for a resolution in favour of unilateral disarmament. It had been put forward by the TGWU. The AEU, NUR and USDAW were among those voting for unilateralism.

These moves had their affect on smaller unions like the NUAW, which in time was to support unilateralism. Edwin Gooch told delegates to the 1960 Biennial that he had supported a motion in the House of Commons which 'rejected the nuclear arms policy which threatened the suicide of Great Britain and the annihilation of mankind.' However, a resolution calling for unilateral disarmament was remitted to the EC.

The Union did not confine its international interests to those of the big powers, but also took a keen interest in third-world countries and former colonies. In the March 1955 *Landworker* there was a feature on the difficulties of the emerging trade unions in the colonies. It was a time of unrest in Kenya and 'tribes were rounded up in trucks like cattle for "screening". The majority have committed no crime, but they were detained like criminals.'

In the same year, the *Landworker* took a brief glance at a former enemy. Rain had brought radioactive dust from the Bikini hydrogen bomb tests on to glasshouses in the 'Lea Valley' of Japan. Japanese scientists said that tea plants were affected by radioactivity, and wheat and rice showed contamination in the heads.

At the Labour Conference at Margate in 1955, delegates rejected, by a heavy majority, a call to oppose the manufacture of the H-bomb, but agreed to a call for action through the UN to secure an immediate reduction in armaments and the banning of hydrogen and atomic weapons.

A *Landworker* editorial in February 1957 condemned Britain's attack on Egypt:

> One morning . . . the nation woke up to the appalling fact that Anthony Eden and his Government, in the name of the British people, was preparing to attack Egypt. Powerless to do anything but protest, it watched the Government lead Great Britain into a state of armed conflict with a much smaller nation. It saw the armed forces, which were kept up to strength in the name of defence, used to commit an act of aggression in flagrant disregard of the United Nations . . . Gradually the strength of public opinion had its effect on Eden and his Cabinet. Using the United Nations as a face saver they finally called a halt to their folly. Our troops were withdrawn . . .

The *Landworker* was reflecting the feelings that ran high in the trade-union movement at the Government-engineered Suez crisis and the subsequent fiasco. Petrol rationing returned to Britain, and unemployment came to factories. Union organisers, who normally covered between 1,000 to 1,600 miles a month, found that to travel across a county late at night without a car was virtually impossible. They had difficulty going to accidents, interviewing witnesses, or taking immediate action to prevent hardship in eviction cases. The supplementary petrol ration granted to the Union meant that only the most urgent calls could be met. Fortunately, as the worst effects of the Government's escapade passed, things returned to normal.

At that year's Labour Conference, partly reflecting the Tory Government's wilful stupidity over Suez, which had brought to the fore the dangers of world war, over a quarter of the 438 motions on the agenda dealt with disarmament and the hydrogen bomb. But the voting against the unilateral banning of the bomb was 5,836,000 to 781,000.

After the Suez Crisis, some of the steam went out of the Cold War, and when the 1958 Biennial met, the suggestion of exchange visits with the Soviet Union was raised in a successful motion by Alf Fooks, Dorset. It said that these would increase goodwill and understanding between nations. Jack Dunman, Oxon, seconded, supported by Wilf Page, Norfolk, and Gordon Dales, Lincs.

Another aspect of Tory Government policy in relation to world affairs was the issue of an official handbook in 1958, on the need to protect agriculture, its families, crops and livestock in a nuclear war. This ludicrous epistle, called *Home Defence and the Farmers*, claimed that fall-out became less dangerous as time went on; and on food for the family, it said that the pods of peas and beans would be contaminated, the actual peas and beans being quite safe. Other vegetables were not so reliable, and only the hearts of such things as cabbages, sprouts and lettuce should be touched. Water should be stored, 'in case anything happens to the mains supply'. For livestock it recommended just sufficient food and water to keep them alive, and that cows should be milked out before being left. As many of the animals should be brought inside as possible, and those outside should be put in a sheltered place – 'Trees would give some protection . . .' Over the years its recommendations were ridiculed by nuclear experts, and subsequent governments were increasingly coy about re-issuing it.

At the 1959 TUC, the debate which aroused the keenest interest was that on nuclear disarmament. There were several motions before Congress. The first called for the endorsement of the policy set out in the TUC-Labour Party statement on disarmament and nuclear war, 'The Next Step'. Another, submitted by the TGWU, rejected the idea of basing defence policies on the threat of nuclear weapons. Yet another called for the renunciation by Britain of nuclear weapons, and a fourth protested against ballistic-missile sites here. Vincent Tewson asked Congress to support the official policy and turn down the other three motions. Delegates agreed with official policy by 5,214,000 votes to 2,695,000. They turned down the TGWU motion by 5,133,000 to 2,785,000, and defeated the motion renouncing nuclear weapons. But by 4,040,000 to 3,865,000 they supported the protest against US missile sites in Britain.

The Labour movement had moved a long way from the early fifties, when the constellation of US airbases amongst the wheatfields of East Anglia had become the pivot of American nuclear war plans. Rows of Thor rockets, all pointing to cities in the USSR, were no longer quite so acceptable to the general public, and that included farmworkers, who were increasingly questioning their purpose.

Much eventually leaked out about US intentions including the fact that plans for the US to 'strike' a first blow against the USSR with atomic weapons were prepared in September 1945, just a month after the surrender of Japan. Public records of the US Joint Chiefs of Staff have since revealed that they would, if need be, 'seize and hold' UK airfields for this purpose. Doubts about the wisdom of acquiescing to nuclear madness continued to grow, and by the eighties, the majority of the trade unions in Britain had affiliated to CND. But before then, in the 1950s, the development of British nuclear weapons began in total secrecy, undeclared in Parliament or to the public, or even to most members of the Attlee Government. NUAW leaders, like Edwin Gooch, are now believed to have been among those not in the know. All this would not have been possible without the stepping up of the Cold War propaganda in the Labour movement, coupled with appeals for wage restraint, because of the cost of rearming.

Moves for Nuclear Disarmament

But to return to 1959 when the *Landworker* set out Labour policy for the General Election in October, pointing out that 'Labour still leads in its belief that East and West can live and work together. Given a Labour Government . . . Britain will set the pace by the ending of nuclear tests.' Its hope for a Labour Government didn't come off – the Tories remained in power.

The vexed question of nuclear arms was discussed at the 1960 Biennial at Chester, when Ted Sales, Dorset, moved, and W. H. Clough, Cheshire, seconded, a motion calling upon the British Government to cease testing, manufacturing and stockpiling all nuclear weapons, at the same time seeking international agreement for total disarmament. An amendment, protesting against providing West Germany with nuclear weapons, was accepted by the mover. Alf Fooks, Dorset, said that the testing of nuclear weapons was polluting the atmosphere and poisoning the food of the world. A. E. Calver, Cambs, said that the Government must be told to clear out every atomic and hydrogen bomb from the country. The EC asked for the motion to be remitted. Conference agreed by 80 votes to 60.

Again, at the Biennial at Bournemouth in 1962, the way to peace was debated, and one thing that the speakers had in common was a passionate desire for peace. Yet the essential dilemma was how to reconcile deeply-held opposing convictions. Ted Sales, Dorset, moved a composite which 'considers the worsening of international relations . . . to be the result of diplomacy based on nuclear war policies.' It called on the British Government to pursue a policy of international agreement for complete and general disarmament in agreed stages and with control and inspection. Meanwhile Britain should renounce the use of all nuclear weapons and prohibit the use of British soil or water for use as bases for such weapons. R. Watson, Norfolk, moved an amendment deleting 'Government' and inserting 'Russian, French and American Governments'. A. Smith, Yorks, believed that Britain should not go it alone. Harold Collison supported the amendment for the EC. The amendment was carried by 80 votes to 40 and then ratified as the substantive motion.

Indicative of the Union's wide-ranging interest in international affairs was its official representation at an anti-apartheid vigil by trade union leaders outside South Africa House in London in 1964 – the year the Biennial adopted a motion appealing to all nations to refuse to supply South Africa with arms.

In July 1965, a Union delegation of five members visited the USSR, and found farming there vastly different from that in Britain. They noted that the USSR Agricultural Workers' Trade Union had 12 million members, which included workers on State farms, agricultural machinery workshops, flour and mixed feed mills, besides agricultural students and officials of agricultural departments. Delegation leader, Lord Hilton, said that the tractor driver got the same wage as a skilled machine worker in a factory. They visited a State farm, where 'living conditions were pleasant though by British standards rather cramped.'

The following year, three visitors from the Soviet Agricultural Workers' Union were hosted by the NUAAW in Britain, where they visited the Royal Show at Stoneleigh, and farms in different parts of the country.

*　　*　　*

At the Labour Conference in 1966 there were again major debates on defence and foreign policy. On the NEC's advice, Conference rejected calls for the Government to disassociate itself entirely from US policy in Vietnam, re-examination with a view to withdrawal from NATO, withdrawal of all nuclear weapons, and the dismissal of Government arms salesmen. The NEC's overseas policy statement was carried, but their advice was not accepted when there were majority votes in favour of decisive reduction in military commitments East of Suez and a stop to the US bombing of Vietnam. The Union's vote followed the NEC line in every case except that of the motion on arms salesmen.

A group of British trade unionists went to war-ravaged Vietnam in 1971, including Joan Maynard, who was not, the *Landworker* carefully pointed out, representing the NUAAW. In an article, Joan described the Vietnamese as having so little in the way of material things, it made the group wonder how they could hold off the mighty USA. They had help from the USSR, and an indomitable will to get the Americans out of their country so that they could rebuild it. Their agriculture reflected years of colonial rule; they had a one-crop economy, rice; they still ploughed with oxen, and did the most laborious things by hand. Joan predicted that the Americans would not win, and said Union members must continue to press the Government to disassociate itself from American policy in Vietnam.

Opposition to American nuclear weapons on British soil increased during the seventies, and at the Biennial at Cromer in 1980, only Edgar Pill, Wiltshire, went to the rostrum to assert NATO's contribution to Britain's defence. The call for the withdrawal of American nuclear weapons from Britain was overwhelming. And in 1981, peace issues were to the fore at the Suffolk area Conference in Ipswich, which opposed the siting of American Cruise missiles 'in any part of the British Isles', and called for the cancellation of Trident.

After the merger with the TGWU, the new trade group affiliated to CND, and its official policy was for the Labour movement to give a lead in positive steps towards world peace, and genuine national security of all nations, both East and West. A far cry from the Cold War days, when many in the Union were reluctant to have anything to do with the 'peace' movement. By the late 1980s, with the advent of Mr. Gorbachev as President of the USSR, there was a sea change in relations between East and West, helped tremendously by a start to the democratisation of the Soviet system, and earlier antagonisms shown by the Union leadership to everything Soviet disappeared.

George Edwards Addressed the Sunday School

Perhaps this might be the appropriate place to take a look at one of the leading Communists in the Union, Wilf Page, often a protagonist in its debates on international affairs.

The highlight of the year for young Wilf Page was when George Edwards addressed his Sunday School class. It was not Wilf's first contact with the

Union. His Sunday School teacher, Billy Furness, who was active in the Union, and saw it as a day-to-day expression of Christianity, related passages from the Bible in Union terms. He declared, 'The Bible says love thy neighbour as thyself, and the Union says an injury to one is an injury to all.'

Young Wilf took it all in, although this kind of practical Christianity soon brought him into conflict with the Tory headmaster of his day school. But the message stuck, and the adult Wilf eventually believed that the Union, and Communism, were a kind of applied Christianity.

And his life bore witness to that youthful grounding. There was much conflict, too, for in his early days as a Union activist he was reviled by some as a Communist, but he finished up holding high office, was respected as an elder statesman of the Union, and on its behalf read the lesson at a harvest festival service in Norwich Cathedral. On his 75th birthday, thousands gathered for the annual rally on the village green to commemorate the Burston School Strike sang 'Happy Birthday Dear Wilfred'. But a lot was to happen before that Autumn day in 1988.

Wilf was born at St. Faiths, Norwich; his father was a horse dealer, his mother a devout Christian. He attended the village school until he was nearly fourteen, when he left because his father had an accident and Wilf was needed to look after the horses. He was later an upholstery apprentice, didn't like it, and went to work in London as a barman, living in. He next joined the RAF, stayed in it for twelve years, became an aerial photographer instructor, served abroad, and was demobbed after the Second World War.

He returned to Norfolk, and wanting to do something positive, went to see Edwin Gooch, who said, 'You're the boys we are looking for, you had better join the Union and the Labour Party.' He did, and Wilf toured the villages with Chris Mayhew, then a local Labour MP, and soon found himself doing a bit of speaking. Edwin then suggested that Wilf should become Labour Agent for North Norfolk, where Edwin was MP. It was obvious that Edwin thought a lot of Wilf, admired his capabilities and began to groom him as heir apparent to his Parliamentary seat. So it was a shock to Edwin when Wilf joined the Communist Party. 'I objected to the way the Labour Government was smashing up the resistance movements in countries like Greece and Malaya, fighting the very people who had fought on our side during the War,' said Wilf when I interviewed him in 1988 in Overstrand, on the Norfolk coast, where he had lived for most of his life. 'Then came Marshall Plan which subjected Britain to US domination. It was too much, so I resigned.'

Edwin was furious and wouldn't speak to Wilf. Some Union officials toured branches warning them not to have Wilf as a speaker as he was out to destroy the Union.

That was in 1950. In addition to being Labour Agent, he had been very active in the Union and was chairman and secretary of Roughton branch. The Tory farmers didn't want to know him either. One told him he could go to Russia and get a job. He was getting desperate as he had a growing family to support, and did various jobs, lorry and bus driving, coastal defence work, was an attendant at a caravan park, and once tried serving teas on the sands to make a living. He finally took a job working on a smallholding for Herbert Harvey, an old Union stalwart who had played a great part in the 1923 Norfolk Strike, and was a prominent Labour Party campaigner. 'No other bugger would employ me,' said Wilf. He had won a seat on Erpingham Rural District Council for Labour, and retained it as a Communist for 24 years, until local government reorganisation in the seventies.

Not for two years did Edwin and Wilf speak to each other. But Wilf admired Edwin's heroic opposition on the Labour Party NEC against German rearmament, and one day saw Edwin walking through Cromer and congratulated him on his stand. Edwin said, 'We didn't lose all those men in the war to have it start all over again my boy,' and they became close friends again.

Wilf was more determined than ever to continue his activities in the Union, but despite his renewed friendship with Edwin, many obstacles were put in his way as the Cold War heightened. When he wanted to go to the Union's schools, the answer was always, 'It's over subscribed.' Jack Wilson, DO for North Norfolk complained to Harold Collison. The following year Wilf got an invitation to go, and was just about to leave for the school, when a letter arrived saying he couldn't go because the school was again over subscribed. Jack Wilson made a special trip to Clacton, where the school was being held, and found that there were four vacancies. He was accepted the next year, without any difficulty.

But that didn't mean Wilf got on any better with the other top men in the Union. He often clashed with Harold Collison, and strongly objected to his remarks at a Norfolk Conference that the Union no longer had organising officers recruiting – all recruiting had been done. They were only servicing. 'In other words,' said Wilf, 'they became social workers. What a stupid thing to say, trying to transform the Union from a leading force into a passive social service institution. This helped prevent the Union being a fighting force in the countryside and was a factor in its decline.

'This fitted in with Collison's objection to wage demos, and we had to fight hard for them at biennials. Eventually we got one in London and about ten selected people walked yards apart, a very strange demo. We've built up on them a bit since then.'

Wilf was in the forefront of the Union's opposition to Britain joining the Common Market. It was the first Union to oppose, and began with a resolution objecting to EEC membership from the Roughton branch, moved by Wilf, and carried by one vote. The EC said derisively, 'one vote, that's not enough for so important an issue,' but when it came up before the Whitley Bay Biennial, proposed by John Hardy (who later became DO for Shropshire) of Roughton, it was carried by a large majority.

Wilf recalled that opposition in the Union against joining the EEC, was that the food was too cheap in this country, and farmworkers were suffering through low wages. Higher-priced food would give farmers higher cash flows and there would be more for farmworkers. Wilf smiled, 'It never worked out that way. The EEC has been a disaster for the Union, and Britain.'

When I called to see Wilf, he was looking tired. He had only a few days before moved from a large terrace house in Overstrand into a fisherman's cottage; two up, two down. It suited Wilf and his wife Christine much better in their 'retirement'. Wilf was still active in the Union, especially for pensioners, and Christine had gone off to a British Legion meeting. Christine had been as active a trade unionist as Wilf. She was prominent in USDAW, was a member of its EC, was awarded the TUC Gold Badge, and got five million votes when she stood for the TUC General Council, although not quite enough to win a seat. They have both been active in the peace movement. Wilf joined CND's symbolic 'snowball' wire-cutting campaign round US nuclear bases in Norfolk, appeared in Court with Lord Melchett (also a Union member) and were both fined.

Looking back on his life's battles, Wilf felt that people in the Union were 'not really nasty, but apprehensive of my political philosophy.'

A change in attitude towards Wilf by the Union's hierarchy began when he joined the EC in 1969 as its first and only Communist member. He said, 'They realised I was a fairly responsible character, and no obstacles were put in my way.' He went on to be elected to the European Farmworkers' Association, and later became its President. He also represented the Union on other bodies, and after the merger, became its representative on the TGWU EC until his retirement.

Referring to the EEC's farm policy, Wilf said, 'Doubts of the NUAAW in early days have been substantiated. We knew there would be a bonanza for the barley barons, but we didn't think that the honeymoon would have lasted as long as it has. We gave it five years, but now the interests of European farmers, with their surpluses, are turning Britain into a dumping ground for these surpluses, at the expense of British agriculture and the housewife. It began with milk quotas, now there's cereal cutbacks, and the Brussels bureaucrats seem to be winning the battle to dismantle the Milk Marketing Board in spite of over a 90% vote by milk producers in Britain to retain the Board. This is all part of Mrs. Thatcher's euthanasia for industrial Britain in favour of the transnational companies, which is what capitalism is all about these days.'

On the Agricultural Rent Act, Wilf said, 'It took so long to get the Rent Act because the forces against abolition of tied cottages were so powerful and the Union's parliamentary campaign so muted, and that, I'm sorry to say, included our sponsored MPs, until Joan Maynard came along. The Act has worked in favour of the farmers, they don't have to pay the legal costs of getting possession, but at least it's prevented people being peremptorily put out on the streets.'

On the merger Wilf said, 'The Union's decline was partly due to bad management by the Union's old hierarchy, and lack of accountability of DOs to members – they could do what they liked, and some did. Also the high cost of servicing a scattered membership. I opposed the merger. I felt the NUAAW might be a small union, but it still had a tremendous contribution to make, and that old Methodist, democratic approach could have sustained it; the strength of a Union is the members' relationship with its leaders and, in a big union, members are divorced from the leadership and it's not a good thing. The trade group has got to start recruiting not only farmworkers, but any rural worker and the self-employed, because so many farmers are forcing their workers to go self-employed.'

At the age of 75, Wilf still looked ahead, 'The only future for British agriculture is to go back to family farming, break up these huge estates and the prairie farmers' thousands of hectares, divide them into viable units and let them to tenant farmers, but encourage them by financial incentives to become co-ops; they wouldn't employ many workers, but the big farms don't employ them now. Some farmworkers could work for a labour committee and be contracted to work for farm co-ops as needed. Farming should return to more natural, organic methods. It's safer for the farmworkers and consumers, and better for the conservation of the countryside.'

17

A Dangerous Place to Work

The first wealth is health . . . health or fulness answers its own ends, and has to spare, runs over, and inundates the neighbourhoods and creeks of other men's necessities.

Emmerson, *Conduct of Life*

The Official Secrets Cover-Up

In the 1890s, it was the hapless village policeman, often at the beck and call of the farming squire, who had the job of looking out for dangerous threshing and chaff-cutting machines. Not until the 1950s was there any major safety legislation for farmworkers.

Yet the early part of this century saw ever-increasing mechanisation, and farm work became a more hazardous occupation. Not that it was ever that safe. Livestock and hand tools had always constituted potential dangers to life and limb, and animal-transmitted diseases were once a major threat to the health of the general population, to say nothing of the farmworker who had the closest contact with them.

One of the long-standing injustices was that farmworkers were denied the protection of the Factory Acts. Yet agriculture had an accident rate second to that of coal mining, and the position got considerably worse with the large-scale use of poisonous chemicals and complicated machinery.

Not only the farmworkers and their families are at possible risk, but even their unborn children. The public, too, can be at risk through eating highly-sprayed fruit and vegetables, and from hormone and similar injections in cattle to stimulate growth, although it is difficult to collect much factual evidence. Little research was done in this sphere, and even less revealed; meanwhile controversy has raged.

It was not until the late 1980s, at the time of the widespread salmonella outbreak in eggs and factory chickens, and listeria in soft cheese, that the general public was allowed to become aware of the risks they ran from chemicalised farming; much of what little was previously known by people in the industry had, with the help of the Official Secrets Act, been kept from the public. Hence calls at the time for a Freedom of Information Act on the lines of the one existing in America; such a step in Britain would stop some of the grosser abuses of both worker and consumer alike.

Before July 1948, the farmworker injured by an unguarded machine had very little chance of getting damages, only weekly compensation. Occasionally he could claim for injury under the Employers' Liability Act, but the difficulty of establishing liability made such claims rare. Since July 1948 the farmworker's position improved so far as claiming a lump sum for damages was concerned, due to the repeal of the Employers' Liability Act, but the lack of statutory regulations severely handicapped farmworkers.

In agriculture, only two Acts provided for proper guards on dangerous machinery: the Threshing Machines Act of 1878 and the Chaff Cutting Machines (Accidents) Act 1897. A penalty of £5 could be imposed for non-compliance, but it is impossible to find on record a single case in which injuries from neglect of the provisions of these Acts was proved, and prosecution ensued.

When the Home Office Committee chaired by Sir Ernest Gowers reported on the health, welfare and safety of non-industrial workers in 1949, agriculture had moved a long way from using the comparatively uncomplicated machinery of the Victorian age. A Union representative gave evidence to the Committee which concluded that no Act could afford farmworkers the same safeguards as those enjoyed by factory workers, but recommended that certain sections of the Factories Acts should be incorporated in a Bill of limited scope to apply to agriculture. They pointed out that 35% of farms in Britain employed no paid workers, whilst a further 28% employed two workers or less. Thus two-thirds consisted of small units where a substantial part of the labour was supplied by the farmer and his family, and consequently employers and employed shared the same risks. A strange line of argument for not bringing in safety measures, if indeed that was their thinking.

However, they did make a number of limited recommendations, including the compulsory provision of washing facilities, protective clothing for workers using certain chemicals, and safeguards against injury from machinery. They proposed that the Threshing Machines and Chaff Cutting Machines Acts should be repealed and that safety devices be compulsory for dangerous machines. A. L. Marriott of the Union's Legal Department thought the recommendations a 'big step forward', but implementation proved extremely slow.

At this time, the Legal Department had been studying the effects of the increasing use of chemicals on the farm, and was particularly concerned about DNOC (Dinitro-orthocresol), an exceedingly dangerous preparation that had already caused the deaths of several workers. A long memorandum on the dangers in using DNOC was prepared and submitted to MAFF and the TUC. It urged that until the compulsory provision of protective measures, DNOC should be banned. The TUC agreed.

By 1953 there were nearly 4,000 tractors on British farms, 16,000 combine harvesters compared with 200 in 1938, and 1,000 grass drying plants where hardly any stood before the war. Machinery was being increasingly adapted for hoeing, planting, beet-lifting and cultivating. Experience showed that the risk of injury in agriculture was then greater than in any other industry.

The only breakdown the Union had of the causes of farm accidents related to 2,022 cases during a period in 1949. The Nuffield Foundation Research Unit found that 33% of the total accidents involved machinery – tractors accounted for 188 accidents; trailers and carts, 141; ploughs, drills and manure spreaders, 55. Of the non-mobile machines: 34 involved threshing drums; 20, balers and pressers; 29, grinders and slicers; and 33, circular saws. Moving heavy objects by hand accounted for 320 cases, of which 74 occurred through carrying sacks. There appeared to be no 'accident' caused by poisonous chemicals. In view of the increasing use of toxic substances, it is unlikely that none occurred – more probably, they were not properly identified.

Harold Collison wrote, 'The Union is increasingly concerned at the delay in implementing the recommendations of the Gowers Committee . . . If the Government continues to refuse to give farmworkers the protection they have so long demanded it will accentuate their drift to town occupations where their health, safety and welfare receive greater consideration.'

At the annual meeting of Liskeard (Cornwall) District Committee in 1953, F. C. Cole, DO, reported that in the first ten months of that year, no fewer than 112 members had accidents at work, entitling them to Union benefit.

A new kind of return was issued by MAFF in 1953. It set out the number of kinds of fatal accidents on farms in the four years 1949–52. Those involving tractors totalled 145, including 30 children; machinery, 70, including eight children; hand tools, by falling objects or by falling, 96. Bulls caused 38 deaths, other animals, 27; electrocution, 25; lightning, 4; gunshot, 38. All told, there were 487 fatal accidents, including 52 children. Only three were recorded as dying of poisons.

The first prosecutions under the Agriculture (Poisonous Substances) Regulations, 1953, were taken the following year when a contractor pleaded not guilty to three charges: (1) Having no register, found guilty, fined £10; (2) For not supplying all the protective clothing required, guilty, fined £25; (3) For permitting the worker to spray when not wearing protective clothing, guilty, fined £40. The employee was fined £10 for not wearing protective clothing. For smoking after he had sprayed, without first washing his hands and face, he was fined £10.

At the TUC at Brighton in 1954, Dr Gordon Evans of the Medical Practitioners' Union, said that of 700,000 accidents at work each year, 290,000 were in industries outside the scope of the Factories Act. Stan Brumby, Lincolnshire DO, said that in 30 years he had never seen a first-aid box on a farm. If this was anything to go by, it meant there were nearly 300,000 farms without one. Not until August 1957 did regulations come into force requiring the provision of first-aid items on farms.

Changes in the regulations protecting workers using certain poisons came into operation on 2 May 1955. A new organo-phosphorus substance, 'Metasystox', was added to the list requiring protecting clothing.

Not all the hazards in the 1950s were due to increased mechanisation or new poisons, as members were reminded by two inquests in 1955 at King's Lynn, where two people died from tetanus. One death followed when a worker pierced his foot with a fork, and the second was the result of a cut finger.

Land workers are more prone to tetanus than many, because tetanus germs are found in the soil, but they shouldn't ask for trouble by catching rats with their bare hands. One member of Chislet (Kent) branch was doing this in 1955, when he was bitten and poisoning resulted. Fortunately tetanus did not set in. He became champion sparrow catcher in a local club, with a total of 3,081 heads in a year, but although he collected 1,171 rats' tails, he was beaten by someone who notched up 1,200. And he couldn't go to collect the cup he won because of the rat bite.

The first 'Workers' VC' awarded to a Norfolk man went to Mark Overson, of Tilney St Lawrence, for going to the assistance of 66-year-old stockman, Arthur Jude, when attacked by three bullocks in 1955. He forced two back with a hoe, but the third would not be deterred. Mr Jude died from severe fractures and internal injuries. The 'VC' was 'The Order for Industrial Heroism' given by the *Daily Herald*, and with it went a bronze medal and cheques for £10 each from the paper and the Union. The 1956 Biennial at Great Yarmouth wanted all cattle de-horned.

'Apparently there are no regulations requiring guards for such flywheels,' commented the coroner at the inquest on L. J. Willett of Canterbury branch. He died when his clothing became entangled in the spindle of a flywheel of a stationary engine. Both his arms were torn off.

In 1955, Harold Davies, Labour MP, Leek, introduced a Bill in the House of Commons to implement the Gowers recommendations. Unfortunately, the Bill was killed by the sudden dissolution of Parliament and subsequent General Election. 'Nonetheless,' said the Union, 'good has been done to precipitate action by the Government, and before the Christmas recess of Parliament, the Minister of Agriculture, Mr. Heathcoat Amory, presented to Parliament the Agriculture (Safety, Health and Welfare Provisions) Bill.'[1]

So, after years of campaigning by the NUAW, a Government-sponsored Bill on farm accidents was 'on the stocks'. The Union had participated in many discussions with the Ministry on its scope. The Bill sought to deal with the wider machinery risks, operations and processes, animal management, training and supervision of young persons, farm buildings, limitations on weights to be lifted and prohibition of children from riding and driving vehicles and machines. The outdated Threshing Machines and Chaff Cutting Machines Acts would be repealed. Enforcement of the new Act would be by inspectors with power to enter and inspect 'at all reasonable hours any land used for agriculture.' The penalty for a breach of regulations would be a fine not exceeding £50.

The *Landworker* wanted to know just how many inspectors would be employed, as the effectiveness of the regulations would depend on their proper enforcement. On the prohibition of children from riding on or using machinery, the journal saw a loophole in respect of children aged 13 to 15, and hoped this matter could be satisfactorily cleared up. It recognised that the Bill would not give an automatic extension of the Factories Act to agriculture, but thought it would 'provide satisfactory standards comparable with those in industry.'

In 1956 the Agriculture (Safety, Health and Welfare Provisions) Act became law. A year later, the Union noted that 'on the matter of the Inspectorate, there are already appointed the Chief Safety Inspector and eight Regional Safety Inspectors, who had been trained and posted. The 39 Wages and Poisonous Substances Inspectors have had supplementary training and are working at divisional level. Additional officers to make up a total complement of 62 in the Inspectorate have also been selected; they are in course of training and should be playing their full part by April, 1958.'[2]

It was a good start, and considerable progress was made over the next few years, but the Union had to wait many more years before it got what became a central feature of its safety campaigns: its own safety representatives on farms.

Alarming Rise in Fatalities

Despite the new Safety Regulations, there was no appreciable drop in accident numbers, and fatal accidents claimed 127 farmworkers in 1956; 112 in 1957; and 109 in 1958. These figures included 45 children under 15. About 50% involved tractors.

In the early 1960s there was an alarming rise in fatal farm accidents. In industry, the death rate was one for every 20,000 workers. On the land it was about one in 5,500. Injuries in the factory were about one in 50, on farms one in 36. And in 1961, 17 more people were killed on farms in England and Wales during the first four months than during the corresponding period of the previous year.

It must have been something of a surprise to the House of Commons, when Edwin Gooch and Albert Hilton moved a 'Prayer', asking that a proposed safety regulation be annulled. The Union had always wanted the maximum weight lifted by a farmworker to be progressively reduced to 1 cwt. In discussions on the new regulation, the Union indicated that it was prepared to agree to an interim compromise at 1½ cwt; but to tell farmworkers that they must, in effect, lift any weight until 1965 when the new proposals would become law, was not good enough. A reduction to one hundredweight could be done before 1965. A Government Minister said that there was an estimated 20 million large sacks circulating in the trade, with a life of around 20 years, and time must be given for replacement. He promised to take note of the farmworkers' objection, and Albert withdrew the motion. Commercial convenience was still to take precedence over health and safety.

In 1960, when new chemicals, including 'Endrin' and 'Endothal,' were added to the list of poisonous substances used on farms, the *Landworker* claimed that the Regulations brought in since 1956 to control these substances had worked well. In fact, since then, no agricultural worker had died as a result of using a poisonous substance.

At that year's Biennial, a composite on farm safety was preceded by statement from the EC by Bill Case. He said that when the Safety Act came in after years of agitation, some may have expected an overnight transformation, but this had not happened owing to the complex matter of making regulations. It was not an easy matter, and credit should be given to the Ministry for what they had accomplished so far, and he accepted the motion on behalf of the EC. Moving the successful motion, C. Button, Lincs, wanted additional measures to minimise hazards associated with animal management, electrical apparatus, vehicle loading, dust in crop-drying operations, and instruction in the safe use of machines.

When he gave evidence the same year to the Research Study Group,* George Hook expressed satisfaction with the apparent effectiveness of the Agriculture (Poisonous Substances) Regulations, but was apprehensive about the continued use of toxic materials. Less than ten years earlier, several deaths were caused through ignorance of the risks and unrestricted use of poisonous insecticides and weedkiller.

In the 1960s, an automatic device came on the market for scaring birds off farmlands. One exploded and killed Brother H. Johnson, of Wootton, Norfolk. At the 1962 Biennial at Bournemouth, a debate on this new hazard aroused such feeling, R. H. Clarke, Norfolk, moved a successful emergency resolution for regulations to make these contrivances safer. Another Norfolk member lost an eye, and L. Miles, Norfolk, said 'They are detestable things' which should be banned. George Hook said that they were a potential danger to children and the public, but a sense of proportion was necessary. Essential implements like tractors also caused accidents. Later that year the makers modified the device.

In 1962, George Hook found the main conclusions of the Research Study Group's Report on Chemicals in Agriculture and Food Storage reassuring, although there was need for more research. 'Our members should be reassured as the Group found no evidence of adverse effects on the health of consumers, and considered that workers were well protected by the Agriculture (Poisonous Substances) Regulations.'[3] During 1946–65 (before the introduction of the regulations) there were eight recorded deaths from toxic chemicals against none for 1956–60. Also, among an average 20,000 non-fatal agricultural accidents annually, less than five were from chemical poisoning. The Group believed that the Regulations had been successful in giving farmworkers protection against toxic chemicals.

---

* Appointed in 1960 by Ministers of Science, Agriculture and Health, to study the need for further research into the effects of using toxic chemicals in agriculture and food storage.

Agricultural workers, the Group thought, were not exposed to pesticides for long enough periods for repeated exposure to cause ill effects. And hazards to passers-by were considered small, because a single exposure to spray drift could 'rarely have a measurable effect on health'. But the Group did recommend that fundamental research should continue into finding less toxic chemicals and into the hazards to field operators. Said George Hook, 'Despite the comforting assurances to allay the disquiet still existing among workers and the public, a fair deduction is that there is neither cause for alarm nor room for complacency.'

In view of later developments in farm chemicals and better knowledge, it would, with hindsight, seem that the Group was unduly complacent. Fortunately, the Union was not. The 1962 Biennial urged the Government to encourage, with all possible speed and means, research into non-toxic substitutes. The next chapter on 245-T deals more fully with poisonous sprays.

When the Commons debated the Agricultural (Field Machinery) Regulations 1962, Albert Hilton deplored the continued use of unsafe machinery and declared that there were 'too few inspectors to ensure that farmers carried out their obligations.' James Prior, Tory MP for Lowestoft, thought that inspectors managed their job very well so far – they had gone over his farm 'with a fine tooth comb'. Pleas for the regulations to be brought forward from 1968 were turned down to allow time for them to take full effect on the manufacture of new machines. The new regulations were formally approved.

But a general complacency still prevailed about chemicals. At the Cambridge Conference on Food Supply and Nature Conservation in 1964, Stan Hall, EC, attended. The main emphasis of the conference was on the control, through toxic chemicals, of the pests and diseases which attack crops. 'There is, so far, little evidence,' reported Stan, 'of serious illness resulting from sprays. But there are danger signs – bacterial diseases are lessening whilst virus diseases are increasing. A watch must be kept.'

However, the Advisory Committee on Poisonous Substances recommended in 1964 that the use of 'Aldrin,' 'Dieldrin' and 'Heptachlor' should, for most purposes cease. The first two were widely used in fertiliser mixtures, sheep dips and sprays. The Committee found no evidence of any serious immediate hazard from the use of pesticides in general, either to human or wildlife – apart from certain species of predatory birds.

Empty First-Aid Boxes

Safety was a major topic at the 1964 Biennial at Felixstowe. E. Pearce, Berkshire, moved a composite calling for more safety inspectors to enable farms to be visited more frequently without notice. 'We hear of first-aid boxes empty and thrown into corners, or locked away in farm offices. You have to have accidents in office hours – often between 9am and 4pm.' Another delegate spoke of dangerous machinery being hidden after notice of impending inspection. And as regards protective masks and clothing, the attitude of many farmers was, 'If you want it, buy it yourselves.'

Bill Case, EC, told delegates that it was six or seven years since the major safety legislation was introduced, but it was too early to judge its impact. Statistics were their principle guide, and although there had been a reduction in fatal accidents in 1963, the number of non-fatal accidents had risen.

In 1963–4, there were 20,800 safety inspections against 14,500 in the preceding period. The total number of farm fatalities – 99 – was the lowest for four years, and the lowest since the passing of the 1956 Safety Act. Another welcome sign was fewer non-fatal accidents in 1963–4, when there were 12,777 accidents in this group. Not until June 1965 was Farmer's Lung recognised as a notifiable disease. Farmer's Lung is a type of allergic asthma, long known to be caused by sensitivity to mouldy hay.

One growing hazard was corn drying. 'If you are on your own and you fall 40 ft into a bin of a corn dryer, there is nobody to save you,' declared F. Oxby, Lincs, at the 1966 Biennial, when moving a successful motion calling for a regulation that two or more men should be in attendance at a corn dryer on nightshifts. R. Clarke, Norfolk, said one morning he could not see his mate. 'I found him in the end at the bottom of the shute where you load the corn.' H. Cocksedge, Hunts, drew a graphic picture of a man who falls into 50 tons of dry corn. 'It is like getting into quick sands.'

A lot of time was devoted at the Conference to health and safety. A resolution was carried that no one should be allowed to work single-handed with large herds of dairy cattle. And the EC weighed in, favouring a resolution that all sacks on farms should be a standard size, and while another motion sought 'shelter from the weather, and a mess hut' for eating out in comfort. One resolution called for better first-aid measures, and for schoolchildren to be taught first-aid in view of accidents on remote farms. Conference wanted farmers to install means of communication in all outlying farm buildings where there was machinery. It was no good when workers had to walk a mile or more to reach a telephone. One resolution sought stricter enforcement of safety regulations with the appointment of more field inspectors. J. Robinson, Yorks, called for stiffer penalties on defaulting employers – not fines of £5 or £50, but three months' imprisonment.

There was a record low in farm fatalities for the year ending September 1965. The total number was 87 compared, with 120 in 1962; non-fatal accidents totalled 10,408, compared with 11,236 in 1962.

It is perhaps not without significance that there was an increase in the number of prosecutions under the Safety Provisions, and very welcome was the fact that 29,500 inspections were made in 1964–5, as against 20,800 in the preceding 12 months, and an extra 70 qualified safety officers joined the Inspectorate, bringing it up to 460. But the 1966 figures were disappointing. There were 115 fatalities – 28 more than the previous year. Forty-two were killed by overturning tractors. The gloom was relieved only by the prospect of fewer fatalities in the years to come as the tractor-cab regulations became operative and curbed the still most deadly killer on the farm, the overturning tractor.

And better times did come. At the end of 1967 there were 520 safety officers. Parallel to this increase there was a drop of 770 non-fatal accidents in 1967 compared with 1966. In contrast, the figures for fatal accidents were still disappointing. During 1966–7 there were 227 fatalities, including 40 children, as compared with 186 (32 children) during the two years ending 30 September 1965.

A Government report dealing with poisonous substances showed no deaths involving agricultural chemicals, but in both 1966 and 1967 there were two deaths from gas poisoning on silo installations. In 1967 there were 11 cases where workers suffered eye injury, mostly while mixing farm chemicals.

It was in 1969 that the Welland and Nene River Authority found it necessary to remind farmers to prevent chemicals reaching water courses, years before nitrate in rivers surfaced as a major problem.

Another new danger, especially to forestry workers, was the use of power saws and mechanical augers. At the Portsmouth TUC in 1969, John Hose, EC, successfully moved that the disease 'Raynaud's Phenomenon' be listed under the Industrial Injuries Act. He explained that power-saw workers developed a numbness of the fingers which spread to the whole hand and forearm, leading to gradual loss of grip. With the increasing incidence of the disease the Union wanted more done to prevent it and to alleviate the distress where the disease had taken hold. John was later able to report that an improved power saw had become available.

At the 1970 TUC, a Union resolution on carbon dioxide poisoning was carried unanimously, with the backing of the TGWU. It expressed concern over the growing risk of death from CO_2 poisoning facing workers in grain silos, and called for stricter safety regulations.

Tractor Safety Cab Made Compulsory

On 1 September 1970, the New Agriculture (Tractor Cab) regulations came into operation, compelling all new wheeled tractors to be fitted with approved safety cabs or frames. Overturning tractors had caused over 30% of fatalities on farms. In Sweden, which had made cabs compulsory much earlier, there had not been a single fatality from an overturning tractor for ten years.

At the TUC Conference at Blackpool in 1971, four more important planks were thrust into the TUC's programme through the initiative of the NUAAW. The Union's motion on chemical farming was allowed to stand on its own, and it was almost identical with a resolution at the Union's 1970 Biennial. A clear example of how a measure, sponsored in the first instance by a small union branch, can, via the biennial and the TUC, be brought to the attention of the Government. The resolution spelt out the dangers arising from chemical farming, especially from aerial spraying.

*   *   *

One of the countless committees of inquiry set up over the years, whose activities could have had a beneficial effect on humanity more than any other, was the Royal Commission on Environmental Pollution, under the chairmanship of Sir Eric Ashby. Reg Bottini was a member of its working party on pollution. He told a conference in 1972 that, despite the increasing attention given to pollution in the media, the threat had not so far been fully recognised. 'Most people no doubt would vaguely acknowledge the debt they owe to farm chemicals for making available much of the food they eat; but it is doubtful if many of them see the grim significance in the fact of a well-known pesticide like DDT – once declared safe by the "experts" – now being phased out by MAFF because other "experts" have discovered a dangerous build-up of this poison in human beings and wildlife.'

Reg also pointed out that millions of fish were dying in our rivers, victims of noxious effluents discharged into waterways. Farm and forestry workers knew what it was all about. That was why resolutions warning of the dangers of chemical farming were passed at their conferences. 'For what profit shall we gain, or our children after us, from social and economic advance if we continue to poison our environment.' He said that 'steps should be taken now to promote an international master plan to combat pollution.'

New Health and Safety Executive

Following protracted investigations into all aspects of Safety, Health and Welfare, the Robens Committee reported in June 1972. It wanted fundamental and far-reaching changes in the structure, administration and powers of safety enforcement agencies, including agriculture.

The Committee, under Lord Robens, received evidence from all the organisations representing employers and workers, including the NUAAW, which demonstrated the low level of safety enforcement in agriculture, and the urgent need for the introduction of additional regulations to cater for new hazards arising through mechanisation and chemical innovation. The most basic of the changes recommended by Robens was for the scrapping of all existing inspectorates and the creation of a single safety and health at work authority. Its immediate effect would be to bring into cover some six million workers then not protected by any form of safety legislation.

Following publication of the Report, farmers wanted agriculture to be excluded from the new proposals. They argued that farming operations were exposed to the natural elements, which could not be controlled, were highly dispersed in small units, and characterised by independent working with minimal supervision. They maintained that the agricultural inspectorate should remain independent, and that the new authority should have no jurisdiction in agriculture.

The Union argued that whilst agricultural safety remained the sole responsibility of MAFF, farmers, by virtue of their powerful political lobby, would be able to delay or prevent the level of enforcement and the introduction of new regulations urgently needed.

After months of discussion, the Government finally introduced a Safety and Health at Work Bill; but they had bowed to the farmers' pressure, and had in all essentials, excluded farming from the new authority. Fortunately, a Labour Government was elected before the Bill became law, and immediately drafted its own Safety and Health at Work Bill, but even so, MAFF maintained that agriculture should be excluded. The new Bill followed the pattern of the previous Government's in excluding agriculture, but eventually the Union's arguments were accepted and agriculture included.

The new Bill established a Health and Safety Commission and provided for workers' representatives on it. The powers of the Inspectors were also substantially increased, and not least that they would be able to stop a hazardous process and seize any hazardous article or substance. They would be responsible to the new Commission, but the existing agricultural inspectorate was not to be disbanded. They would act as agents for the Commission. It was not suggested that the new set-up would solve all the safety and health problems confronting farmworkers.

What the Union did feel, declared Jim Watts in the *Landworker*, was that they had now introduced into the agricultural system uniformity with other industries, and an opportunity to exert a much stronger influence on safety enforcement and the creation of new regulations through worker representatives. All in all the Union had achieved a major policy objective, a signal victory that it was hoped would show, in time, a marked improvement in farm safety.

Jim's hopes were premature. A last-minute footnote read: 'The victory announced in this issue turned out to be a very short-lived affair. Despite the efforts of Lord Collison, the Government were defeated in the House of Lords; and when the Safety and Health at Work Bill came back to the House of Commons on 18 July, the Government was again defeated – this time by only six votes. The opposition majority was gained with Liberal support.'

Although agriculture was not fully included in the later 1974 Health and Safety at Work Act, the Union declared, 'the passing into law of the Employment Protection Act saw that responsibility for agricultural safety, health and welfare is now the full responsibility of the Health and Safety Executive.'[4]

*   *   *

By the early seventies there was a steady decline, not only in the number of farm accidents, but also, encouragingly, in the proportion of accidents to the labour force. Statistics do not enable precise comparison, but non-fatal accidents per 1000 among all groups of workers employed dropped from the rate of 25.3 in 1963 to 17.9 in 1970 and 16.4 in 1971. This trend was not evident in the same period for fatal accidents, although there was a definite improvement during 1972. But the Union was worried that in recent years there had been no reduction in the number of children killed.

*   *   *

Concern at the continued dangers from animals was raised at the 1974 Biennial. George Stephenson, of Kilham, was attacked by a bull in the stockyard, and was lying there for almost two hours before being found. He died in hospital. His story was told by Henry Woodmansy, S Yorks, who said that safety regulations in this sphere were practically non-existent. He moved a successful resolution demanding stricter regulations for the handling of bulls. George's widow would not get a penny because no one could prove negligence.

Another resolution welcomed the regulations covering noise levels in tractor safety cabs, but thought the 90dBA limit too high and wanted it substantially reduced.

Margaret Ward, Hunts, said that according to a local NFU official, cab noises were making farm 'hands' neurotic. It was stated that the EC had sought the noise limit to be 88dBA. In the event, 90dBA set conformed to European standards. The EC wanted the motion remitted so that they could negotiate further, but Conference refused and carried the motion.

Despite the greater safety of tractors because of the cabs, they could still kill. The 1974 Biennial wanted all tractors subject to the same tests as applied to other vehicles under the Road Traffic Acts.

As the Health and Safety Executive launched its campaign for greater safeguards in 1977, farmworkers continued to make their own protests heard. Leicestershire County Conference called for the 'full measures outlined in the Health and Safety Act' to be implemented immediately, and the South Lincolnshire Conference demanded that crop-spraying chemicals be properly tested. That year the Union was very much involved with the Forestry Safety Council, which was developing Codes of Practice for chain-saw felling, low-volume spraying, the use of clearing saws, and so on.

It was the following year, at the Brighton TUC, that NUAAW delegates spoke of the Union's problem in getting their own safety representatives recognised by employers. They pointed out that the Union was not recognised under the Health and Safety at Work Act unless it had individual agreements with each and every employer. Congress called on the Government to amend the Act so that farmers were compelled to recognise union safety representatives.

Union Safety Representatives At Last

October 1978 was a red-letter day for those determined to drive death, injury and disease from the workplace. It was then that the first trade union safety representatives were given the power to combat occupational hazards. Since that date the annual toll of death and injury in Britain has declined. Only one major group of employers turned their faces against this trend: the farmers.

Safety representatives are empowered to inspect the workplace for hazards before they cause accidents. They are entitled to information on machinery and dangerous chemicals from employers, manufacturers and safety inspectors. They were a major factor in raising safety issues in other industries, and gradually the number of farm safety representatives increased. Farmers were finding that they had nothing to fear but plenty to gain in higher standards, which might save their own necks as well as the farmworkers.

Safety representatives were operating on a big Leicestershire farm in the early eighties. The Union issued a 'Safety Representative Credential Card' at the CWS farms at Stoughton. Stoughton CWS had an agreed safety policy, '. . . to involve all personnel: management, supervisory, maintenance and production, in working together to prevent injury and to safeguard the health of all employees.'

All its 50 workers were NUAAW members and branch secretary John Tooley was on the seven-man safety committee, as was Mick Wells, the elected Union safety representative. The committee was chaired by farm manager J. Fort, which was important, as such a body is useless without someone to authorise expenditure to make decisions a reality. Their safety policy also had 17 codes of practice, which covered a far-ranging list of dos and don'ts, involving fire, accident reporting, first-aid boxes, poisonous substances, hygiene, training in use of machinery and safety, machine guards, protective clothing, children, and handling stock – 'at no time will bulls be handled by one man alone.'

Central to the whole safety system at Stoughton was the regular safety checks made before each safety committee meeting. For this purpose a safety representative inspection sheet was drawn up that covered 35 different points embracing tractors, trailers, manure spreaders, silage pits, lagoons, electric generators, ladders, buildings, roofs, first-aid boxes, firepoints, and farm signs. Each listed item had a 'pass' or 'fail' column to tick, and space for comments. The reports formed the basis for the quarterly safety committee meetings whose minutes were sent to each committee member, enabling them to confirm – or complain – that agreed steps had been taken – or not taken – to eliminate potential dangers.

Mr. Fort summed up the CWS attitude by saying, 'I think a farm or estate should be a safe place to work on and we are totally committed to such safety.'

A good example that could be followed elsewhere.

*   *   *

A trail-blazing meeting of farmworkers' unions from all over Europe took place in Geneva in 1982, and could have led to a tightening-up of safety standards in Britain. Delegates from 19 agricultural workers' unions ranging from Denmark to Hungary, including the NUAAW's Chris Kaufman, met to discuss the effects of mechanisation and use of chemicals on farms. There was general agreement that new technologies were of benefit in cutting down on heavy work and increasing production, so long as the workers' interests could be safeguarded.

Chris was struck by how far Britain was behind other nations in farm safety. 'Our laws, regulations and enforcement procedures lag a long way behind most of our European counterparts. They had direct union participation to the extent of stopping the job if the work or system or machine is considered a hazard, or the workers haven't had adequate training. The British system of pesticide control law is a national scandal. Only Portugal and Spain are as bad.'

The conference, organised by the ILO, repeated calls at Union conferences for union safety representatives, and agreed on the need for proper training for farmworkers, and safety designed into machines and work methods. It also wanted national and international action for common standards of testing, transporting, storing and using chemicals, and research into alternative technologies.

At the 1982 TUC in Brighton, the Union again participated in a debate on health and safety. Jack Boddy successfully moved a resolution condemning the farmers' use of a legislative loophole to enable them to refuse to recognise safety representatives, and sought the appointment of union safety representatives in agriculture.

There was no let up in the calls for safety at the 1983 Trade Group Conference, and they brought more speakers to the rostrum than any other issue. Fred Gustke, Cambs, successfully moved a resolution demanding that employers should provide and clean spray-operators' overalls, 'as it is not fair or healthy that their wives should come into contact with contaminated clothing.' Hampshire's Maurice Housden again demanded the end of aerial spraying without a single dissenting vote. A successful Staffordshire motion demanded more visits by Safety Inspectors, without prior notice.

*   *   *

Roy Tapping was baling hay on Home Farm, Kenton, near Chinnor, Oxfordshire, in 1983, when his arm was caught in the machinery. Almost the whole of the limb was torn from his body. He was knocked unconscious and suffered four broken ribs. When he came to he saw the severed arm, picked it up in his right hand and walked nearly a mile to the farm and found help. He was rushed to Stoke Mandeville Hospital, where, using the most advanced micro-surgical techniques, it was sewn back onto his shoulder.

It was not certain at the time whether the operation would be a success, but in 1987, he got back part use of his arm; the use of the hand was gravely impaired. To that extent, the remarkable bravery of 37-year-old Mr. Tapping paid off.

And Mr. Topping was lucky in one respect. He could get immediate surgery. The 55-year-old surgeon, Bruce Bailey, who led the team that operated on Mr. Tapping, told the *Landworker* that Government cuts in the NHS were well on the way to ensuring that hospitals could not afford to perform such operations. 'I am having to beg administrators here to be allowed to admit patients needing micro-surgery,' he said. 'We have the techniques, the surgical staff, the enthusiasm and the commitment. We lack the space in operating theatres and wards, the X-ray and other equipment, the ancillary staff.' He said NHS spending was pitifully inadequate – about half what is spent in other European countries – and patients often cannot get even common and straightforward surgery.

Mr. Bailey said that Mr. Tapping's injury might never have happened if there were enough farm inspectors to check dangerous implements. 'It's not even any sort of economy. You could pay for 20 inspectors for what it's going to cost to put Roy Tapping right again.'

Employment Under Secretary John Selwyn Gummer tried to pin the blame for these accidents on the workers. 'There has been some horrific accidents in the past few weeks involving adult workers using hay balers . . . it may be too late to blame the manufacturer after an accident. Too late even to blame the boss.'

No, never blame the boss. Roy Tapping's employer denied negligence and breach of duty, but at Oxford Crown Court in 1987, Roy Tapping won £45,000, an agreed sum settled six days into the hearing. Little enough for his great loss.

'Do It, or Get Out' Ultimatum

One union activist with every reason to be keen on safety and accident prevention is Howard Wright, whom I interviewed in 1988. Howard was one of nine children living in Amesbury, Wiltshire. His father was a stoker, and his mother took in washing from Boscombe RAF Station. Howard left school at 15 and his first job was as an apprentice saddler, Salisbury racecourse not being far away. He later served in the Merchant Navy for four years, then returned to Wiltshire and worked as assistant herdsman on an arable and dairy farm at Orcheston.

Howard joined the NUAAW the same year. 'I just felt that if everyone was in the Union, we could demand a few more things like safety representatives, better wages and so on.'

Wages were important, for that year he married. 'I don't know how Georgina and I lived, it was pretty shocking trying to make the money last the week.' He worked on other farms in Wiltshire, and in 1972 went up to Cheshire because he couldn't get a job as a herdsman – his ambition – until he had greater experience, and thought that Cheshire's higher production rates would add to his knowledge.

By then, he and Georgina had their first son, Jamie, and one night Howard told his boss that he had got to take two year old Jamie to the doctor because he had stomach pains. The boss said, 'No, you can take him after working.' Howard said, 'I'll take him during tea time.' The boss replied, 'We don't stop for tea, we carry on till eight. If you don't work you haven't got a job here and I'll keep your money.'

Howard took the boy to the doctor's and when he went back to work that evening, his boss told him he didn't want him. 'Georgina and I discussed whether I should throw in the job, but I decided to go back because Georgina thought the boss might just be trying to see what I was made of.'

When he returned to work in the morning the boss said, 'You ain't fooking coming on this place any more,' and Howard had to leave. When he went for his wages on the Friday, the boss said, 'I ain't paying you any.'

Little did that boss know he was moulding a strong Union man, with a keen sense of justice, who was later to become a full-time official. At the time, Howard got in touch with a Union man who brought the DHSS into the affair. The DHSS made the farmer pay a week's wages, and the Union got Howard another week. Howard then moved around farms in Cheshire, as he had a bit of a 'reputation', and he ended up on the Wirral with an old-fashioned type of farmer, with old machinery and 150 cows tied up with chains in byres. He was a tractor driver.

One day his new boss told him to maintain a potato harvester on an outlying farm. The only way to do it was to have it ticking over, but there was no power-take-off guard, so Howard returned to the main farm and explained that he wasn't maintaining it because of the absence of the guard.

'You mean to tell me,' said the incredulous farmer, 'you came up here, all that way, to tell me that. Get back to that machine or get down the bloody road.'

Howard went back. It was a windy day, and he was wearing overalls and a floppy hat. The potato harvester had a little hole to squirt oil in, with the PTO beneath it. 'My hat blew off, and I put my hand on the draw bar to pick it up and the next thing I knew I was taken into the machine. In seconds I was stripped, except for my wellies and underpants. My overalls, sweater, tee shirt, vest, trousers were all a little ball wrapped round the PTO shaft.' His right arm was smashed and his back scorchmarked. In hospital for three months – four months of physiotherapy followed – he finished up with a steel pin in his injured arm. The accident occurred at 2pm, and from then, until the day he went back to work, his boss never paid him a penny.

The Union fought his case, and after a 2½-year battle he was finally awarded £2,500. When Howard did return to work after seven months' absence, his boss handed him one week's wages saying, 'I don't want you any more.'

Once more, Howard started looking for another job, realising that safety on most farms was appalling, with employers forcing men to work in dangerous conditions. 'I considered that 85% of farmers in Cheshire were undesirable to work for.' He believed that the best way to improve farm safety was through the trade union movement.

His next job was near Nantwich with a farmer who was 'not a bad employer as they go in Cheshire.' He was second herdsman. He transferred to the mid-Cheshire branch of the NUAAW and his trade union activities took off. He sat on various committees and ended up as district secretary, and then county secretary. What he found as chairman didn't improve his opinion of most Cheshire farmers. 'The employers wanted to own you body and soul, they wanted to run your life, seven days a week, 52 weeks a year. If you wanted a Christmas Day off, it was taboo. You had to put in for it three years in advance; if you had small children it made no difference. They would have you working up to 10 or 10.30 at night, but if there was no work to be done, they wouldn't find it, you just worked your eight hours and that was it; few could manage on eight hours. The whole attitude of farmers was feudal; forelock touching – this, in the seventies.

'If you were arguing about wages or safety, they always threw the tied cottage at you. They used to imply you would lose your home, and they would think nothing of knocking you up to come in at night, and if you were going on holiday, they'd say "come in". You'd protest, and they'd say, "That's tough."

'My wife couldn't drive, and the youngest had to go to hospital and the boss used to moan and groan whenever I took the boy to hospital, although I always made up the time. To be sick on a farm was a crime, you were only sciving.'

Howard was pleased to return to Wiltshire in 1977, doing a herdsman's job at Orcheston. He became branch secretary, was elected to the West Wiltshire District Committee, became its secretary, and was elected to the county committee, of which he later became chairman. Among numerous other positions he held was membership of Wiltshire Farm Safety Committee. After the merger, on Howard's initiative, a liaison committee between the Trade Group and the NFU on farm safety was set up in Wiltshire.

'There was a farm safety committee in Wiltshire in existence,' explained Howard, 'and on it was the WI, Fire Brigade, Young Farmers, Electricity Board, CLA, and it dealt with everything but farm safety; it might touch on it now and again, but they only met once a year.'

The new liaison committee was set up so that the Trade Group could talk to the NFU across the table to see if they would implement what the workers wanted for safety, and they could do likewise with the workers. 'It does work, and it's done many useful things,' said Howard.

Among Howard's other activities was being secretary of Amesbury Labour Party, and as a member of CND he went on peace marches. But the Union took up most of his time, and he represented Wiltshire at the last Biennial of the NUAAW at Skegness, where Wiltshire fought the merger. 'I opposed,' he said, 'but once the vote was taken in favour we decided to do everything we could to make it a success.' He found divisional committees in the TGWU rulebook and suggested that the new Trade Group should have them. One was formed in Wiltshire when it was decided to scrap district and county committees. 'We have just one divisional committee for Wiltshire, and that's the pattern that has been followed throughout the country, with two delegates everywhere.' Edgar Pill was elected first divisional secretary, with Howard divisional chairman. 'The South West,' said Howard, 'led the way in setting up Regional Trade Group committees,' and Howard was elected to that. From the SW Regional Trade Group Committee, Howard and Peter Woodland were elected to the National Trade Group Committee. Howard was later elected chairman. Three years after this history ends, Howard was made Regional Trade Group Secretary.

Danger of Brucellosis

Following many years of Union representations, it was in 1971 that the Industrial Injuries Advisory Council considered evidence submitted to it in order to advise the Government whether or not brucellosis should be scheduled as a prescribed industrial disease.

For a long time the Union had been concerned over the risk to people, especially herdsmen, of contracting brucellosis, and wanted the disease notifiable as one of the measures necessary to secure its complete eradication. It was in 1965 that the Union first raised the matter with the Government, which took the view that 'prescription' was not necessary as the 'accident provisions of the Act were adequate to cover the disease.' MAFF decided that 'notification' in animals was impractical as the disease often showed no overt symptoms.

Brucellosis was known to cause animals to yield 20% less milk, and a report published in 1967–8 estimated that 59,300 cows had aborted and in addition 49,000 had given birth to fully-formed dead calves. There was very little risk to the public from the disease, as pasteurisation and heat treatment of milk eliminated the risk of infection. The main risk was to farmworkers and those in direct contact with the animals.

In 1967 the Government introduced a voluntary Accredited Herds Scheme. All sides of the industry thought this scheme totally inadequate, and the Government later announced the Brucellosis Incentive Scheme, under which owners of registered brucella-free herds would qualify for incentive payments in the form of a premium: 1¼d per gallon of milk and 36s 6d per head on beef. In 1970 it was made an offence for any person to sell, except for slaughter, animals known to be infected.

It seemed that, at long last, measures were being taken to recognise the disease for what it is, although the Union considered that the only effective way to eradicate it was by a slaughter-and-compensation policy.

In the 1970's, the wife of a stockman at Shipston on Stour went down with brucellosis – she had only washed his overalls and had no contact with the animals. A stiffness crept over her body, she couldn't sleep, and her arms became so weak she couldn't brush her hair. She became breathless, and at times couldn't move from her chair. Yet she was not entitled to a penny compensation.

*   *   *

In the 1970s, a MAFF field officer called at the farm in North Devon to see a farmer about a guarantee payment. He saw a worker using a manure spreader with an unguarded power-take-off shaft. When he pointed out this infringement of the safety regulations, the worker told him, understandably, that he must see the boss. The boss blew his top, insulted the officer, and told a lorry driver unloading poultry feed to go to lunch so that the officer's exit was blocked, but the driver drove off instead. The farmer then drove his own van into the yard to prevent the officer leaving.

A court case followed, and the farmer said that he was worried in case his poultry got fowl pest. The officer had disinfected his boots. Defending solicitor asked the farmer, 'Would it be a catastrophe if you had fowl pest on your farm?' The farmer replied, 'It would.' No one, apparently, thought it would be a catastrophe if the worker got tangled up in the power shaft. The farmer was fined £15 with £5 costs.

Albert Warren, DO, said, 'This is an example of some employers' attitudes towards safety regulations. I wonder if the farmer would have raised any objection had the officer only dealt with the question of guarantee payments?'

*   *   *

Sixty-eight-year-old Albert Warren, lived in retirement in Iddesleigh, Devon, where he was born, in a house overlooking the fields he worked in as a boy. But he was no 'never been any further than the next village' man. He left the village school at 14, and went on a farm as a dogsbody, earning 13s 4d for a 56-hour week. At 15, his wage went up to 14s 10d. Always a bit of a rebel, he wanted to join the Union, but there was no branch in Iddesleigh, so in 1944, he joined one in Dolton, a neighbouring village. In 1956, a branch was formed in Iddesleigh and Albert was 'press ganged' into the secretaryship by Charlie Leathwood, the new DO.

Sitting in his front parlour, Albert recalled those early days when I interviewed him in 1988. 'I didn't mind being pushed into the secretaryship, everyone liked old Charlie. Although the NUAAW was in evidence in North Devon in the early 1900s, it was not until 1956 when Charlie came into the area that it "took off". It was during the next five years under his leadership, and that of Cliff Hardy, that a sizeable membership was built up, probably reaching its peak in 1960–65.'

They had 25 members in Iddesleigh then, and 101 members in 1988 but that included members within a 20-mile radius. Albert recalled that in those early days in the Union, Charlie and Cliff had the assistance of a number of keen and dedicated members in the shape of George Neish, Les Prance, Norman Prouse, Stewart Ridgman, Reg Northey and many others. Albert soon found himself on the district committee, and then the county committee, of which he became secretary.

In April 1963, he was given the new post of Recruiting Officer for Devon. 'I never did any,' said Albert smiling, 'because Roland Hammersley, DO, was

17. Union officials always recognised the importance of social get-togethers, like this branch dinner at Stone-in-Oxney, Kent, in the mid-1960s.

18. A sheep market in 1954. Livestock sales are important events in the agricultural calendar. Farmworkers are kept busy getting animals to and from sales, but the work provides a break from the usual farm routine.

19. At Lodford, Lincolnshire, a distraught family goes through the trauma of eviction from a tied cottage.

20. Jim Watts, head of the Legal Department, gives a lending hand to a farmworker's wife during the family's eviction from a tied cottage in 1972. Other NUAAW members join in the general protest.

21. The Union was always keen on vocational training for farmworkers, and did much to initiate educational courses. In 1953, the first farm apprentice, under a new three-year scheme, was Graham Stride of Bath, seen here driving in fencing on a farm at Chilmark, Salisbury.

22. The Union had many roadmen as members before the coming of machines like the one above, which is spraying verges to destroy weeds at Southam, near Cheltenham, Gloucestershire, in 1951. Their use, together with mechanical hedge slashers, greatly reduced the need for roadmen.

23. Part of the 1950 intake of the Women's Land Army get their first practical lesson: hitching and unhitching, without losing a finger. Large numbers of WLA girls joined the Union.

24. Labour gangs, consisting mainly of women, undertake many arduous tasks on farms. These women, in 1948, break for a much needed snack, which often have to be taken in open fields.

sick and I did his job till he left in 1964, and I was then officially appointed DO for Devon.' Reflecting on the idea of recruiting officers, Albert said, 'I don't think it was much good, because you had one fellow going round the whole county as RO and another servicing members, following in each other's footsteps. It would have been much better for them both to recruit and do the work of DOs.'

Albert was DO from 1964 until the time of the merger; he took early retirement in September 1982. Like most DOs, Albert was much involved in tied cottage cases. Although he managed to avoid any formal evictions, members used to be in and out of some of the cottages like yoyos. One case stuck in his mind. A member had been to Court and had not found any alternative accommodation in the time given by the Judge. He and his wife went out house and job hunting and on returning found the farmer had forced the door of his cottage, changed the lock, and nailed up the back door and windows. They slept that night in a woodshed.

'The same farmer then engaged a new man, whom I managed to recruit into the Union. This man had a heart attack and was admitted to hospital. The farmer went to the hospital and told him he had to get out at the end of the week. The poor chap, who had a wife and family, collapsed and died soon afterwards. His wife disappeared, apparently to relatives, and there was not much else I could do but enrol the next man coaxed into taking the job by the soft-talking farmer. He did not stay long, and was the subject of another court case. I signed up about half a dozen of his new employees, for no one ever stayed long. They were damned glad I had got them to join, for we gave them some protection each time they went to Court.'

As in most parts of the country, Albert found Devonshire farmers, and their wives, to be full of wile. When the last man engaged by this farmer was sacked, his boss, who now had chronic diabetes and could not work, applied for possession, and Albert represented his ex-employee at an ADHAC hearing. 'The farmer's wife came and cried her heart out, saying that she had to do all the work, but it was known that there was a moonlighter working there. Our member was given a council house, and for several years that cottage remained empty.'

Speaking of the Rent (Agriculture) Act, Albert said that before it, local councils were not very fast in providing alternative accommodation, but there had been a dramatic change since it became law. 'They now seem able to find something quite quickly. However, with the recent sale of council houses, the situation has changed again; there's few houses available for sacked farmworkers. So the farmworkers are still in the grip of farmers as long as they are in tied cottages. Tied cottages still need to be abolished. Let them pay proper wages, and then their workers could pay proper rents.'

Devon was not a very militant, Union-minded county and Albert found that the sense of protection the Union gave brought a lot of people into the Union. 'The bosses were so bloody minded, good industrial relations did not exist.' And sometimes, this bloody mindedness was found where it was least expected. He recalled that Roland Hammersley went recruiting on a CWS farm in South Devon and the manager threw a bucket of water over him. But he still recruited there. However, some CWS farms in the West Country had a good relationship with the Union. The management expected their employees to join; the farms were like closed shops. It helped considerably where safety was concerned. They also organised the farm staff at Dartmoor and Exeter prisons.

'There used to be a lot of unpaid overtime on farms at weekends; we stopped most of it, but there's still some today. One chap I know milks cows on Saturdays and weekends, and never gets paid for it.' Albert explained that he milked in the morning up to 10.30, then worked on the farm's sawmill, and milked again at night after leaving work. 'As he comes under an agreement for sawmill workers, it's been impossible to get him paid for his milking. He couldn't claim it as overtime, because he hasn't done eight hours in agriculture.'

Harvest Lung Investigated

A large-scale investigation into dust hazards amongst agricultural workers in Lincolnshire began in the early seventies. It started when Dr. Roe, of East Barkwith, asked Alec Russell, South Lindsey DO, if he would co-operate in an investigation which needed the active support of men working in dust. Dr. Roe, a GP in the heart of cereal-growing Lincolnshire, realised in 1969 that a number of his patients were suffering from out of the ordinary chest complaints. He contacted the chest unit at Sheffield Royal Infirmary and found the specialists there shared his concern. A team of experts, under the leadership of consultant chest physician Dr. C. S. Darke, got working on the problem, including a specialist on disease spores at Rothampstead Research Station. The Union gave full support to the team, and Alec acted as their linkman. One of their surveys revealed that dust from grain is the source of an illness affecting some 15–20% of workers who operate combine harvesters, grain dryers and others who clean out storage bins. In some cases, the symptoms are so acute that it would be dangerous for workers to continue to work in such dust-hazard situations.

From the result of all tests it began to be suspected that the illness, with its symptoms of coughing, wheezing, tightness round the chest and headaches, is not caused by small shattered particles of plant material, but by spores from fungus diseases that attack the ear of the grain. The spores lodge on the bronchial tubes, causing acute irritation.

It is thought that this disease, aptly labelled 'harvest lung' has caused the loss of thousands of working days during harvest time. Dr. Darke considered that very little could be done to prevent the illness, but called for the greater use of good face masks and better ventilation in grain stores.

At the 1974 TUC, an NUAAW motion on dust hazards was composited with a related measure from the NUM which called for all chest diseases, e.g. emphysema and bronchitis, be scheduled as industrial diseases.

Seconding, Wilf Page said, 'The protection afforded to the agricultural worker does not begin to compare to that given to his colleagues on the factory floor, despite the fact that the combine harvester is virtually a mobile factory . . . and . . . the storage of grain gave rise to an obvious dust hazard. Yet there is no mandatory requirement for the fitting of dust-extraction plant, or the provision of adequate masks.'

At this point, Wilf displayed a dust mask which, according to the makers, the workers would 'enjoy wearing'. In fact it was an added hazard. It did not provide adequate protection, and only gave the wearer a false sense of security. Wilf got Congress's unqualified support for the measure.

In 1984, the annual report of the Agricultural Health and Safety Executive showed 63 fatalities. The trend had been downwards since 1979. A big advance was a drop in child deaths; adult deaths were actually up for 1983.

George Neish, DO at Stafford, where a 28-year-old farmworker had recently lost an arm, said, 'We fear for the future; our fears are based on cutbacks in the Health and Safety Executive. In 1979 the total number of inspectors in agriculture was 198. Today it is down to 154 inspectors. Actually, in the field, there are now only 108 inspectors. Less than a year earlier, the retiring Chief Inspector, Jim Whittaker, had said that the then figure of 120 in the field was "inadequate". If that number was inadequate,' declared George, 'what should it be called now?'

Statutory Sick Pay

One aspect of health and safety on farms that greatly concerned the Union was the denial of any statutory sick pay, long after it had been paid to other workers. All agricultural workers were entitled to was the basic National Insurance sickness benefit, and they had been denied that for many years.

The Union began talks seeking 'Wages during Sickness' in 1947. And when the Agricultural Wages Bill 1947 became law, it was thought that the AWB would have power to establish a sick-pay scheme. The AWB began discussions to frame such a scheme, but as a result of a High Court action over a farmworker's sick pay claim, the Board was told by its legal advisers that it had no power to order sick pay. A Union deputation met the Minister of Agriculture to urge that as the power was unintentionally withheld from the AWB, the Act should be amended forthwith. Tom Williams refused.

There was a spate of resolutions demanding sick pay at various NUAAW conferences over the years – at the 1960 Biennial there were no fewer than 30. The passing of the Agricultural Act 1967 enabled the AWB to order a wages-during-sickness scheme, and negotiations began.

When in 1974 an AWB Statutory Sick-Pay Scheme was finally proposed, appointed members would not push the issue and the matter was dropped.

However, an historic victory for the Union came in 1975, when it negotiated a legally enforceable sick-pay scheme – after 30 years' battle. It came into effect on 21 July 1975, and was won at a meeting of the AWB on 24 March when the combined vote of the workers' side and the independents, with farmers opposing, carried a proposal that a scheme be introduced to provide for up to 13 weeks' wages during sickness in any one year. It provided for full-time workers, with 52 weeks or more continuous employment on the same farm or with the same employer, to receive payment for up to 65 days in any calendar year, or in a period of six months commencing 1 October in any year.

Hailed by Reg Bottini as a Union breakthrough, he wrote that the decision meant that alone, among industries whose minimum rates were fixed by statutory wages boards or councils, agriculture would have a legally-enforceable sick-pay scheme. 'We must be proud, as a Union, that our continued efforts over the years have been crowned with success, giving a lead to other Unions involved in statutory wages boards and councils.'[5]

Education, and Safety First

Many leaders of the old Union started off by working in the fields at a very early age – by six or seven they would be crow scaring or picking stones – and came to no apparent immediate harm. What it did to their scant education, and the long-term effect it had on their health, is difficult to quantify: the fields were no place for small children then, and are certainly not today. It is not unreasonable in the 1980s to say, as the Union does, that no child under 16 should work in agriculture.

This is one aspect of health and safety not faced by modern factory workers at their work places; the employment of large numbers of children on farms, or living on them. For the latter, the farms become their playgrounds, something completely foreign to the factory floor. Agriculture is one of the few industries in Britain where children of school age are officially allowed to work, and young and inexperienced teenagers encouraged to operate dangerous machinery; it is not therefore surprising that there is a high accident rate amongst them, sometimes fatal.

In many parts of rural Britain, where farmers' influence was great, education committees had for decades gone out of their way to enable older children to do part-time land work, and holidays were sometimes fitted in with harvest times. In the Fens, the late Autumn break was known as the 'potato-picking holidays'.

In 1949, Edwin Gooch asked the Minister of Education, George Tomlinson, if he was aware of the growing opposition of education authorities to the employment of schoolchildren in gathering the country's crops, and would he guarantee that this was the last year the practice would continue. Tomlinson said he was sending a circular to the authorities that 'it would be necessary to ask for the help of older schoolchildren' to gather the crops, and could not guarantee it would be the last year, although he was anxious to end the practice.

The *Farmer and Stockbreeder* asserted that the children 'enjoy thoroughly' such work, and gave them an insight into farming that must be invaluable in after years. The *Landworker* tersely commented, 'Picking potatoes on a cold, damp October morning is not our idea of recreation for children, nor theirs . . . as for giving them an insight into farming we know of no work more calculated to give them a distaste for farming.'

Edwin and other Union representatives met colleagues of the NUT to discuss possible steps to stop children working on farms when they should be at school, and were favourably received. But there were some strange attitudes. In a letter to the *News Chronicle*, Olive Gordon, a teacher, claimed that the delinquent child 'is far below the average intelligence and . . . when enough reading, writing and arithmetic have been inculcated for him to be able to adjust himself to life, he should, as early as ten years of age, be sent to help on a farm . . . not remain at school to be an annoyance and a bad example to normal children.' Many Union members thought a better sense of values should be 'inculcated' into some teachers.

The May 1951 issue of Labour's *Rural Bulletin* stated that safeguarding the nation's food supplies 'must take precedence over education so long as the existing conditions continue.' This was the 'firm conclusion' of the Secretary of State for Scotland after considering all the evidence. This seemed suspiciously like the Victorian arguments used when children were sacrificed in the mines and factories a century earlier. The Union, declared the *Landworker*, 'did not expect to hear it from a member of the Party which has always prided itself upon its high sense of responsibility in regard to education, the primary condition of the good life among the people.'

'A complete and absolute ramp' was the description applied to the employment of schoolchildren in the potato-picking harvest by a delegate at the National Association of Head Teachers' Conference at Leamington in 1950. The 400 delegates cheered when a headmaster exclaimed, 'to the multifarious people who are using the schools for their own ends our message is "Hands off, get out".' Following a newspaper story, 'Only Children Could Save Us', he successfully moved a resolution seeking the end of school attendance exemption for potato harvesting. He said he knew what happened to people who offended farmers, 'but they can't sack us'.

Again in 1953, the NUAW and the NUT protested to the Ministers of Agriculture and Education against the use of schoolchildren to harvest potatoes during term time. F. A. Speechley, a Grantham (Lincs) headmaster said, 'the children are in no mood for arithmetic and English when they return to school. Last year only 40 out of 230 children of 14 and 15 turned up for lessons during harvest weeks.'

Farmers in County Durham were likened to slave drivers by a Tynemouth High School sixth former who, in the school magazine described his experiences at a harvest camp:

> I don't know whether or not farmers are the same everywhere, but to many of us, those of County Durham seemed like slave drivers. The more prosperous, the more wealthy the farmer, the harder we were expected to work and the less

generous he was in return. The only thing to which we town dwellers could look forward to in a long day was the tea break . . . Eventide found us dirty, exhausted and with only sufficient strength to crawl into the waiting lorry . . .

The Defence Regulations allowing schoolchildren to work on farms during term time were allowed to lapse in 1953. This move was welcomed by the Union. But at the Conference of Labour Women at Eastbourne in 1954, when two Union delegates, Joan Maynard and Mrs. G. Cull (Terrington, Norfolk), submitted a motion demanding that the labour of schoolchildren be completely prohibited, it met with some opposition. One delegate argued that a smallholding needed children to work them. The motion met with reserved acceptance from the platform and was referred to the EC for further consideration.

Although the Defence Regulations had lapsed, no comprehensive legislation was introduced to cover the employment of children on farms, and the danger to children was far from over. At the TUC at Southport in 1955, Union delegates questioned the employment of young persons. W. Martin, EC, said that although the employment of children between 13 and 15 was covered by general legislation in other industries, none of it applied to farms. Statistics showed that 10% of fatal accidents on farms involved children under 15. A motion to stop schools altering holidays to coincide with farming operations was passed.

Fatal accidents occurred that year with vehicles driven by boys. Three men were talking by a Wiltshire farm gateway when a tractor did not turn sharply enough to negotiate the gateway. One was knocked into a ditch and the tractor ran over him. He was Alfred Gebel, of Holt branch. The driver was 12. The farmer said he had not 'allowed' the boy to drive along the route where the accident occurred. At the inquest the coroner said, 'Whenever harvest times come, I have these cases, and this is the third I have had this harvest where boys are driving.' In South Lincolnshire, a lad of 15 employed on a farm since April was given a dumper to drive, something which, naturally, gave him quite a thrill. he was garaging it when he over-ran some bricks used as 'stops' in the shed, his head hit the roof and he was killed.

There were 151 fatal accidents on farms in 1959, and 23 of the victims were under 15. This shameful blot on the industry was revealed in MAFF figures. It is difficult to think of any other industry where 23 schoolchildren could meet their deaths in one year. These figures referred only to fatal accidents. There are no sources giving the number of non-fatal farm accidents involving children.

In 1961, a Bill came up in the House of Commons to reduce the age at which a person could drive a tractor on the roads, from 17 to 16. The Union was opposed to 16-year-olds being allowed to do this, both in their own interests and in the interests of general road safety. Unfortunately, an amendment to the Bill to prevent lowering the age limit was lost.

And Union branches were ever watchful for anything that might harm the education children were getting. Baldock (Herts) District Committee, in November 1960, reported that a number of members' children were being kept in after school and as a result had to walk home. It could be dangerous. They contacted the 'appropriate authority' and the matter was 'rectified'.

When it was noted in the press that Holland County Education Committee proposed closing schools during the potato harvest, the Union's Spalding District Committee held an emergency meeting and passed a resolution of protest. This was issued to the press and got considerable publicity. It played a strong part in the deliberations of the Education Committee, which voted against closing by 195. One member declared, 'We are an education committee, not a farmers' employment bureau.'

John Hebblewhite, Tongue End, Lincs, appeared before the Queen in 1961 when he was awarded the Cornwall Badge known as the 'Scouts VC' for bravery during a long period of hospital treatment. His accident occurred in 1955 when he was only 12, and not, of course a Union member. His father had been in the Union since 1916. John was grievously burned when a tractor caught fire, causing an explosion that drenched him with flaming petrol. He had to undergo skin grafting and the Union obtained for him a settlement of £16,342.

A number of children are killed on farms where they live, or while their mothers are doing farm work. A boy and a girl, aged four and three, played while their mother picked potatoes. They were later found drowned in a pond used for dumping unwanted potatoes. The potatoes covered the surface to such an extent that anyone not knowing could not tell there was water below.

It was difficult to cope with children living on farms, or childish pranks, said the *Landworker*, 'but there are no doubt ways which in retrospect some of these accidents might have been prevented. If enough fuss is kicked up, local authorities may be induced to provide day nurseries for the care of children whose mothers go to work.' There were few day nurseries in rural areas at the time, but in the 1980s, Region 1 of the Trade Group secured creches on some farms where there were mothers working.

In 1974, J. C. Weeks, MAFF Chief Safety Inspector, reported that out of 91 fatal accidents on farms in 1973 in England and Wales, 25 were children under 16. For the previous ten years the total was over 200. This was an increase in accidents to children, all the more tragic when compared with a reduction in fatal accidents to adults.

There has been a fall in fatal accidents to children on farms in recent years:

Fatal accidents to children under 16

'70	'71	'72	'73	'74	'75	'76	'77	'78	'79	'80	'81	'82	'83	'84
34	30	20	28	30	23	21	25	16	24	10	13	13	5	4

That four in 1984 was four too many, and it rose to ten in 1985, and was eight for both 1986 and 1987.

Region 3 has been responsible for initiating a number of developments in the Trade Group. One was opposition to the training of 13-year-olds in tractor driving. Howard Wright, Regional Secretary, is on the Agricultural Advisory Committee and sub-Committee of the HSE. It published a code of practice for children on farms with which the Trade Group agreed, with the proviso that the age at which children would be allowed to drive tractors should be raised from 13 to 16. Subsequently, the NFU took the document and built it into the Approved Code of Practice training for 13-year-olds. They had ignored the proviso and tried to sneak it through, but the Trade Group got it stopped.

The Trade Group, and its parent body, the TGWU, in the eighties continued to vigorously campaign against children working on farms, and issued a leaflet addressed to children answering questions like: 'What's wrong with driving a tractor? I'm big enough.' 'Many young persons might have said the same,' said the leaflet, 'but a lot of them are dead or crippled.'

At Stoneleigh National Agricultural Centre in May 1988, TGWU health and safety specialist Peter Hurst called for a change in the law on children operating farm machinery. 'In the last ten years, 111 children have died in farm accidents. Agriculture is truly the children's killing fields,' he declared. 'The Health and Safety Executive must push for a change in the law to raise the minimum age for children working in agriculture to 16 years in order to bring it into line with the rest of British industry . . . children are open to abuse and exploitation as cheap labour. Society has a duty to protect them and keep them safe. It is time for the law to be changed so that it does this.'

REFERENCES

1. Annual Report, 1955.
2. Annual Report, 1957.
3. *Landworker*, February 1962.
4. Annual Report, 1975.
5. *Landworker*, April 1975.

18

Doomsday Countryside

A land flowing with milk and honey
Old Testament

Very Profitable Farm Poisons

Except during the Second World War, the agricultural policy of British
Governments has never seriously taken into account the relationship between
ill health and poor diet. Yet not only is the national diet increasingly unbal-
anced, much of the food we eat is in contact with poisons used on the farm.
And very profitable poison it has been for the big chemical companies, who
have been acting like drug pedlars with full Government support. We will
now go more fully into some of the problems caused by farm chemicals,
already touched upon in the previous chapter.

Almost 100% of our cereals and vegetables are sprayed with at least one
pesticide between sowing and harvesting, and some wheats receive ten or
more different pesticides before harvesting.

There are no Government regulations to control and limit pesticide
residue in food, but spot checks have found harmful chemicals in produce on
sale in the shops, ranging from mushrooms to blackcurrents and lettuce.
DDT* is one dangerous chemical that finds its way into our stomachs through
the produce we buy. The EEC fixed mandatory limits for some pesticide
residues, but the UK insisted that they should not be imposed here until 1991.

Farm chemicals not only threaten the safety of the food we eat, but are
having an enormous effect on the environment. They have destroyed much
wildlife, birds, mammals and countless insects, many of which were beneficial
to man. Coupled with mechanisation, chemicals have led to prairie-like
landscapes, which are alien to the English countryside.

In 1963, Rachel Carson's *Silent Spring* burst upon the world. In it she
indicted new pesticides for the effect they were having on wildlife. Her whole

---

* 'Dichlorodiphenyltrichloroethane' – a colourless, odourless substance used as an
insecticide.

thesis was attacked as unscientific, and unproven. And that the new pesticides were apparently affecting human life, again unproven. Years later, Rachel Carson's dangers were recognised as real, but the effects on humans had still to be taken into account by some governments, who allowed the profits of the petrochemical industry to take precedence over public welfare.

The public is apt to cheerfully assume that, if a substance does not kill you off pretty promptly, it is harmless. But there is the strong possibility of long-delayed actions, genetic damage and the slow build-up of poisons in the tissues.

Of course, there are genuine doubts in the medical profession; there is no proof that any of the new chemicals are harming humans. The metabolic reaction to the same chemical differs. A chemical that makes one person seriously ill, might have no affect whatever on someone else. As cigarette manufacturers so often remind the public, an association does not prove cause and effect, but when in 1890 an asbestos-weaving mill was built in Normandy, 50 employees died during its first five years of operation. The connection between asbestos and lung disease was observed in Britain in the 1920s, but not until 1931 was asbestosis recognised as an industrial disease, and not until the sixties admitted to cause cancer.

So while the public is kept in the dark on farm chemicals, the effect on people who use them, the farmworkers, has at times been horrific, sometimes fatal. Yet up to the time of writing, the Government refuses to take any effective measures to end the menace.

MAFF has never ceased to behave like a very docile lap-dog of the NFU – even in the late eighties at the time of the salmonella outbreak – except for the usual window-dressing.*

The new pesticide legislation designed to protect consumers and farm-workers is an 'empty gesture' because the Government refused to appoint scientists and inspectors to enforce it, declared the Institution of Professional Civil Servants (IPCS) in 1987. The Food and Environment Protection Act 1986 had laid down for the first time legal requirements for the use of pesticides. Previously, the toxic chemicals were only governed by a 'gentle-men's agreement' between the pesticide manufacturers and MAFF, wrote James Erlichman, Consumer Affairs Correspondent of the *Guardian*:[1]

> In theory, the Government has ordered a safety review on all of the 3,000 pesticides products now in use in the UK. But the IPCS, which represents all the scientists and inspectors in government, says it will take 50 years for Ministry scientists, at present staffing levels, to evaluate the risks.§

---

* 'The Minister of Agriculture had like so many of his predecessors – Labour men like Fred Peart as well as Conservative – become a virtual prisoner of NFU interests.' Teddy Taylor, Tory MP, Southend East, *Daily Mail*, 20 December 1988.

§ This at a time when the Government is cutting down on all Civil Service staff.

The IPCS believed that under the new law, the average farm would only be visited once every 29 years because of the small number of HSE inspectors. The HSE admitted that it had only 144 inspectors in the field, but claimed that the average farm could expect a visit within 15 years. The IPCS called upon the Government to give the HSE the £3 million it had requested to hire more inspectors to enforce the Act, and to hire more scientists to test the safety of approved pesticides.

That call echoed many the NUAAW had made in the post-war years to control and evaluate the use of chemicals, their effect on farmworkers, the consumer and the environment. Calls that were evaded, or if any action was taken, fudged with the connivance of MAFF and the NFU.

Way back on 11 May 1950, General Sir George Jeffreys asked the Minister of Agriculture in the House of Commons whether, if before new insecticides based on the organic phosphorous compound, parathion,* are used on a large scale in Britain, he proposed to take steps to avoid danger, both to users and consumers. Tom Williams replied that the manufacturers provided instructions on precautions to be taken and there should be no dangers to users or consumers. Sir George asked if the Minister was aware that a number of deaths in America had been attributed to this insecticide, and Williams said that they had given all the publicity they possibly could to the dangers.

After, Edwin Gooch asked whether in view of the fact that there had been several deaths in Britain of people using these new insecticides, the Minister would consult with the Home Secretary with a view to completely banning their use. Williams said the situation was being closely watched by the Agricultural Research Council, who were in close touch with the Medical Research Council at the Ministry's Pathological Laboratory. The protective procedure established and the conditions laid down were believed to be effectively and generally observed. Pointed questions and blunted replies, the typical response of Governments reluctant to take effective safety measures.

Weedkiller That Killed Humans

At that year's Conference of trade unions catering for women workers, Mrs. Winifred Chamberlain, Kent, and Miss Eileen Hymes, Chester, NUAW, called for the implementation, without delay, of the recommendations made by the Committee on Health, Welfare and Safety, for sanitary accommodation and safety precautions on farms. Men using weedkillers and insecticides went home blistered, and if without masks and goggles, were really ill. They received the unanimous backing of the Conference.

The deaths on 6 June 1950 of two young men after spraying fields in Yorkshire with DNOC weedkiller underlined the urgency of the Union's

---

* 'Diethylparanitrophenylthio-phosphate.'

campaign. They had sprayed weeds over 40 acres and collapsed after leaving the field. One died on the roadside near the farm, the other in hospital. At the inquest, evidence was given that there was no drug known to provide an effective remedy to DNOC poisoning. Dr. Donald Payne, pathologist, said that there had been five deaths among spraying operatives and one in industry. All the symptoms had been dramatic in onset. A man could be sweaty and thirsty, and dead in two or three hours. Replying to Mr. O. H. Parsons, solicitor for the Union, Dr. Payne agreed that the best thing to do would be to encase operators in rubber. It was said that the men did not appear to realise the danger of the stuff, and had not worn protective clothing supplied, probably because the weather was hot. Verdict: death from DNOC poisoning.

A general discussion on the safety of operators was held on 26 June 1950 between representatives of the Union, the TUC and MAFF officials. This was followed on 11 July by a conference of Union representatives, farmers, manufacturers and contractors which further discussed the adequacy of the usual precautionary measure. This meeting was called largely on the initiative of the Union, which all along took the lead in directing attention to the dangers of DNOC. Edwin Gooch was chief spokesman for the workers, supported by George Hook.

MAFF later set up a small working party to make recommendations for promoting the safety of operatives using toxic substances, and to advise on the related recommendations of the Gowers Committee. Arthur Holness, *Landworker* editor, was appointed to the working party, and the Union and the TUC again demanded that DNOC be banned until adequate statutory precautions were adopted.

At the 1950 TUC Congress at Brighton, the Union had a motion on the agenda on poisonous washes. In view of the 'totally inadequate attempts to deal with the growing menace of poisonous weedkillers and insecticides' it called for the prohibition of DNOC and parathion. It was referred to the General Council.

Another warning on the dangers of DNOC and parathion came in 1950 from Dr. Donald Hunter, physician to the London Hospital, who said they were deadly in their effect on man, and urged strict precautions to prevent harm to handlers.

In reporting a lecture by Dr. Hunter, the *British Medical Journal* said that at least five deaths had occurred in Britain – four of them when men were spraying cereal crops. Deaths and cases of severe intoxication in industry and agriculture had been reported from Europe, USA, India and Africa. 'Fatal cases in industry have occurred, invariably during the hot weather.' Dr. Hunter wanted medical examinations of all DNOC workers at weekly intervals and 'men showing early toxic symptoms, namely, excessive thirst, sweating and loss of weight, should be suspended from work, since there is no way of telling in which individuals severe intoxication and even death may result.'

Referring to Dr. Hunter's warnings, the *Landworker* pointed out that DNOC had been in use since 1892 and is now used on a large scale. Fatalities had followed its use in both medical and agricultural practice. In 1933, DNOC had been used to treat obesity and over-dosage caused three deaths. A leaflet had been issued by MAFF warning that DNOC was poisonous if taken internally in any quantity, that food contaminated with DNOC should never be eaten, and food should not be handled by an operator without washing.

Substantial Damages Secured

The Union secured substantial damages for the widow of a member who died from DNOC poisoning in 1947. Legal restrictions on the purchase of DNOC were made in the 1930s, but exceptions were made for farmers and horticulturalists. The Gower recommendations on protective clothing would have helped to prevent these fatalities, but like those of many other committees, had apparently been shelved.

In 1951, the Report of the working party chaired by Professor S. Zukerman, to review the use of toxic chemicals in agriculture, was published. It made a number of recommendations, some of which would involve legislation. While they were receiving the Minister's consideration, action had already been put in hand by voluntary agreement of safety measures for the current spraying season.

It was not until 1953 that some of the hoped-for measures were set out in the Agriculture (Poisonous Substances) Regulations. Those specifically mentioned were DNOC, dinoseb, parathion, schradan, dimefox, mipafox, TEPP (or HEPT). These could not be used unless certain precautions were observed. It laid down that workers must be thoroughly trained and supervised; those under 18 were prohibited from using them. No more than ten hours could be worked in any one day (or more than 60 hours in seven consecutive days), nor more than 120 in 21 consecutive days. Protective clothing had to be used and warning notices put up on gates to sprayed fields.

In 1955, acute parathion poisoning was diagnosed in an employee of spraying contractors. He wore protective clothing, but his rubber gloves were heavily contaminated with parathion inside. And in Jersey, a 61-year-old farmer was killed by absorbing arsenic through the nose, mouth and skin from a potato spray known as 'Hawmac'. He smoked his pipe whilst spraying, and wore no protective clothing.

Secrecy Hampers Action

One of the problems with the use of farm chemicals in Britain is the secrecy[*] that surrounds them, and did much to hamper Union action. In the USA, where the Freedom of Information Act operates, the perils are at least out in

---

[*] 'Some 400 pesticides are used in the UK. Summaries of the makers' safety studies have been made public for only 13, the Campaign for Freedom of Information disclosed.' *Guardian*, 13 July 1989.

the open. According to the *New York Times*,[2] pesticides contaminate ground-water, rivers and estuaries throughout the USA. In a National Cancer Institute study, farmers in Kansas were found six times more likely to contract lymphatic cancer if exposed to herbicides more than 20 days a year. Three-fifths of the 480 million pounds of herbicides used annually in the USA are agents known or suspected to cause cancer. Some 90% of all fungicides are carcinogenic. Despite increasing expenditure on pesticides, $6.5 billion a year in 1988, insects, diseases and weeds destroy a third of America's crops. That is the same proportion as in the 1940s – and indeed the same as in Europe in the Middle Ages. The same could be happening in Britain, but such facts are not so easy to come by here.

The 1970 Biennial highlighted the dangers of aerial spraying near houses, and requested that it be made compulsory to put up notices warning the public that berries and plants might be contaminated. Yorkshire delegate, W. Linwood, told of an aeroplane which had not turned off the spray in time, and garden crops were wiped out. Colin Hands, DO, successfully claimed compensation.

At the 1972 Biennial, there was yet another resolution on aerial spraying which received unanimous support. Moving it, Gordon Dales, Lincs, did not argue the pros and cons of its economic value, but strongly asserted it was no good to human beings. He said, 'I had some trees in my garden which were smothered in blossom but there was not a bee or an insect of any description to pollinate them. We have got to do it ourselves. I have only seen a couple of hares this year. Soon there are going to be no hares, no rabbits, there is going to be nothing.' F. Brett, E Suffolk, seconding, said, 'In North Suffolk children were in a playing field while a plane was spraying, and had to be carried back into school.'

Jim Watts reminded the Conference that, hitherto, Union policy had been to press the Minister to exercise control over aerial spraying, but now they wanted aerial spraying banned within the vicinity of villages and populated areas.

Proof on Spray Dangers

Of course, it was always hard to get proof that these sprays did any harm, but sometimes the users did get close to admitting responsibility. Enfys Chapman ran a farm with her husband in Royston, and was caught in an organophosphate spray (Hostathion) from a helicopter. She was racked with pain and eventually taken to Addenbrookes Hospital with severe asthma and convulsions. She had positive proof of her exposure through soil and blood tests. In 1983, Enfys received £12,000 compensation in an out-of-court settlement arising from the action she took against the sprayers, backed by Hoechst, manufacturers of the chemical involved. She was supposed not to talk about the case any further, but refused, and was instrumental in setting up the Pesticide Exposure Group of Sufferers to expose the risks of agrochemicals.

Mrs. Chapman was lucky in that she was able to collect the evidence of her exposure to the spray immediately after the incident, before it was washed away, something that is not always possible for a farmworker, unless he has an unusually co-operative employer!*

At the 1972 Biennial, Alan Pullen moved a successful resolution concerned at the increasing health hazards to farmworkers handling chemical additives in animal feeds, and seeking periodical health checks for all such workers. He referred to the widespread use of hormones in broiler production and by sheep farmers, and to the danger of handling hormone preparations.

Another resolution called for far stricter controls of toxic chemicals on farms and the mover, Henry Dellar, Cambs, said that at the previous Biennial he had supported a similar resolution asking for a notice to be put up in a field that had been sprayed, with the name of the chemical and date used. On returning home he had been visited by two farmers and asked if he was mad. He explained that his objections were based on crops being sprayed with chemicals, the effect of which lasted six weeks, but which were harvested within three weeks of spraying. Speaker after speaker spoke of illness and distress, working with toxic chemicals but throughout the debate there was reflected the concern for the impact of such poisons on the earth itself and those who consume the produce of the land.

This early interest in the effect of pesticides on humans and the environment shows the Union at its best, alerting the public to dangers then generally unknown, long before anyone claimed to be an environmentalist.

One possible effect of sprays was highlighted by a survey in Lincolnshire in 1976. A 30-year-old member was in hospital with heart trouble, believed to have been caused by sprays. Vigilant members made a survey and found a number of heart complaints amongst farmworkers. George Curtis, DO, said that 'It's a real shame when a man in the prime of life has a heart attack. We are worried that other members could be getting a gradual deadly build-up of poison in their bodies. There does seem to be a lot of heart complaints among local farmers.' Without official investigation, it was impossible to establish whether it was higher than in non-agricultural workers. Later, one Lincolnshire man died from heart disease after spraying.

Branches and district committees in the seventies continued to call for tougher measures against toxic chemicals, and there was growing evidence in 1976 that Government checks were far from adequate. Some chemicals were listed as dangerous under the Pesticides Safety Precautions Scheme and never to be used without protective clothing, but few Union members had ever seen, let alone used this type of clothing.

But the most widely-used pesticides were not even listed as dangerous, and still caused serious illness to members. One was off work for three weeks after

---

* The Pesticide Exposure Group of Sufferers was still active in the 1990s, seeking information from sufferers, bringing them together, contacting interested organisations and lobbying Parliament. Most importantly it campaigns for adequate NHS tests for pesticide exposure. Address: 10 Parker Street, Cambridge CB1 1JL.

spraying with a 'safe' chemical. In Cambridgeshire, members using metasystox and disystox for controlling aphids, had problems eating and swallowing, their breathing became difficult. Another supposedly 'safe' chemical,
Delancol, produced swelling around the eyes.

The serious risks were underlined by a MAFF scientist working for the
Pesticides Safety Precautions Scheme at the Plant Pathology Laboratory at
Harpenden, Herts. He was seriously ill after contact with a minute amount of
TCD, present as an impurity in one of the most wide-used pesticides, commonly
known as 'Brushwood' killer or 245–T. Some weeks after contact, the scientist
noticed 'an excessive oiliness of the skin, first affecting the nose and then spreading
to the lower part of the cheeks, and then to the neck. Later he developed on his
head and neck huge blackheads giving off a rancid odour. His hair began to fall
out, he had stomach upsets and lost weight. Long black hair grew on his shoulders,
back and hands. And his blood cholesterol level became 'enormous'.

At the time, heart diseases had been ruled out as a result of contact with
farm chemicals. So had cancer, but it was beginning to emerge that some
farm chemicals were cancer-producing.

The 1980 Biennial expressed its horror at the amount of chemicals a
farmworker had to contend with, and the many potentially lethal types of
crop sprays allowed on the market almost weekly, and asked the EC to ensure
that no chemical was released for general use until exhaustive tests had been
made as to its safety. It called for a total ban on 245–T.

'The biggest step forward in farm chemical safety in decades,' was how
Jack Boddy greeted the setting up of a sub-committee of the HSE at its first
meeting on 25 April 1983. Known as the Chemicals in Agriculture Working
Group, it was to investigate the practical problems of users in the field. Unlike
the PAC, it had the priceless asset of including worker representatives. 'This
takes it out of the ivory tower atmosphere of all the other expert committees
packed with academic scientists with no knowledge of what it is like to get
your boots dirty,' declared Chris Kaufman.

The Union bluntly informed the Government that their proposed Pesticides Bill* was simply tinkering with an 'inadequate and unrepresentative
system'. The Union drew up a 'Charter for Action' on pesticides, detailing a
new safety system which would protect agricultural workers, the public and
the environment. A key point was that any safety system must provide a place
for workers' representatives as of right. The Charter outlined the Union's
major policy demands on pesticide legislation. It called for legal controls on
matters such as manufacture, clearance, marketing, uses and applications;
legally enforceable health and safety training for manufacturers and users,
along with medical research; legally enforceable freedom of information on
all data, and policy information.

---

* This became the Food and Environmental Protection Act, 1986, referred to
earlier in this chapter.

The Charter was submitted to MAFF in September 1984, and Reg Green, Trade Group legal officer commented, 'There are far too many reasons for believing that the Government's proposed Pesticides Bill is nothing but a sop to the British agrochemical industry. The one overwhelming reason, though, is the government's failure to tackle the central issues of worker representation and worker access to the necessary information.'

'They know how big a contribution to the pesticides debate this Trade Group and its expert advisers have made. If they keep us out of a new system controlling pesticides it must be because they think the workers might make those controls meaningful.'

But the Union, and its members, were kept out.

A farmworker died from exposure to a herbicide, according to the 1987 HSE Report. The man became ill in 1980 and died in 1986. A coroner recorded a verdict of death from aplastic anaemia, caused by exposure to the herbicide. Yet another long-term victim of farm chemicals, which didn't say a lot for Government controls to date.

Union's Great Victory

In 1982 the Union's case against 245–T was dramatically documented in a book entitled *Portrait of a Poison. The 245–T Story* [3] by Judith Cook and Chris Kaufman, the Union's Research Officer who became a leading figure in the campaign against this chemical.

Reviewing the book in the *Landworker*, Francis Beckett wrote:

> Suppose that the most famous weedkiller in the world turns out to be the most harmless stuff in the world for human beings . . . That when all the scientific evidence is in, it can be shown to be completely innocent, and that the miscarriages, deformed births and cancer deaths for which it has been blamed, have, in fact, nothing to do with it. It's not impossible. None of the anti-245–T campaigners claim to have watertight, copperbottomed scientific evidence that it even harmed anyone. They simply point out the growing consensus of world scientific opinion; the fact that it contains dioxin, the most lethal substance known to man; and the fact that, if it does not do terrible damage to human beings, then there is a tragically high number of strange coincidences, and the people who use it seem to be a singularly unfortunate lot.

He said that if the Government banned it, they would simply lose an efficient weedkiller. But the Government was not going to ban it.

> The Tory Government is treating 245–T in effect, like an accused person in the dock ought to be treated: as innocent until proved guilty. So if it's guilty, what then? Hundreds more people will have died agonised deaths from a rare form of malignant soft tissue cancer while ministers sit on their hands and wait for the evidence. Hundreds – probably thousands – more women will have miscarriages; and as many again will give birth to hideously deformed babies

like those in Vietnam, which was heavily sprayed with 245–T by the American
Army. That's the risk if the Government is wrong . . .

At a press conference to launch the book, Shadow Agriculture Minister
Norman Buchan promised that the next Labour Government would ban
245–T, but a change of administration was a long way off.

The book repeated Union arguments for the job of pesticide control to be
given to the HSE and for the establishment of an Environmental Protection
Agency, independent of government and industry.

It may be appropriate to note here that the use of the main ingredient in
245–T in the Vietnam war, perhaps gives a clue to the British Government's
obsessive secrecy over the use of pesticides, and the real reason why PAC
deliberations are covered by the Official Secrets Act. Most agrochemical
plants could quickly be turned over to making chemical warfare products,
and some top agrochemical experts have connections with the chemical
warfare research station at Porton Down.

In the 1956 list of approved chemicals issued by MAFF, 245–T was
mentioned and, in the late sixties, complaints were made by members working
for the Forestry Commission (FC) about its use. These were drawn to the
attention of the FC by Reg Bottini and Jim Watts, and Tom Healy, TGWU,
when they met representatives of the Commission in April 1970. They issued
an agreed statement that the FC had received no reports of harm to workers
by the chemical, but its use would be suspended pending further enquiries.
When this was reported to the Union's Forestry Workers' Advisory Committee, it was pointed out that the FC had failed to provide suitable protective
clothing, and agreed that as so far there was no concrete evidence of illness
caused by sprays, regular medical checks should be made.

In the early 1970s, the FC made several attempts to re-start its use of
245–T. The Union fiercely resisted, and the FC claimed that it could get
contractors to do the job if necessary.

Labour MP, John Home Robertson, Berwick-on-Tweed, joined the growing
list of MPs in 1980 badgering the Government to do something about the menace
of agrochemicals. He said that 'according to the HSE, in 1976 there were ten
cases only of poisoning reported on farms. In 1977 there were 27, and last year
there were 32. That is the tip of the iceberg. There are many more cases that are
neither reported nor detected, because the effects of small doses are extremely
difficult to diagnose. In 1944 there were only 65 approved chemicals for farmers
and growers . . . Now there are approaching 1,000 products on the market. It is
true to say that virtually every arable acre in Britain is treated with some sort of
chemical . . .' He wanted the use of 245–T suspended.

Jerry Wiggin, Parliamentary Secretary to the Minister of Agriculture, said
some of the accidents involving pesticides resulted from 'sheer carelessness'
and 'Agent Orange', used in Vietnam, contained 450 times as much dioxin
as any product used in Britain. 'May I put the matter in perspective by
pointing out that the highest rate that 245–T is used here, mostly in forestry,

the amount of dioxin distributed is the equivalent to one grain of sugar spread over a football pitch, and if one put together all the dioxin in 245–T formulations used every year in this country it would not fill a salt spoon . . .' Without the use of pesticides the yields of cereals would fall by 45% in three years. 'We must not forget, either, that pesticides earn valuable export revenue, some £130 million in 1978.'

This was typical of the Tory Government's reaction to the problem, nothing was proven as to its dangers, it increased production, and was very profitable.

Complete Ban Sought

A complete ban on 245–T was called for by NUAAW President John Hose at the FC Joint Industrial Council meeting in November 1979. There had been widespread disquiet following incidents in Wales, Somerset and Oregon, USA. Anger mounted when the FC refused, and the NUAAW imposed its own ban on workers using it.

Chris Kaufman thought that the pressure for a total ban, spearheaded by the NUAAW, had reached such an intensity that it could only be a matter of time before the British Government fell into line with the USA, Italy, Holland, Norway and Sweden, in calling a halt to its use. Such is the obduracy of Tory Governments when it comes to workers' safety that no such ban was forthcoming.

Chris had reasonable cause to be optimistic, though. Support for the Union's stand snowballed. Euro MP, Kenneth Collins, Strathclyde East, called on the EEC to extend the ban to all Common Market countries, and the *Daily Mirror* began campaigning for a ban. Messages of support flooded in from worried members of the public, amateur gardeners, environmentalist groups, scientists and doctors.

Evidence against it was building up. There was the horrific incident in Seveso, Italy, when clouds of dioxin released from a chemical plant left 106 children disfigured and 34 women had to have abortions, which had considerable effect in bringing the dangers to public attention.

But the FC still insisted there was no conclusive evidence of its dangers. They said MAFF's PAC had reviewed 245–T eight times, and recently reported that 'it offers no hazard to users, general public, to domestic animals, to wildlife or to the environment generally, if used as directed.'

These assurances no longer sounded convincing. John Hose pointed out that it was not the responsibility of the unions to prove a substance was unsafe, but there was now sufficient doubt to make a ban imperative. However, the FC refused.

The PAC in 1983 gave the 245–T a clean bill of health. However the Government and the chemical manufacturers were in a fast-dwindling minority, who were happy to allow its continued use. Boots the Chemists told the *Landworker* that they no longer retailed brands called 'Nettle Killer' and 'BBN'. Woolworths said they had re-formulated 'Touchweeder' to exclude

245–T, and the company of which Dennis Thatcher was chair, Chipman Ltd, which used to supply British Rail until they ceased using it, now claimed to have stopped producing 'Chipman Brushwood Killer.'

The Trade Group speedily hit back with a denunciation of the latest 'whitewash' and called for workers to keep up their refusal to handle the chemical. At a London press conference, Jack Boddy said, 'I am horrified that this Government is unable to withstand the lobby power of the agrochemical companies who profit from the vast sales of farm chemicals . . . the Government has announced its intention of using Britain as a gigantic laboratory in which to experiment on the millions of workers, amateur gardeners and members of their families who can be exposed to products containing 245–T . . . There is now so much evidence ranged against 245–T that the Minister and his Advisory Committee of academic scientists and civil servants can only be characterised as King Canutes, blind to the flood of evidence which surrounds them.'

A complete ban had been called for by the 1980 Biennial, and it demanded prohibition of paraquat sprays until satisfactory antidotes were found and readily available. Maurice Housden, Hants, said 40 different sprays were in use on the Ministry experimental husbandry farm where he worked, and that establishment was no different from most farms in that respect. Hugh Harnwell, Cambs, said sprays had made one of his branch members impotent and broken up the marriage. Mike Bissett, Herts, said all spray operators should be licensed. Doug Oswick, Norfolk, said, 'When I was a young man, they would work you to death. Now they will poison you.' He had seen protective clothing drop to pieces after being washed. 'Don't let protective clothing lull you into any false sense of security.'

Conference also demanded that aerial spraying should be banned. 'It was more often a miss than a hit,' said Tom Girling, Suffolk. Eric Hudson, Norfolk, said 245–T was probably the worst thing to be loosed on the earth since mustard gas, yet thousands of acres were sprayed indiscriminately. Peter Peck, Ampthill, Beds, said that nothing would grow in a forest after 245–T, but employers refused to blame the chemical, saying the sun or even the rain must be the cause.

Chris Kaufman said 245–T without dioxin was known to cause cancer and birth deformities in animals. 'Despite all details of cases affecting workers, their wives and families and the public, MAFF has hidden behind the PAC . . . And why also did farmworker Eddie Trehearne develop cancer of the neck and die 12 months after a knapsack leaked on to his neck? Why is the onus on the victim to prove that a chemical is dangerous rather than for the people who put it on the market to prove that it is safe? Last year the agrochemical companies' world sales made 10 billion dollars.'

President John Hose declared that the 'biggest blot' in agriculture was the record of safety and health. There was a frightful waste of human resources by accidents, and agricultural employers gave no more than lip service to the need to make farming safer.

Public Support

A wave of public support for the NUAAW campaign for an immediate ban on 245–T followed publication in 1980 of the Union dossier, *Not One Minute Longer*. But Minister of Agriculture Peter Walker, though he ordered a new review of the NUAAW's collected evidence, still refused to suspend use of the herbicide. Whilst he looked the other way, the rest of the world took action. The Scottish TUC and the Women's TUC backed the TUC General Council's call for a total ban. Local authorities like Peterborough, Nottingham, Milton Keynes, South Yorkshire and Lewisham joined Somerset and Avon in imposing their own ban. Railwaymen, local authority workers and many others refused to use 245–T. The National Dairy Producers' Association called for a ban, and the issue was again raised in Parliament. Labour agriculture spokesman Roy Mason repeated the Party's call for a ban.

'Ban it now and let the PAC do its investigations at leisure,' said Jack Boddy, when along with Chris Kaufman, he met Peter Walker, Professor Kilpatrick (chair of PAC) and Jerry Wiggin, after publication of the dossier. 'No' said the Minister of Agriculture, and in one word continued to leave at risk millions of workers and their families.

At Somerset's County Conference, 245–T came under fire from a man whose wife had a miscarriage after he had used the spray. Paul Cobledick told the conference, 'I believe dioxin is transferred through the sperm. My next door neighbour has had the same experience.' The *Landworker* demanded:

> How can the Government continue to refuse a ban in the face of calls from the NUAAW, the TUC, doctors, scientists, MPs and the public, concern about the risks involved . . . there seems no rational explanation. It looks like dangerous lunacy to turn a deaf ear to a demand that says, quite reasonably, 'We think this substance may well cause all kinds of harmful effects. Don't allow it to be used until tests have convinced us that it is safe.' But if we look at the way pesticides are allowed onto the market we begin to get closer to the answer. Peter Walker, is the man who can impose the ban. At present he is dithering. It is his Government department which has responsibility for pesticide control. As the recent Royal Commission on Environmental Pollution Report pointed out, this involves MAFF in a direct contradiction between its efforts to promote agricultural productivity and its efforts to regulate the risks arising from farming in Britain.
>
> Mr. Walker has a misplaced faith in the work of his PAC which has always given 245–T its approval. The NUAAW cannot accept the views of a committee which is so closely tied to MAFF. And what is the PAC ? It is a collection of academic scientists and Government 'experts'. A worthy body you may think. 'Of world-wide repute,' says Mr. Walker. But aren't we missing something ? Where are the workers' representatives ? People who understand the practical difficulties of spraying in the wind and the rain or the hot sun or with the pressing of time, on a steep hill or whatever . . . The PAC may well have a reputation but all the evidence suggests that its fame is growing for the wrong reasons. For its ability to bury its head in the sand.

Consider the way it has been going on. It has ignored data from animal experiments showing that dioxin causes cancer and birth deformities on the grounds that we do not know for sure that these characteristics would be reproduced with humans. Does this mean that human beings are safe ? Yes, says the PAC – without a shred of evidence.

It concluded by saying that trade unionists did not want to be guinea pigs just for the satisfaction of proving a lot of 'experts' wrong.

David Thomas, a Northamptonshire farmworker, wrote to Peter Walker calling for an immediate ban. His letter read: 'Dear Mr. Walker, . . . My wife Margaret has had two miscarriages and two near miscarriages, also one of our daughters was born with a blocked urethra tube and enlarged kidney. A major op was required . . . I have good reason to suspect 245–T as I have used it in my work for at least the past 12 years . . . I have come across other cases . . . They have all used 245–T and had it on their skin . . . All these cases are within a mile or so of where I live . . . You have asked the experts to look into the chemical, but no one has asked us the users what effect it has on us . . . A lot of innocent people will be using 245–T this Summer, how many more miscarriages, deformities and cancer cases do you want to see in next year's dossier ? . . . I plead with you from my heart to order an instant ban today . . . Yours sincerely, David Thomas.'

Extensive Survey

In the most extensive survey of its kind ever undertaken, the NUAAW then launched an investigation into the use and effects of 245–T on workers using it. In marked contrast to the approach of PAC, which appeared to instigate no research of its own, the Union intended to find out just how widely the herbicide was used, the conditions it was used in and the possible medical effects. A questionnaire, drawn up with the assis- tance of scientists, doctors and trade union colleagues, was circulated to all branches. It asked members for what purpose they were told to use it and whether they were provided with protective clothing and washing facilities.

Later, in 1980, the Union's campaign gathered further strength. It went international; the Union asked the European Farmworkers' Association to hear the case for a Europe-wide ban. The NUAAW fact-finding survey was going well. The replies provided a wealth of data indicating possible medical effects on users.

The NUAAW finally got to grips with the PAC, or at least, its scientific sub-committee. A Union delegation was led by Jack Boddy and Chris Kaufman, and included scientific back-up in the shape of doctors Jenny Martin, Charles Clutterbuck and Alistair Hay. And showing the concern of other unions were Dave Gee, GMWU, and John Matthews, ASTMS. They were not impressed with the sub-committee after spending four hours discuss-ing with them the scientific evidence on toxic effects of 245–T.

These exchanges only went to confirm the NUAAW and TUC view that the PAC's days ought to be numbered. After the meeting Jack Boddy called for its winding up, declaring, 'This committee . . . has repeatedly told the public that there is nothing to worry about. Yet members of the scientific sub-committee showed themselves to have little idea of the practical problems of spraying . . . It is time that these decisions were passed to the HSE, which has the merit of including representatives of the people in the firing line. One has to wonder about the competence of the PAC which informs the world that only three tonnes of 245–T is being used in Britain every year. We know that imports are more like 150 tonnes.* When we met the committee they were greatly surprised by this revelation. We are alarmed at their approach. In their eyes, the scientific evidence proving the hazards of a chemical has to be made absolutely watertight. In our view the decision has to be made on the balance of probabilities. When people's health and indeed lives may be at stake a responsible body cannot wait – as was the case with asbestos – until there is a sufficiently impressive death toll . . . The committee admits that they are in the dark as to the real effects of 245–T and its incredibly toxic contaminant, dioxin, on human beings.'

By that time about 60 local authorities had banned 245–T. Labour-led Worcester City Council joined the growing list. Worcester was the Parliamen-tary constituency of Peter Walker, who refused to ban it.

A joint working party was set up in the Brendon Forest, Somerset, to study the use of chemical sprays, following the refusal of Union members to use Strykol (Gamma BHC) because those using it had had upset stomachs. 'They also say it is unpleasant to use,' said Barry Leathwood, DO, who held talks with FC officials.

In 1980, the Union sent more evidence to the PAC in support of its demand for a ban. But the bosses hit back, repeating claims that there was no danger from 245–T if properly used. The British Agrochemical Association (BAA) and the CBI, of which the NFU is a member, were the organisations disputing the Union's evidence with no more than assertions.

The experimental data given the PAC included American animal research which showed tests on rats and mice with minute quantities of the 245–T contaminant, dioxin, causing cancer. Other animal tests had already demon-strated birth deformities, abortions, miscarriages and liver and skin diseases in experiments using pure 245–T and dioxin separately. A study of Swedish workers had suggested confirmation of some of these effects on those using this type of herbicide. The NUAAW was at pains to explain that it could not prove cause and effect – but there were an awful lot of coincidences. New

---

* In answer to Joan Maynard in the House of Commons, a Government spokesman admitted that 151 tonnes were imported in the 12 months ended May 1980.

cases cited included a Northamptonshire man working on a British Rail 245–T spray train; he was drenched by the chemical as he stuck his head out of the cab. A son was born with no holes in his ears and a cleft palate. Amid speculation in Whitehall that the PAC was about to recommend a ban, the PAC came up with the usual refrain, 'We need more time to look at the evidence.'

Meanwhile pressure for a ban grew. All English and Welsh water boards joined BR in saying that they would not use 245–T. And several more local authorities joined the 60 or so councils who had already halted its use.

But the PAC appeared to have gone to ground. The long-awaited report from this committee which had been examining the NUAAW evidence remained long awaited. When a delegation from the NUAAW met the PAC and Peter Walker in August, it was assured that a recommendation on what to do about the pesticide would be produced in September. Since then there had been nothing but silence. Jack Boddy believed that the PAC was about to come out with another 'whitewash' report. There was speculation that Walker was waiting for the furore to die down before giving a decision.

An example of the campaign against 245–T: Tom Rampling of Oxfordshire let the world know exactly what the Union's objections to it were. As secretary of Banbury Trades Council, he sent the NUAAW dossiers not only to the local MP, to the four Banbury members of Oxfordshire County Council, the 20 members of Cherwell Rural District Council, and the three local papers, but also to the Banbury Council of Churches. Captain Gordon Kitney, the churches' social responsibility committee chair, straightaway took the issue up with Cherwell RDC and asked them to ban 245–T.

Towards the end of 1980, the British Agrochemical Association, alarmed by the success of the NUAAW campaign, sent a letter to authorities throughout Britain. It said, 'We accept that the trade union movement and others are free to pursue their objectives of seeking direct influence in the control arrangements governing all pesticides. However, to damn the safety arrangements governing all pesticides in pursuit of that objective is unfair and to create groundless scare stories about specific products is deplorable.'

Chris Kaufman commented, 'That's very big of them. But what they call "scare stories" we call human tragedies which we have every reason to believe may have their origin in use of pesticides whose effects are still not fully understood. To dismiss them in this way illustrates very well why we have no confidence at all in a system in which we have no say.'

At the time the number of local authorities banning 245–T rose to more than 70, and Shropshire Woman's Institutes urged a ban on aerial spraying of similar chemicals.

Another important development was when the TUC General Council vote unanimously to stop supplies of 245–T coming into Britain.[4] As 245–T was not made here because the process was considered too dangerous, the TUC decided to check where supplies came from and contact trade unions abroad asking them to stop work on it.

Praise for the NUAAW's campaign came from a leading American scientist, Dr. Samuel Epstein, a pathologist who studied the toxic effects of pesticides. On a visit to London he said the campaign was being followed by many Americans concerned with the effects of 245–T.

Dr. Epstein was an advisor to the US Environmental Protection Agency when it banned 245–T. Among its reasons was that dioxin is present in commercial preparations of 245–T of about 100 parts per billion; dioxin is the most potent known cancer-producing agent and preliminary information on a group of Monsanto workers involved in a dioxin accident had found an excess of lymph cancers among those dying since 1969. There was also increasing evidence of large-scale public exposure to 245–T, including the identification of dioxin residues in beef fat.

'Wind up the PAC. It can't do the job it's supposed to do.' That was the message of a press conference held at the TUC in January 1981. Three major unions' general secretaries explained why they had no faith in the PAC: Jack Boddy, Clive Jenkins (ASTMS) and Bill Whatley (USDAW). Clive pointed out that the agrochemicals industry was a multi-million pound concern; this explained the resistance the unions were experiencing to what was a reasonable demand to play safe. Bill reported the concern of his members. 'Packets can break open. Tops of cans can come loose. Labels can come off.'

In 1981, the Labour Party NEC sent a deputation to see Walker to argue for a ban on 245–T, and for responsibility for pesticides to go to the HSE.

Later in the year, the NUAAW demanded a complete overhaul of the system for the control and safe use of pesticides. The call was made at a press conference to launch the Union's reply to the Government's whitewash of 245–T. It was a report called *Pray Before You Spray*.

At the conference, Chris Kaufman held up the 1980 list of approved chemicals and compared it with the 1970 one. The 1980 list was three times as fat – graphically illustrating the chemical 'population explosion'. With him was chemical expert, Dr. Jenny Martin. Pointing out that 12 million TUC members and two million European farmworkers had backed the NUAAW campaign, the report said that the trade union movement had no confidence in the Government committee of 'experts' which continually played down the risks to workers. In it, the Union again called for the winding up of PAC and wanted clearance for the safe use of pesticides to be taken over by the HSE, which did not have the conflicting responsibility of MAFF – of maximising food production against operator safety – and had workers representatives. It also wanted to end the voluntary Pesticides Safety Precautions Scheme; the removal of unnecessary confidentiality of industrial safety data, and an accessible safety data bank open to the workers engaged in their use, and proper training for workers.

Chris introduced *Pray Before You Spray* by quoting the words of the US Environmental Protection Agency:

> It is impossible to ascertain a safe level of human exposure to dioxin. Because science has not established that there are threshold doses for chemical carcinogens below which there is no cancer risk, even very low levels of exposure to dioxin must be regarded as creating some risk. The quality, quantity and variety of data, demonstrating that the continued use of 245–T contaminated with dioxin present risks to human health, is unprecedented and overwhelming.

The world-wide pressure, spearheaded by the NUAAW, led to the ending of large-scale manufacture of 245–T by 1983. But existing stocks remained a hazard. So the Trade Group continued to campaign for a total ban, until the Government, in the words of Jack Boddy 'sees sense'. Another breakthrough left the British Government even more isolated: the ending of 245–T manufacture at Chemie Linz plant in Austria early in 1983, which meant that all European production ceased. It followed similar moves in West Germany. There had been no 245–T production in Britain since 1976, when Coalite learnt the lessons of the Seveso explosion.

An investigation by the *Landworker* led it to believe that the only known 245–T producer was a company in New Zealand called Ivan Chemicals, a subsidiary of the American Dow Chemicals. 'I am 95% sure that it is still being produced in New Zealand,' said Mr. Jackman, Agricultural Attache to the New Zealand High Commission in London. But however much was produced in New Zealand, it was thought unlikely to fill the gap left by the Western World's pull out. It was estimated that stocks in Britain would run out, and the ban on the use of 245–T first pursued by the old NUAAW would become a fact.

Dr. Jenny Martin again helped draw up the confidential TGWU questionnaire which would assist in evaluating the evidence of people in contact with 245–T. Replies showed that apart from those who had suffered relatively minor problems, such as rashes and headaches, there were five cases of soft tissue cancer, two of which were fatal. Two were in very young men, and there were congenital defects in babies. One father, who had used 'SBK Brushwood Killer', had a daughter with club feet, deformed hips, mitten-shaped hands, short arms with webbing in the elbow joints and deformed shoulders. The fibia was missing from each leg and she had a weak chest.

A boy was born with deformed limbs, total deafness and multiple handicaps. His father actually made 245–T in the 1950s. A woman who tested 245–T in laboratory conditions suffered six miscarriages afterwards. Eventually she had one premature child and suffered ill effects herself. Another worker who used 'SBK Brushwood Killer' had a daughter with a cleft palate, harelip and weighed only 4lbs 8oz; another woman who handled 245–T produced a baby with spina biffida. All these malformations were the same as those which appeared in Seveso after the explosion there.

In July 1984 there was a new call upon the Government to ban the sale of 245–T. A new Union report, *How Many More?*, was issued. It gave details of 27 further cases of people suffering from cancer, birth deformities, miscarriages and skin diseases following contact with 245–T.

Chris Kaufman said that it was a national scandal that Britain had not joined other countries in banning 245–T. 'The Union has had to step in where the Government has failed to do any research into the medical effects on people exposed to this chemical. The cases we have unearthed are uncannily similar to those Vietnam war veterans who have just received a 180 million dollar pay-out from American chemical companies.'

So ends, for the purpose of this history, the Union's virtual victory over 245–T in Britain, despite the Government's obstinacy in not ordering an official ban.

The age of chemical pesticides is far from over, but the sooner farmers lessen their dependence on chemicals and switch to alternative controls the better. One useful technique would be encouraging pests' natural predators, and to introduce pest-resistant plants. The latter promise to be cheaper and far more sparing of the environment and farmers, than the brutal technology of chemical pesticides. The chemical companies do not like the idea, and will do their best to impede such biotechnology, so the Trade Group must remain ever vigilant.* Today's mono-culture enables pests to multiply enormously when presented with unlimited quantities of their favourite foods. A return to more mixed farming would also help lessen the number of pests – another move that would be welcomed by farmworkers.

Disaster: Foot and Mouth

A large-scale disaster hit many British farms in October 1967 – foot-and-mouth disease – and the Union unhesitatingly rallied to the national cause as well as looking after the interests of its members, some of whom lost their jobs.

The first outbreak was confirmed on the farm of Richard Ellis, in Llanyblodwell, Shropshire, on 25 October, and no one could have guessed at the devastation which followed.[5] It was market day at Oswestry, a few miles away, where some 7,000 head of stock were sold, including two of Mr. Ellis's cows. From midnight on 25 October, an area of ten miles around Llanyblodwell was declared an infected area, and restrictions imposed on the movement of animals in neighbouring counties. MAFF officials set about the difficult task

---

* 'Levels of dioxin in the breast milk of British mothers are 100 times higher than the Government's own guidelines permit, according to Sir Donald Acheson, Government Chief Medical Officer. He said there was no evidence the babies were at risk. "We are on an amber light, not a red light." The mothers accumulate the dioxin from animal fats they eat.' *Guardian*, 30 June 1989.

of tracing all animals that had passed through Oswestry on the crucial day. But the job was done, and by 30 October standstill restrictions were lifted in the whole area. Mr. Ellis's two cows were not carrying the infection and no harm had been done, it seemed. But even as the restrictions were being lifted, reports were coming in of further outbreaks, at Darnhall in Cheshire, and another at Borwick on the borders of Lancashire and Westmorland. New restriction orders were made, and thereafter news of fresh outbreaks came thick and fast. By 2 November, 40 outbreaks had been confirmed in Shropshire, Cheshire, Denbighshire, Flintshire, Lancashire and Montgomeryshire. By 4 November, 4,858 cattle, 4,404 sheep and 1,697 pigs had been slaughtered.

The movement of cattle was banned in the whole of northern England and Wales – from Merioneth to the Humber. Farmers were stunned as 100 MAFF vets fought the epidemic from headquarters set up in the police station at Oswestry. The first standstill order on 25 October had been imposed within ten minutes of the confirmation of the outbreak at Llanyblodwell. Some 3,000 animals were still there, and most of them went to the slaughterhouse.

Arguments soon raged as to how the disease,* caused by a virus, had spread so rapidly, and the usual culprits, gulls, starlings and foxes were pinpointed, but no one really knew. The subsequent pattern of cases suggest that the disease could have been windborn.

The accepted method in Britain to control outbreaks was by slaughtering the affected animals, and then burning and burying the carcasses in huge pits.

Many specialists believed the human agency to be a means of spreading the disease, and the Union took every practicable measure to help the authorities prevent this happening. The first important event to be postponed was the Nottingham and Derbyshire Conference; postponement of other county conferences quickly followed. Organisers in the affected areas were advised by head office to work in harmony with MAFF and NFU officials. And on 27 November, the General Purposes Committee decided that there should be a countrywide ban on Union meetings and functions. The December meeting of the EC was cancelled and the 1968 Winter School postponed.

Meanwhile, herds of infected cattle were slaughtered, burnt and buried. Their owners were well compensated. Fred Peart told the House of Commons that these methods of eradicating the disease had paid off in the previous 75 years. Whilst modern vaccines gave a degree of protection for cattle and sheep, the annual vaccination required would be extremely expensive with

---

* The disease causes nasty blisters round the animals' feet and mouth, accompanied by high fever; the animal produces excessive amounts of foamy saliva and cannot eat. Pregnant cows are liable to abort and the milk dries up. It is extremely contagious, and is the most infectious animal disease known, and once it gets hold, rages like a forest fire. The virus can survive on almost every material, including clothing, rubber boots and dairy implements.

our animal population of 45 million. 'I have arranged for a supply of vaccine to be stored in this country so that a vaccination programme could be adopted as a second line of defence. But I shall not use this unless our present programme breaks down.'

Harold Collison met Peart to discuss the impact of the disease on farmworkers and an agreed statement was issued, saying, 'Particular consideration was given to problems affecting farmworkers whose jobs have been jeopardised or earnings seriously reduced by the outbreaks.' Peart said that he would consider the practical questions raised, and appreciated the part farmworkers had played in tackling the emergency.

By January 1968, a growing number of farmworkers were being dismissed or having their earnings substantially reduced as more and more cattle were destroyed. With a gradual abatement of the epidemic bringing a decline in the miserable work of disinfecting, burning and burial, the employment of affected farmworkers grew worse. John Hockenhall, DO, Cheshire and Flint, estimated in his area alone over 1,500 workers were employed on farms that had the disease, and wrote to S. Schofield Allen, MP for Crewe, seeking his help on behalf of workers who had been dismissed or suffered a reduction in wages. 'If their inherited skill and loyalty are thrown away, then it will be a sad day for the countryside,' wrote John. Following a voluntary agreement between John and the Cheshire NFU, the latter's secretary, F. Cureton, advised farmers to retain their workers where possible and pay them their usual wage.

MAFF was reminded by the Union that so far nothing had been done to compensate those workers who had lost their livelihood, and difficulties were increasing for those employed in affected areas. There were, for example, two workers living in the affected areas who were told by a MAFF official not to travel to their work on a farm in a free area. There were also disputes about clearing up pay. Differing rates were paid in various areas, and a number of farmworkers were not receiving the 8s 6d an hour farmers received in re-imbursement from the Ministry.

Harold Collison proposed to Peart that it was in the interests of the industry, as well as the workers, that a means should be found to enable farmers to continue to employ their men at the old rates of wages, and to take into account the increase in wages that they would have expected from 5 February.

The Union's Emergency sub-Committee met on 3 January and, noting an abatement in the number of foot-and-mouth cases, modified some of the severe restrictions the Union had placed on its activities in infected areas. In all other counties, normal Union activities could be resumed.

At the 1968 Biennial, W. Stubbs, Cheshire, moved a resolution regretting the complete lack of security for farmworkers when foot-and-mouth struck an area. It sought 'justice for the workers by demanding from the Government that arrangements be made that all workers on affected farms should have the right to continue employment without loss of earnings.' He said that in

Cheshire alone, 500 workers had been made redundant. Others had had their earnings reduced. J. Langford, Salop, pointed to dissatisfaction caused because employees of contractors disposing of dead animals received up to £47 a week, while farmworkers got one third of that amount. Harold Collison said the worst hit areas were Cheshire, Staffordshire and Shropshire, and DOs from infected areas would give oral evidence to the Northumberland Committee of Inquiry that had been set up. The Union would continue to press the need for accepting 'consequential losses' to the Committee. The resolution was carried unanimously.

MAFF turned down the Union's request to take special steps to enable farmers affected by the epidemic to continue to employ their workers and pay them the old wage rates. No satisfactory compensation for the farmworkers who lost out because of the epidemic was ever obtained. The great epidemic finally petered out in February 1968. The totals of animals slaughtered were: cattle 208,811; sheep 100,699; pigs 113,423. Total cost of the epidemic was over £100 million, of which £35 million was paid by the Government to farmers who had animals slaughtered.

REFERENCES

1. *Guardian*, 1 September 1987.
2. Reprinted: *International Herald Tribune*, 15 November 1988.
3. Pluto Press, 1982, £2.95, available to Union members at £2.20 from T&G Publications, Transport House, Smith Square, London, SW1V 3JB.
4. *Landworker*, January 1981.
5. Ralph Whitlock, *The Great Cattle Plague*, John Baker (Publishers) Ltd, 1968.

19

Horticulture and Marketing

Nothing will ever be attempted if all possible objections must be first overcome.
Dr. Johnson

Diddling the Small Producer

In the early fifties, a smallholder in St. Mary's Cray, Kent, was getting 9d or 1s for a net of cauliflowers. Depending on the size of the cauliflowers, each net contained up to 25. Not surprisingly, he was finding it difficult to make a living. Angry, too, because he believed that in the shops each cauliflower was selling for far more than he got for a full net.

He and a sub editor on the Labour *Daily Herald* decided to do a little unusual market research. They hid twenty notes in some cauliflowers and duly dispatched them to market. The notes read: 'Dear Housewife, I'm a smallholder, and have a job making a living. I believe you pay a lot more for these cauliflowers than I get for them. Would you please let me know where you bought them, and how much you paid?' There were six or seven replies. The cheapest was bought in the East End of London at 1s 3d, the dearest cost 2s 4d in Knightsbridge. All prices were well above that of a single net!

The sub editor had told of the experiment to *Herald* editor, Percy Cudlipp, keen to do an exposure of the gigantic mark-ups of middle-men. These people often sold the produce to each other over the phone, without even seeing it, to the detriment of the consumer, the producer and ultimately, the NUAW members who worked for him.

But the story did not appear. An embarrassed editor explained, 'We decided it was too risky. It would upset the wholesalers, and that would upset the directors of Odhams (who then controlled the *Daily Herald*), which rents out premises to them in Covent Garden.'

I tell this story because it is a first-hand account – I was the sub editor – and it deals with one of the problems affecting horticulture that were still largely unsolved in the eighties, and indeed have grown and increased in stupidity.

*   *   *

The Union has always organised horticultural workers (it very early on took over the old National Union of Horticultural Workers) and some of its members did varied jobs. In fact, horticulture – the art of cultivating gardens – includes fruit growing, glasshouse production and much more. Over the years, the Union improved the pay of horticultural workers, but like that of farmworkers, it still lagged behind that of the average industrial worker.

As with agriculture, the NUAW was concerned with the marketing, or non-marketing of horticultural produce. Often cauliflowers, tomatoes and many fruits are destroyed to keep up the prices in the shops, and the producers mainly the smaller ones, go on getting a lot less than the retail prices.

The Agricultural Market Acts of 1931 and 1933 provided for statutory marketing bodies, and when the Lucas Committee* reported in 1948, it claimed there was no need for protection against marketing monopolies. It did, however, recommend a system to market produce on public utility lines by organisations representing 'not any section interest, but the community in general.'

'The weakness of agricultural policy is the absence of an efficient and comprehensive scheme of marketing and distribution,' Edwin Gooch told the Guild of Agricultural Journalists on 16 April 1948. 'I think there is an unanswerable case for public control of the handling of food supplies. The first principle should be to initiate community control, not to hand out State guaranteed controls to private interests. The Lucas recommendation that Commodity Commissions should be established to market the products, in respect of which the State has guaranteed consumer prices, is in accordance with the sound principle that the State, in return for that guarantee, has a right to ensure that all avoidable intermediate costs in handling farm produce are eliminated and the product transferred to the taxpayer (the consumer) . . . with no greater increase in price than an efficient and economical market system requires.'

Lucas Report Welcomed

On the whole, the Union welcomed the Lucas Report, which failed to get the sympathy of the farmers. Most of its recommendations were a long time being carried out, if ever. However, the Marketing Act of 1949 was one result; the Milk Marketing and Potato Marketing Boards resumed their powers in 1954, and the Wool Marketing Board was established in 1950.

But the Boards were not as satisfactory as they might have been, and G. D. H. Cole, the Labour historian, noted that they are 'chosen by the producers of the products concerned and thus represent profit-seeking as against consumer or public interest.'[1] He said it had been proposed that they

---

* A Government Committee on agricultural marketing, presided over by Lord Lucas.

25. Safety on the farm was always a prime concern of the Union, but its importance often took second place to the need for speed. Haysel begins on a farm at West Bolton, Wensleydale, with two children near the cutter bar. The boys are probably too young to recognise the danger, but what of the farmworker who is using a fork while the machine is in motion?

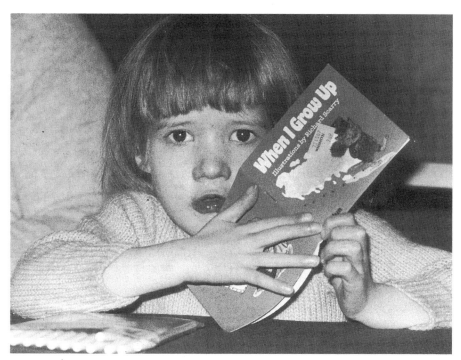

26. Little Kerry Hogben never did get the chance to grow up: the Union's campaign against 245–T in 1980 came too late to save her life. Her mother, Mrs. Irene Hogben, was a typist at Burts and Harvey Ltd, Belvedere, Kent. She typed out hundreds of invoices for 245–T. Men handling bags of 245–T would come into her office covered in powder. She was told it was not poisonous. Kerry was born with a massive hole in her heart and a defective pulmonary artery, and her lungs, liver and kidneys were too small. Similar defects were found in babies born in Vietnam, where the US military sprayed 'Agent Orange' (which contained 245–T).

27. Farmworkers planting early potatoes in the Valley of Gulval, Penzance, in February 1949. Not many decades later this work was done by machinery, operated by one, or sometimes two men. A back-breaking job had been made unnecessary; so had many of the workers who did it.

28. Spraying main crop potatoes on a farm at Aldsworth, Gloucestershire, with sodium arsenate to kill the tops and destroy blight which might develop and spread. This huge spraying machine being used in 1957 was a foretaste of the technological advances that were to revolutionise farming after the Second World War.

29. Precautions to prevent the spread of foot and mouth disease are stringent.
Sgt. McPherson of Bolton Police is seen dipping his boots in disinfectant before leaving
Wicken Lees Farm, Chew Moor, Lostock, near Bolton, Lancashire, where an outbreak of the
disease occurred in December 1957. Straw was also put down as a precautionary measure.

30. Outbreaks of foot and mouth disease in cattle led to thousands of farm animals like these
being slaughtered in 1972, and either being burnt in giant pyres on the farms, or buried in
huge pits, beneath mounds of quick lime.

31. The Union's 'Buy British' campaign during the closure of poultry factories in 1981 caught the public imagination and received much support. Union members are gathered outside a supermarket in Ipswich selling foreign poultry, and Pip Snell, EC, is talking to a passerby.

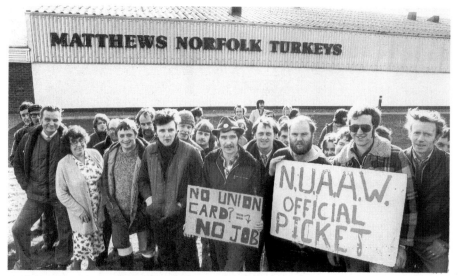

32. The strike in 1982 at Bernard Matthews' turkey processing plant in Norfolk was a milestone in the Union's post-war militancy. A. J. Rudd, its leader, is seen holding the 'No Union Card' placard amidst this group of strikers outside the factory.

should be reconstituted so as to represent public and consumer, as well as producer interests. 'Farmers, however, vigorously oppose such a system and in the name of self-government, claim the right to make compulsory regulations for their own trades.'

Union members were also concerned at production costs. At the Union's Oxford Conference in 1951, Michael Madden, county secretary, successfully moved a resolution that while approving guaranteed markets, deplored that they 'enable so much of the industry to be operated at a low level of technical efficiency and at high average production costs.' It called on MAFF to pursue 'an enlightened policy for compulsory farm reorganisation.' Michael believed that any further wage increase 'may well depend on our ability to reduce the cost of producing food.' Three delegates spoke against bigger agricultural units and thought smaller ones would be better for the country, a view more in keeping with the Green policies of the eighties than the produce-more-at-all-cost drive of the fifties.

Among the Union's members were hospital staffs, whose pay was negotiated by the National Joint Council for Staffs of Hospitals and Allied Institutions. They were divided into three groups; London, urban and rural. In 1949, London men got £5 10s (women £4 6s), urban men £5 4s (women £4 19s); and rural men £5 1s (women £3 18s) for a 48–hour week. This was better than AWB rates, an advantage maintained over the years.

There was no separate national negotiating machinery for horticultural workers who, generally, were paid in line with AWB orders. Local negotiations, especially in relation to production bonuses, sometimes improved rates. With the Ministry of Labour as 'arbiters', attempts were made in 1948 to establish joint negotiating machinery. They continued into 1949, but came to nothing.

Pay and marketing of horticultural products, were just two of the Union's concerns. At the TUC at Bridlington in September 1949, during a discussion on equal representation on agricultural bodies, Bert Huson said that in the Union's view, the establishment of a Development Council for the horticultural industry was 'an urgent necessity' and that on it representation of employers and workers should be equal.

That year, MAFF submitted a plan for a voluntary Development Council for Horticulture, with the Union and NFU having equal representation. The NFU refused to co-operate, and while the Union pressed the Government to go ahead with the plan, it came to nothing.

At the Biennial at Margate in 1950, F. W. Moore, Sussex, moved a resolution calling for steps 'towards control and organisation of the vegetable and marketing system and implementation of the recommendations of the Lucas Report.' Another resolution sought a system of marketing on the lines suggested in the Lucas and Williams reports. G. C. Varndell, Sussex, supported, as the present system was chaotic, 'It seems wrong that tomatoes and other produce from our district, sent to Covent Garden, should come back to Worthing to within a few yards of where it was grown.' Both resolutions were carried unanimously.

The Union had a large number of members in the Worthing area, where the average holding was three acres of 'outside' ground with about a dozen green-houses. There was also a handful of large holdings each employing about 200 workers. The area produced a lot of tomatoes, strawberries and flowers.

One or two firms experimented with profit-sharing schemes. One firm paid a bonus on profits to every member of the staff, who was given a proper balance sheet every quarter. This firm had ten nurseries, and the workers elected a delegate from each to a committee which met every month to discuss ways of increasing productivity and to deal with complaints from the workers. Another small firm gave a bonus on actual production. If in one year 100 baskets of tomatoes were marketed, and the next year the number rose to 120, the bonus was increased.

Worthing members were, however, far from satisfied with the marketing of their products. They disliked growing stuff for which the grower got 4d, and they then saw it on sale in local shops at 8d or 1s. They also wanted a shorter working week and fuller consultation about their work.

At the Labour Conference at Margate in 1950, Alfred Dann stressed the need for immediate action to overhaul the marketing of horticultural produce. He said the nation could not afford the present system, and the difference between the price received by the producer and that paid by the consumer, was staggering. It was not uncommon to pay 10d for a lettuce, and on the same day to read that farmers were ploughing lettuces in because the markets were 'glutted'. He wanted municipal and public ownership of modern whole-sale markets. Under such authorities it would be possible to control prices. He called for a quick decision on the Lucas Report. The NEC agreed to accept 'with caution' the resolution calling for a complete overhaul of marketing. In fact, the Government moved in the opposite direction, and ended regulations controlling the sale of such products.

At the 1954 Biennial at Cheltenham, Tom Gasgoyne, Yorks, successfully moved a motion that the Government's return to 'free markets' was a 'retrograde step which can only be of benefit to auctioneers and middlemen.' It wanted produce to be marketed through publicly-controlled commodity commissions. Harold Collison said that the 'EC stood firmly in line with the motion.'

Middlemen's Profits

That individual members of the NUAW took a keen interest in middlemen's profits, was illustrated by a letter in the *Landworker* from H. Crofts, Worthing, who saw sprouts in a greengrocers at 9d per lb. 'I . . . found that they were grown in Bedfordshire and sent to Covent Garden where they made 9s a bushel. The wholesalers then sold them in Worthing at 12s 6d per bushel and they retailed at 21s per bushel.' Allowing for transport, commission, etc, it was 'reasonable to assume that the grower received about 7s a bushel. As they were retailed at 21s, it means that 14s had been taken by middlemen for

28lb of sprouts.' This showed farm profits were mostly going into the pockets of people 'who never see the land'.

Meanwhile, the Union had been pressing ahead with its efforts in the Lea Valley, celebrated for its countless acres of glasshouses. Being just north of the huge London market, these glasshouses were very prosperous. A system of bonus payments had developed over the years, but the amounts varied considerably, likewise the basic weekly rate. There was a great need for some degree of uniformity.

Nursery workers for the large CWS operation in the Lea Valley enjoyed a guaranteed bonus system and fairly good working conditions, which was more than could be said for many Lea Valley workers, who had to put up with poor sanitary or working facilities. Lea Valley was only a small part of the Co-operative movements interests in farming and horticulture: the CWS is the biggest farmer in Britain, and the Union had secured wages and conditions agreements with it over many years. Very often the Lea Valley led the way; an agreement for CWS workers in 1949 was: males £5 11s 8d, and females £4 4s for a 47–hour week, with overtime at time and a quarter and six statutory holidays with pay. Sick pay was for two weeks a year. Outside the Lea Valley, in rural areas, the rates for glasshouse workers were: males £5 4s and females £3 14s for a 47–hour week. The CWS agreed in 1956 to pay the adult male rate at 20, but rejected a claim for a 15s increase for its Lea Valley workers, which was referred to the National Conciliation Board for CWS Employees. The Board failed to agree, so the chair awarded an extra 11s 3d for men and 7s for women.

Over the years, the Union pressed for better overtime pay and other bonus payments for CWS employees and workers in the other horticultural establishments, including such things as heat money for cucumber workers, which in 1957 was 6s per week for the growing season of 26 weeks.

In 1961, when CWS nurseries attempted to increase the footage of glass worked by tomato growers from 400 to 450 feet, members resisted and the CWS backed down for the time being. In 1963, discussions began on a 5–day week for nursery workers for part of the year, but it was not possible to reach total agreement. However, a 5–day week for part of the year was introduced by agreement at Marden Nursery, Hertfordshire, in 1964.

In 1965, wages for tomato and cucumber growers continued upwards on the basis of AWB rates, but from then onwards CWS workers relied mainly on the AWB to determine pay increases.

Over the years, as London stretched further and further out, much land was taken for house building; many of the nurseries of the Lea Valley were sold off, and the remainder became shadows of their former selves, with very few workers, and Union membership in the area declined considerably.

In 1968, the CWS closed its remaining Lea Valley nurseries, and was left with three nurseries in County Durham, Shropshire and Herefordshire, although it kept its huge farm and horticultural establishment at Coldham in Cambridgeshire.

Marketing Council Set Up

In 1959, the Government had announced new measures to help the industry in the form of grant aids to producers, the establishment of a Horticultural Marketing Council, and the setting up of a Covent Garden Marketing Authority. Horticultural holdings large enough to take up the whole of a person's time could obtain one third of the cost of providing or improving plant and equipment, plus financial help for marketing co-operatives. These steps were recommended by the Runciman Committee,* after taking evidence from various sources, including that of the TUC.

The Union had submitted a memorandum to the TUC and the submissions made by it were very similar to those put forward by the Union, and followed the views expressed in the NUAW policy document, *Health and Wealth Under Our Feet* – including the need for a central authority to control markets.

Runciman's main recommendations were for a Horticultural Marketing Council and a London Markets Authority. However, the suggested functions and powers of this Council lay mainly with market intelligence and research, whereas the TUC had felt that the Council should be able to take positive action in marketing and distribution. Another point on which the Unions were critical was the inadequate representation for workers and the public on the Council.

When the Government set up a Horticultural Marketing Advisory Council in 1958, C. R. Allcorn, DO, who had wide experience of the Lea Valley glasshouse industry, was appointed to it. And by June 1959, this Council recommended that a permanent council should be established, financed by the Government for the first two years, and afterwards to be self-supporting by a levy on sales. The new Council received a £250,000 Government grant for two years, and were provided three out of its 28 seats. Said the NUAW, 'It seems that notice has been taken of the views on co-operation that the NUAW and the TUC put to the Runciman Committee, and also of the views of workers' representation and the ability of the Council to undertake trading on an experimental basis. So that though the new proposals leave a lot undone – as compared with the suggestions of the Union – they do form a useful basis for further improvement.'[2]

It was short lived; the Council was wound up in March 1963. The industry could not agree on how to finance it after Government funding ended. 'This brought to an end the only practical result (apart from the measures to re-site and re-organise Covent Garden Market) of the recommendations of the Runciman Committee.[3]

---

*　The Runciman Committee was set up in 1955 by the Conservative Government and reported in 1957.

Following the Council's demise, the NFU and other trade organisations set up a Joint Consultative Council to try to continue the work of the HMAC. The NUAW recognised that this could not be as effective as the HMAC, but wished to be associated with it, and nominated G. S. Hall, EC, to be its representative on it.

The Union set up a National Horticultural Advisory Committee in 1963 to review problems of members in horticulture. Both the 1963 and 1964 Annual Reports make no mention of this committee, but the 1965 Report lists 'the members of the HMAC appointed for the second two-year term, which met twice during the year' as: J. Carter, C. Sneath, F. W. Butler, T. Barker, C. Winter, C. Love, W. Jenkins, F. Hollingsworth, E. Nettle, W. Rouffignac, S. Pike, T. Furnell, with Reg Bottini as secretary.

At the 1964 Biennial, when the Agricultural Horticultural Act came into force, Edwin Gooch said that the Government had belatedly realised that Britain's agricultural policy could not be fashioned in isolation from production in the rest of the world. The result was the new Act to control the flow of food from other countries, and to establish grades of fruit and vegetables, something the Union recommended to the Runciman Committee eight years previously.

Later, in 1965, the Government announced its plan for the development of horticulture and agriculture. Its White Paper, *The Development of Agriculture*, echoed the Union in pointing out that owing to the inadequate size of many farms – they could not provide a decent living to the farmer 'at prices which the taxpayer and consumer could afford' – the Government was to offer help to enlarge farms where practical, to expand co-operative enterprises in order to secure bigger scale production; and to resettle or retire farmers (with grants) who wanted to leave the industry. The aim was to secure the voluntary amalgamation of smaller farms – these were often of a 'horticultural' nature – to produce a 'commercial' unit capable of giving full-time occupation to a farmer employing one worker, or family helper. Grants of 50% were proposed on all operations essential to amalgamation.

This did not, however, in any way face up to the Union's desire to see more farm land in public ownership; it simply led to bigger and more profitable farms in private hands. The *Landworker* said, 'The Union welcomes the Government's proposals . . . For years we have been advocating that measures should be taken to make grants to farmers wishing to leave the industry, in principle, follows almost precisely the recommendations that were made in *Farming for the Future*.'

When the Apple and Pear Development Council was established in 1966, appointed members included Stan Hall, EC, and Cliff Hardy, DO, the latter being replaced by Chris Morris in 1970.

In 1968, Reg Bottini was appointed to the Central Council for Agricultural and Horticultural Co-operation established the year before; it was intended to help agricultural co-operatives.

Concern over EEC

In 1972, the National Horticultural Advisory Committee was concerned at the effect of entry into the EEC on horticulture. That there would be problems was clear and may be the reason why at the end of the year, the new Minister of Agriculture, Joseph Godber, wound it up.

He probably did not want it on his back, as glasshouse growers were having increasing difficulty in meeting competition from the EEC – at the height of the tomato season, it was often impossible to buy British tomatoes in many parts of London, only tasteless Dutch ones – and in 1975 the NHAC drew attention to the need to restore Government subsidies for oil heating in glasshouses to meet this EEC competition. Their pleas fell mainly on deaf ears, and many English growers were forced to curtail their operations, or to close down. This led to a considerable drop in Union membership in this sector as the labour force fell further.

In 1976, the NHAC considered the changing needs of members, and drafted a new constitution and committee structure, which it hoped would more fully represent modern commercial horticulture. The NHAC was reconstituted, and nominations for membership sought for the different sections, ranging from glasshouse crops to landscape gardening.

After the merger, the NHAC, now the Horticultural Workers' Advisory Committee, continued its campaign against subsidised Dutch produce which was further threatening British jobs. 'Negotiations for horticultural workers continued throughout 1983 at local level despite claims from the employers that the industry was in dire straits.'[4]

In 1984, there was a big improvement in horticulture, but it was not felt by the remaining workers in it. They were still subject to AWB rates, and that year's award 'was seen as wholly unsatisfactory.'

The horticultural industry continued on the up grade in the mid-eighties, but the employers were like the farmers – hostile to pay increases – and their workers continued to be denied an adequate and just wage.

*   *   *

From the mid-sixties, the Union had been recruiting on a large scale in the fast developing mushroom sector, especially in East Anglia. By 1966-67, it had negotiating rights[5] with ten companies involved in mushroom production. Wages in most mushroom factories appear to be that the smaller number of men got slightly above AWB rates, while the women got the AWB minimum.

One major producer, Country Kitchen Foods (CKF), recognised the Union in 1971 and an agreement was signed for workers at its three main factories: Churchill, Somerset; Buxton, Derbyshire; and Ipswich, Suffolk. This gave men from £17.50 to £28 per week, against the AWB minimum of £16.20. Women were on piece-work and many only part time. The Annual Report makes no reference to piece rates for part-timers, but in 1973 negotiations led to an increase in time rates in line with AWB increases, and a comprehensive wages structure came into operation. This gave men: (a) £19.50–£21; (b) £21.50–£23; (c) £23–£27; (d) £24.50–£29; and (e) £28 plus. The AWB male ordinary rate was £21.80; women's rates ranged from £15.60 to £21 plus, against an AWB basic of £17.44.

There had been a gradual move towards equal pay and, from January 1977, basic rates for both men and women were in line with the AWB rate of £39, and parity with AWB rates was maintained in 1978. A plussage system enabled workers to get slightly above AWB rates.

Other mushroom growers with whom the NUAAW had agreements in the sixties and seventies included: Valley Farm Mushrooms, Hoxne, Norfolk; East Suffolk Mushrooms, Woodbridge; Blue Ribbon Mushroom Farmers, Cromer (later amalgamated with Middlebrooks); Broadland Mushroom, Marham, Norfolk; Catfield Mushrooms, Norfolk; A. G. Linfield, Sussex; and Darlington Mushrooms, Surrey.

In 1979, Middlebrooks, Cromer, announced that it was to close with the loss of 250 jobs. This brought out the fighting spirit of NUAAW members, who held big demonstrations against the closure, and roused the people of this small resort and surrounding villages in support. Shop stewards Dave Buttle and Alan Lundie had a willing team, collecting 2,000 signatures on a protest petition. They wanted to keep the factory going either by starting their own co-op, or finding a buyer willing to operate the plant. They received enthusiastic support from their local EC member, Wilf Page. They met MPs and Ministers, but their efforts were to no avail and it finally closed. Many of the 250 workers remained unemployed for a long time.

Vegetable Packers Organised

Another post-war development was the setting up of firms packing vegetables and other produce. By the early eighties, this had grown to a sizeable sector, packing not only British produce, but walnuts from China, produce from North and South America, and the EEC. Many people working in these plants were women, some were in the Union, but many were not.

In 1966, talks were held to secure negotiating rights with the following companies who were pre-packing vegetables, bulbs and plants: Geest Industries, Spalding; Marshall Bros., Boston and H.C.C. Tinsley and Sons, Holbeach. Marshall Bros. signed an agreement that wages would be determined by the AWB, and recognised the Union. In 1967, Geest agreed to basic rates for men aged 20 and over, £12 10s 3d for a 42–hour week; and for women aged 18 and over, £7 14s 0d for 40 hours. Hard on the heels of that agreement, came one with Tinsley & Sons, making their basic rates those of the AWB.

Throughout the late 1960s, membership and Union activities in the packing side had continued to expand '. . . in various aspects of commercial horticulture and over a range of ancillary industries.'[6]

Union activities now covered vegetable packing, bulb and plants, fruit packing, seeds, specialist rose growing, egg packing, and even workers at Paignton Zoo in South Devon. A range of agreements and pay rates was reached, the Union negotiating individually with companies. Often the basic wages were set at the AWB minimum, but some were lower, with 'attendance bonuses' and plus rates negotiated locally.

By 1971, the Union had negotiated wages and conditions with the following companies involved in vegetable packing or other ancillary activities: East Kent Packers, Faversham; Norfolk Fruit Growers, Hoveton; Waveney Apple Growers, S Norfolk; Morse Roses, Norfolk; Marshall Bros, Lincolnshire; H.C.C. Tinsley and Sons, Lincolnshire; Bees, Cheshire; Geest, Lincolnshire; Devon Growers, Cullompton; Settle Creamery, Lancashire; Goodenough's, Berkshire; Northern Dairies, E Yorkshire; and Paignton Zoo.

The rates at Bees Seeds were lower in 1969 than the AWB minimum. It was £11 18s 6d for 20-year-old men, and £8 2s 6d for 20-year-old women, against £12 8s and £9 6s AWB rates respectively. In 1970, the Bees men did catch up with the £13 3s AWB rate, but the women got £8 19s as against the £9 17s 6d women's rate.

Dissatisfaction with wages at Bees in 1973 resulted in two short stoppages of work, and lengthy negotiations. The wages of warehouse operatives (over 20) were raised to £22; machinery operatives and packers went up to £15.44 plus £2 after 12 months, and section leaders got £19.50. In addition, the company provided free bus facilities, 'representing a saving of 60p per week'. These rates compared with the AWB minimum of £19.50 for men and £15.60 for women.

By 1976, the Union involvement in ancillary industries ranged from meat packing in Cambridgeshire to peat extrication in Cumbria. By 1977 the meat packing included the Halal Meat Company of Worcestershire, which packed for Muslims.

After the merger with the TGWU, the involvement with packaging and allied industries continued, but slimmer annual reports give few details as to the wages won for these workers. The HWAC was reconvened for the first time in Spring 1984, and much work lay ahead of it.

REFERENCES

1. G. D. H. Cole, *Post-War Conditions of Britain*, Routledge & Kegan Paul, 1956.
2. *Landworker*, December 1959.
3. Annual Report, 1963.
4. Annual Report, 1983.
5. Annual Report, 1966.
6. Annual Report, 1971.

20

New Sphere to Organise

What is food to one may may be fierce poison to others.
Lucretius, *De Rerum Natura*

The Coming of the Factory Chicken

As the pattern of agriculture changed, new areas opened up for the Union which offered an opportunity to organise the workforce. One of the biggest, and most successful from the Union's point of view, was the rapid development in the late fifties and sixties of intensive poultry production – the introduction of large units raising millions of birds on 'battery' systems, both for eggs and meat production.

Some of the Union's most militant industrial action in the post-war period ensued, leading to better pay, conditions and hygiene for the workforce, if not better conditions for the birds being processed.

In the run up to the late sixties, British eating habits changed. Much farm produce, backed by heavy advertising, in conjunction with the supermarkets which were spreading throughout the country, was prepacked. This prepacking had a revolutionary effect on poultry production. For some time since the end of the Second World War, chicken meat was still a luxury dish for the urban wage-earner, often only eaten on special festive occasions. By the early sixties, for the average town family, the weekly chicken had become commonplace. A three or four pound bird reached the modern kitchen neatly prepacked in cellophane, ready for the oven.

So, to meet the huge demand for broiler fowls, a big new industry grew up. Some thousands of workers, mostly women, found new employment, and joined the Union.

How it was done was explained to me in 1990 by Terry Hammond, TGWU DO at Newcastle upon Tyne, who was appointed NUAW Durham and Northumberland DO in August 1967. He immediately became involved with poultry processing at Buxteds Chicken Factory in Hartlepool, which opened in October that year. Terry told me, 'Recruiting Officer Eddie Collinson and I recruited at the Labour Exchange even before the factory opened. It grew over the years, and when it closed we lost 350 members.'

Next they turned their attention to the Glenrothes factory. 'Eddie and I travelled to the new Eastwoods factory the day it opened. There were about 100 employees to start and practically all joined the Union.' He then discovered that Eastwoods had a large farming enterprise nearby which had opened 18 months earlier. As was the Eastwoods' practice, in addition to growing grass for drying, for use in their feed mill, they were into cereals and livestock, and had a huge egg-producing unit, as well as a hatchery and breeding farms. Said Terry, 'I set about organising the labour force on this side also; I think that eventually we had about 1,100 members at Eastwoods in Fife.

'The General Manager at Eastwoods in Fife, Reg Chapman, suggested to D. B. Marshalls that they might like to do business with us and contact was made. In late 1971, a team of us moved in – Eddie Collinson, by then head of the Organising Department, Tom Carlile, his deputy, Graham Humphreys, DO for Lancashire, Davey Scotland, our senior shop steward at Eastwoods and myself. In four days we recruited about 1,000 new members and eventually we probably had around 2,000 members at Marshalls at their factories at Newbridge, Coupar Agnus, Cambuslang and Coatbridge (a few years later), and at their hatcheries, breeder, grower and broiler farms, plus the farm side and feed mill.

'Although the NUAW was not the relevant Union for Scottish agriculture, we had had a few members over the border for many years, but it was the rapid growth of the poultry-processing industry which gave us the opportunity to develop north of the border.'

One firm with which the Union became closely associated was the Buxted Chicken Company Ltd, with headquarters in Sussex; it controlled hatcheries and factories in various parts of Britain. On full capacity the company could by 1963 supply some 600,000 chickens a week. Their Horstead Keynes, Sussex, hatchery, was said to be the largest in Europe, with one million eggs incubating at any one time. These eggs were collected from 70 farms in Southern England. Hatching took 21 days – the same as a dozen eggs under one hen. Setting machines held some 90,000 eggs. After 18 days the eggs were placed in special hatchers and three days later the chicks were ready for despatch. The birds had a carefully controlled nine-week growing period and were then delivered to one of the firm's five factories to be processed.

There was a number of other firms besides Buxteds, many modest in size, but some other big ones too, such as J. B. Eastwood in Nottinghamshire. Some firms strongly resisted unionisation, and did not change their attitude till strike action was threatened by the often militant women workers. Others, like Buxteds, quickly adapted to having Union members in their workforce, and installed a new canteen and other up-to-date facilities for their Dalton, Yorkshire, factory. This was progress in any language.

Development of the 'broiler' industry, as it became known, had really taken off by 1960, and Eastwoods raised broilers in 12 or 13 weeks and then killed, plucked, dressed and packed them in the factory on their Nottinghamshire farm. By 1961, the factory was dealing with an average of 23,000 to 25,000 birds per day. It was staffed solely by women, with one male foreman; nearly all were in the Union.

For 18 months the Union tried to get an agreement with the company on wages and conditions. At first, Eastwoods declined, but eventually accepted the 'principle' of recognition. However, nothing happened, and members insisted on recognition. In March 1961, strike notices were handed in on behalf of over 100 women. Reg Bottini and C. Barker, DO, went to the company's offices on 10 March and delivered a formal one week's notice of withdrawing labour, making it clear that they were available for further discussions in an effort to avert a stoppage. On the day the strike notice was due to expire, the firm recognised the Union and the strike was cancelled. This was the first of many victories in the broiler industry, secured without a strike, thanks to the enthusiastic loyalty to the Union shown by the women, and 100% membership.

An increase in the basic hourly rate of 1d and payment of the adult rate to all girls at 18 instead of 21 was secured. This meant for girls 18, 19 and 20, a 3d an hour increase. The new basic rates began at 1s 10½d an hour at 15, rising to 3s 2d at 18. The standard working week was reduced from 44 to 42 hours, to be worked in five days. Twelve days annual holiday was also won, plus six public holidays.

Following this big breakthrough, there was a rapid increase in Union membership at the Yorkshire Chicken Packers Ltd. Likewise, the majority of workers at the broiler factory of Pollastra Packers Ltd, Eye, Suffolk, joined the Union, and at the small broiler factory of Country Stile Ltd in Yorkshire a majority of workers became members, and the Union was recognised. Yorkshire Chicken Packers agreed to substantial improvements in wages and conditions.

It was not until 1963 that recognition finally came at Pollastra Packers, Suffolk, and then only when strike notices were handed in on behalf of 60 members after 21 months' effort to secure recognition. There had been several meetings with the management, but no progress had been made. Finally, in November 1963, the chairman wrote to the Union, saying that 'The Board decided not to grant your Union or any Union the "Recognition" of negotiating rights that you desired.'

The Union gave one week's strike notice on Friday evening, 30 November, and four days later the Company chairman addressed the employees in the canteen. He stressed the 'happy family' aspect of the firm and implied that if the Company were forced to recognise the Union it would be shut down completely. On Thursday, 6 December, the chairman sponsored a 'secret ballot' in which the workers were asked, 'Are you in favour of striking in support of the recognition of the Union?' No Union officer was invited to give the workers any explanation as to why the EC had called for strike action. Not surprisingly the 'guidance' given by the chairman produced an overwhelming vote against strike action. Members were invited to a Union branch meeting on the Friday. It was well attended, and a secret ballot showed a clear majority in support of the original strike decision.

On Saturday 8 December, the chairman made the first approach, suggesting that the Company and the Union should jointly conduct a secret ballot. On Monday, the chairman and John Stewart, DO, each addressed the workers. Then came the ballot, with a clear majority in favour of Union recognition. The Company conceded, and negotiations began on wages and conditions.

At the time, the Union was also seeking negotiating rights with Bernard Matthews at Great Witchingham, Norfolk, which employed many members. Its chairman, Bernard Matthews, had recently joined the board of Pollastra Packers. Talks with Pollastra went speedily ahead, resulting in pay increases, and a sickness pay scheme.

Doctor Checks a Chicken Factory

Jack Brocklebank, North Yorkshire DO, told me in 1988, 'I never had a strike other than lightening strikes in chicken factories. We had some large factories and we got them all in the Union, two-thirds were women and we were making women shop stewards who had never seen a Union card before. We had opposition from the bosses, but persevered. One boss said "Jack, this is the best thing we've done here to bring the Union into our factory, you've removed all the irritants that caused a lot of small disputes, life is much easier now." '

But it wasn't always like that in Yorkshire. In 1969 there was an outbreak of skin complaints among employees of Eastwoods at Stokesley, so Jack visited it, accompanied by Jim Watts and Dr. Robert Murray, the TUC's medical adviser. They met E. Braithwaite, a shop steward, and several women workers.

Dr. Murray took a great interest in the whole process, noting that Stokesley handled 30,000 birds daily. On arrival, the birds were lifted out of their cages by a team of girls called 'hangers on', who suspended them by the legs from metal holders in a continuous conveyor. He noted, 'It is a tricky job and very smelly and dusty from the fluttering of wings and the smell of chicken manure. In addition, there is a risk of minor injury from beaks and claws.'

The chickens went on the conveyor line past an electric stunner and then to a rapid series of operations in which the throat is cut, the bird necked, defeathered, cropped, vented and eviscerated. The giblets are separated from the offal and the bird goes into a washing tank in which it is cooled. Next it is weighed, graded and priced, wrapped, blast frozen at 40°, packed into cartons and put into cold storage.

Dr. Murray continued, 'it was considered inadvisable . . . to reveal my profession so the investigation had to consist of a very perfunctory interrogation and examination of the hands of a few girls in the canteen during a break.' He found 'marked evidence of an infective skin condition, though in most cases these were in the late stages of healing.' It was difficult to get an accurate estimate of the total number of girls affected, but 57 was the figure quoted by Jack Brocklebank. It was accepted that the 'epidemic' was on the decline, presumably because a new method of treating skin punctures and abrasions. A nurse had been employed for this treatment. 'Nevertheless, the appearance of the hands was striking. They were abnormally calloused in the palm, especially at the roots of the fingers, and one girl showed a slight generalised contracture of the hand. There were four cases of paronychia, an abnormal number to see in a casual look at a few hands, and two older women had recently had to have their wedding rings removed, leaving a circular, indented, livid, infected depression. The purplish colour of the lesions was striking and did not appear to be due entirely to cold.'

Dr. Murray believed that there was 'some fairly specific type of infection' from either pecks or scratches or from contaminated water.' Rubber gloves were later provided.

Five girls, without any questions on Dr. Murray's part – which he was careful to avoid – volunteered that they suffered badly from a chest condition. They were all 'hangers on' and attributed their condition to the dusty nature of the job.

At the time there had not been much investigation into health problems of chicken workers, although a medical inspector in the North East had investigated skin infection which appeared widespread. Dr. Murray wondered whether this was related to antibiotic resistant organisms in feeding stuffs containing antibiotics, and thought it ought to be investigated bacteriologically. He commented, 'Whatever might be our personal feelings about the production of battery chickens, no one could pretend that the process is an elevating one. Mr Watts spoke of a "brutalising" influence on the girls, and while those I spoke to seemed to be reasonable types, there was a toughness and insensitivity which appeared to affect those on the first half of the production line more than the second . . . perhaps the most striking impression of the visit was the sight of a nipper of 15 years and 4ft 6ins whose job consisted in standing and snipping the excess skin from the necks of carcasses as they came past him at the rate of one or two per second. A dim occupation prospect!'

Everyone took seriously Dr. Murray's report, investigations followed, and brine was found to be causing much of the trouble. Steps were taken to avoid the processors coming into contact with so much brine, and the earlier skin conditions lessened.

Other firms which recognised the Union were Golden Produce Ltd, Lymington, Hampshire, and Waveney Valley Packers, Diss, Norfolk. But it was the threat of strike action by 21 women at Kenton Chicken Packing Station, Debenham, Suffolk, which brought recognition there. The dispute followed the dismissal of three workers for failing to work overtime. Members complained that the employer paid plain time-rates for overtime. The firm refused to discuss the matter, and said they would dismiss Union members in dispute that evening. The Union promptly made the strike official. Often all

24 women involved appeared on the picket line. In the third week discussions led to recognition and no one was victimised. The basic rate for women was increased.

Women played a very big part in getting the Union firmly established in the broiler industry, and it was Sister L. Spencer, secretary of Eastwood Broiler branch, in the early sixties, who was the first-ever woman to win the Union's plaque for enlisting 100 members.

Recognition at Bernard Matthews

Further important advances came in 1964. Bernard Matthews recognised the Union and signed an agreement on wages and conditions. After negotiations lasting nearly two years, the agreement, effective from 12 October 1964, provided basic rates for males of 20 and over at £10 a week, falling to £4 16s for boys starting at 15. Girls got 3s 6d an hour at 18, falling to 2s 3d for those of 15. Standard weekly hours were 45 for males and 42½ hours for females.

In December that year, further agreements led to increases for many hundreds of workers at three poultry packers. At Eastwoods, wages went up by 12s to £11 19s 8d for men of 20, with proportionate increases for younger men. Women's rates went up by 9s to £8 1s 6d at 18, with similar increases for younger women. At Bernard Matthews, there was an increase of 12s for men of 20, making a wage of £10 12s, with proportionate increases for younger men, and the female rate was increased by 2½d an hour, making 3s 10½d at 18 with proportionate increases for younger women. At Waveney Valley Packers, men of 20 got 4s 7d an hour, women of the same age 3s 7d, and in addition won a 7s 6d attendance bonus.

In November 1965, notice of strike action was served on J. P. Woods Ltd, of Craven Arms, Shropshire, following the firm's refusal to recognise the Union. A week later the company did so. In 1966, pay increases were secured, which produced a 40-hour week, wages of £11 12s for adult males and £8 0s 9d for adult women.

At another chicken packing factory, Lloyd Maunders, Tiverton Junction, Devon, a substantial number of workers joined the Union. It was recognised in 1966, and improved pay followed, giving a top rate of £12 12s for a 44-hour week for men of 20. Women had increases of 5d to 4d an hour.

In 1968, Eastwoods offered the Union facilities to recruit at their new plant at Glenrothes, Scotland, employing 600 people. The Union felt that if it did not undertake the Glenrothes organisation, the TGWU might step in, and having secured negotiating rights there, it could then spread them to chicken plants in England and Wales, where the NUAAW held sway. There was an agreement between the TGWU and the NUAAW on agriculture in Scotland generally, and the NUAAW did not organise there. When Eastwoods opened in Wales, the TGWU had argued their right to organise; but had set out to displace the NUAAW in the processing field, and had succeeded. So the

Union decided to organise at Glenrothes and inform the TGWU. This was done, successfully.

By 1968, there was 130 poultry stations listed by the National Association of Poultry Packers; most were small, but at 24 larger plants the NUAAW had agreements. 'We deliberately concentrated on organising the larger packing stations',[1] thus taking a leaf out of the larger union's books.

At the end of 1967, the Union had 1,629 members in the 24 stations mentioned, but only about 50% of the workers were organised in the factories where the Union had agreements; in some the figure was as low as 25%. The TGWU, GMWU and USDAW had sole negotiating rights in a few establishments.

First Poultry Workers' Conference

The first representative conference of members in poultry packing was held in Harrogate on 28 July 1968. Representatives from 12 of the northern factories covered by agreements with the Union were present and were, of course, mostly women. Consideration was given to problems of organisation, the collection of subs and the varying standards of management. The General Secretary emphasised the importance the EC attached to the Union's poultry packing membership.

'A Good Settlement' was a headline in the *Landworker* in January 1969. It referred to an increase of £1 a week for men and 15s for women after talks with Bernard Matthews at Great Witchingham. It meant that men of 20 would get £12 16s 7d and women at 18, £9 9s 5d.

The poultry packing industry continued to grow during the sixties, and when *The Changing Structure of Agriculture* (HMSO) was published in 1970, it noted that the most dramatic change had occurred among poultry enterprises. In England and Wales, the average size of broiler enterprises increased by 22% a year between 1960–68 (by 36% between 1960–63), and the average laying flock by 12% a year from 1965–69.

With poultry becoming an increasingly important sector of the national food industry, the National Diploma Board for Poultry said in 1973 that the industry faced an acute manpower shortage. This was not surprising, considering the poor pay and obnoxious conditions in many factories.

The value of poultry output was running at £150 million per annum, and coupled with eggs, accounted for 13% of the gross output of British agriculture. In 1971–72, Ross Poultry and Eastwoods together sold 99 million birds, around 30% of the market. Midland Poultry Holdings (J. P. Woods) came sixth in the league table and, with seven other companies, including the Sun Valley parent, Union International Company, and D. B. Marshall (Newbridge), contributed to a 40% share of sales. In all these enterprises the Union had secured agreements.

But the expected labour shortage did not fully materialise, for by the mid-seventies some of the smaller packers were experiencing financial problems, although the doyens of the trade, Eastwoods kept striding ahead. In 1974 they could report sales up from £85.25 million to £106.18 million, and by then were employing 5,500 workers throughout Britain.

Some big companies did not take kindly to the wage increases. The annual meeting of Ross Poultry (part of Imperial) was reported in the *Guardian* in 1975 thus: 'Sir John Partridge, retiring chairman of the Imperial Group (salary £30,000 a year), had some harsh words about rampaging wage inflation . . . The day of serious reckoning was at hand, he said, if output didn't keep pace with pay. Imperial, of course, had done its bit "by belt-tightening wherever practicable".' The prudent economies did not apparently extend to the salaries of executives, 40 of whom were paid between £10,000 and £12,500 a year. Six directors passed the £25,000 mark. One could guess where the economies were made.

In 1978, Imperial made a takeover bid for Eastwoods, and, by then, 4,000 of Eastwoods 5,000 employees were Union members. Shop stewards met and 'accepted' the merger provided no redundancies resulted. The NUAAW believed that the advantages of an enlarged group, for efficiency and future employment prospects, outweighed theoretical reduction in competition and consumer choice. Imperial finally bought Eastwoods for £38 million.

Sir John Pile, chairman, Imperial, launched a verbal assault on trade unions in his 1979 annual report. He said, 'It is apparent that there are wreckers who have demonstrated their power and who are at work in our country in the hope of one day completely changing our democratic society into a tyranny. It is tragic that successive governments have, by enacting ill-considered legislation given opportunities to such people and led us to the point of industrial anarchy.'

Replying to the chairman of the biggest single employer of NUAAW members, Jack Boddy said it was a 'destructive and ill-informed attack.' Adding, 'The Imperial group, because of its ownership of Eastwoods and Ross/Buxted, now employs 6,000 NUAAW members. I am therefore, very disturbed that its chairman seems to have little understanding of the purpose of trade unions and – even more sinister – of employment legislation . . . This Union spent 70 years fighting to ensure some security and some dignity for the workers it represents. We are not going to see that taken from us at the behest of one powerful industrialist who seems, if his recent statement is anything to go by, to want to reduce them to nineteenth-century conditions or near feudalism. I shall therefore be happy to meet him . . . to explain the real nature and purpose of trade unions and employment legislation . . . it is important to 6,000 of my members in poultry that their management should not be so resentful, blinkered and bitter.'

No such meeting ever took place, and it was not the workforce that was to bring trouble to the chicken factories, but other factors, including membership of the EEC, and in the eighties, the salmonella poisoning scare.

Sir Richard Body, the outspoken Tory MP for Holland with Boston, revealed in 1988, at the time of the salmonella scare, that measures designed to clean up the plants were thwarted by MAFF on cost grounds in the seventies. 'These included rejecting at least 90% of the poultry sent for processing because they were salmonella infected.' He declared, 'Hundreds of people in my constituency work in egg and poultry businesses which do not allow trade unions. I am particularly worried about their health.'[2]

The more unpleasant side of working in poultry factories was very much the concern of the Union which, by 1980, had nearly half its members working in factories of one sort or another, poultry plants predominating.

Herbert Wilson, Attleborough branch (Buxted Poultry), found many workers were soured by factory work, and said in the *Landworker*, 'The first factory I worked in had the luxury of windows: only recently did I realise, it was a luxury. There is a short period near Christmas, when daylight does not enter the life of a factory worker. The worker arrives in the dark, leaves in the dark and has artificial light all day. Annie Besant, the factory reformer at the beginning of the century, would have found the modern factory where I was employed had individual machines and was repetitive enough. But when there is a belt, the need to get variety into the work is not always appreciated by the worker. You are droned by the nature of the work into acceptance . . . the factories I have worked in have been slow to modernise. Yet low productivity is blamed on the worker. Modernisation is not wrong, only the way it is implemented.' He referred to the frustration and pride that produced more unofficial disputes than any spoken reasons, with the management treating the workers as children.

Confirmation of Herbert's criticisms rapidly came from Twydale Turkeys in Yorkshire. Rules forbade going to the toilet other than at tea breaks, and special permission had to be obtained from departmental managers.

Later, in 1980, the Ross group shut down all its poultry and egg production in Scotland, making 300 NUAAW members jobless. When Imperial took control of Ross the previous year, they promised there would be no closures. They now blamed EEC competition for the decision to close some of their new acquisitions.

These closures were part of a crisis developing in the UK egg and poultry industry, affecting jobs, sales and profits. Social trends had become unhelpful, too. Domestic cake baking had declined, and the cooked breakfast the exception rather than the rule. The result was a decline in domestic egg consumption. But people were eating more poultry instead of expensive red meat. Poultry consumption prior to 1980 had been increasing 3% annually, but the industry was geared up to increase output by more than 3% a year, and as a result the UK was marginally more than self-sufficient, and stocks were accumulating in cold stores. The quantity held in public stores increased from 11,000 tonnes in 1975 to 30,000 in 1979.[3] By 1980, eight million chickens and two to three million turkeys were in store.

If the increasing problem of cheap imports from France or Holland were added to British production, the net effect was to reduce the UK workforce and throw hundreds of NUAAW members out of work. It was ironic that poultry imports rose from 8,500 tonnes in 1975 to 32,000 in 1979, almost exactly the same amount as had to be dumped into cold stores.

The Union did all it could to prevent closures, or at least obtain the maximum financial compensation. Every effort was made to find a buyer for the Buxted Glenrothes factory; for example, representations were made to local MPs and to Ministers, and meetings held to try to save over 300 jobs. Lengthy negotiations, with the companies concerned, secured severance pay above the State redundancy payment scheme.

Attempt to Set Up Co-operative

Jim and Isobel Hendrie were among the displaced workers who joined over two million other people on the dole. They worked at Buxted Chicken (Attleborough) which closed in November 1980. The sacked workers tried to set up a co-operative to run the plant, but DHSS officials ruled that redundant employees could not claim unemployment pay until they had spent their redundancy money. This meant that when they had paid off their debts they would have nothing to live on, let alone any spare cash to help set up the co-operative.

Keeping members from destitution was a continual worry. 'We took one member to the DHSS because he had no money – not a penny. They told us it would take 14 days to assess whether he was in urgent need,' said Jim Hendrie.

As for Buxteds, they announced that they would not allow the factory to be used for chicken production by anyone else, and started moving the equipment out as fast as possible.

The personal tragedy following the closure was spelt out by Jim. 'Vast numbers of Buxted employees were school-leavers, handicapped, widows and one-parent families. It was impossible for them to get the required number of National Insurance stamps to entitle them to unemployment benefit. Their only redress was supplementary benefit, which had been denied them. I am daily receiving calls of distress about payments that cannot be made for electricity, fuel, rent, children's clothes and so on . . .'

In the early seventies, Jim and Isobel moved from London to the pleasant little Norfolk town of Attleborough to escape the rat-race. Although Jim had a good job as an engineer, with three children to bring up they found the going tough. So Isobel decided to get a job. She had previously worked as a secretary, but there was no job like that in Attleborough, only vacancies at Eastwoods, so she started as a packer.

Although she had been around a bit, Isobel had never worked in a factory before. It was a shock. 'You can't get much lower than a chicken factory,' she said, when I interviewed her in 1988. 'It's the pits. Within a few weeks your hands begin to swell, but you have to keep going, with the conveyor belt moving so fast. And the smell, it was unbelievable.'

Isobel, a neat, rosy-cheeked woman with greying hair, told me she was glad she wasn't on the killing line, but was involved in the gutting. 'I often felt like giving up. I don't know how I stuck it, but I just had to.'

It was totally unlike the life she was used to. Her father, a Scot from Edinburgh, was a paper maker. His job took him round the world, and at times Isobel lived with her parents in Peru and Norway, later in Bolton, Cardiff and Kent. Despite all this travelling, she matriculated on leaving school. It was in Kent, when she was 23, that she met Jim, a Londoner, and she was not as she put it 'in any way union minded'.

Isobel didn't join the Union immediately she started at Eastwoods. She explained, 'The fact that people had to work there in such conditions, how fast and hard they had to work, seemed to me like slavery for a pittance, and this prompted me to join.' Some of the young girls had to work so quickly putting rubber bands on the chickens, that they got tenosynovitis, which meant that their fingers remained bent and locked, almost claw-like. Their arms were also affected. 'One arm would get thinner than the other. I don't think they ever recovered if they had been on an eviscerating line a long time – arthritis sets in. Their hands are under spraying water for cleaning. Water everywhere.'

Gradually, Isobel became active in the Union, and finished up as branch secretary and shop steward. She began recruiting. The management had no objection to the 250 workers, mostly women, joining, and they appeared to prefer the NUAAW to a more militant union, but there was a problem. Application forms were not being filled in properly, applicants details were often sparse; sometimes the only writing on the form was the applicant's signature.

'I didn't realise till then that many of the workers couldn't read or write. It was the personnel officer who told me. I felt very saddened by this, and this is why I decided to fight all the harder for these women.'

The personnel officer helped complete the application forms, and when things got rough, this ill-educated workforce was ardent in its support of Isobel. 'They were the most loyal group of women I've ever come across,' she said. 'It was a shame that the standard of education dished out by the Tory-controlled County Council was so terrible.'

The personnel officer continued to be helpful, and when a closed shop was established, did a lot behind the scenes to try to get agreements without the women having to strike. 'When I joined Eastwoods, the conditions were really bad,' said Isobel, 'but by the time the factory closed in 1980 conditions had changed. Most of the workers regretted they had to go; it had become almost home from home for most of them.'

'What sort of changes,' I asked. 'They used to wear terrible white aprons which sort of wrapped round you like a sack. They got covered in blood and muck, but eventually we had yellow check overalls which made the whole place look brighter. The supervisors mellowed, too; it was not so much "You must do this", it was more "Will you" or "Can you". We got a staff shop, and the personnel officer and I went to wholesalers and bought whatever the workers wanted, and they got stuff a lot cheaper. There was a totally different atmosphere. People would be laughing at work, something which never happened when I first went there – everybody looked grim.'

Health and safety practices improved as they got their own safety representative, and the Attleborough Public Health Officer was a great help. 'He started pressurising the firm to improve things, and it became a safer, as well as happier workplace. When we had an accident, we always managed to get some compensation. It helped show the management that they had to care.'

Jim, who had previously worked at Jeyes in Thetford, had moved to the chicken factory as maintenance supervisor, and had become the engineers' shop steward.

Isobel went on a TUC shop stewards' course. 'They're very good,' she said. 'I came back much wiser. We were always balloting people in the factory to see what they wanted. They were never keen on strikes because they couldn't afford to lose the money. Unfortunately, many workers seemed to think the Union could do everything for them and didn't realise that they had to do a lot of things for themselves, with the help of Union officials. Younger members, who could read and write, became more independent and did do things for themselves; they could think for themselves, too.'

Most of the workers were bussed in from surrounding villages, leaving home at 6 am and returning at 6 pm. Sometimes the buses in Winter were late arriving, and the Union arranged for the workers to have tea from the canteen if they were more than half an hour late. 'They were greeted with a cup of warm tea, which was much appreciated after standing about in the biting wind in some villages,' said Isobel.

Although the idea of forming a workers' co-op was no hare-brained scheme, but carefully planned and costed, Isobel would be among the first to admit, with hindsight, that it was probably a non-starter. 'Perhaps we were a bit unrealistic and it would never have worked, but we tried,' she said. 'All the time we seemed to be getting nearly there, and the co-op would be formed, but we never quite made it. You wondered why. It may be silly, but it made me think that these big chicken firms have got a lot of pull; they didn't want further competition, but we'll never know. We approached banks. They were willing to help with loans, but said the workers must be thoroughly committed by putting money in. They didn't understand that these women hadn't any money, only their skill to offer.'

They approached the Co-operative Development Agency in London, which sent them leaflets. 'That was all the help we got from them, it was absolutely useless, but we got an awful lot of help from John McGregor, Tory MP for South Norfolk.*

---

* Later to become Minister of Agriculture.

At the time of the proposed co-op, the bottom had dropped out of the frozen chicken market, and it was decided that the co-op should produce fresh poultry on a smaller and more efficient scale. Buxteds would not let the factory to them as it would defeat their main objective in closing it, which was to reduce the number of birds on the market and so keep the price up. South Norfolk District Council offered to lease them an empty factory at Wymondham. A company, Breckland Poultry Ltd, was formally set up by six or seven of the workers, each with a £1 share, but it didn't stop there for Isobel and Jim. They offered to mortgage their home to raise more capital. They carried out extensive market research and two places were won at Manchester Business School. Isobel and another girl attended, and the head of marketing told them their fresh chickens plans had the best chance of succeeding. They were also going to make soups, pies, sell the feathers to pillow makers and the blood to fertiliser firms. They even arrived at a price for birds, 46p per lb, with giblets. And in documents they drew up it was agreed that Mrs. Hendrie, who was going to be secretary and book-keeper, 'can work in any part of the factory where required to make up any shortages of staff.'

The factory was then being run by Banham Poultry Products, but none of the former workers had been taken on by the new owners. Jim applied for job after job, but he never got another in Attleborough. His age was partly against him, so he started his own engineering business. 'People didn't pay,' said Isobel. 'We were conned, laughed at, and lost thousands of pounds. We lost our house. It is difficult not to feel bitter. But I don't feel bitter about the co-op, and never regret helping the women in the chicken factory.'

Isobel, who was still in the Trade Group and a member of Wymondham and Attleborough Trades Council, added, 'We sometimes see them in town and we always chat. Some of the women, and the men, have never worked since the closure.'

*   *   *

At the time of the Attleborough closure, 1,700 workers at Bernard Matthews' plants in Great Witchingham and Halesworth (Suffolk), rejected the latest pay offer of 12%, minus the Christmas bonus. A previous offer of 11% had led to a walk-out by more than 100 members. NUAAW branch secretary Glenn Bate said, 'We have accepted low pay offers in the past on the understanding that we were helping to build up the Company. Now B. Matthews is the biggest turkey producer in Britain, with profits last year of £3.8 million. Our members are not prepared to see the stuffing knocked out of their living standards any further. We have never taken industrial action before, but it's got to the stage that we won't put up with low wages any longer.' The basic minimum at Matthews was £61 per week. After threats of further walk-outs, the 1,700 workers settled for a three-pronged agreement which gave them 11% on basic pay, a Christmas bonus and profit sharing. A working party, including NUAAW convenors Glenn Bate and Billy Draper, George Barnard and Peter Medhurst, DOs and Union finance experts, were to work out the profit-sharing scheme.

A number of chicken factories began to close, including six belonging to Buxteds. Jack Boddy said, 'The poultry industry is suffering from the twin attacks of Thatcherism and unfair EEC competition. But I cannot believe that the vast Imperial Group does not have the resources to maintain jobs and production, rather than leave the market completely open for foreign imports.'

One alleged reason for the crisis in poultry processing was the row over EEC regulations. UK processors claimed that the inspection system here is more expensive to run and that imports from EEC countries did not come up to UK standards. Jack Boddy wanted government action to get the EEC to remove anomalies and ensure that conditions affecting British producers were brought into line with their European counterparts. The British Poultry Federation claimed that the EEC hygiene inspection system had added 'dramatically' to the costs, compared with the British system – sometimes by 20 to 30 times.

'Buy British' Campaign

As the crisis worsened, blockades of ports through which subsidised French poultry entered the UK, and lightning swoops on shops selling them, were among proposals to save the industry. Ironically, the French subsidies threatened French jobs as well. The subsidies went towards creating ultra-modern plants – and thousands of jobs in the older plants were at risk. The NUAAW's efforts to stop French poultry imports had the full support of the French Farming and Forestry Union. The two Unions agreed on a joint campaign against the building of a huge turkey factory in Brittany, which would be able to sell birds 10p a pound cheaper than British turkeys.

In 1981, the NUAAW's 'Buy British' campaign came to a triumphant end when the Government banned most imported poultry, except from Ireland, Sweden and Denmark. But MAFF went to extraordinary lengths to deny the ban had anything to do with the NUAAW campaign. Its strange press notice was tersely headlined, 'Newcastle Disease in Poultry'. It opened with self-congratulations about how little Newcastle Disease there was in the UK and outlined steps British producers must take to ensure that this desirable state of affairs continued. It went on about slaughtering flocks where the disease occurred, and in the last part came to the point. Only countries which insisted on vaccination, as the UK would do in future, would be allowed to export poultry to the UK. France, Holland and the USA did not have a slaughtering policy. Their producers were allowed to vaccinate instead, but it was not obligatory.

The Government would have been in difficulty if it had announced that it was banning foreign poultry to save the UK industry. It had always insisted that it would not interfere in industry, either by offering subsidies or granting import controls. That was the central plank of Tory economic dogma. And it would have been in trouble with its EEC partners, for import controls to protect home industries were against EEC rules. Import controls on health grounds were permitted.

The moment it heard of the ban, the NUAAW called off its planned picket of shops and ports. A Union statement said it was 'delighted', but added, 'We'll now be watching the British poultry producers like hawks. They must not use this good news as an excuse to go back to the bad old ways of two or three years ago, when many of them were failing to innovate, and were closing factories and making redundancies at the first hint of trouble.'

The NUAAW initiative in launching the 'Buy British – Save Jobs' campaign received a lot of media publicity. Coverage in national and local papers, radio and TV was high, with Union members much in demand to appear before cameras and microphones, for the campaign caught the public imagination. Tremendous support from shoppers for the case put by NUAAW members distributing leaflets, car stickers, posters and lapel badges was experienced by pickets up and down the country.

It was one of the Union's most imaginative campaigns of recent years. Within a week of the start of the campaign, Marks and Spencer started putting British poultry stickers on all UK-produced poultry they sold, and a director said this was in direct response to the NUAAW campaign. Marks and Spencer gave Union chiefs a guarantee that they were phasing out the 9% of their poultry that came from France. 'Just as fast as we can train UK producers to turn to the cuts we want, we will bring our business back home,' their food director told the Union. Turner's Turkeys of Lincolnshire were given by a leading store an order for 100,000 turkeys which was to have gone to France. Ray Turner said that this was a direct result of the NUAAW campaign. Ironically, this was one of the few companies not to recognise the Union. Bejams stated that once they had sold the last of their American poultry they would stick to British. Bernard Matthews' shares shot up 22p.

All very nice for the producers. What of the workers? 'It certainly adds up to a more secure future for poultry workers,' said Jack Boddy. 'The producers are going to have to take their workers more into consideration in future. If, after all this, there is one single job lost in the industry, I shall want to know why. And I cannot think of an answer that would satisfy me.'

All told, the ban and its outcome was a splendid victory for the Union and did much to safeguard 20,000 jobs. But the industry's management still needed to buck up its ideas, to innovate and not leave the growing market for poultry cuts to its foreign competitors. And too often the workforce had been let down by complacent managements, so the Union needed to remain ever vigilant.

Not So 'Bootiful' Strike

A significant event in the history of industrial relations in the poultry industry began to take shape early in 1982. Industrial action by NUAAW members at Bernard Matthews turkey units had been rumbling on ever since what was described as 'the shortest wage negotiations in history.' Mass meetings and a ban on overtime had followed an offer to 1,200 workers at Holton and Great Witchingham plants, which amounted to £5 across the board – a take-it-or-leave-it offer made in three-and-a-half-minutes. The workforce decided to 'leave it', with chairman of the joint committee, Billy McBeath, backed by Pat Woodyard and Alan Deare, convenors, saying, 'unless the Company starts negotiating properly we will have no alternative to taking action.'

There was a series of officially-backed lightning stoppages, culminating in a full-scale strike on 15 February, with 1,200 workers taking part. In March, the *Landworker* reported that 30 workers at Matthews' Bawsey Mill, which made feed, were sacked for supporting the strike. It declared, 'Bernard Matthews' massive profits hit as his workers say "We've had enough of serfdom" . . . There'll be no settlement until they're taken back.' Five of them, Philip Bray, Karl Creed, Alex McGivern, Derek Poole and Steven Mendham, were pictured in front of the feed mill where they worked, 'which Bernard Matthews keeps so cold that stray birds drop out of the rafters frozen to death.' The 1,200 workers in the main plants were still on strike, and showed no sign of weakening. Matthews was still refusing to talk about their grievances, so peace was as far away as ever. Matthews' claim one day that the strike was folding, was exploded the next morning when just 50 people turned up for work – and most of them were office boys and supervisors.

Before the strike started, the workers had spent months trying to persuade Matthews to discuss their pay claim. Two days before, Jack Boddy went to Great Witchingham in a last-minute attempt to avert a strike. He offered negotiations. He offered arbitration by ACAS. He was turned down. So Matthews' workers had to choose. Either they accepted the £5 pittance, half the amount the farmworkers settled for that year, or they struck. There was no third way. The minimum adult wage at Matthews was £67.71 for a 40-hour week, and 16-year-olds worked the same hours for £48.46.

All the same, the workers were prepared to compromise on their 25% pay claim. Hearing that Mr. Matthews would not negotiate until they moderated it, they reduced the claim to 15%. Mr. Matthews found another excuse for refusing to listen to the men and women who produced his £4½ million profit the previous year. An appeal was made to other trade unions and the NUAAW for extra funds for the strikers.

Discontent at Matthews had been brewing for years, and low wages were only part of the cause. Matthews was one of the worst employers in the country, declared the *Landworker*. Speeds on the production line were increased to impossible rates in order to maximise profits. Workers made themselves ill trying to keep up. '. . . We've put up with this sort of treatment for years, and watched Matthews make massive profits . . . and jump to the demands of the bosses in fear of losing our jobs,' said Billy McBeath. 'We'll stand no more of it.'

The *Landworker* said:

Money is the immediate issue. When a man can work there for 27 years and still be taking home £53.56 for a hard and unpleasant week on the eviscerating line, there's something wrong. When he works for a company which has told him that he gets what he's given or else he gets out, discontent will be fuelled. And when the company refused to discuss wages, the discontent may well boil over into the sort of anger which has led the men and women whom Bernard Matthews regards as serfs to say "Enough is enough". Yet perhaps if Bernard Matthews wasn't quite such an appalling employer in other respects as well, he could have got away with all of that. Which brings us to the underlying cause . . . he's consciously climbed to wealth and power over the backs of an overworked and despised workforce. Just listen to some of them: "We've worked harder here than we've ever worked before. Matthews told us that and then kicked us. The only thing they provide is a tea machine. They used to give us two pence to put in it. They've withdrawn that now." . . .He's the sort of employer who's constantly forcing them to work faster and harder, destroying their health for the sake of an extra buck. He's the sort of employer who provides nothing and expects everything. He's the sort of get-rich-quick merchant who regards the men and women who work for him rather as Roman emperors regarded their slaves. That's why there's a strike there. It's not because left-wing troublemakers are stirring up the workforce, as Mr. Matthews claimed. No troublemaker, left-wing or otherwise, could have made them as angry as he's made them . . . Now the strike is on, it's got to be won. Other employers in the poultry industry have not treated their workforce like dirt in the way Mr. Matthews has. But if he gets away with it, who knows whether it might give them ideas. Which is why we're asking readers to help. Picket lines are cold and sometimes lonely places, especially when you're fighting an employer who's decided to use every dirty trick his vast wealth can buy in order to break your spirit. Go and join them if you can. The money to keep up the fight will be found, but it's not going to be easy. And Matthews is paying for full page advertisements in the local papers, threatening like a playground bully. So send some money to the strike fund . . . There's no use reasoning with a man like Matthews. He'll treat his workers like dirt if he can. Like any other conscience-less dictator, he has to be beaten.

Chris Kaufman, *Landworker* editor, visited the picket lines and found 'the tremendous spirit and solidarity of the NUAAW members taking this action as strong as ever "despite" a stream of misleading statements by the Company.' One striker told him that 'nearly all the married men here are having to claim Family Income Supplement. I am one of the highest-paid shop floor workers. I've only one kid and I have to claim. I'm supposed to pay £20 a week rent but my wage is so low. I'm only able to pay £5 . . . I have to get the rest back in rebates. I'm a senior charge hand with 17 years' service. Do you know what I would take home if I did a flat week? £62. I think 17 years of my life worth more than that . . . The Profit Sharing Scheme? That's a farce. He's got to make £31½ million before you get a look in and then you get a percentage of a percentage. We've had nothing. Anything we've got was knocked off the Christmas bonus. He says he pays the highest wages in the industry. That's a load of rubbish . . . At last year's wage negotiations he told us if we didn't think the wage was good enough to apply for Family Income Supplement. He told us that! All we're asking for is a decent wage. Let the Government spend public money where it's needed on schools and hospitals instead of subsidising Bernard Matthews.'

As the strike got under way, Matthews made great play in the press that the effects of cutting off feed to the turkeys would mean them starving. He conveniently forgot that there was still feed getting through to them and that he had made a fortune by fattening them up faster than was good for them in order ഛ slit their throats in the fastest possible time. One striker said, 'Those turkeys are putting into our strike fund. This strike is prolonging their lives.'

'It was claimed during the strike that a good 10% of the birds miss the stunner and they had their throats cut while they're flapping away like mad till they died,' said one employee. 'And the man slitting their throats couldn't lift them off because the line was going so fast. He had to kill them or they went into the boiling hot water while they were still alive. Once a man got caught in the stunner himself because they had been working him too hard and he got too close. He fainted or got knocked unconscious and about 40 birds went through the boiling hot water. They were boiled alive.* We've worked harder here than we've ever worked before . . . People will tell you they work so hard that all their knuckles swell up. They're injured for life with arthritis . . . It happens when you're hanging up and have your hands stuck in water all day. 24,000 a day . . . that's a lot of turkeys. It used to be 16,000. Now they're increasing it . . . They give you three minutes to go to the toilet. If you're not out by then someone comes after you. Any longer and you get a quarter-of-an-hour attendance bonus knocked off.'

Everything in the garden wasn't 'bootiful' for Mr. Matthews any longer. As news of the stand being taken by Union members spread, messages of support from the public poured in. Practical help came with attempts to cut

---

* At that time, the firm staunchly denied that any turkeys were boiled alive, and obtained a High Court injunction preventing Jack Boddy from 'publishing any allegation to the effect that the plaintiffs [Bernard Matthews] cause or permit live turkeys to be put into boiling water . . . instead of their being killed humanely.' When Matthews applied for the injunction to be extended, the Union's QC, Patrick Milmo, pointed out that Boddy had never said the words complained of, and Matthews' lawyers later withdrew the injunction. A victory for the Union, it would seem, but Matthews had achieved a major objective – keeping the allegation out of the national newspapers.

off supplies. The TGWU blocked the movement of soya through ports, and oil from various sources. Cold stores were alerted not to handle Matthews' products and a consumer boycott was being considered.

Strike pay was £12 per week. The *Landworker* published a dramatic picture of the afternoon shift coming to work in a bus. Only one lady was visible in the bus. Matthews claimed that 287 came in that day. The *Landworker* saw this coachful of one and a minibus – full of another.[4]

The strike lasted six weeks, the biggest ever in the poultry industry, and ended when the workers at the two factories voted for a 9% settlement. Jack Boddy sent the strikers a message: 'We're proud of you.' Announcing the vote to return to work, Billy McBeath said, 'There are no winners or losers in a situation like this, but our members have reached what they consider to be a suitable compromise for a return to work.'

The achievements of the Matthews' workers have to be seen against the background of the employers at first refusing point blank to negotiate in what was regarded as a determined effort to undermine the NUAAW's organisation in the company. The strikers fight for fair wage was boosted by the flood of support from other NUAAW branches and national unions, who chipped into the strike fund with anything from pub collections to a donation of £1,000 from the seamen's union. The courageous stand of these men and women who stood in freezing picket lines around the clock and had to scrape and borrow to keep going, won the respect of thousands of people throughout the country and made a deep impression on their fellow inhabitants of Norfolk and Suffolk. That year's annual Conference congratulated the EC on a successful campaign to protect jobs in the poultry industry. (See Chapter 22, 'Union Leadership Goes Left', for the financial repercussions of the Matthews' strike on the Union.)

More Strikes

Before the year was over, a lockout brought Buxteds' factory at Gainsborough to a standstill. The trouble was triggered off by an 8% pay offer in August, and the company made it clear they would not budge, though the offer was below the rate of inflation for workers who earned less than the average anyway.

The dispute started relatively mildly, with no hint of the bitter confrontation that was to follow; workers merely banned overtime and worked to rule. Alec Russell, DO, said, 'These are not militant people, just ordinary people who are fed up.' Hopes of a peaceful settlement were torpedoed one day when the day shift arrived to find the factory gates locked. The night shift responded by coming out in support. Nearly 500 workers were by then outside the factory gates, and the company seemed to be preparing for a long dispute. For nine days of the lockout, workers mounted a 24-hour, 7-days-a-week picket. A new management initiative was needed. Eventually it came in the form of a restructured pay offer and the strike ended after the majority of some 400 workers voted to return to work.

Before the year was out, Buxteds closed not only their Gainsborough factory, but also West Hartlepool and Buxted plants, making 1,700 workless. These closures followed the Government's lifting of its ban on poultry imports, a move that met with a considerably muted response, considering the noisy campaign that went into getting the ban in the first place. The British Poultry Federation stayed strangely silent. The TGWU was remarkably mute. Even the NFU limited itself to statutory mutterings about the danger of Newcastle Disease. Presumably, they all felt there was no way they could get the ban re-imposed.

Meanwhile, in Norfolk, at the end of 1982, a remarkable change came over Bernard Matthews' management: it made a 10% pay offer. Staff also got a Christmas present – a turkey. 'We are doing well and there is no reason why employees should not share our success,' said Mr. Matthews. It was a spirit welcomed by the Union negotiators. 'In the long term the strike was good for industrial relations,' said the two Union officials involved, Peter Medhurst and George Barnard. 'The Company realised its workforce was not willing to be kicked around and seems to have stopped trying to do so. We welcome that.'

At the 1983 TGWU Conference the first ever attended by the newly-formed Agricultural Trade Group, the blacking of foreign fowl imports was won in dramatic fashion. A resolution was carried seeking the 'blacking [of] all poultry meat imports at their source of entry into this country.' Roger Shutt, of Sun Valley Poultry, Hereford, in an emotional appeal for support, won it overwhelmingly on a show of hands.

National Poultry Advisory Committee Formed

February 1984 saw the final stage in the establishment of the Union's National Poultry Advisory Committee. Delegates from poultry firms met in London to discuss current problems and the industry, beleagured by imports and beset by price anomalies, dominated by large companies and increasingly controlled by the power of the multiple retailers. Half the workforce was subject to agricultural wages and conditions, the other half negotiated directly with the employers. The imports issue was very much in the news, as the European Court of Justice had just ruled that Britain must open its markets fully to poultry imports, making the possibility of a new campaign to black poultry imports hopeless. However, a powerful programme of action to save the British poultry industry was drawn up at the Conference, and poultry advisory chairman, Denis G. Chiappa, said, 'The future of this industry – and its defence against subsidised imports – should not be left to the workers and their trade-union representatives. But if it is up to us to make sure the industry survives, then we accept that responsibility.'

The Poultry Advisory Committee agreed to go back to the producers once more to involve them in a campaign to boost British poultry sales. If there was no satisfactory level of involvement from retailers, to picket key establishments selling foreign poultry; to publicise the 'country of origin' marks on wrappings to help family purchasers buy British; and to open discussions with other TGWU trade groups to pinpoint key ports of entry of foreign products.

As thousands of tons of highly-subsidised poultry flooded into the country, nearly 8,000 out of 40,000 jobs in the industry were threatened. Denis G. Chiappa said they had to act and 'that's why we are tightening the noose.' They had approached dockers to try to stop these imports.

At the Suffolk Sovereign poultry plant in Eye, 200 night-shift workers were told on arrival that they were to be made redundant. They immediately walked out. After talks, Peter Medhurst, DO, announced that the management had agreed to a new shift system which reduced the numbers on the night shift to just over 100, but also agreed to increase numbers on day shift. 'I don't like losing any jobs, but believe the workforce and the stewards are to be congratulated for saving a hundred jobs we might have lost if our resolve had failed.' said Peter.

The position of the British poultry industry has continued to change, with the squeezing out of the few remaining independent producers, and much of the industry controlled by the transnational companies, answerable to no one in Britain.

Its one aim is profit, and nothing must hinder that aim, neither the consumer, the worker, or the health of both. This latter is again best illustrated by the salmonella scare in the late eighties, when it was believed that a large quantity of eggs and chickens were infected. Millions of eggs had to be destroyed, and the Government quickly prepared a rescue package, not for the victims, but for the producers. Said *Today*, 'Whether the egg industry has got too much compensation or too little . . . you have to admire the speed with which it has winkled £19 million* out of the Government. Other victims should be so lucky! When it comes to compensation for accidents, criminal damage or medical error they have to wait years for the law to grind out a judgment. For quick results, it's still best to belong to a powerful lobby like the NFU.'

A former tester for salmonella with one of Britain's largest poultry producers told me, 'It was known by the laboratory staff that the directors did not like us to find salmonella infection above a rate of 15%. Sometimes we found it as high as 20%. We made correct returns. But the laboratory chief never put in returns above 14% so as not to upset the directors and make them feel that something had to be done about it.'

---

* The final figure was less.

'Does this still go on,' I asked. 'Oh no,' she said, 'they closed the laboratory down, and appointed two or three quality control inspectors instead. They can't test for salmonella, but they can help to make things look good.' That was after she was sacked for joining a union.

There remains much to be done in the poultry industry, for both workers and consumers.

REFERENCES

1. Minutes of Organising Sub-Committee, February 1968.
2. *Guardian,* 19 December 1988.
3. MAFF figures.
4. *Landworker,* March 1982.

21

Trees – Britain's Great Asset

If every just man that now pines with want
Had but a moderate and beseeming share
Of that which lewdly-pampered luxury
Now heaps upon some few with vast excess,
Nature's full blessings would be well dispenc'd
In unsuperfluous proportion.

Milton

Establishment of the Forestry Commission

Long before every concerned citizen became an environmentalist, the NUAAW recognised the importance of trees to Britain, not only as an invaluable part of our ecological system, but of economic importance to the national economy. Our climate is peculiarly suited to growing trees, especially softwoods. They grow faster here than in most other European countries, yet few of them grow less timber than we do. The 4.6 million acres (2.2 million hectares) of forestry in this country is only about 8% of the land surface. This makes little economic sense in a situation in which timber ranks as our third biggest import at over £1,500 million a year – some 92% of home requirements.[1]

It would be economic commonsense for any government of whatever political hue, to ensure as far as practical, that the UK supplies its own timber needs. For in addition to its primary use as timber, it could in future be a main source of chemicals at present derived from fossil fuels. It would seem unwise, if not immoral, for British governments not to exploit to the full, for the benefit of the nation, Britain's ideal conditions for growing timber, but they have done just that. At times, we have had in this respect, a number of highly immoral governments.

For decades the Union campaigned on such matters, not only in the interests of the country as a whole, but on behalf of its members. The Union had long represented forestry workers, especially since the establishment of the Forestry Commission in 1919, and many of them rose to high rank within the Union; notably John Hose, an able young forestry craftsman who was to become the Union's president.

Forestry workers had a similar struggle to better their wages and conditions to that of their agricultural comrades, but some of them had a significant advantage; those employed by the FC had to deal with one employer throughout Britain. The FC was set up to guarantee Britain's native timber supplies, and is both a nationalised industry and the national forestry authority. By 1950, its trade receipts were over £1½ million a year, and rapidly growing. Many of its powers were whittled away in later years by Conservative governments, to benefit private landowners and the big timber interests. And the public money which goes on State forestry is but a fraction of that given to privately run agriculture, especially by Tory governments, ever ready to put publicly-owned industries into financial strait jackets as a preliminary to privatisation.

In the 60 years since 1919, the area of forest plantations and woodlands in the UK doubled, half being owned by the FC. The FC was given powers to buy land in the open market, afforest it and sell the resulting timber, and since 1967 has had a responsibility to cater for public recreation and enhance the beauty of the countryside.

The Union always supported the FC as the rightful custodian of the nation's woodland, but it has been an uphill battle, with many fierce fights with the Commission with regard to the welfare of its workforce, and some of its development policies. In 1972, a major review of FC policy by the Treasury produced a devastating cost-benefit programme which claimed that new planting was not economically or socially justified; the Union was horrified by what this would mean in the way of retrenchment of publicly-owned forests and subsequent job losses. However, the FC repulsed the Treasury's assault by making social and environmental arguments, mainly that afforestation stemmed rural depopulation, and provided valuable access and recreation for the public in the countryside.

Yet the would-be despoilers of the FC did not give up, and since the late 1970s, the FC budget has been squeezed by successive public expenditure cuts, resulting in job losses. It has also been the subject of Tory calls to privatise it, especially as many of its trees were reaching maturity and becoming highly profitable; the Forestry Act 1981 gave the FC the right to sell land, previously it could only buy land. The Minister was also empowered to transfer FC profits to the Treasury, presumably to nip in the financial bud any further developments the Commission had in mind.

The large-scale sales of FC woodland to the private sector which followed were at a high cost to the public purse, as the private sector is heavily subsidised by the State. That the Government should support the private sector whilst severely curtailing the FC's activities had a Tory ideological bias, rather than being pure Tory monetarist economics. The State supported private forestry with grants and concessions on income and capital gains taxation. People who had no knowledge of forestry, including pop stars, moved into private forestry, so rich were the pickings. Some didn't even know where 'their' forests were. Then in the mid-1980s, some curbs were placed on this kind of tax-avoidance.

There were never any such riches for forestry workers. In 1947, the adult male Grade I forestry worker received £4 15s; Grade II, £4 12s 6d; Grade III, £4 10s; women, £3 8s, as against £4 10s for men, and £3 8s for women farmworkers. Both did a 47-hour week.

In the early post-war years, women represented 50% of the forestry labour force, and like the WLA on the farms, they did everything – felling, planting and nursery work – but it was a long time before they got equal pay, and by then, few still worked in British forests.

Inflation set to work, and although wages generally never caught up, there were some fairly big pay rises, and by 1984 forestry craftsmen were on £87.60, with a basic £77.05, compared with £82.80 for farmworkers, both on a 40-hour week.

Lengthy negotiations led to improvements in 1964. Grades I, II and III, were replaced by two grades: skilled forestry workers and forestry workers. This meant that most workers moved into the top grade. Before the review there were 3,503 Grade I workers (56%); 1,416 Grade II (22%); 1,390 Grade II (22%). Afterwards there were 5,117 skilled forestry workers (81%); 315 forestry workers (5%), and 877 basic grade (14%). Lead rates were improved and lorry drivers no longer tied to rates fixed by the Road Haulage Wages Council, but fixed by the Forestry Commission Industrial and Trades Council (FCITC).*

Under a scheme ratified by the Joint Co-ordinating Council for Government Industrial Establishments, a number of established posts were allotted to the FC. An initial quota of 3,250 'established' posts in the FC was more than enough to cover employees eligible for establishment. This scheme provided for pensions on retirement of one-eighteenth of the yearly wage; a gratuity of three-eighteeths of the year wage of each year up to 40; a death grant; and for early retirement due to ill health with a gratuity. There was also a sick-pay scheme. These changes represented a considerable improvement in conditions for forestry workers.

*   *   *

Among the guests when the Kielder Forest village was opened on 27 May 1952 was NUAW member George Rome, who as a lad of 16 had planted the first trees in the Kielder Forest 26 years earlier. In that time it had become the major part of the 170 square miles of FC land in Northumberland, the largest afforestation area in Britain, and the largest man-made forest in Europe. Some of the trees George had planted into bare hillsides had grown 40 feet.

---

*   A joint management and Union committee. In the late 1980s, the trade group representatives were Barry Leathwood, Bill Brack, David Blackie and Ivan Monkton.

George, the only remaining member of the original forest workers, was at the opening with his wife Margaret, a former schoolteacher. His wages in the early days were only 32s 6d a week, and he had to do all the heavy ploughing and drainage work by hand. Now, largely owing to the efforts of the Union, pay had been raised 400%, and mechanical power does all the heavy work.

Kielder village was to be the first of five in the vast forest, intended to provide homes for 2,000 forest workers. Lord Robinson, FC chairman, said at the opening that by 1970, Kielder and its companion forests would provide the country with 1 million tons of timber.

Forestry was of great importance to many upland areas where, because of lack of work, social amenities were scarce, schooling inadequate, and the small family farms, despite schemes of improvement introduced by post-war Labour governments, proving unviable. Thousands of workers in these areas were leaving for the towns, resulting in a further run down in amenities.

One man faced with these problems was Gwilym Davies, North Wales DO, and he attended in 1952 a special panel established by the Council for Wales and Monmouth to investigate rural areas of mid-Wales. The story unfolded was a tragic one of derelict farmsteads and houses, insanitary conditions, a lack of piped water and electricity in most of the existing hamlets, no public transport and means of social intercourse. One of the most feasible suggestions to rehabilitate such areas was afforestation. 'As work in the new forest developed, entirely new villages could be established complete with all modern amenities, and the provision of full cultural and social development,' Gwilym declared. 'We have a vital interest in this, because the majority of the 2,800 workers employed by the FC in Wales are Union members.'

The Welsh Forestry Workers' Committee meeting at Aberystwyth was told that the FC's activities in the principality envisaged a target of 800,000 acres with a working force of 15,000 to 20,000 men and women. Forestry, and its ancillary trades, would become one of the major Welsh industries and 'our villages and hamlets would once again re-echo to the song and laughter of a happy people,' Gwilym declared.

Later, special Union forestry conferences were held in Wales, and at one in 1954, G. B. Ryle, Director of Forestry for Wales, told delegates that expanding Welsh forests would undoubtedly prevent the drift from rural areas. Among the 16 resolutions passed was one calling for the establishment of industries to utilise forestry products in areas where forests are established, in order to ensure well-balanced rural communities.

Alas, all the summits of afforestation envisaged by Lord Robinson at Kielder and campaigned for by the Union in various parts of Britain, were never fully scaled, owing to changes in government policies and cutbacks in finance.

Only two of the other four FC villages envisaged in the Kielder Forest were built, Byrness and Stonehaugh, and by the 1980s, with Kielder village, all three were in decline. Terry Hammond, DO, told me, 'Because of job cutbacks, FC employees no longer occupy all the houses, and the FC is getting local authorities to take over various services; it is all very sad.'

Not that the Union ever gave up its campaign for forestry workers. At the Biennial at Cheltenham in 1954, F. W. Ward, Cardigan & Pembroke, successfully moved a resolution calling upon the Government to implement without further delay the policy of rehabilitating rural Wales by improving forestry and agriculture.

But such wholehearted support for the FC never eased the Union's wages negotiations with that body. In 1954, the basic wage for forestry workers of £6 2s for 47 hours compared unfavourably with other rural industry, and the FC refused an increase.

From the inauguration of the FCITC until 1951, the official side insisted that forestry wages were governed by the AWB. The unions wanted wages to be freely negotiated within the ambit of the FCITC. The Industrial Court supported the unions, and subsequent FCITC discussions indicated the bad grace with which the official side accepted this decision. They refused to view forestry wage rates against other comparable industries; the only comparison they would consider was farm rates, which were lower. For a number of years the Union pressed for the introduction of Industrial Civil Service pay rates for forestry workers, and a break from AWB rates, but by 1990, had still not succeeded in effecting any change.

*   *   *

Who were the men who made forestry a career, and membership of the Union an important part of their lives? They are a diverse crowd, judging by some I met.

Lachie McAlister, a married man of Saddell Village, Campbelltown, Argyle, had been a forestry worker for 24 years when I was introduced to him in 1984, and holds strong views on safety. He was very critical of the contracting-out by the FC of the felling of standing timber, which he believed has led to an increase in accidents.

Lachie worked in Achaglachgach Forest, near Tarbert, Loch Fyne, and recalled one contract team there: a mother working a power saw felled a tree onto her son of about 20. 'The couple had no safety gear, they didn't even wear helmets. The boy had a head injury, but he worked on for half an hour and then had to stop because he was suffering from concussion. Within half an hour he was paralysed. They tried to take him to hospital in their car, but the throttle broke and they couldn't even get to the road. Finally an ambulance was called. I don't know what became of the lad.'

It couldn't have happened if they had worked under FC rules. When an FC man is felling, he has got to be two tree-lengths from the next worker, must wear a safety helmet and a lot of gear.

Lachie complained, 'When the FC gives out these felling contracts, the safety regulations are in small print and they don't enforce them.' He added, 'FC workers go through strict safety training. Private forest owners don't give a damn. Everything is done to get the private work done quickly, and safety goes by the board. Only the Union enforces safety regulations.'

One man who took a different view of many things, was Frank Percy Lewis, a foreman on the Chillington Estate in the Midlands, owned by Peter Gifford, one time CLA President. This estate included about 700 to 800 acres of woodland, where Frank was foreman, worked by seven full-timers and three part-timers.

Over the years the question came up on the estate – 'machinery or men?' Frank preferred men, because men were adaptable and could be switched to all sorts of jobs. 'At times we had Manpower Commission lads working here and kept three on. Also we took on another young man because we wanted a lorry driver.'

Frank looked upon Mr. Gifford as a very fair employer. 'When I went for the interview, I told him I was NUAAW Shropshire county chairman, and he said, "that's up to you". He wants a lot of work done, but couldn't afford the £50,000 needed for a sawmill, for instance, and was quite happy to increase the workforce, which has worked out well.'

When he first went there in 1972 they used to work on Saturday mornings, and half an hour at night. 'We cut it out about 1974,' said Frank, who was completely against overtime. 'We don't see any need for it,' he said. 'Maybe once a year there's a rush order and I ask the lorry driver to come in on a Saturday morning, but that's all.' He was very conscious of safety matters. 'It's the employer's duty to have safety equipment available, but you cannot always make the workers wear it; I would like the law changed to make wearing it compulsory.'

At Chillington, the estate supplied all-weather clothing, such as donkey jackets, wellies, safety gloves, and the first-aid box has everything in it. 'We've had minor accidents, but we've always got them to a doctor, nothing serious,' said Frank.

Frank had been in the Union for 43 years, having joined in 1940 when he started work on a farm. 'I've always agitated for better conditions, and my job as foreman has never made any difference,' he said. 'I believe in having a go and using our branch as a weapon. Do that and a lot can be achieved. You must have respect of people in the area.'

A firm believer in keeping politics out of Union affairs, Frank was on the Board of Featherstone Prison, having been nominated by the local Tory MP. He also served as a governor of the Girls' High School in Wolverhampton, where he had one son in the police force.

One man firmly opposed to the privatisation of FC land was 66-year-old Eric Hudson of Norfolk. Eric, who was born at Burgh, one of three sons of a farmworker, left school for general farm work with a wage of 10s 6d, and later joined the Royal Artillery. When demobbed he went felling for a private firm, and joined the FC in 1953. There used to be a lot of FC land in North Norfolk, but by the time he had retired in 1983, much of it had been sold off.

'When I came to Marsham there were 43 FC workers in the Wensum Forest, now there's only seven. The run down was mostly due to mechanisation; once where young trees were being established, they had to be hand weeded. You would see up to 30 people doing that in a plantation, then spraying and tractor weeding came in, and three men can now do what 30 once did. Felling was all done with bow saws and axes, then we had power saws; now you can get as much timber felled with five men as it once took 15 to 20. Planting is also all done now by machine.'

Eric went on to give many more instances of the cutbacks in the labour force. The upkeep of 'rides' was always done by hand, now done by a tractor swipe. The wire fences were once hand weeded, now it's one man with a spray. And they're not even bothering to fence the plantations now. When he first joined the FC, three warreners kept down the rabbits; those jobs have been abolished. He pointed out another difference between then and now, perhaps only perceptible to forestry workers. 'You'll never see the same quality of crop as when I started,' he said, 'because there's nothing now to stop vermin attacking them; they take the tops out of young trees which subsequently grow deformed.'

Safety practices within the FC were very good according to Eric, until they started to sub-contract. 'I did my damnedest to stop that sort of thing,' he said. 'Anything I saw wrong I stepped in as safety representative for the area. I was going along a public road once and I saw a chap run out of the forest, look both ways and then run back into the trees. In the next instant a tree dropped right across the road. It was a busy road and anything could have happened. I reported it to our head forester, who stopped it immediately. When the FC felled roadside trees we always had to have two people keeping look-out on the road, but not with these private contractors.'

Most of the forestry work round North Norfolk since the eighties has been done by contract workers. 'I've seen people with power saws in action wearing only light shoes, instead of metal capped felling boots. On hot days people don't like wearing the heavy protection gear, but it's dangerous not to, and if our FC workers didn't wear it, they could be suspended. There is no one to suspend the private contractor. They don't seem to care.'

Eric and his wife Vanda still lived in Marsham, and he hoped that the FC will be allowed to carry on for the sake of the people who used the woods for pleasure, if nothing else. And he had noticed a change of attitude among top FC people. 'When we first began to fight privatisation, we didn't get much backing from the top, but it's changed lately. When woodlands are being sold off now, we find voices from high up supporting our opposition.'

A tall, sturdy man, who retired at the age of 62 because he was fed up with what was happening in the FC, he still represented the Union on health tribunals, and regretted the merger with the TGWU, but felt it was inevitable. 'I feel the only real hope for the rural working class now is to see that we get a Labour Party that is fit to govern, and that means the Labour Party and the trade unions have got to be seen working together.'

Conflict in the Uplands

There was sometimes conflict between upland farmers and the advocates of afforestation. This came to light in 1955 during the introduction of the Agricultural (Improvement of Roads) Bill in Parliament, which was to make £4 million available to improve roads in livestock rearing areas. This specially applied to Welsh upland areas where farmers had difficulty in getting the maximum out of their land, but many opposed letting some of it go for afforestation.

At the TUC Congress at Southport in 1955, Tom Daniel, Hampshire, DO, spoke on an NUAW motion calling upon the Government to make a determined effort to develop Britain's forest acreage. He wanted large areas of bracken and scrub afforested to enable the FC to increase its employees from 13,000 to 40,000. It was carried without dissent.

In order to improve organisation amongst forestry workers, the EC in 1955 instituted biennial regional conferences for them. Reg Bottini said, 'Until we have 100% membership among FC employees we shall not reach the desired goal of equality in wages and conditions with general industry.'

As another step in that direction, the Union's national Forestry Workers' Advisory Committee (FWAC) was set up in 1956 with seven members: J. Bradshaw (N West); A. H. Ebenezer (N Wales); G. Evans (S Wales); F. Trout (S West); F. Shippey (N East); A. Harbord (East) and F. H. Peachey (S East). Due to a lot of hard work, the Union did achieve almost 100% membership of FC forestry workers, together with the TGWU and GMWU.

At the Biennial at Yarmouth in May 1956, John Hose (Notts) moved a successful resolution seeking a minimum of £8 for a five-day week for forestry workers. He said that the FC was running at a loss, and one reason was that instead of selling pit timber direct to the Coal Board, sold it to a private dealer who converted it 'and makes at least 230% profit'.

At the 1965 TUC, the Union moved a successful resolution urging that the Government make a determined effort to develop the forest acreage in Britain. Not long after, MAFF revealed that the FC was falling a long way behind what was planned in 1943, the annual acreage planted dropping since the peak year of 1954.

In 1957, whilst private contractors were given work in State forests, the FC continued to sack its own employees, contrary to a pledge given a few years earlier. Few denied at the time that this was part of the Government's policy to encourage private contractors, and John Hose, who worked in one of the affected areas, was a vociferous opponent. He asked, 'Are we to accept the idea that as more woods become fully established and profitable, the Commission will find more men redundant in these areas? And then suggest that they move to more remote spots to pioneer new forests, whilst the result of their earlier work and State investment become profitable concessions to money-grabbing private enterprise firms?' He hoped not, and wanted action to safeguard the future of forestry, and his long fight for action played no small part in his rise to the presidency of the Union.

It was in 1957 that the Union submitted a claim for a 44-hour week. The FC offered 46, and the Union took the matter to the Industrial Court, which ruled in favour of the FC. The Union did, however, win an improvement for foresters working in water; their plus payments were raised from 1d per hour to 2d, and standby rates for night fire-fighting duties were increased. And even more important, the Union agreed with the FC on the introduction of a 5-day week (February–October) and a 5½-day week (November–January).

The 1960 Biennial called for a minimum of two-thirds of a year on piecework, to give FC workers a chance of adding to the minimum wage. John Hose wanted the EC to be 'more active' in its public speaking to safeguard the living of forestry workers. Reg Bottini said his motion implied criticism of the EC, but they should remember that other unions were involved and past action had been taken on a majority view. The motion was carried.

In 1961, forestry workers were affected by the Government's Wages Pause Policy; a wage increase of 8s 6d per week was agreed in December, but it was not paid until April 1962.

There was a big battle in 1963 for a reduction in the working week from 43 to 40 hours. The FC refused any reduction, despite the Union cutting its request to 42 hours, which the FC finally conceded.

On a suggestion of the FWAC, John Hose replaced E. Pigott on the FCITC, and the following year John replaced Percy Schofield, chairman Cheshire County Committee, on the EC.

When in 1965 the administration of the FC was reorganised, Reg Bottini, Tom Healy (TGWU) and Jack Eccles (GMWU) met Fred Willey, Minister of Land and Natural Resources, to protest at the ignoring of the trade-union side of the FCITC. They also complained about the FC's shortfall in planting and land acquisition, and deplored the increasing use of private contractors. The Minister confirmed that as at September 1964, the FC's industrial employees numbered 10,973 as against 11,200 a year earlier. He 'hoped' the numbers would increase by about 650 over the next five years, as the FC was now entering into marketing and processing.

Union members hoped the changes would lead to the extra jobs Mr. Willey forecast, and at the 1965 TUC at Brighton, the Union submitted an amendment to a Civil Service Union motion dealing with the expansion of the FC and the need to end the use of private contractors. John Hose said that in 1954 when FC thinnings and fellings amounted to 26 million hoppus feet,* the amount handled by contractors rose sevenfold, to over 15 million hoppus feet. Congress unanimously supported the amended motion.

There was a long debate on forestry at the 1966 Biennial. John Hose listed a number of improvements, especially that of the grading scheme, and hoped

---

* The cubic measurement of a tree before metrication.

that the Labour Government would see to it that the profit now coming out of the woodlands would revert to the people who paid for it in the first place – the taxpayers. The Conference wanted a review of 'the whole structure of FC schemes, wages and conditions which at present is heavily loaded in favour of administrative staff, to the detriment of our members.'

'If the FC had sat down deliberately to invent a means of causing the greatest annoyance, frustration and anger to their workers, they could hardly have come up with anything more calculated to do it than the private contractors,' declared D. Harrison, a young forestry worker from Hants, when moving a successful composite against private contractors. The majority of contractors left the woods in a very untidy state which had to be corrected by FC staff, adding to the cost. Contractors left a tornado of rubbish scattered through the countryside.

Moving a successful resolution calling for all work-study investigations by the FC to be done by independent consultants or by a team with equal trade-union representation, Fred Peachey, Hants, said that they were not opposing progress or modernisation, but objected to work-study schedules being arrived at by FC officials 'on which the forestry worker has at no time been allowed an opinion'. Fred, FWAC chairman, predicted an acute timber shortage in Europe by 1970, and Conference once more called for an expansion of the FC's activities.

In 1967, during wage negotiations in which no advance was made because of 'severe wages restraint' by the Labour Government, the FC tried to break national bargaining by proposing differential rates for Scotland, England and Wales. The Union wisely opposed this retrogressive policy. A TUC deputation to the Minister of Agriculture reflected the deep concern of FC workers about their future prospects, and at that year's TUC, John Hose continued the campaign against private contractors.

That matters were worsening for FC employees was made devastatingly clear in 1968 when the Commission said it would reduce the labour force by 2,000 by September 1972. Despite a vigorous protest by the NUAAW and two other unions, the Minister of Agriculture accepted the recommendation that 1,490 jobs, or 19.3% of the labour force, would go by 1972.

At that year's Biennial at Aberystwyth, a wide-ranging speech was made by Prime Minister Harold Wilson, but not once did he mention forestry. This omission was taken up by John Hose, who said this was worrying at a time when we needed an expansion of the industry in order to save foreign exchange. Redundancy, he said, threatened nearly one quarter of FC workers, and Fred Peachey moved a successful resolution demanding that the Labour Party be reminded of their many promises regarding a secondary form of employment in rural areas. D. Wanklyn, S Wales, said there was the highest percentage of unemployment in the Welsh valleys, and the present forestry policy would aggravate this situation; conference wanted all private contractors barred from FC work. The Union, at that year's TUC, moved a successful motion deploring the run-down in FC jobs.

In 1969, a delegation from the TUC saw the Minister of Agriculture on FC policy, but little satisfaction was gained. This came after a House of Commons debate on the FC at the end of 1968, when figures given showed that in 1957, 35% of the work done in Commission forests was done by contract labour, which increased to 58% by 1963, and in 1967 was 50%. John Parker, MP for Dagenham, was concerned at the big drop in the FC workforce. He wanted the Commission's work to be planned ahead so that it could use its own labour and not contract unless absolutely essential. Replying, John Mackie, Minister of Agriculture, said that the reduction in labour had been necessary because of important technical progress. He announced more planting in Scotland, but was less hopeful for the South West and East Anglia.

FC Financially Disadvantaged

In 1970, the Union pressed the Government to change the financial support system under which the FC is seriously disadvantaged compared with private forest syndicates, but there was virtually no hope of a change for the better when Labour was defeated and Edward Heath installed as Prime Minister.

An explanation of this disadvantage was given in one of the most severe verbal assaults ever made in the Commission's 50-year history, when John Hose at the 1970 Biennial declared, 'One has the impression that the FC has the death wish on it, that it is determined to go just as fast as it possibly can.' He said the Government's policy on the FC had seen a further reduction in the labour force; there were about 1,500 fewer workers than 18 months earlier. Only about 100 had been sacked. Many left of their own accord, 'disgusted with the attitude, not only of the FC, but of the Treasury at the back of them, and the Government at the back of them.' He said that the FC's efforts to acquire land had been scotched by the Treasury. Meanwhile the Government's fiscal policy had given the private sector a huge tax advantage over the Commission.

He instanced the case of some 250 acres in Cumberland, where the owner played the State foresters off against the private sector. The FC's offer was acceptable to the owner, but because the Commission could not afford to buy the inbye land and buildings, the Economic Forestry Group bought the lot. The Group immediately sold off the inbye land and buildings, planted the upper land with the aid of an FC grant, and left it completely without staff.

John gave another example of how the private sector found it financially attractive to take on land and 'outwit Government departments'. The establishment cost of clearing, fencing, draining and planting of an average 1,000 acres of land would be about £57,000 over 20 years. For this, the private owner would get a grant of £33,000, leaving him to find £24,000 over 20 years to establish the wood. In fact, the tax system meant he need find at most about £14,000; if he were in the surtax bracket he would have to find less than £2,000 – and that was for a plantation that after 20 years would be worth £180,000.

His speech was a curtain raiser for a motion moved by Fritz Berthele, Northumberland, who wanted a searching inquiry into the FC by the Union, the TUC and through the Forestry Group of Labour MPs. Fritz said there was a lot of dead wood in the FC, but it was at the top of the ladder. The labour force consisted of three workers to one official and this was 'deplorable'. Nearly £4½ million was spent in 18 months by the Commission on administration alone.

Ron Taylor, S Wales, said that the perilous position of the FC was the deliberate result of Government long-term policy aimed at winding up the Commission and handing it over to the private contractors. And E. Hudson, Norfolk, declared that the high proportion of staff meant high overheads resulting in the FC being unable to compete with the timber merchants. In the 18 months in which industrial staff had been cut by 1,441, non-industrial staff was reduced by 45; a ratio of 32 to one. The motion and an addendum, that the managerial side be thoroughly inspected with regard to expenditure and manpower, were both carried.

At the 1970 TUC, John Hose again took up the cudgels on behalf of forestry workers, and challenged the truth of the replies from Cledwyn Hughes, former Labour Minister of Agriculture, on the occasion of meetings and correspondence with him in 1969. The Unions had pressed for faster forestry expansion, but the Minister had replied that we must maintain a proper balance between hill farming and forestry. 'What he didn't tell us,' said John, 'is the stark fact that although the FC is expected to maintain this balance by not planting hill land, no such restriction is placed on the private sector. One such private company increases the amount of its managed plantations by 20,000 acres a year.' The Minister had also claimed that very little FC work was put out to contractors, but members knew otherwise.

Output per FC worker had risen by 90% since 1960, and during the same period there was an increase of 80% in the average hourly wage rates, according to the 50th Annual Report of the FC in 1970. It was clear that the increased productivity of forestry workers in recent years had been far in excess of their increased earnings. The FC declared that the enhanced output per worker had been partly due to simplification of the products made in the forest, and the larger trees now being worked. Pity the compilers could not bring themselves to give the workers some credit for this splendid productivity record.

The Report confirmed that non-industrial staff as a proportion of industrial staff continued to rise. Of the former, 83 left during the year ended 31 March 1970, to leave 2,617 (13 more than in 1957). Industrial staff who left in 1970 numbered 7,487, after a fall of 834, of whom 10% were sacked. Despite increased costs, Government aid for the year was £15.1 million, almost £½ million less than the previous year, and included £3,382,941 in subsidies to private forestry. The Report referred to 'informal round table discussion' with the private sector 'held in confidence'. What, wondered Union members, was being covered up?

This FC Report was no surprise to the Union, as the Tory Government had given absolutely no sign that they would take any action whatsoever to reduce the considerable disquiet among forestry workers. Early in 1971, the FWAC met the Minister of Agriculture, James Prior, and there had been frank talks about the acute anxiety among members about the FC's deliberate policy of reducing the workforce, and hiving off some of the more profitable State enterprises to the private sector. Prior was unable to guarantee that there would not be any further contraction in FC operations.

At the Suffolk County Conference in 1972, Bert Hazell attacked the Government's forestry policy. He referred to the alleged loss in 1971 of some £3 million by the FC. Pointing out that the total grant aid to the FC since its inception in 1919 amounted to less than total Government subsidies to agriculture in any year since 1947, Bert declared, 'Of course, like the farmers, the Commission with three million acres are in business, but what is so frequently overlooked is the recreational facilities . . . for picnics, pony trekking, camping and fishing. It is impossible to put a cash figure to the amenity value of the FC's services, but they would be sadly missed by the public if they were not available.'

Referring to the £2 million in grants to private woodland owners in the previous year, Bert reiterated the truth that, commercially, the FC was obliged to compete on disgracefully unequal terms with private forestry. He hoped that MAFF would take account of all this in the Review of Forestry Policy so long promised.

He had some time to wait. It had still not been issued by the time of the Union's Biennial which condemned the Government's policy of gradual disengagement from State forestry. Basil Finney, Cumberland, mover of the resolution, said that '. . . thousands of acres of unproductive moors used solely for the benefit of rich gunmen should be purchased and brought into production.'

Finally, the Review was published as a White Paper later that year, and surveyed the FC's financial position, the returns on capital invested and the benefits in providing work and recreational facilities. The Government agreed that it would be unfair to expect forests to provide a return of capital greater than 3%, and where there was need to provide employment, a rate of 1% might be considered reasonable. This was a far cry from the 10% that had been expected for many years. Although difficult to put a cash value on the use the public makes of State forest for recreation, the Government recognised the importance of this and expected the current £1½ million costs of recreational purposes to rise to £6 million over the next decade.

When the Review made comparisons with the private sector, it confirmed much of what the NUAAW had been saying for years – that Government aid and tax benefits were of greater value than the private woodland owner admitted – but the Government was not prepared to see any enlargement of the FC estate.

John Hose welcomed the Government's acceptance of the FC role as a provider of recreational facilities, but thought the Government should make greater use of the existing powers under the Forestry Act 1947, and move into milling, pulping, etc. Summing up he said, 'We shall continue to press for expansion rather than decline, for permanent employment in the forest as opposed to redeployment to suit planting and felling programmes and for better marketing and management systems than at present.'

The early 1970s saw a continued stream of resolutions at biennials concerning the FC's lack of large-scale planting, and a new concern was noted. The FC had been under attack for some years for its unsightly geometric grids of quick-growing pine and spruce, which conservationists said spoilt upland areas; and tried to appease them by ringing some plantations with deciduous trees. Some Union members saw these criticisms as a danger to the industry, and at the 1974 Biennial when the conservationists came under attack it was claimed that they 'now only have to lift a finger and the Commission do as they wish'. Since then, there is little to show that planting a greater variety of trees has significantly harmed the FC financially, or caused job losses. And by the 1980s, Union members and conservationists were more likely to be working hand-in-hand than fighting each other.

When a Labour Government was returned in October 1974, Gavin Strang, Parliamentary Secretary to the Minister of Agriculture, met another Union delegation putting the case for expansion of State forests, but the following year, Minister of Agriculture Fred Peart expressed doubts as to whether this was possible in the current economic climate, and very little expansion ever took place. Throughout the 1970s, forestry workers were again victims of various government schemes to restrict pay increases, and there were still no substantial alternative forms of employment.

Technical Innovations

As with agriculture, there had been a tremendous mechanisation of forestry by the 1970s, and many skilled mechanics were required to take advantage of technical innovations which went far beyond the chain saw. However, in the actual planting of trees, spade or mattock were still much in evidence. Even here, on suitable sites, deep ploughing enabled a man to plant thousands of trees where once he planted hundreds in the course of a week's work. Weeds that checked early tree growth were still controlled by hand, but more and more mechanical and chemical weeding made for a higher productive force. Most timber cutting was now done by power saw, as was the initial conversion to sawn timber, and specially-designed tractors and haulage vehicles opened up land that would have once been uneconomical for forestry.

All this called for a highly-skilled workforce, and apart from the campaign for better wages and conditions, protective clothing and safety helmets, NUAAW representatives on the Forestry Training Council pressed for forestry skill tests to be recognised by the National Proficiency Test Committee, well above the basic rates then enforceable. One aspect of forestry, ahead of agricultural workers, was safety. Not only did forestry workers have active safety representatives, but they also had a say in drafting safety policies.

When the new Tory Government came to power in 1979, the Union feared that there would be a slashing of the FC. It was not long in coming. In 1980, the Government announced plans to sell off more FC woodlands. This asset-stripping – in line with that of the worst of predatory sharks in the City – would raise about £100 million over the next three years, although the Union did not expect the FC to be wound up. The Government's Forestry Act 1981 included legislation for the sell-off.

John Hose denounced the Government's policy as 'a doctrinaire measure designed to dispose of publicly-owned land to private interests ... Their main interest will be a return on investment rather than the diligent management of a valuable asset for the good of the whole community ... The new Bill is a licence to exploit this investment by the taxpayers. It is a chance for the fly-boys to buy mature woodland, planted and maintained at public expense, and to denude it of trees.'

Campaign to Save Public Forests

Branches and area conferences condemned the Government's policy, and after meetings of the FWAC, the Union launched a big campaign to save Britain's publicly-owned forests, declaring that privatisation would lead to 'No Entry' signs and miles of barbed wire surrounding private forests.

The NUAAW joined with other unions in forestry in campaigning to stop the sales. The campaign was co-ordinated by TGWU official, Arthur Mills, who would gladly sell anyone a 'Stop Forest Sales' T-shirt for £2.59 or hand out leaflets to picnickers in a forest. The campaign aroused a lot of public support; it had no immediately discernible effect on Government policy, but did perhaps play a part in the later slowing down of forest sales.

In 1983, the FC put another 25 plantations on its 'for sale' list, totalling 15,000 acres, and that year, Labour's manifesto for the next General Election promised to reconstitute the FC as an expanding public enterprise. Labour failed to win the election.

Forestry workers' anger boiled over in May when men from several North Eastern forests staged a one-day stoppage over lack of progress on their annual pay claim and the threat of redundancies from sales of FC land. An offer by the FC of a 4% rise was dismissed as 'too little, too late' by the Union side on 17 May. This paltry offer would have produced a new weekly basic of £71.25 (£2.75 increase) for unskilled workers and £81 (£3.10 increase) for craftsmen, some £7.71 behind craftsmen in private woodlands.

This increase should have taken effect on 1 February 1983 – after five months' delay – and Arthur Mills, the Union negotiator, said they were tired of endless delaying tactics by the FC, 'We are going to contact the Minister direct.' The Union had first notified the FC of its claim in October 1982, and heard nothing till May 1983. The 4% increase would leave forestry workers worse off in real terms. The FC said they had to abide by Government guidelines.

Jack Boddy, John Hose and Arthur Mills met the new Minister of Agriculture, Michael Jopling, and sought to impress upon him just how serious the situation had become. Jack forcefully told him that the FC, on instructions from the Treasury, was trying to reduce the pay award in real terms by deductions from superannuation contributions. The delegation also pointed out that, in the past, the FC had always related its offer to the settlement reached by the AWB, an alignment always opposed by Union negotiators. however, this year, the FC was back-tracking on the usual procedure.

Finally, eight months later, the FC came up with a pay offer the workers could accept. An extra 5% from February 1982, 3% more in September. It meant an unskilled forest worker earning £68.50 a week would get £71.90 backdated to 1 February, and £74.08 backdated to 1 September. A craftsman earning £77.90 got £81.79 backdated to 1 February, and £84.24 backdated to 1 September.

A TUC delegation met Government ministers on 18 October to express concern at the Government's policy on State forestry. Bryn Davies, S Wales DO, and Stuart Neale were in the group which told ministers that the new land planted by the State and private sector was well below the target of the 1981 Forestry Act, and wanted to know if failure to reach Treasury target sales of £82 million by 1985 would lead to FC land being sold at give-away prices. The ministers were quite open about the Government's intention to shift the balance from State to private hands, but claimed that it was only 10% of FC land up for sale or already sold.

Arthur Mills and Stuart Neale, accompanied by members of other forestry unions, two television cameras and newspaper photographers, marched up to No 10 Downing Street and handed in the gift of a Christmas tree. Stuart was in full safety-gear and carried a chain saw. When a small group of onlookers saw him, there was an ironic cheer. Did they mistake the purpose of his call on Mrs. Thatcher? The gift was meant as a reminder to Mrs. Thatcher that the policies of her Government threatened the very future of the nation's trees.

Next came a lobby at the House of Commons. The presence of more than 60 MPs must have made it one of the more successful Parliamentary campaigns that the Trade Group had been involved in, and showed the concern felt by MPs. The lobby was chaired by Falkirk's Labour MP, Dennis Canavan, who said that the 1981 Act gave the Government power to sell more and more. Mrs. Thatcher 'knows the strength of feeling among MPs about those increases [sales], and that's why she has not the guts, honesty or decency to come back to the House and debate them.' Labour's new agricultural spokesman, Bob Hughes, said, 'we fully support this campaign against the sales.'

In February 1984, the *Landworker* disclosed that a formal MAFF statement just published, but not publicised, revealed the true nature of the Government's Forestry Act. Liberal MP, Stephen Ross, had asked for a simple listing of all woods sold or listed for sale since the 1981 Act came into effect. Those lists demonstrated that dramatic impact of privatisation. There were more than one thousand names on the list. In Powys, for example, 32 separate woods or plantation blocks were being sold off at the end of the 1981–2 financial year – only eight months after the 1981 Act became law. Another 24 Powys names were listed under the heading of completed sales by November 1982, but only a few of these names appeared as 'in the process of being sold' in the previous March. Most were clearly additional sales. Another 40 Powys plantations were listed as being sold at November 1983. So some 100 separate woodlands in Powys alone had been privatised since July 1982.

This scale of asset-stripping was repeated in most of the FC heartlands. The list of sales in Dyfed and Clwyd, Strathclyde, Highland, Grampian, Dumfries and Galloway, Northumberland, North Yorkshire and all Eastern conservancies in England were equally dramatic. Arthur Mills said that they brought home the realities of privatisation. 'We can now measure the impact in a way people understand rather than quote pretty meaningless figures.'

In the House of Commons the Government said it had no plans to increase the current disposal programme of £82.1 million, but the period over which it was to be achieved had been extended by one year to 31 March 1987. Thus the Government announced a climbdown. There would be no further sales for the time being once that £82 million had been reached. The Union had won a great victory, albeit temporary, for there are still a lot of forests that could be put on offer.

Welcoming the news, Arthur Mills said, 'It is the Union's belief that the sales are still part of Tory dogma. A vigorous campaign and the united opposition of Labour, Liberal and SDP MPs has helped to curb the Government's excesses, but the real opposition has come from the ordinary people of Britain. Only when all the FC woodlands are returned to the British people will we celebrate a victory.'

Later in 1984, the Trade Group launched a national petition to keep Britain's forests open to the public, and 20,000 petition forms were distributed from Headland House. Thousands of signatures were collected, and the forms were plonked down on a ministerial desk to ram home the point.

'Secret' forest sales by the FC were condemned in 1984 by one of the most influential political bodies in the country. MPs on the Public Accounts Committee, with a built-in Tory majority, told the Commission that secret woodland sales were no longer acceptable to Parliament and demanded a 'full explanation of sales policy and practice'. They wanted to know why the FC refused to make public the price they had sold nationally-owned assets for. In a report of the Committee, it was clear that Labour, Social Democrat and even Tory MPs were shaken by the extent of the secrecy surrounding woodland sales since the passing of the 1981 Act. It showed that the FC had kept secret reserve prices, below which the Commission claimed they refused to sell; secret buyers, with no names published, even after the sale; secret selling prices, again even after sales were complete. The MPs obviously felt that they had stumbled across an extension of the Mafia where Omerta (silence) is law. The Committee formally recommended that the FC should publish the price of land when sold. Once again, the Trade Group's stand had been vindicated.

Later in 1984, the *Landworker* was able to analyse FC figures on FC land sales, which were beginning to show a pattern. It gave a good idea of where, and why, the forests were being sold. In the three years up to 9 July 1984, just over 27,000 hectares of forest were sold. As many as 17,500 hectares went in Scotland. In Scotland, 15 individual sales over 400 hectares constituted 76% of the land sold; in Wales, 97% of the sales were in parcels of less than 40 hectares. This lent weight to the suggestion that the major beneficiaries were wealthy landowners with already large estates. In England, the picture was more diffuse; some 5% of East Conservancy land was sold, but less than 10% in the North East. Twelve separate sales of more than 100 hectares accounted for 36% of land sold in England. Following a statement in Parliament in July 1984, it appeared that the average price from July 1981 to June 1984 was £873 per hectare. It was believed by the Union that the same Commission land, not for special tracts, was making as much as £1,800 per hectare, which meant that great chunks of FC land had been sold at knock-down prices. Landowners and private companies did very well out of these sales.

Although the FC sales programme in 1984 was increased, Tory plans for a wholesale sell-off were shelved. Forestry Minister George Younger said that the Government had decided that the sales programme was to be extended to 31 March 1989, and that its 'main purpose should be the rationalisation of the estate with a view to improving the Commission's efficiency and . . . commercial effectiveness . . .' G. D. Holmes, director general of the FC, described the statement as 'a vote of confidence by the Government in the future of the FC.'*

Whether forestry workers could have equal confidence was another matter. The past record was clearly not good. In the late sixties, as we have seen, there had been big cuts in its programme, with many job losses, even when Labour was in office. By 1984, wages for FC workers were still low compared with other industrial workers. By 1985, the forest craftsmen's wage had risen to £93.65, and the basic wage to £83.35, compared with AWB wages of £89.70.

And the way forward for the Union? The new Trade Group national secretary, Barry Leathwood, says, 'The selling off by the FC of woodland, and the use of contract labour is not popular with those who value what is an extremely important public asset. Now more than ever before, we have to

---

*   In June 1989, the Tory Government announced that it wanted the FC to sell off another 100,000 hectares to raise £150 million over the next 10 years. This is 11% of FC holdings. Since 1981, 75,000 hectares of plantable land were sold, netting £130 million for the Tory Government to dish out in tax cuts to the very wealthy.

link up with the environmental, conservation and recreational organisations in a massive campaign to keep British forests public, to provide good secure employment and an environmentally sensitive management policy, and giving access to the public.'

President with a Difference

John Hose was born in Nottingham, one of three children of a railwayman. He attended a State school, then gained a place at the esteemed Blue Coat School in the city. He left in 1943, worked in an architect's office until he became a sapper in the Royal Engineers. He was engaged on bomb disposal, but left the Army with the rank of corporal, determined never to work indoors again. For a year he dug trenches for Nottingham Corporation Waterworks, then went to the FC training camp at Grizedale in the Lake District. There he joined the Union, went to Sherwood Forest in 1949, married twice, and retired in 1988. A lot happened to John between those two dates.

In Sherwood Forest he became very active in the Union as secretary of the Annesley, Arnold and Woodborough branches, and, taking a great interest in education, represented the Union on the regional council of the WEA. He finished as the last president of the NUAAW before the post disappeared after the merger. He became chairman of the Trade Group and later, after his retirement, received the Group's Gold Badge.

John did a variety of jobs for the Union. Especially noteworthy was his work for the forestry workers; appropriately, for 'relaxation', he went fell walking, and when he could not get near the fells, walked across London to Union conferences. The day I met him in 1990 he had walked from St. Pancras station to Transport House.

John also liked to relax with a book – his house was stuffed full of them – and was especially interested in military history and biography. Another way of relaxing was with a beer, and listening to Irish folk music in his local pub.

Looking back over the years of Union work, he believed one of its failures has been the inability to reach firm decisions. 'To sit in at a meeting, by the hour, the day, the week. Then ask what have we achieved – nothing. Decisions were needed. I think this is one of the failings of trade unions, generally.'

Recruitment to the NUAAW failed, he believed, because its leaders were too busy doing other jobs. 'We were always a parochial organisation. DOs were a law unto themselves. Norfolk and Lincolnshire were the basis of the old NUAAW. Belonging was a step upwards; keep your nose clean, and you were a parochial power in the land. It was a step towards the county council, being a JP. Ultimately you might make Parliament or the House of Lords.

'You believed in trade unions, but there was a breaking point. If you became a DO, you continued to do everything you had been doing as a lay officer; it became a paid job. I've never had a paid job in the Union.

'Recruitment failed because some DOs convinced the EC that they were so busy representing the membership, that they couldn't find the time to recruit. This failure to recruit applied from DOs to people at the top. I know people doing "outside" jobs felt that what they were doing helped their members, but it took up a lot of their time. There was one full-time officer on 93 committees, which were not in my view directly connected with his agricultural membership. What time did he have left for Union work after attending those 93 committees!'

His attitude was in contrast to that of George Edwards, the Union's founder, who believed that members, and presumably officials, should be in on everything. John represented the Union in Europe on the IFPAAW, but this did not come within his category of 'outside' jobs.

John had another criticism of the old Union. 'It needed dragging back from being friendly-society orientated, to being a proper union, so that we could organise the whole of the membership to the same extent that we had got my local forestry group organised. We negotiated our own piece-work rates. If we had all done this, we would have been a better union. We were spending more money on funeral benefits than we were on education. What did the old Union banner say: "Organise, agitate and educate". We should have stuck to that.'

John strongly backed the recruiting officer scheme, which had forceful opposition in the Union, and as already related, was abandoned. He said, 'Eddie Collinson, a former insurance salesman, recruited like mad, including some good people. I believe three of them are now TGWU officials. Rural people are difficult to recruit, but once in, not difficult to retain. Some of my members I haven't seen for 20 years. You have to write to them to keep in touch, but the subs come in. If an RO worked with a group of DOs the scheme worked. If you retained a member for ten years, you got more than the £5 cost of recruitment. Some DOs couldn't service the new members because of their outside interests. If pressure had been put on from the top, the RO scheme would have been a complete success.'

Another scheme John backed was the computerisation of membership records, also abandoned as a failure. He said, 'You had DOs who opposed it, because they opposed centralised control; people failed to sort out the mistakes, so the scheme failed. We possibly tried to bring it in too early, but we are computerised now on a TGWU regional basis, and it works, although mistakes still need sorting out. I don't regret our earlier attempt to save money and be efficient.'

John believed the three greatest successes of the Union in the post-years were to get Raynaud's Phenomenon listed as an industrial disease, the campaign against 245–T, and the forestry training scheme. The listing of Raynaud's disease changed the whole of the chain-saw industry. Chain saws were fitted with anti-vibration devices, operators had to wear anti-vibration gloves and the job was much safer. He believed that the State forestry sector gave the lead to the whole industry on 245–T, and the FC training scheme was the envy of other industries.

He was unique as President. He was not a member of the Labour Party, or any other party come to that. Did he find it a disadvantage? 'No. Some might have thought it curious, but it's never been any problem to me, I never gave it a thought. I could criticise anybody I wanted. I pointed out to conference that it was a Tory Government which stopped forestry being used for tax fiddles.'

John was interested in party politics, but not as a joiner; he had a 'plague on all your houses' attitude. And he was vehement on one thing: 'Trade unions should use politicians, not let politicians use the unions.'

Not the sort of man to give up, John continued to work for the Trade Group locally on his retirement, and nationally continued his battle against forestry privatisation through his work on the joint union committee against disposals of FC land.

REFERENCE

1. *Outlook for Agriculture and its Environment*, Union policy document, 1976.

Union Leadership Goes Left

For if the trumpet give an uncertain sound,
who shall prepare himself to the battle?

New Testament

A Quaker Who Loved Farm Work

One man, Jack Boddy, beginning as an ordinary member and ending as General Secretary at the time of the merger, knew the Union intimately throughout the turbulent post-war years that this history covers. Jack was a man of the left; former general secretaries during and after the Second World War were mainly right-wing. Let us spend a little time with Jack, his experiences, his views and his beliefs as to what went right in the Union, and what went wrong.

When Jack Boddy left the City of Norwich Grammar School in 1939 and told his teacher that he was going to be a farmworker, the astonished man exclaimed, 'Do you mean you're going to waste your education?' But Jack (and few who knew him as an adult would agree it was any sort of a waste – quite the contrary) contributed much to the struggle of the agricultural workers of Britain.

I went to see Jack in Swaffham, Norfolk, where he had lived for many years. He was short in stature, but not in energy or commitment. He had a ready smile, five cats and one dog, and had when I called, not long since mourned the death of his wife Merle, a frequent visitor to biennials. He has since remarried.

Jack, whose dark hair was then greying, was a diabetic, but that had not lessened his hard work for the trade union and Labour movement, something he imbibed almost from the cradle. He was born in Norwich of Quaker parents, his father was a bricklayer at Coleman's Carrow works and the first chairman of Carrow works' council. Both parents were active in the Labour movement; his father was a Norwich city councillor and later High Sheriff. Characteristically, his father died addressing a public meeting. His parents' house was regularly used as committee rooms during elections, and Jack's first political activity was running between polling stations with electoral registers, checking off the voters. At the age of 10 he was addressing envelopes during a general election.

Before he won a scholarship to the grammar school, Jack briefly attended a CoE school, but the CoE Creed was unacceptable to his parents and he was excused religious instruction. Once, when he was sent to another room for this reason, the teacher automatically assumed he had been sent for punishment, and made him stand in a corner with his hands on his head. His mother was furious, in a polite way.

His desire to work on the land came about because at three, as Jack put it, he was 'supposed' to be delicate, and the doctor advised that he should get into the country as much as possible. His parents took him camping on farms at every opportunity. 'I loved it, particularly being with horses,' said Jack, 'and that's all the work I wanted to do.' He would have liked to become a vet, but his parents couldn't afford the expense, so he began on a farm at Salhouse and quickly became a cowman. His first pay was fairly good, 18s a week, milking at 2am and 2pm, half a day off one afternoon per week. He stayed with the same farmer, a decent sort, for several years and became his farm manager at 22. Later he moved to a 700-acre farm, Standfield Hall, at Wymondham and became farm foreman.

Immediately Jack left school his father got in touch with Jack Quantrill, DO, and his son was signed up in the Union. Every worker on his first farm was in the Union, and Jack was soon collecting dues. As a boy, Jack had been a regular attender at Quaker meetings, and continued to be so. He noticed a new girl at these meetings, which no doubt pleased her, for it appears that her main purpose in attending was to see Jack. It was Merle, a school teacher. She had been CoE, but converted to the Quaker faith, became as active in the trade union and Labour movement as Jack, and was twice mayor of Swaffham.

On moving to Wymondham, she and Jack soon won seats for Labour on Wymondham District Council, and Jack next won a seat on Norfolk County Council from the local doctor, and was appointed a JP, at the time believed to be the youngest magistrate ever.

It was about then that Jack decided that politics were of greater importance to him than farm work. 'I loved the farm, but clearly I couldn't do both. I looked upon Union work as being part of politics, and that was important to me.' He applied for the job of DO for the Holland Division of Lincs, and got it. The Boddys moved to Holbeach, with four children. A little apprehensive of his new responsibilities, Jack went to see Edwin Gooch and told him he didn't know whether he could do the job, as he didn't know anything about it. Edwin said, 'It's easy, all you need is administrative skill.' As a job description, that was quite an understatement.

The first job he found himself doing was representing members before tribunals. A new law, Seasonal Workers Regulations, had been enacted on the initiative of Barbara Castle; anybody unemployed for the same period each year was disallowed dole after three years, and in order to obtain benefit had to have a quarter of his or her off-season in employment. This particularly affected women workers, and every week Jack was representing 20 to 30 women members, desperate to get their dole, often in the Winter when no work was available. 'In the early days we frequently won their case, but eventually the regulations became so fixed, it was virtually impossible to win,' said Jack.

Jack gained an enormous amount of experience in Lincolnshire. The EC expected DOs to attend three branch meetings a week. 'I was very nervous attending meetings,' said Jack. 'I was physically sick, but I got over it.' And he had enough members to keep him busy. Membership in Holland was then about 16,000, now it is numbered in hundreds. And as a Norfolk man, he was made extremely welcome, which says something about Jack, for a Norfolk man in Lincolnshire was looked upon with a certain degree of suspicion. One possible reason for this was that things were done differently in Lincolnshire from the way they were in Norfolk. The bulk of the work in South Lincolnshire was piece-work; over in Norfolk there was less piece-work. Lincolnshire then led the country with top piece-work rates. 'We operated a piece-work system in Lincolnshire which enabled a man to earn 145% of the basic rate for every crop. This was negotiated with the NFU.'

While in Lincolnshire, Jack became a member of local councils. He had many friends there, but the yearning to get back to Norfolk was strong and in 1960 he applied for the DO vacancy in West Norfolk when Albert Hilton was elected MP. He got the job, and remained S W Norfolk DO until he became General Secretary. He became a member of Norfolk County Council and eventually leader of its Labour Group. He was also appointed a member of local hospital management committees, and chairman of one. He also became a member of the East Anglian Regional Hospital Board and member of the Regional Board for Industry, but not without opposition from the Union's EC.

Jack was not popular with some members of the EC. When he was appointed to the hospital authority he was asked by the EC to either resign from the authority or as Organiser. They claimed he couldn't do both jobs. Jack challenged them to show that as a result of his 'outside' activities his members were being neglected. They couldn't. 'I was never at home at night, and I was working all hours God sent and told them that my activities on the health authority benefitted Union members.'

At the time, the EC was also embroiled with another organiser, Sid King, and didn't want him to take up his appointment with the Trent Regional Authority. Later, the EC admitted that Boddy and King were officers 'of long standing and considerable competence and could not be dismissed without damaging the Union,' and a formal notice to end King's appointment was rescinded. Nothing more was done to get Jack out of his Organiser's job. When Reg Bottini was considered by the S E Electricity Board for a part-time vacancy, the EC decided to take no action after he had raised it with them. Yet the EC later tried to stop Jack joining the East Anglian Economic Planning Council. Their inconsistency was apparent, and Jack ignored them and became a member of the Council.

These were not Jack's first brushes with the EC. Earlier, when he was asked to stand as Labour candidate for Central Norfolk, the EC declared his 'political attitude did not reflect the official Union policy'. I asked Jack if he could enlighten me on this statement. 'That was at the time when Albert Hilton, who was on the EC, was hounding me, and I was on the carpet all the time. I was on the left and Albert was very right-wing. I was anti-nuclear, and it was alleged that I was using my position as DO to propagate my views in opposition to the Union's right-wing policy.'

Jack said that if he differed from the Union's official policy, he never said anything publicly. He never did contest Central Norfolk, but he quickly gained the confidence of Union members in Norfolk, and during one of his conflicts with the EC they threatened to resign *en masse* if he were sacked.

Another of Jack's jobs often brought him into conflict with the EC. He was vice-chairman of the Organisers' Association, which meant he was one of those negotiating wages and conditions of employment with the EC. Jack explained, 'They used to appoint DOs from active members, but once you became a DO, some EC members seemed to assume you were out to do the Union down, and this led to many conflicts. Because the Union subs were paying the DOs, the attitude was to keep DO wages down and keep the DOs working as hard as possible. An absolutely capitalist outlook. Some EC members thought if a DO was only paid as much as a farmworker, it would give him an incentive to get better wages for the members. DOs were kept isolated from each other and were not allowed to go to each others' areas without permission from the EC. Like any employer, they did not want workers, in this case DOs, getting together and offering any united opposition to the EC. Some EC members seemed like some of the worst possible farmers in their attitude to their employees.'

Jack's job as DO in Norfolk covered the Royal Estate at Sandringham. A new Estate Agent stated his intention 'to make the estate pay' and one of the means he adopted was to raise the rents of its tied cottages to their 'economic' value. This meant that rents rose from 6s by varying amounts up to £3, putting all the rents above the statutory maximum deduction from wages. Jack raised this with the Estate Agent, for although the law of the land did not apply to Royal estates, nevertheless it was a recognised practice that they did adhere to the law. Jack persuaded the agent to accept the same means of assessment as the ordinary farmer and have the cottages inspected by the County Wages Committee, on which there were NUAAW members, as well as farmers and independents. He told Bert Huson, one of the Union representatives on the inspecting team, 'Don't be overawed by the Royal Estate, keep the rents as low as possible.' The Committee cut the rents, some to 3s – they were in such a bad state – and many to the statutory 6s, and allowed a few up to £1. The agent then reduced all the rents accordingly and repaid the tenants' money which had been incorrectly deducted, amounting to about £1,000. They subsequently stopped charging any rent at all!

Some time later Jack, with other representatives of the working class, was invited to a party on the Royal yacht moored at Felixstowe, and the Queen and the Duke of Edinburgh were present. Jack was wearing his NUAAW badge and Prince Phillip asked, 'Who are you?'

'I'm NUAAW DO for West Norfolk, and I look after the workers on your estate at Sandringham,' replied Jack.

Prince Phillip responded, 'Ho, ho, no you don't, we do that.'

Jack, remembering some 'improvements' to the workers' cottages, which involved making a toilet and bathroom immediately adjacent to the kitchens with no passage between them as is required by law, told the Duke of this. Prince Phillip replied, 'In all the houses I live in, the toilets open directly on to the living accommodation.'

'I know,' said Jack. 'I've been to Buckingham Palace.' [Jack had been there to receive the MBE from the Queen Mother.]

Prince Phillip said, 'We do the best we can. Get in touch with me.'

Jack asked, 'How do I do that?'

Prince Phillip replied, 'Ring me up; no, better not, write to me.'

But before Jack could do that, he received a letter from Buckingham Palace addressed 'Dear Mr. Boddy', in which Prince Phillip wrote that he had checked and found that all the cottages not scheduled for sale or demolition were last modernised five years ago and had bathrooms and W.Cs. He said that it was obviously not possible for them to conform exactly to the Parker/Morris* standards of newly-constructed cottages. Perhaps he had misunderstood the nature of Jack's complaint, and would be happy to look into any questions he cared to raise. The letter was signed 'Yours sincerely, Phillip'. Jack did write again, but heard nothing further.

Although Jack was retired in 1988 when I interviewed him in a day-long mardle, as befits Norfolk, he was still active in Union and Labour Party work. While I was at his house, the phone rang. It was from a man he was trying hard to get into a council house. The cottage the man was living in was in a bad state, and his only water supply was from a nearby drain. Still no tap water towards the end of the 20th century!

Relations with the Labour Party

Reviewing the Union's relations with the Labour Party over the years, Jack said, 'We always submitted our policy documents to the Labour NEC; to what extent they paid any attention is debatable. Union policy was always for public ownership of the land, but as far I know this was never included in Labour policy statements. Nye Bevan introduced the idea of taking over large estates, but that's about as far as it went.' He did not think there was much evidence

---

*   The Parker/Morris standards are those laid down by law.

of 'any concrete influence', adding, 'Joan Maynard, Edwin Gooch and Bert Hazell were members of the NEC. Joan was on the left and Edwin and Bert on the right, so what impact they had is less obvious, because the NEC was right-wing anyway, and none of Joan's socialist philosophy was acceptable to them.'

However, despite the disappointments over the tied-cottage legislation, Jack believed that the 1976 Act which abolished the worst evils of the tied cottage was the Union's greatest achievement since the Second World War, followed closely by improvements in holiday entitlement and the legislation to make safety cabs on tractors compulsory.

Although many members must have been profoundly disappointed with successive Labour Governments, very few ever contracted-out of paying the political levy (which amounted to 1d or 2d per week) to the Labour Party. But Jack recalled that 'where we had one or two Conservative branch secretaries, we sometimes received contracting-out forms for every member of that branch.'

The coming into the Union of the newly established poultry factory workers made a great difference to the Union. They made a substantial contribution to its income when subscriptions from farmworkers were slumping because of the fall in the farm workforce. 'But,' said Jack, 'in some ways our attention to the basic agricultural worker became more relaxed, in that in a factory it was relatively easy to enrol members, whereas the farmworker still had to be recruited on an individual basis, and it was easier to go for the easy option.' The militancy of the poultry worker did not spin off on to farmworkers. 'It's easy to be militant when there's, say, 300 of you in a factory, but not so easy when you are one or two farmworkers, working alongside the boss. The poultry workers, with the help of the Union, did score some notable victories.'

Wages for farmworkers were never anything near what Jack would have liked them to be. But rates of pay while Jack was General Secretary and Trade Group Secretary rose by £56.20 over a 10-year period, which was as much as they had done in the previous 40 years.* This increase coincided with Thatcher's 'keeping down' of wages and inflation. 'Although inflation accounted for some of that increase,' said Jack, 'she can't have been as successful as she would have us believe.'

Another profound criticism of Labour governments was their various attempts to restrict wages. Jack said, 'I'm in a dilemma. I've supported Labour all my life, but I hesitate to comment on what I believe to be basic failures of the labour movement to do for workers what they should and could have done.' He recalled Barbara Castle's introduction of the Seasonal Workers Regulations, which 'denied the dole to many who had been made unemployed through no fault of their own, and I could see no logic in the decision to introduce and maintain this particular piece of legislation.'

---

* Wages in 1956 were £6.75 per week; in 1966, £10.50; 1976, £36.50; 1978, £43.00 (when Jack became Secretary); 1987, £99.20.

Neither could he see much logic in Mrs. Castle's policy document, *In Place of Strife*. 'I never believed it was going to get off the ground as far as the trade union movement was concerned, because it hit against the workers' interests. It didn't, but it enabled the Tories when they came to power to quote in support of their anti-working class legislation the decisions taken by the previous Labour administration, and eventually paved the way for the vicious attack on the unions by Mrs. Thatcher. It also helped her to find excuses to make the monstrous charges for various DHSS services, at the same time as reducing the efficiency of the National Health Service. Strange to say, when Heath was premier and introduced cost-of-living pay settlements, the agricultural workers were able to maintain and slightly improve their incomes relative to other workers in a way in which had not been possible under some Labour administrations. While farmworkers were getting the same increase as everyone else under Heath, the gap between their pay and that of other workers was being reduced.'

The strike at Bernard Matthews' poultry plant cost the Union £75,000 at a time when the Union's finances were in a disastrous state. 'I think that £75,000 sealed the Union's fate as far as merging with another union was concerned,' said Jack. 'I don't regret having the strike; there was no alternative. The situation was forced upon us, negotiations had reached an impasse and according to agreements with the firm, I was called in as part of the procedures. Bernard Matthews said he was prepared to meet me on my own, an offer I rejected. Matthews eventually agreed to meet me accompanied by three shop stewards. In the discussion which followed he indicated he was not prepared to make any offer above that already made, which the members had rejected. We left the meeting and reported to the remaining shop stewards, who decided to recommend to a mass meeting that notice be given of strike action in accordance with the agreement. The workers were out for six weeks and Matthews made a number of offers and ACAS was involved. Members had begun drifting back, although the strike was still substantial, and a mass meeting agreed to a return to work with no victimisation. We made a gain on the original offer, but it was not as substantial as we might have hoped. It was not until subsequent negotiations, in which I was not involved, that we saw the success of the strike. They got a better settlement than on previous occasions.'

Financial Decline

Jack attributed the earlier financial decline of the Union to two things: the rebuilding of Headland House and all the associated expenditure, and the attempt to bring the Union into the 20th century by over-involving branch secretaries in the computerisation of the membership records. It was a mistake to attempt to involve branch secretaries in basic, yet important work connected with computers, which placed too big a strain on them. 'We spent an enormous amount of money in setting up computers and lost a large number of branch contributions as a result,' said Jack. He was not against some computerisation. When he became General Secretary, he persuaded the EC to agree to install a computer of a simplified type in the finance department to maintain records, but it did not involve branch secretaries in its operation and it worked very well.

'When I ran for the general secretaryship I had no inkling of the bad financial state of the Union, as I later found it. My reaction was that I had to do something about it as a matter of urgency. I entered into discussions with solicitors acting for the Union with a view to their accepting responsibility for some of the work being done by the Legal Department, which was costing the Union a lot of money.

'I involved the Publicity Department in preparing posters, leaflets, etc., to make it easier for recruitment, but the situation was against us and it was virtually impossible to achieve savings in expenditure and the increased income to keep the Union independent. It was clear that we could not continue along the road we were travelling without substantial staff cuts, which I felt would decrease services to membership. Some thought we should cut the number of DOs, but my experience told me that this would so reduce the service as to be self-defeating in maintenance and recruitment of membership. There was no alternative to joining up with some other union.

'I had been a member for 40 years and was unhappy at the prospect of the Union ceasing to be an independent organisation. My discussions with other unions were all designed to ensure that we were able to continue to exist with as independent a set up as was possible. In my initial discussions with Moss Evans of the TGWU, he indicated that the agricultural workers had been at the forefront of the establishment of trade unions in Britain and his view was that our organisation should continue as an entity of its own. This has not worked as well as I hoped. It was my idea that the agricultural section should organise small groups of rural workers such as quarrymen, small rural industries, foundries, furniture workshops, garages and similar groups, which the bigger unions have never organised, but we with our experience of organising isolated workers, could organise. But this never materialised.

'If the Trade Group is going to succeed, I'm convinced it has still got to do this, as I can see a continued decline in the agricultural labour force. So for the sake of the countryside and the rural worker generally, the Trade Group's activities have to be extended, with the positive encouragement of the EC of the TGWU.'

In an afterthought, Jack said, 'The future of farming at present is being decided in Europe and the problems of the rural worker are to a large extent ignored. British agriculture has to some extent become the victim of its own success, and one of the problems of European agriculture has been that for years the EEC has been endeavouring to produce a policy which will ensure the survival of the French, Italian and West German small farmer, while we have tried to make that same policy suit the large British farm units. This has led to problems with EEC policies, huge surpluses which cost fantastic amounts to store or destroy, and I don't think that it is possible to maintain a modern agricultural system in Britain with a uniform policy such as this. Our future lies in a greater diversification within the agricultural policy of the whole of Europe.

'What is required in Britain is equal emphasis on research, to devise a system of agriculture which suits current needs, as was put into the research and development of past successes. This is an objective which is being disregarded by the current Tory Government, which is persistently running down research establishments or placing them in private hands. We need research into lower input and lower output farming, which could be as profitable as maximising production, and at the same time maintain a viable labour force. This must entail less use of chemicals, particularly nitrogenous fertilisers, and a substantial reduction in the use of pesticides which are currently doing so much damage to the environment and wildlife, to say nothing of what they are probably doing to the people who use them, and ultimately, the consumer.'

1984 – The Year of Newspeak

In his opening address at the Trade Group's annual conference at Eastbourne in May 1984, John Hose said it was almost impossible that year for any trade unionist not to compare the industrial and political relationships obtaining 150 years earlier, at the time of the Tolpuddle Martyrs, and the present time. He declared that 1834 'was a time of reactionary anti-working class attitudes, opposed to those who would better themselves by banding together against the actions of rapacious employers . . . 150 years has brought us full circle, and the gains made so painfully over that time are, it seems, to be sacrificed on the altar of autocracy and nepotism as the placemen and office seekers are replaced by self-seeking men and media manipulators.'

By 1984, Britain was becoming the squalid and selfish society thrown up by a new breed of boastful Toryism, that of Margaret Thatcher. John said, 'The present Government is . . . intent on destroying democracy not only in the trade unions but within the country as a whole . . . the Government of this country has taken upon itself to remove power from local government – and Parliament, under the guise of good economic management. The year of Newspeak is upon us.'

His allusion to Newspeak was a reference to George Orwell's prophetic *1984* tale of Big Brother watching the humbled workers. Orwell had written his satirical and nightmarish tale before women's liberation, and had not envisaged Big Sister, and the threat to liberty was more subtle than Orwell prophesied. Instead of blatant Newspeak, we had the manipulation of the news by 'unimpeachable' sources, and whilst we had no Ministry of Plenty with its fake figures, we had the massaging of employment figures, readjustment of economic forecasts – anything from interest rates to that of inflation. A kind of kid-glove, sophisticated Newspeak if you like. Much of it was enveloped by an obsessive secrecy beloved by Margaret Thatcher.

It was all so cleverly done that, for a long time, some of the poorer sections of the community thought it was in their interest, whether it was the attacks on the trade unions, or the sale of council houses. Later, many realised that the unions were no longer able to fight, for example, for safety standards in industry; or that house 'owners' found that they could not pay the mortgages on their newly-acquired council houses.

The Tory Government's attacks on the trade unions was openly questioned by the ILO, representing government, unions and employers. It said that Britain was in breach of international conventions on eight counts, and called for legislation to bring Britain into line with the minimum requirements accepted by other countries.[1]

The Catholic Church strongly criticised the Thatcher Government for undermining trade union rights. A church working party stated that the Government's belief 'that there is no such thing as society, only individuals and families . . . runs contrary to the belief of Christians'. It sought to encourage Catholics to join unions.[2]

The new laws did seriously weaken the unions, including the TGWU, but the old NUAAW had gradually run down from the heights it scaled in the early post-war years, and it is right to ask whether this loss of strength could have been avoided, how much it was its own fault, and how much the fault of others.

It never succeeded in winning the majority of farmworkers into its ranks; the innate difficulties in organising very small groups of workers over large areas partly accounts for this failure, but not entirely. Despite hard and spirited campaigning on many fronts, it failed to raise agricultural wages to a rate comparable with those in industry generally. Although it secured many improvements, it failed to raise conditions on farms to any great degree for many years, and not until the advent of Joan Maynard in Parliament did it manage to ameliorate the tied cottage system. These were failures, but on no account should it be doubted that wages and conditions would have remained immeasurably worse if the Union had not existed. To that extent, the Union was a godsend to the farmworkers, even if many did not realise it.

These failures should not be entirely attributed to the Union's own weaknesses, or the lack of militancy amongst its members. One prime reason for its failures in the post-war years was that it was badly let down by the Labour governments of those days. They backed the farmers, and short-changed farmworkers at every opportunity.

Whilst these Labour governments showed no keenness to meet the workers' demands, they were not entirely their own masters. Britain was in hock to the United States, which dictated the terms for economic aid as it did to third-world countries in the sixties and seventies. For most of the Second World War, Britain was broke, and received aid at a heavy price. Winston Churchill, in 1940, drafted a telegram to Roosevelt complaining that the USA was behaving like 'a sheriff collecting the last assets of a helpless debtor'. He never sent it. Instead he put a brave face on it, bluffed everyone by talk about a splendid partnership, while in truth Britain was little more than a client state, albeit a very useful one.[3] The early post-war Labour governments continued in the same manner, hence their relationships with the unions were never all they might have been. Not getting justice, many NUAAW members lost heart and drifted away over the years, while other farmworkers were never stirred to join.

Even had the unions fared better, the NUAAW would still have faced a massive loss of members due to the greatly reduced numbers working in the industry, and in the sixties and seventies, the Union failed to streamline its organisation to fit slimmer and changing times.

Another factor which may have kept some workers out of the Union in the post-war years was that, although the Labour Government frequently sought the aid of the Union to help increase food production, it did not pass the notice of some that it did so without giving the Union any real say in policy making. As far back as 1949, the fact that the Labour Government did not heed the views of the workers occasionally slipped out. That loyal Labour man, Edwin Gooch, complained to Norfolk County Committee that 'The Minister [of Agriculture] does not consult the workers.'[4]

Yet another reason, although a lesser one, which may have weakened the Union, was the post-war leadership's inability to accept criticism, or be receptive to new ideas, unless they fitted in with their own preconceived notions of the best policies for the Union. Go-ahead DOs were frequently kept on a short rein, and an example of the EC's distrust of critics can be seen in its reaction to the analytical history of the Union written by Michael Madden (secretary of a county committee) who, after going to Ruskin, won a scholarship to Queen's College, Oxford, where he gained a BA in philosophy, politics and economics. His history, which has already been quoted in this volume, was considered to be a 'misrepresentation of their policies and criticism of their leadership' which revealed 'prejudice in the mind of Bro. Madden'.[5] They refused to back its publication. Michael left the Union, went on to edit the staff magazine of the Southern Electricity Board, and joined NALGO.

In the years immediately before the merger, some Union members believed the EC to be divided and demoralised, when membership and financial losses were mounting at a frightening rate. John Hose does not accept this. 'We were, however, divided,' he told me, 'divided on political grounds. We were divided between ex-officials coming onto the EC and lay members, we were divided on whether subs should be raised, and there was a big divide on the redeployment of staff.'

Contrary to most people, Edgar Pill saw the recruitment of poultry workers as leading to a weakening of the Union. He believed the Union was being swamped with food processors rather than producers. Said John Hose, 'I think that happened. I think it was a bad thing. Edgar preferred a craft union, and thought workers should be organised in their own groups.'

Whatever the pros and cons of craft unions against general membership, there can be no disguising the huge influx of cash the poultry and 'allied' workers brought to the Union, and many contend that this kept the Union independent during its last years. Whether, without this dilution, more farmworkers would have been recruited, is doubtful.

It is not without interest to note that those who were the strongest advocates of the merger in the 1980s were often those who earlier had fought against raising contributions to an economic level. Would this have lost members? It might, considering the low rates of pay, but it is a fallacy to believe that higher contributions alone would have enabled the Union to survive as an independent body.

Ken Tullett (Swanland branch), who attended the 1980 'merger' conference, told me that he refused to be mandated by his branch on the subject. 'Like many others, I went to Cromer with an open mind. It was only when I saw the paucity of ideas in the pro-independent party, who dabbled mainly in nostalgia, and the absolute financial collapse staring us in the face, that I voted for the merger, believing there was no alternative.'

Much heat was raised over one 'alternative'. Selling Headland House and moving into cheaper premises in a country town, say Peterborough. Was it feasible? I doubt it – at the time it was suggested. A small number of unions have successfully made such moves, but they were in a much stronger financial position than the NUAAW when they did so. Additionally, most of their wage negotiations were conducted with employers all over the country; the NUAAW's main negotiations take place in London, and they would have had to have paid frequent visits to the capital for that purpose, and for lobbying ministers, which would have been very costly.

Also, it was said at the time of the merger, Headland House was worth well over £1 million. This might have seemed a modest sum, considering the cost of offices in London, but in reality it was worth much less. In 1982, the auditors insisted on a revaluation of Headland House by independent valuers. They valued it at £770,000, as it was partly tenanted and could not be sold with full vacant possession. This sum could have been swallowed up by redundancy payments, as many head office staff would not have wanted to move.

As President, John Hose refused to sign the transfer of engagements agreement with the TGWU. He told me, 'We failed to stay independent because we did not fully organise. If we were 100% organised we could have taken on the bigger, individual farms, as we did the forests, and won.'

John admits to being bitter about the merger. 'It was a political decision. We could have stayed independent if DOs had accepted reorganisation in the counties, and regionalisation of offices – there were stacks of ways of saving money. We could have raised contributions; we would have lost some members, there is always somebody waiting for an excuse to leave any organisation. But subs went up when we joined the TGWU, but we didn't lose any members in my branch.'

He added, 'Of course I was disappointed over the merger. I think events have proved me right, but now as part of the TGWU, it is still my Union.'

Barry Leathwood, who was secretary of the Organisers' Association at the time of the merger, commented, 'I was asked by the EC to obtain the views of the officers towards the merger: two-thirds accepted it as a necessity, the rest were unsure. Some thought we could go on independently. They were all very concerned about the future.'

Barry denied rumours at the time of the merger talks that some DOs were so worried about the Union's financial crisis, that they rang head office to enquire if they would get their wages. 'I'm sure I would have heard of it, had that happened,' he said.

Commenting on John Hose's belief that the Union could have remained independent if DOs had accepted reorganisation, Barry said, 'That would have been possible if it had been done by the early 1970s, but by the time of the merger, it was too late; there was no option but to merge. Jack Boddy found things in a bad way when he took over the general secretaryship.'

Barry recalled that in the early seventies, on his own initiative, he circulated proposals to the EC on the reorganisation of the counties and regionalisation. He never got a reply. 'But I did get the unofficial comment, "If he's got time for this, he's not doing his job properly". I felt then that we could have remained independent, but when the EC failed to address the issue, I was convinced that one day we would have to merge.'

Somerset, for which Barry was DO, supported the merger, against the rest of the West Country, an indication of the regard in which many counties held their DOs, and the fact that he campaigned for the merger in the county, and went round with slides showing why it was necessary.

My own conclusion is that there was no real alternative to the merger when it came about, as unhappy as many members were with it.

Barry, when I interviewed him in 1990, had some more pertinent comments to make about the Union practices, which may have helped it to lose its independence, but first, in the next chapter, let us find out a little more about the man himself.

REFERENCES

1. *Guardian*, 28 April 1989.
2. *Guardian*, 1 May 1989.
3. Clive Ponting, *1940: Myth & Reality*, Hamish Hamilton, 1990.
4. *Landworker*, September 1949.
5. EC Minutes, May 1957.

23

The TGWU Trade Group and Its Future

Remember this also, and be well persuaded of its truth:
the future is not in the hands of Fate, but in ours.

Jules Jusserand

New Man at the Helm

Barry Leathwood, who was to take over the leadership of the Trade Group when Jack Boddy retired, was born in Sandbach, Cheshire, the son of Charlie Leathwood, a popular DO who worked in various parts of the country, including Devon, Yorkshire and Kent. They were the only father and son to be DOs at the same time since the Union's foundation.

His father had worked on a farm, and Barry was the eldest of five children. Barry started his education at the CoE School in Sandbach, but as his father's organising took him to different parts of the country, he went to a number of schools, and left at 16.

Barry's earliest memories are of his father doing trade union work, and almost as soon as he was big enough to ride a bike and be let out on his own, he was riding round collecting union subs. He never worked on a farm, except during school holidays, but his father soon enrolled him in the NUAW and he became a member of the AEU when he was apprenticed as a toolmaker. He worked as a toolmaker for 17 years, including a long time with the International Harvesters, Doncaster, and ICI. He became a district commit-tee member of the AEU, and chairman and trustee of a branch having more than 500 members. He was very interested in education and youth work; became a youth club leader, was active in the Labour Party, was a county councillor, and as such, vice-chair of the council's children's committee and chair of its youth committee. Barry married in 1963, and he and his wife Ann, have a daughter, Sarah.

On his 30th birthday, Barry started thinking about his life, and what he wanted to do. At the time, in addition to his Labour Party and AEU work, he was doing a lot for the NUAW. 'Many NUAW members used to contact me about Union matters, because they knew me, and when my father had a heart attack, Ann and I ran the area, dealt with correspondence and everything; more of my time was spent doing outside work than the time I put in as a toolmaker,' he said.

'It was a question of whether I wanted to become a full-time social worker or trade union official. It was getting obvious that I couldn't do both. I was accepted as a trainee probation officer and as Somerset DO in October 1973, and decided on the latter. It was a difficult choice. I was concerned about having political freedom, and working for the probation service, I wouldn't. I was reluctant to work for the NUAW because father did, there might be accusations of nepotism, but I put such thoughts aside, and it never happened. I enjoyed working for the Union. I can't think of anything else I would prefer to do. Never a single moment's boredom – frustrations, problems, irritations, anger, but never boredom, often sheer pleasure.'

When Jack Boddy retired as national Trade Group secretary in 1987, Barry was appointed to the job by the General Executive Council of the TGWU. The main contenders for it included Tony Gould, Ivan Monkton, Geoff Beer and Peter Medhurst.

Barry believes greater militancy in the post-war years might have saved the Union as an independent body, but is careful to spell out what he means by militancy. 'I think,' he said, 'that as a Union we invested too much authority in the DOs, and didn't do enough to build the confidence of lay activists. The Union would have been strengthened if they had been encouraged; we behaved too much as a friendly society. Some lay activists were discouraged, especially bright young activists, who could create problems for officials wanting a quiet life. There was a philosophy abroad that the DO was the font of all knowledge and that the DO could resolve problems that occurred, rather than help the local activists to resolve them.'

When Barry was appointed DO at the age of 32, he went to Headland House. 'There I was told by Reg Bottini to "get off to Somerset and build your kingdom". Many of the old brigade had this way of thinking. Some old DOs would tell branch secretaries as little as possible, they kept knowledge to themselves, knowledge was power. I wouldn't like it to be thought every DO was like this, but some were, and lost their lay activists.'

Barry commented on the low pay of DOs, which had drawbacks other than the obvious ones. 'When I started, I earned less than I did as a toolmaker. DOs were encouraged to take on part-time jobs with remuneration. Some had to do it to manage. Some DOs had too many commitments outside the Union, I suspect that many were nominated by the EC for these jobs.'

This belief conflicts, to some extent, with the strenuous opposition the EC had to some DOs taking outside jobs. Probably, the EC preferred DOs with their viewpoint on outside work, and encouraged some to do it, but not others. Also, outside appointments were easier for NUAAW members than those of other unions. NUAAWers were not thought likely to be militant, and therefore, more malleable by the local or national establishment.

Poor working conditions didn't help DOs either. 'When I started,' Barry said, 'I worked from the front bedroom of my house, with very little equipment, and no secretary. Ann did some of the work. I learnt to type, this hindered real work.' Later he got a small office, but it was poorly equipped, with only a part-time secretary.

Barry is convinced that the potential of members was never properly harnessed to give the Union the strength it needed. 'The biennials demonstrated the tremendous talent of many lay members. Yet it was never encouraged in terms of industrial organisation. It was an elderly Union with an ageing workforce, and often elderly people feel threatened by bright young people. I'm certain the EC often felt like that.

'It seems to me we never seriously encouraged people to organise at the farm gates; this could have been done at some of the large farms, quite effectively. We relied totally on the AWB nationally, whereas we should have used the wage award as a basic rate and tried to negotiate higher sums locally. This would have given us the right to formal recognition and safety representatives.'

Another weakness of the old Union, in Barry's view, was the time spent by DOs filling in forms for members. 'We should have been using our resources to help them to do it themselves. DOs had a different role from officers in other unions. If there is a group of you together, there is a collective wisdom, but our members were denied that.

'We should have spent more on education, then members would have been better able to help themselves. This form-filling was very time consuming, very costly and sometimes unnecessary,' he said. 'Frequently, someone who lived two miles from the office, and was mobile, would send for you. Perhaps he only wanted a form, but he sent for the DO! Often they could have filled them in themselves, then the forms only needed checking. We couldn't have gone on as we were, whether we merged or not.

'We were a very centralised Union and spent the bulk of our money in London. The EC was always telling DOs to save money. I did some research, and found we spent a bigger proportion of our money in London than in the districts.'

That must have meant another black mark for Barry from the old EC, if he bothered to send them his findings, after his earlier rebuff on reorganisation.

Final Months of NUAAW

When the Union started in 1906 with 56 branches, it had an annual income of £166, expenses of £120, leaving a balance of £46. In 1979, just before the 1980s which saw the end of the Union as an independent body, it had 2,471 branches (its highest number was 3,700 in 1949), an income of £1,000,916, with expenses of £1,047,106. It had never exceeded one million pounds a year in income before; in 1949 it was only £173,621. Inflation was largely responsible for the much higher figure.

Falling membership was taking an increasing toll by 1979, and DOs were doing the job of many branch secretaries, who were increasingly difficult to replace. One DO was declared redundant and no new ones were appointed that year, in accordance with the EC's policy of cost cutting.

The Annual Reports and accounts of the early 1980s make sombre reading, and are indicative of the malaise affecting the Union. The 1980–1 Report says that there was a 'significant loss of membership in the poultry processing industry through the closure of many of Ross Buxted factories . . . but a potential remains among the "spent bird" processors', many of whom were anti-union, resisted official approaches, and needed 'organisation from within'. It went on: 'Reduction in membership unfortunately continues', with recruitment disappointing.

By 1981 the number of branches had fallen to 2,293; income had risen to £1,271,975, expenses were £1,357,049 – a dangerous excess of expenditure over income. That year, the Union's auditors noted that contributions received should have been £148,000 more than shown, and 'this may have been because of an accelerated reduction in numbers in the second half of the year, or to delays in remittances by branches.' Whatever the reason, it didn't help.

Then came the merger with the TGWU, already recounted. The 75th Annual Report in 1982 was the first of the agricultural workers as a national Trade Group of the TGWU. It recognised that 'one of our major problems is undoubtedly the regional organisation by which the TGWU is administered and that it is important that all Trade Group members play their full part in regional affairs . . .'

No full report on NUAAW finances for 1982 was possible, as from 1 May, its financial records were transferred from Headland House to the TGWU regional offices. However, upto 1 May, total income from all sources was £418,289 for the four months, and total net assets of the Union on 30 April 1982 were £728,768. This was below the value of Headland House, because of liabilities of £226,740.

The slimmed-down annual reports of the 1980s were mere shadows of their former selves, and in 1983, the Landworker Publishing Company, normally run at a loss by the NUAAW, was formally wound up, as its finances were merged with the TGWU.

Another stage in the merger was completed in 1983. The last set of registers and membership cards issued by the NUAAW expired at 31 December, and the remaining branches being serviced by Headland House were transferred to the regional office of the TGWU in North London. From 1 January 1984, the financial administration of all branches was dealt with by the appropriate regional offices, and the financial machinery at Headland House closed.

In 1984, when this history formally ends, the Annual Report spoke of the many problems facing the Trade Group during the transitional period into membership of the TGWU as 'being ironed out'. For the first time the Trade Group had an Irish representative from Region 11 (Northern Ireland).

Members of the Trade Group national committee who had the job of steering it through a difficult year were: J. Hose, chair; T. Baptie, W. Brack, J. Brown, D. Chiappa, R. S. Cooke, V. Cross, K. Feeley, R. Gamwell, M. Hancock, D. Halstead, D. Maltby, I. Monkton, W. Page, B. J. Salmon, P. Shearman, D. Sheppard, P. Stockton, P. Webster, H. Wright, P. Woodland, J. R. Boddy, national secretary.

The Trade Group was given the go-ahead to hold its traditional Winter schools at the TGWU's splendid centre at Eastbourne, and Bryan Moss, DO, became liaison officer with the education office at Transport House to assist in the organisation of future schools.

As a result of making the *Landworker* free, the print run in 1984 was increased from 22,000 to 34,500. It continued as one of the brighter of Britain's trade union journals, and was in growing demand. The Union's long established annual diary got a new look in 1984, thanks to Sue Longley, and sales were higher, but then sales resistance arose, some members preferring the cheaper TGWU diary. This problem was later solved by making them both the same price.

There was a total of 62 tied-cottage cases in 1984 and, in some, the new Legal/Health & Safety Department was able to convince solicitors acting for landlords to withdraw proceedings or have the matter dealt with under ADHAC procedure. But it was clear that 'the fines which may be imposed (but rarely are) under the Rent (Agriculture) Act 1976, are totally inadequate to deter landlords from abusing the system especially in view of the massive profits to be made by selling cottages as second homes.'[1]

In 1984, Brian Beard, of Morpeth, suffered from 'harvest lung'. He became ill after working on a drying unit on a farm at Stannington. As a result he lost both his job and his tied cottage. His case was taken up by the Trade Group, and five years later, 63-year-old Brian received agreed damages of £140,000 at Newcastle upon Tyne High Court.[2]

Agriculture still maintained its unenviable record as the third most dangerous industry in Britain, and in the majority of cases the Union still enjoyed no statutory recognition for appointing safety representatives, amid signs that the Tory Government intended further weakening what few safety provisions existed in agriculture. Regrettably, the Trade Group had still not won its long fight to have the age raised at which children were allowed to drive tractors.

Reg Green carried on much of the work of Chris Kaufman on farm chemicals, and in 1985, when the work of the Legal/Health & Safety Department was taken over by the TGWU legal services, it was fortunate that matters concerning agricultural workers were dealt with by Reg, who had joined the parent body's Legal Department.

Safety was still of over-riding importance to the Trade Group. From 1977 to 1984, a total of 576 males and 44 females were killed in agriculture, horticulture and forestry. Ages ranged from a few months to 90 years. The trend was downwards, but allowance must be made for the big decline in the workforce.

In 1984, Angela Shariff and Gladys Holding represented the Trade Group at the 59th Conference of Labour Party Women in Swansea, and did their best to ensure that the rural case was heard, despite agriculture and rural life not being noticeably high on the agenda. A Trade Group amendment to a transport resolution to ensure that the specific needs of rural women were met was debated and carried.

Despite all its efforts, the Trade Group was able to obtain an increase of only £3.60 in pay, making the weekly rate of £82.80 for 40 hours. An application for a substantial increase and for a 35-hour week failed to get the support of the independent members of the AWB. The annual conference wanted £130 for a 35-hour week, thus agricultural workers were still badly paid compared with industrial workers.*

One thing, however, changed for the better. Farmworkers had an improved image amongst the general public. They were no longer regarded as forelock-touching, unskilled labourers, doing jobs best suited to those low in talent and education. The Union helped to achieve this change of view, but overwhelmingly, it altered because the evidence that this was plainly not the case, was there for all to see – fields full of complicated machinery, bags of pesticides that could kill a crop if wrongly applied, together with all the attendant paraphernalia of spraying techniques, to say nothing of the demanding computers tucked away in farm offices, which had to be understood and worked. This change in public opinion did not, however, lessen its poor view of farmwork as a desirable job; pay was still too low, and working and social conditions still relatively bad compared with those of 'town' jobs.

From this brief résumé of events in the early eighties, it will be seen that a lot remained to be done for agricultural workers in the areas of employment legislation, tied cottages, health and safety, wages and conditions. Yet farming was still very profitable. Lord Carter, a Labour agricultural spokesman, shed valuable light on its finances when he revealed that from the early 1970s until 1984, farming had made a return in some cases of 30% to 35% on tenants' capital (averaging 20%).[3]

The Future for Agricultural Workers

That something should be done for the workers was ever more pressing in the Britain of the mid-eighties, with the country well into the Thatcherite version of Toryism, with its credit-card consumerism, unemployment, and homelessness; an economy geared solely to money-making come what may, and

---

*   Patrick Bond, Trade Group researcher, analysed later MAFF figures and found that the number of farmworkers below the poverty line rose substantially in 1988. The Council of Europe's low pay threshold for 1988 was £145.57 and the Low Pay Unit's £143.67. The average pay was £142.12. This meant that 45.6% of adult full-time men in England and Wales, and 70.5% of adult full-time women, fell below this threshold.

barely-concealed contempt for moral, spiritual, intellectual and social values. So what does the future hold for the Trade Group and its small membership? This cannot be considered without taking a long view of agriculture, ecological matters and the needs of the British people, and how best they are served.

With few exceptions, the changing nature of rural society is rooted in the changes which have taken place in agriculture. A 1984 Government survey found that only 14.1% of those working in rural areas were involved in agriculture. And the WI found that 54% of villages had no doctor's surgery, 75%, no chemist and 84%, no dentist. Bearing in mind that in 1985 almost 40% of British households had no regular use of a car, and only 31% of women could drive, this lack of medical facilities causes immense problems for many rural families. Add to this the lack of affordable housing, inadequate schools, transport and leisure facilities. To enjoy living in the countryside you have to be well-provided for financially, and most farmworkers' families are not, nor are many other rural poor.

Yet agriculture has made immense, very profitable strides since the thirties, but at a terrible, and partly unknown, cost. In the 1930s, Britain was only 30% self-sufficient in food. Rapid growth after the war ensured that self-sufficiency rose to 62% by the time we joined the EEC in 1973, and by 1984 we were 78% self-sufficient in eggs and potatoes, and an over-producer of cereals.[4] But at what cost? An immense tonnage of chemicals was poured over the land, and as we now know, sometimes to its detriment, and to the detriment of the people of Britain.

Emotional responses are not the answer to humanity's present problems; we need practical plans for our proper stewardship of the world's resources, especially that of the land. We need a sustainable agriculture.

Modern, intensive farming, with its soil exhaustion and high chemical input, is part of the environmental sickness that infects much of our planet today. Britain needed to boost its agricultural output, but need it have been done so recklessly? And why did we do it in the way we did? One answer partly lies in the immense profits to be made in supplying farm chemicals.

When the principle of guaranteed prices was established during the Second World War, that great supplier of farm chemicals, ICI, began to give special attention to MAFF.

'No company has been more politically minded than ICI: it has seen the advantage of maintaining strong links with Ministers, MPs, and in all the departments which have responsibilities touching its activities. Many years ago it set up a Government Affairs department, and under the redoubtable Mr. C. F. Thring – better known in Westminster and Whitehall as Peter Thring – it acquired considerable influence. Mr. Thring belonged to the Carlton and Reform Clubs: in the first he entertained politicians; in the second, Government officials; and it was at the Reform he was often to be seen in the company of Sir Frederick Kearns, the Permanent Secretary of MAFF. To be able to call by their Christian name hundreds of men and women in public life was the claim Peter Thring could make.'[5]

The use of farmyard manure seemed doomed. ICI fertiliser bags were seen all over Britain's farms, and by the 1980s, ICI fertiliser sales had climbed to over £1,300 million annually.*

Ninety-nine per cent of our cereals and vegetables are sprayed with one or more pesticides between sowing and harvesting, and there is no statutory system of controls to limit the pesticide residue in food. The Royal Commission on Environmental Pollution considered that DDT was so dangerous that its use should be banned. That was in 1970. But its use has continued. The EEC has introduced two directives which fix mandatory limits for some pesticide residues, but the UK has insisted that these limits should not be imposed here before 1991.[6]

The pros and cons of chemical farming will doubtless be discussed for decades to come, but that it has already done some harm to the environment, and hugely slashed the farm labour force, cannot be denied. Nor can it sensibly be denied that some chemicals will be needed in farming, if we are to maintain reasonable production levels, for a long time to come. Especially if we are to feed ourselves in Britain, and not lessen by our own consumption the food available to the world population, which could increase by another billion in the 1990s. The UN Population Fund says the current world population is 5.3 billion, and increases by about 250,000 a day. This could have catastrophic consequences for the environment, and agriculture.[7]

But it should not be accepted that only the big chemicalised farms are efficient; small mixed farms, which are likely to employ more labour, can be both highly efficient and productive, and, without the excessive use of chemicals, environmentally more acceptable.

Lou Howson, a retired farmer and member of the NFU's working party on smaller farms, in an article decrying the disappearance of small well-run efficient family farms said, 'There was evidence to suggest that the most efficient resource allocation in agriculture is in countries where production units are predominantly of a size which can be managed by the farmer, his family, and perhaps some hired help.' He quoted the EEC's Deputy Director for Agriculture as saying, 'We believe that the modest-sized family farm is a key element in a healthy agriculture and a sane rural world.' He condemned the Tory Government for repeating the *canard* about 'inefficient small farms' and not encouraging them.[8]

It is arguable as to whether the extra hired labour, which might not amount to much, would put up production costs measurably (there would be a lot less spent on machinery and chemicals), but if it did, a rational, civilised society should not find it too difficult to balance out the extra cost against less paid out in dole money.

---

* 'Following environmental pressures to use fewer fertilisers and the impact of cutbacks in EEC farm output, the ICI sold off its fertiliser business to a Finnish company after it sustained large losses.' *Guardian*, 27 July 1990.

That the public, as it becomes better educated in health and environmental matters, will demand a lesser use of chemicals, should not be doubted. In the United States, at the time of writing, more than 30 food-safety bills are before Congress, at least eight states are imposing regulations of their own, and growers are changing their methods to reduce the use of chemicals. And there is a revolution in eating habits; Americans are demanding fresh, rather than frozen or processed meats, fruits and vegetables, and they are consuming more raw foods than ever.[9]

That sort of thing will surely happen in Britain, too, and is foreseen by the bigger food retailers. The Co-op – that pioneer of unadulterated food – is upgrading its image further as a supplier of quality foods, while Joe Barnes, joint managing director of Sainsbury's, told farmers in 1990[10] that after the 'convenience' food vogue of the 1980s would come the 'considerate' habits of the 1990s. Whereas, in the 1980s, consumers were concerned with their own health and were interested in food ingredients and nutritional value, in the 1990s, they would focus on how food is produced, on its quality, its variety and its naturalness. All trends that will profoundly affect farmworkers.

Also affecting Britain is the fact that the world demand for coarse grains is rising strongly, disappointing as it must be for the health-conscious. Coarse grains are those fed to farm animals, and people in the Near or Far East are spending some of their increasing cash on meat. The International Wheat Council said that in 1990 consumption of coarse grains could outstrip production for the fourth consecutive year, reducing stocks to their lowest level since the mid-1980s.[11]

Such reduced stocks could affect Britain eventually, so production would have to be kept up here; possibly even bringing more land into cereal growing, although a lower consumption of meat would be a better alternative, with the grain being used more directly for human consumption.

Another problem facing world agriculture is the environmental one, and global warming in particular. The latter could have a drastic effect on Britain. If the sea does rise by almost a metre over the next 50 years, large areas of our most productive farmland, especially in Lincolnshire and the low-lying Fens of Cambridgeshire and Norfolk, could be lost to the sea for ever, if no means (and the immense amount of money) can be found to stem the waves. In addition, the remaining cereal growing areas of East Anglia and the South could become too hot and dry to grow corn, and alternative crops would have to be found.

On top of this, world food shortages could get worse. In 1989, for the first time in its history, the USA failed to produce enough cereal for its own needs. This might mean that Britain could no longer import hard grain from Canada for breadmaking.

Such developments would make nonsense of the Thatcher Government's set-aside bribery, to say nothing of the need for alternative crops – one of which might be fast-growing wood plantations for power stations, wood being an ecologically acceptable fuel, for when burnt it only emits the same amount of carbon dioxide as a tree takes in during its lifetime. Experiments with a wood-fired power station are taking place in Sweden at the time of writing.*

The immensity of the changes that must come in the countryside should not be underestimated. And that there will be social, political and economic pressures on farming to change its ways, was predicted by Professor Peter Wilson, principal of the East of Scotland College of Agriculture, at a meeting at the Edinburgh Science Festival. He said that these pressures would mean farming techniques would take an 'entirely different direction' from those of the past.[12]

Labour's agricultural spokesman, Dr. David Clark, promised in 1989 that Labour's new agricultural policy would be 'the greenest agricultural policy in Europe'. This would include tougher pollution laws, tighter pesticide controls, the payment of green premiums to all farmers prepared to conduct their work in an environmentally sensitive manner and incentives for conversion to organic farming. He said that this move to organic and low input farming would allow farmers and farmworkers to do what they do best, not run ice cream parlours or whatever other diversification schemes might be on the cards.

But much more is needed. To restore a proper balance between city and rural life, is perhaps one of the greatest tasks facing modern society; it is not just farming methods that are in need of attention. And the Trade Group can play its part. High agricultural yields at any cost are no answer to the evils of mass unemployment; the over-crowding of cities can only be halted if the level of rural life is raised, with each community offering a wide variety of jobs to its members.

To fit in with the changes that are ahead will need a new kind of Trade Group. It cannot go on as it is. By 1990, it was down to 37,000 members. The full-time labour force in agriculture had dropped to 86,000. Even if it enrolled every single one of them, it would still not have a rosy future.

And a further decline in the full-time labour force to 67,000 by 1998 is projected by the National Economic Development Council's Agricultural Ad-Hoc Sector Group, although this is based on further curbs on agricultural production, which may prove undesirable.[13]

At their 1990 Trade Group Conference at Eastbourne, delegates decided to change the name of the group, so that they could enrol all rural workers; they could not fix upon a suitable title, that was left until later. But there was a strong feeling that the word 'rural' must be included.

This proposed name change was a sensible move. To recognise a problem is the first step towards the wisdom necessary for its solution. Nearly all the forerunners of the NUAAW had the word 'rural' in their titles, and although farmworkers predominated, they organised all kinds of workers. Now that

---

* The set-aside scheme, launched in 1988, offered farmers up to £200 a hectare if they agreed to set aside at least 20% of their arable land for five years.

there is an even greater number of non-agricultural workers in rural areas, and must be more in the future, the need for an organisation they can join is greater than ever. They need someone to protect them, or rather organise them to protect themselves. Yet there is no specifically 'rural' union in Britain catering for their needs.*

Barry Leathwood said, 'But we are not going to attract a wider range of people unless we identify with other industries in rural areas. That is what many of our members want, especially the young, and go-ahead officials, many of whom have experience of organising members outside the farmworkers, poultry and forestry workers.

'We don't want to poach from other unions, but there are lots of unorganised people in rural areas, and we, with our rural experience, could recruit them into the Trade Group and provide a basis for a much bigger TGWU membership. People in rural areas have a lot in common. We are a campaign group, we would provide an organisation for them. School caretakers, the rural mechanics, shop assistants, they could all be their appropriate trade group in the TGWU, but serviced by us, as the rural wing of the TGWU.

'It should be possible to recruit more agricultural workers; the problem of the Trade Group is that most of our members are serviced by composite officers, who have other industrial commitments. They are under pressure to recruit more members, and agricultural workers are not the easiest to recruit in great numbers, but we have got to try.

'Organic farming will help stem people leaving the land. But it's difficult to see how there could be considerably more people employed. We are not thinking of going back to hoeing fields of carrots, but of modern methods of organic farming.

'We've got to work a lot harder to encourage people to do things. We are the victims of our own past successes; we've secured a great deal of protection from eviction, and even though wages and conditions are not marvellous, there are things like three months' sick pay, even for part-timers, which we have won, so some people no longer feel the need to be in the Union. That's a wrong assumption. If the Trade Group were to collapse, those things would fade away very quickly.

'Above all, we've got to carve ourselves out as a dynamic, campaigning organisation in rural areas, concerned with industrial, social, environmental, food safety and rural issues. We would be open to all people interested in such matters.

'I'm an optimist. I think that providing we can get our act together, put over this rural concept of an organisation for everyone in the countryside, we can win a bigger membership. We are the only rural workers' organisation. We are badly needed.'

---

* This change of name was done in December 1991, and it became the Rural Agricultural and Allied Workers' Trade Group.

Hopes are high. By the advocacy of such principles and the carrying out of such a policy, I believe the Trade Group will ultimately be able to realise not only these new hopes, but also the hopes of the old pioneers, obliterate poverty of both body and mind in the countryside, lead the way forward to a fuller life, and no matter how hard the going, enable all men and women to work and rejoice in the needs of both hand and brain, produce food that is safe to eat, win the fullness of the earth and, if carefully husbanded, its resources.

REFERENCES

1. Annual Report, 1984.
2. TWGU's *Record*, December 1989.
3. *Rural Socialism*, No 26, published by the Socialist Countryside & Agriculture Group, April 1990.
4. Charlie Pye-Smith and Chris Hall (eds.), *The Countryside We Want*, Green Books, 1987.
5. Richard Body, *Red or Green for Farmers (and the rest of us)*, Broad Leys Publishing, 1987. (Mr. Body is Conservative MP for Holland with Boston, already mentioned earlier in this volume.)
6. *The Countryside We Want*, op.cit.
7. *Guardian*, 15 May 1990.
8. *Rural Socialism*, No 26, op.cit.
9. *International Herald Tribune*, 8 May 1990.
10. Winegarten Memorial lecture, Agriculture House, 23 May 1990.
11. *The Independent*, 8 May 1990.
12. *Scotsman*, 9 April 1990.
13. *Work in the Countryside*, NEDC, 1989.

Postscript

Further changes have taken place in farming since the writing of this history ended in 1990. Mostly for the worse. By 1993, some 35 people were leaving the land every day, adding up to 12,775 a year. Many joined Britain's 3 million (4 million – unmassaged) dole queue, and the future of the Rural, Agricultural and Allied Workers' Trade Group cannot be divorced from the dismal state Britain finds itself in after 13 years of Conservative rule.

A pay increase of £3.60 (2.75%) on the basic wage, making it £138.21, was wrung out of the AWB in March 1993, but it will not go far to meet rising living costs. It left farmworkers £70 below the average industrial wage. Then came the 17½% tax on fuel, and increased taxes on cars, an essential form of transport for most rural dwellers. This contrasts with the £6,700 a week (54%) rise of Sir Patrick Sheehy, head of the tobacco and insurance giant, BAT. No doubt it is all part of Prime Minister John Major's classless society, a nation 'at ease with itself'.

One nasty part of the pay settlement was that it incorporated 'flexible' hours, including possible working on Sundays. This effectively ends the cherished five-day week.

Although British farming was hit by EEC dictats, the bigger farmers were still doing nicely. In 1992, farming income rose by 23.7% to £1,837 million, helped along by falling interest rates, devaluations of the Green Pound and lower labour costs. Productivity continued upwards.

The Conservative Party won the 1992 General Election with the aid of barefaced lies, whilst Labour snatched defeat from the jaws of victory aided by spin doctors, and Neil Kinnock resigned as leader. Trade Group members were dismayed; they had hoped to see an end to the Tory attacks on living standards.

But the beginning of the 1990s was not all gloom for the TGWU, which was streamlined to cut costs following an inevitable fall in membership during the biggest depression in Britain since the 1930s. The aim was to make it more efficient in protecting members' interests, and in so doing, those of the general public.

Also, there was a definite change of attitude to trade unions by that public. John Major's attempt to give Conservatism a human face soon wore thin. The moistening cream dried and cracks revealed the same old Tory machine bashing away at the NHS, schools, public transport, pensions and the like. The great achievement of Labour's post-war Welfare State was to remove fear from people's lives. If people were old or ill they knew they would be cared for. The Tories brought back fear.

Then came the decimation of Tory councillors in the May 1993 local elections, when the Conservatives lost control of all but one of the traditionally 'true blue' English shires. It was the worst result for them since the counties became administrative bodies in 1880.

Large sections of the public had begun to see through Tory policies. Many Tory voters were upset. When Michael Heseltine made his savage attack on the miners in 1992, the public responded magnificently. Who in the 1980s, when Arthur Scargill was the *bête noire* of most of the media, would have envisaged him being presented with a bouquet by a well-wisher in Park Lane, and being cheered by thousands, as miners staged their protest march.

This new perception of trade unions was not without its effect on the Trade Group. After years of being attacked by successive governments, members' spirits rose.

There was much to be done as Tory asset-stripping of the nation's property continued and taxes increased because of the dire state of the nation's finances. It need not be. One seldom-mentioned source of funds is there for the taking – the Peace Dividend. For several decades, the leaders of the TGWU had courageously sought to secure this dividend for the benefit of the nation. By 1993, the time had never been more ripe. The Cold War was over, and money spent on running the Trident nuclear submarine fleet – £380 million a year – would pay the annual costs of 20 hospitals, or a year's salaries for 10,000 nurses. And this is but a fraction of the savings available if the whole useless nuclear weapons programme was scrapped.

Other immense savings could be made if Britain ate more of its own produce. We imported £12.3 billion worth of food in 1992. Lettuces were brought 1,500 miles, beans 1,800 and tomatoes 500. Some came from the famine-stricken areas of Africa, which should be growing food for their own consumption. Trade Group members would like to see our growers and distributors getting their act together, to enable all of us to eat British. An added bonus would be to ease our balance of trade deficit problems.

The Trade Group continued to keep a wary eye on farm chemicals, and bovine spongiform encephalopathy (mad cow disease) was added to its concerns. For the first time ever a member received £750 compensation after being kicked by a BSE infected cow. The danger of BSE infection spreading to humans remains unknown. The Trade Group wants more research done on it.

Abolishing the Milk Marketing Board after pressure from the EEC may lead to job losses, and there are fears that CAP policy of taking land out of production means more job cuts. Barry Leathwood said, 'While farmers are compensated for taking land out of production, displaced workers get no compensation.'

One development much concerning the Trade Group is the move to distance the Labour Party from the unions. The Labour Party is the child of the unions, and these proposals are not the adolescent cutting of apron strings, but something more fundamental. This is not what most Trade Group members, accustomed to working with the Party, want. These moves are designed to weaken the influence unions have on Labour, steps long advocated by the anti-union press. They met opposition from many union leaders, including TGWU General Secretary Bill Morris.

So 1993 finds the Trade Group in good heart, still determined to work towards a more just, compassionate Britain, as envisaged by its founders nearly 100 years ago.

May 1993

Abbreviations

AAC	Agricultural Apprenticeship Council.
ADHAC	Agricultural Dwelling Houses Advisory Committee.
AEC	Agricultural Executive Committee (earlier known as WAEC, War Agricultural Executive Committee).
AEU	Amalgamated Engineering Union.
ASTMS	Association of Scientific, Technical and Managerial Staffs.
ATB	Agricultural Training Board.
AWB	Agricultural Wages Board.
CAWU	Clerical and Administrative Workers' Union.
CLA	Country Landowners' Association.
COHSE	Confederation of Health Service Employees.
DO	District Organiser.
EC	Executive Committee of the NUAW and NUAAW.
EEC	European Economic Community, or Common Market.
FC	Forestry Commission.
FWAC	Forestry Workers' Advisory Committee.
GMWU	General and Municipal Workers' Union.
HSE	Health and Safety Executive.
IFPAAW	International Federation of Plantation, Agricultural and Allied Workers.
ILO	International Labour Office.
IPCS	Institute of Professional Civil Servants.
MAFF	Ministry of Agriculture, Fisheries and Food.
NAG	National Association of Grooms.
NATO	North Atlantic Treaty Organisation.
NEC	National Executive of the Labour Party.
NFU	National Farmers' Union.
NJIC	National Joint Industrial Council.
NUAW	National Union of Agricultural Workers until 1968, *when it became the*
NUAAW	National Union of Agricultural and Allied Workers.
NUPE	National Union of Public Employees.
NUR	National Union of Railwaymen.
NUT	National Union of Teachers.

PAC   Pesticides Advisory Committee.
RAAW   Rural, Agricultural and Allied Workers.
ROSPA   Royal Society for the Prevention of Accidents.
SOGAT   Society of Graphical and Allied Trades.
TGWU   Transport and General Workers' Union.
TUC   Trades Union Congress.
UN   United Nations.
USDAW   Union of Shopworkers, Distributive and Allied Workers.
WI   Women's Institutes.
WLA   Women's Land Army.
YOP   Youth Opportunity Programme.
YTS   Youth Training Scheme.

Currency Conversion Table

shillings	shillings	pennies
(20/– = £1)	10/– = 50p	12d = 5p
	9/– = 45p	11d = 4.5p
20/– = 100p	8/– = 40p	10d = 4p
19/– = 95p	7/– = 35p	9d = 4p
18/– = 90p	6/– = 30p	8d = 3.5p
17/– = 85p	5/– = 25p	7d = 3p
16/– = 80p	4/– = 20p	6d = 2.5p
15/– = 75p	3/– = 15p	5d = 2p
14/– = 70p	2/– = 10p	4d = 1.5p
13/– = 65p	1/– = 5p	3d = 1p
11/– = 55p		2d = 1p
	(1/– = 12d)	1d = 0.5p

Name Index

Note: Page numbers in **bold** type indicate major references to the life and/or views of the person. Page numbers in *italics* refer to the illustrations appearing between those pages.

and poultry workers 376, 382, 383, 384, 387

and Union merger 115–21 *passim*, 124–9, 130, 132–3

views of other members 73–4, 83

and wages battles 173, 243, 244–5, 247, 269, 272, 406

Boddy, James (W Norfolk) 112

Body, Sir Richard 286, 376–7

Bolton, Brian *136–7 (ill. 14)*

Bolton, J. (Somerset) 60

Bond, Fred (Finance Officer) **70–1**

Bones, Freddie (Kent) 153

Bontoft, Revd. R. A. 34

Booth, Albert 165

Bottini, Reg 46, 53, **84**, *136–7 (ills. 10, 11)*, 365, 371

and the Common Market 263, 264, 266, 269

as General Secretary 84, 85, 104

and health and safety 319, 346

and Industrial Relations Act 101–2, 237, 238

as moderate 84, 97, 185

and public expenditure cuts 160, 165

relations with other members 104, 108, 111, 414, 426

and tied cottage fight 185, 199, 201–2, 204, 280

and Union financial problems 93–4, 101, 128

and wages battles 178, 234, 237, 238, 239, 399

and water supplies 178, 179

Boulton, W. (Lancs) 118

Bowen, Jack (Yorks) **17–19**

Boyt, C. G. (Dorset) 300–1

Brack, Bill 138, 429

Bradshaw, Jim EC 62, 398

Braithwaite, E. (Yorks) 372

Brannigan, F. 3

Bray, Jeremy MP 78

Bray, Philip 384

Brett, Fred (E Suffolk) **141–2**, 342

Britton, Professor D. K. 52

Brocklebank, Jack EC **108–11**, 124, *136–7 (ill. 15)*, 166, 292, 296

activities as DO 3–4, 107, 279, 372–3

and rural housing 3–4, 73–5, 149

and Union left/right polarisation 68, 73–5, 92–3

Broughton, A. (Lincs) 234

Brown, Charles (Berks & Oxon) 115

Brown, Fred EC 29, 34, 68, 141, 226

Brown, G. (Bucks) 95, 96

Brown, George MP 40, 194, 290

Brown, J. 429

Brumby, Stan EC 42, 47, **88–9**, 104, 178, 253, 312

critical of old guard 69–70, 74–5

Buchan, Norman 346

Buckton, Ray (TUC) 143

Burt, Caroline (NAG) 284

Bush, Alan 114

Butcher, Phillip (NFU) 245

Butler, A. (Yorks) 234

Butler, F. W. 365

Butterfield family (Essex) 275

Buttle, Dave 367

Button, C. (Lincs) 315

Cailliau, Kay and Michael 184

Callaghan, James 53, 83, 108, 241

Calver, Ted EC 53, 80, 124, 136–7 *(ills. 14, 15)*, **179–82**, 200–1, 304

and the Common Market 261–2, 264

and land nationalisation 289, 291

in Union elections 77, 78, 86

Campbell, Jim (NUR) 301

Canavan, Dennis MP 406

Carey, R. 161

Carlile, T. (Organising Dept) 116, 370

Carr, Robert 235

Carson, Rachel 337–8

Carter, J. 365

Carter, Lord 430

Case, W. A. J. EC 9, 30, 31, 83, 255, 317

honours received 12, 57

Castle, Barbara 233–4, 413, 417–18

Cater, John (Wilts) 137

Cave, W. E. 39

Chamberlain, Mrs. Winifred 339

Chamberlain, Ted 264

Chandler, C. H. EC 9, 29, 38, 218, 289

Chapman, D. (S Devon) 116, 234

Cherrington, John (*Financial Times*) 52, 293

Chester, Sir George (TUC) 187

Chiappa, D. 245, 388–9, 429

Childs, Ronald (Hants) 199

Churchill, Winston PM 36

Clark, Dr. David 434

Clarke, R. H. (Norfolk) 72, 78, 83, 315, 317

Clayton, Edgar (Yorks) **17–18**

Clayton, Hugh (*The Times*) 294

Clough, W. H. (Cheshire) 226, 304

and gang labour 285–6

and land nationalisation 289–91, 292, 296

left-wing views 66, 92, 97–8, 102, 417

as MP 55, 101, 102, 139, 166

in Presidential elections 97–8, 112, 117

and role of women 275, 277–81

and tied cottage fight 185, 193, 195–6, 198, 200–6 *passim*, 280, 421

and Union merger 116, 119–20

and vice–presidency 70, 78, 86, 92, 94–7

and wages battle 225, 237, 239–41 *passim*, 244–5, 280

Medhurst, P. DO (Suffolk) 112, **139–41**, 142, 237, 426

and the Common Market 263

and poultry workers 382, 388, 389

Mendham, Steven 384

Mickleburgh, H. and family 45

Midgelow, Harold EC 255

Miles, L. (Norfolk) 67, 315

Miles, Prof. Charles (AWB) 245

Miles, Robert (Glasgow University) 219

Millar, A. D. (N Cumberland) 129–30

Milligan, Stephen (*Sunday Times*) 272

Mills, Arthur *136–7 (ill. 14)*, 405–6, 407

Mills, Dorothy (Kent) 116

Minett, A. (Cambs) 116, 120

Monckton, I. 426, 429

Monks, A. E. DO 22, 30, 169, 170, 225

Moore, A. 37

Moore, F. W. (Sussex) 231, 361

Morgan, W. J. (Devon) 299

Morris, Bill (TGWU) 439

Morris, Chris E. EC **62–5**, 158, 160, 256, 264, 365

and rural transport 155–6

and tied cottage fight 200–1

Morris, Iris (Kent) 277

Morrison, Herbert MP 23

Moyle, Richard 165

Murray, Dr. Robert 372–3

Murray, Len (TUC) 100, 114, 135, 143, 240

Naginton, David (Salop) 61, 86

Neale, Stuart (S Wales) 136, 256, 271, 406

Neate, Bill (Finance Officer) 71, **75–6**

Neatherway, A. (Sussex) 96, 200–1

Neish, George DO (Devon) 251, 328, 331

Nethercott, Ron 144

Nettle, E. 365

Neville, Mrs. Marian (Redhill) 103

Newens, Stan MP 200

Newman, B. S. (Berks) 22

Noble, F. G. (Salop) 177

Norman, Mrs. Sarah (Norfolk) 275

Norman, P. (Sussex) 229, 230

Northey, Reg (Devon) 328

Oakden, Mrs. L. E. (Derbys) 275

Oakes, Gordon 165

O'Reilly, Kevin (Members Services) 252, 253

Orme, Stanley MP 164–5

Oswick, Doug (Norfolk) 120, 200–1, 293, **296–8**, 348

Overson, Mark 313

Owen, David MP 265–6

Oxby, F. (Lincs) 317

Page, Wilf EC 95, *136–7 (ills. 15, 16)*, 269, 302, **305–9**, 367, 429

and battle for fair wages 230, 237

communist views 48, 53, 97, 103

and health and safety 331

and land nationalisation 291, 292, 296

and tied cottage fight **190–1**, 200–1

in Union elections 78, 86, 97

and Union merger 124, 137–8

Paget, Jack EC 166

Paget, R. T. MP 33–4, 85

Pannell, A. E. EC 9, 62

Parry, Ted (Hunts) 83, 192

Parsons, O. H. 340

Paul, J. EC 9, 83

Payne, Dr. Donald 340

Peachey, Fred (Hants) 78, 173, 262, 263, 398, 400

Peacock, Ellen (Lincs) 276

Pearce, E. (Berks) 316–17

Pearson, Harry DO (Kent) 41

Peart, T. F. MP 70, 79–80, 261, 404

and foot-and-mouth outbreak 356–7

and tied cottage fight 194–5, 203

Peasegood, A. DO 188

Peck, Peter (Beds) 348

Peden, Mrs. E. (Essex) 103

Pedley, W. H. 295–6

Phillips, J. F. (NFU) 185

Phillips, Morgan (Labour Party) 299

Phillips, Wogan (Glos) 289

This book was commissioned from the author in September 1983 by the TGWU, and completed in May 1990. It was published on 5 July 1993 by the TGWU and Frontline States Ltd in an edition of 2000 copies, of which 800 copies were specially presented to delegates at the TGWU's Biennial Delegate Conference.

The text was typeset on 10.5/12 point Monotype Baskerville by Carnegie Publishing Ltd, Preston. The proofs were read by Dana Captainino; the name index was prepared by Margaret Cronan; and the illustrations researched by Charlotte Lippman. The cover artwork was prepared by Peter Hammarling at Artworkers Management Ltd, London. The book was printed and bound by Redwood Books, Trowbridge, Wiltshire.

LA
VIDA EMPIEZA
CADA DÍA

ANNE IGARTIBURU

LA VIDA EMPIEZA CADA DÍA

**366 reflexiones para
estar presente**

Edición a cargo de Francesc Miralles

Papel certificado por el Forest Stewardship Council®

Primera edición: noviembre de 2022
Primera reimpresión: febrero de 2023

© 2022, Anne Igartiburu
© 2022, Penguin Random House Grupo Editorial, S. A. U.
Travessera de Gràcia, 47-49. 08021 Barcelona

Diseño: Penguin Random House Grupo Editorial / Yolanda Artola y Marta García

Edición a cargo de Francesc Miralles

Printed in Spain – Impreso en España

ISBN: 978-84-03-52367-8
Depósito legal: B-16.732-2022

Compuesto en Mirakel Studio, S. L. U.

Impreso en Gómez Aparicio, S.L.
Casarrubuelos (Madrid)

AG 2 3 6 7 8

A todos los que me habéis acompañado en este camino.
A mis hijos, sois mi luz.
#zuekinnagobeti

ÍNDICE

BIENVENIDA

Querido lector o lectora:

Con estas letras quiero agradecerte que te hayas animado a iniciar este camino conmigo para explorar 366 maneras de vivir en plenitud cada día.

A través de estas páginas, quiero ayudarte a que descubras que cada amanecer es una oportunidad de empezar de nuevo, y que despertar a la consciencia depende de ti, momento a momento. Ojalá pueda acompañarte en ese despertar con aquello que he ido aprendiendo, leyendo y reflexionando en mi propia senda.

La vida es lo que sucede aquí y ahora, en este preciso –y precioso– instante. Tú eres vida, luz y energía. Empápate de ella y compártela.

Gracias a todos los que me habéis animado a hacer realidad este libro y me habéis ayudado en ello, especialmente a Francesc Miralles y Silvia Quiroga, ¡sparrings fieles!

Avanzamos con cada latido.

ANNE IGARTIBURU

PRÓLOGO

de Sergi Torres

Seguro que ya te has dado cuenta de que solemos vivir la vida con un ojo mirando al pasado y el otro mirando al futuro. De hecho, lo vemos como lo más lógico del mundo, ¿cierto? Pero, en realidad, sin darnos cuenta, al vivir de este modo nos perdemos la vida, porque la vida solo existe en este mismo instante, en el presente.

En una ocasión, yendo a trabajar en moto, mientras esperaba a que se pusiera el semáforo en verde, me di cuenta de algo tan aterrador como profundamente liberador. Allí, detenido frente al semáforo y con cierta ansiedad porque llegaba tarde, me estaba imaginando que me despedían. Pero a pesar de imaginármelo con calidad de imagen 4k y sonido envolvente, de repente, me di cuenta. ¡Me di cuenta de que estaba imaginando! No estaba viendo mi despido, simplemente estaba imaginándolo. Y es que me estaba perdiendo vivir lo que sucedía en ese momento de mi vida, semáforo en rojo incluido, por el mero hecho de imaginar una tragedia laboral que ni siquiera sabía si iba a suceder.

Este suceso no quedó entre el semáforo y yo. A lo largo del día, estuve tan atento como pude a cuántas veces imaginaba en lugar de vivir. Y, aquí viene lo aterrador: descubrí que casi todo el día lo pasaba imaginando, ya fuera recordando o anticipando acontecimientos. Este fue el primer paso, profundamente liberador, de un camino que me sacaba de la burbuja de mi propia realidad imaginada y me devolvía de nuevo a la vida tal cual era. Vamos, algo así como pasar de mi metaverso interior a la vida real, la de verdad.

Dentro de nuestra cultura de las prisas, del hacer y del tener, hemos convertido el presente en el gran ignorado. Los recuerdos, los resentimientos y los remordimientos del pasado, junto a las expectativas, los temores y los deseos del futuro, gobiernan nuestra vida. Y todo esto sin darnos cuenta del sinsentido que supone, porque todo el sentido se encuentra en la vida e, insisto, la vida se encuentra en el presente.

Solemos buscar cómo recuperar la frescura de vivir, la pasión por descubrir cosas nuevas y, sobre todo, la sensación de estar vivos. Pero yo me pregunto: ¿por qué lo buscamos donde no está? Muy pocas personas miran al presente como la respuesta, o al menos como la puerta a la mirada espontánea, inocente y luminosa de cuando éramos niños. Porque sí, es cierto que la vida empieza cada día, pero para vivirla primero debemos ponernos de pie ante ella. No obstante, no te preocupes porque la vida lo tiene todo pensado.

¿Recuerdas esa fuerza o impulso que, de niños, llegado el gran momento, nos llevaba de gatear a ponernos en pie? Pues esa misma fuerza es la que nos pone en pie ante la vida. De hecho, esa fuerza no se detiene jamás y nos impulsa a levantarnos en muchas otras facetas a lo largo de la existencia. A levantarnos emocionalmente, por ejemplo. Pero tampoco se detiene ahí, porque su objetivo es llegar a la parte más profunda del ser humano y, cómo no, ponerla en pie. Me refiero a su corazón. Es decir, aprender a amar incondicionalmente, a disfrutar de quienes somos, a brillar en nuestro máximo esplendor y a compartirlo con los demás en gratitud. ¿Te parece difícil?

Este libro que tienes en tus manos es sencillo y natural, pero poderoso. En nuestra sociedad actual, tan a menudo complicada y artificial, sencillez y naturalidad se confunden con pobreza e insuficiencia. Pero algo que es sencillo y natural y que además nace del corazón se convierte en algo muy poderoso. Y si no, miremos a la naturaleza.

Si pudiéramos contemplar el cielo estrellado de una noche sin luna con la mirada de un universo, seguramente veríamos la sencillez, la naturalidad y el amor en el que vivimos. Si pudiéramos contemplar nuestras relaciones con la mirada de la vida que nos llevó a encontrarnos, seguramente veríamos la sencillez, la naturalidad y el amor en el que vivimos. Y así, tantas cosas...

A Anne, un día esa fuerza le alcanzó el corazón, y la impulsó a ponerlo en pie y dar un nuevo paso ante la vida. Un paso que curiosamente nos devuelve de regreso a nosotros mismos y al presente también. En mi caso a la moto, frente al semáforo, llegando tarde. Y alguien pensará, *pues en ese caso prefiero que no me devuelva a ninguna parte, gracias,* pero en verdad a mí me estaba devolviendo a la vida.

Anne nos comparte, con una mirada de niña maravillada, todo lo que esa fuerza le ha mostrado por el camino. Y así es como yo conozco a Anne, una mujer viva y con un gran corazón de niña aventurera. Con este libro ella nos regala muchas pistas y herramientas para convertir este *ponernos de pie* en algo sencillo, natural y amoroso.

Y es que, a pesar de que no todos los momentos son agradables, están llenos de vida y nuestro corazón solo quiere vivirlos, porque para eso existe, para vivir.

Después de millones de años evolucionando y de tantos logros tecnológicos, aún no sabemos sentir, ni pensar ni relacionarnos humanamente entre nosotros. Todavía nos superan nuestras propias emociones; parece incluso que nos aplastan. Y algunos de nuestros propios pensamientos no se marchan de nuestra cabeza por más que queramos, como si fueran ellos los que se piensan a sí mismos ahí dentro.

Para regresar a la vida tenemos el presente y nuestra honestidad. Nuestra parte es cultivarlos. Aquí tienes en tus manos 366 maneras de hacerlo. Sí, de forma natural y sencilla, pero poderosa.

Esta fuerza de la que he hablado, y de la que nace este libro, puso en pie a toda una especie, transformándola de *Homo habilis* a *Homo erectus*. Quizá hoy, en el continuado empeño de esta fuerza, estemos frente a la transformación del *Homo sapiens sapiens* a *Homo amare*. Quién sabe.

Por cierto, ese día no llegué tarde al trabajo, sino que volví a nacer, porque sí, es verdad, la vida empieza cada día.

SERGI TORRES

1
HOY EMPIEZA TODO

Hay un concepto del zen, el *shoshin*, que en japonés se traduce como *mente de principiante*. Es la actitud de quien no da nada por sabido, como si el mundo recomenzara a cada instante.

Eso es lo que sucede cada mañana cuando abrimos los ojos en un nuevo día. No importa lo que sucedió ayer. No importa lo que nos espere mañana. Hoy es una hoja en blanco que solo tú puedes escribir, si no haces pronósticos y te dejas sorprender por la jornada.

En su libro *Mente zen, mente de principiante*, el maestro Shunryu Suzuki afirmaba:

> *Cuando la mente está vacía, se encuentra siempre dispuesta para cualquier cosa, abierta a todo. A la mente del principiante se le presentan muchas posibilidades; a la del experto, pocas.*

¿Estás listo para empezar el día con espíritu *shoshin*? En ese caso, todo puede suceder. ¡Feliz inicio!

CON OJOS NUEVOS

Marcel Proust decía que la creatividad está en la mirada, en saber observar el mundo con ojos nuevos. Como ejercicio inicial, te propongo que contemples lo que tienes delante ahora mismo —tu casa, la oficina, cualquier lugar donde estés— como si fuera la primera vez.

¿Qué descubres que no habías visto hasta ahora?

2
PASA DEL *RUNRÚN*

A lo largo de la jornada, habrá momentos en los que tu mente se hará escuchar a través de ideas recurrentes o incómodas. No hay nada malo en ello, puesto que se ha calculado que tenemos unos noventa mil pensamientos al día.

Yo llamo *runrún* a ese parloteo de la mente que me lleva a lugares insospechados que no me gustan, guiada por mí, porque somos así de inquietos. Sé por experiencia que no debo darle importancia, ya que si trato de rechazar estos pensamientos, aún se refuerzan más.

Cada vez que te asalte el *runrún*, date cuenta de que tú no eres tus pensamientos. Ellos vienen y van. Se proyectan en tu mente y luego se marchan, a no ser que quieras retenerlos o expulsarlos. Solo tú sigues aquí.

NUBES PASAJERAS

Los meditadores definen los pensamientos como nubes pasajeras antes de que el cielo vuelva a ser azul. Para frenar el *runrún* propio de tener muchas cosas en la cabeza, solo debes calmarte y poner tu atención en un único foco: la respiración.

- Deja todo lo que te preocupa para centrarte únicamente en el aire que entra y sale por tus fosas nasales.

- Cada vez que acuda un pensamiento, no lo juzgues. Simplemente déjalo pasar como una nube que flota en el cielo de tu mente.

Con la práctica, te irá resultando más fácil disociarte de tus pensamientos y, así, conquistar la serenidad.

3
¿CUÁL ES TU *FLOW*?

En la reflexión anterior vimos cómo disociarnos de los pensamientos reiterados o invasivos. Además del ejercicio de atención en la respiración, también podemos lograrlo poniendo nuestro foco en una actividad que nos permita fluir.

Cuando estás en modo *flow*, tu inconsciente empieza a crear nuevas posibilidades porque está más relajado. Sucede lo contrario cuando te hallas en alerta: tu mente está solo para defenderse o para escapar, no para crear.

Si queremos generar nuevas opciones, tendremos que buscar alternativas a aquello que nos está bloqueando. Para ello, nuestra mente necesita estar *entretenida* y contenta haciendo cosas que nos gusten.

No es algo que suceda de hoy para mañana. Al incorporar a tu día a día la rutina de estar relajado y fluyendo, con el tiempo crearás un hábito y en tu vida se dibujarán nuevas posibilidades.

REQUISITOS PARA FLUIR

¡Busca en tu vida esas cosas que te hagan sentir el *flow*! Según Mihály Csíkszentmihályi, el autor de *Flow* que falleció durante la pandemia, la experiencia de flujo tiene estos ingredientes:

- *El tiempo vuela.* Tal vez has estado largo rato haciendo algo, pero sientes que ha sido un instante.

- *Estás totalmente concentrado.* No hay distracciones que valgan.
- *No es muy fácil ni muy difícil.* En el primer caso, te aburrirías enseguida; en el segundo, la dificultad te bloquearía.
- *Apenas sientes el cansancio.* Lo que amas hacer no te supone esfuerzo.

4
LA FELICIDAD DE CAMINAR

Existe una relación directa entre mover el cuerpo y la felicidad. Cuando me siento apagada o los problemas del mundo me pesan demasiado, me pongo mis zapatillas y salgo a andar.

Con cada paso que doy, siento que la mochila de mis preocupaciones se va aligerando, hasta que al final ya solo estoy pendiente de cada músculo de mi cuerpo, de mi peso al pisar, levantar el pie y volver a pisar.

Puro *mindfulness* en movimiento, en el que están implicadas también otras sensaciones de consciencia plena que nos permiten conectar con nuestro cuerpo.

Las señales físicas inciden en la mente, igual que las de la mente se reflejan en el cuerpo. Del mismo modo que las emociones se somatizan, podemos transformar nuestro estado emocional al mejorar nuestra forma física.

Como aconsejaba el filósofo Friedrich Nietzsche: «Hay que sentarse lo menos posible y no creer en ningún pensamiento que no haya surgido al aire libre, estando en movimiento».

¿A QUÉ TE COMPROMETES?

Probablemente, tu móvil tenga una aplicación que cuenta cada zancada que das durante la jornada. Muchos *walkers* —caminadores— urbanos se fijan un determinado número de pasos al día, que realizan en el camino al trabajo, de compras o disfrutando del simple placer de respirar y moverse bajo el cielo.

Para mí, más que alcanzar un determinado número de pasos, se trata de decidir a qué te comprometes en lo que respecta al movimiento de tu cuerpo. Cada persona tiene sus propios límites, sus propios compromisos consigo misma.

¿Cómo lo vas a hacer? ¿Cuándo lo vas a hacer? ¿A qué te comprometes? Y, no menos interesante, ¿cómo lo vas a celebrar tras cumplirlo?

5

NO PODEMOS GUSTAR A TODO EL MUNDO

A menudo no nos damos cuenta de hasta qué punto vivimos para agradar a los demás. Es una actitud que tenemos en piloto automático, como una inercia que nos lleva por caminos que no son el nuestro.

La necesidad de gustar a todo el mundo forma parte de nuestro instinto de supervivencia y tiene su origen en cuando éramos cazadores y recolectores.

Nuestro pensamiento primitivo interpreta que si no somos aceptados por el grupo —si no caemos bien—, podemos ser abandonados por este. Y eso nos pondría en riesgo de morir. Es una interpretación totalmente exagerada, puesto que ya no vivimos de la misma manera ni dependemos de la tribu.

Sin caer tampoco en el egoísmo o la arrogancia, entender que no podemos gustar a todo el mundo nos libera, ya que nos permite ser coherentes con lo que sentimos y pensamos y elegir estar a gusto con nuestra propia vida.

NO ESTÁ MAL CAER MAL

En su libro *Atrévete a no gustar*, los filósofos japoneses Ichiro Kishimi y Fumitake Koga afirman que la verdadera libertad personal tiene como peaje no gustar a todo el mundo e incluso caer mal a algunas personas.

Esta es una regla práctica que podemos recordarnos cada vez que estemos actuando por *complacer*.

En sus propias palabras: «La única forma de ser libre es darte permiso para ser lo que quieres ser, no lo que esperan los demás de ti».

6
LO QUE OBTIENES ES LO QUE VES

En casi todas las experiencias, un 10 por ciento corresponde a lo que en realidad sucede y un 90 por ciento a lo que nosotros interpretamos. No somos conscientes de cómo nos contamos nuestra propia película sobre un acontecimiento, por eso hay que tomar distancia y ser lo más objetivo posible al observarlo.

Si lo que sucede es, sobre todo, nuestra interpretación de lo que sucede, el remedio está claro: ser lo más objetivos posible. Cuando nos llegue cualquier *input* que nos contraríe, el remedio es analizarlo de forma racional y relatarnos qué ha pasado.

Imagina que llega un correo electrónico escueto en el que tu jefa o jefe te pregunta cómo llevas una determinada tarea. Sea por la brevedad del mensaje o porque nos sentimos susceptibles, la mente puede activar el *runrún* del que hemos hablado en páginas anteriores, lanzando interpretaciones como: *¿Por qué me escribe un mensaje tan corto? ¿No tiene ganas de saludarme? ¿Habrá perdido la confianza en mí? ¿Piensa reemplazarme?*

Contra las hipótesis fantasiosas que ocupan mucho espacio mental y roban toda nuestra energía, la objetividad del mensaje: solo nos han preguntado por el estado de una tarea.

El hecho es el hecho, y el resto es la interpretación del hecho. Como dice Tina Turner *What you get is what you see*, lo que obtienes es lo que ves. Pero hay que tener en cuenta con qué gafas ves, miras o interpretas tu vida.

—— RELATA LO QUE HA SUCEDIDO SIN METER EMOCIÓN ——

Cuando sientas que un acontecimiento te desborda emocionalmente, haz el ejercicio de describirlo con objetividad, como si lo vieras desde el exterior sin imponer un juicio. Deja fuera cualquier emoción que hayas sentido. Hazlo por escrito o de manera mental, pero de una forma objetiva en la que puedas relatar los hechos. Lo que es, es.

7
ELIGE TUS BATALLAS

Una de las causas por las que a menudo nos sentimos sobrepasados es porque intentamos atender demasiados frentes al mismo tiempo.

Sin duda, si te paras a pensar, verás muchas cosas que desearías que fueran distintas, pero tratar de abordarlas todas simultáneamente es como si un pescador intentara pescar dos peces a la vez.

Para elegir tus batallas, tienes que discernir aquello que es prioritario en tu vida, aquí y ahora, y que depende de ti hacer.

Con el fin de saberlo, puedes preguntarte: ¿Qué asuntos me aportan y cuáles me están restando energía y no aportan nada bueno a mi existencia?

Si eliges de forma inteligente las batallas que merece la pena librar, no perderás tiempo ni energías en cuestiones secundarias o innecesarias.

Aférrate a aquellas que te aportan y descubrirás cómo, sorprendentemente, se abrirán nuevos campos de acción de lo más ilusionantes. Y también recuerda que al librar una pequeña batalla y salir adelante, se solucionan los problemas en otros frentes.

DECIDE UNA O DOS BATALLAS

Intentar atajar todas las *batallas*, además de ser una locura, nos lleva a comprobar al final que, de este modo, la guerra no se gana.

En este ejercicio voy a invitarte a que elijas uno o dos asuntos que considerses prioritarios y en los que quieres involucrarte:
- BATALLA 1.....................................
- BATALLA 2.....................................

Te propongo que no abras nuevos frentes hasta que cierres estos dos.

8
VENTANAS A LA FELICIDAD

Para mí, la lectura es un oasis que me aporta inspiración y serenidad a partes iguales. Mi familia tenía una librería y, ya de pequeña, al pasear los ojos por las portadas y los lomos de los libros, sentía admiración por aquellos autores y autoras capaces de plasmar tantas ideas, conceptos y bellas historias.

Este es uno de los motivos por los que entrevisto a tantos escritores que me estimulan. Cada libro te permite mirar en otras vidas y paisajes, por lo que es un excelente remedio contra los días grises.

En nuestra era digital, tal vez por el predominio de los contenidos audiovisuales, estamos leyendo menos de lo que necesita nuestra mente y nuestro espíritu.

Los libros son ventanas a la felicidad porque nos regalan otras visiones, otros razonamientos y conclusiones, amplían nuestra percepción y nos hacen viajar más allá de nuestra zona de confort. Leer es una apasionante aventura que podemos emprender desde el sillón de casa.

Recuerda que nunca es tarde para iniciar una rutina de lectura, porque la vida empieza cada día, es una historia que comienza cada día.

Te recomiendo, de vez en cuando, leer en voz alta para ti o para otros algún relato o poema que te estimule.

EL MEJOR SOMNÍFERO DEL MUNDO

El doctor Eduard Estivill, especialista en medicina del sueño, asegura que no hay remedio tan poderoso para dormir como el libro de papel.

En las horas previas a acostarnos, en cambio, desaconseja las pantallas de cualquier tipo, incluido el e-book, ya que la estimulación lumínica en el nervio óptico nos desvelará y no gozaremos de un descanso de calidad. Te reto a probar durante una semana y a ver los resultados.

9

SI PUEDES HACERLO AHORA...,
¡SIMPLEMENTE HAZLO!

L os seres humanos nos orientamos de forma natural hacia el placer.
Por eso hay ciertas tareas que son ineludibles, pero van quedando
relegadas y ocupan espacio mental.

A casi nadie le gusta hacer papeleo y gestiones burocráticas, por ejemplo.
Sin embargo, si no las atendemos, la bola se va haciendo más grande.

Los expertos en gestión de tiempo, de hecho, recomiendan empezar
las tareas del día por aquella que nos da más pereza. Justamente por eso
es liberador hacerla, ya que dejamos de cargar con ella el resto de la jornada.

Para introducir el hábito de atajar las cosas en su debido tiempo, es
útil el sistema GTD (*Getting Things Done*) del consultor norteamericano
David Allen, que dice que hay que programar las acciones cuando aparecen, no cuando expiran. Es decir, tener control de nuestro calendario en
lugar de ir a remolque.

Estos son hábitos que van creando una forma de proceder, por eso hay
que insistir en ellos. Hacer aquello que puedas YA te permitirá ir más ligero de quehaceres.

LA REGLA DE LOS DOS MINUTOS

De manera parecida a otras técnicas de gestión del tiempo, como la regla de los sesenta segundos, Allen establece ese tiempo en dos minutos. En sus palabras: «Si puedes hacer una tarea en menos de dos minutos, deberías hacerla ahora mismo. Si por el contrario te supone más de dos minutos, resérvala para tu lista». Resumiendo: HAZLO AHORA. ¿Crees que durante el día de hoy podrías intentar llevar a cabo esta regla?

10
DEMASIADO OCUPADO

Hay una frase que se ha atribuido a Bill Gates y a Warren Buffett, entre otras personalidades. Y es *Busy is the new stupid*. Es decir, estar ocupado es la nueva forma de ser estúpido.

¿Por qué estúpido? Pues porque para tener buenas ideas es necesario disponer de tiempo para que puedan surgir.

Así como una artista no podría pintar en un lienzo totalmente lleno, si no te das tregua, si no te das un respiro para detener la actividad frenética, no podrás crear nada nuevo en ningún ámbito de tu vida.

Esta es la razón por la que los expertos en gestión del tiempo dicen que alguien siempre ocupado no puede ser productivo. Como mucho irá atendiendo urgencias con el piloto automático puesto.

Reconozco que de jovencita yo estaba enganchada a la actividad. Tal vez por lo que me decía mi padre: «Si quieres que algo se haga, encárgalo a alguien muy ocupado». Y como yo siempre lo estaba, no paraba de adquirir compromisos.

¿Y si incluimos en la agenda el noble arte de desconectar?

LA FILOSOFÍA NIKSEN

Para salir del permanente *too busy* —demasiado ocupado— y refrescar tu cuerpo y tu mente, te propongo que practiques el *niksen*, como los holandeses llaman al arte de descansar de forma consciente. Aunque solo sea veinte minutos al día, un respiro libre de obligaciones te recargará las pilas y nutrirá tu creatividad.

No se trata de no hacer nada, sino de hacer cosas distintas que te relajen la mente, como salir a correr o regalarte una lectura que te ayude a *cambiar de canal*.

11
EL SÍNDROME DEL IMPOSTOR

Seguro que conoces esta sensación: estás haciendo algo y oyes una vocecilla que te dice: *No soy capaz, tengo miedo.* Y no te atreves a hacer lo que deseas a causa de ese temor. Eludes el reto o compromiso porque piensas que no te va a salir bien y tal vez porque crees que te juzgarán.

También puede que se sume a eso el pensamiento de *Yo no me merezco triunfar.* Y es que existe un miedo a brillar, como si lo que has conseguido hubiera sido por un cúmulo de casualidades o pura suerte. Incluso tal vez creas que, en realidad, no te lo has *currado* suficiente y que al final se darán cuenta de esa verdad de la que te alerta la vocecilla: *Te van a pillar. No eres tan excelente.*

Esa es la base del síndrome del impostor. Te asalta la idea de que eres menos de lo que crees que eres. Hasta que oyes a los demás señalando lo bueno que ven en ti y que tú no puedes ver.

A muchas personas nos cuesta aceptar lo valiosas que somos, y eso nos frena para seguir avanzando y asumir nuevos retos. Es como si nos costase más manifestar nuestro talento o los logros que hemos conseguido.

¿Y si fueras tú quien te da ese *feedback* apreciativo? ¿Hasta qué punto te permites brillar?

DESACTIVA EL BOICOT INTERIOR

Igual que cuidas cómo hablas a otras personas, cuida tu lenguaje interior, cómo te hablas a ti. Es bien sabido que no hay peor crítico que uno mismo, por lo que debes prestar atención a los mensajes que te dices. Cada vez que te sorprendas siendo demasiado duro contigo, pregúntate:

- ¿Cómo puedo tratarme como a una persona querida, tal y como lo haría con un hijo?
- ¿Cómo puedo tener el mismo cuidado y delicadeza hacia mí mismo?

12
¿DEMASIADO AUTOEXIGENTE?

Con qué rasero te mides? ¿Cuántas cosas te pides a ti mismo que no le pedirías a nadie? ¿Te has dado cuenta de lo que agota la autoexigencia?

Es importante diferenciar el cumplimiento de pequeños hitos y el propósito entusiasta –constante y comprometido– de la autoexigencia –continuada y desmesurada– que nos convierte en autómatas.

Para bajar nuestro nivel de autoexigencia es muy recomendable diseñar un plan de acción alcanzable y, sobre todo, medible y asequible.

Recuerda que esto del bienestar emocional es una carrera de fondo en la que los pequeños logros son dignos de ser celebrados. Nuestro nivel de tolerancia y mimo son la mejor manera de aprender y evolucionar.

La excesiva autoexigencia o el perfeccionismo pueden llegar a bloquearnos. Para evitar esa trampa, lo mejor es pararse a observar y ser muy realista e identificar todo lo conseguido hasta el momento. En lugar de machacarte –no hay nada más cansado que esa sensación de no ser suficiente ni merecedor de lo que posees–, toma conciencia de todo lo que has conseguido, superando dificultades. Si entonces lo lograste, puedes hacerlo de nuevo. Más y mejor.

PIDE *FEEDBACK* DEL BUENO

Este *feedback* es el que pueden darnos las personas que nos quieren y saben lo que valemos. Si te cuesta ver tus méritos, pregunta a tu entorno: *¿Qué crees que me hace valiosa o valioso?*

Limítate a escuchar su respuesta, sin restarte méritos, y da las gracias.

De este modo podrás verte a través de otros ojos y ratificar que, efectivamente, tienes mucho que ofrecer.

13
SIMPLEMENTE, RESPIRA

Se cuenta que una de las cosas de Yoko Ono que enamoró a John Lennon fue una tarjeta que ella le entregó en la exposición en la que se conocieron donde, sencillamente, ponía *RESPIRA*. Por aquella época, el ya exBeatle llevaba una vida de drogas y agitación que lo tenía sin aliento. El consejo de la artista japonesa tenía todo el sentido del mundo.

Desde hace milenios, sabemos que los beneficios de la respiración consciente son incalculables: conectas contigo de una manera directa y rápida. Respirar conscientemente te permite seguir tu cuerpo, tu cadencia, a la vez que te alejas de cualquier otro pensamiento. Al estar concentrado en la acción de respirar, la calma y la serenidad llegan de forma natural.

La investigadora Nazareth Castellanos hace énfasis en la relación entre la respiración y nuestro rendimiento mental. Como demuestra en un estudio de neuroanatomía de 2017, «según cómo estemos respirando, tendremos más capacidad de atención o de memoria. Y, no solo eso, sino que el patrón respiratorio influye también en cómo expresamos la emoción».

También subraya que nuestra capacidad de memoria aumenta cuando inspiramos por la nariz, respecto a cuando lo hacemos por la boca.

TRES TÉCNICAS DE RESPIRACIÓN

En su libro *Namaste*, Héctor García y Francesc Miralles mencionan en el capítulo dedicado al *Pranayama* —la expansión de la energía vital a través del yoga—, tres ejercicios de respiración para tres usos distintos:

1. Si te sientes letárgico, con falta de energía, y deseas activarte: *la fase de inhalar debe durar más que la de exhalar.*
2. Si sientes mucha ansiedad y quieres relajarte: *la fase de exhalar debe durar más tiempo que la de inhalar.*
3. Si no te puedes concentrar y estás algo inquieto: *la fase de exhalar e inhalar deben durar lo mismo.*
Te propongo practicar estas tres respiraciones que pueden ayudarte.

14

AMA LO QUE ES

Admiro especialmente a Byron Katie, la autora de *Amar lo que es*. Su camino de descubrimiento no fue recto ni fácil. Tras una larga depresión que la llevó a encerrarse en su casa, desconectada del mundo y de sí misma, llegó a pensar en acabar con su vida. Afortunadamente, un fogonazo de lucidez llegó en el momento perfecto.

¿Qué descubrió Byron Katie que la sacó del sufrimiento? Una idea muy simple y poderosa a la vez: que sufrimos, sobre todo, cuando no aceptamos *lo que es*, es decir, lo que la vida pone en nuestra mesa aquí y ahora.

Tomar conciencia de eso la transformó. Se dio cuenta de que el dolor que sentía no venía del mundo, sino de su mirada reactiva sobre el mismo. En palabras de Katie: «Los pensamientos que hieren son aquellos que no van de acuerdo con lo que es, con la realidad». Para neutralizar los pensamientos negativos hay que abrazar y amar la realidad. Desde el amor y la aceptación podremos sumergirnos plenamente en la vida.

CUATRO PREGUNTAS Y TRES INVERSIONES

Byron Katie elaboró su método *The Work* para desarmar cualquier pensamiento dañino invasivo:
1. *¿Eso que pienso es verdad?* (Si la respuesta es *No*, pasa a la tercera pregunta).
2. *¿Puedo saber absolutamente que eso es verdad?* (*Sí* o *No*).
3. *¿Cómo reacciono cuando creo en ese pensamiento?*
4. *¿Quién sería sin ese pensamiento?*

Tras estas cuatro preguntas, Katie sugiere pasar nuestra creencia por tres inversiones. Si la idea invasiva es, por ejemplo, *Él no me quiere*, debes decirte:
1. Él me quiere (hasta donde puede o sabe).
2. Yo le quiero (¿lo acepto realmente como es?).
3. Yo me quiero (¿soy capaz de hacerlo?).

15
¿DESDE DÓNDE INTERPRETAS LO QUE TE PASA?

Te animo a que te hagas esta pregunta cada vez que algo que te ha sucedido afecte de manera importante a tu estado de ánimo. Puede ser que lo hagas desde el corazón, las tripas o la cabeza.

¿Lo has interpretado desde la emoción y la visceralidad, o has sido racional al respecto? Si le prestas atención, el cuerpo te puede ayudar a saber dónde lo has recibido.

Saber desde dónde interpretas lo que te pasa te permitirá entender por qué te está afectando y de qué manera.

¿Lo que te ha sucedido corrobora o ratifica alguna verdad en la que habías puesto toda tu fe? ¿Te ayuda a comprender o empatizar con algo? ¿Te ha puesto en los zapatos de otra persona?

La interpretación que hacemos del mundo parte de una creencia que, como unas gafas tintadas, tiñe cómo ves lo que te rodea.

Yo te recomiendo que filtres siempre desde el corazón, ya que, desde ese lugar, con calma y una respiración consciente, puedes darle una vuelta de tuerca y reinterpretar cualquier hecho en clave positiva.

¿QUÉ GAFAS TE HAS PUESTO HOY?

Si todo depende del cristal a través del que miras, como afirma el dicho popular, es útil definir el color de nuestra mirada. Tres ejemplos:
- *Gafas del pesimismo:* los cristales son tan oscuros que ensombrecen cualquier motivo de alegría a nuestro alrededor.

- *Gafas del escepticismo y la duda:* estas lentes lo cuestionan todo, lo cual hace imposible tomar decisiones y disfrutar de la vida.
- *Gafas de la felicidad:* como en el libro de Rafael Santandreu, es nuestra mirada más brillante y generosa sobre la realidad.

16
EL MOMENTO DE PARAR

Cuando notes que hay mucho ruido en tu mente, experimentes agitación o te sientas *pasado de revoluciones* es importante que pares antes de perder el control.

El monje coreano Haemin Sunim, autor del ensayo *Aquello que solo ves al detenerte*, aborda esta cuestión planteando una pregunta fundamental: «Cuando todo a mi alrededor se mueve tan rápido, me detengo y me pregunto: ¿es mi mundo el que está frenético o es mi mente?».

Muy probablemente sea lo segundo. En ese caso, te aconsejo que procedas así:

1. Fuerza la quietud, deja de correr o de hacer lo que tienes entre manos ahora mismo.

2. Para detener esos pensamientos frenéticos, respira lenta y profundamente, hasta que sientas que regresa la serenidad.

3. Si estás yendo hacia algún sitio, ralentiza tus movimientos y sonríe. ¡No te puedes ni imaginar lo que ayuda!

UNA PAUSA ACTIVA

Ovidio, el gran poeta romano, recomendaba hace dos milenios: «Tómate un respiro; el campo que ha reposado da una cosecha más abundante». Cada vez que necesites una pausa, piensa que no es una pérdida de tiempo, sino una inversión para luego dar más y mejores frutos.

17

TUS FORTALEZAS

En una ocasión, preguntaron a Jim Clifton, presidente de Gallup, una gran empresa de encuestas de opinión, cuál era el mejor consejo que le habían dado en su vida. Dijo que fue uno de su padre: «Piensa que tus debilidades no se desarrollarán mucho más, mientras que tus fortalezas seguirán creciendo infinitamente».

Este consejo me parece muy relevante, porque a menudo estamos tan atentos a lo que nos falta que desdeñamos las fortalezas que tenemos de manera innata y que nos han traído hasta donde estamos.

Tenemos que desplegar esas fortalezas, hacerlas efectivas y activar ese *ON* a través de la experiencia vital.

Todo empieza por identificar cuáles son. Para llevarlo a cabo, podemos recorrer nuestra trayectoria vital y ver los momentos complicados de la vida en los que aplicamos nuestras habilidades.

TU CAJITA DE TESOROS Y HERRAMIENTAS

Pregunta a las personas que mejor te conocen cuáles fueron, desde su punto de vista, los momentos de tu vida en los que se manifestó una fortaleza tuya: una conducta, una costumbre o un hábito que ha hecho de ti una persona más sabia y valiosa. Se trata de identificar las cosas que te han rescatado en momentos complicados de la vida.

Toma nota de esos pequeños logros que alcanzaste sin darte cuenta. Son una cajita de tesoros y herramientas de las que echar mano siempre que lo necesites.

18
AFIRMACIONES

En la década de los ochenta, Louise Hay convirtió su libro *Usted puede sanar su vida* en un inesperado best seller que cambió la manera de pensar –y de hablarse– de millones de personas.

La autora parte de que el amor es una cura milagrosa, por lo que si te amas a ti mismo, vivirás milagros. En el extremo opuesto, las personas que alimentan ideas y creencias negativas sobre ellas mismas sufren toda clase de trastornos y problemas.

Si el tono de nuestros pensamientos configura nuestro presente y, por tanto, también nuestro futuro, es fundamental prestar atención, ya que lo que creemos de nosotros y de la vida acaba siendo nuestra verdad y realidad.

A partir de la idea de que el universo nos apoya en todo lo que decidimos pensar y creer, Louise Hay afirma:

Si me digo que el amor está en todas partes, y que soy capaz de amar y digna de amor, y me adhiero a esa nueva afirmación y la repito frecuentemente, esa llegará a ser mi verdad. En mi vida aparecerán personas capaces de amar, las que ya forman parte de ella demostrarán más amor, y yo descubriré lo fácil que me resulta expresar mi amor a los demás.

EMPIEZA LA JORNADA CON AFIRMACIONES

Escribe tres afirmaciones positivas sobre tres ámbitos en los que quieras influir —por ejemplo: tu autoestima, el trabajo y el amor— y empieza el día leyéndolas antes de que te arrastre la vorágine de tareas. Tienen que ser en primera persona, en positivo y cortas y fáciles de recordar.

Un par de ejemplos:
- *Me quiero tal y como soy.*
- *Doy lo mejor de mí cada día.*

Este sencillo ejercicio de leer tus afirmaciones hará que sintonices un canal positivo en tu emisora mental para empezar el día.

19
¿CÓMO LE PIDES AL UNIVERSO LO QUE DESEAS?

D e las afirmaciones vamos a pasar a los deseos. Prácticamente todo el mundo tiene algún deseo que le gustaría materializar.

En uno de los pasajes más célebres de *El alquimista*, Paulo Coelho afirmaba que «cuando quieres realmente una cosa todo el universo conspira para ayudarte a conseguirla».

Esto ha llevado a pensar a más de uno que basta con pedir al universo lo que quieres para obtener esta ayuda. Sin embargo, yo te propongo llevar esta cuestión más allá. Cada vez que le pidas algo al universo, pregúntate para qué deseas eso con tantas ganas. ¿Eso que quieres es lo que realmente necesitas?

Si es algo que de verdad te falta, analiza cómo puedes programar tu plan de acción, poniendo el foco en lo que deseas conseguir y siempre desde la apertura a nuevas posibilidades, no desde la carencia.

Quizá lo que en este momento ves como una necesidad se diluya en el tiempo y llegue otra cosa mucho más importante que ahora ni siquiera sospechas.

¿QUÉ ESPERA LA VIDA DE MÍ?

Más allá de nuestros deseos y supuestas necesidades, la vida nos manda señales que son invitaciones a recorrer determinados caminos. Para contestar a la pregunta de este pequeño ejercicio, presta atención a tus capacidades y talentos. ¿Dónde, en qué y cómo puedo ser más útil en este momento de mi vida?

20
ENTRENAR NUESTRO CEREBRO

Quisiera confesarte algo que me ocurre a veces, ya que creo que puede servirte si te encuentras en esta situación.

En ocasiones, me cuesta recordar el nombre de algunas personas, el título de un libro o de una película. Si, además, me pongo nerviosa, me resulta aún más difícil y me bloqueo. Lo que sí recuerdo es la emoción que me evocan esas personas, pero eso da para otra reflexión.

Depende de la situación, puede ser un poco violento; sin embargo, cuando me lo tomo con humor, enseguida me viene el dato que estaba buscando. ¿No es fabuloso?

Esto no me ocurre ni con las canciones ni con los poemas. Tal vez por mi trabajo tenga la parte audiovisual más desarrollada.

Con el tiempo he aprendido que la clave está en rebajar la presión, no obsesionarme con recordarlo al instante y saber que mi mente, a veces, también tiene días malos. Para enfrentarme a esta carencia, practico unos ejercicios de agilidad mental creados por mi querida Catalina Hoffmann, que forman parte de su método *Neurofitness*.

DOS CONSEJOS PARA UN CEREBRO SANO

Catalina Hoffmann, especialista en estimulación cognitiva y en entrenamiento cerebral, recomienda dos sencillas medidas que podemos seguir:

1. *Hidratación*. Dado que el cerebro se compone mayormente de agua, es importante hidratarnos bien, antes incluso de tener sed.

2. *Oxigenación*. Inspirar por la nariz, elevando el pecho, el diafragma y el vientre, para expulsar luego el aire suavemente por la boca, como si apagáramos una vela.

Así que recuerda: para cuidar tu cerebro, cada mañana, al levantarte, bebe un buen vaso de agua y oxigénate tres veces siguiendo este modelo.

21
SABER OBSERVAR

En contraposición a lo que te he contado en la reflexión anterior acerca de la manera en que soy incapaz de recordar algunos nombres, me considero una gran observadora.

Tengo facilidad para leer lo que me rodea, así como las emociones y energías que se manifiestan. Esa es una información *distinta* que recibo de la persona que tengo delante, del autor que leo, de la obra artística que contemplo o de la música que escucho. Es algo que me sucede desde niña.

Me quedo con detalles muy pequeños que a otros se les escapan. De esto me di cuenta al descubrir lo mal que me oriento y lo que me cuesta interpretar un mapa. ¡Los planos, en cambio, se me dan bien!

¿Te consideras una persona observadora? Si eres capaz de prestar atención a los detalles, ganarás capacidad perceptiva en tu universo cotidiano.

UN EJERCICIO DE OBSERVACIÓN

En la habitación o el espacio donde lees este libro, te propongo que mires a tu alrededor como si vieras por vez primera el lugar donde estás. Fíjate en algún detalle que hasta ahora te había pasado desapercibido. ¿Qué te dice este descubrimiento? Puede que llegues a la conclusión de que pasamos buena parte de la vigilia dormidos.

22
MAESTROS COTIDIANOS

Reconozco que nunca he sido muy social. Ni siquiera de niña lo era. Sé que me muevo en un entorno en el que parece complicado no serlo, pero me las arreglo siempre para descubrir entre la multitud a alguien con quien tener una conversación cercana y emocionante. Eso me llena y da sentido a mi vida.

Me lo tomo como un regalo, porque, a partir de la gente que tengo la fortuna de conocer, aprendo y me siento más alegre con lo que tengo y soy. Me genera calma y gratitud conocer esas historias de vida.

Sin embargo, otras veces, especialmente en mi profesión, me encuentro frente a gente con la que siento que comparto poco.

Hoy te animo a que pienses con gratitud en el primer grupo, el de esas personas que se cruzaron en tu camino y que, sin que esperases nada, al final te procuraron una lección valiosa para la vida.

EL SÉQUITO HACE A LA REINA

Esta variante del *hábito hace al monje* podría haber sido pronunciada por el empresario y conferenciante Jim Rohn, que afirmaba que somos la media de las cinco personas con las que pasamos más tiempo.

¿Quiénes son en tu vida esas cinco personas y cómo las puntuarías en un valor que te interese desarrollar? ¿Qué media obtienes a partir de todas ellas? ¿Conoces personas de valor que podrías incorporar a tu círculo para *subir nota*?

23
EL ESPEJO DE LOS DEMÁS

Has observado alguna vez que, en los malos momentos, atraes a personas de signo negativo, así como sucede lo contrario cuando estás en paz contigo?

Ya en la antigüedad, Hermes Trismegisto decía que «como es adentro, es afuera»: cuando una persona no se acepta y no se ama, ese mismo desequilibrio se traduce en sus relaciones con otras personas.

Los demás nos hacen de espejo. Muchas veces nos molesta algo de alguien, justamente porque compartimos ese mismo punto a mejorar. Por el contrario, reconocer lo que el otro hace bien a veces nos da vergüenza o apuro. Sin embargo, en cuanto empiezas a hacerlo, no solo descubres la belleza del reconocimiento, sino que te sientes parte de aquello que admiras.

Al reconocer cosas en los otros, también aprendes a verlas en ti. Siguiendo la ley del espejo: sé generoso con los demás y los demás lo serán contigo.

¿Qué dice el mundo que te rodea, en este momento vital, de cómo estás por dentro?

HAZ LAS PACES CONTIGO

Si queremos sanar el mundo, debemos empezar sanándonos a nosotros mismos. Para ello, merece la pena chequear cómo estamos por dentro:

- ¿Cómo puedo aceptarme como soy y estar donde quiero estar?
- ¿Cómo me doy permiso para ser imperfecto, como toda persona en crecimiento?
- ¿Cómo puedo perdonar lo que no me gusta de mi pasado?
- ¿Cómo puedo ser consciente de mis valores y talentos?

24
EL SEGUNDO ACUERDO

Naciste con el derecho de ser feliz. Naciste con el derecho de amar, de disfrutar y de compartir tu amor. Estás vivo, así que toma tu vida y disfrútala», decía Miguel Ruiz, el autor del clásico *Los Cuatro Acuerdos*.

Inspirado en la sabiduría tolteca, este autor afirma que los acuerdos más importantes son aquellos que establecemos con nosotros mismos. Recordemos cuáles son los que él propone:

1. Sé impecable con tus palabras.
2. No te tomes nada personalmente.
3. No hagas suposiciones.
4. Haz siempre lo mejor que puedas.

El Segundo Acuerdo resuena a muchas personas porque la mayoría de las fricciones con los demás vienen de no cumplir con él. En palabras de Miguel Ruiz:

Nada de lo que los demás hacen es por ti. Lo hacen por ellos mismos. Todos vivimos en nuestro propio sueño, en nuestra propia mente; los demás están en un mundo completamente distinto de aquel en que vive cada uno de nosotros.

LIBRE DE OPINIONES

Sobre esto, el guía espiritual Sergi Torres nos ofrece un sencillo ejercicio para tener en cuenta: nunca te tomes en serio nada que piensen los demás o tú mismo. Asume que se trata simplemente de opiniones, de interpretaciones, no de la realidad.

25
INCERTIDUMBRE POSITIVA

Hablemos de la incertidumbre. Es una sensación que, hoy en día, nos es muy familiar. Convivimos con ella a menudo, especialmente a partir de los grandes cambios que ha sufrido el mundo en los últimos años.

A la mayoría de nosotros nos asusta, pero la verdad es que todo o casi todo es incierto en esta vida. También las cosas buenas son inciertas, no sabemos si llegarán o no. Por eso es importante que la incertidumbre no nos bloquee. ¿Cuáles son las claves para gestionarla y superarla?

Andrés Pascual, autor de *Incertidumbre positiva*, establece la siguiente distinción:

Incertidumbre = incapacidad para predecir tu futuro.

Incertidumbre positiva = capacidad para crear tu futuro.

Ciertamente, en las situaciones de más incertidumbre resulta imposible saber qué pasará, pero al mismo tiempo es el momento más interesante para hacer cambios vitales y aprovechar las nuevas oportunidades que brinda toda crisis.

Cuando el mundo parece haber perdido el rumbo, la manera que tenemos de predecir el futuro es crearlo.

VIVIR EN TIEMPO PRESENTE

Si sientes que el futuro te abruma, y que reina el caos y la confusión, el remedio para recuperar la calma es enfocarse en este día. Quizá no puedas saber qué pasará en un año, ni siquiera en unos meses, pero lo que suceda hoy está en tus manos. Y, al final, el futuro se construye con la suma de muchas jornadas como hoy.

26
EMPATÍA

Si hay algo que nos hace sentir vivos es la conciencia de pertenecer a algo más grande que uno mismo, poder conectar de forma profunda con las personas que nos rodean.

Dicho de otra forma: tener empatía.

Personalmente, esta es una de las cualidades que más valoro en cualquier persona: la capacidad de ponerse en el lugar del otro y acompañarlo desde la emoción, sin juicios ni prejuicios. Es sentir que, de alguna manera, lo que sea que le ocurre nos está ocurriendo también a nosotros.

En el budismo, un término cercano a la empatía es la compasión, que no significa tener lástima por alguien, sino unir nuestro sentimiento al suyo. La gran experta en religiones Karen Armstrong lo define así: «Cuando sentimos con el otro, nos destronamos del centro de nuestro mundo y ponemos a otra persona ahí».

Y lo mejor es que, al hacerlo, no solo ayudamos a la otra persona, sino que nos sentimos mejor, más conectados a la humanidad y al universo entero.

Sobre esto, la profesora norteamericana Brené Brown señala: «La empatía es la escalera que nos saca de un mismo agujero».

SAL DE TUS ZAPATOS

Un ejercicio básico para entrenar la empatía consiste en elegir a una persona a la que te resulte difícil entender o te genere rechazo. Dedica quince minutos a imaginar cómo es su vida, las dificultades a las que se enfrenta día a día, sus frustraciones y deseos insatisfechos. Camina con ella imaginariamente durante ese tiempo y estarás más cerca de comprenderla.

27
EL PODER DE LA GRATITUD

En esta reflexión quiero hablarte sobre el poder de la gratitud. Hay dos maneras básicas de relacionarse con el mundo: a través de la queja o del agradecimiento.

La primera nos instala en la carencia y la negatividad. La segunda, en la abundancia y la gratitud.

Practicar esta última te permite sintonizar con el lado amable de la vida, de modo que, cuanto más agradeces, más motivos encuentras para dar las gracias. Es un estado de consciencia elevado que te proporciona energía creativa.

Prueba de ello es un estudio llevado a cabo por los investigadores Emmons & McCullough, que midieron el bienestar de un grupo de voluntarios después de diez semanas escribiendo un diario de gratitud, frente a un segundo grupo que se centró en los problemas cotidianos, y un tercero que relató los acontecimientos vividos de forma neutral.

El resultado fue que el primer grupo se sentía un 25 por ciento más feliz que el resto y manifestó mayor optimismo de cara al futuro.

ELABORA TU DIARIO DE GRATITUD

Hoy te invito a que escribas al principio de cada jornada tres cosas por las que te sientes afortunado por este nuevo día. Antes de acostarte, escribe lo mejor que te ha sucedido hoy y expresa tu agradecimiento. Esto te permitirá cultivar la gratitud y sintonizar cada vez más fácilmente con esta poderosa energía.

28
COMPARTE TU LUZ

E res una persona valiosa. Tienes cualidades que te hacen única y auténtica. Sobre esto, el violoncelista Pau Casals nos legó una bella reflexión que quiero compartir:

Cada segundo que vivimos es un momento nuevo y único del universo, un momento que jamás volverá... Y ¿qué es lo que enseñamos a nuestros hijos? Pues, les enseñamos que dos y dos son cuatro, que París es la capital de Francia. ¿Cuándo les enseñaremos, además, lo que son? A cada uno de ellos deberíamos decirle: ¿Sabes lo que eres? Eres una maravilla. Eres único (...) Debes esforzarte –como todos debemos esforzarnos– por hacer el mundo digno de sus hijos.

Ese esfuerzo supone no quedarte con tu luz: debes compartirla con los demás, para contribuir a su iluminación. No te quedes nada para ti. Compártelo, por pequeño que sea.

El mundo está necesitado de tu generosidad y, por lo tanto, también de tu genialidad y autenticidad. Al final, cuanto más compartes tu don, más lo desarrollas, multiplicando y expandiendo su efecto a la vez.

¿CUÁL ES TU ELEMENTO?

Esta es una pregunta que nos formulaba sir Ken Robinson, el gran experto en educación fallecido en 2020. Así como el agua es el elemento del pez, cada persona tiene un determinado entorno o situación donde se desarrolla con más facilidad y puede brillar con luz propia.

Piénsalo. ¿Cuál es el tuyo?

29
LOS TRES FILTROS

Se cuenta que un alumno de Sócrates fue a verlo para decirle que acababa de oír algo acerca de uno de sus discípulos.

–Espera –lo frenó el sabio–. Antes quiero que pases la prueba de los tres filtros.

–¿Los tres filtros?

–Sí, y el primero es el de la verdad. Necesito que me digas si estás seguro de que lo que vas a contarme es cierto.

–Bueno... lo acabo de oír y no sé si...

–Es decir, que no lo sabes –dijo Sócrates–. Entonces vayamos al segundo filtro: el de la bondad. ¿Lo que quieres contarme es bueno para mi discípulo?

–¡Me temo que no! Al contrario.

–Entonces... pretendes contarme algo malo sin saber si es cierto. Bueno, aún podrías pasar el tercer filtro: el de la utilidad. ¿Esto que quieres contarme, me va a ser útil?

–Pues, sinceramente..., ¡creo que no!

–Entiendo. Si no es cierto ni bueno ni útil... ¿para qué contarlo? –concluyó Sócrates.

EL VALOR DE CALLAR

Esta historia atribuida a un pilar de la filosofía griega nos aporta una herramienta muy valiosa que puede sernos útil cuando tengamos una información que podría herir a alguien. Si no pasa la prueba de los tres filtros, lo mejor es que desestimemos la información y no digamos nada.

30
PENSAMIENTOS POSITIVOS

V olvamos a hablar de una de las científicas más brillantes de este país, por lo que respecta a neurociencia y a la conexión entre el cerebro y el cuerpo: Nazareth Castellanos.

Al contrario de lo que suele creerse, afirma que el cerebro recibe y gestiona mejor y retiene más tiempo los mensajes positivos que los negativos.

Además, Castellanos resalta el hecho de que podemos adelantarnos tanto a los buenos como a los malos mensajes: «Según la literatura científica, el cuerpo sabe lo que la mente aún no. Por eso, si tenemos consciencia corporal, podemos conocer la reacción antes de expresar la emoción».

Esto es especialmente interesante, porque nos da la clave para definir cuál queremos que sea el tono de nuestra vida.

¿Y si en lugar de amargarnos con informaciones negativas, que nos provocan ansiedad y desesperanza, comenzamos a promover mensajes de signo opuesto?

Si empezamos a hablarnos con frases que nos hagan sentir mejor, al mismo tiempo estaremos creando una actitud a favor de lo que pueda venir. De manera inconsciente, además, estaremos preparados para los inconvenientes que nos traiga la vida.

EN CLAVE POSITIVA

Te propongo que escribas cinco cosas positivas en un papel. Luego, léelas en voz alta y piensa cuál de ellas vas a tener más presente en el día de hoy.

¿De qué manera vas a honrarla?
¿Con quién la compartirás?
¿De qué manera convertirás esa clave positiva en un bello recuerdo?

31
DECÍDELO CON CALMA

S e atribuye a san Ignacio de Loyola esta regla: «En tiempo de desolación nunca hacer mudanza». La recomendación de este religioso guipuzcoano que fundó la Compañía de Jesús encaja con uno de los conceptos clave de la sabiduría china: el *Wu Wei*.

Traducido como *no hacer*, este concepto apunta a que hay momentos para la acción y otros para la prudencia y la observación, en especial cuando vivimos épocas turbulentas.

En las relaciones interpersonales, por ejemplo, cuando los ánimos están muy crispados, conviene dejar que los nervios se relajen y encontrar una ocasión más oportuna para reconducir las cosas. En estos instantes, el *Wu Wei* es lo mejor que se puede hacer.

Para las grandes decisiones o cambios drásticos, espera a estar bien: en calma y en un momento más feliz.

DALE 24 HORAS DE TIEMPO

El popular consejo de *consultarlo con la almohada*, cuando se trata de una decisión importante, me parece de lo más acertado. ¿Cuántas veces nos dejamos llevar por la impulsividad y luego lo lamentamos?

La próxima vez que tengas que tomar una decisión muy relevante, no digas *sí* o *no* de inmediato. Date 24 horas para, desde la calma, optar por la opción más inteligente.

32
VISUALIZA TU OBJETIVO

A menudo nos sentimos bloqueados ante algo que queremos conseguir, pero que no sabemos con precisión qué es. Eso ocurre porque no le hemos dado aún forma.

Para dársela, lo mejor es llevar a cabo una visualización.

Antes de cerrar los ojos, prepara el ambiente: puedes poner una música para inspirarte o tal vez prefieras el silencio; puedes hacerlo a la luz de las velas o en un lugar en penumbra. Personalmente, a mí me ayuda mucho la música y una respiración muy pausada.

A la hora de comenzar, es importante estar en calma. Desde ahí, imagina cuál sería y qué forma tendría ese objetivo que quieres alcanzar.

Cuando aparezca una idea, lo recomendable es bocetarla desde la calma, sin presión. Dibuja o describe ese objetivo en un papel. Cuanto más en detalle lo plasmes, mejor. Especifica su forma, sus características, los objetos y las personas que lo rodean; puedes incluso asignarle un color. ¡Tú decides!

LA MAGIA DE LO EMOCIONAL

Algo que saben muy bien los publicistas es que las ideas o imágenes que dejan huella son las que tienen impacto emocional. A la hora de decidir aquello que quieres visualizar, elige algo que despierte en ti una emoción positiva y motivadora. Al nutrirla a través de tu imaginación, te preparas para alcanzarla.

33
CRONOBIOLOGÍA

S omos naturaleza. Somos parte de los ciclos de la vida y de los cambios que hay en nuestro entorno.

El paso de las estaciones, las plantas, los animales, el agua de la lluvia, el viento... Formamos parte de todo eso y a veces lo obviamos, pero la realidad es que, como naturaleza que somos, cada persona experimenta cambios y debemos integrarlos, darles la bienvenida y convivir con ellos.

La moderna cronobiología nos enseña que nuestra salud y vitalidad dependen de nuestra capacidad para adaptarnos a los ciclos de la vida. Nuestro reloj interno necesita sincronizarse con el de la naturaleza, que se expresa mayormente por la luz, por lo que las personas más longevas suelen levantarse con el sol, comen a horas determinadas y se acuestan con la oscuridad.

¿Llevas tu reloj interno sincronizado con el de la vida?

CELEBRA LAS ESTACIONES

Honra y celebra los ciclos de las estaciones. Te propongo acciones para dos momentos clave del año:

- *Solsticio de verano.* En muchos países, la verbena de San Juan da la bienvenida a la nueva estación y se encienden hogueras. Escribe en un papel lo que quieres hacer desaparecer en tu vida y quémalo.

- *Solsticio de invierno.* Crea tu propio ritual para recibir esta estación tan adecuada para el recogimiento y la reflexión. Por ejemplo, con una infusión caliente, puedes anotar en un papel los principales acontecimientos que has vivido este año y tus proyectos para el siguiente.

34
¿CÓMO TE HABLAS?

Hoy me gustaría invitarte a prestar atención sobre cómo te hablas a ti mismo.

¿Cómo te expresas? ¿De qué manera cuentas tu historia? ¿Qué palabras y expresiones utilizas? ¿Cómo conjugas los verbos?

Hay personas que utilizan, sin darse cuenta, un lenguaje negativo al contar su realidad o describirse ellas mismas. Hablan en clave de carencia, de lo que les falta, y no de lo que tienen, lo cual les pondría en la senda de la gratitud.

Otras conjugan sus verbos en pasado, como si estuvieran de vuelta de todo..., o fían su suerte al futuro, ignorando el ahora.

Es importante saber cómo hablamos, porque en el lenguaje laten nuestras creencias y nuestra forma de relacionarnos con el mundo.

Tanto si hablas a otros como si te hablas a ti mismo, sé consciente de las palabras que eliges, porque a través de ellas defines tu realidad. Opta por un lenguaje que te permita tener un discurso positivo, abierto y generoso contigo.

ABANDONA EL CONDICIONAL

Una forma sutil de procrastinar es usar el tiempo futuro o condicional en lugar de una afirmación: *Si tuviera..., entonces podría...* o bien *Cuando..., entonces podré...*

Como pequeño ejercicio, te voy a proponer que cada vez que te descubras utilizando el condicional o un futuro incierto, cambies esta fórmula que sitúa el poder fuera de ti por una afirmación en la que tú eres el protagonista: *Voy a...*

35
ERES INCOMPARABLE

En los tiempos que corren, en los que parece que nuestra vida es un escaparate y tenemos que intentar estar a la altura, debemos tener muchísimo cuidado a la hora de compararnos con los demás. Es algo que hacemos de forma habitual y que constituye un gran error. Muy probablemente saldremos perdiendo en comparación con lo que vemos en otros. Y esta manera de castigarnos solo conduce a dañar nuestra autoestima.

Cada persona es como es y sigue su camino, a su propio ritmo. Lo que les sirve a los demás quizá no sea lo más adecuado para ti. O quizá sí y te ayude a ver por dónde avanzar, pero hay que ir con cuidado.

Es normal que esto suceda, porque nos lo han inculcado desde muy pequeños con mensajes como: *Mira, tu hermano ha terminado toda su comida; mira Fulanito, qué bien se porta.*

Estos mensajes de la infancia nos impulsan hoy, de forma inconsciente, a compararnos con los demás, casi siempre a la baja. Pero incluso cuando son para bien, las comparativas son siempre arriesgadas y engañosas.

Como cantaba Sinéad O'Connor, «nothing compares to you».

EL CONSEJO DE JORDAN PETERSON

Uno de los autores más respetados en Estados Unidos nos recomienda en su cuarta regla para la vida: «Compárate con quien eras tú ayer, no con quien alguien es hoy».

Cuando te quitas la responsabilidad y el peso de compararte con los demás, es cuando verdaderamente eres libre.

36
ROMPER CON LOS PATRONES

Te has preguntado alguna vez por qué hay determinados *errores* que repetimos una y otra vez? En la mayoría de los casos es porque no somos conscientes de ello.

Cuando te das cuenta de que has tomado las mismas decisiones poco acertadas, ya tienes media solución en tus manos. La otra media es pasar a la acción y cambiar tus hábitos o actitudes.

Para adquirir consciencia, podemos tomar alguno de esos momentos en los que repetimos un patrón. Por ejemplo, en relaciones de pareja. Imagina que una persona elige de forma reiterada parejas que no respetan su libertad personal.

Si echa la vista atrás, tal vez relacione este patrón con un padre o madre que coartaba su libertad, pero a quien estaba muy apegado y de quien necesitaba su aprobación.

Al desvelar el argumento primigenio, el motivo original por el que nos comportamos así, entonces podemos desactivar el patrón. Si es necesario, incluso buscando la ayuda de un terapeuta.

El primer paso para cambiar nuestra forma de hacer las cosas es cuestionar el motivo original por el que nos comportamos así. Hacer consciente la parte inconsciente que hay detrás de una creencia es un punto de partida clave para cambiar un patrón.

EL ELEFANTE Y LA ESTACA

Uno de los cuentos más célebres de Jorge Bucay tiene como protagonista a un elefante a quien de pequeño ataron a una débil estaca y, siendo ya mayor, sigue atado a ella porque no sabe que es lo bastante fuerte para arrancarla.

Aplica esta metáfora a tu vida y pregúntate:
- ¿A qué estacas ya no debería estar atado?
- ¿Qué hábitos o actitudes tenían sentido en el pasado pero ya no lo tienen en mi presente?

37

EXPRESA LO QUE NECESITAS

Con los años he descubierto lo importante que es comunicarnos bien con las personas que tenemos delante, empezando por darles la información que necesitan de manera correcta y clara.

Unas veces no sabemos expresar lo que queremos y otras no entendemos lo que el otro quiere decirnos o bien no nos atrevemos a preguntar. O simplemente no le damos importancia a un momento crítico para el otro.

El remedio a todas estas situaciones puede resumirse en una sola palabra: comunicación. Pero no cualquier clase de comunicación.

El psicólogo Marshall Rosenberg acuñó la CNV, la Comunicación No Violenta, para referirse a una forma de expresarnos que, sin herir al otro, pone en claro nuestras necesidades, como veremos en el ejercicio que se propone a continuación.

TRANSFORMA EL REPROCHE EN EXPRESIÓN DE TU NECESIDAD

Si en lugar de reñir o señalar al otro, con lo cual solo logramos que se ponga a la defensiva o que contraataque, expresamos de manera clara y amable lo que nos hace falta, lo difícil se vuelve fácil.

Un ejemplo práctico:
En lugar de decir a tu pareja *estoy harto de que estés ausente todo el tiempo,* puedes decir *necesito que pasemos más tiempo juntos.*

38
ORDEN Y CONCIERTO

Cómo es el espacio en el que vives o trabajas? ¿Te inspira calma o es un lugar caótico en el que pierdes mucho tiempo buscando dónde están las cosas?

Personalmente, cuando lo tengo todo en su sitio, me siento más tranquila y serena. Por ese motivo me gusta dedicar tiempo a ordenar mis espacios. Desde mi despacho, los papeles, los libros, la agenda... hasta el frigorífico.

He comprobado que, cuanto más ordenado se encuentra tu entorno, así como tu imagen, tu mente en general está también más ordenada y armónica.

A mí me gusta llamarlo *orden y concierto*, porque todo está en su sitio y *concertado*, lo que quiere decir que tiene un volumen, un espacio y una luz particular. Hay un equilibrio y eso me permite también, a la hora de sentarme y visualizar, tener una claridad y una perspectiva mucho más adecuada para lo que necesito hacer.

EL MÉTODO KONAMARI

El popular sistema de Marie Kondo para mantener la casa en orden tiene unos principios muy básicos y eficaces:

- El orden empieza por eliminar todo aquello que no necesitas.
- Cuanto menos cargada de cosas está una casa, más habitable es. Eso influye de forma positiva en tu estado de ánimo.

- Decir adiós a lo inútil es una forma de decir adiós al pasado y purificarse.
- En caso de duda, pregúntate si un determinado objeto te produce felicidad. Si la respuesta es *no*, puedes desprenderte de él.

39
DESDE EL SILENCIO Y LA CALMA

Seguro que has vivido situaciones de estrés o irritación en las que el tono de las voces que discuten va subiendo. En estos casos, no solo no se arreglan las cosas, sino que suelen empeorar.

Mantener el silencio en una situación delicada es mejor que dar opiniones que no te han pedido.

Cuando se produce una discusión o enfado entre varias personas, me parece interesante observar lo que sucede desde la calma y el silencio. Me limito a recibir lo que me llega a través de los sentidos sin juicios, de la forma más objetiva posible.

Al estar en calma y en silencio, ayudamos a no crispar más la discusión, favoreciendo un clima de concordia.

Para llevarlo a cabo solo necesitas aportar una mirada serena, estar presente para acompañar a quien se encuentra en un momento difícil, sin entrar a valorar nada.

CUIDADO CON LOS CONSEJOS NO SOLICITADOS

El conferenciante Joan Antoni Melé, impulsor de la banca ética en España, advierte del peligro de dar consejos a quien no nos lo ha pedido. Esto puede crear incomodidad en el otro por varias razones:

- Muy probablemente, la persona solo quiere que la escuchemos y comprendamos, no que le demos nuestras soluciones.
- Lo que nosotros haríamos no tiene por qué coincidir con lo que necesita hacer la otra persona, porque somos mundos distintos.
- Decir al otro lo que debería hacer a menudo se percibe como soberbia, no hay una equidistancia entre las partes.

40

SLOW LIFE

E stamos tan acostumbrados a la cultura de lo instantáneo, en la que todo se logra con un clic, que hacer las cosas despacio se ha convertido en un reto.

Me parece todo un arte la capacidad de observar, comer, bailar, caminar, pensar y sentir despacio, disfrutar de la pausa o la cadencia con la que hacemos las cosas.

Y no se trata de pegar frenazos cuando nos sentimos colapsados, para luego volver a correr, sino de vivir de forma un poco más lenta para poder apreciar los regalos que nos brinda la existencia.

Me gusta llamar *el baile de la vida* al hecho de ir más despacio. Un truco para promover este ritmo puede ser poner una música un poco más lenta de la que solemos escuchar, para incorporar esa lentitud a nuestro cuerpo.

La *slow life* no se limita solo a cómo nos movemos o al tiempo que dedicamos a cocinar un plato con cariño, sino que también incluye una gestión más tranquila de nuestros pensamientos y emociones, poniendo atención a lo que decimos y hacemos.

Lentamente, pero sin perder la cadencia, la vida nos ofrece toda su belleza y sus matices.

CINCO MEDIDAS CONTRA LAS PRISAS

Carl Honoré, autor de *Elogio de la lentitud*, nos propone algunas iniciativas para vivir de manera más relajada y atenta:

1. No sobrecargues tu agenda, prescinde de todo lo que puedas.
2. Cuando estés con tu familia o con tus amigos, desconecta el móvil.
3. Tómate tu tiempo para comer y beber, tu cuerpo lo agradecerá.
4. Pasa tiempo contigo mismo, no temas al silencio.
5. Si has contraído el virus de la prisa (es una epidemia mundial), intenta curarte.

41

VITAMINA C DE CURIOSIDAD

Te has parado a pensar alguna vez en los regalos de la curiosidad? Esta *vitamina* para la imaginación es fundamental en la vida de cualquier ser humano. Desde niños desarrollamos un sentido de la curiosidad que, poco a poco –desde mi punto de vista–, se va apagando en la mayoría de las personas.

Cuando damos las cosas por sabidas y nos quedamos con lo obvio, la falta de curiosidad nos cierra muchas puertas: limitamos la imaginación y el aprendizaje, perdemos nuestra capacidad de sorprendernos con las cosas y preguntarnos qué hay más allá.

Para volver a nutrir tu curiosidad, cuestiónate cualquier cosa que des por sentada. Desafía la visión que tengas del mundo y de ti mismo.

UN RETO PARA MENTES CURIOSAS

Para aportar esta vitamina C a tu mente, te propongo el siguiente reto mensual:
- Entabla conversación con al menos una persona de tu trabajo o entorno con quien nunca te has parado a charlar.
- Lee un libro de un autor o una autora que no conozcas.

- Visiona un documental sobre un país o una época de la historia que no te resulte familiar.
- Pasea por una calle o zona del lugar donde vives en la que nunca hayas estado.

42
ACEPTA LA AYUDA

Prácticamente todo el mundo disfruta ofreciendo su ayuda a los demás. Sentirnos útiles eleva nuestra autoestima y puede incluso sacarnos de un momento delicado de nuestra propia vida.

–¿Qué puedo hacer cuando esté desanimado? –se dice que preguntaron a Teresa de Calcuta.

–Anima a otro –respondió.

Lo interesante es que a muchas personas les cuesta hacer el camino contrario: dejarse ayudar. Sea porque tienen la creencia de que al dejarse ayudar son más débiles, o por el deseo legítimo de no molestar, niegan al otro este privilegio.

Así que, además de ayudar a quien lo necesite, es fundamental que te dejes ayudar y acompañar, especialmente cuando te encuentres en un proceso de cambio.

Ya se trate de un amigo, un familiar, un profesional, un maestro o de tu pareja, deja que los que te quieren te ofrezcan ayuda y se sientan útiles. Asume que eres importante para los demás.

¿QUIÉN PUEDE SER MI *SENPAI*?

En las empresas japonesas, la persona nueva que entra queda al cargo de un *senpai* que la guiará. Se trata de un mentor con muchos años de experiencia en esta tarea concreta que ayuda al *kohai*, el discípulo, a crecer y superar los retos que encontrará en su nuevo puesto.

En cualquier faceta de tu vida, si te enfrentas a una dificultad que no sabes cómo resolver, busca a una persona con experiencia en ese campo o situación. Muy probablemente se mostrará feliz de ser tu *senpai*.

43
NADIE COMO TÚ PARA CUIDARTE

Tal como sucede con la ayuda, también nos resulta más fácil cuidar de los demás que de nosotros mismos. Tendemos a ponernos muy abajo en nuestra lista de prioridades. Como decía el novelista Robert Louis Stevenson: «No hay deber que descuidemos tanto como el de ser felices».

Si nadie cuida a la persona cuidadora —algo que corresponde a uno mismo—, esta ve menguada incluso su capacidad de cuidar a los demás.

Por eso es importante tener detalles contigo, ya sea un poco de tiempo personal, un masaje o cualquier otra actividad que te regale bienestar.

Al cuidarte, celebras la vida y la intimidad con tu ser. Comprarte un libro, escuchar una canción que te gusta, hacerte la manicura, darte un baño o pasar tiempo con alguien a quien quieres mucho. ¡Todo esto te da vida!

Los pequeños instantes de autocuidado hacen que, de repente, la existencia adquiera más sentido. Son granitos de arroz para demostrarte que eres importante para ti mismo.

ELIGE TU PREMIO

Si estás haciendo una tarea que te resulta especialmente larga y pesada, fíjate una gratificación para celebrar que has terminado. Puede ser un regalo espiritual, intelectual o incluso físico, darte un pequeño placer para celebrar que lo has hecho bien y que la vida no son solo obligaciones.

44
ASERTIVIDAD

Saber decir *no* es igual de importante que decir *sí*. Cada vez que nos negamos a algo que sentimos que no debemos hacer, ponemos límites y damos oxígeno a nuestros anhelos, priorizando lo que consideramos que es mejor para nosotros.

Sin duda, decir *no* nos cuesta muchas veces, porque tememos herir los sentimientos de los demás o no cumplir sus expectativas. Pero un *no* a tiempo facilita las relaciones y la vida en general, ya sea a nivel personal o profesional.

Hay muchas formas de decir *no,* ahí reside la clave, como veremos en el ejercicio de esta reflexión.

En todo caso, al rechazar lo que no nos resuena, decimos «sí» a otras cosas importantes, damos la bienvenida a otros espacios, personas y posibilidades. Y no se trata de negarnos a todo, sino de encontrar el equilibrio entre lo que necesitamos y lo que los demás necesitan.

Jim Carrey, en su divertida comedia *Di que sí* encarna a un empleado de banca que tras años dando negativas, pasa por un seminario de autoayuda y se propone durante un tiempo decir *sí* a todo, con consecuencias catastróficas.

Se trata, al fin y al cabo, de encontrar el perfecto equilibrio.

NO, PERO...

Los especialistas en asertividad ofrecen técnicas para negarnos con una sonrisa y sin sentirnos culpables. Una de ellas es acompañar el *no* con una alternativa para quien solicita ayuda.

Dos ejemplos:

No puedo cuidar de tu hijo este sábado, pero te paso el teléfono de un excelente canguro.

No tengo tiempo para hacer la tarea que me pides, pero puedo ponerte en contacto con una especialista en la materia.

45

EL VALOR DE LAS PREGUNTAS

Cuando uno tiene dudas, es importante dejarlas en reposo y preguntarte a ti mismo antes de lanzarlas al mundo. Quizá solo tú puedas darles respuesta.

Una fábula tradicional cuenta que había un rabino que insistía a sus seguidores en que debían aprender por sí mismos. Sin embargo, siempre había gente que acudía a él esperando que les diera respuestas.

Cansado de esta situación, una mañana decidió fijar un cartel delante de su casa donde se leía: *SE CONTESTARÁN DOS PREGUNTAS POR 100 $.*

Tras pensárselo un buen rato, uno de sus discípulos más adinerados decidió llamar a su puerta para formularle dos importantes preguntas. Le pagó de antemano la cantidad fijada y le dijo:

–¿No son cien dólares una cifra desorbitada para dos preguntas?

–Sí –respondió el rabino–. ¿Cuál es la segunda pregunta?

DEJA DESCANSAR LAS PREGUNTAS

El rabino quiere animar a su discípulo a que indague y responda él mismo a sus cuestiones. Te habrá sucedido alguna vez, sin embargo, que hay preguntas para las que no tienes *todavía* respuesta. En estos casos, puedes seguir este procedimiento:

1. Escribe tu pregunta en un cuaderno o en una hoja de papel doblada y guárdala 24, 48 horas o incluso una semana, según su dificultad.
2. Durante este periodo, no hagas ningún esfuerzo en hallar la respuesta.
3. Transcurrido el *tiempo de descanso vuelve a ella y escribe libremente lo que te venga a la cabeza. Con toda probabilidad, el inconsciente habrá tenido tiempo de plantear nuevos caminos.*

46

TU PAREJA, TU MAESTRO

El filósofo Paul Tillich decía que el primer deber del amor es escuchar.

Las relaciones que tenemos nos ayudan a crecer. Nosotros mismos, a la hora de escoger pareja, buscamos a alguien que nos comprenda. Y muchas veces eso nos ayuda a sanar heridas del pasado. En la pareja proyectamos nuestras necesidades, por lo que esta se convierte en un medio para el autoconocimiento y a su vez en una maestra de vida, ya que el hecho de que sea distinta a nosotros y tenga su propio camino nos enseña algo diferente a lo que somos y sabemos.

Es muy importante la escucha activa para resolver las fricciones que puedan darse. De otra manera, minarán nuestra relación.

Tanto si tuviste pareja en su momento y ya no está en tu senda, como si sigue contigo y te despiertas a su lado cada día, es importante valorarla y dar las gracias, porque es un espejo de tu evolución espiritual y una escuela constante para tu vida.

LAS LECCIONES DE TUS MAESTROS/AS DE VIDA

Si te sientes con ánimos de practicar arqueología personal, te propongo que hagas este ejercicio con las parejas más importantes que has tenido.

Pregúntate en cada una:

• ¿Qué me enseñó esta relación sobre la vida y sobre mí mismo?
• ¿Cuál fue la creencia que descubrí en mí en esta relación?
• ¿Quién he llegado a ser gracias a esta experiencia?

47

MODELA TU REALIDAD

Hay veces en las que envidiamos sanamente a las personas que logran algo que nosotros deseamos. El ejercicio del modelado consiste en identificar a esa persona y pensar: ¿Qué hacía o hace y tú no?

Recuerda que modelar no es imitar, sino hacer tuyo todo eso, desde tus modos y tu forma de ser genuina. Se trata de integrar en tu modo de ser lo que hizo que esa persona fuese exitosa en lo que tú te propones ahora.

La idea es descifrar —incluso consultar a esa persona si tenemos la posibilidad— y conocer cómo ha alcanzado su objetivo.

Para ello necesitaremos indagar:

1. Cómo actúa
2. Qué rutinas tiene
3. Cuáles son sus hábitos
4. Qué libros ha leído y qué fuentes ha consultado

Fíjate bien en todo lo que sea relevante del proceso que ha seguido para alcanzar aquello y úsalo a tu favor.

EL MÉTODO FRANKLIN

Benjamin Franklin pasó de ser un chico humilde —decimocuarto de dieciséis hermanos— a uno de los padres fundadores de Estados Unidos. ¿Cómo lo logró? Gran lector de biografías, de cada personaje que admiraba se preguntaba qué virtud suya le faltaba a él. Llegó a identificar trece, y dedicaba una semana a la práctica de cada una de ellas.

Si quieres seguir el Método Franklin:
1. Anota las virtudes que admiras y te gustaría desarrollar.
2. Dedica una semana a incorporarlas a tu vida. En una hoja con siete columnas, pon una cruz por cada día en el que hayas llevado a la práctica esta virtud.
3. Cuando logres siete cruces seguidas, pasa a la siguiente.

48
TOMA UN BAÑO DE BOSQUE

Como muchos expertos aseguran, la naturaleza nos permite establecer una conexión con nosotros mismos. Este es el motivo por el que las personas que viven en grandes urbes y no salen nunca al campo gozan de menos salud y energía que quienes se permiten, al menos semanalmente, un baño de bosque.

En japonés se llama *shinrin-yoku* y se ha convertido en una tendencia mundial desde que se publicaron los resultados de investigaciones científicas que se iniciaron en la década de 1980 y que concluyeron que, aunque se trate solo de una salida semanal de cuatro o cinco horas al bosque, los efectos en nuestra salud física y mental son notables:

- Refuerza el sistema inmunitario, en especial, las células NK (del inglés *Natural Killer*), que combaten las células tumorales.
- Baja la presión sanguínea y el ritmo cardiaco.
- Reduce los niveles de estrés y de cortisol.
- Mejora el estado de ánimo y promueve la serenidad.
- Favorece un sueño reparador.
- Potencia la libido y la energía sexual.
- Mejora la salud visual.

INSTRUCCIONES PARA HACER SHINRIN-YOKU

1. Elige preferiblemente bosques centenarios, con senderos que sean transitables para personas de cualquier condición física.
2. Desconecta el teléfono móvil u otros dispositivos antes de empezar.
3. El paseo ha de tener un destino prefijado. Se trata de dejar que te lleven los pies, deteniéndote a descansar cuando te apetezca.
4. Los ejercicios de respiración o de meditación en movimiento ayudan a potenciar el *shinrin-yoku*.

49

DORMIR BIEN PARA ESTAR DESPIERTOS

magina que ya has regresado de tu baño de bosque. Cenas temprano para acostarte a una hora prudente, sincronizada con los ciclos de la vida. Pero ¿qué sucede los días laborables, cuando volvemos a casa tarde y con todo el estrés del trabajo? Muchas personas duermen poco y mal, porque gozan de un sueño superficial y poco reparador. Normalmente dormimos en ciclos de unos noventa minutos en los que se van sucediendo estas fases:

Fases I y II. Adormecimiento que sucede en los primeros diez minutos, y sueño ligero, que ocupa cerca del 50 por ciento de cada ciclo.

Fases III y IV. Relajación profunda y sueño Delta, que ocupan el 20 por ciento del ciclo.

Fase V (rem). Supone un 25 por ciento del ciclo. Hay mucha actividad cerebral y es cuando soñamos. Es vital para que la memoria se consolide.

Es muy importante poner atención a cómo vivimos las horas previas a acostarnos. ¿Cuál es tu nivel de inquietud o de agitación? Si es alto, una pequeña meditación te ayudará a lograr un poco de calma antes de dormir.

FACTORES QUE ESTROPEAN EL SUEÑO

En las 2-3 horas previas al descanso nocturno es importante resolver las tareas sencillas de menos de un minuto y que nos roban la tranquilidad. Y conviene evitar:

- Discusiones familiares o laborales. Es mejor trasladarlas a otro horario, al igual que los emails.
- Noticias catastrofistas o estresantes. Elige otra clase de contenidos.
- Pantallas. Como sabemos, merman la calidad de nuestro sueño.
- Comidas tardías o copiosas, que se traducirán en una digestión pesada.

50

SANAMENTE VULNERABLE

B rené Brown, a quien ya hemos mencionado en una reflexión anterior, tiene una charla y también un libro llamados *El poder de la vulnerabilidad*. En ellos nos invita a celebrar los beneficios de mostrar nuestro lado menos conocido, pero que precisamente nos ayuda a conectar con los demás de una manera más cercana y emocional. Veamos cómo define la vulnerabilidad esta gran especialista:

> *Ser vulnerable es exponerte y ser visto, pero es difícil hacerlo cuando estamos preocupados por lo que la gente pueda ver o pensar de nosotros. Ser perfeccionista no es lo mismo que tratar de ser lo mejor posible. El perfeccionismo no es un logro saludable ni implica crecimiento; es simplemente un escudo.*

Cuando tendemos puentes para mostrar nuestras dudas, temores e inseguridades, creamos un vínculo de confianza con el otro, además de promover el acompañamiento mutuo.

Lejos de ser una muestra de debilidad, la vulnerabilidad se torna en lazo de unión entre las personas.

—— **LA VULNERABILIDAD AYUDA A CONSTRUIR VÍNCULOS** ——

Te propongo que pienses en momentos en los que te has sentido vulnerable.
- ¿Sentiste que eras «tú» más que nunca?
- ¿De qué manera te ayudó a tener empatía hacia otras personas?
- ¿Cuál es la unión más profunda que has tenido con alguien desde el dolor compartido?

Al mostrar que somos personas vulnerables, los demás nos perciben más humanos, auténticos y sinceros.

Mostrarnos tal como somos nos permite ser transparentes y conectar con los otros a un nivel mucho más profundo y genuino.

51

LA MILLA DE MÁS

Hay un concepto anglosajón muy poderoso, *The Extra Mile*, que podríamos traducir como *la milla de más* y hace referencia a superar nuestros propios límites.

Cuando vamos más allá de ese techo de cristal que nos hemos autoimpuesto, descubrimos talentos ocultos y aparecen nuevas oportunidades. La milla extra implica dejar de depender de la suerte, de las circunstancias externas, y asumir el cien por cien de responsabilidad sobre nuestro destino.

Si quieres ampliar tu ámbito de aprendizaje, desarrollar tus capacidades y tus recursos a nivel intelectual y emocional, es interesante recordar la idea de la milla de más.

Primero toma conciencia de hasta dónde has llegado.

Luego piensa qué más puedes lograr y aportar.

La clave es ir poco a poco, con la idea de mejorar la gestión de tus habilidades.

Piensa, ¿cuál es esa milla de más que puedes recorrer en este momento de tu vida?

KAIZEN EMOCIONAL

Esta célebre expresión japonesa que se traduce como *mejora continua* es aplicable también a la gestión de nuestras emociones y capacidades. No podemos esperar un cambio radical de un día para otro, pero sí conseguir, poco a poco, un progreso paulatino.

Algunas ideas:

- Intentar estar un día sin enfadarte o hacer comentarios negativos.
- Felicitarte al final de la jornada por lo que has conseguido, aunque hayas dado solo un pequeño paso en la dirección correcta.
- Concretar de forma práctica una cosa que querías hacer y que hasta ahora solo estaba en tu mente.

52
PREPÁRATE

Os voy a contar un truco muy fácil para dejar de aplazar aquellas cosas que deseamos hacer, pero que, por algún motivo, nos cuesta empezar.

Personalmente, he aprendido que muchas veces una preparación a conciencia, previa a esa actividad que se nos resiste o nos da pereza, es fundamental para el resultado que estamos buscando. Sin olvidar que debemos dejar un margen para los imprevistos que pueden modificar el resultado final. Estos pasos previos sirven para allanar el terreno y que no nos queden excusas para no arrancar.

En mi caso, ya se trate de hacer deporte, de estudiar o de acudir a un lugar determinado, el simple hecho de tener preparada desde el día anterior la ropa, el desayuno o lo que necesite para el viaje facilitará que haga lo que me he propuesto.

Sin embargo, la preparación debe ceñirse a lo indispensable, a aquello que realmente necesitamos, para no desequilibrar la balanza entre los preparativos y la acción.

Apliquemos la consigna clásica de los corredores: *¡Preparados, listos, ya!*

EL ARMARIO DE STEVE JOBS

Para no perder tiempo por las mañanas pensando cómo iba a vestirse, Steve Jobs tomó una decisión radical: utilizar una misma prenda todos los días: un mismo polo negro con cuello de cisne diseñado por Issey Miyake del que tenía un centenar en su guardarropa.

Sin llegar a ese minimalismo extremo, te propongo que identifiques cuáles son las dos o tres prendas con las que te sientes más a gusto para tenerlas siempre a mano. Otra opción es preparar la noche antes lo que quieres ponerte y así no perder tiempo por la mañana.

53

LA TRAMPA DE ESTAR HIPEROCUPADO

Estar ocupados a todas horas es algo a lo que nos hemos acostumbrado. Sin embargo, la pregunta que me hago es: ¿Es necesaria toda esta actividad o hay compromisos de los que podría prescindir?

Y esta hiperocupación no es exclusiva de los adultos, ya que muchas veces la trasladamos a los hijos. Como señala la psiquiatra Marian Rojas, «Los niños de hoy tienen agenda de ministros». ¿Y todo eso por qué?

Y es que a veces, aunque parezca mentira o de primeras puedas sentir rechazo por lo que voy a decirte, parece que estamos encantados de estar muy ocupados.

La sociedad actual da gran importancia a la actividad permanente, como si no hubiera otra forma de vivir. Y verbalizar este agobio que muchas veces nos creamos nosotros mismos es una manera de estar *a la moda*. La hiperactividad es sinónimo de éxito. Sin embargo, eso no significa que sea recomendable.

Sopesa si tu estilo de vida es sostenible, si es bueno a largo plazo y qué precio estás pagando por ello.

TOMA UN CAFÉ CONTIGO MISMO

Este es el título de un popular ensayo que publicó hace un par de décadas el doctor Walter Dresel. Es una invitación a tomarte una pausa y, así como das cita a todo el mundo, concedértela a ti en exclusiva. Una hora de tranquilidad, en casa o incluso en un café en compañía de tu libreta, puede hacer milagros.

Como aconseja este médico uruguayo: «No esperes más: haz un hueco en tu desbordada agenda para dialogar contigo mismo».

54
NUESTROS MAYORES, NUESTRO LEGADO

S omos lo que somos, en gran parte, gracias a nuestros mayores y también a pesar de ellos.

Sin embargo, poco les honramos, pocas veces les decimos lo importantes que son para nosotros y poco les agradecemos lo que han hecho por nosotros.

Hoy puede ser un buen momento para hacerlo. Te propongo que pienses en alguien hacia quien te sientas especialmente agradecido.

Abuelos, tíos, padres... Ellos son nuestros maestros, porque además de transmitirnos su experiencia nos inculcaron valores y aprendizajes, nos acompañaron y nos impulsaron para llegar a ser quienes somos.

Muchas veces los dejamos de lado, ya sea por las prisas o porque miramos más hacia delante que hacia atrás.

Hoy es un día perfecto para honrar la figura, el recuerdo, la persona y la compañía de algún maestro o maestra de nuestra vida.

¡GRACIAS POR TANTO!

Te propongo que escribas una carta de agradecimiento a alguien que haya sido un referente en tu existencia, viva o no todavía. Si te ha transmitido valores que has seguido, dale las gracias por ello y manifiesta los cambios y progresos que has logrado con su inspiración.

55
AMAR NO ES DEPENDER

Muchas relaciones de pareja se vuelven tóxicas porque una parte responsabiliza a la otra de su felicidad o de su infelicidad. Y es que en el momento en que para estar bien necesito que el otro haga o sea determinada cosa, pierdo el dominio de mí mismo.

Esta es una cuestión que exploró el médico y psicoterapeuta Fritz Perls, creador de la terapia Gestalt junto con su esposa, Laura Posner, y que escribió la siguiente declaración para reivindicar la autonomía:

Yo soy Yo
Tú eres Tú.
Yo no estoy en este mundo para cumplir tus expectativas.
Tú no estás en este mundo para cumplir las mías.
Tú eres Tú
Yo soy Yo.
Si en algún momento o en algún punto nos encontramos
será maravilloso,
si no, no puede remediarse.

FELICIDAD EN PRIMERA PERSONA DE SINGULAR

No se trata de volvernos egoístas, sino de dejar de depender de lo que hagan o digan los demás para sentirnos completos.

Para ejercitar el desapego, puedes hacer este sencillo ejercicio:
• Enumera las cosas que puedes hacer por ti mismo, sin ayuda de nadie más, para sentirte mejor.

• Cada vez que te sientas desanimado o falto de energía, recurre a esa lista y haz algo que te cargue las baterías del entusiasmo, sin depender de terceros.

56

COSAS QUE NO SALEN
A LA PRIMERA

La historia de las grandes mujeres y hombres demuestra que hay una relación directa entre la tolerancia a la frustración y el éxito. Si Edison hubiera abandonado su propósito al fracasar con los primeros filamentos, el mundo habría tardado mucho más en conocer la luz eléctrica.

Este es un aprendizaje que podemos aplicar en nuestra vida cotidiana. En ocasiones, las cosas no salen como desearíamos, se nos resisten o, simplemente, no son tan fluidas como esperamos. Cuando eso ocurre, yo siempre me digo que no es el momento. Lo mejor es no forzar.

En ocasiones, dejar que las cosas *no* sucedan es lo más inteligente que podemos hacer. Solemos orientarnos hacia los resultados, pero muchas veces el resultado también puede ser no obtener ningún resultado.

Seamos como el bambú, cuyas raíces crecen en silencio durante años y, cuando han profundizado lo bastante en la tierra, de repente la planta crece en cuestión de días.

Si sientes que algo se te resiste, no te impacientes. Confía en que es lo mejor que puede suceder en ese momento.

ENTRENA LA MIRADA A MEDIO PLAZO

Para superar la cultura de lo instantáneo, en la que todo se consigue con un clic, enfócate en propósitos que lleven su tiempo:
- Aprender un idioma que puedes hablar con soltura en 2 o 3 años.
- Un plan de negocio a cinco o más años vista.
- Introducir hábitos de los que al principio no ves sus frutos, pero que a medio plazo van a transformar tu vida.

57
ESCULTOR DE TU PROPIO CEREBRO

Ramón y Cajal decía: «Todo ser humano, si se lo propone, puede ser escultor de su propio cerebro». Y la buena noticia es que esto es algo que podemos hacer a cualquier edad.

La neuroplasticidad nos permite cambiar nuestra forma de funcionar en cualquier momento de nuestra vida.

Nuestro cerebro tiende a ahorrar energía y, por lo tanto, opta siempre por el camino más fácil. Es decir, acude por defecto a respuestas y conclusiones que ya conoce para resolver cualquier situación. Automatiza todo lo que puede y por eso a veces se dice que funcionamos con el *piloto automático*. Sin embargo siempre tenemos la libertad de retomar el mando.

Podemos crear nuevas rutas neuronales cambiando rutinas y hábitos que acabarán transformando nuestra forma de pensar y vivir.

Dicho de forma fácil: si quieres que las cosas cambien, hazlas de manera distinta.

REDISÉÑATE

Al incorporar nuevas rutinas a nuestra vida, conectamos con nuevas posibilidades y creamos nuevas rutas neuronales que nos permiten ser escultores de nuestro propio cerebro.

Desde esa certeza, pregúntate:

- ¿Qué hábitos me gustaría cambiar para vivir de otro modo?
- ¿Qué debo hacer de forma repetida para implantar ese hábito?
- ¿Qué premio me concederé cuando lo haya conseguido?

58

CUANDO LA VIDA SE PONE CUESTA ARRIBA

Hay ocasiones en las que sabes perfectamente que se acercan momentos complicados en los que vas a necesitar una porción extra de energía, valor y coraje.

Reserva siempre una buena dosis de todo ello para cuando llegue la *cuesta arriba*. Como en el coche, reduce antes de una curva, calcula el combustible que queda, mete una marcha más corta en las rampas y siéntate de manera correcta para manejar la situación lo mejor posible.

Ya estás listo para lo que venga, y con la reserva llena.

Alguien dijo que las dificultades son el desayuno de los campeones. Tómatelo como un punto de referencia para saber en qué momento te encuentras, qué capacidades has desarrollado, cuál es tu nivel de resistencia y resiliencia. Y, sobre todo, date cuenta de que la dificultad, como la cuesta arriba, es temporal. Luego volverás a ver el horizonte desde la planicie e incluso encontrarás preciosos valles.

DEL POZO AL TÚNEL

La psiquiatra Marian Rojas dice que una forma de ganar esperanza y energía es dejar de pensar que estás en un pozo. En el pozo hay oscuridad y no se puede salir de él. En lugar de eso, piensa que estás en un túnel y que, una vez lo atravieses, habrá luz al otro lado.

59
DOLOR Y SUFRIMIENTO

Tal vez la frase más citada de Buda sea la de: «El dolor es inevitable y el sufrimiento es opcional». ¿Qué quiso decir Siddhartha Gautama, hace ya dos milenios y medio, con esto?

Básicamente, que una cosa es el dolor, que forma parte de la propia vida, y otra es el sufrimiento, que obedece a nuestra interpretación de lo sucedido.

A lo largo de la existencia, además de vivir cosas muy agradables, vamos a sufrir pérdidas, accidentes y crisis de todo tipo. Eso no lo podemos evitar, forma parte del camino. Lo que sí depende de nosotros es la manera en que lo gestionamos.

Una cosa es lo que vivimos y otra el impacto emocional con el que lo vivimos. La misma situación puede generar reacciones muy distintas según el grado de control que tengamos sobre las propias emociones. Y ello depende en gran medida del autoconocimiento.

Entender cómo somos, cuáles son nuestras fortalezas y debilidades, nos ayudará a ver y sentir ese acontecimiento desde otros parámetros y paliar así el sufrimiento.

¿TENDRÁ IMPORTANCIA DE AQUÍ A UN AÑO?

Esta es una pregunta que les planteaba a sus pacientes el psicólogo Richard Carlson, autor del clásico *No te ahogues en un vaso de agua*. Cada vez que sufras por algo que ha sucedido, sigue su método:

1. Responde con sinceridad a esta pregunta: ¿Tendrá esto importancia de aquí a un año?
2. Si la respuesta es no o albergas serias dudas, deshazte del problema ahora mismo y deja de sufrir.

60

MAESTROS DE LO DIFÍCIL

En una de sus reflexiones más célebres, el dalai lama razona así: «Se dice que nuestro enemigo es nuestro mejor maestro. Al estar con un maestro, podemos aprender la importancia de la paciencia, el control y la tolerancia, pero no tenemos oportunidad real de practicarla. La verdadera práctica surge al encontrarnos con un enemigo».

La variedad de caracteres y sensibilidades humanas es tan rica que, sin duda, no habrá día en el que no tengamos oportunidad de practicar con estos singulares maestros de vida.

En su libro *Cómo tratar con personas difíciles*, los psiquiatras Christophe André y François Lelord señalan que hay multitud de personalidades complicadas que pueden perturbar la vida cotidiana. Sin embargo, todo el mundo tiene la capacidad de aprender a convivir con esos rasgos espinosos, empezando por los de uno mismo.

Si somos conscientes de que todos somos o hemos sido difíciles para alguien, nos resultará más fácil entendernos con los demás.

NO HAY PERSONAS TÓXICAS, SINO RELACIONES TÓXICAS

El psicólogo Rafael Santandreu se muestra contrario a la etiqueta de *personas tóxicas*, ya que —según afirma— lo que existen son relaciones tóxicas, bien sea porque las distintas partes no son compatibles o porque han establecido una relación asimétrica.

¿Tienes una relación de este tipo en tu vida?

En ese caso, lo aconsejable es renunciar al vínculo —o rebajar la frecuencia de trato— para el bien de ambas partes.

61
VOLVERÁ (SI TIENE QUE SER)

Hay cosas que no debemos empeñarnos en retener. Es bueno dejarlas ir y confiar en que volverán a nosotros cuando sea necesario. Puede tratarse de un amigo que ha sido importante en una época de nuestra vida, pero al que ahora notamos lejano o distraído. No hay que enfadarse por ello ni forzar las cosas. Si nuestros caminos han de coincidir de nuevo, volverá.

También a veces perdemos temporalmente una pasión. Algo que antes nos gustaba mucho deja de provocarnos interés o no nos seduce con la fuerza de antes. Si estamos destinados a retomar esa pasión, volverá.

Incluso cuando nos olvidamos de un proyecto o de una idea... ¡volverá! Quizá lo haga con más intensidad, para mostrarte nueva información sobre ti o sobre el mundo. Ahora no es el momento.

Recordemos este bello pasaje del Eclesiastés:

Hay un tiempo de llorar y un tiempo de reír;
un tiempo de lamentar y un tiempo de bailar;
un tiempo de esparcir piedras y un tiempo de juntarlas (...)
un tiempo de buscar y tiempo de perder.

Al dejar ir, creamos un espacio para que lleguen cosas nuevas, confiando en que lo que tenga que volver, volverá.

--------------- DEJA IR Y DEJA VENIR ---------------

La llamada Teoría U, del profesor del MIT Otto Scharmer, se sustenta en dos principios que en inglés son *Let it go & Let it come*: solo si *dejas ir* el pasado (lo cual incluye viejos prejuicios e ideas preconcebidas) crearás espacio para que puedan venir cosas nuevas.

¿Qué es, en este momento de tu vida, lo que estás reteniendo y deberías dejar ir?

62
PURIFÍCATE

Para iniciar una nueva etapa con respecto a un asunto que te duele especialmente, debes tener el valor de empezar de cero, recomenzar de una forma pura.

¿Cómo hacerlo?

Primero debes purificarte, es decir, limpiar la lente con la que ves la vida de cualquier suciedad o resto de una época o situación que ya no es la tuya. Así podrás disfrutar del presente y preparar el futuro con una mirada nueva.

Luego, entre una etapa y la siguiente, quizá sea necesario que atravieses desiertos. Tómatelo con espíritu de aventura, con voluntad de aprender. Para ello solo tienes que afrontar la vida y entregarte a la experiencia con la mejor disposición.

Como recomendaba el pintor del siglo XIX Eugène Delacroix, se trata de «Desear lo mejor, recelar lo peor y tomar lo que venga».

GRACIAS Y ADIÓS

Un sencillo ritual de purificación para algo que consideres que ya no te corresponde vivir puede ser:
- Escribe en una hoja de papel aquello que ha dejado de tener sentido en tu vida.
- Colócalo en un recipiente seguro y dale las gracias por las lecciones que ha aportado a tu vida.

- Acto seguido, enciende el papel con una cerilla o mechero y contempla cómo se deshace entre las llamas.
- Desde la gratitud, despídete de lo que ha sido y, una vez apagado, asume que empiezas de cero sin esa carga.

63
FRENTE AL ESPEJO

Quisiera recomendarte algo. Especialmente, si eres mujer. Concédete un tiempo a solas delante del espejo, desnuda y en calma... ¿Estás dispuesta a descubrir la belleza de tu cuerpo? Préstale atención como lo que es: tu vehículo para la vida.

Tu cuerpo es un templo que contiene tu divinidad. Es un regalo increíble y por eso merece que, después de este ejercicio de apreciación, te comprometas a mimarlo todo lo que puedas.

Es el cofre de todo lo que atesoras. Desde la cabeza hasta los pies: obsérvalo todo: tus ojos, tu boca, tus brazos, tus piernas, tus hombros, tu vientre...

Tu cuerpo y tu mirada sobre él son una preciosa herramienta para comprometerte con tu bienestar y celebrar lo que eres, con todo tu amor y cariño.

EL ESPEJO DE TU AUTOESTIMA

Aprovechando que estás teniendo un encuentro con tu propia imagen, te propongo que realices el siguiente ejercicio:
- Haz unas cuantas respiraciones profundas.
- Describe en voz alta lo que ves en el espejo, pero con una mirada apreciativa.

- ¿Cómo es la persona que ves en el espejo? ¿La conoces bien? ¿Qué es lo que más te gusta de ella? ¿Qué posibilidades aún no realizadas ves en ella?

64

CAMBIA DE PERSPECTIVA

En 1985, el médico y psicólogo maltés Edward de Bono publicaba *Seis sombreros para pensar*, que parte de una idea provocadora: ¿Y si pudiéramos vernos –a nosotros y a las cosas que nos preocupan– desde distintas perspectivas como quien cambia de sombrero?

Imaginemos que tenemos seis sombreros de diferentes colores, cada uno con un modo de pensar:

- *Blanco*: pensamiento neutro y objetivo. Nos atenemos a los hechos. ¿Qué ha pasado?
- *Rojo*: pensamiento emocional. ¿Qué sentimientos me despierta este asunto?
- *Negro*: pensamiento cauteloso. ¿De qué manera me puede perjudicar esto?
- *Amarillo*: pensamiento optimista. ¿Qué beneficios me puede procurar esta situación?
- *Verde*: pensamiento creativo. Se trata de dejar fluir la imaginación. ¿Qué me sugiere esto, más allá de lo obvio?
- *Azul*: pensamiento integrativo. ¿Qué puedo sacar de los cinco sombreros para mejorar mi vida?

CAMBIA DE SOMBRERO

Practica lo que acabamos de ver cada vez que te sientas bloqueado. ¿Cómo pintan las cosas desde otras miradas? ¿Qué te dice cada sombrero que te pones (de forma figurada)? Atrévete a pensarte y sentirte desde distintas perspectivas.

65

EL TAO DE LOS CAMINOS

Seguro que más de una vez te has preguntado si vas por el camino correcto, cuando algo se te resiste pese a intentarlo una y otra vez. Puedes llegar a sentirte agotado y muy desmotivado. ¿Por qué insistir en ese camino?

Déjame decirte algo: Si no fluye, si no es fácil, si hay que forzar para que encaje, entonces no es el camino.

Hay una frase misteriosa de Lao-Tsé, el fundador del taoísmo, que nos da una clave al respecto: «Si no cambias la dirección, puedes terminar donde has comenzado».

¿Qué quería decir con eso este sabio que vivió en China hace dos milenios y medio? Básicamente, que los caminos que no nos permiten avanzar nos paralizan y nos hacen agotar nuestra energía en vano.

Cuando te sientas así, cambia de dirección.

UN PASO ATRÁS, UNA ZANCADA ADELANTE

Otra idea poderosa de Lao-Tsé es: «Si no puedes avanzar una pulgada, retrocede un pie». Con ello se refería al valor de reconocer los errores, sin por ello avergonzarte o sentirte menos. Cada equivocación asumida puede parecer un paso atrás, pero si aprendemos la lección, supone una gran zancada hacia delante.

¿Qué paso atrás has dado que luego ha resultado una zancada hacia delante?

66

LA MEJOR PARTE

Al igual que sucede con una canción, una película o un momento compartido, siempre recordamos la mejor parte de las cosas. Rescatamos aquello que nos hace sentir más vivos, más conectados con nosotros mismos.

Te propongo que hagas lo mismo con la vida. Cuando te asalte el desánimo o la apatía, pon de relieve lo mejor de todo lo que te aporta la existencia. Puede ser una parte de tu trabajo que te gusta especialmente (aunque otras te puedan resultar aburridas). O tal vez sea un encuentro semanal con amigos que esperas con ilusión. O aquel libro que vas degustando poco a poco, porque lo disfrutas tanto que no quieres que se acabe.

En lugar de focalizarte en lo que no funciona, en lo que te crea desazón, dirige tu mirada hacia lo mejor de la vida, aquello por lo que merece la pena ser vivida.

¿Cuál es tu trozo favorito de la tarta de la felicidad?

ICHIGO-ICHIE

Esta expresión japonesa significa literalmente *una vez, una oportunidad* y se exhibe en una tablilla en los salones de té para invitar a las personas a poner los cinco sentidos en la ceremonia, ya que no volverá a repetirse nunca del mismo modo.

Si quieres convertir lo que estás viviendo en la mejor parte de tus recuerdos, ponle todo tu amor y atención.

67

EL PRIVILEGIO DE ELEGIR

El pensador estadounidense William James dijo en una ocasión que «cuando debemos hacer una elección y no la hacemos, esto ya es una elección».

Sin duda, no aprovechar nuestra capacidad para decidir es una postura vital que nos lleva a funcionar en piloto automático. Simplemente, dejamos que las cosas sucedan.

Poder elegir en cualquier aspecto de nuestra vida es un privilegio del que pocas veces nos damos cuenta. Sin embargo, cuando se hace de manera consciente y libre, es un regalo que solo puede dar satisfacciones. Incluso cuando la decisión acabe siendo la menos acertada.

Porque toda decisión, sea o no la mejor, trae consigo los regalos del aprendizaje.

El acto de elegir nos otorga el mando de nuestra vida. Y lo mejor es que no se trata de una ley absoluta e inquebrantable. Siempre podemos rectificar y cambiar de dirección, probar algo nuevo, algo mejor. ¡Tú decides!

DECIDIR MEJOR

En su libro *Decidiendo en tiempos de paz y de guerra,* David Cabero, que dirige la compañía BIC en Europa, aporta numerosas ideas para tomar mejores decisiones.

Algunas de ellas:

1. Pregúntate cuáles son las razones para *no* tomar esa decisión.
2. Genera el máximo de opciones para elegir.
3. No delegues en otra persona, si te corresponde a ti decidir.

Cabero añade que «quien no decide, no se equivoca» y que «si no arriesgamos, no aprendemos». Por eso merece la pena decidir.

68
EL POTENCIAL QUE HAY EN TI

Proponía Gandhi: «Sé el cambio que quieres ver en el mundo». Y yo añado que no te puedes imaginar la capacidad que tienes para cambiar el mundo.

Desde las pequeñas cosas a las más trascendentales. Cada uno de tus actos, palabras y pensamientos tiene un impacto en los otros, en el mundo. Cuando te das cuenta de ello, nada vuelve a ser igual.

Toda persona modela su realidad y contribuye a modelar la de todos. Dicho de otro modo, tu potencial para el cambio es increíble, para tu vida y la de los demás.

Date cuenta de ello. Sé el puente, el canal entre las cosas que te apasionan, que conoces bien y con las que puedes ayudar a otros que te necesitan. Así, el camino solo puede ser gozoso.

¿Qué huella quieres dejar en el mundo? En lugar de adoptar un enfoque maximalista, asume que cada decisión, acto y palabra tuya cuentan.

EL PODER DE LO PEQUEÑO

Se atribuye a Anita Roddick, la fundadora de The Body Shop, la frase:

«Si crees que eres demasiado pequeño para producir algún impacto, trata de irte a la cama con un mosquito en la habitación».

Reformulando esta idea en positivo, podemos concluir que cualquier cosa que hagas por ti misma y por los demás, por pequeña que parezca, acaba teniendo impacto en tu presente y en tu futuro, así como en el de los otros.

¿Cuál quieres que sea tu pequeña gran aportación en el día de hoy?

69
EL CIEGO Y LA LÁMPARA

Un relato tradicional de Oriente cuenta que un hombre, al despedirse por la noche de su amigo ciego, le entregó una lámpara.

–Yo no necesito una lámpara –dijo el ciego–, pues para mí no hay diferencia entre claridad u oscuridad.

–¡Cierto! –repuso su amigo–, pero si no la llevas, otras personas pueden tropezar contigo.

–Tienes razón.

Tras andar un rato en la oscuridad, de repente el ciego tropezó con alguien.

Ambos gritaron de dolor.

–¿Es que no has visto mi lámpara? –dijo el ciego, muy enfadado.

–Tu lámpara está apagada, amigo...

NO HAY PEOR CIEGO QUE EL QUE NO QUIERE VER

Esta fábula me hace pensar en las personas que consideran que todo el mundo debería ver lo que ellos ven, aunque lleven la lámpara apagada.

Cada vez que creas que llevas la razón, pregúntate: ¿Puede haber más de una realidad o versión sobre el mismo hecho?

Solemos apegarnos a nuestra versión porque nos encanta confirmar lo que queremos creer y, por eso, acudimos a las fuentes que lo avalan y corroboran...

¿Y si te das el beneficio de la duda?

Atrévete a cuestionarlo todo, aunque sea como un juego. Te relajarás y ampliarás horizontes.

70

UN INVENTO DE MIL PASOS

Vivimos en la era de lo instantáneo, en la que todo se consigue con un clic. Sin embargo, no hay que olvidar que la vida tiene sus tiempos.

Es fácil ser arrollado por la impaciencia, pero no te llevará muy lejos. Lo común es querer llegar ya, alcanzar el objetivo. Pero no te puedes saltar pasos... Un paso viene tras otro. Así ha sido siempre en cualquier ámbito de la vida. Los atajos no sirven cuando buscas la excelencia.

Se cuenta que cuando, tras inventar la luz eléctrica, preguntaron a Edison cómo se sintió con el millar de fracasos antes de dar con el filamento correcto, el inventor declaró: «No fueron mil intentos fallidos, fue un invento de mil pasos».

En sus palabras resuena también la máxima de Lao-Tsé: «Un viaje de mil millas comienza con un paso».

Dar ese primer paso es ya un éxito en sí mismo.

LA REGLA DE LAS 10.000 HORAS

En su ensayo *Fuera de serie*, el periodista Malcolm Gladwell calcula que son necesarias 10.000 horas para llegar a ser un verdadero maestro en algo. Si te propones alcanzar ese nivel, te hago un sencillo cálculo de lo que puedes tardar en acumularlas:

8 horas diarias × 5 días a la semana = 5 años
4 horas diarias × 5 días a la semana = 10 años
2 horas diarias × 5 días a la semana = 20 años
1 hora diaria × 5 días a la semana = 40 años

71
RESILIENCIA

Hace décadas que en psicología se habla de la resiliencia. Este término se usaba originalmente para referirse a los materiales, en concreto a su capacidad de regresar a su forma inicial tras haberse aplicado una fuerza sobre ellos.

Trasladado a la vida humana, la persona resiliente es no solo aquella que es capaz de sobreponerse a las dificultades sino que además aplica los aprendizajes logrados a través de esa experiencia.

El neurólogo francés Boris Cyrulnik es experto en este tema. Su vida misma es ejemplo de resiliencia: de familia judía, sus padres fueron asesinados en el Holocausto y él mismo sufrió los campos de concentración de niño. Logró escapar y tuvo que vivir el resto de su infancia en casas de acogida.

En sus palabras: «La resiliencia es el arte de navegar por los torrentes. A veces la vida nos hiere y nos lleva por direcciones que no habríamos deseado. Sigue adelante, más sabio, humano y más fuerte».

Cada vez que superamos un obstáculo, sacamos un aprendizaje para el futuro, además de demostrarnos nuestra capacidad de seguir adelante.

CONFÍA EN TUS CAPACIDADES

Los desafíos que nos pone la vida son la única forma que tenemos de conocer nuestro nivel de resiliencia. En este ejercicio, te propongo que analices la última gran prueba que te puso la vida. Pregúntate:

1. ¿Cuál fue la principal dificultad que tuve que superar?

2. ¿Qué recursos personales utilicé para hacerle frente?

3. ¿De qué manera me sentí reforzado después?

Acuérdate de todo eso la próxima vez que te encuentres ante un gran obstáculo.

72

LAS PIEDRAS Y EL ARCO

Se cuenta que, en los viajes a Oriente de Marco Polo, en una ocasión, quiso describirle al emperador mongol Kublai Kan un puente especialmente bello.

Sin entender por qué el veneciano describía la construcción piedra por piedra, el emperador le preguntó:

—Pero, entonces..., ¿cuál es la piedra que sostiene el puente?

—No está sostenido por esta o aquella piedra —le explicó Marco Polo—, sino por el arco que forman entre todas.

Kublai Kan reflexionó en silencio unos momentos y luego añadió:

—¿Por qué me hablas, entonces, de las piedras, si el arco es lo que importa?

—Sin piedras no hay arco —se limitó a decir el viajero.

Este relato nos procura un mensaje importante: cada uno de nuestros actos y decisiones son una piedra con la que construimos nuestra vida. Tal vez no les damos importancia por separado, pero la suma de todos ellos es nuestro futuro.

¿CUÁLES SON LAS PIEDRAS GRANDES DE TU VIDA?

La gestión del tiempo es como un frasco que vamos llenando de piedras. Primero hay que poner las piedras grandes, luego las pequeñas, y aún cabría arena e incluso agua.

Si no pones las piedras grandes al principio, luego no cabrán. Es decir, si perdemos la vida en actividades o preocupaciones poco relevantes, no nos podremos ocupar más tarde de las cosas que son realmente importantes.

¿Cuáles son las piedras grandes de tu vida?

73

KINTSUGI

El concepto japonés de *kintsugi* hace referencia al arte de recomponer un objeto de cerámica roto en pedazos, uniendo sus piezas con barniz de resina a veces mezclado con polvo de oro, plata o platino. Y lo más bello es que, aunque el objeto no es el mismo, una vez bien restaurado adquiere aún más valor. ¿A qué se debe? Los expertos en *kintsugi* dicen que es porque, tras la reconstrucción, el objeto tiene una historia que contar y brilla en los lugares rotos.

Aplicado a las personas, las más interesantes son aquellas que han pasado por muchas aventuras y desventuras, han aprendido y tienen mucho que contar.

¿Cuáles son las rupturas o heridas que te han hecho ser quien eres? Si sientes que tu alma está por recomponer, ¿cómo te gustaría restaurarla para que sea tan valiosa como tu experiencia?

UN CV DE APRENDIZAJES

En Estados Unidos, cuando un candidato a un cargo manda su currículum, incluye las cosas que no han salido bien. Si fue despedido de una empresa o si se arruinó en un proyecto empresarial propio, lo refleja en el informe, ya que se considera un valor. Son errores que le han enseñado y que no volverá a cometer.

¿Te atreves a escribir tu CV de fracasos y aprendizajes?

74
BE WATER, MY FRIEND...

A veces no es necesario cambiar ni intervenir en el camino de las cosas... Es preferible fluir con ellas. Ya lo decía Bruce Lee con su «Be water, my friend».

La frase fue utilizada para un anuncio de coches y pertenece a la entrevista más larga que le hicieron a Bruce Lee, hacia el final de su vida. Sin embargo, es muy interesante saber qué dijo justo antes:

> Se como el agua, abriéndote paso a través de las grietas. No seas cabezota, adáptate al objeto y encontrarás un camino alrededor o a través de él. Si nada dentro de ti es rígido, las cosas del exterior se revelarán ellas mismas.
>
> Vacía tu mente, no tengas forma.
>
> Sin forma, como el agua.
>
> Si pones agua en una taza, se transforma en la taza. Pones agua en una botella y se transforma en la botella. La pones en una tetera, se transforma en la tetera. Ahora, el agua puede fluir o puede colisionar.
>
> ¡Sé agua, mi amigo!

ADÁPTATE A LA VIDA

En lugar de luchar contra los elementos, te doy algunas ideas para fluir:
- No trates de corregir el rumbo de alguien que está muy excitado. Déjalo expresarse o que se quede con su enfado. Ya habrá tiempo de hablar más adelante.

- Percibe cuándo las personas están abiertas a proyectos o cuándo están a la defensiva y actúa en consecuencia.
- Cuando sientas fatiga, dale descanso a tu cuerpo en lugar de forzarlo, y canaliza de forma inteligente tu energía cuando te sientas pleno.

75
ÚTIL PARA LA FELICIDAD

H ay una frase atribuida al escultor francés Auguste Rodin que dice: «Útil es todo aquello que nos da la felicidad».
Me parece un interesante punto de partida: deberíamos mantener y nutrir todo aquello que aporta felicidad, alegría, bienestar o calma a nuestra vida.

Puede ser un determinado hábito o actividad, una persona que te alimenta el alma, o incluso un lugar que te hace sentir especialmente bien.

¿Qué es lo que te procura verdadera felicidad, por pequeño que sea?

El poeta alemán Bertolt Brecht se hizo esta pregunta y respondió con la siguiente lista: La primera mirada por la ventana al despertarse, el viejo libro vuelto a encontrar, rostros entusiasmados, nieve, el cambio de las estaciones, el periódico, el perro, la dialéctica, ducharse, nadar, música antigua, zapatos cómodos, comprender, música nueva, escribir, plantar, viajar, cantar, ser amable.

MIL COSAS QUE ME GUSTAN

Mi querida y admirada Sol Aguirre, que tanto me inspira, tiene un reto con toda su comunidad que consiste en identificar mil cosas que te gustan (#1000cosasquemegustan), apuntarlas y descubrir la grandeza de las pequeñas cosas que nos gustan y que nos hacen vivir de una manera más plena. Te invito a que te unas.

76
FRAG MEN TAR

H as pensado alguna vez que puedes *frag men tar* tu vida en etapas para poder observarla desde fuera y planear lo que vas a hacer en cada fase?

El empresario chino Jack Ma dio en una conferencia su visión sobre las etapas de la vida óptima, en relación con la carrera laboral:

- Hasta los 20 comete todos los errores posibles, no tengas miedo a fallar, y gana experiencia.
- De los 20 a los 30 aprende de alguien a quien admires. Hasta los 30 no importa en qué compañía trabajas, si no a qué jefe sigues.
- De los 30 a los 40 deberías estar trabajando ya para ti, si lo que quieres es emprender.
- De los 40 a los 50 es hora de centrarte en hacer las cosas en las que eres bueno.
- De los 50 a los 60 trabaja con los jóvenes, porque sin duda lo harán ya mejor que tú.
- A partir de los 60, usa el tiempo para ti. No sabes cuánta vida útil te queda, disfruta de cada día.

UN EXCEL VITAL

Transportemos esto a la vida personal. Si piensas llegar a los 100 años, programa tus próximas etapas en un Excel u otra hoja de cálculo.

Anota en cada etapa lo que es indispensable para ti para así poder priorizarlo.

77
CREE Y CREA

El ser humano tiende a anticipar los sucesos y a pensar en resultados concretos. Sin embargo, por fortuna, la vida no es ciencia exacta y las cosas no suelen suceder como esperamos. Tal como cantaba John Lennon en una canción dedicada a su hijo: «La vida es aquello que te va sucediendo mientras estás ocupado haciendo otros planes».

Ciertamente, no hay un credo establecido de la vida, pero la vida es ya un credo en sí misma. Creer en ella es parte del ejercicio diario de cohabitar con los acontecimientos que suceden.

¿Qué es lo que crees de ti y de la existencia? ¿Qué estás dispuesto a creer para crear la vida que quieres?

¿QUÉ CREAS CON TU MENTE?

Si tu realidad toma forma a través de las creencias que tenemos sobre ella, estaría bien que hicieras la siguiente revisión de tus archivos internos:

1. ¿Qué creencias tengo sobre el éxito y el dinero?

2. ¿Qué creo sobre el amor y sobre mis relaciones con los demás?

3. ¿Cuáles son mis creencias sobre la vida?

Si algunos de estos *credos* son negativos, empieza a sustituirlos por creencias que vayan a tu favor.

78
LAS CUATRO CLAVES DEL BUEN SEXO

Hablamos demasiado poco de la importancia del sexo en nuestra vida. Es una cuestión muy personal y parte del conocimiento de las propias necesidades.

Sin embargo, a nivel general, según el psicólogo Antoni Bolinches, hay cuatro claves que debemos respetar para tener buen sexo:

1. *No hagas nada que no quieras.* Complacer a la otra persona no debe llevarte a prácticas o situaciones en las que no te sientas cómodo.
2. *Haz todo lo que quieras.* Desde el respeto y la libertad, el sexo es una forma más de expresarte y de gozar de la vida.
3. *Hazlo desde el propio deseo.* Saber qué es lo que de verdad te gusta es una premisa esencial para el buen sexo.
4. *Hazlo de acuerdo con tu escala de valores.* Además de desear lo que se hace, hay que ser fiel a uno mismo. Disfrútalo de manera sana, bonita y alegre.

No desperdicies la oportunidad de conocerte a través del sexo. Decide bien con quién compartes algo tan sagrado y valioso. Es un regalo de la vida.

DISFRUTA Y CUIDA EL SEXO QUE VIVES

Si tienes una pareja sexual, ábrete y verbaliza aquellos deseos, anhelos y fantasías que te apetecen y, si hay coincidencia en alguna de ellas, según las cuatro claves que hemos visto, podéis hacerla realidad.

79
ESTAR A BUENAS CONTIGO

C reo que esta es una de las grandes lecciones que aprendemos demasiado tarde: *No podemos complacer a todo el mundo*. A veces lo intentamos, pero con ello solo provocamos que la situación se complique y sea más retorcida de lo que al principio pensábamos.

Por eso, en cualquier interacción con los demás, es importante no ir contra los propios deseos, prioridades y valores.

Yo misma, cuando me doy cuenta de que algo no está yendo por donde me gustaría, o no avanza de manera ágil y fluida, me hago la pregunta: Pero ¿realmente quieres hacer esto o estás cumpliendo las expectativas de otros?

Una creencia que ha estado muy presente en mi vida y es posible que también en la tuya es la de *tengo que estar a buenas con todo el mundo*. Ahora me digo, desde el respeto y el cariño, que no puedo vivir otra vida que no sea la mía. Y si eso implica ganarse la antipatía de alguien, no pasa nada. La autenticidad es mucho más importante que la opinión que puedan tener de ti.

Se trata, más bien, de estar a buenas contigo mismo.

ESCUCHA TU CUERPO

Muchas veces, cuando hacemos algo con lo que íntimamente no estamos de acuerdo, el cuerpo nos lo comunica de forma sutil a través de sensaciones de incomodidad. Si estás atento a estas señales, lograrás vivir de manera más coherente contigo mismo.

80

LA ORACIÓN DE LA SERENIDAD

E s muy posible que alguna vez te haya llegado este texto breve e inspirador:

> *Señor, concédeme serenidad para aceptar*
> *todo aquello que no puedo cambiar,*
> *valor para cambiar lo que soy capaz de cambiar*
> *y sabiduría para entender la diferencia.*

Conocida como la Oración de la Serenidad, fue escrita por el pastor Reinhold Niebuhr hacia 1943, durante una misa de domingo en la localidad de Heath, Massachusetts.

Esta plegaria ha penetrado tanto en la cultura popular que incluso forma parte de los doce pasos del programa de Alcohólicos Anónimos y Neil Young la incluyó –en latín– en la contraportada de un álbum suyo en 1981.

¿Qué sentido tiene para ti en este momento de tu vida?

DOS PREGUNTAS VITALES

A partir de la Oración de la Serenidad, te sugiero que contestes a estas dos cuestiones:

1. ¿Qué es aquello que no puedo cambiar, porque no depende de mí, en este momento vital? ¿Cómo puedo aceptarlo?

2. ¿Qué es lo que puedo cambiar, porque depende de mí, y debo cambiar? ¿Cuándo voy a hacerlo?

81
LO MEJOR DE TI

En cada cosa pon lo mejor de ti. Es tan sencillo como hacer las cosas bien, hacerlo lo mejor que sabes y convencido de que es lo correcto. Hay personas que aplican la ley del mínimo esfuerzo y otras que no empiezan jamás aquello que deberían hacer porque les bloquea el miedo a no hacerlo perfecto.

Sobre esto, el entrenador de fútbol americano Vince Lombardi decía:

«La perfección no es alcanzable, pero si perseguimos la perfección podemos alcanzar la excelencia».

Es como el cuento del arquero que apuntaba a la luna: no llegó jamás a acertar en ella, pero se convirtió en el mejor arquero de su tierra.

Da lo mejor de ti y superarás tus límites.

TU KAIZEN COTIDIANO

La filosofía japonesa de la mejora continua es una herramienta perfecta para «apuntar a la luna». En aquello que estés haciendo, plantéate qué puedes hacer hoy un poco mejor que ayer para subir un escalón más hacia la excelencia.

82
SER FELIZ O APRENDER

Hay una célebre frase, atribuida al humorista británico Marcus Brigstocke, que dice: «Prefiero ser feliz a tener razón».

Sin embargo, yo creo que podemos ir un poco más allá. Si le damos otra vuelta, podríamos preguntarnos: ¿Qué prefiero: ser feliz o aprender?

A veces podemos estar tentados a callar, a no expresar lo que sentimos, porque así creemos preservar la paz. Pero la felicidad que obtenemos así es solo temporal, porque en el fondo no estamos de acuerdo.

Aunque al pronunciarnos sobre algo corramos el riesgo de equivocarnos, incluso si eso sucede, estaremos aprendiendo. Sobre nosotros y sobre los demás.

No hay nada malo en tener una opinión diferente a la del resto. Ni hay tampoco nada malo en cambiar de opinión si después vemos que no llevábamos la razón. Todo son aprendizajes que nos llevarán a una felicidad mucho más duradera que el breve alivio que nos produce quedarnos en silencio.

CÓMO SOSTENER EL CONFLICTO

Un freno a la hora de ser asertivos es que nos aterra estar molestos con los demás y perder su consideración. Algunas claves para dejar de sufrir por este motivo:
- Podemos comunicarnos con delicadeza y ser claros al mismo tiempo.

- En general, las personas que se muestran sinceras y asertivas son más valoradas y respetadas que el resto.
- Si la otra parte se enfada, porque esperaba otra cosa, piensa que el enfado pertenece a él o ella, no a ti.

83
MÁS ALLÁ DEL LÍMITE

Si has practicado yoga, sabrás que al realizar los asanas solemos llegar al límite de la postura poco a poco. Cada sesión supone un reto con uno mismo a través de la respiración y la consciencia corporal. Cuando llegas a ese límite de la postura es donde empieza lo interesante, porque ahí está el punto de inflexión, de aprendizaje y evolución.

Siempre sin forzar, pero entendiendo ese trabajo que te lleva más allá de tus supuestas limitaciones.

Descubrir que podemos superar ese techo es una valiosa lección para cualquier situación de la vida cotidiana. Cuando superamos el límite empezamos a aprender y a conocernos de verdad.

¿Qué limitaciones te has fijado en lo que estás viviendo ahora mismo? ¿Cómo puedes rebasar ese límite, poco a poco y sin hacerte daño, tal como se hace en el yoga?

LA MURALLA DEL MIEDO

El escritor y conferenciante David Fischman dice que «el miedo es una muralla que separa lo que eres de lo que podrías llegar a ser». Si quieres motivación para derribar ese muro, pregúntate las veces que necesites:

¿Qué seré y haré cuando supere este miedo?

84

VOLVER A PASAR POR EL CORAZÓN

Recordar es volver a vivir. Aprender es recordar.
La palabra *recordar* viene del latín *recordare* y significa *volver a pasar por el corazón*. Volver a sentir, a vivir de la manera que fue. ¿No es fascinante?

Nuestro inconsciente no distingue de tiempos ni de modos. Así que, si crees que lo necesitas, vuelve a pasar por el corazón. Hazlo con aquello que te dio vida, que te acerca también al coraje, a la valentía de poner el corazón por delante.

Un ejercicio que puede ayudarte a ello es pescar recuerdos felices que creías olvidados. Puedes hacerlo a través de viejas fotos o mediante un ejercicio de indagación personal. Con los ojos cerrados, trasládate a una época especialmente brillante, a un encuentro memorable o a un viaje que te dejó huella.

Trata de rescatar escenas y momentos mágicos.

Vuélvelo a pasar por el corazón.

UN CUADERNO DE RECUERDOS INSPIRADORES

Te propongo que trabajes en un cuaderno donde almacenar momentos felices para volver a ellos cuando te sientas apagado. Puedes poner allí imágenes, notas, descubrimientos, trozos de conversaciones, cualquier cosa que te devuelva a ese instante mágico.

Lo ideal es que ese cuaderno tenga muchas páginas para que quepan numerosos *greatest hits* de la felicidad.

85
LA NOCHE OSCURA

San Juan de la Cruz habla en su poema *La noche oscura del alma* del camino hacia una nueva visión de la propia vida.

Y es que muchas veces no es hasta después de tocar fondo cuando empezamos a vislumbrar una nueva y mejor vida. Para salir airoso de la tristeza o la ansiedad a veces primero hay que atravesar desiertos, avanzar por sendas guiadas por un corazón que arde.

Así como el desierto esconde vida y procura valiosas lecciones al caminante, en la tristeza de hoy crecen las semillas de nuestra futura felicidad.

Sobre esto, en 1953 el escritor existencialista Albert Camus escribía:

> *En medio del odio me pareció que había dentro de mí un amor invencible. En medio de las lágrimas me pareció que había dentro de mí una sonrisa invencible. En medio del caos me pareció que había dentro de mí una calma invencible.*

> *Me di cuenta, a pesar de todo, de que en medio del invierno había en mí un verano invencible. Y eso me hace feliz. Porque no importa lo duro que el mundo empuje en mi contra, dentro de mí hay algo mejor empujando de vuelta.*

──────── ¿CUÁL ES TU NOCHE OSCURA? ────────

Es importante conocer y reconocer nuestra propia *noche oscura* para salir reforzados desde la esperanza.

Puedes explicársela a un buen amigo, a un terapeuta, o incluso a ti mismo a través de un diario personal.

86

CELEBRACIONES

Cuántas veces te dijeron que no habías hecho las cosas del todo bien o que las habías hecho mal? ¿Cuántas veces te negaste un premio al pensar que no eras merecedor de él?

Tantas que te lo has creído. Tantas que, incluso, cuando quizá merecías un pequeño reconocimiento, ni siquiera te diste cuenta.

Eres merecedor de atención, afecto, reconocimiento y cariño siempre. ¿Por qué no empiezas por reconocer tus cualidades y señalar las cosas que sí haces bien?

Sé consciente de todo lo que haces para enriquecer la vida –la tuya y la de los demás– y, si además lo necesitas, empieza por celebrarlo contigo mismo.

Orientados a solucionar problemas o a tapar agujeros, muchas veces nos olvidamos de premiarnos. Tal vez porque esperamos grandes acontecimientos, cuando la vida nos procura diariamente pequeños regalos.

CELEBRA LAS PEQUEÑAS COSAS

Una manera de cargar nuestra vida de energía positiva es celebrar las pequeñas cosas.

Cada gesto de celebración, cada brindis, es un ritual que será recordado, y eso hará que el cerebro retenga más tiempo el motivo de la celebración.

Como decía Robert Brault: «Disfruta de las pequeñas cosas, porque tal vez un día mires atrás y te des cuenta de que eran las grandes».

·87

LOS SIETE MONOS

La doctora en psicología Jenny Moix, que ha publicado recientemente la fábula *La cueva del mono*, trabaja con el concepto zen de la *mente de mono*, que muestra siete características acerca de cómo pensamos:

1. *El mono saltador.* La mente tiene tendencia a saltar al pasado y al futuro, lo que nos produce tristeza y miedo.
2. *El mono circular.* La mente siempre anda por los mismos sitios, y el surco puede convertirse en un hoyo sin salida.
3. *El mono juez.* La mente tiene un libro donde tiene anotado cómo debería ser la realidad.
4. *El mono culpabilizador.* En ese libro está también la emoción que deberíamos sentir en cada situación.
5. *El mono cegador.* Entre la belleza y nosotros se interpone la mente y no nos deja verla, porque no para de parlotear.
6. *El mono hipnotizador.* Nos mete dentro sus películas. Muchas emociones no son consecuencia de la realidad, sino de nuestros pensamientos.
7. *El mono soñador.* De día y de noche, la mente crea nuestra realidad. Nuestra tarea es despertar.

─────────────── **EL PERRO NEGRO** ───────────────

En su libro anterior, *Mi mente sin mí,* Jenny Moix cuenta que Winston Churchill se refería a sus momentos de depresión como al *perro negro,* para separarse de sus emociones y estados de ánimo. Cuando estaba desanimado, advertía a sus colaboradores: «Hoy vuelvo a tener el perro negro caminando a mi lado».

Esta clase de metáfora te servirá para entender algo muy liberador: *no eres tus pensamientos.* Puedes dejar de identificarte con el mono.

88

EL REGALO DEL PRESENTE

Un relato judío cuenta que alguien preguntó a un sabio rabino:
—¿Cuál ha sido el día más especial de su vida y quién fue la persona más importante?

—El día más especial de mi vida es HOY —respondió—. Y la persona más importante es con la que ahora estoy hablando.

Proyectarnos al pasado o al futuro suele acarrear emociones dolorosas, como hemos visto. En el pasado viven la tristeza, la culpa y el resentimiento. En el futuro viven la ansiedad, el temor y la incertidumbre.

La alegría y la paz mental pertenecen al presente. Quizá por eso, esta palabra significa también regalo. El presente es un regalo.

Cuando quieras dejar atrás tus miedos o los recuerdos que te llevan a la melancolía, el apego o la tristeza, céntrate en vivir con intensidad lo que está sucediendo aquí y ahora de manera consciente con todos tus sentidos.

Además de liberarte de las suposiciones que te hacen sufrir, estarás construyendo los buenos recuerdos del futuro.

¿EN QUÉ TIEMPO VIVES?

Un ejercicio interesante para saber cuánto presente hay en tu vida es observar, al hablar, si utilizas más el tiempo pasado, futuro o presente. Eso te dará una idea de dónde estás y te ayudará a volver al aquí y ahora.

89
SONRÍE, POR FAVOR

No hay un gesto tan sencillo y que tenga un poder equiparable al de la sonrisa. En su libro *Reír y vivir*, la actriz y *coach* Imma Rabasco la define así:

La sonrisa arquea nuestros labios hacia arriba, un gesto lleno de belleza que puede tener varios orígenes. Tal vez brota por la voluntad del alma de asomarse a una forma de vida optimista, alegre y conciliadora. O puede responder a un enamoramiento –de una persona o de la vida–. Lo importante es que no desaparezca. O que, si se va, vuelva.

Con independencia de donde venga, cada sonrisa atrae más sonrisas, porque este gesto de bienestar y felicidad evoca pensamientos agradables en nuestro cerebro.

La sonrisa tiende puentes y ayuda a expresar que venimos no solo en *son de paz* sino además en *son de amar*.

LA SONRISA DE BUDA

En el libro que titula el ejercicio se cuenta que un hombre muy pobre le dijo a Buda que era totalmente infeliz. Ante esto, el Iluminado le contestó que para ser feliz debía dar algo a los demás, ser caritativo. Sorprendido, el hombre le dijo que no poseía nada. ¿Qué podía ofrecer?

Entonces Buda le dijo:
—Sí tienes algo, tienes tu sonrisa. Ofrécesela a la gente y empezarás a ser más feliz.

Te propongo que ofrezcas tu sonrisa y amabilidad a las personas que lo necesitan. Además de iluminar su vida estarás alegrando la tuya.

90

ENVIDIA DE LA BUENA

Con admiración y cariño, siempre intento tomar ejemplo de quien me inspira. Tal y como os conté anteriormente que hacía Benjamin Franklin con las biografías que leía, yo tomo nota de aspectos que me gustan de las personas inspiradoras de mi vida y hago un plan para desarrollar esas cualidades en mí. Aunque conozco a alguien que termina la ducha con agua muy fría y reconozco que es algo que aún no he conseguido hacer...

Sí, es envidia de esa que despierta curiosidad, motivación y admiración. No me refiero a la envidia maliciosa y destructora del relato de Caín y Abel, sino a la que nos hace descubrir esa hambre que nace en nosotros al compararnos con otros, que nos permite localizar nuestras insatisfacciones internas y repararlas.

Es lo que se llama *envidia de la buena*. De la que se basa en la admiración y no en la crítica, la que usamos para construirnos a nosotros y que nos ayuda a convertirnos en personas mejores.

Así que, por qué no, cultivemos la buena envidia y quitémosle esa pátina negativa a la palabra para aportarle una nueva utilidad: que sea un detector de puntos de mejora, nos ayude a descubrir pequeñas grietas y poros en nuestros cimientos para poder repararlas, afianzar nuestras fortalezas y convertirnos en nuestra mejor versión.

QUIÉN QUIERES SER

El best seller de James Clear, *Hábitos atómicos*, sustituye las *to do lists*, las listas de lo que hay que hacer, por el desafío de decidir QUIÉN QUIERES SER a partir de ahora. La mecánica es sencilla:

1. Decide QUIÉN QUIERES SER a partir de ahora (tal vez inspirado en alguien a quien admiras).
2. Empieza a actuar como ese QUIÉN, con hábitos que confirmen tu nueva identidad.

91

DUDAR ES DE SABIOS

Decía sir Francis Bacon, un intelectual inglés del siglo XVI: «Si comienza uno con certezas, terminará con dudas, mas si acepta empezar con dudas, llegará a terminar con certezas».

¿Quién no ha conocido a personas ignorantes que creen saberlo todo y tratan de imponer su opinión?

Si dudar es de sabios, permítete cuestionar y cuestionarte como una excelente manera de avanzar. Quien va con certezas, le cierra las puertas a las infinitas posibilidades que nos ofrece la vida.

Con todo, para ser saludable, la duda debe tener un límite. Es bueno invitarla a pasar cuando estamos en una encrucijada, pero no podemos darle habitación y dejar que se quede en casa.

Al final hay que tomar decisiones, aunque sean erróneas, ya que al menos nos permitirán descartar opciones y seguir adelante.

AUTODUDA Y PROCRASTINACIÓN

William Knaus, uno de los asesores de Bill Clinton en su presidencia, aseguraba que las personas que posponen por sistema padecen el llamado *síndrome de autoduda*. Creen que están dudando, pero en realidad se trata de una excusa para no empezar nunca las cosas, porque tienen baja tolerancia a la presión que imprimen las grandes metas.

Cuando sientas que estás dudando demasiado, pregúntate si tu vacilación oculta en realidad el miedo a empezar.

92
PREPÁRATE PARA LO BUENO

S i aceptamos que *lo que crees es lo que creas*, concluiremos que hay que estar siempre preparado para lo que pueda llegar, anticipando y dando la bienvenida a aquello que puede ser digno de nuestra vida.

Deja un espacio a lo que llegue sin avisar y sin esperarlo apenas. Prepara tu vida para acoger todo lo que anhelas.

Si lo que deseas, por ejemplo, es el amor, solo llegará si tienes la puerta abierta. Hay una canción de Daniel Johnston, *True Love Will Find You In The End*, que habla de eso.

Traducida, viene a decir:

El amor verdadero te encontrará al final. Esta es una promesa con una trampa, ya que solo si estás buscando podrás encontrar. Porque el amor verdadero te está buscando también, pero ¿cómo podrá reconocerte a menos que des un paso hacia la luz? (...) Por eso, no te des por vencido hasta que el amor verdadero te encuentre al final.

—————— **DEFINE POR ESCRITO LO QUE NECESITAS** ——————

Ya se trate del amor verdadero, de un trabajo distinto o de cualquier otra cosa que anheles, hay más posibilidades de encontrarlo si lo defines con detalle.

Si escribes en una ficha qué características concretas debe tener lo que esperas, tu radar interior se orientará para encontrar justamente eso.

93
LOS DOS MIEDOS

E s común que temas perder lo que tienes, y también no ser capaz de conseguir lo que anhelas. El primer temor provoca inseguridad y ansiedad; el segundo, más miedo, frustración y desolación.

Si ambas clases de miedos no estuvieran tan presentes en nuestra vida, nos encontraríamos en el camino hacia la felicidad.

¿Cómo podemos librarnos de ellos?

En cuanto al primer miedo, se trata de entender que solo poseemos de verdad lo que tenemos en este preciso momento, ya que la vida es cambio constante. Si no eres capaz de disfrutarlo ahora por miedo a perderlo, entonces ya lo has perdido, porque tampoco lo tienes en el ahora.

En cuanto al segundo miedo, se puede mitigar anhelando solo aquello que depende de uno mismo. Si con esfuerzo y constancia lo consigues, entonces solo debes temer perder las ganas.

DEL MIEDO AL MEDIO

Para este ejercicio, haremos una transposición de letras. Cada vez que tengas miedo a perder algo o a no conseguir algo, cambia ese *miedo* por el *medio* necesario.

1. Si tienes *miedo* a perder algo, busca el *medio* de conservarlo y, sobre todo, de disfrutarlo aquí y ahora.

2. Si tienes *miedo* a no lograr algo, busca el *medio* de conseguirlo por tus propios *medios*, valga la redundancia.

94

ACEPTA LO QUE ES

Los grandes maestros saben que el amor y la sabiduría parten de la aceptación: de ti mismo, de los demás, del mundo, de la naturaleza, de la realidad.

Eckhart Tolle dice:

> *Tu aceptación de lo que «es» te lleva a un nivel más profundo (...). Cuando dices «sí» a la vida tal como es, cuando aceptas este momento como es, puedes sentir dentro de ti un espacio profundamente pacífico. Superficialmente puedes seguir sintiéndote feliz cuando hace sol y menos feliz cuando llueve; puedes sentirte feliz si ganas un millón de euros e infeliz si pierdes todas tus posesiones. Sin embargo, la felicidad y la infelicidad ya no calan tan hondo. Son olas en la superficie de tu Ser. La paz de fondo que hay dentro de ti permanece inmutable en cualesquiera que sean las condiciones externas.*

Cuando abrazamos *lo que es*, fluimos con la vida, con cualquier forma que tome, y nos adaptamos a los cambios –externos e internos– con la misma naturalidad que aceptamos la salida del sol y su puesta.

UN PASEO ADVAITA

Para experimentar *lo que es*, te propongo que des un paseo sin juzgar absolutamente nada, ni lo que te rodea ni tampoco a ti mismo. Limítate a caminar, siente la gravedad con cada paso, percibe la temperatura, la brisa y la luz, pero no lo etiquetes como *bueno, malo, bonito o feo*. Experimenta la no dualidad que define la espiritualidad advaita. Abraza *lo que es* momento a momento.

95
ADICCIONES INCONSCIENTES

S i entendiéramos la causa profunda de nuestro malestar, sonreiríamos con la misma compasión con la que miramos a un niño que se asusta al ver un chispazo por primera vez, antes de arroparlo con ternura.

En el documental *The Wisdom of Trauma*, el profesor Gabor Maté asegura que debajo de muchas formas de sufrimiento late una adicción: complacer a los demás, trabajar sin descanso, preocuparse de forma constante... Para reconocerlas y diagnosticarlas, propone que contestemos a la pregunta: *¿Quién está a cargo, el individuo o su comportamiento?*

O podemos plantearnos una pregunta más simple todavía: si te das cuenta de que te estás haciendo daño a ti mismo o a los demás, ¿estás dispuesto a parar?

Si no puedes renunciar a ese comportamiento o mantener la promesa que te has hecho, es una adicción, asegura Maté en su libro *In the Realm of Hungry Ghosts*.

¿PASIÓN O ADICCIÓN?

Siguiendo el hilo de este médico y autor de origen húngaro, cuando no sepas discernir entre algo que te apasiona hacer y una adicción, recurre a las siguientes preguntas:
- ¿Siento que tengo el control sobre mis actos? ¿Tengo la libertad de parar cuando lo deseo?
- ¿Domino esta conducta sin que la conducta me domine a mí?
- ¿Cumplo mi promesa cuando decido hacer algo distinto a lo que me empuja esta pasión?

Si contestas *no* a una o más de estas preguntas, se trata de una adicción de la que debes deshacerte.

96
LA CARROZA VACÍA

Un relato tradicional cuenta que una niña paseaba con su abuela por un plácido prado y se detuvieron en una curva del camino. Su abuela entonces le preguntó:

−¿Oyes lo mismo que yo?

La niña aguzó el oído y finalmente dijo:

−Oigo el ruido de una carroza.

−Así es −dijo la abuela−. Es una carroza vacía.

−¿Y eso cómo lo sabes? −preguntó la niña−. Aún no ha llegado para que podamos verla...

En este punto, la anciana sonrió y dijo:

−Es fácil saber si una carroza esta vacía. Cuanto más vacía va la carroza, mayor es el ruido que hace.

Este cuento es una alegoría perfecta de las personas que hablan demasiado e interrumpen la conversación de los demás, aunque realmente no tengan nada importante que decir. Cuanto más vacía va la carroza, más estridente es su ruido.

COMPARTIR EL SILENCIO

Un proverbio hindú reza: «Cuando hables, procura que tus palabras sean mejores que el silencio». Esto es algo que podemos practicar estando en compañía. De hecho, un signo de intimidad y armonía entre dos o más personas es cuando son capaces de compartir el silencio sin sentirse mal por ello.

97

ESPERAR CONTENTO

La paciencia parte del convencimiento de que cada cosa tiene su momento y que en la espera también se encuentra la importancia de aquello que ha de llegar.

Yo suelo decirles a mis hijos que *paciencia es esperar contento*.

Jugando con la palabra paciencia, un periodista decía que es *la ciencia de la paz*. Sin paciencia, la cultura de lo inmediato nos hace estar ansiosos e irritables, y nos agotamos fácilmente. Con paciencia, evitamos precipitarnos y no ponemos un *deadline* a lo que debe suceder.

Cuando dejamos atrás las prisas y las exigencias, el mundo se vuelve un lugar mucho más amable y placentero. De repente, sentimos que tenemos más tiempo, porque gozamos de cada minuto y de cada hora.

Esperar contento significa no impacientarse porque las cosas no sucedan hoy y, simplemente, disfrutar del camino.

EJERCICIOS DE PACIENCIA

Hay muchas prácticas que nos ayudan a ejercitar el músculo de la paciencia.

Veamos tres de ellas:

- Encarga un libro en una pequeña librería y espera a que te lo traigan en lugar de pedirlo con un simple clic.

- Acude a restaurantes de *slow food* donde todo tarda más porque cocinan alimentos frescos.

- Escucha con atención lo que te están diciendo en lugar de interrumpir o empezar a pensar lo que vas a contestar. También eso requiere paciencia.

98
SI VOLVIERA A NACER...

Una especie de epitafio falsamente atribuido a Borges empezaba así:

Si pudiera vivir nuevamente mi vida, en la próxima trataría de cometer más errores. No intentaría ser tan perfecto. Me relajaría más. Sería más tonto de lo que he sido. De hecho, me tomaría muy pocas cosas en serio.

Más allá de quien escribiera este texto, me sirve para preguntarte: ¿Qué harías diferente si volvieras a nacer?

Personalmente, creo que si volviera atrás en el tiempo, dedicaría más tardes y noches a convocar a personas que conversen en torno a mi mesa.

Disfrutar de la compañía de personas bellas, de seres humanos ricos en experiencias, es un auténtico regalo al que muchas veces no damos el valor que merece.

La buena noticia es que no necesitas volver a nacer para hacer todo eso. Puedes empezar a disfrutar de lo mejor de la vida a partir de ahora.

¿CUÁNTO SE TARDA EN CAMBIAR?

En el documental *No soy tu gurú,* Tony Robbins se dirige a una nutrida audiencia y les dice algo así: aunque llevéis diez años intentando cambiar, eso no significa que el cambio os lleve diez años. Cambiar es cosa de un instante, solo que a veces tardamos diez años en decidirnos a hacerlo.

¿Qué cambio deseas introducir ahora mismo en tu vida?

99

LOS HIJOS COMO ESPEJO

Nuestros hijos son un espejo de quienes somos. Nos modelan con sus enseñanzas vitales y también nos muestran mucho de nosotros mismos.

Si eres padre o madre, seguro que más de una vez te has sorprendido reconociendo en tus hijos gestos y actitudes que tenías o tienes tú mismo.

Si no hemos tenido descendencia, podemos hacer el mismo ejercicio fijando la mirada en nuestros padres. ¿Qué hemos heredado de ellos, con independencia de que nos guste más o menos?

La relación entre padres e hijos es un camino de ida y vuelta lleno de autoconocimiento. Tanto si nos reflejamos en el espejo de nuestros padres como en el de nuestros hijos, ver en el otro aquello que somos nos aporta una luz que, justamente, nos permite cambiar de perspectiva.

AYUDAR NOS AYUDA

Bert Hellinger, el creador de las *Constelaciones Familiares*, decía: «Los humanos dependemos, en todos los sentidos, de la ayuda de otros. Únicamente así podemos desarrollarnos. Al mismo tiempo, también dependemos de ayudar a otros».

Si para crecer se necesita ofrecer y recibir ayuda, por una parte, debes plantearte qué necesita de ti tu hijo, una madre o padre, un hermano o un familiar que te permita desarrollar tus capacidades; por otra, debes aprender a pedir ayuda cada vez que la necesites.

100
COSAS QUE HACER ANTES
DE MORIR

Seguro que alguna vez ha caído en tus manos una obra o artículo sobre las cosas que hay que hacer antes de morir, los 100 libros que todo el mundo debería leer o las 100 películas que de ningún modo deberías dejar pasar.

Sin embargo, eso son solo listas ajenas que no tienen por qué coincidir con tus gustos y prioridades. Me parece más interesante que escribas tu propia lista de lo que deseas hacer en esta vida.

Tal vez se trate de un viaje, de escribir un libro, de aprender un idioma o a tocar un determinado instrumento. Cualquier cosa que palpite fuertemente en tu interior merece estar en la lista. Y deberías poner los medios para intentar cumplirla.

Como decía el novelista Mark Twain: «Dentro de veinte años te arrepentirás más de las cosas que no hiciste que de las que llegaste a hacer. Por lo tanto, ya puedes levar el ancla. Abandona este puerto. Hincha las velas con el viento del cambio. Explora. Sueña. Descubre».

¿Y si empiezas poniéndolo por escrito?

BUSCA TU TESTIGO

Además de plasmarlo por escrito, una manera de materializar un determinado sueño de tu lista es nombrar a un amigo, pareja o familiar como testigo de tu propósito. Confíale la fecha de inicio y lo que te comprometes a hacer para lograrlo. Por su parte, tendrá el papel de supervisar si lo estás cumpliendo y reñirte cariñosamente si es necesario.

101

UNA BELLA SOLEDAD

E res una buena compañía para ti mismo?
La soledad es un sentimiento, un estado y, a la vez, un espacio de libertad. Un vacío y un todo al que recurrir para serenarte y llenarte de tu esencia.

En esa quietud solitaria apreciarás los regalos que llegan desde el interior y que, quizá, la compañía de elementos externos (no solo personas) te impide identificar.

La soledad te conecta con lo más profundo de ti mismo y, al mismo tiempo, con todo lo que existe fuera. Los japoneses llaman *Yugen* a esos momentos en los que nos damos cuenta de que no somos algo separado del universo, sino que *somos el universo*.

Desde la observación hacia fuera hasta la integración de lo externo, es necesario pasar ratos de soledad para luego caminar ligero hacia aquellos que te necesitan.

Se atribuye al existencialista Jean-Paul Sartre la frase: «Si te sientes solo cuando estás solo, estás en mala compañía».

─────────── **PRACTICA LA SOLOSOFÍA** ───────────

El último libro de la psicóloga Nika Vázquez, *Solosofía,* acuña una palabra nueva para designar el arte de estar solo en buena compañía con uno mismo. El *solósofo* o *solósofa* sabe disfrutar de actividades en soledad, tenga o no una pareja o una familia.

Te propongo algunas:

• Ir solo al cine, con la libertad de levantarte y marcharte si no te convence la película.

• Darte cita en un café o en un parque para revisar, tal vez con una libreta y bolígrafo, las cuestiones de tu vida que ahora mismo te interesan.

• Atreverte incluso a hacer un pequeño viaje en solitario, en el que descubrirás muchas cosas sobre ti mismo. ¿Puede haber mayor aventura?

102
DEJA PASAR EL PASADO

M ás allá del juego de palabras, hay personas que no logran vivir el presente con plenitud y hacer planes de futuro porque siguen ancladas al pasado.

Hay muchas formas en las que el pasado nos puede retener, incluso sin darnos cuenta: viejos rencores de los que no nos hemos desprendido, sentimientos de culpa por cosas que podríamos haber hecho mejor o de manera diferente, una nostalgia excesiva por una época en la que fuimos felices...

Para levar estas anclas, solo tienes que darte cuenta de que el pasado ya es pasado. Lo que has aprendido gracias a él y lo que amas de ese tiempo quedó atrás.

Puedes desear con todas tus fuerzas volver a esos lugares felices, igual que huyes de los lugares poco agradables que te hicieron sufrir. Pero todo, todos ellos, son pasado.

Suéltalo y sentirás que tu vida arranca.

--------- **EL CONSEJO DE PABLO D'ORS** ---------

En su exitosa *Biografía del silencio*, este sacerdote y escritor español nos da una clave para liberarnos de la culpa hacia algo que hicimos o fuimos en el pasado:

Desde mi presente (...) no puedo condenar a quien fui en el pasado por la sencilla razón de que aquel a quien ahora juzgo y repruebo es otra persona. Actuamos siempre conforme a la sabiduría que tenemos en cada momento, si actuamos mal es porque, al menos en ese punto, había ignorancia.

Por lo tanto, perdónate. Con lo que ya has aprendido, vas a hacerlo mejor a partir de ahora.

103
DESPREOCÚPATE

Según un estudio realizado en la Universidad Estatal de Pensilvania, el 90 por ciento de las cosas que nos preocupan nunca se hacen realidad.

Se llegó a este porcentaje aproximado a partir de un grupo de personas que padecían ansiedad y que, a lo largo de un mes, fueron escribiendo todo lo que les preocupaba.

Se demostró que, en 9 de cada 10 casos, sus temores eran totalmente injustificados, ya que no se reflejaron en su vida. Por tanto, se trataba de fantasías, proyecciones infundadas de su mente.

Darse cuenta de esto las ayudó a desactivar los ataques de ansiedad.

Si eres una persona con tendencia a preocuparte, toma nota de este estudio y empieza a utilizar tu tiempo en ocuparte, en vez de pre-ocuparte.

TERAPIA OCUPACIONAL

El psicólogo y escritor Antoni Bolinches asegura que la mejor manera de desactivar las preocupaciones es teniendo ocupaciones. Estar ocupados nos permite somatizar menos, baja nuestro nivel tensional, tenemos menos hipocondría...

Cada vez que te asalten las preocupaciones, puedes aplicar la terapia ocupacional. Ocúpate bien, haz cosas que te gusten o te interesen.

El lema debe ser: más hacer y menos pensar.

104

AUTOCONOCIMIENTO

La buena gestión emocional tiene que ver con el conocimiento de uno mismo. Al igual que no puedes amar a alguien sin reconocerlo y aceptar quién es, sin desear que sea otra cosa, el amor por uno mismo empieza también por la aceptación.

Cuando conoces y aceptas tus emociones, tu forma de relacionarte con el mundo, tus sueños y prioridades, entonces puedes decir que tienes amistad contigo mismo.

Eso te dará paz mental, a la vez que te permitirá evolucionar y vivir con más libertad.

Invierte tu valioso tiempo en saber quién eres, qué eres y decide qué quieres hacer con tu vida. Hazlo de manera honesta y celebra cada avance, porque solo las personas valientes como tú vivirán de manera plena y consciente.

¿QUIÉN SOY YO?

Un místico que tenía su *ashram* en Arunachala, en el sur de la India, daba esta pregunta a todos sus estudiantes, pero la respuesta no podía ser el propio nombre ni la profesión ni la procedencia familiar ni cualquier otra convencionalidad.

¿Te atreves a interrogarte de este modo? Justamente un proverbio indio dice que «uno solo posee aquello que no puede perder en un naufragio». ¿Qué es lo que no podrías perder en un naufragio? En la respuesta te encontrarás a ti mismo.

105
DENTRO DE TUS POSIBILIDADES

En una reflexión anterior vimos cómo las personas a las que admiramos nos pueden servir de inspiración para la automejora. Basta con fijarnos en sus virtudes y preguntarnos: ¿qué hace esta persona que yo no hago?

Sin embargo, es muy posible que eso que ves en la otra persona esté ya en ti. Lo único que sucede es que te resulta más fácil verlo en el otro.

Cuando identifiques algo extraordinario en alguien, pregúntate cuánto de esa cualidad hay en ti. Sea positivo o no tan agradable, por la ley del espejo, si lo ves en otros, es muy posible que esté también en ti, por pequeño que sea.

Solo puedes ver aquello que conoces y solo puedes trabajar en ello cuando lo reconoces.

Acerca de eso, el emperador y filósofo Marco Aurelio decía:

Aunque tus fuerzas parezcan insuficientes para la tarea que tienes ante ti, no asumas que está fuera del alcance de los poderes humanos. Si algo está dentro de los poderes de la provincia del hombre, créelo: también está dentro de tus posibilidades.

¿QUÉ HARÍA EN TU LUGAR?

En momentos de bloqueo o agobio ante una situación que te sobrepasa, imagínate que eres alguien que es un referente para ti. Puede ser incluso un personaje histórico o de ficción. Pregúntate: ¿Qué haría X en mi situación? Una vez tengas la respuesta, obra en consecuencia.

106
NADA ESTÁ PERDIDO

Cuando crees que lo has perdido todo, la vida te sorprende. Quizá con recursos propios que descubres y no sabías que tenías, o bien personas que te recuerdan lo valioso que eres.

A veces hay que tocar fondo para darse cuenta de que somos como el Ave Fénix, capaces de renacer de nuestras cenizas.

Julio Cortázar lo explicó de manera especialmente bella, al decir que «nada está perdido si se tiene por fin el valor de proclamar que todo está perdido y que hay que empezar de nuevo».

Como en un proceso de alquimia, ese *todo* del que habla el escritor argentino se transforma y crea nuevos *todos,* nuevas capacidades y prioridades.

AHORA PUEDO VER LA LUNA

Un aforismo a veces atribuido al zen, pero que al parecer pertenece a Karl Marx, dice: «Mi granero se ha quemado. Ahora puedo ver la luna».

Cuando sufras algún percance, pregúntate:

- ¿Qué gano con esta pérdida?
- ¿Qué puedo ver ahora que antes no veía?
- ¿Qué fortaleza tengo de la que solo ahora soy consciente?
- ¿Qué personas han demostrado ser importantes en este momento difícil de mi vida?

107
DISCIPLINA

A medida que aprendo sobre mí misma, me doy cuenta de que necesito tanta disciplina y orden como relajación y naturalidad. Puedo explicarlo con una imagen gráfica: para mí, la disciplina es como soltar el hilo de la caña de pescar y tensarlo lo justo para que esté siempre lista para la vida. No muy suelto en el carrete, para que el hilo esté firme y visible en el horizonte. Así, con el corcho a la vista y flotando, me dejo llevar por las corrientes más apetecibles que llegan desde otros mares. Quiero descubrir y aprender de ellas.

Al igual que el pescador a la captura de lo inesperado, necesito las rutinas que hacen de mí alguien constante y con esa capacidad de ver lo nuevo para aprender de la vida.

EL CUERPO, PRIMERO

A menudo relacionamos las rutinas con lo mental: actividades que tienen que ver con la organización, la creatividad o la buena gestión del tiempo. Sin embargo, una rutina saludable debe de empezar por nuestro vehículo para la vida, y eso implica:

- Una alimentación equilibrada y saludable.
- Ejercicio suave para tonificar el cuerpo.
- No escatimar horas de sueño.
- Regalarnos vida social y actividades de ocio para relajarnos.

108
LO QUE DEPENDE DE TI

Ante una crisis o un dilema, te darás cuenta de que hay asuntos que no dependen directamente de ti para solucionarse. Si inviertes energía en ellas, será en vano.

En lugar de eso, pregúntate qué puedes hacer tú con las cuestiones que sí dependen de ti y ponte manos a la obra cuanto antes.

Hace ya un par de milenios, el filósofo estoico Epicteto lo explicaba así:

> De todas las cosas que existen en el mundo, unas dependen de nosotros, otras no dependen de nosotros (...)
>
> Las cosas que dependen de nosotros son por naturaleza libres, nada puede detenerlas, ni obstaculizarlas; las que no dependen de nosotros son débiles, esclavas, dependientes, sujetas a mil obstáculos y a mil inconvenientes, y enteramente ajenas.

Tomemos estas sabias palabras para ocuparnos de lo que sí depende de nosotros y no gastar fuerzas allí donde no tenemos influencia.

--- **CUATRO VIRTUDES ESTOICAS** ---

Para esta escuela filosófica, hay cuatro virtudes cuya práctica nos ayudará en el arte del buen vivir. Son las siguientes:

1. *Sabiduría*. Para saber lo que depende de nosotros y lo que no.
2. *Templanza*. Para no tomarnos a la tremenda lo que sucede ni dejarnos llevar por el primer impulso.
3. *Justicia*. Para gestionar nuestro trato a los demás, pero también a nosotros mismos.
4. *Coraje*. Para no amilanarnos ante los cambios y desafíos y actuar desde lo que depende de nosotros.

109
NUESTRA PIEDRA DE TOQUE

L as cosas que más se nos resisten son también las que más nos enseñan, porque nos muestran cuál es nuestro punto a trabajar. En ese
sentido, las dificultades son nuestra *piedra de toque*.

En su sentido original, la piedra de toque es una piedra dura y oscura
que sirve para conocer la pureza de un material. Por ejemplo, al rascar el
oro o la plata. En una segunda acepción, la piedra de toque es aquello que
nos permite evaluar nuestro valor preciso. Por ejemplo, la de un navegante
será la primera gran tormenta a la que se tiene que enfrentar al mando de
la nave.

A nadie le gusta que las cosas se tuerzan, pero con el tiempo acabare-
mos dando las gracias por haber pasado por determinadas situaciones.

El gran regalo de los obstáculos es que, una vez superados, nos hacen
conscientes de qué somos capaces, de cuál es nuestro valor.

¿CUÁL ES TU PRÓXIMO RETO?

Dice el escritor y conferenciante
Álex Rovira que el coraje no es la
simple ausencia de miedo, sino
la consciencia de que hay algo
importante por lo que merece la pena
arriesgarse.

En este ejercicio, te pido que te
preguntes qué desafío tienes ahora
ante ti que te empodera para ir más
allá de tu miedo.

110
AUTOAMABILIDAD

Aunque no es una palabra que estemos acostumbrados a oír, la *autoamabilidad* es una vía óptima y demostrada para el bienestar emocional.

¿Te vas a permitir ser amable contigo mismo o quieres seguir cuestionándote, juzgándote y castigándote, como quizá has aprendido desde pequeño?

Hace poco Nazareth Castellanos compartió un estudio realizado en 2021 sobre el cerebro y la autoamabilidad. En concreto, sobre los cambios cerebrales y los cambios psicológicos asociados que produce cultivar la autocompasión.

Sobre estos últimos, concluyó que gracias a la autoamabilidad:

- Disminuye nuestra autocrítica y autojuicio.
- Paliamos el aislamiento y nos relacionamos más y mejor con los demás.
- Mejora nuestra capacidad de tener atención plena.

En suma, ser amable contigo mismo te aporta paz mental, concentración y buenas relaciones.

EL EFECTO PIGMALIÓN

Al igual que, según el Efecto Pigmalión, la visión negativa sobre alguien condiciona que nos dé una respuesta igualmente negativa, si quieres recoger belleza y amabilidad en tu vida, empieza cultivando esa visión de ti mismo.

Cuando te des cuenta de que te estás tratando con dureza, haz este cambio de perspectiva.

111
LO QUE DABA EL ÁRBOL

Un relato tradicional cuenta que había un rey que mostraba con mucho orgullo su jardín. Hasta que un noble visitante se atrevió a preguntarle:

–Es muy bonito, pero ese árbol solitario de allí, junto al lago... ¿qué fruto da?

Tras pensarlo un rato, el rey reconoció:

–Pues me temo que ninguno.

–¿Ninguno? ¡Qué árbol más vago!

Consternado, hizo llamar al jardinero para decirle:

–No puede ser que ese árbol no dé frutos. No quiero vagos en mi reino. ¡Tálalo!

El jardinero cumplió la orden muy a su pesar, ya que tenía cariño por aquel árbol.

Aquel mediodía, el rey salió a pasear por el lago. Hacía tanto calor que deseó pararse a descansar, pero no supo dónde. Entonces se dio cuenta de que, si bien el árbol no daba frutos, daba algo más importante: sombra.

Todos y todo lo que nos rodea nos da algo, y depende de nosotros saberlo valorar y apreciar.

LA GRATITUD HACE AMIGOS

Está demostrado que las personas que muestran su agradecimiento a los demás tienen más facilidad para hacer amigos y sus relaciones son más duraderas. ¿A quién y por qué puedes darle las gracias hoy?

112
TÓMATE TU TIEMPO

No permitas que te metan prisas. A veces es necesaria una pausa para decidir las cosas, sean o no importantes. De hecho, nuestro propio cuerpo nos informa de cuándo necesitamos frenar o pararnos a mirar el paisaje; otra cosa es que lo escuchemos.

Cuando sientas que estás cansado o confundido, tómate el tiempo que necesites. Nadie debería presionarte.

Sobre los ritmos cambiantes de cada persona, el novelista Marcel Proust decía:

> Los días quizá sean iguales para un reloj, pero no lo son para un hombre. Hay días empinados e incómodos, que cuesta un tiempo infinito coronar, y días en cuesta abajo, que pueden bajarse fácilmente cantando. Para recorrerlos, las naturalezas –particularmente las que son un poco nerviosas– disponen de diferentes velocidades, como los automóviles.

RELÁJATE EN UN MINUTO

- Si te sientes fatigado o estresado, respira lentamente y aguanta el aire 4 o 5 segundos.
- A continuación, libéralo de golpe. Puedes emitir un suspiro.

- Mientras exhalas, relaja la mandíbula y los hombros.
- Repite esta serie seis o siete veces y te sentirás mucho mejor.

113

CHEQUEA TUS RELACIONES

Tienes relaciones que alimentan el alma? Examina cuál es tu red de amigos y relaciones en este momento de tu vida, las personas con las que intercambias mensajes y convives a diario. ¿Con quiénes interactúas más y de qué manera? ¿Qué tipo de energía envías y recibes y cómo te dejan al cabo del día? ¿Echas de menos otro tipo de relaciones, otro tipo de conexión? ¿Cómo podrías establecer esta clase de relaciones de alta calidad?

Somos lo que vivimos, pero sobre todo cómo y con quién lo vivimos. Por lo tanto, nuestro bienestar, energía e incluso nuestro éxito dependen de la clase de vínculos que creamos con los demás. Yo lo llamo *crear redes bonitas*.

TRES TIPOS DE VÍNCULO

Josep Pla, un escritor catalán de la segunda mitad del siglo xx muy apreciado por sus crónicas y ensayos, decía que hay tres clases de personas con las que nos relacionamos: *amigos, conocidos* y *saludados*.

Una forma de gestionar nuestros vínculos de manera sana es no confundir estas categorías y ser selectivos en el apartado de los amigos, ya que son las personas que más inciden en nuestra felicidad.

114

MEJOR HECHO QUE PERFECTO

Esto se les suele decir a aquellas personas que, de tan perfeccionistas, tienden a alargarlo o postergarlo todo, llegando incluso a lo que se conoce como *parálisis por análisis.*

A veces nuestro ideal de excelencia es tan complejo y ambicioso que acabamos por no hacer nada. En este caso, el perfeccionismo es solo una excusa para no avanzar.

Contra ese síndrome, las personas expertas en productividad recomiendan empezar por lo que se conoce como *mínimo viable.*

El mínimo viable es lo mínimo que necesitas para ponerte en marcha. Sin embargo, no debes quedarte ahí. A partir de este punto, puedes ir mejorando lo que haces porque ya estarás en movimiento.

Por lo tanto, la clave está en el equilibrio: ni quedarnos parados por miedo a no hacer algo perfecto ni conformarnos con lo primero que nos salga. Eso sí, partiendo siempre del mínimo viable como el primer peldaño hacia la excelencia.

TRES PREGUNTAS PARA PROGRESAR

Cuando te quedes paralizado, te propongo estas tres preguntas para ponerte en marcha:

1. ¿Por qué es importante para mí lo que estoy haciendo?
2. ¿Qué nivel o meta deseo alcanzar?
3. ¿Cuál es el siguiente paso en esa dirección?

115
LA UTILIDAD DEL MIEDO

El miedo tiene muchos detractores en el ámbito del bienestar emocional. Y es cierto que a menudo nos impide avanzar y nos limita, pero también es una defensa contra posibles amenazas.

Incluso cuando tenemos un temor injustificado, si lo examinamos con atención nos dará pistas sobre qué lo origina. Por lo tanto, nos resultará útil para conocernos mejor. Si nos aliamos con él, una vez comprendido, puede ser una catapulta para ir un poco más allá de nosotros mismos.

Pero ¿cómo hacerlo? Dando las gracias al miedo por todo lo que nos ha enseñado y protegido hasta ahora y retándole, incluso, a quedarse durante un tiempo para explorar otras áreas de nosotros que desconocemos.

La admirable Marie Curie se expresaba en estos términos al respecto: «Nada en la vida debe ser temido, solamente comprendido. Ahora es el momento de comprender más para temer menos».

TERAPIA DE EXPOSICIÓN PROGRESIVA

Según la psicología conductista, en lugar de evitar lo que tememos —eso solo refuerza el miedo—, la mejor manera de superarlo es exponernos de forma progresiva a lo que lo causa. Por ejemplo, alguien con fobia al metro puede empezar bajando al andén un par de minutos en compañía; luego hacerlo solo; tomar el metro y recorrer una estación. Y así sucesivamente, hasta que la huella positiva haya sustituido la que ha provocado la fobia.

¿Con qué probarías tú esta terapia en tu vida?

116

AHORA YO

Decía Francisco de Quevedo: «Vive solo para ti si pudieres, pues solo para ti si mueres, mueres».

Y tenía mucha razón, pues nadie puede vivir nuestra existencia por nosotros.

Por eso mismo, no significa ser egoísta ni egocéntrico decir *ahora yo*. A nadie más le corresponde escribir nuestra propia historia. Cuando nos damos cuenta de eso, empezamos de verdad a ser guionistas, actores y directores de nuestra vida.

Piensa, ¿eres quien verdaderamente lleva la dirección de tu película o tiras de inercias e influencias externas a la hora de tomar tus decisiones?

El *ahora yo* implica elegir, asumir riesgos, corregir el rumbo cuando sea necesario, empezar de nuevo. En definitiva: vivir.

TU PRÓXIMO PUNTO DE INFLEXIÓN

Visualiza tu biografía como si fuera una película. Date cuenta de todos los momentos en los que has tomado decisiones que han supuesto un punto de inflexión en tu historia.

Cuando llegues a tu momento actual, pregúntate cuál va a ser el próximo punto de inflexión. Ponte manos a la obra para acompañarlo con tus actos y pensamientos.

117

EL CAMINO DEL CORAZÓN

M uchas veces nos encontramos en una encrucijada vital y no estamos seguros de qué camino deberíamos tomar. En esos momentos, hay una brújula que todos tenemos incorporada que nos puede ayudar a marcar el rumbo.

En su clásico *Las enseñanzas de Don Juan*, Carlos Castaneda recibía del indio yaqui el siguiente aprendizaje:

> *¿Tiene corazón este camino? Si lo tiene, el camino es bueno; si no, de nada sirve. Ningún camino lleva a ninguna parte, pero uno tiene corazón y el otro no. Uno hace gozoso el viaje; mientras lo sigas, eres uno con él. El otro te hará maldecir tu vida. Uno te hace fuerte; el otro te debilita.*

Lo que te dicta el corazón suele ser lo más auténtico, un impulso que te da fuerza para emprender cualquier viaje o proyecto con coraje y determinación.

No dejes de poner atención a los mensajes que te envía tu corazón en su latir y aparta cualquier distracción que te impida escucharlo alto y claro.

ATIENDE TUS CORAZONADAS

Definida como *la sensación o sospecha de que algo va a ocurrir*, la corazonada es una señal que surge del inconsciente, cuando este cuenta con una información superior a la que maneja la mente consciente. Es importante escuchar estos mensajes de la intuición, porque muchas veces demuestran ser acertados. Escúchalos.

118
EL RÍO DEL CAMBIO

Joe Dispenza, doctor en quiropráctica y estudioso de la neurociencia y la epigenética, enseña en sus cursos a crear nuevos caminos neuronales a través de la meditación.

Cuando esos nuevos caminos están ya formados, llega el momento de llevar ese cambio a la realidad. Entonces viene el verdadero reto. Dispenza lo explica diciendo que el cambio es un río, y al cruzarlo te enfrentas a dos peligros:

1. *Los demás*, a quienes, acostumbrados a que actuemos y seamos de determinada manera, nuestro cambio les genera inquietud. Por eso, mientras nadas hacia la otra orilla, algunos te gritarán: *¡¿Adónde vas, loco?! ¡Vuelve!*

2. *Tus propios miedos.* Cambiar es tan incómodo como sumergirte en un río de agua helada. Puede que cuando llegues a la mitad del río, pienses *¡qué frío está!*, y te sientas tentado a regresar a tu zona de confort.

Dispenza aconseja que no escuches a nadie y mucho menos a tus propios temores cuando decidas cambiar.

¿QUIÉN ERES SIN TU MIEDO?

Nuestros temores limitan y determinan el espacio que podemos ocupar, las cosas que podemos llegar a hacer. Por eso, cuando decidimos desafiarlos y nos lanzamos a la piscina, descubrimos quiénes somos realmente.

¿Te atreves a probarlo?

119

EL MOMENTO ADECUADO

A menudo esperamos el momento adecuado para lanzarnos a hacer algo, pero parece que ese momento nunca llega. De hecho, es muy posible que creas que nunca llegue.

Vamos a darle la vuelta a esa idea.

Hay veces que es el propio momento el que te espera a ti, desde hace mucho tiempo ya. Lo sabes y lo intuyes. Solo tienes que dar el paso.

Atrapa ese momento que te está mirando con ganas –quizá sea este precisamente– y te está diciendo que no debes esperar más.

La vida no espera.

No esperes el momento adecuado y lánzate.

Haz todo aquello que estás llamado a hacer antes de morir.

—— LOS CUATRO CONSEJOS DE ELIZABETH KÜBLER-ROSS ——

Esta psiquiatra y escritora que trabajó la mayor parte de su vida con moribundos nos da estos valiosos consejos para la vida:
1. Vive de tal forma que al mirar hacia atrás no lamentes haber desperdiciado la existencia.
2. Vive de tal forma que no te lamentes de las cosas que has hecho ni desees haber actuado de otra manera.
3. Vive con sinceridad y plenamente.
4. Vive.

120
CADA INSTANTE VIVIDO

Cómo podemos medir la calidad e intensidad de nuestra vida? Tal vez la mejor manera de hacerlo sea con la consciencia de cada instante vivido.

A cada respiración, a cada mirada, a cada sentir le corresponde el poder de otorgarte una vida plena y de aprendizaje que no es comparable con ninguna otra.

Cuando vivimos el presente con ese grado de consciencia y realización, entonces el camino al futuro se convierte en un agradable viaje lleno de descubrimientos. Sobre esto, Mihály Csíkszentmihályi, a quien ya hemos mencionado, añade:

Cada uno de nosotros tiene una idea, aunque sea vaga, de lo que le gustaría conseguir antes de morirse. Lo cerca o lo lejos que lleguemos a estar de ese objetivo se convierte en la medida de la calidad de nuestra vida.

Sin embargo, ese camino al futuro se compone de millones de instantes vividos, cada cual único e irrepetible. ¿Estás disfrutando de tu momento presente?

PRACTICA EL FOCO

Aprovecha lo que vayas a hacer ahora mismo para ejercitar la atención plena. Pon los cinco sentidos en esa actividad, por muy cotidiana o incluso aburrida que pueda parecer. Conviértela en una meditación, demostrándote a ti mismo que eres capaz de convertir esa acción y ese momento en el centro de tu universo.

121

LO BUENO DE SER BUENO

Aunque no abundan en los medios, debo reconocer que me emocionan las buenas noticias. Me conmueve la bondad, la generosidad, la empatía y el amor del ser humano hacia lo que le rodea: personas, animales, naturaleza...

Descubrir a héroes cotidianos que se preocupan por el bienestar de los demás me devuelve la fe en la humanidad. Me hace sentir viva y me recuerda que, en el fondo, soy una niña que cree en la capacidad del ser humano para amar, reparar y acompañar en el dolor.

Si tú también experimentas a veces esta agradable sensación, te propongo un reto: ¿Y si asumes tú el papel de héroe cotidiano, aunque sea con una pequeña acción, para dar esperanza a los demás?

¿CUÁL ES TU GRANO DE ARENA?

La madre Teresa de Calcuta decía que muchas veces sentimos que lo que podemos aportar es solo un grano de arena en el desierto, pero que el desierto sería menos sin ese grano. Desde esa filosofía, te planteo pequeños retos:

- ¿Qué puedes aportar en el ámbito de tu familia para que todo vaya un poco mejor?

- ¿Cuál puede ser tu grano de arena en tu profesión para facilitar la vida a los demás?
- Y, no menos importante, ¿qué pequeña mejora puedes hacer por ti mismo para cuidarte y sentirte mejor?

122
ESTRELLAS INVISIBLES

Ayer vi amanecer por primera vez junto a mi hijo. Volvíamos de pasar la noche en Urgencias. Mientras regresábamos con el coche, solo se veía una estrella en el firmamento. Entonces el sabio niño dijo:

–Hay estrellas que no vemos en el cielo, ¿verdad, mamá?

Me emocioné al escucharlo, porque tenía toda la razón: ¡cuántas cosas por descubrir!

Paramos el coche al margen del camino y nos bajamos en un descampado para observar mejor el cielo nocturno.

Gracias a una aplicación en el teléfono que te da el nombre de los astros, descubrimos todo un baile infinito de constelaciones.

Todas estaban ahí, también las que no se veían. Luces por descubrir que nos pueden servir de guía en el momento menos esperado.

Lo mismo sucede en la vida cotidiana: hay maravillas que están ahí, aunque no las veamos, esperando ser descubiertas.

——— EL DISOLVENTE UNIVERSAL DE LOS PROBLEMAS ———

La doctora en física cuántica Sonia Fernández-Vidal, autora de muchas obras de divulgación científica, afirma que estudiar el cosmos —a través de un libro, de un documental o de la simple observación— nos abstrae de los pequeños problemas de la vida diaria. Además, alimenta nuestra curiosidad y capacidad de sorpresa, lo cual es un aliciente más para levantar la cabeza hacia el cielo.

123

LA VIDA ETERNA ES AHORA

El jesuita y terapeuta Anthony de Mello, gran conocedor de la India y autor de numerosos libros de relatos, nos legó esta reflexión sobre la velocidad:

El día en que ustedes paren de correr, llegarán (...) La vida eterna es ahora, está aquí, pero te han confundido hablándote de un futuro que esperas mientras te pierdes la maravilla de la vida que es el ahora. Te pierdes la verdad.

De Mello dice que no debemos «ni temer ni tener esperanza en un futuro juntos», porque ambas son proyecciones, al igual que el pasado, y añade:

Las cosas solo serán cuando deban ser, por mucha prisa que te des (...) Tienes que vivir libremente el ahora, separado de los recuerdos, que están muertos; solo está vivo el presente y lo que tú vas descubriendo en él como real.

VUELVE

El gran enemigo del ahora son las proyecciones. Cuando tu conciencia viaja al pasado o al futuro, por la razón que sea, dejas de disfrutar de lo que te ofrece el presente.

Cada vez que te des cuenta de que eso sucede, puedes decirte ¡*vuelve*!

y poner los cinco sentidos en lo que pasa aquí y ahora. Al principio puede costarte, pero a medida que practiques, te será más fácil regresar al ahora.

124
ÚNICO

Quizá nadie te lo dijo cuando eras un niño, pero vengo a recordarte algo: eres un ser único. Único en todo lo que haces, sientes y piensas. ¿No es extraordinario?

Cuando tomas conciencia de ser un fuera de serie, te empoderas para protagonizar tu propia historia.

En tu autenticidad y carácter genuino está tu fuerza para evolucionar y dar lo mejor de ti en cada fase de la vida, con los retos que comporta. Para ello, debes practicar el autoconocimiento y la comprensión de tus capacidades.

¿Qué piensas hacer con tu vida? ¿Te vas a quedar con las ganas de descubrir todo lo original que hay en ti, con lo que podrías cambiar el mundo?

PARA DESCUBRIR LO GENUINO EN TI

- Cada mañana, cuando te levantes, recuerda que no hay nadie como tú y que eres responsable de conducir esa vida única.
- Cuando te descubras admirando una cualidad de alguien que crees que te falta, dale la vuelta al asunto y pregúntate qué tienes tú que la otra persona no posee.
- Date cuenta de aquello que es tuyo y solo tuyo. ¡Celebra tu carácter único!

125

DAFO

En el mundo de la empresa se utiliza el denominado *Análisis DAFO,* una herramienta para conocer la situación de una empresa o proyecto, aunque también se puede aplicar a la persona. Veamos qué significan estas siglas:

- **D**ebilidades
- **A**menazas
- **F**ortalezas
- **O**portunidades

Algo que diferencia a las personas exitosas del resto es el hábito de revisar periódicamente su situación. Para ellas, el análisis es también parte de la toma de decisiones. Puede que en ocasiones no todo llegue del *universo.*

Plantéate de vez en cuando un DAFO para saber dónde estás y cómo estás. Mientras lo haces, indaga y busca visiones alternativas sobre el asunto. Sin duda, te procurará informaciones que pueden llevarte a nuevos caminos y soluciones que ni siquiera imaginas.

────────────── **TUS PREGUNTAS DAFO** ──────────────

Elige una determinada cuestión o tema que te preocupe actualmente y hazte las siguientes preguntas:

1. ¿Cuáles son mis puntos débiles en esta situación? ¿Cómo puedo compensarlos?
2. ¿Qué amenazas se ciernen en el horizonte si no hago algo para evitarlo? ¿Qué es lo primero que debería hacer?
3. ¿Cuáles son mis puntos fuertes que debo potenciar a mi favor? ¿Por dónde debo empezar?
4. ¿Qué oportunidades me ofrece esta situación?

126

SINCERICIDIO

Quizá hayas oído hablar de la expresión *sincericidio* referida a una situación en la que queremos ser tan sinceros que acaba siendo un homicidio de la autoestima o del orgullo de los demás. Puede ser ofensivo darle nuestro parecer a aquella persona que no nos lo pide.

Muchas veces nos lanzamos a aportar nuestra visión sobre las decisiones o circunstancias ajenas, por el mero hecho de reafirmarnos en lo que pensamos. Sin embargo, el problema es que no se trata de nosotros, sino de otra persona con una experiencia y perspectiva sobre la vida totalmente distinta.

Si nadie te ha pedido que seas sincero, cuida cómo y a quién le das opiniones y consejos sobre su vida, porque puedes hacerle más mal que bien.

En caso de duda, acompañarás mejor con una mirada amable, un silencio o tu presencia que con palabras *omnisapientes*.

PEDIR PERMISO

Se dice que los japoneses, antes de contar un problema, piden permiso al interlocutor para enturbiar su paz mental. Podemos aplicarnos esta misma medida a la hora de meternos en la intimidad de otra persona. Antes de lanzarnos, es prudente preguntar: *¿Te gustaría que te diera mi parecer sobre lo que estás viviendo?*, o bien, *Si en algún momento quieres saber lo que pienso sobre esto, solo me lo has de pedir.*

127
DEMOS LAS GRACIAS

ontra el síndrome de pensar que todo va mal y que no hay nada de lo que alegrarse, una mirada positiva es capaz de desmontar cualquier fatalismo.

Un viajero que atravesó toda Rusia sin apenas dinero explicaba que su secreto era no tener expectativas. Si llamaba a una casa y le permitían dormir bajo el porche, lo celebraba. Si le abrían la puerta del establo, era ya una fiesta. Y si, además, le ofrecían algo de beber o de comer, se sentía bendecido por los dioses.

Todo tiene que ver con las expectativas.

El solo hecho de estar vivos, con todas las posibilidades a nuestro alcance, debería inspirarnos gratitud.

Hace dos milenios y medio, Buda lo expresaba así a los monjes que le acompañaban en su peregrinación:

Demos las gracias, porque si hoy no aprendimos mucho,
al menos aprendimos un poco,
y si no aprendimos un poco, al menos no enfermamos,
y si enfermamos, al menos no morimos,
por tanto, demos las gracias.

WORST CASE SCENARIO

Hay una estrategia que emplean los estadounidenses cuando se enfrentan a una dificultad. Se hacen la pregunta: *¿Qué es lo peor que podría pasar?* Una vez asumes el peor escenario posible, cualquier cosa que suceda por encima de ese umbral te parecerá positiva.

128
¿CON QUÉ TE IDENTIFICAS?

La actividad profesional y la personal cada vez tienen una relación más estrecha y muchos pueden elegir trabajos que los llenan, los hacen más felices y convierten las horas laborales en algo creativo y gratificante. No siempre es así, pero por fortuna en muchas ocasiones sí.

Es bien conocido el pasaje bíblico que dice: «Por sus actos los conoceréis». Y a partir de aquí planteo las preguntas: *¿Somos lo que hacemos? ¿Cómo nos aferramos a nuestra identidad profesional?*

Muchas veces asociamos identidad y ocupación. Sobre esto, la escritora afroamericana Toni Morrison explicaba en la revista *New Yorker* las conclusiones a las que llegó tras pasar por empleos que le resultaron frustrantes:

1. *Tú haces el trabajo; no es el trabajo el que te hace a ti.*
2. *Tu vida real es la que vives con tu familia.*
3. *No eres el trabajo que haces; eres la persona que eres.*

Demasiado a menudo nos aferramos a lo que hacemos y muy poco a lo que somos y sentimos. Ese apego no debería limitarte en la expansión de la consciencia de lo que eres.

—————— MODO HACER Y MODO SER ——————

En su ensayo *Mindfulness*, el doctor Mark Williams y la doctora Danny Penman resumen así lo que sucede en ambas actitudes vitales:

Modo Hacer	Modo Ser
• Automatismo	• Capacidad de elección
• Pensar, analizar	• Sentir
• Luchar, juzgar, comparar	• Aceptar, observar
• Te identificas con el pensamiento	• Te desidentificas de él
• Evitas emociones dolorosas	• Te acercas a ellas y las reconoces
• Su tiempo: el pasado y futuro	• Su tiempo: el presente
• Pérdida de energía	• Recarga de energía

129
EL CREDO DEL LOBO

Hay nueve leyes para la vida, atribuidas a los indígenas norteamericanos, que están inspiradas por los lobos. Son las que siguen:

1. *Respeta a los mayores.*
2. *Enseña a los jóvenes.*
3. *Coopera con el clan.*
4. *Juega siempre que puedas.*
5. *Caza cuando sea necesario.*
6. *Descansa entre medio.*
7. *Comparte tu afecto.*
8. *Da voz a tus sentimientos.*
9. *Deja tu huella.*

Te propongo que reflexiones sobre cada una de ellas, entendiendo de qué manera se traduce a tu vida actual. ¿De qué manera los lobos nos enseñan a vivir mejor?

—————— **LA PREGUNTA DE CLARISSA PINKOLA ESTÉS** ——————

En una de las obras más celebradas de la literatura inspiracional, la autora de *Mujeres que corren con lobos* recurre, simbólicamente, a este animal para despertar la intuición y creatividad innatas en nosotros.

Te comparto, para que trates de responderla, una de las preguntas más provocadoras que encontramos en el libro:
«¿Qué debo matar hoy para generar más vida?».

130

HAZLO POR TI

Cuando vivimos en piloto automático en lugar de escuchar nuestros propios impulsos y prioridades, acabamos haciendo las cosas de cara a la galería.

Desde pequeños, buscamos el reconocimiento de nuestros mayores, su aprobación para cerciorarnos de que lo estamos haciendo bien. El problema es cuando, de forma inconsciente, seguimos alimentando esa conducta en la vida adulta.

Para evitar ser esclavos de la aprobación ajena, debemos reafirmarnos y reforzar los pasos que damos sin darle demasiada importancia a lo que puedan decir los demás.

¿Para quién haces lo que haces? Espero y deseo que sea por ti.

Por mucho que consigas el reconocimiento externo, lo importante es que siempre camines hacia lo que de verdad te llena. Cuando haces eso, todo adquiere sentido.

--- **EJERCICIO DEL ESPEJO** ---

Ponte delante de tu reflejo y plantéate las siguientes preguntas:

1. ¿Soy sincero y consecuente con mis deseos, planes y prioridades?

2. ¿Me doy el primer lugar o vivo en función de los deseos de los demás?

3. ¿Cómo puedo ser más Yo y menos lo que mi entorno quiere que sea?

131
EL TIEMPO ES RELATIVO

E l tiempo es una mera percepción y, por ello, cada persona lo vive de manera distinta, aunque parezca que es igual para todos.

Se cuenta que una vez le pidieron a Albert Einstein que explicara de forma sencilla la relatividad del tiempo, y respondió que cuando una persona realiza una tarea que le desagrada especialmente, un minuto puede parecerle una hora, pero que, en cambio, cuando fluimos con algo que nos apasiona y nos aporta felicidad, una hora parece un minuto.

De este ejemplo deducimos que hay un tiempo cronológico y otro psicológico. Si elegimos actividades que nos hagan disfrutar, el tiempo adquiere otra calidad.

Somos el tiempo que vivimos y cómo lo vivimos.

LA PRUEBA DEL MINUTO

Para darte cuenta de lo subjetiva que es la percepción del tiempo, si tienes a mano un reloj de agujas con segundero, te propongo que sigas con la mirada una vuelta completa de la manecilla más fina. Experimentarás el minuto más largo de tu vida.

Esto te demuestra que la atención influye en la percepción y calidad del tiempo.

132

SOY SUFICIENTE

Aleja de ti la autoexigencia por un instante. Regálate la posibilidad de sentir que eres suficiente, más allá de lo que hagas o dejes de hacer. Quizá así te liberes de obstáculos que te impiden avanzar en tus relaciones y objetivos anhelados.

Tenlo claro. Afírmate con este mantra: *soy suficiente.*

Celebra lo que has hecho y no lamentes lo que no pudiste hacer.

El filósofo del siglo XIX Ralph Waldo Emerson, pionero de los libros de desarrollo personal, recomendaba: «Termina cada jornada sin remordimientos. Has hecho lo que has podido y mañana será otro día».

No seas duro contigo mismo. En lugar de enfocarte en lo que no has hecho todavía o en lo que te falta, celebra cada cosa que hayas llevado a buen fin. Eso te dará motivación para seguir avanzando.

LA FÓRMULA DE CARY GRANT

En una ocasión le preguntaron a este actor del Hollywood clásico cuál era su secreto para sentirse satisfecho con su vida. Su respuesta, que nos podemos aplicar como principio vital, fue la siguiente: «Mi fórmula para la vida es muy simple. Me levanto por la mañana y me acuesto por la noche. Entre medio, trato de ocuparme lo mejor que puedo».

133
EL PRINCIPIO DEL CAMBIO

L a posibilidad de cambiar tu vida empieza en el mismo instante en el que has decidido que lo vas a hacer.

El cómo lo vas a hacer es personal y dependerá de las herramientas que tengas en tu mano. Es, en todo caso, una aventura fascinante llena de descubrimientos y avances.

Aquello que debas o quieras hacer no lo pospongas. Hazlo ahora mismo, ya que has puesto atención en lo que te gustaría cambiar y te estás haciendo preguntas sobre ello.

Este ya es el principio del cambio. No te detengas.

Todo cambio exige una determinación y voluntad férreas. Para armarte de esa fuerza, indaga hasta llegar al motivo profundo que te mueve al cambio. Cuanto más clara tengas la razón por la que quieres cambiar, más fácil será dar el paso.

¿QUIÉN Y QUÉ SERÁS CUANDO LO LOGRES?

Esa es una buena pregunta que puedes hacerte cada vez que sientas que decae tu motivación para afrontar un cambio. Piensa en quién te convertirás y qué nueva situación tendrás cuando hayas cumplido lo que deseas alcanzar. Con ese objetivo en mente, sigue adelante.

134
EL ENFADO DEL BARQUERO

A l monje vietnamita Thích Nhất Hạnh, que falleció durante la pandemia, le gustaba explicar esta historia:

Un hombre estaba remando por un río en su bote, corriente arriba, durante una mañana muy brumosa. De repente, vio que otro bote venía corriente abajo sin intentar esquivarlo.

Avanzaba directo hacia él, así que gritó *¡Cuidado! ¡Cuidado!*, pero el bote le dio de pleno y casi le hizo naufragar.

Furioso, el hombre empezó a gritar maldiciones al otro navegante para que se enterara de lo que pensaba de él. Sin embargo, cuando observó el bote más de cerca, se dio cuenta de que estaba vacío.

El mensaje de esta fábula es que muchas veces nos enfadamos por cosas que no son culpa de nadie, son simple obra del azar. Si lo asumimos, evitaremos gritar en balde a una barca vacía.

EL CARBÓN CANDENTE DEL ENFADO

Cada vez que sientas que la furia se apodera de ti, recuerda la frase de Buda:

«Retener la ira es como asir un trozo de carbón candente con la intención de arrojarlo contra alguien; tú eres quien se va a quemar».

Para preservar tu calma y *no quemarte*, no prolongues el enfado y pasa página.

135
HÁBITOS

Para muchas personas, la sola idea de crear nuevas rutinas y hábitos se les hace cuesta arriba, les resulta un compromiso difícil de acometer. ¿Cómo romper ese bloqueo que a veces nos impide transformar nuestra vida?

Por una parte, tenemos la motivación de cómo te sentirás cuando lo hayas logrado. Ese aliciente te dará fuerzas para seguir adelante, porque esos nuevos hábitos son los que te llevarán a una vida nueva y libre.

Por otra parte, sustituir unos hábitos por otros es una cuestión de prioridades. Al igual que al llenar tu cesta de la compra dejas fuera los alimentos tentadores pero que no te convienen, mantén lejos aquellos hábitos que no te llevan a ningún sitio. Aquellos que solo logran desestabilizarte y te alejan de lo que quieres ser y conseguir.

UN DIARIO DE HÁBITOS

1. Hazte con un cuaderno exclusivo para tu trabajo con los hábitos que quieres depurar.
2. En todas las páginas, en la parte izquierda, anota los hábitos negativos de los que te quieres desprender y tus avances en ese sentido.
3. En las de la derecha, escribe aquellos nuevos hábitos que quieres incorporar.
4. No quieras cambiarlo todo simultáneamente. Céntrate en un solo tema y no pases al siguiente hasta que no hayas consolidado dicho cambio.

136
TIENES TALENTO

Todos tenemos algún talento. Lo que ocurre es que podemos no ser conscientes de él, tenerlo escondido bajo el miedo, las dudas y los juicios externos e internos.

Sir Ken Robinson decía que es absurdo enseñar a todos los niños por igual, en una educación uniformada, sin preocuparnos antes por averiguar cuál es la capacidad especial de cada pequeño.

¿Cómo desentrañar, aunque sea de adultos, esos dones que te mostrarán el camino original de quién eres?

Según Robinson, un camino es la prueba y error de la ciencia: «Si no estás preparado para equivocarte, jamás llegarás a nada original».

Atreviéndote a probar distintos caminos, llegarás a descubrir tu talento especial, aquello que siempre quisiste ser.

NUNCA ES TARDE

Puede que no hayas desarrollado todavía tu genialidad porque alguien te convenció de que lo que querías hacer era solamente un sueño inalcanzable. Tú se lo compraste, casi convencido. Te lo hizo creer así, porque en el fondo, esa persona también tenía sus propios miedos, dudas y juicios.

¿Y si te das una nueva oportunidad?

Como afirmaba la novelista George Eliot: «Nunca es tarde para ser lo que deberías haber sido».

137
LA CATEDRAL

Hay una historia que se cuenta sobre la construcción de la catedral de Londres que me parece muy significativa porque habla de la fuerza del propósito.

Su arquitecto, Christopher Wren, decidió visitar de incógnito la cantera para observar a los picapedreros. Se fijó en tres de ellos. Uno trabajaba de forma deficiente, el otro con corrección y el tercero con una fuerza y pasión extraordinarias. Intrigado, se aproximó al primero y le preguntó:

–Buenos días, ¿a qué se dedica usted?

–¿Es que no lo ve? Trabajo de sol a sol picando piedra. ¡No veo la hora de terminar!

El arquitecto repitió entonces su pregunta al segundo, que contestó:

–Me gano un salario honradamente para mantener a mi esposa y mis hijos. Lo hago lo mejor que puedo.

Finalmente, se dirigió al tercero:

–Buenos días, ¿a qué se dedica usted?

El picapedrero levantó la cabeza y, lleno de orgullo, le dijo:

–Estoy construyendo la catedral de Londres, caballero.

QUÉ, CÓMO Y POR QUÉ

El conferenciante Simon Sinek dice que hay tres niveles de excelencia en aquello que hacemos:
1. Hay personas que saben QUÉ hacen. Es el nivel más bajo.
2. Otras saben CÓMO lo hacen. Es un escalón intermedio.
3. La excelencia pertenece a aquellas que saben POR QUÉ lo hacen.
   Cada vez que hagas algo realmente importante, pregúntate en cuál de los tres niveles estás operando.

138

LET IT BE

E n la escuela nos enseñan a adquirir conocimientos, a aprobar exámenes y a establecer relaciones con los demás, pero también deberían enseñarnos a perder, a dejar ir.

A medida que avanzamos en la vida, nos damos cuenta de que hay personas a nuestro alrededor que no son las más adecuadas para vivir en calma. Bien sea porque nos alteran en nuestro día a día o porque necesitan seguir su camino para crecer.

A veces debemos dejar ir a alguien que amamos, alejarnos de esa persona, aun sabiendo que la echaremos de menos. Será bueno para ambas partes. Y más si, además, expresamos con cariño el deseo de dejar ir.

Paul McCartney escribió *Let it be* tras soñar con su madre, que le aconsejó que *dejara ir* aquello que, tras años de felicidad, le estaba pesando a él y a sus compañeros. Sería el fin de The Beatles.

TRES PASOS PARA CERRAR

Si sientes que tienes que dejar ir una pareja, un amigo o un proyecto compartido, puedes hacerlo de forma bella y saludable, aunque al principio no seas comprendido:

1. Explica con serenidad las razones por las que no deseas seguir.

2. Agradece todo lo que habéis vivido y aprendido juntos.

3. Desea de corazón una feliz andadura a la otra parte en aquello que emprenda.

139
AUTOLIDERAZGO

M e gusta decir que un líder es generoso cuando comparte sus conocimientos e inquietudes e influye en quienes le rodean a través de la empatía y el entusiasmo.

Esto no es exclusivo del mundo de la empresa. Todos hemos tenido a algún profesor o profesora que nos contagió de este modo el amor por su asignatura.

Sin embargo, el liderazgo no termina ahí. Puedes aplicarlo a tu propia vida. Practicar el autoliderazgo significa ser generoso, empático y entusiasta contigo mismo. De este modo, podrás vivir lleno de inspiración.

Trátate a ti mismo como lo que eres: el maestro y guía de tu propia vida.

Quien no sabe liderarse a sí mismo tampoco podrá hacerlo con los demás. Por consiguiente, empieza tomando el mando de tu propia vida.

EL LIDERAZGO SEGÚN JACINDA ARDERN ───

La neozelandesa que, con 37 años, se convirtió en la primera ministra más joven de la historia fue calificada por la prensa internacional como la *líder más eficaz del mundo*. Esta es su definición de liderazgo:

Para mí, el liderazgo no se trata necesariamente de ser el más ruidoso en la sala, sino de ser el puente, o lo que falta en la discusión y tratar de construir un consenso a partir de ahí.

140

MADUREZ

El profesor Juan José Zacarés, cuyo doctorado versó sobre la madurez psicológica, expone que el verdadero sentido del crecimiento es la transformación en lo que cada cual realmente es.

Eso implica el desarrollo de nuestras potencialidades, de todo aquello que nos hace únicos e irrepetibles. En sus palabras:

> *La madurez como plenitud de la existencia no es una etapa o fase más del desarrollo, sino una conquista individual. Todos los individuos alcanzan la edad adulta, pero no todos consiguen la madurez personal.*

Alcanzar esa madurez implica actuar desde la libertad y la responsabilidad, tomando conciencia de los resultados de nuestras decisiones.

Asimismo, una persona madura no depende de la aprobación de los demás y sabe mantener la calma en medio de las tempestades.

LAS CINCO CLAVES DE LA MADUREZ

Para evaluar el grado de madurez de una persona, empezando por uno mismo, según un estudio publicado en la revista *Annals of Psychology* deben darse estas cinco cualidades:

1. *Realismo.* Ser capaz de mirar de frente los acontecimientos sin dejarse llevar por interpretaciones.
2. *Equilibrio.* Las emociones no suben y bajan como una montaña rusa.
3. *Naturalidad.* Mostrarse como se es, no pretender aparentar otra cosa.
4. *Entusiasmo.* Facilidad para motivarse ante un proyecto.
5. *Capacidad de adaptación.* Ser flexible y saber improvisar.

141
EL PASADO PRESENTE

Eres de los que se anclan al pasado o, por el contrario, tiendes a enfocarte en el futuro? En este segundo caso, tu energía mental se proyecta en lo que te gustaría crear. Pones mucho foco en un porvenir prometedor. Sin embargo, ¿estás seguro de haber soltado el pasado?

Tal vez haces planes basándote en un conocimiento viejo, a partir de resultados que ya obtuviste. En ese caso, debo decirte que quizá no has soltado el pasado del todo.

Recuerda: el futuro nunca llega si el pasado está presente.

Para proyectarte hacia el futuro, desde el aquí y ahora, libre de cargas y expectativas, imagina que tu vida es una hoja en blanco, el primer capítulo de un nuevo libro.

Haz limpieza de todo aquello que ha sido para ti un impedimento para avanzar. A fin de cuentas, el futuro se construye desde el presente coincidiendo todo finalmente en uno, con cada pequeña acción, palabra y pensamiento.

HAZLO SMART

En un modelo iniciado en la década de 1980 por George T. Doran, la palabra que en castellano traducimos como *listo* o *inteligente* sirve para definir las cinco características de los planes que funcionan:

ESPECÍFICO (en inglés, *specific*). Es decir, lo más concreto posible.

MEDIBLE. Nuestro progreso hacia ese objetivo ha de ser cuantificable.

ALCANZABLE. Entendido como realista y asumible.

RELEVANTE. Ha de ser motivador, empoderador, que resulte importante e incluso retador.

TEMPORALIZADO. Ha de tener fecha de inicio y de finalización.

142
APUNTA A TI MISMO

Para los que nos empeñamos en la imposible tarea de cambiar a los demás, hay un libro zen que da una importante pista sobre dónde debemos poner el foco de la excelencia.

Se llama *Zen en el arte del tiro con arco* y su autor, el alemán Eugen Herrigel, publicó en 1948 las principales lecciones aprendidas como discípulo de un gran maestro de *kyudo*, como se llama esta disciplina en Japón.

Esta es una conclusión a la que llega el autor, que vivió varios años en el país nipón:

> *El arquero se apunta a sí mismo y se dispara a sí mismo, y así llega de forma simultánea el arquero y la diana, el golpeador y el golpe (...) Entonces sucede el milagro supremo y definitivo; el arte carece de arte, disparar es no disparar, disparar sin arco ni flecha; el profesor vuelve a ser aprendiz, el maestro un principiante, el final un principio y el principio perfección.*

Con ello indicaba que la verdadera *diana* a la que hay que apuntar, si quieres un mundo mejor, es a uno mismo.

¿CUÁL ES TU DIANA PARTICULAR?

De todos los ámbitos de tu vida —economía, familia, cuidado personal, carrera, espiritualidad...—, determina cuál tienes más desatendido. Dirige tu arco, a través de las flechas de los hábitos, hacia el centro de esa área en la que quieres mejorar.

143
ELIGE LO MÁS DIFÍCIL

En momentos de cambio, tendrás que tomar decisiones complicadas. Son momentos en los que lo que hagas determinará tu nuevo rumbo vital.

Por este motivo, si inicias una nueva andadura, si vas a crear otra vida, de todas las opciones que has diseñado, elige primero la más difícil de llevar a cabo. Solo así te acostumbrarás a superarte y tus límites ampliarán cada vez más su margen.

Hay un dicho atribuido al cuerpo de ingenieros de Estados Unidos que reza: «Lo difícil lo hacemos de inmediato, lo imposible llevará un poco más de tiempo».

Me parece un lema espléndido para los momentos de gran exigencia que nos brinda la vida, ya que sitúa lo *difícil* en el ámbito de la normalidad, y lo *imposible* en el de lo posible con un poco más de tiempo y experiencia.

DESMONTA LA DIFICULTAD

Como si sentaras al reto al que te enfrentas ahora en el diván, puedes interrogarlo de la siguiente manera:
1. ¿Quién ha decidido que esto es *difícil*?
2. ¿Es difícil para cualquier persona o solo es difícil para mí?
3. ¿De qué manera actuaría una persona para quien no es difícil?
4. ¿Qué necesito para actuar del mismo modo y hacer fácil lo difícil?

144

UNA MIRADA AMPLIA

Conjugar el mundo en primera persona del singular tiene algo de perverso. Siento ser así de directa. A estas alturas de la vida, ¿vas a permitir que tu mente aplique una sola mirada a tu alrededor? Mirar la realidad desde una sola perspectiva es como escuchar en *mono* una sinfonía que tiene múltiples matices y texturas.

En el fondo, todos sabemos que el juego va de otra cosa. Va de observar, entender, integrar y evolucionar con el aprendizaje. Va de hacerle la 13-14 a tu mente para responderle que tú eres algo más que tus circunstancias, que tienes capacidad de elección y una mirada amplia sobre todas las percepciones posibles.

PONTE EN SUS ZAPATOS

Según Ken Wilber, escritor y pionero de la psicología transpersonal, «la persona más evolucionada es aquella que es capaz de ponerse en los zapatos de todo tipo de personas».

Cada vez que te sientas irritado o decepcionado con alguien, trasládate a su historia personal y a su situación. Eso te permitirá comprender por qué piensa, habla y actúa como lo hace.

145
EL DON DE INSPIRAR

T ienes el don de influir en todo lo que te rodea. En más personas de las que te imaginas. Tienes la capacidad de expandir tus talentos e inspirar a los demás.

Sin embargo, para compartir todo esto que te ha sido dado, primero has de saber conectar de manera inteligente con los otros. En su clásico *Cómo ganar amigos e influir sobre las personas*, que se viene reeditando desde 1936, Dale Carnegie nos da algunas recomendaciones:

- En las relaciones, se logran mejores resultados elogiando de forma inteligente que censurando.
- Si quieres corregir a alguien, hazlo contigo mismo.
- Dejar hablar a tu interlocutor e interesarte por sus problemas es la llave a su corazón.
- Se hacen más amigos interesándote por la otra gente que intentando que la gente se interese por ti.

EVITA CRITICAR

Una regla de oro en el método Carnegie es no censurar nunca a los demás, ya que solo se consigue que la otra persona se ponga a la defensiva y se justifique, albergando además resentimiento. Según sus palabras: «Cualquier tonto es capaz de criticar, condenar y quejarse. Y la mayoría lo hacen».

146
ENERGÍA QUE SE TRANSFORMA

Sea lo que sea que estés sintiendo, date cuenta de que es temporal. Este es el momento para empezar a soltarlo. Puedes dejar ir, y al hacerlo te vas a sentir mejor.

Las emociones son una energía que se transforma y les debes dar la bienvenida. Si las arrojas fuera del escenario de tu vida, ignorándolas, volverán para que les *eches cuentas,* cual vecino quejoso que necesita ser escuchado.

Atiéndelas y recuerda que mandas tú.

Sea lo que sea lo que te duele en este instante, se irá. Sonríe, ¡tú, a lo tuyo! y sigue adelante. Como decía Marilyn Monroe en unas bellas notas personales: «Mantén tu cabeza en alto y, lo más importante, mantén la sonrisa, porque la vida es hermosa y hay mucho por lo que sonreír».

DOCE MÚSCULOS MILAGROSOS

Cada vez que sonreímos movemos doce músculos que activan una verdadera alquimia en el estado de ánimo. Según diferentes estudios realizados, al sonreír se reduce el estrés y el dolor, promovemos la confianza y aumentamos incluso nuestra propia respuesta inmunitaria.

Por lo tanto, ¡sonríe por favor!

147
¿CUÁL ES EL SECRETO DE LA FELICIDAD?

Esta es la pregunta que se hace el protagonista de *El viaje de Héctor*, una novela escrita por François Lelord en la que un joven psicoterapeuta se propone descubrir por qué sus pacientes no logran ser dichosos.

Con este fin, empieza a viajar y a hablar con todo tipo de personas que parecen vivir con alegría. Así es como descubre que la felicidad, entre otras cosas, es...

- algo que muchas veces llega por sorpresa
- una caminata por montañas desconocidas
- estar junto a las personas queridas
- tener un trabajo que te guste
- sencillamente: pasártelo bien
- una manera de ver las cosas
- hacer felices a los demás

Tal vez esta última clave sea la más importante, y además todos podemos llevarla a cabo de diferentes maneras.

UNA PERSONA AL DÍA

Si hacer felices a los demás nos procura felicidad, te propongo que cada día busques de forma consciente una ocasión para hacer feliz a alguien. Tienes mil maneras a tu alcance, te pongo cuatro ejemplos:
- Escuchar y animar a alguien que está pasando por un mal momento.
- Regalar un libro a quien necesita inspiración.
- Hacer reír a tu entorno con una historia graciosa.
- Expresar a una persona cercana lo que te encanta de ella y lo importante que es para ti.

148

TU CAPACIDAD DE PENSAR

M i admirado Sergi Torres nos invita a acoger esta idea por un instante: «Tu capacidad de pensar es infinitamente mayor de lo que piensas».

Y añade: «El ser humano desconoce su capacidad de pensar porque está atrapado en su forma de pensar. Tu capacidad de pensar es distinta a tus pensamientos».

Una cosa es aquello que somos, otra lo que podemos ser, y lo mismo sucede en la esfera del pensamiento. Que hasta ahora hayamos funcionado de determinada manera no significa que no podamos hacerlo de otra.

Podemos actuar de forma más brillante y profunda.

Solo me queda añadir *Amén* y seguir mi existencia aplicando la mayor consciencia.

─────── **LAS TRES PREGUNTAS DE SERGI TORRES** ───────

En su libro *Saltar al vacío*, este joven maestro dice que «aparentamos saber mucho de la vida, pero no pasamos ni las tres primeras preguntas del test». Son estas:
1. ¿Quién eres?

2. ¿Por qué estás vivo en este mundo?
3. ¿Cuál es tu función dentro de la vida?

Haz el ejercicio de contestarlas para expandir tu pensamiento.

149
ENTRAR EN ZONA

Hay un estado óptimo a la hora de ejecutar cualquier tarea, en el que todo parece fluir de manera impecable. Todo sale rodado. No quieres detenerte porque te das cuenta de lo bien que avanza justo en ese momento.

Yo lo llamo *entrar en zona*.

Me gusta identificarla, aprovecharla y, si puedo, anclarme a ese instante, integrando las sensaciones que me llegan, tanto en lo físico como en mi mente.

Intento averiguar qué ha podido suceder. ¿Qué acontecimientos se han dado para haber entrado en esa zona tan productiva?

Te animo a que descubras tú también qué te hace *entrar en zona*, qué necesitas para lograr ese grado óptimo de concentración y fluidez en lo que haces.

PON TODA TU ATENCIÓN

Según Mihály Csíkszentmihályi, el autor de *Flow* de quien ya hemos hablado, «es imposible disfrutar de un partido de tenis, de un libro o de una conversación, a menos que la atención esté totalmente concentrada en la actividad».

Esta es también una de las claves para *entrar en zona*. Por lo tanto, aparta cualquier distracción (pon el teléfono en modo *no molestar)* cuando vayas a hacer algo valioso para ti.

150
EL PROPÓSITO DE LA VIDA

Últimamente se habla mucho de la importancia de encontrar el propósito vital. Tal vez por eso, quienes no terminan de encontrarlo se frustran y sienten no estar del todo realizados.

Para lograrlo, podemos avanzar desde lo pequeño hasta lo grande, dar al instante presente la posibilidad de que nos inspire desde la cotidianidad más sencilla. El propósito de la vida empieza, muchas veces, con pequeñas cosas que podemos hacer todos los días.

En lugar de agobiarte pensando en horizontes inalcanzables, deja que lo cercano sea el punto de partida.

Vivir es, ya de por sí, una gran motivación. Es expandirse y sorprenderse cada día. Por lo tanto, entiende que el propósito ya te ha sido dado, aunque tú quizá lo estés buscando.

Tal vez si dejas de buscarlo lo encuentres en las cosas más sencillas. Deja que el propósito te tome la mano y, mientras tanto, acércate a lo que más te inspire.

CINCO VÍAS PARA DESCUBRIR TU *IKIGAI*

Francesc Miralles y Héctor García, coautores del best seller *Ikigai*, proponen diferentes caminos para encontrar el propósito vital:
1. Haz un ranking de las actividades que te producen *flow*. La que esté más arriba puede ser tu *ikigai*.
2. Determina cuál es tu elemento, la actividad o situación en la que das lo mejor de ti mismo.
3. Escribe todas las cosas que detestas hacer. ¿Qué tienen en común? Vete al opuesto. A través de lo que no te gusta se llega a lo que te gusta.
4. Recuerda quién eras y qué soñabas en la infancia, ya que los niños están naturalmente unidos a su *ikigai*.
5. Practica el *prueba y error* de la ciencia. Ábrete al máximo de experiencias y conoce a personas nuevas.

151
RECUPERAR LOS SUEÑOS
DE INFANCIA

E n una de las charlas más emocionantes e inspiradoras de los últimos tiempos junto a la de Steve Jobs en Stanford, el profesor de realidad virtual Randy Pausch se dirigió a los estudiantes de la Universidad Carnegie Mellon para ofrecerles una última lección.

Tras explicar que padecía un cáncer terminal, su conferencia trató sobre cómo hacer realidad los sueños de la infancia, a lo que Pausch dedicó los últimos meses de su vida. En sus palabras:

La primera vez que hice una lista con mis sueños tenía solo ocho años. Treinta años después, esta lista me continúa sirviendo para muchos propósitos. Y sé cuál es el truco: no se trata de saber cómo hacer realidad tus sueños, sino de vivir tu propia vida. Si diriges tu existencia en la dirección adecuada no tendrás que perseguir nada, porque los sueños vendrán hacia ti.

RESCATA UN SUEÑO INFANTIL

Siguiendo el emotivo ejemplo del autor de *La última lección,* como se tituló el libro sobre su charla, te propongo que hagas una lista de los sueños que tenías en tu infancia. Elige al menos uno, el que te parezca más motivador, para cumplirlo en este momento de tu vida.

152
LA TERAPIA DE LOS ARMARIOS

L lamo así al hecho de organizar mis armarios, porque cuando ordeno, planifico, decido, priorizo, cribo, retiro, aparto, ordeno, limpio
y reubico siento que lo hago también con mi vida. Como dos vasos
comunicantes, el orden exterior propicia el interior.

Ya mencioné a Marie Kondo en otra parte del libro al hablar de orden y concierto, pero con la terapia de los armarios vamos a bajarlo a la
práctica.

Sé que es algo muy personal, pero, poniendo las cosas en su sitio, re-
tirando lo que ya no uso, logro apreciar lo que atesoro. Doy a cada cosa la
importancia que tiene y, en muchas ocasiones, esta actividad me permite
hacer sitio para cosas venideras.

Sin miedo, atrévete a darle sentido a esas perchas, cajones y estante-
rías en todos los aspectos de tu vida. Sé la Marie Kondo de tu propia vida.

EL MÉTODO DAVE PARA LIBERAR ESPACIO

En su libro *Simplifica tu vida*, Elaine St. James comparte este truco para dejar de acumular y crear nuevos espacios:

Nuestro amigo Dave avala la utilidad de este método para deshacerse de cosas que ya no necesita, pero que no soporta tirar. Guárdelas con una etiqueta que indique una fecha a dos o tres años vista, pero no apunte su contenido. Guarde la caja en el altillo, o en el sótano, o donde usted crea conveniente. Una vez al año examine las etiquetas. Cuando llegue a una caja cuya fecha se ha sobrepasado, tírela sin abrirla. Como no sabe qué hay dentro, nunca lo echará en falta.

153
HASTA QUE LA MUERTE NOS SEPARE

L as obras románticas clásicas hablan del amor eterno entre dos seres humanos. Pero ¿qué hay del amor que te debes a ti mismo? Oscar Wilde decía que «amarse a uno mismo es el comienzo de una aventura que dura toda la vida». De hecho, sin esta clase de amor tampoco pueden existir relaciones sanas con los demás.

Hablemos, por lo tanto, de amarte para toda la vida, del trato que has hecho con tu propio ser.

En el juego de la vida, esta es una regla fundamental: Si vas a vivir contigo (con tu cuerpo, tu mente y tu espíritu) hasta que la muerte os separe, en la salud y en la enfermedad, cual historia de amor inquebrantable, ¿prometes cuidarte y amarte para siempre?

TRES CUIDADOS PARA LA AUTOESTIMA

Para cumplir con este propósito, es bueno que cada cierto tiempo hagamos un chequeo de cómo estamos tratando nuestras tres dimensiones como ser humano:

1. CUERPO. ¿Me estoy nutriendo de forma sana y consciente? ¿Ejercito mi cuerpo y le doy el descanso que merece?

2. MENTE. ¿Mantengo lubricado el músculo de la curiosidad? ¿Me doy tiempo y espacio para aprender cosas nuevas?

3. ESPÍRITU. ¿Busco espacios para cultivar el silencio y la conexión con la naturaleza, con el universo?

154
ENVEJECER Y CRECER

En uno de los muchos textos que nos legó Osho hacía la siguiente reflexión:

Cualquier animal es capaz de envejecer; crecer es la prerrogativa de los seres humanos (...) Crecer significa sumergirse en cada momento más profundamente hacia el principio de la vida.

Sin duda, uno de los privilegios de envejecer es que adquirimos una mirada más sabia sobre la vida y sobre nosotros mismos. Este controvertido maestro y a la vez brillante escritor hindú lo explica con gran belleza:

Para crecer simplemente observa un árbol. A medida que el árbol crece hacia arriba, sus raíces se estiran hacia abajo, más hondo. Hay un equilibrio. Cuanto más se eleva el árbol, más profundo penetran las raíces. No puedes tener un árbol de cuarenta y cinco metros de altura con raíces pequeñas, no podrían sostener a un árbol tan enorme. En la vida, «crecer» significa crecer en profundidad dentro de ti; es allí donde están tus raíces.

———— LOS REGALOS DE LA MADUREZ ————

Para darte cuenta de cómo estás creciendo por dentro, puedes plantearte las siguientes preguntas:
1. ¿Qué cosas temías o te preocupaban de más joven y ahora no te inquietan?

2. ¿Cuáles eran tus prioridades entonces y cuáles tienes ahora?
3. ¿Qué es lo más importante que has aprendido con la madurez?

155

LA SABIDURÍA DE ACOMPAÑAR

Ciertamente, debes buscar tu propio camino y entenderte. Estar contigo a solas y crecer en esa consciencia. Pero ¿qué más espera de ti el mundo?

La sabiduría es la intersección entre lo que tú esperas de la vida y lo que la vida espera de ti.

Probablemente ya llevas un largo camino recorrido y comprendes que esto no va solo de sentirte bien y *encontrarte*. Va también de acompañar a otros para entender su camino y, de paso, de sentirte útil, de entender el tuyo.

Un maestro zen decía que retirarse del mundo, vivir en lo alto de un monte como ermitaño, es mucho más fácil que mezclarse con la gente en la ciudad. Tu nivel de consciencia lo marca cómo son tus relaciones, tu comprensión y capacidad de ayuda, ya que los demás son un espejo de quién eres hoy.

TU CÍRCULO ÍNTIMO

El experto en comunicación Ferran Ramon-Cortés propone el siguiente filtro para saber qué personas forman parte de tu entorno más íntimo y cuáles son amistades o relaciones para otro tipo de situaciones.

Según el autor de *La isla de los 5 faros*, tu círculo íntimo lo forman las personas que invitarías a comer en la cocina de tu casa.

¿Cuántas amistades de esta calidad tienes ahora?

156
EL SENTIDO DE LA VIDA

S i hay un autor en el siglo XX que habló en profundidad sobre el sentido de la vida fue Viktor Frankl.

Tras perder a casi toda su familia en el Holocausto, dio nacimiento a la logoterapia, convencido del poder sanador de encontrarle un sentido a la existencia. Tal y como escribió él mismo en 1942 en el campo de concentración de Theresienstadt:

> *No hay nada en el mundo que capacite tanto a una persona para sobreponerse a las dificultades externas y a las limitaciones internas como la consciencia de tener una tarea en la vida.*

Tal vez por eso la pregunta más importante que podemos hacernos es: ¿Cuál es mi tarea en la vida?

Frankl afirmaba que «el éxito, como la felicidad, es el efecto secundario inesperado de la dedicación personal a una causa mayor que uno mismo».

El autor de *El hombre en busca de sentido* encontró el significado de su vida en ayudar a otros a encontrar significado a la suya. ¿Qué da sentido a tu existencia en este punto de tu vida?

COMO SI VIVIERAS POR SEGUNDA VEZ

Para desarrollar la propia responsabilidad y coraje, Viktor Frankl aconsejaba lo siguiente: «Actúa como si vivieras por segunda vez y la primera lo hubieras hecho tan desacertadamente como estás a punto de hacerlo ahora».

¿Cómo quieres que sea esta nueva vida que te dispones a empezar?

157
NÓMADA

Hay épocas en las que sentimos que nuestra existencia está estancada, como si la energía no se moviera y, no sabemos por qué motivo, *no suceden cosas.*

Un error común es pensar que el mundo vendrá a nuestro encuentro, que las cosas sucederán mientras permanecemos sentados en el sofá. No es así como funciona la dinámica de la transformación. La energía fluye con el movimiento. Hazte un poco nómada para permitir los cambios que anhelas y que no sabes exactamente de dónde deberían venir.

Con ser nómada no me refiero a que debas dejar tu casa, tu ciudad, tu trabajo, para llevar una vida bohemia e itinerante. Se trata solo de abrir la mente a otras posibilidades, de moverte en nuevas direcciones para aportar frescura y espontaneidad a tu día a día.

IDEAS PARA AÑADIR NOMADISMO A TU VIDA

1. Evita hacer las cosas siempre de la misma manera. Cambia la ruta para ir al trabajo o para visitar a tu familia y amigos.
2. Deja entrar a gente nueva a tu vida que te aporte visiones distintas.
3. Descubre nuevos libros y películas, acude a exposiciones y conferencias. Incluso sin moverte del lugar donde vives, la vida puede convertirse en una aventura.

158

UNA ESTRELLA INTERIOR

L a filósofa y escritora Ayn Rand, nacida en San Petersburgo y nacionalizada estadounidense en 1931, nos dejó a mediados del siglo pasado poderosas inspiraciones sobre el arte de vivir.

Quiero compartir esta reflexión suya sobre el destino de cada cual y la búsqueda de la felicidad:

Cualquiera que sea el camino que yo tome, la estrella que me guía está en mi interior; la estrella que me guía y la brújula que señala el camino. Señalan en una única dirección. Señalan hacía mí.

No sé si esta tierra en la que estoy es el corazón del universo o si no es más que una mota de polvo perdida en la eternidad. Ni lo sé ni me importa. Pues sé qué felicidad puedo alcanzar en esta tierra (...) Mi felicidad no es el medio para fin alguno. Ella es el fin. Es su propio objetivo. Es su propia razón de ser.

HAZ BRILLAR TU ESTRELLA INTERIOR

Para poder seguir esa estrella interior que guía y que señala el camino, debes limpiarla de todo lo que le resta resplandor:

1. Ideas limitantes sobre lo que *no puede ser* o lo que *debe ser* tu vida.
2. Opiniones y expectativas ajenas.
3. Miedos irracionales.
4. Pronósticos sobre lo que va a suceder antes incluso de haberlo vivido.
5. Otras estrategias (muchas veces inconscientes) de autoboicot.

159
GRADOS DE INDEPENDENCIA EMOCIONAL

S er feliz por ti mismo no significa dejar de lado a las personas de tu entorno. Significa relacionarte con los demás desde tu autonomía y poder personal. Es tomar conciencia de tu propia grandeza, independientemente de lo que suceda ahí fuera.

Según el maestro en psicología transpersonal José María Doria, hay cinco grados de dependencia emocional respecto a una pareja:

Dependencia pura. Cuando no somos correspondidos por la otra persona, lo cual crea un anclaje enfermizo.

Co-dependencia. Dos personas que dependen entre sí con todos sus controles, celos y reproches.

Independencia. Se da en relaciones basadas en la autonomía emocional, con intimidad, pero sin apegos excluyentes.

Co-independencia. Un nivel por encima, se produce entre personas totalmente independientes que comparten su amor.

Inter-independencia. Supera el ámbito de la pareja, ya que hay relaciones de afecto y cooperación a cada instante, incluso con quienes no conocemos íntimamente.

───────── **PEQUEÑO TEST DE DEPENDENCIA EMOCIONAL** ─────────

1. ¿Necesitas que él o ella te confirme su amor a menudo para tener la seguridad de que está contigo?
2. ¿Vigilas el tipo de relaciones que establece con los demás?
3. ¿Te preguntas a menudo qué estará haciendo cuando no os encontráis juntos?

4. ¿Sientes a menudo celos o la frustración de no ser lo más importante de su vida?

Si has respondido *sí* a una o más preguntas, debes examinar tu dependencia emocional y buscar algunas maneras de liberarte de ella.

160
PUNTOS DE VISTA

Es curioso. No sé si a ti te pasa, pero algunas personas me dicen que pongo distancia o que puedo incluso resultar fría. Me lo suelen comentar ante mi sorpresa.

En realidad, no es así exactamente. Simplemente, soy muy respetuosa y prudente en los primeros contactos.

Tampoco están en lo cierto quienes me dicen que soy muy cariñosa y afable siempre con todos. Tan solo estoy atenta a lo que me rodea y doy lo que intuyo que se necesita de mí.

Si te ofreces al mundo con lo mejor que puedes dar, más allá de cómo te perciban los demás, seguro que estás en el camino acertado, con independencia de la imagen que te digan que proyectas, porque, además, nunca será la misma para todos.

DECIR Y HACER

Tal como concluye Álex Rovira en una de sus obras, en el territorio del amor hay personas que dicen y no hacen, con lo cual las suyas son palabras vanas; otras hacen, pero no dicen, tienen problemas a la hora de expresar su amor. El grado más saludable de integración sería *decir y hacer* de una manera honesta en nuestras relaciones con los demás.

161
ESTAR PRESENTE

M e lo recuerdo cada día y quiero compartirlo contigo. Quizá sea la clave de casi todo lo que tiene que ver con el arte de ser feliz: *la vida es lo que está sucediendo aquí y ahora. En el presente.*

Levanta la mirada por un instante y observa alrededor de ti. Después cierra los ojos y respira profundo.

Otra vez.

Es esto. Es ahora.

Demasiadas cosas suceden y se nos escapan mirando atrás o hacia adelante, más allá en el horizonte.

Cuando vives aquí y ahora, tiempo y espacio convergen en una línea vertical imaginaria que te atraviesa de arriba abajo para que te dejes ser y sentir.

—————— **EJERCICIO DE ESCRITURA EN EL AQUÍ Y AHORA** ——————

John Cheever, maestro norteamericano de los cuentos, proponía a sus alumnos un ejercicio que nunca falla para escapar de la dispersión que nos produce proyectarnos al pasado o al futuro.

En su taller de escritura proponía lo siguiente: *Escribe una carta de amor desde un edificio en llamas.*

¿Te atreves a ponerte en situación y escribir esa carta, aquí y ahora, a la persona o personas que más quieres?

162

ENCONTRAR Y BUSCAR

Con la novela *Siddhartha*, el premio Nobel de Literatura Hermann Hesse divulgó en todo el mundo el orientalismo.

Su protagonista, que tiene el mismo nombre de pila que quien devendría Buda, sale de viaje para encontrar la sabiduría, algo que resulta ser más difícil de lo que cree, como vemos en este fragmento:

Cuando alguien busca —dijo Siddhartha—, suele ocurrir fácilmente que sus ojos solo ven la cosa que anda buscando; este alguien no puede encontrar nada, no deja entrar nada dentro de él, porque siempre está pensando en la cosa buscada, porque tiene un fin, porque está poseído por este fin. Buscar significa tener un fin. Pero encontrar quiere decir ser libre, estar abierto a todo, no tener fin.

DÉJATE SORPRENDER

Siguiendo esta reflexión de *Siddhartha*, de vez en cuando suspende el modo *buscar* para poder verdaderamente *encontrar*. Un par de ejemplos:

- Si estás en un restaurante nuevo, en lugar de buscar en la carta aquello que puede gustarte, deja que el camarero te sorprenda con su plato favorito.
- De vez en cuando, pide a un amigo en el que confíes que te recomiende qué deberías leer o ver en televisión. Aparta el juicio y deja que las sorpresas te encuentren.

163

UN REGALO DEL PASADO

A veces, un instante se convierte en un regalo. El recuerdo de lo vivido contiene un universo de sensaciones y aprendizajes que regresan como un bálsamo.

Ese momento felizmente no se ha perdido. Quedó en el bolsillo, cual piedra bella que recogiste en la orilla y que, al secarse, dejó de interesarte.

Pero está de vuelta para que recuerdes esa playa, aquel *tú* que vio belleza en ese trozo minúsculo de mar y quiso atesorarlo en el bolsillo.

Aquí está de nuevo en tu mano, pidiendo que la mojes en la ola del presente para enriquecer el ser humano en el que te has convertido hoy.

Lo dicho: un regalo lleno de sentimiento que te hace sonreír sin decir nada más.

TU MAGDALENA DE PROUST

La monumental obra del escritor francés, *En busca del tiempo perdido,* se despliega a partir del recuerdo que le despierta al narrador tomar un poco de té con una magdalena que le da su madre.

¿Qué olores, sabores o lugares tienen en ti el poder de recuperar tesoros del pasado?

Utilízalos para gozar de estos regalos memorables que son una reserva de felicidad.

164

BOOMERANG

Una de las frases más lúcidas de Carl Gustav Jung es: «Lo que aceptas, te transforma; lo que niegas, te somete». Durante toda su carrera, el médico y psicólogo suizo insistió en integrar la sombra, hacer nuestra aquella parte que no queremos ver.

Aquella parte de ti que rechazas vuelve a ti una y otra vez, te recuerda que hay asuntos que están pendientes de solucionar. Mientras no lo afrontes, volverá cual *boomerang*.

Esa parte de ti no dejará de llamar a tu puerta hasta que le prestes la atención que reclama, la comprendas y le des la bienvenida. Una vez entendido el porqué de su visita podrás agradecer el aprendizaje que te brinda.

Hecho esto, por fin puedes dejarla ir para siempre.

HAZ AMISTAD CON TU SOMBRA

Según C. G. Jung, la sombra es la parte de nuestra personalidad que está oculta o reprimida. No aceptamos que forma parte de nosotros, ya que queremos vernos como seres siempre buenos y nobles.

Dos claves para hacer las paces con tu sombra:

1. Cuando sientas emociones de las que no te sientas orgulloso —rabia, odio, deseos inconfesables—, en lugar de rechazarlas, acógelas para entender cuál es su raíz. Siéntalas en el diván.
2. Cuando algo te irrite sobremanera de otra persona, más de lo que sería razonable, pregúntate si ese defecto o actitud está apuntando hacia una zona de sombra de ti mismo.

165
NO TE RINDAS

Mario Benedetti es uno de los autores más entrañables y motivadores que ha dado la literatura hispanoamericana. Además de escribir novelas llenas de belleza como *Primavera con una esquina rota*, es también un maravilloso poeta. Este texto tan inspirador del que comparto unos fragmentos popularmente y por error se atribuye a él, aunque realmente no es suyo, sino que pertenece al argentino Guillermo Mayer, que lo escribió para sí mismo en un momento vital duro:

No te rindas, por favor no cedas, aunque el frío queme, aunque el miedo muerda, aunque el sol se esconda, y se calle el viento. Aún hay fuego en tu alma. Aún hay vida en tus sueños. Porque la vida es tuya y tuyo también el deseo (...)

Porque no hay heridas que no cure el tiempo. Abrir las puertas. Quitar los cerrojos. Abandonar las murallas que te protegieron. Vivir la vida y aceptar el reto. Recuperar la risa, ensayar un canto, bajar la guardia y extender las manos desplegar las alas e intentar de nuevo (...)

Aún hay fuego en tu alma. Aún hay vida en tus sueños. Porque cada día es un comienzo nuevo. Porque esta es la hora y el mejor momento.

—— TRES FIGURAS GEOMÉTRICAS A EVITAR EN LA VIDA ——

Además de poeta y novelista, Benedetti tenía una constante conexión con los problemas existenciales del ser humano. En una de sus reflexiones más célebres, Benedetti dijo: «En la vida hay que evitar tres figuras geométricas: los círculos viciosos, los triángulos amorosos y las mentes cuadradas».

166
MÁS Y MEJOR

No *puedo hacer más con lo que me ha sido dado.* ¿Te has sorprendido alguna vez diciéndote algo así?

Pensar que has recibido menos de lo que necesitabas en su momento tiene una ventaja: te permite entender que, quizá, tus decisiones fueron las mejores que podías tomar.

Pero ¿y ahora? ¿Qué tienes en tu mano para mejorarlo?

Un proverbio árabe dice que no importa lo que has sido, sino lo que serás a partir de ahora.

Sorpréndete de todo lo que has aprendido, en especial de tus errores y fracasos, casi sin darte cuenta. Aplica toda la sabiduría de tu madurez en el momento presente, sin lamentarte ni un segundo más.

Quizá en el pasado te faltaron recursos y experiencia para hacerlo distinto, pero ahora eres más y mejor.

INNOVAR Y APRENDER

Los especialistas dicen que no es posible innovar sin cometer errores. Sin embargo, para progresar es necesario no volver a cometer *los mismos errores*, porque eso implica que no hemos aprendido.

¿Hay errores que sigues repitiendo? Pregúntate por qué no sales de esa rueda, qué necesitas cambiar para salir de ella.

Toma cualquier nuevo fracaso como una oportunidad de aprendizaje, pero recoge la lección cuanto antes.

167

INFINITAS POSIBILIDADES

Siempre me digo que sería necia si pensara que todo empieza y acaba donde yo lo concibo. Porque la vida es mucho más, hay infinidad de cosas por descubrir.

Nuestro mundo no empieza ni acaba en el metro cuadrado en el que estás ahora ubicado. Ni este espacio ni este tiempo te pertenecen en realidad. Son circunstancias cambiantes. Eres mucho más.

Has llegado a la vida para dejarte sorprender por ella y ser poroso con lo que te regala el mundo.

Los parámetros que utilizamos para entender el universo no son más que instrumentos limitados para conocer un poco mejor nuestro paso por este espacio y tiempo.

Más allá de lo que vemos y creemos, albergamos infinitas posibilidades. Celebremos esa riqueza que nos queda por descubrir.

EL MITO DEL 10 POR CIENTO

Una declaración atribuida a Einstein, posiblemente de forma errónea, es que solo usamos el 10 por ciento de nuestro cerebro. Pero desde un punto de vista puramente físico, las resonancias magnéticas no aprecian que, salvo accidente o enfermedad, haya zonas de nuestro cerebro que estén inutilizadas. Otra cosa es cómo usamos nuestro cerebro. Podemos aumentar su rendimiento:

- Focalizándonos en una cosa a la vez, en lugar de dispersar nuestra atención.
- Evitando distracciones, como el *scrolling* en las redes, que no nos aportan nada, ni siquiera placer.
- Cambiando los pensamientos recurrentes y no productivos por una atención que esté orientada a las soluciones y al aquí y ahora.

168

PALABRAS PARA JULIA

H ay un poema que José Agustín Goytisolo escribe a su hija y que me cantaba mi padre, en la versión de Paco Ibáñez. Se llama *Palabras para Julia*, me emociona desde niña y ahora aún más.

Es una oda al amor para que recuerdes que alguien piensa en ti y que todos nos encontramos, al fin y al cabo, en el camino. Nunca estamos del todo solos.

Ha sido mi credo en muchas ocasiones. Aquí comparto un fragmento:

> *Nunca te entregues ni te apartes*
> *junto al camino, nunca digas*
> *no puedo más y aquí me quedo.*
>
> *La vida es bella, ya verás*
> *como a pesar de los pesares*
> *tendrás amor, tendrás amigos.*

─────── **SOLO SE PUEDE VIVIR HACIA ADELANTE** ───────

El poema original de Goytisolo, empieza diciendo: «Tú no puedes volver atrás / porque la vida ya te empuja / como un aullido interminable».

En este arranque lleno de belleza late la sabiduría de Søren Kierkegaard, el filósofo danés considerado padre del existencialismo. Este decía: «La vida solo puede ser entendida mirando hacia atrás, pero tiene que ser vivida hacia delante».

Por lo tanto, comprendamos lo que hemos sido y aprendido, y vivamos en la única dirección posible: la que nos lleva de este momento hacia el futuro.

169
LA VERDADERA ABUNDANCIA

Quienes no tienen una visión restringida de la abundancia, limitada a la riqueza económica, tienen más fácil alcanzar la plenitud y el éxito en todos los sentidos de su vida, incluida la prosperidad material que necesitan.

De hecho, los directores de felicidad de las empresas –lo de *recursos humanos* se empieza a quedar obsoleto– saben que el salario emocional es tan importante o más que el puramente financiero. Este incluye:

- El reconocimiento profesional y humano que reciben en la organización.
- La capacidad de crecer como seres humanos por los retos que les procura la empresa.
- La aportación que hacen al mundo gracias a su actividad.

Los profesionales más valorados solo permanecen en una compañía si se sienten *bien pagados* emocional y espiritualmente.

CUANTIFICA TUS RIQUEZAS

Más allá de lo que ingreses cada mes o tengas en el banco, en este ejercicio te propongo que midas:
- Cuántos buenos amigos y personas queridas tienes.

- Cuántas ideas eres capaz de generar, el número de proyectos que tienes vivos en tu cabeza.
- Tus existencias en materia de sueños que esperan ser cumplidos.

170
TAN CERCA

Un relato tradicional cuenta que un pez muy joven le preguntó a otro más adulto lo siguiente:

—¿Qué es el mar? Hace tiempo que oigo hablar de él, pero no sé dónde está ni qué es exactamente.

El pez mayor sonrió y le respondió:

—El mar es justamente lo que está a tu alrededor, chico.

—Vaya... pero, entonces, ¿cómo es que no puedo verlo? —preguntó el pequeño pez.

—Porque te rodea y está en todas partes. De hecho, tú eres parte del mar, porque aquí naciste y aquí morirás. Siempre nadas en él. Seguramente es por eso, porque está tan cerca, por lo que te cuesta verlo.

El mensaje de esta pequeña fábula es claro: muchas veces buscamos lejos cosas que en realidad tenemos muy cerca.

EL CONSEJO DE PAUL AUSTER

El autor de *La trilogía de Nueva York*, entre otras obras, y marido de la escritora Siri Husvedt, comenta lo siguiente en sintonía con la historia que acabamos de conocer:

Dicen que tienes que viajar para ver el mundo, pero yo a veces pienso que, si estás quieto y con los ojos bien abiertos, verás todo lo que puedes manejar.

171
PERSPECTIVA

L levo casi treinta años mirando a una cámara, sabiendo que hay personas al otro lado, reconociendo el poder de difusión que tiene una imagen en la pantalla.

La manera más efectiva de relativizar y darme cuenta de que yo soy un mero canal, un puente para *contar historias*, es observar el monitor de referencia que hay en un lado del estudio.

En ese me veo, desde la distancia, y me observo desde fuera para tener constancia de lo que estoy siendo en ese momento y así relativizarlo todo.

Tomar perspectiva es una herramienta muy poderosa para darnos cuenta de quiénes somos en cada momento de nuestra vida.

PREGUNTAS PARA CONOCERTE Y RESETEARTE

¿Te has observado en la distancia alguna vez? ¿Qué ves?

¿Cómo gestionas el verte desde fuera?

¿Qué aprendes?

¿Qué te gusta de ti? ¿Qué cambiarías?

¿Por dónde vas a empezar?

172
FUERA DE LA CELDA

ay ocasiones en las que no encontramos recursos para salir de una determinada situación o bucle emocional. En estos casos, podemos llegar a sentirnos en una celda oscura imposible de abrir. No obstante, ¿es eso real?

La llave del cerrojo la tenemos nosotros, pero no siempre es fácil de encontrar.

Empieza asumiendo que las circunstancias te llevaron ahí. Y ahora ya sabes que esas circunstancias tienen mucho que ver con tu interpretación de los hechos. Por eso, lejos de castigarte más, te invito a que busques la llave.

Como un viejo cuento, tal vez la puerta ni siquiera esté cerrada y eres tú quien cree que es así. ¿Has probado a abrirla?

Para salir de donde te encuentras bloqueado, te será muy útil bajar el nivel de autoexigencia y recuperar la certeza de que tu vida te pertenece. Fuera de la cárcel, te espera un mundo casi infinito, como lo eres tú. Como lo somos todos los que un día estuvimos en esa celda.

SEMÁFORO ROJO, SEMÁFORO VERDE

Hay un momento del libro *Greenlights,* las memorias de Matthew McConaughey, en las que el actor dice que muchas personas se quedan detenidas en los semáforos rojos de su vida, obviando que hay otros verdes que les invitan a pasar.

A partir de esta reflexión, dos preguntas muy sencillas y directas:
- ¿Cuál sientes que es ahora el *semáforo rojo* de tu vida?
- ¿Cuál es el *semáforo verde* en forma de camino u oportunidad que no estás aprovechando?

173
NADA PERMANECE

Una de las mayores fuentes de sufrimiento, según el budismo, es empeñarnos en que sean permanentes cosas que no lo son. Para darnos cuenta de que todos, personas y cosas, somos aves de paso, quiero compartir un cuento zen:

Un discípulo rompió accidentalmente un jarrón de mucho valor que pertenecía a su maestro. Antes de que este viniera, recogió a toda prisa los añicos y los escondió en su hábito.

Cuando el maestro llegó para impartir sus enseñanzas, el discípulo le preguntó:

–¿Por qué morimos, maestro?

–Es natural –respondió–. Todo lo que existe tiene un principio y un final. Cada cosa y persona debe vivir el tiempo que le ha sido dado. Luego, tendrá que morir.

Al escuchar eso, el estudiante dejó caer al suelo los añicos de jarrón y declaró:

–Maestro, a su jarrón le ha llegado la hora de morir.

MUERTES Y RENACIMIENTOS

A lo largo de la vida, experimentamos diferentes muertes y renacimientos. Termina una época y empieza otra. Algunos amigos dejan de estar, pero llegan otros con nuevas propuestas. Darnos cuenta de esto nos quita la tristeza de *perder*, ya que estamos perdiendo unas cosas y ganando otras todo el tiempo.

¿Cuál fue tu última muerte? ¿Y tu actual o próximo renacimiento?

174
LA TEORÍA DE DUNBAR

El ser humano es eminentemente social. Necesita tener conexión con los demás y se proyecta así, a través de las personas que le rodean.

Según la teoría del antropólogo británico Robin Dunbar, el ser humano, para desarrollar su dimensión social, tiene como máximo:
- 5 personas fundamentales
- 15 buenos amigos
- 150 conocidos

Para calcular esta última cifra, Dunbar se basó en el número máximo de personas en las sociedades de cazadores y recolectores. Y es trasladable a los grupos actuales que componen una oficina, fábrica o incluso una comuna.

Por encima de esa cifra, el número de conocidos deja de ser manejable.

Estos cálculos nos pueden ayudar a revisar quiénes componen nuestro entorno social y qué jerarquía tienen en nuestras prioridades.

LLEGADAS Y SALIDAS

Más allá de estos datos, que son estadísticos, las personas que integran estos tres grupos van cambiando. Hay llegadas y salidas, como en los aeropuertos. Este es un ejercicio interesante que puedes hacer cada año o fin de curso:
- ¿Qué personas importantes han salido de mi vida?
- ¿Cuáles han entrado?

175
COMPROMISO

Si estás motivado con algo, quizá ya tengas claro alguno de tus objetivos inmediatos. Ahora bien, para alcanzarlos no solo necesitas un plan de acción, una hoja de ruta a seguir. También deberás sopesar hasta qué punto te comprometes con ese objetivo y si estás dispuesto a realizar el esfuerzo que requiere.

Sobre esto, Abraham Lincoln decía que «el compromiso es lo que convierte una promesa en realidad».

Sin compromiso, es difícil que los planes trasciendan los límites de lo mental o que, una vez en marcha, no bajemos los brazos ante la primera dificultad.

Por su parte, el *coach* Tony Robbins añade: «El único límite a tu impacto en el mundo es tu imaginación y compromiso».

Habla en serio sobre esto contigo mismo. Solo así, comprometiéndote en la gesta que vas a emprender, podrás superar los obstáculos que encontrarás en el camino.

UN CONTRATO CONTIGO

Para afianzar tu compromiso con aquello que has decidido hacer, te sugiero que escribas un contrato contigo mismo donde fijes:
1. Qué te propones hacer.
2. Cuándo empezarás de forma efectiva.
3. Qué deberás hacer diariamente para lograr tu objetivo.
4. Fecha en la que completarás tu proyecto.
   Fírmalo debajo como el contrato que estás suscribiendo con tu compromiso.

176
ENFÁDATE BIEN

P ermítete enfadarte de vez en cuando y no guardes solo para ti lo que te corroe por dentro. Hay ocasiones en las que debemos estallar. Acaba siendo terapéutico, porque después de la tormenta llega la calma.

Permítete un poco de vehemencia en caso necesario. Si estás acompañado, avisa a tu entorno de cómo te sientes para que esté al tanto de ese sano desequilibrio.

Si el enfado es con otra persona y necesitas expresarlo, toma nota de lo que decía Aristóteles en su *Ética a Nicómaco*:

> *Cualquiera puede enfadarse, eso es algo muy sencillo. Pero enfadarse con la persona adecuada, en el grado exacto, en el momento oportuno, con el propósito justo y del modo correcto, eso, ciertamente, no resulta tan sencillo.*

CAMINAR LIBERA EL ENFADO

Salir a caminar o correr es un gran bálsamo para procesar el enfado. Sobre esto, la escritora estadounidense Lucy R. Lippard describe en su libro *Overlay. Contemporary Art and the Art of Prehistory* este ritual de las gentes del norte, citado por Anna Sólyom en su *Pequeño libro de magia cotidiana*:

Una costumbre de los esquimales para aliviar a alguien de su enfado consiste en que esa persona camine siguiendo una línea recta a través del campo. El punto en que el enfado es conquistado es marcado con una vara, como testimonio de la fuerza o la duración del enojo.

177
DESIERTO Y OASIS

W alt Whitman, el gran poeta de la modernidad en Estados Unidos, tiene un texto que es una luminosa hoja de ruta para vivir día a día. Empieza así:

No dejes que termine el día sin haber crecido un poco, sin haber sido feliz, sin haber aumentado tus sueños. No te dejes vencer por el desaliento. No permitas que nadie te quite el derecho a expresarte, que es casi un deber. No abandones las ansias de hacer de tu vida algo extraordinario.

El autor de *Hojas de hierba* es consciente de que «la vida es desierto y oasis». Ser humano es aceptar que la vida nos lastima y enseña, pero eso no nos hundirá mientras seamos protagonistas de nuestra propia historia. Whitman concluye:

Disfruta del pánico que te provoca tener la vida por delante. Vívela intensamente, sin mediocridad. Piensa que en ti está el futuro y encara la tarea con orgullo y sin miedo (...) No permitas que la vida te pase a ti sin que la vivas.

EL CLUB DE LOS POETAS VIVOS

Probablemente recuerdas la película *El club de los poetas muertos*, con un estelar Robin Williams como profesor que contagia a sus alumnos el amor por la poesía.

Como ejercicio para esta reflexión, te propongo que compartas tus poemas favoritos con las personas que amas. ¿Qué tal un encuentro en el que cada cual aporte su texto preferido?

178
SÉ COMO UN CAMALEÓN

Soy camaleónica, ¿y tú?

Me adapto al entorno de una manera bastante ágil y efectiva. Y te confieso que eso me divierte. No siempre fue así, pero cuando le perdí el miedo a ser porosa y acepté todos los registros que mi persona atesoraba, me di cuenta de que esta cualidad me ayuda muchísimo a conectar de verdad con las personas. Me permite comprender a quienes han tenido distintas vivencias a las mías y tienen mucho que aportarme.

La buena noticia es que este don camaleónico puede entrenarse con estos ingredientes:

Curiosidad. Todo empieza por llevar la mirada más allá del mundo conocido, de nuestra zona de confort.

Observación. ¿Qué hacen los demás que yo no hago? ¿Qué puedo aprender de quienes no son como yo?

Empatía. El tercer paso es trasladarnos al punto de vista del otro, para contemplar la vida desde su perspectiva.

ZELIG Y LOS ROMANOS

Ser camaleónicos en exceso nos puede llevar a las situaciones que vive Woody Allen en *Zelig,* la historia de un hombre sin personalidad propia que se funde con quien tiene al lado. El punto de equilibrio sería la reformulación de un viejo dicho latino: «Si vas a Roma, haz como los romanos, pero sin dejar de ser tú mismo».

179
TRILOGÍA DE LA COHERENCIA

Decía Gandhi que «la felicidad es cuando lo que piensas, dices y haces están en armonía».

Yo lo llamo *la trilogía de la coherencia*, ese hilo rojo de la serenidad que lo une todo cuando, efectivamente, hablamos y actuamos como pensamos, o *triceversa*.

Si piensas una cosa y dices otra, estás engañando al otro y a ti mismo. Si dices una cosa y haces otra, vives en las falsas promesas.

Las tres partes deben estar en perfecta armonía para sentir que llevamos una vida coherente.

Y, para mí, ese hilo conductor lleva una frase grabada en toda su extensión: *pon siempre amor*. Lo más importante es que esta coherencia se construya desde el amor.

UN BARÓMETRO PARA LAS AMISTADES

Puedes aplicar la trilogía de la coherencia para medir la calidad de las personas de las que te rodeas. No puedes saber cómo piensan, pero entre todas las virtudes que puedan tener, aquellas que hacen lo que dicen pertenecen a una élite que merece la pena cultivar.

180

INTELIGENCIA EMOCIONAL

Desde que, hace tres décadas, empezara a divulgarse en todo el mundo la importancia de la inteligencia emocional (IE, como se conoce por sus siglas), esta ha llegado a todos los ámbitos. Daniel Goleman la definía así:

> *El conocimiento de uno mismo, es decir, la capacidad de reconocer un sentimiento en el mismo momento en que aparece, constituye la piedra angular de la inteligencia emocional.*

Aquel que no sea capaz de gestionar sus emociones y estados de ánimo, de identificar lo que le está pasando —así como lo que siente el otro—, le costará mucho más progresar en la vida.

Hoy es algo de sentido común que, poco a poco, se comienza a impartir en los colegios y está al alcance de todos. La IE debe practicarse sobre todo en las situaciones de dificultad, como advierte el propio Goleman:

> *Dominar el mundo emocional es especialmente difícil porque estas habilidades deben ejercitarse en aquellos momentos en que las personas se encuentran en peores condiciones para asimilar información y aprender hábitos de respuesta nuevos, es decir, cuando tienen problemas.*

EJERCICIO BÁSICO DE IE

Cuando choques con alguien y no puedas comprender por qué actúa así, pregúntate:
- ¿Cómo se está sintiendo esta persona ahora mismo?
- ¿Cómo me siento yo ante su acción o reacción?
- ¿De qué manera puedo ayudarle a que me cuente cómo se siente y por qué se siente así?

Aplicando la IE, los conflictos duran mucho menos o se desactivan directamente, con lo que todas las partes se sienten mejor.

181
EL ARTE DE ESCUCHAR

M e llaman mucho la atención las personas que no solo no escuchan, sino que además hablan muchísimo y suelen llevar la conversación a su terreno. Confieso que en este tipo de situaciones termino por desconectar.

Intento no hacer nunca lo mismo. Sé que no hay nada más bonito y agradable para un ser humano que sentirse escuchado, acompañado y comprendido, incluso en su silencio.

Según el filósofo hindú Jiddu Krishnamurti, hay pocas personas que dominen este arte debido a lo siguiente:

Nuestro escuchar es siempre con una idea preconcebida o desde un punto de vista particular. No escuchamos simplemente; se interpone siempre la pantalla de nuestros propios pensamientos, de nuestras conclusiones, de nuestros prejuicios (...). Para escuchar tiene que haber quietud interna, una atención relajada; hay que estar libre del esfuerzo de adquirir.

PROFUNDIZA EN TU ESCUCHA

La naturaleza nos ofrece un buen campo de práctica para este arte del que habla Krishnamurti. Si nos acostumbramos a poner atención plena en lo que sucede a nuestro alrededor, nos resultará más fácil escuchar a los demás o a nosotros mismos. Es así de sencillo:
- Ve a un lugar lo más alejado posible del mundanal ruido.
- Quédate quieto, cierra los ojos y capta los sonidos que te rodean.

- Suspende tu pensamiento para prestar atención a todo lo que pasa por tus oídos. ¿Escuchas el viento? ¿Se oye también su fricción en las hojas? ¿Hay pájaros, insectos que tienen su canción? Sumérgete en ello.
- Dedica al menos un par de minutos a esa escucha antes de volver al ruido del mundo.

182

CHANOYU

H enri Brunel, que ha sido maestro de yoga durante más de treinta años y divulgador de la cultura japonesa, describe así cómo es
una ceremonia del té tradicional, llamada *chanoyu*.

El maestro de té lleva a cabo los gestos rituales con eficacia, lentitud, cui-
dado y amor. La conversación va transcurriendo, apacible; se habla de
poesía, de historia, de arquitectura. Muy suavemente se va apagando el
ligero ruido de las voces, y todos contemplan en silencio los boles familia-
res, una flor del campo; se oye a lo lejos el canto de un pájaro. El tiempo se
encuentra en suspenso; armonía, serenidad.

No es necesario vivir en Japón, ni siquiera que te guste el té, para compartir la belleza del *chanoyu*. Lo esencial de este acto es hacerlo con atención plena para convertir el encuentro en un oasis de calma y armonía.

──────────── **REGLAS PARA UNA CEREMONIA DEL TÉ** ────────────

1. El lugar debe ser silencioso, libre
de ruidos de tráfico, televisores o
conversaciones ajenas.
2. Las personas que participan en el
chanoyu dejarán sus problemas
y preocupaciones fuera, lo
que incluye desconectar los
dispositivos móviles.
3. En la conversación se evitan temas
que puedan crear incomodidad,

como política, rivalidades
deportivas o conflictos del mundo.
4. Se promueve, en cambio, la charla
sobre cualquier forma de arte, la
naturaleza o la calidad del té.
5. La reunión debe tener un espíritu
Ichigo-ichie, es decir, hacerlo con
consciencia de que este encuentro
no se volverá a repetir.

183
NO TAN EN SERIO

Soy la primera en tomármelo todo muy en serio. Me hago cargo de las situaciones y no me resulta baladí ningún trabajo o compromiso. Pero de un tiempo a esta parte, modifico ese gesto que pongo de vez en cuando, con el ceño casi fruncido y cara de concentración, para hacerme a mí misma un guiño y darme un beso ante el espejo, a lo *selfie* adolescente, mientras me digo, *no es para tanto, mujer.*

Permítete relajarte y aflojar la tensión a la que llevas acostumbrado demasiado tiempo. No es recomendable tomártelo todo tan en serio. Comprometidos sí, pero con alegría y alguna que otra risa, por favor.

Sobre esto, decía Eduardo Galeano:

> *El humor tiene la capacidad de devolverte la certeza de que la vida merece la pena. Y uno se salva, a veces, por el chiste, por el mágico sonido de la risa, que puede no ser tu risa; por la escondida capacidad de tomarte el pelo, de verte desde afuera y reírte de vos mismo.*

ACTIVA EL HUMOR

Volviendo a Eduardo Galeano, cuando las cosas se pongan demasiado graves, aplícate este lema suyo: «No te tomes en serio nada que no te haga reír».

Una buena risa a tiempo te ayudará a descargar la tensión, tomar distancia y, con ello, encontrar mejores soluciones para la situación que estás afrontando.

184

CAMBIAR A LOS DEMÁS

Casi todos intentamos en algún momento cambiar a otros, con la esperanza de que sean como a nosotros nos gustaría que fueran. Aunque sea por su bien, porque vemos que sus elecciones vitales les perjudican, no nos corresponde a nosotros liderar su cambio. Como decía lúcidamente Andy Warhol:

> *Cuando las personas están preparadas, entonces cambian. Nunca lo hacen antes, y a veces mueren antes de dar el primer paso. No puedes hacer que nadie cambie si no quiere, del mismo modo que, cuando alguien quiere cambiar, es imposible detenerlo.*

Cada persona cambia cuando quiere y puede. Además, ¿quién soy yo para pretender que dejes de ser tú, si no me has pedido que lo haga?

Cuando he entendido que es más fácil asumir lo que sucede sin forzar nada ni a nadie, mi vida ha ido por caminos por los que lo natural y lo orgánico toma las riendas.

INSPIRAR EN VEZ DE CAMBIAR

Como acabamos de ver, no es posible cambiar a nadie que no ha decidido hacerlo por sí mismo, pero sí podemos inspirar con nuestro ejemplo.

Un caso típico serían los padres que quieren que sus hijos se despeguen de las pantallas, cuando ellos están todo el día pendientes del móvil.

Lo mismo sucede con la lectura: no podemos obligar a un niño a que le guste leer. Sin embargo, si nuestra casa está llena de libros y nos ven a menudo leyendo, antes o después se acercarán a este hábito.

185
UN POEMA PARA VIVIR

Roberto Abadie Soriano, maestro muy querido en Uruguay y autor de numerosos libros que leen los niños de su país, a los noventa y dos años redactó esta receta para la longevidad en forma de poema:

Vida sana y ordenada.
La comida, moderada.
No abusar de los remedios.
Buscar por todos los medios.
No alterarse por nada.
Ejercicio y diversión.
No tener nunca aprehensión.
Poco encierro, mucho trato
y continua ocupación.

Merece la pena aplicarnos estos consejos como resumen de la sabiduría para la larga vida. ¿Cuántos de estos puntos sigues en tu rutina?

EL ARTE DE ESTAR FELIZMENTE OCUPADO

Esta es una traducción libre que se da del término *Ikigai,* que vimos páginas atrás. Ahora, ¿qué significa estar felizmente ocupado? Algunas pistas:

- La decisión de mantenerte activo viene de ti, no es una imposición.
- Esta actividad te produce *flow,* no se te hace larga ni pesada.
- Lo que haces tiene un propósito, te ayuda a sentirte mejor o aporta algo al mundo.

186

EL RITMO DE LOS DEMÁS

Cuando estás listo para desempeñar un proyecto en equipo y parece que todo confluye, que te sientes motivado y totalmente enérgico, ¡cuidado!

Comprueba si la otra parte está lista y si es su momento. Como bien sabes, los tiempos de cada uno son distintos. Coincidir en el momento es clave para el éxito de los asuntos en común.

Observa, calibra, busca la manera de que todos vayáis a una. No siempre tu momento coincidirá con el del resto del equipo.

Esto también es aplicable a la pareja. Tal vez, por ejemplo, tú sientas que es hora de dejar la ciudad para irte a vivir al campo, pero tu pareja de vida necesita un poco más para madurar un cambio de tanto calado.

LA DIAGONAL DE EVOLUCIÓN

Cuando alguien te desespere por su falta de iniciativa, por su torpeza o por cualquier otra razón, piensa que cada persona está en un punto diferente de evolución personal.

Imagina que la vida es una pendiente de crecimiento. Hay quien se encuentra en la parte baja de la cuesta, con lo cual, actúa y reacciona desde donde está. Quien está en la parte superior de la diagonal, en cambio, puede hacerlo desde una sabiduría y madurez mucho mayor.

187
HALLAR EL NORTE

Recuerdo cuando, de pequeña, salía al monte con mi padre. Aún no había navegadores en el móvil. Un mapa cartográfico, una brújula y descubrir dónde estaba el norte eran todo un reto para mí, que soy muy despistada y no me oriento del todo bien.

Un rato juntos y mirar al mapa me bastaba para saber hacia dónde debía ir, para descubrir ese norte tan importante entonces.

Siempre lo conseguía, pero confieso que en gran medida era por la confianza que mi padre depositaba en mí.

Ahora, varias décadas después, me gusta saber que el norte de mi vida puede variar. Soy capaz de seguir mi rumbo gracias a la confianza en mí misma y a la depositada en mí por parte de aquellos que me amaron y a quienes amo.

UN MAPA PERSONAL

Hace años se puso de moda crear *un panel de visualización propio* para que la mente se oriente hacia lo que quiere conseguir. Básicamente se hace pegando en una cartulina imágenes que representen aquellos logros que son importantes en este momento de nuestra vida.

El panel de visualización debe colgarse en un lugar a la vista, de modo que cotidianamente estemos en contacto con ese *norte* al que queremos llegar.

188
¿SE PUEDE DECIDIR EL DESTINO?

Un relato tradicional japonés cuenta que, en el curso de una batalla, un general ordenó atacar, aunque su ejército contaba con muchos menos hombres que el del enemigo.

Llenos de temor, mientras iban camino de la guerra, los soldados quisieron parar en un templo. Tras rezar con ellos, el general sacó de su bolsillo una moneda y anunció:

–Voy a lanzar esta moneda al aire. Si sale cara, ganaremos la batalla. Si sale cruz, perderemos. ¡Dejemos hablar al destino!

Dicho esto, arrojó la moneda al aire y los soldados miraron con gran tensión lo que salía. Fue cara. Contentos y confiados, atacaron con gran moral al enemigo y lograron la victoria.

Terminada la batalla, un oficial comentó al general:

–No se puede cambiar el destino.

–Eso es cierto –contestó el general.

Luego mostró al oficial la moneda: tenía cara en ambos lados.

Este cuento ilustra el poder de la convicción en todo lo que emprendemos. Aquello que queremos hacer realidad, primero debe ser real en nuestra mente.

EJERCICIO DE ANTICIPACIÓN

Entre las técnicas de proyección para lograr resultados, una de las más sencillas y realmente efectivas es la siguiente:

1. Decide de manera clara qué es lo que quieres conseguir.

2. Visualiza a continuación cómo alcanzas tu objetivo y cómo te sientes por ello.

3. Quédate con la sensación de que ya lo has logrado para empezar a dar pasos en esa dirección.

189

LA ZONA GRIS

Existe lo que yo llamo *zona gris* para designar esos momentos en los que no estamos ni en la luz ni en la oscuridad. Es una tenue penumbra en la que puedes permanecer casi desapercibido *ad eternum*.

¿Sabes a qué me refiero? A ese estado intermedio en el que no te posicionas ni tomas decisión alguna para no equivocarte.

La zona gris puede resultarnos cómoda, pero, créeme, a largo plazo, no solo te agota, sino que te apoltrona y te limita a una onda de mediocridad de la que cada vez te costará más salir.

¿Te conformas con ser una persona gris en una zona gris y renuncias al arcoíris?

Sobre esto, Renoir dijo una vez: «Una mañana, a uno de nosotros se le terminó el negro y ese fue el nacimiento del Impresionismo».

¿Y si decides sacar el negro y el gris de la paleta de colores con los que tiñes tu vida?

MEJOR MAL QUE NINGUNA

Los especialistas en toma de decisiones afirman que, muchas veces, una mala decisión es mejor que ninguna, cuando nos encontramos en un momento de crisis. Aunque nos equivoquemos, eso nos mostrará enseguida que ese camino no es válido y veremos otras opciones efectivas para salir del atolladero.

190
TAL COMO ERES

Cuando llevamos demasiado tiempo ocultando quiénes somos, podemos olvidar quiénes éramos y, aún peor, quiénes estamos llamados a ser.

Tal vez al principio fue por timidez. O, en el caso de ser extrovertido, taparas tus inseguridades con risas y conversaciones banales que te alejaban de tu esencia, sin darte cuenta de lo que te perdías al no preguntarte en silencio si ibas por el mejor camino.

Muchos nos alejamos de la propia senda porque la sociedad nos mandó el mensaje de que destacar, preguntar, cuestionar, dudar y equivocarse era poco recomendable.

La buena noticia es que siempre estás a tiempo de redescubrirte, de conectar con tu autenticidad y mostrarte al mundo tal como eres.

EL LEMA DE FRIDA KHALO

La pintora más brillante del siglo xx tuvo que lidiar contra los prejuicios y rigideces de su época. Aun así, decidió seguir siempre una senda propia. En sus palabras:

Tan absurdo y fugaz es nuestro paso por este mundo que solo me deja tranquila el saber que he sido auténtica, que he logrado ser lo más parecido a mí misma.

¿Qué puedes hacer para vivir de forma más auténtica y fiel contigo mismo?

191
TRES PRINCIPIOS PARA LA VIDA

K yong Ho fue un célebre maestro espiritual que, a finales del siglo XIX, renovó el budismo en Corea. Nos legó estos tres principios sobre el arte de vivir:

1. No desees una salud perfecta. En la salud perfecta hay codicia y exigencia. Como dijo un viejo maestro: *haz del sufrimiento de la enfermedad una buena medicina.*
2. No aspires a vivir sin problemas. Una vida fácil lleva a una mente perezosa que emite juicios. Como dijo un viejo maestro: *acepta las ansiedades y dificultades de la vida.*
3. No esperes que tu práctica se vea siempre libre de obstáculos. Sin impedimentos, la mente que busca la iluminación puede quemarse. Como dijo un viejo maestro: *logra la liberación a través de los trastornos.*

LOS OBSTÁCULOS COMO TRAMPOLINES

Según la visión de este maestro, las dificultades y problemas son trampolines que nos permiten ir más allá de nosotros mismos. Cada vez que la vida ponga un obstáculo en tu camino, pregúntate: ¿De qué manera lo que estoy viviendo es una oportunidad para ser mejor?

192

ABRIR EL ABANICO DE POSIBILIDADES

Durante mi formación de *coaching* para acompañar a personas en cambios vitales, tuve un profesor que me dio pautas muy interesantes para aplicar en momentos de duda.

Alfonso Medina fue mi tutor en la fase de la certificación MCC de ICF (International Coaching Federation) y me impresionaba gratamente su pulcritud a la hora de escuchar y poner atención en ese acompañamiento.

Recuerdo que insistía en la importancia de abrir el abanico de posibilidades al *coachee*, o cliente, para después concretar e ir cerrando ese abanico hacia una solución más detallada.

Al abrir el espectro de posibilidades que tenemos ante nosotros, nuestra mente puede crear nuevas opciones ante una toma de decisiones.

Te invito a que indagues sobre ellas a fondo, ya que muchas veces tienes mucho más poder de elección del que crees.

LA INVERSIÓN CREATIVA

En los cursos de *creative writing* de Estados Unidos, cuando un novelista se bloquea a mitad de la trama, se le pide que escriba todo lo que *no va a suceder* en esta historia.

Esta técnica la puedes aplicar a tu propia vida cuando te sientas paralizado ante una encrucijada:

- ¿Qué es lo que no voy a hacer?
- ¿Qué es lo que no va a suceder?

A través de la inversión creativa, por eliminación, empezarás a clarificar tu abanico de posibilidades.

193
NO DEJES DE DIVERTIRTE

R epasando mis valores fundamentales, un día descubrí que quería incluir más diversión en mi presente.

Si no lo había hecho hasta entonces era porque tenía la creencia de que una persona divertida carece de credibilidad. Cuando me di cuenta de que era un prejuicio, supe que me estaba perdiendo demasiadas cosas y que necesitaba la diversión más que nunca.

A partir de entonces, me reté a incluir de forma cotidiana algo divertido y que me sacara de mi zona de confort.

¡Los que somos padres tenemos unos grandes aliados en nuestros hijos! Ahí di rienda suelta a actividades varias: desde saltar a la piscina vestida hasta mojarme bajo la lluvia hasta calarme entera, entre muchas otras cosas.

Me alegro de haberlo hecho, porque ahora soy consciente de la creatividad y el cambio de actitud ante la vida que conlleva trabajar la diversión.

¿Y si empezamos a divertirnos un poco más?

LOS TRES SUPERPODERES HUMANOS

Según la actriz y coach Imma Rabasco, autora del libro *Reír y vivir*, «los mortales tenemos tres superpoderes y sabemos (o intuimos) que sin ellos estaríamos perdidos: la risa, la sonrisa y el humor. La risa distiende, la sonrisa une y el humor relativiza».

¿Qué puedes hacer hoy para dar más espacio a estos tres superpoderes en tu vida?

194
UN SOLO GRAN PENSAMIENTO

Así como los árboles más altos nacen de una semilla, de un brote, las grandes transformaciones de nuestra vida tienen como punto de partida una idea, un pensamiento.

Si sabemos regarlo y cultivarlo, podrá llevarnos a cotas inimaginadas. Sobre esto, el escritor y motivador John F. Demartini dice:

> *Casi todas las historias de personas que han triunfado comienzan con un solo gran pensamiento que ha sido alimentado con fe. Y muchas de las que han alcanzado los mayores éxitos también se han enfrentado a las mayores adversidades. Cuando Walt Disney se presentó a solicitar trabajo de dibujante en los periódicos, lo rechazaron de plano. Un director incluso le dijo que no tenía talento y que se buscara otra cosa que hacer en su vida. Pero él tenía una idea que transformó en visión, perseveró y continuó creyendo en sí mismo.*

TU VIVERO DE IDEAS

Para cultivar tu futuro, es útil que tengas un cuaderno donde anotes esas ideas y proyectos que pueden crecer con el tiempo. Apunta aquí cualquier iniciativa que vaya surgiendo y repasa las anteriores para ver cuál está reclamando tu atención y cuidados en este momento.

195
LA MAGIA DEL AGUA

Pocas maravillas de la naturaleza tienen el poder del agua, que además de darnos vida, tiene la capacidad de pulir y dar forma a las rocas más duras.

¿Te das cuenta de que no podríamos vivir sin ella, al igual que sucede con el aire? ¿Celebras como merece este elemento que te refresca y revitaliza?

Echemos mano de lo que se nos ofrece de manera natural. El agua es esencial para la vida y nos procura una conexión especial con el entorno. Por eso es un privilegio disfrutar de este elemento en plena naturaleza.

Sentir el agua, interna y externamente, es fuente de bienestar. El agua purifica, hidrata y emociona.

Tanto si nos bañamos en una playa o en un río como si gozamos de la lluvia que fertiliza la tierra, celebrar el agua es celebrar nuestra propia vida.

LA ALQUIMIA DEL AGUA

Masaru Emoto, el investigador japonés que dedicó gran parte de su vida al estudio del agua, afirmaba que el pensamiento humano, las palabras y la música influyen en la calidad del agua y la hacen cambiar. Si eso le sucede al agua —reflexionaba—, nosotros, que estamos compuestos por un 70 u 80 por ciento de agua, también somos susceptibles de esa alquimia. Según este principio, pregúntate:
- ¿Qué clase de pensamientos y palabras te dedicas a ti mismo?
- ¿Utilizas la música para modular tu estado de ánimo?

196
EMOCIONES NEGATIVAS

Daniel Goleman, el divulgador de la inteligencia emocional del que hablamos en páginas anteriores, asegura que «las emociones perturbadoras y las relaciones tóxicas han sido identificadas como factores de riesgo que favorecen la aparición de algunas enfermedades».

Esto es así, según este doctor en psicología de Harvard, porque «las emociones negativas intensas absorben toda la atención del individuo, obstaculizando cualquier intento de atender a otra cosa».

Debemos entender que recurrimos a los pensamientos negativos de manera automática para protegernos del peligro. Es un impulso ancestral de cuando, como cazadores recolectores, vivíamos en un estado de alerta y con miedo. Sin embargo, ya no necesitamos estar atentos a ningún peligro que amenace nuestra vida. Es un *automatismo* que nos ha guiado durante milenios, pero podemos desactivarlo. Es momento de bajar la guardia.

Saquemos de nuestra vida los pensamientos que nos perturban para dejar espacio a otros que nos motiven y nos aporten calma.

RECONOCER Y DEJAR PASAR

El primer paso para desprenderte de un pensamiento negativo es tomar conciencia de que lo estás teniendo.

Tras reconocerlo, en lugar de aferrarte a él o luchar contra él, déjalo pasar simplemente sin juicios, como un visitante ocasional.

Si insiste en quedarse, puedes diluirlo con un pensamiento de signo contrario: algo que te provoque placer, bienestar o ilusión.

197

DESDE EL CORAZÓN

Hay una frase de Séneca, el filósofo estoico latino nacido en Córdoba, que dice: «Nada es honesto si se ejecuta a disgusto. Toda acción honesta es voluntaria».

Así debería ser. Haz aquello que te llama desde el corazón. Nada debería ser obligatorio, sino hecho desde la convicción de que esto es lo que debemos y queremos hacer.

¿Cuántas personas conocemos que siguen una existencia que no es suya? Bien sea porque viven para cumplir las expectativas de los demás o para mostrar una determinada imagen de cara a la galería, muchas personas están desconectadas de lo que realmente son.

Atrévete a vivir desde el corazón y haz de tus prioridades el eje de tu vida.

LO URGENTE Y LO IMPORTANTE

Una de las lecciones que nos dejó Stephen Covey, el autor de *Los 7 hábitos de la gente altamente efectiva*, es que la mayoría de las personas entregan su tiempo a lo urgente, que es importante para los demás, pero no para uno mismo. Lo importante es aquello que es significativo para ti, aquello que nadie te impone, y por eso no suele tener un lugar en tu agenda. Una vida equilibrada, según Covey, es aquella en la que hay equilibrio entre lo urgente y lo importante.

¿Qué es lo importante que debes realizar ahora en tu vida?

198

LUZ

Al igual que, como hemos comentado ya, a veces obviamos el agua, a menudo damos por hecho algo tan esencial y necesario como es la luz.

La claridad natural, fuente de calor y energía, marca nuestro ciclo vital diario, como nos recuerda la cronobiología. También tiene una gran influencia en nuestras emociones. La luz cambia la percepción que tenemos de la vida y de los desafíos que nos presenta.

¿Cuántas veces algo que nos parecía irresoluble por la noche aparece bajo una *nueva luz* por la mañana?

Exponerse a la claridad solar, además, parece ser una de las claves de la longevidad. Las personas que viven en las zonas azules pasan gran parte del tiempo al aire libre, con lo que sincronizan sus relojes internos con el del astro rey.

Incluso cuando hace frío, merece la pena brindarles a nuestro cuerpo y alma los beneficios de la luz.

SALUDO AL SOL

Muchos practicantes de yoga empiezan el día con la serie de asanas conocida como *Saludo al sol*. Si no lo conoces, puedes aprenderlo fácilmente en un breve vídeo de YouTube; mi querida Xuan Lan tiene tutoriales y clases magníficas.

Otra manera de celebrar la luz y el calor que nos da vida es, simplemente, abrir la ventana por la mañana y darle las gracias al sol por alumbrar un día más.

199
APRENDER DE TODO

Un cuento judío tiene como protagonista a un rabino que enseñaba a sus alumnos cómo la sabiduría está en todas las cosas, incluso en los inventos de la modernidad.

–De todo se puede aprender algo –afirmaba el rabino–. No hay nada en el mundo que no pueda darnos una enseñanza de valor. Y eso incluye todas las cosas que el ser humano ha fabricado. Todas ellas nos enseñan algo importante.

Uno de sus alumnos le preguntó entonces:

–Maestro, pero... ¿qué es lo que puede enseñarnos el ferrocarril?

–Que por un segundo podemos llegar tarde y perder nuestra oportunidad.

–¿Y el telégrafo? –intervino otro alumno.

–¡Que cada palabra cuenta!

–¿Y el teléfono? –preguntó un tercero.

–¡Que allí se oye todo lo que aquí decimos!

EXTRAE TUS ENSEÑANZAS

Siguiendo el cuento del rabino, te propongo que elijas tres objetos que se encuentren en el espacio donde estás ahora. Atribuye a cada uno de ellos una enseñanza para la vida cotidiana. Puedes hacer este ejercicio con amigos o incluso con tus hijos, como un juego divertido e iluminador.

200
MEMENTO MORI

Opina mi querida y admirada Isabel Coixet que, al menos por lo que respecta a sus películas, «la felicidad queda fatal en cámara. La tristeza y la soledad sí quedan bien».

Una de las obras en las que reflejó esa idea es *Mi vida sin mí* –está entre mis películas favoritas, con un fantástico Marc Ruffalo, por cierto–, donde la protagonista, a quien le queda poco tiempo, hace una lista de cosas que quiere hacer antes de morir.

Es una película triste y al mismo tiempo muy bella porque nos conecta con lo esencial. El hecho de reconocer nuestro propio fin nos permite, justamente, saborear la vida en toda su plenitud.

Sobre esto, los antiguos romanos se repetían la expresión *memento mori* –recuerda que morirás– como antídoto contra la soberbia y la vanidad. Este mismo lema nos sirve para recordar que la vida no espera y que merece que extraigamos todo su jugo.

------- **VIVE COMO SI FUERAS A MORIR MAÑANA** -------

Ponte en la situación de la protagonista de la película de Isabel Coixet para dotar de significado y profundidad a tu vida:
- ¿Qué cosas importantes harías si supieras que tu final está cerca?
- ¿Qué desórdenes arreglarías?
- ¿Qué cosas inacabadas completarías?
- ¿Qué les dirías a las personas que amas?

201
EL DIFÍCIL PRIMER PASO

A veces necesitamos tomar decisiones drásticas que, de entrada, nos resultan difíciles de afrontar. Podría ser dejar la relación con alguien que no te hace bien, desprenderte de alguna pertenencia, erradicar algún hábito o tener una conversación delicada.

Sobre esto último, el consultor y escritor Tim Ferriss asegura que «el éxito de una persona en la vida se mide por la cantidad de conversaciones incómodas que está dispuesta a mantener».

Esta puede ser una buena motivación para hacer aquello que, en el fondo, sabemos que debemos hacer. Cada vez que te preguntes *¿Qué haría yo si de verdad pudiera...?* se revelará aquello que necesitas hacer.

No hay cambio importante sin incomodidad. Por consiguiente, esa decisión difícil, pero a la vez meditada, tiene la clave para tu nueva vida.

El primer paso suele ser el más difícil, pero el hecho de darlo despliega un nuevo universo de posibilidades en tu vida.

LA HORA DE LAS DECISIONES

Si eres de los que se preocupan tras adoptar una decisión importante, te aconsejo que no la tomes justo antes de acostarte, en especial si implica mandar un correo electrónico o wasap del que nos llegará una respuesta, ya que te quedarás con la cuestión dando vueltas en tu cabeza.

Este tipo de resoluciones es mejor tomarlas de buena mañana, para que cualquier tipo de reacción te llegue en medio de la actividad.

202
QUITAR LO QUE SOBRA

S e cuenta que una vez le preguntaron a Miguel Ángel cómo lograba crear sus maravillas de mármol. El gran escultor del Renacimiento respondió que se limitaba a «quitar lo que sobra» en el bloque, pues él ya veía la obra que contenía la mole.

Aplicado a la propia existencia, este método puede ser muy eficaz, ya que muchas veces lo que necesitamos es depurar nuestra vida de aquello innecesario o directamente perjudicial, lo cual incluye algunas actitudes y hábitos.

Sobre esto, el filósofo Plotino –probablemente Miguel Ángel lo había leído– ya recomendaba hace casi dos milenios:

> *Entra en ti mismo y mira. Si no te encuentras bello, haz como el creador de una estatua a la que debe conferir hermosura, quitando por aquí, alisando por allá, suavizando tal línea, haciendo más pura tal otra... (...) quita todo lo que sobre, pon recto lo torcido, ilumina lo oscuro y encamina tus esfuerzos a que todo brille (...) Nunca dejes de labrar tu estatua.*

RESTA PARA SUMAR

Siguiendo el método que hemos visto, pregúntate:
- ¿Qué hábitos o actitudes podría eliminar para reducir la complejidad y los conflictos en mi vida?

- ¿A qué gastos innecesarios puedo renunciar para unas finanzas más saludables?
- ¿De qué compromisos puedo prescindir para liberar tiempo y espacio para mí?

203
TU VIRTUD ESCONDIDA

Te has preguntado cuál es tu mayor talento o has pensado, tal vez, que no tienes una virtud especial? En este último caso, muy probablemente te equivocas.

Te invito a que desentierres tu virtud, como el arqueólogo que extrae del fondo de la tierra el mayor tesoro. Y es que a veces nuestros talentos son mucho más visibles en la infancia y juventud y, como si de fósiles se tratara, los vamos cubriendo con el polvo de la vida, con la tierra de los años y la rutina, perdiendo en nuestro interior lo más valioso que tenemos.

Haz arqueología. Llegaste con ese talento a la vida, aunque no seas consciente de él, y tu misión es entregarlo al mundo para aportar belleza o nuevas soluciones a tu entorno.

Descubre esos pequeños tesoros que hacen de ti un ser increíble, digno de amar y de ser amado.

¿CUÁL ES TU GENIOTIPO?

El empresario Tony Estruch presenta un nuevo modelo sobre el talento en su libro *Geniotipo*, traducido ya a media docena de idiomas, incluido el japonés. Estos son algunos de los más comunes, identificado cada uno por una figura geométrica:

- INFINITO: Tu propósito es educar y mostrar nuevos caminos a los demás.
- CUADRADO: El geniotipo de los buenos gestores que ponen orden al caos.

- ELIPSE: Tu don es la creatividad en cualquiera de sus formas.
- TRIÁNGULO: Es la genialidad de los grandes vendedores o comunicadores.
- CÍRCULO: Tu *leitmotiv* es el amor y entrega a los demás.
- PENTÁGONO: El talento de los médicos, terapeutas y científicos.

Entre estos perfiles, ¿cuál dirías que es tu tipo de genialidad?

204

EL VALOR DEL TIEMPO

Es cierto que no podemos volver atrás en el tiempo, pero esto no debería ser motivo de desánimo. Si descubres que se te ha escapado como arena entre los dedos, sin tú darte ni cuenta, piensa que a veces es necesario que así sea.

Hay muchas cosas que solo apreciamos en todo su valor cuando las perdemos, y una de ellas es el tiempo.

Cuando nos damos cuenta de que cada hora, minuto y segundo son preciosos, porque ya no volverán, entonces empezamos a emplear el tiempo como lo que es: nuestra divisa de mayor valor.

En el tiempo vivimos y atesoramos nuestras experiencias, que nos recuerdan la grandeza de la vida y lo voraz de cada instante.

LOS LADRONES DE TIEMPO

En su libro *Time Mindfulness*, la economista Cristina Benito identifica estos vampiros de nuestro bien más preciado para que podamos evitarlos:

- *Gente desocupada*. «Está comprobado que quienes más pierden el tiempo son expertos en consumir el de los que menos tienen», dice la autora.
- *Compromisos sociales*. No pierdas el tiempo acudiendo a reuniones o eventos solo por obligación o por quedar bien.
- *Compras de última hora*. Una mala organización doméstica hace que tengamos que escaparnos —y perder tiempo— para adquirir aquello que nos falta.
- *Grupos de Whatsapp, Messenger o similares* que no son necesarios, pero que bombardean nuestro móvil a todas horas.

205
LA BELLEZA DE LO DIFÍCIL

E n su clásico *Un camino sin huellas*, M. Scott Peck empezaba con una frase osada para un libro de autoayuda: «La vida es difícil». Este psiquiatra norteamericano explica después por qué la dificultad no debe frustrarnos, sino suponer un acicate para ser aún más proactivos. En sus palabras:

> *Es humano —y sabio— temer a lo desconocido, ser al menos un poquito aprensivo al embarcarse en una aventura; pero solo de las aventuras aprendemos cosas importantes.*

¿Tienes espíritu aventurero? ¿Cuál fue la última gran dificultad a la que te enfrentaste? ¿Qué aprendizaje importante adquiriste?

Scott Peck nos recuerda que «nuestros momentos más sublimes es más probable que se produzcan cuando nos sentimos profundamente abatidos, infelices o insatisfechos. Pues es solo en estos momentos, empujados por la insatisfacción, que somos capaces de salir del camino trillado y empezar a buscar respuestas más verdaderas en otros senderos».

PON NOMBRE A TU AVENTURA

Cambiar la palabra *problema* o *crisis* por *aventura* nos coloca en el papel de héroe o heroína de nuestra vida, en lugar de ser la víctima. Para ello, en este ejercicio te pido lo siguiente:

1. Pon nombre a la última *aventura* a la que te enfrentaste (por ejemplo, LA AVENTURA DE ENCONTRAR UN TRABAJO MEJOR).
2. Dale un título a la aventura que tienes ahora por delante.
3. Haz un mapa con las diferentes etapas que debes superar en este viaje.

206
TU MEJOR COMPAÑÍA

Vas a vivir contigo toda tu vida, ese es un matrimonio que no admite traiciones ni divorcios. ¿Cómo vas a engañar a esa increíble persona que te acompaña y que es tu mejor aliado? ¿Qué mejor compañero para caminar hacia la felicidad y la realización que la versión más honesta de ti mismo?

Hay mucho que podéis hacer juntos para construir una vida que merezca la pena.

El primer paso para comenzar a andar ese sendero a la par es sincerarte, reconciliarte con lo que eres y abrazar a ese ser maravilloso que cada día tiene el privilegio de respirar, amar y sentir. Y que no es otro que tú mismo.

Solo si vives en armonía contigo mismo, fiel a tus principios y deseos, serás capaz de amar a otros y ser amado. Esto es ya en sí un poderoso motivo para potenciar tu autoamor.

¿CÓMO COCINAS TU FELICIDAD?

Hay muchas recetas de distintas autoras y autores, y en este libro encontrarás algunas, pero te propongo que en este ejercicio seas tú quien establezca los ingredientes que necesitas para llevarte de la mejor manera contigo mismo:

1....................................
2....................................
3....................................
4....................................
5....................................

Ahora que ya tienes la receta, ¡manos a la obra!

207
EXPRESAR LAS EMOCIONES

M e costó un tiempo entenderlo, pero ahora sé que es muy positivo expresar las emociones. Hay muchas maneras de hacerlo: compartirlas con alguien que escuche bien, cantarlas, dibujarlas, escribirlas...

¿Cuál es tu forma más natural de expresar lo que sientes?

Sacarlo y canalizarlo por cualquier medio ayuda a que lo que sentimos baje de intensidad y podamos observarlo desde fuera. Así podemos entenderlo mejor, integrarlo y dejarlo ir poco a poco. Evitaremos que las emociones se queden ahí y que reaparezcan una y otra vez.

Estoy agradecida a todas las personas que supieron acompañarme en la gestión de aquellas emociones que me impedían avanzar, las que me dieron pautas y las que escucharon sin juzgar, haciéndome ver que solo yo poseía la llave de mi libertad.

--- **ARTETERAPIA** ---

El arte no es algo para unos pocos, puedes usarlo como una conversación contigo a través de la que descubrir lo que llevas dentro. Puedes elegir la vía de expresión más cómoda o que más te guste:
- Practica el dibujo libre cuando te invada una emoción. Trata de plasmar en el papel lo que sientes.

- Escribir puede tener el mismo efecto terapéutico. A través de las palabras, da rienda suelta a lo que piensas, sientes o deseas.
- La música, la fotografía, la danza... Puedes probar distintas maneras de expresarte y elegir aquella con la que fluyes más fácilmente.

208
LA VIEJA CAJA

En su celebrado ensayo *El poder del ahora*, el maestro Eckhart Tolle explica una fábula que deseo compartir contigo:

Un mendigo estuvo junto a una carretera durante más de treinta años. Un día, un desconocido pasó por allí.

—¿Una limosna? —murmuró el mendigo, alargando mecánicamente su gorra de béisbol.

—No tengo nada que darte —dijo el desconocido. A continuación preguntó:

—¿Sobre qué estás sentado?

—Nada —respondió el mendigo—. Solo una vieja caja. He estado sentado en ella desde no sé cuándo.

—¿Has mirado dentro alguna vez? —preguntó el desconocido.

—No —dijo el mendigo—, ¿para qué? No hay nada dentro.

—Echa una mirada —insistió el desconocido.

El mendigo consiguió abrir la tapa. Con infinita sorpresa, incredulidad y dicha, vio que la caja estaba llena de oro.

Este relato nos enseña, de forma simbólica, que muchas veces tenemos tan cerca nuestra riqueza que no sabemos verla.

LA VIDA ESTÁ AQUÍ

En su juventud, el escritor checo Milan Kundera escribió *La vida está en otra parte*. En esta novela cuenta la historia de un hombre que siempre cree estar viviendo en el lugar y momento equivocados.

¿Y si intentamos que no nos suceda como al protagonista y abrimos los ojos para darnos cuenta de que la vida está aquí y tiene mucho que ofrecernos si dejamos de mirar a otra parte?

209
LA REGLA DE LOS 5 SEGUNDOS

Muchas veces hay que hacer cosas que nos apetecen poco o nada para lograr aquello que tanto queremos. Sin embargo, también sabemos que es la única forma de acercarnos a ese objetivo.

¿Cómo podemos superar la pereza que nos da esto que necesitamos realizar?

Hazlo sin pensar. Esta es la solución que propone mi adorada Mel Robbins con su «Regla de los 5 segundos»:

- Levántate y disponte a hacerlo ahora mismo.
- Verbaliza la cuenta atrás de los cinco segundos −5... 4... 3... 2... 1...− y siente cómo tu cuerpo y tu mente van cortando, con ese ritual, cualquier intento de procrastinación.
- Celebra que por fin lo has hecho.

CÓMO Y CUÁNDO APLICAR LA REGLA DE LOS 5 SEGUNDOS

1. Puedes recurrir a la cuenta atrás siempre que tengas que hacer algo y notes en ti cierta resistencia.
2. Aplícala en cualquier tarea cotidiana que no te apetezca hacer, pero que sabes que necesitas hacer.

3. Mel Robbins aconseja actuar con el espíritu de *quemar las naves*. Es decir, como si no hubiera ninguna otra opción ni plan B.

210
BELLEZA Y HUMANIDAD

Me encanta impregnarme de lo bello, ya sea música, pintura, afectos, miradas, plantas, animales... La belleza me inspira y me pone contenta.

Pero no limito esta experiencia a un paisaje o a una obra de arte. También me atraen las personas bonitas de corazón. Aquellas que son sencillas, claras, abiertas, nobles y generosas.

No hace falta que digan nada, me basta con su actitud y su energía. A veces ni siquiera las conozco y simplemente me siento a su lado o las observo con disimulo.

Puede ser un padre en un parque, una alegre quiosquera, una joven que sale con sus amigas del instituto... Da igual. Si me miran, yo sonrío y luego me voy.

Necesito la belleza del mundo y la de las personas para vivir. Quiero gente luminosa a mi lado para contagiarme de su resplandor.

BELLEZA Y ESPIRITUALIDAD

Según afirma el teólogo y filósofo Francesc Torralba en su ensayo *Inteligencia espiritual,* las personas con esta clase de inteligencia tienen más facilidad para apreciar la belleza del mundo y la de los demás. Por este motivo, los artistas suelen ser profundamente espirituales.

Así pues, tu capacidad para capturar la belleza que te rodea es un indicador de tu inteligencia espiritual.

211
UNA AVENTURA APASIONANTE

A lo largo del libro hemos hablado de la importancia de cuestionar nuestras creencias. Esto conlleva un ejercicio de valentía, ya que desprenderte de tus verdades absolutas hace que entres en un terreno de incertidumbre nada cómodo.

Sin embargo, cuando abandonas el mundo conocido, empieza una exploración muy interesante que te permite abrirte a nuevas versiones de ti mismo y romper con los viejos paradigmas. Esa aventura puede llevarte a un lugar nuevo y más confortable.

Al salir de la zona de confort, a veces sentirás que pasas por un bosque oscuro y lleno de tinieblas, pero no temas por ello. No hay lobos que te devoren ni ladrones que te asalten.

Jugar a no ser nada, a no ser nadie, y no llevar ninguna certeza por bandera despliega ante ti un sinfín de posibilidades a la vez que te libera de la cárcel de lo absoluto.

¿¡Y TÚ QUÉ SABES!?

En 2004 se estrenó un singular documental con este título que mezclaba física cuántica, consciencia y espiritualidad. Entre las muchas inspiraciones que se dan, una de ellas es: «El verdadero truco de la vida no está en el conocimiento sino en el misterio».

¿Te atreves a soltar las certezas y abrazar el misterio de la vida y sus maravillas?

212

DESAPEGO

Este es un concepto fundamental en el budismo, así como en la psicología moderna. De hecho, en uno de los manuales más influyentes de los últimos cincuenta años, *Tus zonas erróneas*, el psicoterapeuta Wayne Dyer afirma:

> *La independencia psicológica implica no necesitar a los demás. No digo no desear tener relaciones con los demás; lo que digo es no necesitarlos. En el momento que sientes esa necesidad te vuelves vulnerable, eres un esclavo (...) La sociedad nos enseña a ser dependientes de una cantidad de gente empezando por los padres; y podría ser que tú sigas aún con la boca abierta esperando a que caigan los gusanos de muchas de tus relaciones más significativas. Mientras pienses que tienes que hacer algo porque es lo que se espera de ti en cualquier relación, y el hacerlo te provoca resentimientos contra esa persona y el no hacerlo te carga de culpa, puedes estar seguro de que tienes que ocuparte de esta zona errónea.*

PEQUEÑO TEST DE DESAPEGO

1. Antes de tomar cualquier decisión importante para ti, piensa: ¿te preocupa que pueda causar molestias o desaprobación?
2. ¿Sueles estar pendiente de lo que los demás opinan de ti?
3. Cuando publicas un post en las redes sociales, ¿te entristece cuando tiene pocos *likes* y comentarios?
4. ¿Te cuesta ir en contra de la corriente?

Si has contestado afirmativamente a dos o más de estas preguntas, tienes que trabajar el desapego, dejar de depender de lo que opine el mundo.

213
RESETEA TU CEREBRO

No soy tu madre ni te diré que te vayas pronto a la cama, pero te recuerdo que el descanso es esencial para el reseteo de tu cerebro. Y no solo cuentan las horas que dormimos, sino la calidad del sueño. Se aconseja dormir en una habitación tranquila, sin ruidos y con la temperatura adecuada, con una cama que se adapte bien a lo que necesita tu cuerpo.

Como dicen los especialistas en sueño, solo quien descansa suficiente está del todo despierto en la vigilia. Un sueño reparador hará que tus neuronas se regeneren y que tu cerebro esté en forma para un nuevo día.

Te invito a que pongas atención a ese tercio de nuestro tiempo, el que pasamos durmiendo, para que en los otros dos tercios goces de energía y calidad de vida.

SEIS TRUCOS PARA DORMIR MEJOR

Según un informe de la Clínica Mayo, podemos mejorar nuestro descanso nocturno con estas seis medidas:

1. *Sigue un horario fijo de sueño.* Nada altera más el descanso que la irregularidad a la hora de acostarnos.
2. *Presta atención a lo que comes y bebes.* No tomes excitantes después de las seis de la tarde ni hagas cenas pesadas justo antes de acostarte.
3. *Crea un ambiente de descanso.* Aleja de la cama móviles, tabletas y ordenadores. Tu cerebro debe relacionar tu espacio con la desconexión.
4. *Limita las siestas diurnas.* Si son demasiado largas, puedes pagarlo en insomnio.
5. *Realiza actividad física como parte de tu rutina diaria.* Mover el cuerpo, cansarlo de forma saludable, ayuda al descanso.
6. *Controla las preocupaciones.* ¡No te las lleves a la cama! Aquello que no hayas podido resolver hoy, déjalo para mañana.

214
EXPLÍCATE, EXPRESA Y COMPARTE

Cuando llegue el momento de iniciar una andadura sentimental junto a alguien –pareja o amigo–, o si quieres refrescar o relanzar la relación en la que estás ahora, empieza explicando el momento en el que te encuentras, cuáles son tus deseos y cómo estás por dentro.

Expresa lo que necesitas y lo que buscas para que la otra parte entienda mejor tus actos y palabras. Comparte lo que te mueve desde el corazón.

Sé generoso en este aspecto e indaga, además, lo que la otra parte necesita de ti para saber si tú puedes corresponderle.

Acércate así, generoso y abierto. Será la mejor forma de crear un camino conjunto y evitar malentendidos y falsas expectativas.

EL BUEN AMOR EN UNA FRASE

Uno de los aforismos más apreciados del psicólogo Antoni Bolinches es «El secreto de una buena relación es casarse con el otro sin divorciarse de uno mismo». Es decir, que no hay nada malo en complacer al otro, siempre que eso no implique perjudicarte a ti mismo o traicionar tus principios.

215
KOĀNS

H as oído hablar alguna vez de los koāns, los acertijos que deben resolver los estudiantes de zen? El discípulo recibe una pregunta enigmática por parte de su maestro y la medita durante días, suspendiendo el pensamiento racional, para llegar a una respuesta espontánea.

Tal vez por eso también son usados en los programas de creatividad para desarrollar el pensamiento lateral. El orientalista holandés Janwillem van de Wetering lo definía así:

> *Un koān es una pregunta que se plantea a un nivel distinto de las preguntas que surgen diariamente, y perdemos el tiempo si pretendemos resolverla mediante los métodos ordinarios. Ni la inteligencia ni la experiencia nos ayudarán. Sin embargo, el maestro pide una respuesta. Te mira e insiste en que hay una respuesta.*

TRES KOĀNS PARA PRACTICAR EL PENSAMIENTO LATERAL

1. ¿Cuál es el sonido de una palmada ejecutada con una sola mano?
2. ¿Cómo puedes salvar a un unicornio?
3. ¿Cuál era tu rostro original antes de que te dieran a luz tus padres?

216
TREINTA CENTÍMETROS

Treinta centímetros. Eso es lo que aproximadamente separa el cerebro del corazón. Es curioso que en ese corto espacio se produzcan, me atrevería a decir, la mayoría de las disfunciones y desencuentros con nuestro propio ser.

¿Qué sucede para que la conciliación entre emoción y pensamiento sea tan complicada?

Hemos hablado ya de que no atendemos lo suficiente lo que sentimos. Este es un punto que me interesa especialmente, ya que si partimos de la base de que se piensa con el cerebro y se siente con el corazón...

¿Qué pasaría si pudiéramos sentir más con el cerebro y pensar con el corazón? ¿Conseguiríamos unificar esa dicotomía que nos desconecta de nosotros mismos?

——— CÓMO ACTIVAR LA INTELIGENCIA DEL CORAZÓN ———

Annie Marquier, matemática e investigadora de la conciencia, explicaba en una entrevista que el corazón contiene un sistema nervioso independiente y bien desarrollado con más de 40.000 neuronas.
Eso le permite tomar decisiones independientemente del cerebro.

Según esta autora, podemos activarlo...
• Abriéndonos al prójimo.
• Escuchando más y mejor.
• Practicando el arte de la paciencia.
• Cooperando con los demás.
• Aceptando las diferencias.
• Cultivando nuestro coraje.

217
EL ENCUENTRO MÁS IMPORTANTE DE TU VIDA

Decía Pablo Neruda: «Algún día en cualquier parte, en cualquier lugar indefectiblemente te encontrarás a ti mismo, y esa, solo esa, puede ser la más feliz o la más amarga de tus horas».

¿Cuántas personas evitan ese encuentro porque no se sienten a gusto con ellas mismas?

Solo desde uno mismo puede conducirse con éxito cualquier cambio vital. Únicamente lo que tú hagas desde el más profundo convencimiento y anhelo será efectivo. Ese será el revulsivo infalible para tirar adelante en los momentos complicados.

Nadie vendrá a descubrirte algo de lo que solo tú tienes: tu fórmula magistral para impulsarte un paso más allá.

¿Estás preparado para el encuentro más importante de tu vida?

TRES MANERAS DE ENCONTRARTE CONTIGO MISMO

1. Permanecer en silencio, sea en la naturaleza o en una habitación tranquila, es una de las formas más sencillas de reencontrarte.

2. La meditación en todas sus modalidades es una vía tradicional para profundizar en ti.

3. Un viaje en solitario es otra magnífica forma de conocerte mejor y descubrir cómo eres y reaccionas ante los cambios.

218
ESTELAS EN EL MAR

Cuando te sientas abatido y todo se te haga cuesta arriba, cuando creas que no puedes más, date cuenta de todo lo que has recorrido hasta ese momento. Así aceptarás, con tranquilidad de espíritu, estar exhausto y abatido. Te permitirás descansar, observar lo logrado y celebrarlo, para tomar impulso mucho más motivado y creyendo en ti.

El poema más célebre de Antonio Machado puede servirte de inspiración en un momento así:

Caminante, son tus huellas
el camino y nada más;
Caminante, no hay camino,
se hace camino al andar.
Al andar se hace el camino,
y al volver la vista atrás
se ve la senda que nunca
se ha de volver a pisar.
Caminante, no hay camino
sino estelas en la mar.

LA LÍNEA DE LA VIDA

Este es un ejercicio muy utilizado en *coaching* para tomar conciencia de nuestro recorrido personal:

1. Traza, en una hoja dispuesta en horizontal, una línea recta que simbolice tu vida.
2. Marca con rayas verticales los acontecimientos más importantes: nacimientos, muertes, matrimonios, rupturas, cambios de trabajo, de vivienda, de país...
3. Incluye en esa línea de vida los momentos de crisis que te han fortalecido y te han hecho ser quien eres.
4. Analiza tu historia en perspectiva y date cuenta de todo lo que tienes por dar y por vivir.

219

LA VIDA NO ES UNA COMPETICIÓN

E n uno de los libros más bellos e inspiradores publicados, *Martes con mi viejo profesor*, el periodista Mitch Albom se reencuentra con un docente que marcó su vida y que, en el cenit de su existencia, se aviene a darle –cada martes– unas últimas enseñanzas sobre el arte de vivir.

Algunas son tan básicas como esenciales: *Lo más importante en la vida es aprender a dar amor y permitir que el amor venga a ti.*

Este profesor entrañable protagoniza una anécdota muy significativa. Estando en un partido de baloncesto estudiantil, al escuchar los cantos: «*¡Somos número uno, somos número uno!*», Morrie sorprende a todo el mundo al abandonar su asiento y plantarse en medio de la cancha para preguntar, levantando la voz:

–*¿Qué problema hay en ser el número dos?*

TRES PREGUNTAS SOBRE EL ÉXITO

Esta anécdota nos sirve para hacernos preguntas importantes cuando nos pongamos en un modo competitivo que nos lleva al estrés:
- ¿Por qué debería medir mis logros respecto a lo que consiguen otros?
- ¿Esto que pretendo alcanzar es importante para mí, o es solo un éxito de cara a la galería?
- ¿Cuál es mi verdadero objetivo, que no implica competir con nadie que no sea yo mismo?

220
SIN PRISA

N adie te persigue. No hay prisa. No te atrapa nada. No te arrolla nada. Solo aceleraste sin saber hacia dónde ibas exactamente. Te pusiste a correr por inercia.

Para cuando te has dado cuenta y has mirado para atrás, has descubierto que no había nadie pisándote los talones. Que te arrollabas a ti mismo. Así que, calma, está todo controlado en cuanto a premura se refiere.

Alguien te dijo, quizá, que corriendo se llegaba antes. Pero ¿correr *pa qué?* me decían en Cuba, cuando era joven. Y es verdad.

Varios estudios demuestran que las personas capaces de ralentizar su actividad manejan mejor el exceso de información, cumplen más con sus compromisos y se distraen menos en el trabajo.

Por todo ello, acostúmbrate a ir más despacio. Verás qué bien sienta.

PRACTICA EL EJERCICIO SUPERLENTO

La lentitud también ha demostrado ser muy eficaz en la práctica deportiva, en especial para perder grasas acumuladas. El llamado entrenamiento LISS (*Low Intensity Steady State*) se realiza así:
- A diferencia de otras prácticas deportivas, el ritmo cardiaco no debe superar el 60-65 por ciento de su capacidad total.
- Para compensar, dedicaremos más tiempo al ejercicio lento: un mínimo de 45 minutos.
- Puedes practicar LISS pedaleando lentamente o caminando en una elíptica, o bien dar un paseo a un ritmo constante hasta lograr un determinado objetivo de pasos.
- En el LISS los *picos* de actividad se cambian por la constancia y el bienestar del ejercicio relajado.

221

TU AJEDREZ VITAL

Quizá a veces sientas que no estás en el mejor momento ni en el mejor lugar, pero eso no significa que no te puedas mover. Como en el ajedrez, lo que importa en esos casos es tu siguiente movimiento. Tomar la mejor decisión con el ingenio y los recursos a tu alcance.

En su libro *El juego de la vida*, Adriana Hernández Planillas ve en este ejercicio una metáfora de la vida:

> *El futuro (...) es la suma de muchas pequeñas causas y efectos que parten de uno mismo. Cada movimiento que hacemos en la existencia tiene sus consecuencias, y a su vez, estas provocan reacciones y nuevas acciones, como en el efecto mariposa. Justamente de eso va también el ajedrez (...)*
>
> *Trasladado a la vida, las personas que van a la deriva son aquellas que no son conscientes de las consecuencias de sus actos, ni para ellas ni para los demás (...) El arte de vivir consiste en comprender todos los mecanismos —favorables o perjudiciales para nuestros intereses— que activamos cada vez que movemos pieza.*

───── **LA ESTRATEGIA DE KASPÁROV PARA LA VIDA** ─────

Este juego intelectual, que ha aumentado su popularidad desde la emisión de la serie *Gambito de dama*, tiene como uno de sus grandes maestros a Garry Kaspárov, quien en su libro *Cómo la vida imita al ajedrez* explica que un estratega «empieza con un objetivo para un futuro lejano y trabaja retrocediendo hasta el presente».

¿Eres capaz de hacer este ejercicio con tu propia vida, midiendo todos los pasos que te llevan desde el ahora hasta esa meta futura?

222
LAS SOLUCIONES ESTÁN DENTRO

Uno de los filósofos más destacados —y a menudo difíciles— de la filosofía contemporánea, Ludwig Wittgenstein, exponía esta alegoría sobre las soluciones que muchas veces buscamos para nuestra vida:

> *Un hombre puede hallarse prisionero en una habitación con una puerta que no está cerrada, sino que se abre hacia dentro; y no saldrá de ella hasta que no se le ocurra tirar de ella en lugar de empujarla.*

Es una explicación muy gráfica de lo que nos sucede muchas veces. Esperamos que cambie la situación desde fuera: que llegue un cambio económico, un mentor, una pareja, un golpe de azar que nos abra esa puerta que nos separa de lo que deseamos.

Pero, como dice el filósofo austriaco, esa puerta se abre hacia dentro. Busca dentro de ti. Tienes todo lo que necesitas para la aventura que deseas iniciar.

REVOLUCIÓNATE

Una frase célebre de Wittgenstein es «Revolucionario será aquel que pueda revolucionarse a sí mismo».

La pregunta aquí sería: ¿Qué puedes hacer, aquí y ahora, para revolucionar quién eres y cómo vives?

223
PEQUEÑAS COSAS

Me gusta poner flores cortadas en casa y plantas en el jardín. Los animales los prefiero en el campo, aunque sueño con tener un gato perezoso cerca.

Me gusta abrir un vino con amigos y degustar un buen queso. Hacer un pastel una tarde y cocinar pasta mientras escucho ópera o descubro nuevas músicas. Ordenar armarios y escuchar el pódcast de gente que me inspira. Curiosear tiendas bonitas y librerías pequeñas. Mirar a la gente y pensar en lo que harán cuando llegan a casa. Peinar las trenzas de mi hija, ponerme los collares de mi madre y pedir una receta a mi tía por teléfono. Planear viajes soñados y jugar a cartas en invierno. Ponerme una mascarilla en el pelo o en la cara y dejar pasar un rato mirando al techo. Escribir cosas cortas y leer novelas de mujeres.

--------------- **HAZ UNA LISTA DE PLACERES SENCILLOS** ---------------

En su libro *El primer trago de cerveza y otros pequeños placeres de la vida*, Philippe Delerm mencionaba delicias cotidianas como ir a comprar cruasanes recién hechos o ver el Tour de Francia en el calor del verano.

Como este autor francés, te propongo que elabores tu propia lista de pequeñas cosas que te devuelven la vida. Cada vez que te sientas desanimado, léela como recordatorio de las cosas que te hacen renacer.

224
TU PROPIA RUTA

Tal vez el pasado no salió tal y como esperabas, porque te faltaba experiencia o recursos. Quizá carecías de la fortaleza y la energía requeridas para abordar los proyectos que tenías por delante. Puede que el ambiente no fuera el adecuado. Sin embargo, hoy no es entonces.

Eres adulto y tienes poder de decisión sobre tu existencia. No hay nadie a quien culpar o responsabilizar de lo que te suceda a partir de ahora.

Tu vida sigue una ruta marcada por ti y para ti. Puedes dar la vuelta en cualquier momento, parar a repostar, pensar o mirar el mapa otra vez. Puedes cambiar de dirección, aminorar la marcha o acelerar la velocidad hasta retar a la luz.

No tienes que seguir la misma senda y mucho menos las indicaciones de quien viaja a tu lado. Tuya es la decisión de elegir la compañía o la soledad, observar el paisaje o cerrar los ojos un instante para imaginar nuevos horizontes, sentir la brisa y el calor o pararte a mirar la lluvia caer.

Lo único que necesitas es tu propio ser como vehículo, libre de cargas, sano de motor y fuerza. Te esperan miles de kilómetros apasionantes de autodescubrimiento y entrega.

--- **EN LA AUTOPISTA DE TU VIDA** ---

Siguiendo con la metáfora del coche, imagina que tu existencia es un viaje en coche en el que solo tú decides tu rumbo. ¿Cómo llamarías el destino al que te diriges?

225
ELOGIO DE LA SOMBRA

E n su pequeño libro *Elogio de la sombra*, el autor japonés Junichiro Tanizaki nos sorprende hablando de la belleza de lo menos brillante.

En una casa japonesa, la opacidad, lo mate, la penumbra, lo oscuro conforman esa estética extraordinaria que tanto admiramos en su arquitectura, así como en la iluminación de los espacios...

Esta visión estética se puede trasladar a una filosofía de vida y una actitud que me parece muy interesante. Más allá de lo superficial y aparente, el elogio de la sombra supone un guiño a la discreción, al misterio y a la sabiduría encubierta que toda persona posee.

Además, sin sombra no hay luz ni reflejos.

No todo debe ser deslumbrante, luminoso y reluciente. Es mucho más interesante y atractivo brillar desde la sombra, dejar que los demás imaginen aquello que no alcanzan a ver.

EL SECRETO DE SOFÍA LOREN

Al ser preguntada una vez sobre el secreto del *sex-appeal*, la gran actriz italiana dijo: «Consiste un 50 por ciento en lo que tienes, y el otro 50 por ciento en lo que las demás personas creen que tienes».

Esa visión del misterio como atractivo está en sintonía con la obra de Tanizaki. Por lo tanto, en lugar de mostrar abiertamente lo que somos, como hombres o mujeres anuncio, os invito a dejar que los demás imaginen los tesoros que esconde nuestra sombra.

226

SUPOSICIONES

Un relato de autor desconocido cuenta que una mujer esperaba su vuelo en un gran aeropuerto y, como aún faltaban un par de horas para entrar en el avión, fue a comprar un libro y un paquete de galletas.

Tras sentarse en una butaca de la sala VIP, dejó en el asiento de al lado su bolso y las galletas. Al momento, el asiento siguiente fue ocupado por un joven viajero.

La mujer se comió una galleta mientras leía y advirtió, asombrada, que el joven tomaba otra del paquete. Cada vez que ella comía una galleta, el joven hacía lo propio.

Y, por si aquello fuera poco, cuando quedaba solo una galleta, el joven tomó la mitad, dejándole a ella el resto.

A punto de explotar de indignación, la mujer cerró el libro y se dirigió a la puerta de embarque. Cuando por fin ocupó su asiento en el avión y abrió el bolso se dio cuenta, avergonzada, de que su paquete de galletas estaba dentro, aún por abrir.

NO PRESUPONGAS

Esta sencilla historia nos da tres lecciones prácticas para la vida diaria:

1. Antes de enfadarnos con alguien, nos tenemos que asegurar de que las cosas son tal y como imaginamos.

2. Muchas cosas que nos asombran tienen una explicación muy distinta a la que dicta nuestra fantasía.

3. Todo tiempo invertido en crear resentimiento hacia algo o alguien es tiempo malgastado.

227
BALONES FUERA

E s cierto que no todo depende de nosotros, pero la tendencia a echar balones fuera puede hacernos perder el control de nuestra vida. Pregúntate cuántas veces depositas en circunstancias externas la responsabilidad de lo que te sucede. Te muestro algunos indicadores para que te des cuenta de cuándo lo haces:

- Utilizar expresiones como *a ver si* o el famoso *es que* para justificarnos y trasladar la responsabilidad al exterior.
- Hablar en condicional: la promesa de que haremos algo *cuando* se den determinadas condiciones.
- Esperar que sea un ente o poder ajeno el que resuelva un problema o un conflicto.
- Adjudicar responsabilidades a terceros cuando las cosas no salen como deseamos.

AFIRMACIONES PARA ECHAR *BALONES DENTRO*

En cambio, puedes utilizar estas frases:
- Soy responsable de mi vida y me ocupo de las cosas que dependen de mí.
- Prefiero ponerme en marcha a esperar la ayuda de otros.

- No hay circunstancias más favorables que las que yo creo en mi vida.
- Parafraseando a Henry Ford, tanto si creo que puedo como si creo que no puedo, estoy en lo cierto.

228

WORK IN PROGRESS

Desde la infancia, buscamos el reconocimiento del grupo para reafirmar nuestra valía. Es natural en los niños, ya que forma parte de nuestra integración en la sociedad.

Pero también de adultos seguimos necesitando –en mayor o menor grado– la confirmación de que lo que hemos hecho está bien, la celebración del logro excelente y, así, cada vez más.

En el fondo, en toda nuestra vida sigue latiendo el deseo de ser aceptados. Sin embargo, la única aceptación que verdaderamente necesitas es la tuya propia.

Nadie puede validar tus logros, tu evolución, tu actual estado de las cosas, más que tú mismo.

Sé generoso y amable contigo, a la vez que inconformista y capaz de seguir soñando. Todo ser humano es un *work in progress* que avanza hacia la plenitud.

ELABORA UN MAPA DE PROGRESOS

1. Establece qué áreas de tu vida necesitan mejora y asigna a cada una de ellas una tarjeta u hoja de cuaderno.
2. Cada vez que logres un avance significativo, anótalo en su lugar. Puedes ilustrarlo con una imagen o gráfico para que resulte más visual.
3. Revisa de vez en cuando los distintos progresos en cada sección. Eso te motivará para marcarte nuevos retos.

229
MOMENTOS DORADOS

En el fútbol universitario de Estados Unidos hay un premio especial, el Trofeo Heisman, que se da al deportista que exhibe más excelencia e integridad.

La novelista Shauna Niequist hace al respecto la siguiente reflexión:

Los grandes momentos se encuentran en cada hora, cada conversación, cada comida, cada reunión.

El ganador del Trofeo Heisman lo sabe. Él sabe que su gran momento no fue cuando le dieron el trofeo. Fueron las mil veces que fue a practicar en vez de ir a la cama. Fueron los kilómetros recorridos en días de lluvia, las comidas saludables cuando una hamburguesa sonaba como el cielo. Que el gran momento se representa y se apoya en una base de momentos que habían llegado antes.

--- **¿CUÁL ES TU ÍTACA?** ---

En uno de los poemas más célebres de la era moderna, *Viaje a Ítaca*, Constantinos Kavafis hace la siguiente recomendación:

Ten siempre a Ítaca en tu mente.
Llegar allí es tu destino.
Mas no apresures nunca el viaje.

Sin duda, la precipitación estropea la belleza de cualquier proyecto que tengas, que debe apoyarse en los momentos dorados y en ese destino final que ilumina tu ruta.

230
ABRAZA A TU NIÑO INTERIOR

El niño que tienes dentro, y que ha pasado algún que otro momento traumático en su vida, hoy tiene en ti a un gran aliado.

Yo misma he sido testigo de emocionantes cambios en personas que, en algún momento de su proceso personal, han buscado a su niño interior para abrazarlo y acogerlo.

El proceso consiste en identificar al niño que fuiste para reconciliarlo con el adulto que eres hoy. Ubicar el episodio traumático que supuso un obstáculo en tu infancia y que te ha marcado. Una vez encontrado, hay que recuperar el pasado a través de la visualización de ese momento y, en ella, abrazar a tu *yo niño* y ofrecerle de manera explícita la protección de tu *yo adulto*.

A partir de ese momento, ese niño tendrá siempre en ti al mejor de los protectores y nada malo le sucederá.

VUELVE A SER NIÑO POR UN DÍA

Anímate a hacer tu viaje para reencontrarte con tu niño interior, trasládate a la infancia y pregúntate:
- ¿Qué te gustaba hacer?
- ¿Cuál era tu juego o juguete favorito?
- ¿Tenías un miedo determinado?

- ¿Qué clase de futuro imaginabas para ti?

Una vez revivas a tu *yo niño*, podrás abrazarlo, comprenderlo mejor y brindarle la protección del *yo adulto*.

231

CONFIANZA

C*onfianza* es una palabra clave cuando se trata de hablar de bienestar emocional. Es una de las que más me gustan, lo confieso. Este es el motivo por el que he decidido dedicarle una serie de cuatro reflexiones dentro de este libro.

Me gustaría empezar indagando sobre el significado del término: es la garantía que depositamos en algo o alguien.

Si se trata de una persona, implica que podemos compartir con ella cualquier proyecto o situación íntima, sabiendo que rema a nuestro favor.

Si tenemos un proyecto en ciernes, supone la capacidad que poseemos de fiarnos de que este se da en el momento adecuado y de que estamos preparados para ello. Sabemos que las circunstancias externas no dependen de nosotros, pero lo compensamos con nuestra intención, con la confianza —valga la redundancia— en que todo saldrá bien.

PROFECÍA DE AUTOCUMPLIMIENTO

Reciben este nombre las predicciones que hacemos —muchas veces en negativo— sobre lo que esperamos que suceda en una determinada situación. Antes de que vivamos el resultado, ya lo estamos anticipando, lo cual hace que inconscientemente facilitemos que eso ocurra. Por eso se llama profecía de autocumplimiento.

¿Tiendes a elaborar pronósticos negativos o positivos sobre lo que te va a suceder? En el primer caso, te recomiendo cambiar tu forma de predecir o, al menos, adoptar una mirada neutra sobre el futuro inmediato.

232
CONFÍO EN TI

E n esta segunda reflexión dedicada a la confianza, profundizaremos un poco más en aquella que depositamos en alguien, ya sea nuestra pareja, un amigo o un colaborador.

Al confiar en alguien, le estamos adjudicando garantías y valor a una persona que, entendemos, es digna de credibilidad. Hacerlo no es condescendencia ni un favor, sino más bien la actitud de un alma agradecida.

Hay algo característico de la confianza, y es que no se puede tener a medias. O confías o no confías en la otra persona.

Pero, nos preguntaremos, ¿qué suele implicar la confianza en alguien?

- Saber qué puedes esperar de esa persona en una situación importante.
- Poder *confiarle* un secreto y tener la seguridad de que no hará un mal uso de esa información.
- No necesitar de muchas palabras para comunicaros. Tu persona *de confianza* enseguida entenderá lo que estás viviendo y sintiendo.

LA PRUEBA DEFINITIVA

En referencia a los diferentes grados de amistad y confianza, el escritor Oscar Wilde situaba esta en primer término: «Cualquiera puede simpatizar con las penas de un amigo; simpatizar con sus éxitos requiere de una naturaleza delicadísima».

¿Cuántas relaciones tienes con esta calidad?

233
CONFÍA EN MÍ

En la tercera reflexión quiero hablar de la confianza que otros depositan en nosotros, ya que puede ser fuente de muchos malentendidos. A menudo no somos conscientes de las expectativas que tienen los demás sobre nosotros. Es interesante estar atento a ello, ya que lo que esperan quizá sean quimeras imposibles con las que no podamos lidiar. En ese caso lo natural es comunicarlo al otro para evitar un desengaño.

Hay personas que creen que somos adivinos, que sabemos lo que sienten sin que se expresen al respecto, pero no es así. Un ejercicio saludable para medir la confianza del otro es preguntarnos o incluso preguntarle:

- ¿Qué significa para él o ella que seas merecedor de esa confianza?
- ¿Qué espera de vuestro vínculo?
- ¿Te acepta esta persona en tu totalidad, con tus virtudes y defectos?

Responder a estas preguntas te ayudará a comprender el tipo de relación que estáis construyendo.

EL WABI SABI DE LAS RELACIONES

La expresión japonesa *Wabi Sabi* significa *la belleza de la imperfección*, y no se aplica solo a las artes, sino también a los vínculos humanos. Veamos sus tres leyes aplicadas a las relaciones, tal y como las plantea Nobuo Suzuki en su libro *Wabi Sabi para la vida cotidiana*:

1. NADA ES PERFECTO. Aceptar tu propia imperfección te ayuda a aceptar la de los demás y a amarlos como son.

2. NADA ESTÁ TERMINADO. Al igual que la naturaleza, las personas están en constante cambio. Si hay amor, debemos acompañar y ayudar al otro en su proceso.

3. NADA ES PARA SIEMPRE. Hay relaciones que simplemente se terminan, al igual que hay otras que empiezan. Evitemos dramatizar.

234
AUTOCONFIANZA

Completaremos esta serie de reflexiones sobre la confianza tratando la clase más importante para el bienestar personal: la autoconfianza.

Además de confiar en otras personas y de ganarnos su confianza, es indispensable que tengamos fe en nosotros mismos. Podemos creer en nuestras capacidades e incluso darnos cuenta de nuestros logros, pero quizá aun así no confiemos del todo en nosotros mismos.

Esta carencia puede hacernos sentir miedo o incluso síndrome del impostor, la sensación de no merecer la suerte o los méritos que nos atribuyen.

Para reforzar la autoconfianza, observa todo lo que has logrado en tu camino hasta aquí y que quizá nunca celebraste. Ahora es el momento de traerlo al presente y valorarlo. No fue fruto de la casualidad. Fuiste tú quien hizo todo eso, la misma persona que va a seguir haciéndolo más y mejor.

———— ¿CUÁL ES TU NIVEL DE AUTOCONFIANZA? ————

Para conocerte mejor en ese sentido, estas preguntas te ayudarán a reflexionar:
1. ¿Necesitas que otros validen tus logros o eres capaz de darte cuenta por ti mismo?
2. ¿Sabes aceptar un halago o reconocimiento sin disculparte o sentirte incómodo?
3. Cuando las cosas se tuercen, ¿te sientes capacitado para darle la vuelta a la situación?

Como práctica extra, te propongo que cada vez que tengas dudas o conflictos que te paralicen, te repitas la palabra confía. Confía en la vida, confía en que llegarán cosas mejores, confía en que esto sucede para algo, confía en que esto es algo que conviene, aunque no lo entiendas ahora.

235

LAS LEYES DE STEVENSON

Robert Louis Stevenson, conocido en todo el mundo por novelas como *La isla del tesoro*, consideraba que nunca encontraremos mayor riqueza que nuestra propia felicidad.

Para promoverla, formuló algunas leyes prácticas como estas:

1. *Nadie lo tiene todo.* Cada persona alberga algún dolor que a la vez mezcla con la alegría de vivir. El truco es hacer que la risa supere a las lágrimas.

2. *No dejes que otros establezcan tus normas.* Sé tú mismo.

3. *Haz las cosas que te gusta hacer,* pero no te endeudes en el proceso.

4. *No pidas prestados los problemas de los demás.* Las cosas imaginarias son más difíciles de soportar que las reales.

5. *Ten muchos intereses.* Si no puedes viajar, lee acerca de otros lugares.

6. *Mantente ocupado en algo.* Una persona bien ocupada no tiene tiempo para ser infeliz.

AYUDAR TE AYUDA

Una última ley de Stevenson es «*Haz lo que puedas por aquellos que son menos afortunados que tú*». Y el novelista anglosajón no lo decía solo para alimentar un espíritu cristiano o compasivo. Sabía que ponernos al servicio de los demás nos aporta coraje, sentido y realización.

¿Cuál es tu mejor oportunidad de ayudar y ser útil en este momento?

236
CONTRA LA DESIDIA

Jostein Gaarder, el autor de *El mundo de Sofía*, decía en una entrevista que se consideraba optimista porque había descubierto, según sus palabras, «que los pesimistas son unos vagos».

A mí me gustaría añadir que la desgana llama a la desgana. Cuanto más nos dejamos arrastrar por la desidia, más nos cuesta salir de ella porque, así como los músculos de la constancia y la motivación se ejercitan, también las tendencias negativas se refuerzan con el uso.

Si sientes que has caído en una espiral negativa de algún tipo, pregúntate qué te hace falta para salir de ahí.

Para superar la desidia, te será útil averiguar qué beneficio obtienes a cambio de tu esfuerzo, al igual que el pesimista se libra de luchar por lo que cree que no va a cambiar.

Conoce a tu *saboteador* y desmonta sus argumentos para cambiar el signo de tu vida.

¿CÓMO QUIERES SER RECORDADO?

Esta pregunta es un buen disparador para cambiar una actitud negativa por otra positiva.

1. Imagina que tu vida ha transcurrido ya y que has dejado tu legado en el mundo.

2. ¿Qué recuerdo te gustaría que tuviera de ti la gente que te conoció?

3. ¿Qué cualidades o logros te gustaría que destacasen?

Una vez sepas cómo quieres ser recordado, se trata de obrar en consecuencia para dejar esa huella en el mundo.

237
TODO ES CUESTIÓN DE MESURA

Un viejo dicho reza que la caridad empieza por uno mismo, así que no lo dudes: a la hora de tomar decisiones, antepón tu persona y tu bienestar.

Eso no significa que debas dejar de lado a las personas que te rodean, pero sí respetar también tus necesidades y deseos.

Nos educan para ser generosos, considerados y amables con nuestro entorno; sin embargo, como dijo un médico de la antigüedad: el veneno está en la dosis.

Cuando llevamos nuestro deseo de ser complacientes fuera de los límites de lo razonable, nos olvidamos de nosotros mismos. Ocurre, por ejemplo, a menudo con las madres y las cuidadoras en general, sobre todo mujeres, aunque también hay muchos hombres con ese perfil.

Ser solícito en extremo te puede llevar a sentir que tu vida no tiene sentido, acumular rabia o agotamiento, mientras otras personas se aprovechan de ti sin darse cuenta del perjuicio que te supone.

--------- **UN TRUCO PARA LOS DEMASIADO AMABLES** ---------

Si eres de las personas que siempre tiene un *sí* por respuesta, cuando te pidan algo mínimamente costoso —en tiempo o dinero— haz lo siguiente:
1. No des una respuesta inmediata. Así evitarás seguir ciegamente tu impulso altruista. Retrasa la contestación, si es por escrito, o comunica a la persona que le dirás algo en 24 horas.

2. Calcula lo que supondrá para ti hacer lo que te están pidiendo. Aunque no sea cuestión de dinero, evalúa qué tiempo y energía deberás invertir.
3. Valora si realmente deseas hacer esa inversión, y si no será un impedimento para otras cosas que tú quieres hacer.

238
¿ESTÁS REALIZADO?

En psicología se cita a menudo a Abraham Maslow y su pirámide de las necesidades humanas.

Según Maslow, en la base están las necesidades fisiológicas, aquello imprescindible para vivir: aire, alimento y agua. En el segundo nivel, las necesidades psicológicas: seguridad, amor y autoestima. Y el nivel superior corresponde a la autorrealización.

Las personas realizadas presentan, según Maslow, estas características:

1. Tienen una percepción clara de la realidad.
2. Se aceptan tal como son.
3. Actúan espontáneamente.
4. Saben centrarse en el problema que les ocupa.
5. Buscan periódicamente la soledad.
6. Son autónomas.
7. Tienen valores éticos.
8. Son sociables por naturaleza.
9. Tienen sentido del humor.
10. Dan rienda suelta a su creatividad.

CHECK LIST PARA REALIZARTE

Analiza cuántas de estas diez características que menciona Maslow cumples. En las que *suspendes*, pregúntate qué puedes hacer para que formen parte de tu camino hacia la realización.

Te invito, asimismo, a que añadas alguna otra característica a la lista.

239
NO MENDIGUES

Sin darnos cuenta, a veces esperamos cosas que no llegan, como el cariño o reconocimiento de alguien, y nos mantenemos a la expectativa, con ojos tristes, a ver si por fin *cae algo.*

¿Te resuena esto?

En principio, nunca deberíamos mendigar afecto o reconocimiento, ya que, si mendigas, solo te llegará lo que le sobra al otro.

Las cosas importantes te son dadas con naturalidad, porque te las mereces. El amor y el afecto son algo con lo que llegas *de serie* al nacer, para después hacerlo crecer de manera generosa. Como adulto que eres, date tú ese cariño verdadero de primera mano, sin rogar a nadie que lo haga.

INDAGA EN LA CAUSA

Muchas personas mendigan amor de adultas porque en su infancia les faltó el amor de su padre o de su madre. Otras buscan el cariño desesperadamente porque tienen un mal autoconcepto de sí mismas y necesitan la validación del otro.

Ve a la causa de tu dependencia emocional y, una vez comprendida, llena tu depósito de amor propio.

240
LA MIRADA DE LOS NIÑOS

Me gusta observar a los niños. Escucho lo que me dicen y estoy atenta a su forma de argumentar sobre los asuntos cotidianos. Me encantan las respuestas que me dan cuando comento un problema doméstico o cuando charlamos sobre cuentos, estrellas, el mar, la lluvia, el hambre en el mundo, el amor o cualquier otro tema que les preocupe.

Sus preguntas son directas. Los *¿por qué?* o los *¿qué pasaría si...?* me descolocan y me hacen sonreír, porque me descubren todo lo que me pierdo por tener una mente más adulta.

Admiro su aptitud para resolver problemas desde la pureza y la imaginación, su capacidad de ser porosos a la información que les llega y de preguntar sin miedo.

Los niños exhiben una curiosidad insaciable y aportan ideas que abren un universo de posibilidades, por descabelladas que sean.

Quisiera poseer siempre su apertura al mundo. Cuando llegue algo nuevo a mí, no defenderme ni tener miedo. Estar atenta a las novedades y dejar volar sin límites mi imaginación.

TRES COSAS QUE NOS ENSEÑAN LOS NIÑOS

El escritor Paulo Coelho afirma que hay tres cosas que un niño siempre puede enseñarle a un adulto:
1. A ponerse contento sin motivo.
2. A estar siempre ocupado con algo.
3. A saber exigir con todas sus fuerzas.

241
LO EFÍMERO

Cuentan que, en el siglo pasado, un turista norteamericano fue a una ciudad de Oriente Medio para visitar a un anciano famoso por su sabiduría.

El forastero se sorprendió al comprobar que el hombre habitaba una humilde choza llena de pilas de libros. No había más mobiliario que una cama, una mesa y un banco.

—Pero... ¿dónde están sus muebles? —se atrevió a preguntar el turista.

—¿Y dónde están los tuyos? —se apresuró a decir el sabio.

—¿Los míos? ¡Yo estoy aquí solo de paso!

—Pues yo también —resolvió el sabio.

El mensaje de esta fábula es diáfano: la vida es efímera, pero muchas personas viven como si el tiempo fuera infinito, desaprovechando la oportunidad de ser felices.

SIENTE MÁS

Cada vez que escuchamos eso de *estamos de paso*, nos damos cuenta de que nuestro camino tiene inicio y final en esta vida que conocemos o creemos conocer. Cuando te vayas de aquí te llevarás poco o nada, además de lo vivido y compartido.

Por todo eso, mi consejo es: evita aferrarte a los logros materiales y experimenta y siente más.

242
LA GRANDEZA DEL *NO SABER*

S i te gusta indagar sobre el autoconocimiento, enhorabuena. Tal vez lleves tiempo sondeando los cielos desde tu atalaya o explorando tu interior en busca de tesoros ocultos.

Quizá no hayas encontrado todavía lo que anhelas. No te desanimes. La espiritualidad no es un objetivo medible, sino una forma de vida. Y la verdadera exploración se hace sin expectativas ni juicios. No se programa ni se calcula.

Sentirás que avanzas cuando lo hagas desde la humildad y la calma, sin sentirte mejor o distinto a los demás al pensar que has alcanzado un estado de consciencia más elevado.

Como decía el maestro Sawaki, «No importa cuántos años lleves sentado en la práctica del zazen. Nunca te convertirás en nada especial».

Deja que tu corazón te guíe en tu viaje desde la grandeza del *no saber*.

TU LISTA DEL *NO SABER*

Si la verdadera sabiduría, como decía Sócrates y los maestros de zen, viene de darse cuenta de todo lo que no se sabe, en este ejercicio te propongo que escribas todo lo que no sabes sobre...

1. Ti MISMO
2. LA VIDA
3. EL UNIVERSO
4. DIOS (O EL NOMBRE QUE QUIERAS DARLE).

Puedes llevar un cuaderno del *no saber* como exploración espiritual.

243
EL JUEGO DE VIVIR

ay un juego que se hizo muy famoso en los años ochenta. Se llamaba *Merp*. Como otros juegos de rol, te invitaba a desempeñar un papel y a tomar decisiones según lo que el maestro iba relatando, a partir de lo que los dados determinaban.

Así, tu destino en el juego dependía de las decisiones que tomabas, pero en base a lo que los dados mostraban en sus caras.

La sensación de vivir tu aventura por bosques y escenarios llenos de imprevisibles acontecimientos era algo divertido, además de una metáfora de la vida misma.

El filósofo Ortega y Gasset decía: «Yo soy yo y mis circunstancias». Las circunstancias las marca el azar, pero cómo te mueves en ellas depende de ti.

Aprovecha tus recursos para avanzar en esta vida que, a ratos, es como un juego en el que aprender, sorprenderse y divertirse compartiendo con los demás.

───────── **LA VIDA COMO JUEGO DE ROL** ─────────

Si no te gustan los escenarios fantásticos, atrévete a imaginar cómo podría ser tu vida si tomaras otras decisiones. Practica el *qué pasaría si...* en situaciones que hasta ahora has vivido como unidireccionales.

244

¿DE QUÉ TIENES HAMBRE?

E l cantante brasileño Titãs habla en su canción *Comida* del alimento
que va más allá y nos pregunta:

> *¿De qué tienes hambre?*
> *¿De qué tienes sed?*
> *No solo queremos alimento y beber.*
> *Tenemos hambre de diversión y arte.*
> *[...] De placer que alivie el dolor.*

Y yo te pregunto: ¿De qué tienes hambre ahora, además de alimentarte y beber? ¿Cómo sacias esa sed y esa hambre? ¿De qué te nutres y qué necesitas? ¿Qué te alimenta cuando tus necesidades básicas están cubiertas?

FLORES PARA VIVIR

Se atribuye a Confucio este texto: «¿Me preguntas por qué compro arroz y flores? Compro arroz para vivir y flores para tener algo por lo que vivir».

En este ejercicio te pido que investigues cuáles son tus *flores para vivir,* aquello que necesitas hacer o experimentar para nutrir tu alma.

245
TODO PUEDE SUCEDER

El maestro Lee Lozowick, que continuó la tradición india de los baúles –artistas y filósofos itinerantes–, afirmaba que para liberar el alma de las cargas de la rutina necesitamos escapar de lo convencional y practicar la *sabiduría loca*.

En sus palabras:

> *La vida es mucho más amplia que las limitaciones que queramos ponerle, y necesitamos estar en permanente romance con ella. Si no lo hacemos, corremos el riesgo de quedar enterrados bajo nuestras circunstancias personales. Es fácil convertirse en un autómata que se levanta de la cama, trabaja como un buey y dedica un tiempo a las prácticas espirituales, pero todo esto son hábitos mecánicos (...) Para librarte de ellos tienes que encarar la vida con una mentalidad infantil, sentirte siempre un principiante y creer en milagros como: «Cada día puede suceder cualquier cosa».*

INCORPORA ESTE MANTRA

Siguiendo esta inspiración de Lozowick, cada mañana repítete este mantra: «Hoy puede suceder cualquier cosa» y sal al mundo con esta mentalidad abierta e infantil de la que ya hemos hablado en páginas anteriores. Empieza el día de este modo durante al menos tres semanas y comprueba qué cambios observas en tu vida.

246

BANDA SONORA

Cuando paso por un aeropuerto, vivo el ritmo frenético de los pasajeros que vienen y van. Paseo entre la multitud, escuchando con mis cascos la música que lo envuelve todo.

Absorta por la melodía, veo gente aquí y allá que corre de un lugar a otro. Observo las caras y, en especial, sus miradas. A veces me suenan familiares y me recuerdan a otras personas que conocí en el pasado.

En ocasiones, siento incluso que quieren decirme algo, recordarme alguna cuestión pendiente.

La música siempre me conecta con el inconsciente y me acerca a lugares emocionales curiosos. Y más, si me pilla despistada y aturdida en cualquier aeropuerto con cara de sueño.

Es como si fuera parte de una película.

¿Qué te hace vivir y sentir tu música preferida?

VIAJA CON LISTAS TEMÁTICAS

Si tienes una plataforma de distribución de música, puedes hacerte listas para promover un determinado estado de ánimo. Estas son algunas categorías en las que puedes poner piezas que te hagan sentir así:

1. *Para empezar el día.*
2. *Motivación total.*
3. *Descanso y relajación.*
4. *Se acabó el trabajo (por hoy)*
5. *La hora de la melancolía*
6. *Alegría y agradecimiento*
7. *Camino del sueño.*

Crea tus propias etiquetas y llena las carpetas con tus temas favoritos para ese viaje musical.

247
EL REGALO QUE MERECES

Cuando te enfrentes a un reto especialmente difícil de conseguir, imagina el regalo que te vas a hacer cuando llegues a meta. No se trata de gastar mucho dinero. Tal vez ni siquiera sea algo que deba ser comprado. Quizá se trate de cocinar tu receta predilecta, organizar un encuentro con viejos amigos o regalarte un día libre para pasear por tu lugar favorito y leer bajo los árboles.

Visualizar el premio o la recompensa te dará fuerzas para seguir adelante.

A veces el mejor galardón está, simplemente, en completar lo que te habías propuesto. No hay nada que te detenga ante un deseo profundo. Y, de hecho, no hay mejor presente que el que te haces a ti mismo al cumplir un reto.

El solo hecho de superarte será ya un regalo que te llene de felicidad y orgullo.

LA FÓRMULA DE HELLINGER

Bert Hellinger, el creador de las constelaciones familiares, del que hablamos en otra parte del libro, decía que los seres humanos tenemos dos obligaciones en la vida: *trabajar* y *celebrar*.

No dudo de que trabajas mucho y bien, pero... ¿dedicas el tiempo que mereces a celebrar? En caso negativo, empieza a introducir celebraciones en tu agenda.

248

DESINFOXÍCATE

T e sientes abrumado por el bombardeo de datos y estímulos que recibes a diario? Me pregunto cómo hemos llegado a este punto.

La información constante a ritmo vertiginoso acaba convirtiéndose en lo que Alfons Comella llamó *infoxicación*, porque no podemos digerir todo lo que nos llega por los dispositivos móviles, entre otros medios.

Tenemos tantos distractores en nuestro día a día que es difícil no olvidarse de *a qué venía yo*, como se suele decir.

Dicen que allá donde pones la atención, va tu intención. No obstante, no podemos tener atención de calidad en medio del llamado IFS (*Information Fatigue Syndrome* o síndrome de fatiga por la información). Sus síntomas son confusión, ansiedad y miedo al colapso.

Es necesario hacer una criba para ganar foco en lo que de verdad es importante, ¿no te parece?

DIETA DIGITAL

En Estados Unidos, cada vez más gente está tomando conciencia de la *infoxicación* y, para evitar la IFS, practican esta dieta digital que puedes seguir:

1. No te conectes la primera hora del día. Dedícala a asearte con calma, a hacer ejercicio o a desayunar sin bombardeo de datos (puedes poner música).

2. Establece un horario fijo de conexión y desactiva los datos después de esa hora. Desde la hora de cenar hasta la de acostarte deberías hacer dieta digital y no reconectar hasta una hora después de despertarte.

3. Elige un día a la semana (tal vez el domingo) que sea totalmente *off line*. Disfruta de la sensación de salir a pasear sin móvil o, al menos, llevándolo en modo *no molestar*.

249

UNA VIDA ZEN

Hay muchas visiones sobre el arte de vivir con armonía y plenitud, pero es especialmente lúcida esta del autor japonés Shoyen Shaku:

Observa lo que dices y, digas lo que digas, ponlo en práctica. Cuando se te presente una oportunidad, no la dejes escapar. Sin embargo, piénsatelo siempre dos veces antes de actuar.

No te lamentes por el pasado. Dirige tu mirada hacia el futuro. Mantén la intrépida disposición de un héroe y el corazón cariñoso de un niño.

Al acostarte, duerme como si se tratara de tu último sueño. Al despertarte, sal inmediatamente de la cama como si tirases un par de zapatos viejos.

CREA TUS PROPIOS RITUALES

Las personas más creativas y eficaces tienen a lo largo de la jornada sus propios ritos, que les ayudan a estructurar el día y a no olvidar las cosas importantes. Siguiendo su ejemplo, te propongo que hagas lo siguiente:

1. Decide cómo quieres empezar las mañanas para no perder energía en este momento radiante de la jornada.

2. Fija algunas pausas a lo largo del día para hacer algo creativo, aunque sea leer un capítulo de un libro. Establece cuáles son tus oasis.

3. Crea tu propio ritual para acostarte libre de estrés y de preocupaciones.

250
EFECTO MARIPOSA

Un viejo proverbio dice: «El débil aleteo de una mariposa puede causar un huracán a miles de millas de distancia», y ha dado lugar a lo que conocemos como *efecto mariposa*.

Cada uno de nuestros actos, por irrelevante que parezca, acaba teniendo consecuencias por la concatenación de causas y efectos que se despliegan de él.

Todo está mucho más relacionado de lo que creemos. Aun pareciéndonos nimios, los micromovimientos que se producen en nuestro entorno no caen en saco roto, y los que nosotros hacemos, tampoco.

Aun así, saber que cada acción tiene consecuencias porque todo está interconectado no debe resultarnos amenazador. Al contrario: la magia del *efecto mariposa* nos dice que todo lo que hacemos, por pequeño que parezca, es valioso y trascendente.

EL MILAGRO DE LO PEQUEÑO

Jean Giono cuenta en el clásico de la literatura de desarrollo personal *El hombre que plantaba árboles* la aventura de un humilde pastor que, al quedar viudo, decide convertir un valle desértico en un vergel con la única ayuda de un bastón con el que va agujereando el suelo para plantar bellotas.

Este relato conmovedor demuestra el valor supremo de las pequeñas acciones que, practicadas con constancia y amor, acaban obrando milagros.

¿Cuál es la bellota que tú deseas plantar en tu vida y en la de los demás?

251
DALE AL *NEXT*

Decía un texto de la brasileña Martha Medeiros: «Muere lentamente quien pasa los días quejándose de su mala suerte o de la lluvia incesante».

Sin duda, quien vive instalado en las lamentaciones consume gran parte de su energía mental en ello. Abonarse a la queja, además de ser una actitud poco constructiva, tiene una repercusión fatal en nuestro estado anímico.

Es cierto que en ocasiones sentimos que nada es justo. Incluso podemos creer que el mundo va en nuestra contra, pero se trata solo de una opinión subjetiva, porque no vemos el mundo, solo vemos *nuestro mundo*.

Al mirar las cosas solo desde nuestro punto de vista, no podemos apreciar lo complicada que es también la vida de los demás. Perdemos la posibilidad de relativizar las cosas y darle al *next* de nuestro cerebro, pasando automáticamente a un estadio en el que seremos más empáticos, considerados y menos víctimas.

CARGA CONTRA LA SILLA

La psicoterapia moderna utiliza a veces una silla vacía para que el paciente se descargue y le diga todo lo que siente a una determinada persona, o incluso al mundo.

En lugar de destilar quejas a lo largo de toda la jornada, como un pernicioso veneno, si tienes mucha rabia acumulada te recomiendo lo siguiente:

1. Sitúate frente a una silla vacía e imagina que allí se encuentra el objeto o persona de tus quejas.
2. Por espacio de diez minutos, como máximo, ves soltando todo lo que tienes dentro y que tanto te indigna.
3. Terminada la sesión, deja las quejas allí para poder reemprender tu vida sin esa pesada mochila.

252

EL CIELO NO PUEDE ESPERAR

Cuando yo era niña, estrenaron la película *El cielo puede esperar*, dirigida e interpretada por Warren Beatty. En ella encarna a un jugador de fútbol americano al que, al sufrir un accidente, un ángel le sustrae el alma antes de que se certifique su muerte.

Para reparar el error del ángel, el jugador podrá reencarnarse en distintas personas para volver al mundo.

El título de esta película me hace pensar en una canción de C. Tangana que dice: «Antes de morir quiero el cielo. El ciento por ciento, por cierto».

¿Te gustaría disfrutar del cielo ya en la tierra, y no en un hipotético después?

Me gusta la idea de no dejar el disfrute para más tarde y creer que lo merecemos en esta vida, que somos ya merecedores de la gloria. Eres digno de aquello para lo que has sido llamado: el cielo de la vida.

El cielo puede esperar, como le sucede a Warren Beaty en su aventura, pero tú no.

--------- **¿QUÉ ES PARA TI EL CIELO DE LA VIDA?** ---------

Puedes responder a esta pregunta en diferentes apartados, ya que no hay una sola fuente de placeres celestiales:
- ¿Qué plato te hace sentir como los dioses del Olimpo?
- ¿Qué lugar te infunde una serenidad celestial?
- ¿Qué actividad te procura un placer indescriptible?

Toma nota de tus respuestas para poner cada semana —y si es posible cada día— un poco de cielo en tu vida.

253
PLATA Y ORO

C asi todo el mundo recuerda a un abuelo o abuela que fue un referente especial en su vida. Esta persona quizá mostraba una paciencia o atención que no encontrábamos en nuestros padres. Y, a la vez que compartía con nosotros su sabiduría, nos animaba a desplegar nuestra creatividad.

Gabriel García Márquez recordaba a su abuelo, con quien convivió hasta los ocho años en el pueblo que le inspiraría Macondo, de este modo: «Ha sido la figura más importante de mi vida. Desde entonces no me ha pasado nada interesante».

Si hemos tenido un abuelo o abuela de esa importancia, es un buen ejercicio recordar conversaciones que tuvimos o algún consejo que nos dio.

Como reza un aforismo de autor desconocido: «Un abuelo es una persona con plata en el pelo y oro en el corazón».

LA INSPIRACIÓN DE LOS MAYORES

Si hace demasiado tiempo que tus abuelos partieron o bien no pudiste disfrutar de un referente de este tipo, te aconsejo que prestes atención a las personas mayores con las que te cruzas día a día:

• Dales conversación y, si esta persona te resuena, pídele que te cuente alguna gran aventura que haya vivido.

• Pídele su opinión sobre algo que te preocupe actualmente. Su larga experiencia y la proximidad de la muerte hace de las personas excelentes consejeros.

254

ESCAPAR DE LAS REDES

En la era de los *social media*, estamos tan expuestos al mundo que corremos el riesgo de caer en las *redes* de las redes, quedarnos atrapados haciendo *scrolling* sin tener siquiera la intención.

Esos momentos de *piloto automático* te alejan de tu vida, ya que las redes sociales te muestran otras realidades que te atrapan, pero que no son la tuya.

Tu existencia es única, quizá singular, rara, a ratos complicada o, a tu parecer, incompleta, pero es la tuya.

Lo que a otro le sirve y lo que muestra al mundo no tiene nada que ver contigo.

En lugar de envidiar la supuesta suerte de otros y compararte con ellos, sé curioso y auténtico. Crea tu día a día desde la aceptación de tu grandeza. A fin de cuentas, por mucho que compartieras y mostraras tu vida, los demás no podrían vivirla.

¿No es eso maravilloso?

NO HAY NADIE COMO TÚ

Para este ejercicio, te pediré que enumeres cuatro o cinco particularidades que hacen de ti la persona que eres. En esa lista puedes incluir algún hábito singular, rituales hechos a medida que forman parte de tu vida o incluso alguna capacidad curiosa de la que eres consciente.

¡Celebra lo que hay en ti de único y especial!

255
SOLUCIONES PROVISIONALES

S i en algún momento adviertes que estás optando por la alternativa más cómoda, porque no estás preparado para la verdadera solución, ponle la etiqueta de *provisional* y esfuérzate en hallar la definitiva.

Sé honesto contigo mismo y no te conformes con lo que, aquí y ahora, es solo un parche que habrá que remendar tarde o temprano.

No hay nada malo en adoptar una solución provisional, siempre que no sirva de excusa para el conformismo.

Sería tan peligroso como, tras pinchar la rueda del coche, poner la de repuesto y olvidarnos del asunto. Si no llevamos la rueda para su reparación definitiva, la próxima vez que pinchemos nos quedaremos tirados en la carretera.

Asume cuándo una solución es temporal y decide, desde ya, cuál será el siguiente paso para arreglar esa situación que no te deja vivir en plenitud.

EJEMPLOS DE SOLUCIONES PROVISIONALES
---

1. Una mesa que cojea puede compensarse, para tener la cena en paz, con un poco de cartón o un pliego de periódicos, pero tendrá que ser calzada más pronto que tarde para que no siga bailando.
2. Un imprevisto económico puede resolverse con la tarjeta de crédito, pero eso no puede convertirse en norma si queremos vivir con serenidad.
3. Podemos camuflar un malentendido o situación incómoda durante cierto tiempo, sobre todo si no tenemos confianza con la otra persona, pero si se repite, tendremos que afrontarlo de forma definitiva.

256
EL DON DE LA QUIETUD

C huang Zhou, el filósofo más importante del taoísmo después de Lao-Tsé, contaba la siguiente historia:

Un hombre tenía miedo de la sombra de su cuerpo y de la huella de sus pasos. Para liberarse de ello, decidió huir. Pero, cuantos más pasos daba, más huellas dejaba. Por rápido que corriera, su sombra no lo dejaba. Persistiendo a pesar de todo en creer que la adelantaría, corrió tanto y tanto que acabó muriendo.

¡Qué insensato! Si se hubiera sentado en un lugar cubierto, su cuerpo no habría proyectado ninguna sombra; si hubiera estado quieto, sus pies no habrían producido huellas. Solo habría tenido que estar tranquilo y todos sus males habrían desaparecido.

Esta fábula nos enseña que muchos de los problemas que padecemos se solucionan simplemente deteniéndonos.

DIGITOPUNTURA CONTRA EL ESTRÉS

También llamada *acupresión*, esta técnica antiestrés tiene la ventaja de que puedes aplicártela tú mismo en cualquier momento y lugar. Una de las más sencillas de poner en práctica en momentos de ansiedad:

1. Presiona con el pulgar el centro de la muñeca, entre los tendones.
2. Mantén la presión unos 15 segundos.
3. Luego realiza este mismo ejercicio en la otra mano.

257

DESPIDE AL JUEZ INTERIOR

E l pensamiento racional guía la mayor parte de nuestros actos y, por lo tanto, nuestra vida. Todo pasa por este filtro que nos lleva a analizar los pros y contras muy rápido.

Las conclusiones pueden ser acertadas o no.

Estas cavilaciones varían según nuestro estado de ánimo puntual y llevan la carga de lo que hemos experimentado en el pasado. Por lo tanto, son totalmente subjetivas.

¿Te gustaría liberarte, aunque sea a ratos, de ese juez interior que no para de dictar sentencia?

Para ello solo necesitas recordarte que *no eres tus pensamientos*, como vimos en la reflexión dedicada a la *mente de mono*.

En vez de creer a tus pensamientos y opiniones, como leyes a obedecer, obsérvalos como algo externo a ti.

Te recomiendo, además, que observes tu capacidad de pensar.

LO ÚNICO QUE FALTA EN TU VIDA ERES TÚ

La frase es de la doctora Jenny Moix, de quien hemos hablado un par de veces en este libro, y nos invita a hacernos varias preguntas para quitar capas a la cebolla y llegar al corazón del ser:

- ¿Qué serías sin las opiniones y juicios de los demás?
- ¿Y qué serías sin tus propias opiniones y juicios?
- ¿Quién hay, en esencia, más allá de tu mente racional?

258
SER LUMINOSO

Hay personas de corazón radiante que nos hacen sentir bien con su sola presencia.

Tienen esa cualidad quienes son capaces de iluminar y guiar no solo su senda, sino también la de los demás. Me atraen esas personas llenas de generosidad innata, ya que la luz les nace de dentro.

Quiero pensar que todos la tenemos y que desplegamos ese poder cuando nos conectamos desde el corazón. En la película *Avatar* se define como «una red de energía que fluye a través de todos los seres vivos (...) toda la energía es solo un préstamo que algún día hay que devolver».

¿Te atreves a brillar —en tu vida y en la de los demás— con toda tu luz?

¿CÓMO ENCONTRAR A UN GURÚ?

La maestra budista Pat Enkyo decía que para elegir a una persona que nos aporte su luz y nos contagie de ella, antes debemos hacernos tres preguntas:

- ¿Puedo tomar riesgos delante de este/a maestro/a?
- ¿Puedo ser ignorante delante de este/a maestro/a?
- ¿Puedo decir *no lo sé* a este/a maestro/a?

Si contestas afirmativamente a las tres preguntas, probablemente es un buen gurú para ti.

259
IR HACIENDO

De pequeña, cuando no tenía claro si empezar alguna actividad, en casa me decían: «Tú ponte y ve haciendo».

Ahora, de mayor, me sigue pareciendo un buen consejo. En caso de duda, *vamos haciendo, y luego ya vemos*. Lo importante es no quedarse paralizados por las dudas.

Hazlo. Hagámoslo. Sin miedo a equivocarnos. Con la alegría de intentarlo y aprender. Lo importante es probar y ver sensaciones.

A ver qué pasa. No te quedes con las ganas.

Nadie nace sabiendo en qué quedará esto o aquello. En mi caso, he practicado deportes varios como la escalada o el *running*, actividades distintas como el coro o la cerámica, y he conocido a gente estupenda en encuentros increíbles.

Todo esto ha hecho de mí alguien un poco más inquieto y feliz. Por eso, agradezco que me dijeran aquello de *ponte a ello y vas viendo*.

KEEP ON TRUCKIN'!

Esta expresión anglosajona viene de la época hippie, cuando muchos jóvenes hacían autostop y eran recogidos por camioneros, como reflejó Jack Kerouac en su novela *On the road*.

El sentido de la frase —*truck* significa camión— es que no dejes de subirte a las oportunidades que te brinda la vida y que te llevan, literal o metafóricamente, a otro lugar.

De lo que se trata es de seguir experimentando y aprendiendo.

260
RITUALES PARA EL ALMA

S obre la importancia de los ritos, un relato oriental cuenta que un hombre estaba poniendo flores en la tumba de un familiar, cuando vio llegar a otro visitante del cementerio.

Al llegar a una tumba cercana, vio que depositaba con gran reverencia un plato de arroz.

Sin poderse contener, el primero le preguntó:

–Disculpe mi pregunta, buen hombre, pero ¿de verdad cree usted que el difunto vendrá a comerse el arroz?

–Sí –respondió el otro–, vendrá cuando el suyo venga a oler sus flores.

Esta pequeña historia demuestra que siempre debemos respetar los rituales y costumbres de los demás. Aunque no los comprendamos, para la otra persona tienen todo el sentido del mundo.

TRES CONSEJOS DEL *FENG SHUI* PARA ATRAER LA FORTUNA

Más allá de los ritos funerarios, la cultura ancestral china tiene, a través del *feng shui,* indicaciones muy precisas para atraer la suerte desde nuestro hogar. Veamos tres básicas:

1. *Mantén limpia y despejada la casa.* El desorden promueve el caos y entorpece las energías de la prosperidad.

2. *Evita fugas de agua.* Y no solo porque se verá reflejado en la factura, sino porque el *feng shui* lo relaciona con la pérdida de otros recursos.

3. *Ventila los espacios cada mañana.* Al abrir las ventanas, se da la bienvenida a las buenas energías y a la abundancia.

261

SI NO TENGO AMOR, DE NADA ME SIRVE

Seguro que has escuchado en alguna boda la carta de san Pablo a los Corintios que dice:

Si no tengo amor, de nada me sirve hablar todos los idiomas del mundo, y hasta el idioma de los ángeles. Si no tengo amor, soy como un pedazo de metal ruidoso; soy como una campana desafinada.

Puede que hayamos prestado poca atención a este pasaje, pero la primera frase es, a mi modo de ver, una lúcida verdad sobre el arte de vivir.

¿Podrías entender tu mundo sin amor?

El amor es para vivirlo, sentirlo, darlo, hacerlo, entenderlo, aplicarlo en cada acto, en cada conversación, en cada mirada y, ante todo y sobre todo, ¡serlo! Porque el amor, de todo y para todo sirve.

—— SIETE CLAVES PARA MANTENER LA LLAMA DEL AMOR ——

Así como se dice que es más fácil llegar a la fama que mantenerse en ella, también el amor necesita de un esfuerzo para que no mengüe. Veamos algunas claves prácticas que sintetizan temas que hemos ido visitando:

1. Amar lo que el otro es, no lo que debería ser.
2. Comunicarnos más y mejor.
3. Poner atención a las pequeñas cosas.
4. Desear la felicidad del otro.
5. Mostrar reconocimiento a la pareja por sus logros.
6. Buscar la igualdad y la reciprocidad.
7. Aceptar, entender y avanzar juntos.

262
TODO ES CUESTIÓN DE TIEMPO

En ocasiones, nos atascamos en un conflicto emocional que nos provoca un sentimiento de impotencia, ya que somos incapaces de saber cómo afrontarlo.

¿Te has parado a pensar que tal vez ese asunto ha llegado antes de que puedas gestionarlo?

Si en alguna ocasión ves que la situación te supera, no desesperes. Solo necesitas un poco más de tiempo para lograrlo. No debe ser motivo de frustración; simplemente, *todavía* no es el momento.

Pasado un tiempo, lo verás todo mucho más claro y te alegrará el alma deshacer ese nudo. De hecho, se habrá desenredado de manera fácil y sin esfuerzo.

Este es el momento adecuado, ni antes ni después.

Como dice la canción *Timing*, de Kevin Johansen, «el tiempo oportuno es la clave del éxito».

¿CÓMO PUEDO SABER SI ESTE ES EL MOMENTO OPORTUNO?

Te doy algunas pistas:
1. Las dificultades que veías en el pasado ya no están ahí o se ven mucho más pequeñas.
2. No tienes miedo a fracasar, o ese miedo es menor que las ganas de intentarlo.
3. Encuentras recursos nuevos para tu propósito: otras personas, ideas y estrategias que te ayudan en tu cometido.
4. Te sientes lleno de energía, como si te hubieras cargado de ganas e ilusión.

263

LA VIDA ES UN VIAJE SIN META

H emos hablado de Eckhart Tolle en páginas anteriores, pero en esta me gustaría profundizar un poco más en este guía espiritual nacido en Alemania.

La vida es un viaje lleno de devenires, dice. Y la llegada al destino es un momento puntual, breve y efímero que te llevará a la búsqueda del siguiente objetivo.

En ese sentido, la vida es un viaje sin meta. Un descubrimiento lleva al siguiente.

Si te focalizas demasiado en un determinado objetivo o resultado, te perderás casi la totalidad de tu vida.

Si tu tendencia mental es no estar presente, no podrás apreciar ese destino. En palabras de Tolle:

Cuando te haces amigo del momento presente te sientes como en casa donde quiera que estés. Si no te sientes cómodo en el ahora, te sentirás incómodo dondequiera que vayas.

EL RESULTADO NO NOS PERTENECE

Este es un lema terapéutico que el autor de *El poder del ahora* reformula así: «El fruto ya se verá cuando corresponda». No obsesionarte con las metas te permitirá:

- Disfrutar de cada experiencia por sí misma.
- Desarrollar tus capacidades sin la presión de si te llevan al éxito o al fracaso.
- Suprimir la ansiedad de la espera.
- Crear un espacio para la sorpresa y la celebración cuando el resultado llegue.

264
LA FELICIDAD PARA QUIEN LA TRABAJA

a tierra es para quien la trabaja fue un lema de la revolución mexicana liderada por Zapata.

¿Se podría aplicar esa misma lógica a la felicidad? Parece ser que sí.

El doctor Gonzalo Hervás se expresaba al respecto con estas palabras:

La felicidad se trabaja, no se puede esperar sentado en casa. Por ejemplo, aquellas personas que realizan deporte regularmente son felices cuando lo hacen porque el cerebro segrega serotonina y oxitocina y genera una sensación que te hace feliz. En resumen, hay que buscar lo que nos hace felices.

¿Cómo puedes trabajar tú por tu felicidad?

CÓMO GENERAR OXITOCINA

Además de practicar deporte, como menciona el doctor Hervás, hay otras maneras igual de naturales de generar oxitocina:

- Conversar con personas afines
- Reír
- Abrazar
- Practicar sexo
- Meditar
- Acariciar una mascota
- Ser generoso con los demás

265
AIRE

Así como hemos hablado del agua y la luz, ahora quiero hablarte del aire, otro elemento indispensable para vivir.

Cuando se habla de los signos de aire en el zodiaco, se refiere su carácter soñador y lunático, que les cuesta tocar de pies en el suelo y tienen espíritu seductor.

Independientemente de nuestro signo, todos somos aire de una u otra forma. Somos expansión, fuerza, capacidad de movimiento y de influencia. Tenemos el don de reforzar y empujar a otros, así como de soplar lejos todo lo malo.

Ser aire te permite elevarte o servir en silencio.

Imagínatelo. Eres eso y mucho más porque eres parte de la naturaleza.

EL AIRE ES VIDA

Así como el *feng shui* considera que el aire atrae la prosperidad, el refranero español dice que «donde entra el aire y el sol, no entra el doctor».

La salud es una razón más para airear las habitaciones en las que pasamos más tiempo.

266
EL PELIGRO DE REFUGIARSE

Es importante reconocer cuándo una determinada ocupación o hábito tiene como fin evitar cosas que no queremos ver de frente. Refugiarte en actividades que suplen una carencia es una trampa que irá a más si no tomas las riendas.

Algunos ejemplos comunes:

- Quedarte a trabajar más de la cuenta en la oficina, sin ser imprescindible que lo hagas, en lugar de afrontar las necesidades de tu vida familiar o personal.
- Alejarte de tus amigos, porque no te sientes cómodo o no sabes cómo comunicarte en este punto de tu vida, y quedarte en casa.
- Buscar relaciones fuera de tu vínculo de pareja, en vez de tratar de solucionar los problemas que os alejan.
- Dedicar horas en un juego o en las redes sociales, como evasión del mundo que hay al otro lado de la pantalla.

En fin, entretenerte y dispersarte en vez de poner foco en lo que debe ser atendido.

SALIR DEL REFUGIO

Todo aquello que haces para evadirte puedes identificarlo cuando te das cuenta de que te aleja de una verdad que molesta. Para desenmascararlo y salir del refugio, puedes preguntarte:

¿Qué estoy tratando de ocultar o evitar con esta actividad que hago de forma inconsciente o repetitiva?

267
¿CÓMO ES DIOS?

E n una de las anécdotas más bellas para entender la creatividad en los niños, sir Ken Robinson, de quien hablamos anteriormente en este libro, explicaba lo que sigue:

Escuché una gran historia hace poco, me encanta contarla, sobre una niña en clase de dibujo. Ella tenía seis años y estaba en la parte de atrás, dibujando, y la profesora contó que esta niña casi nunca prestaba atención, pero que en la clase de dibujo sí.
La profesora estaba fascinada y se acercó a ella para preguntarle:
−¿Qué estás dibujando?
Y la niña contestó:
−Estoy dibujando a Dios.
La profesora dijo:
−¡Pero nadie sabe cómo es Dios!
Entonces la niña concluyó:
−Lo van a saber en un minuto.

─────────── **DIBUJO Y *MINDFULNESS*** ───────────

Para conocer tu inconsciente o llevar tu creatividad por nuevos caminos, te propongo estos tres ejercicios:
1. Improvisa un dibujo con la mano *mala*. Si eres diestro, hazlo con la mano izquierda.

2. Dibuja lo primero que te venga a la mente con los ojos cerrados (o apaga la luz de la habitación).
3. Trata de dibujar un concepto abstracto. Por ejemplo: Dios, eternidad, impaciencia, anhelo...

268

LO QUE ILUMINA TU VIDA

E
s curioso cómo quedan atrás las sombras cuando miras a la luz de frente. Quedan atrás en el tiempo y en el espacio, justo donde comienzan tus pasos, que avanzan hacia algo más claro y radiante.

Cuánto más te orientes hacia lo que ilumina tu vida, menos *chance* le darás a esa sombra que desluce tu existir.

Atrévete a caminar hacia el sol, así como a dejar que brille la luz dentro de ti.

William Bridges decía en su ensayo *Dirigiendo el cambio*:

> *En tu interior hay capacidades por explotar, intereses y virtudes que debes descubrir (...) ¿Qué es lo que, en este punto preciso de tu vida, está esperando pacientemente detrás del telón para salir a la luz?*

TUS ZONAS DE LUZ

Parafraseando el ensayo de William Bridges en el sentido inverso, te propongo que hagas un mapa con los aspectos más luminosos de tu vida. Eso incluye:

- Tus talentos más útiles para los demás.

- Las cualidades que despliegas cuando estás de buen humor.
- Actividades y situaciones en las que *alumbras* tus mejores ideas.

Ser consciente de ello te ayudará a pasar más tiempo en tus zonas de luz que en las de sombra.

269
BENEFICIOS DE CONOCERTE

En su clásico *El arte de la guerra*, el estratega chino Sun Tzu decía:

Si conoces al enemigo y te conoces a ti mismo, no debes temer el resultado de cien batallas. Si te conoces a ti mismo, pero no al enemigo, por cada victoria obtenida también sufrirás una derrota. Si no sabes nada ni del enemigo ni de ti mismo, sucumbirás en todas las batallas.

Esto es aplicable a cualquier batalla que libres en la vida cotidiana. Todo empieza por el autoconocimiento que te ayuda a saber dónde estás y qué es lo que puedes dar en cada situación.

Desde ese conocimiento podrás crecer y expandirte para avanzar y sacar lo mejor de ti.

Desarrollar la consciencia te capacita para superar cualquier imprevisto, entender lo que te sucede o cuidar de tu salud de manera óptima. También te ayuda a entender a los demás y pedir lo que necesitas amablemente, además de mitigar la inquietud ante lo desconocido.

Como decía Sun Tzu, si te conoces bien a ti mismo, también te adaptarás al entorno de una manera más armoniosa.

TRES PREGUNTAS DE AUTOCONOCIMIENTO

- ¿Cuál es tu prioridad en este momento?
- ¿Qué es lo que te da más miedo en esta época de tu vida?

- ¿Cuál es tu mejor herramienta, aquí y ahora, para superar ese miedo?

270
TUS ÓRDENES SON DESEOS

Me gusta invertir la frase *tus deseos son órdenes* por *tus órdenes son deseos*. Me hace acordarme de lo que decía Epicteto: «Subordiné mi impulso a la divinidad. Quiere que consiga algo: yo quiero. No quiere: no quiero».

Hay una concepción muy taoísta del mundo en esta reflexión. Cuando, en lugar de nadar contra corriente, fluimos con las fuerzas de la vida, la fortuna se pone a nuestro favor.

¿Y si deseáramos las órdenes del universo?

¿Y si le mostráramos que acatamos lo que nos propone como algo que deseamos de verdad y estuviéramos a disposición de lo que llegue?

Si lo haces, la calidad de tu vida e incluso los resultados que obtienes mejorarán totalmente.

PARA DISFRUTAR DEL TRABAJO

Con esta misma filosofía, alguien dijo que si no encuentras un trabajo que te guste, hagas que te guste el trabajo que tienes. Para ello:

- En lugar de quejarte, céntrate en los aspectos positivos de tu trabajo.
- Trata de establecer relaciones amistosas con tus compañeros.
- Márcate pequeños retos como pruebas de superación.
- Busca el sentido y utilidad para los demás en todo lo que haces y lo que acontece en tu vida.

271
LA HORA MÍSTICA

Decía el religioso norteamericano Thomas Merton:

Tiene que existir una hora al día en la que el hombre que habla enmudezca. Tiene que existir una hora en la que el hombre de las decisiones deje sus decisiones aparte para aprender algo nuevo: distinguir el sol de la luna, el mar de la tierra firme y el cielo nocturno de la curvatura de una colina.

Este monje trapense ponía énfasis en la importancia de encontrar un oasis de contemplación, de hecho, para cualquier persona.

Y nos da la receta para hacerlo en nuestra vida diaria:

Para mantenernos en comunión con lo que nos rodea, todo lo que debemos hacer es simplemente sentarnos un rato y no hacer nada. Sin embargo, para un hombre que se ha dejado arrastrar completamente por la actividad, nada resulta tan difícil como sentarse y estar quieto, no haciendo nada en absoluto. El solo hecho de descansar es el acto más valiente y difícil que él pueda hacer.

DESCANSA CON LA TÉCNICA POMODORO

Estas pausas tan necesarias para el reposo del espíritu pueden realizarse incluso a lo largo de la jornada de trabajo. La denominada *técnica pomodoro*, que recibe este nombre por los cronómetros de cocina con forma de tomate, funciona de la siguiente manera:

1. Distribuye el tiempo de trabajo en periodos seguidos (sin distracciones) de 25 minutos.
2. Realiza una pausa de 5 minutos cada 25 minutos de trabajo.
3. Cada cuatro *pomodoros* puedes premiarte con una pausa larga de 15 minutos.

272
LA LIBERTAD NO ES GRATIS

Es curioso cuánto anhelamos la libertad. Y también es curioso que los ingleses llamen *free* a ser libre, un término que también significa *gratis*.

Sabemos que la libertad no siempre es dada gratis. Para alguien que tiene un trabajo fijo en una empresa, por ejemplo, y que se lanza a la aventura de ser *free lance*, o autónomo, su libertad se paga –al menos al principio– con inestabilidad económica y más horas de trabajo.

Es solo un ejemplo, ya que la libertad significa algo diferente para cada persona y se materializa de formas muy distintas.

Desde un punto de vista psicológico, la libertad es la no dependencia de las emociones, así como el no sometimiento a cualquier creencia. A partir de aquí, cada cual puede vivir su libertad como la interprete.

¿Qué es lo que a ti te da libertad?

LOS CUATRO INGREDIENTES DE PLATÓN

El filósofo griego la definía así:

La libertad consiste en ser dueño de la propia vida, en no depender de nadie en ninguna ocasión, en subordinar la vida a la propia voluntad solamente y en dar poca importancia a las riquezas.

¿Cuáles de estos cuatro ingredientes tienes en la receta vital de tu libertad?

273
LA GENERACIÓN INSTANTÁNEA

L o cantaba mi querida Christina Rosenvinge: «*Hago ¡chas! y aparezco a tu lado*».

En esta era digital tan vertiginosa, retamos al tiempo y al espacio tratando que todo sea instantáneo. Con un clic compramos cualquier cosa o establecemos contacto con cualquier persona del planeta.

El tiempo y el espacio parecen no existir en la pantalla.

Nos envenenamos de falsa eficiencia, creyendo que tenemos miles de amigos o que sabemos lo que les gusta a los demás. Luchamos por acortar tiempos y distancias, como si todo bien estuviera en lo instantáneo.

Sobre esto, el protagonista de una película de Woody Allen se reía así de la cultura de la velocidad y la prisa:

> *Hice un curso de lectura rápida y fui capaz de leerme* Guerra y paz *en veinte minutos. Creo que decía algo de Rusia.*

COSAS VALIOSAS QUE REQUIEREN SU TIEMPO

- Leer un libro con placer, extrayendo de sus páginas todo su jugo.
- Construir una bella amistad o una relación amorosa.
- Preparar un plato delicioso, como los que hacen las abuelas.
- Criar a un hijo y acompañarlo en todas sus etapas.
- Vivir.

274
SEGUIR JUGANDO

Según John Byers, zoólogo de la Universidad de Idaho y especialista en el juego de los animales y los humanos, las actividades lúdicas nos ayudan a esculpir el cerebro, algo que sigue siendo importante en la adultez. En sus palabras:

Al jugar imaginamos y experimentamos situaciones totalmente distintas y aprendemos de ellas. Podemos crear unas posibilidades que antes no existían. Establecemos nuevas conexiones cognitivas en nuestra vida cotidiana, aprendemos valiosas lecciones y habilidades sin poner nuestra vida en peligro.

Todos recordamos los juegos favoritos que nos absorbían en la infancia, pero ¿has encontrado la manera de seguir jugando en tu vida actual?

ORGANIZA UNA SESIÓN DE JUEGOS

A diferencia de los niños, los adultos raramente quedan para jugar, a no ser que practiquen el golf o algún otro deporte.

Más allá de las típicas citas para comer o cenar, ¿qué tal si reúnes a unos cuantos amigos alrededor de una mesa para jugar?

Podéis rememorar las partidas de Monopoly o atreveros con juegos más proactivos que nos desafían a representar distintos roles.

275
LO QUE SEA PARA MÍ

uisiera compartir contigo un texto de autor desconocido que encontré y que me parece que resume muy bien lo que pienso:

Que lo que no sea para mí, siga su camino.
Que lo que sea para mí, se muestre.
Que lo que sea para mí, llegue.
De manera perfecta y en armonía para todos.
Gracias. Gracias, gracias.

Según mi filosofía de vida, es importante dejar ir aquello que ya no forma parte de nuestra vida, así como estar atentos a las nuevas personas y oportunidades que se presentan.

EL FRASCO DE LA GRATITUD

Además de soltar lo que no nos pertenece aquí y ahora y de acoger lo que llega a nuestro día a día, este ejercicio te ayudará a apreciar lo que ya tienes:

1. Busca un frasco o bote vacío y ponlo en un lugar visible de tu casa.
2. Cada vez que te sientas agradecido por algo de tu vida, escríbelo en una tira de papel y ponlo dentro.
3. Cuando te sientas desanimado o veas el vaso medio vacío, acude al frasco de la gratitud y lee los motivos que contiene para estar agradecido.

276
SOY DE MIS HIJOS

Nuestros hijos no son tanto nuestros como nosotros de ellos. Siempre que me preguntan *¿Son tus hijos?*, respondo *Más bien yo soy de ellos* y sonrío.

Porque así lo siento, que soy suya, su referente y dadora de amor infinito, y soy consciente de que mi labor es acompañarlos, guiar a personas bonitas en su desarrollo emocional. Por ellos debo y quiero estar bien, abierta y completa para dedicarles parte de mi vida con alegría.

Muchos padres se preguntan con ansiedad qué más pueden hacer por la felicidad de sus hijos. La respuesta la tienen en ellos mismos. Los niños también se preocupan por nuestro bienestar, así que no hay nada que necesiten más que vernos como personas felices y realizadas.

AMAR ES DIVERTIRSE JUNTOS

Contra el modelo rígido de la autoridad sin risas, la etóloga Jane Goodall decía: «Una cosa que aprendí de observar a los chimpancés con sus pequeños es que tener un hijo debería ser algo divertido».

A través del humor y la ligereza, ayudamos a los hijos —aunque no solo a ellos— a sobrellevar mucho mejor los problemas y la gravedad del mundo.

277
SOLTAR LASTRE

Para avanzar con agilidad en cualquier aspecto de tu vida, vas a tener que dejar mucho equipaje pesado aquí y ahora.

Los lastres solo te van a quitar energía y capacidad de decisión. Esto es aplicable a las relaciones personales, a nuevas andaduras profesionales o a tu propio desarrollo como ser humano.

Lao-Tsé decía que solo puede ganar el mundo quien es capaz de dejarlo ir.

Yo hace tiempo que descubrí que el *agua pasada* no mueve ningún molino y que el motor de mi vida debe ir sin el peso que supone un obstáculo suplementario.

Aferrarme al pasado es reafirmar que la vida pesa. Soltarlo es bailar al son y ritmo de una música siempre nueva.

CUATRO PASOS PARA SOLTAR LASTRE

1. Examina si hay algún ancla —consciente o inconsciente— que frena tu marcha hacia el futuro.
2. ¿Está justificado que sigas cargando con esa mochila?
3. Si la respuesta es *sí*, resuelve ya, con los recursos que tengas ahora, esa cuenta pendiente.
4. Si la respuesta es *no*, déjalo ir de una vez.

278
EL HIJO DEL VECINO

U na historia tradicional cuenta que un campesino perdió su hacha y enseguida sospechó del hijo de su vecino.

Furioso, se dedicó a espiar la forma de caminar del chico, y le pareció que lo hacía sigilosamente como un ladrón. Luego estudió su expresión, igual que la de un ladrón; también en su forma de hablar reconoció la jerga que utilizan los ladrones.

Todos sus gestos le revelaban que era culpable del robo.

Mientras pensaba en todo esto, el campesino encontró su hacha en el bosque, en el lugar donde la había olvidado.

Cuando volvió a ver al hijo del vecino, le pareció que todos sus movimientos y palabras destilaban honestidad.

─────── **ASÍ ES, SI ASÍ OS PARECE** ───────

Esta es una traducción del título de Shakespeare *As you like it*. Si las cosas son para nosotros tal y como las vemos —o tal y como somos—, para una existencia más positiva hemos de empezar limpiando nuestra mirada de prejuicios e ideas preconcebidas, como las que tiene el campesino del cuento.

279
PEINE DE LOS VIENTOS

Al igual que no concibo la vida sin música, me cuesta entenderla sin las artes plásticas. Me conmueven desde lo visual o incluso desde el tacto, en el caso de la escultura.

Acariciar el Peine de los vientos un día de lluvia en Donosti, y descubrir a través de una de esas púas un Cantábrico vivo me llena de energía y me permite ver y sentir la fuerza de la naturaleza.

Según el propio Chillida, esta escultura encarna la conexión del ser humano consigo mismo y con el cosmos, con la naturaleza.

Cuando me encuentro allí, aprecio el espacio que me rodea, el color, el tacto, la temperatura, el volumen de la escultura... Intento fundirlos con el sonido del mar para enlazarlo con los latidos de mi corazón o el vaivén de mi respiración.

Gracias arte, gracias naturaleza.

MUSEOTERAPIA

Aunque vivas lejos de Donosti, seguro que cerca de ti hay un museo o escultura al aire libre para poder conectar con la belleza y el sentido de las obras de arte. Te aconsejo que dejes tus preocupaciones atrás y te sumerjas en lo que transmite cada pieza sobre la vida, la naturaleza y el significado de ser humano.

280
SIEMPRE ESTOY EMPEZANDO

Cuando te lanzas a una nueva experiencia o te espera un encuentro precioso, muchas veces te sentirás nervioso, tal vez incluso el alma te tiemble de emoción.

Antes de entrar por primera vez en esa cama, o de descubrir cuánto hay de nuevo en ti el día de hoy, despliega en tu mente toda tu capacidad de sorpresa.

Suelta el freno de mano y deja que lo que vas a vivir te inunde y enseñe todo lo que tiene que ofrecerte. Porque nadie ni nada merece ser vivido a medias y porque tú te mereces un presente lleno de descubrimientos.

Se cuenta que una vez preguntaron a Buda qué era la vida, al fin y al cabo, y su respuesta fue: «Siempre estoy empezando».

CUATRO OBSTÁCULOS PARA LA SORPRESA

1. Ir con la expectativa de que las cosas sean de determinado modo.
2. Juzgar o analizar todo lo que percibes y vives.
3. Tener la cabeza en el pasado o en el futuro.
4. Cerrar los sentidos a lo que está sucediendo.

281

DE CINE

A veces, el mejor remedio para un mal día es elegir una película positiva, o al menos entretenida, que nos cambie el estado de ánimo.

Si tenemos un cine a mano, viviremos una experiencia inmersiva que nos abstraerá de nuestras preocupaciones mundanas. Si por nuestra ubicación u horario no nos resulta posible, una sesión de cine terapéutico en casa puede servir.

En palabras del psiquiatra Enrique Rojas Marcos:

Una buena película actúa como un Valium, porque es relajante, rebaja la tensión psicológica y hace olvidar los problemas. Es decir, distrae ensoñando. Por otro lado, las películas actúan sobre el subconsciente, un océano que se esconde en el fondo de la personalidad y que dirige nuestra conducta sin que lo sepamos.

TU BOTIQUÍN DE PELÍCULAS

Según los gustos y sensibilidad de cada cual, podemos hacernos nuestra propia lista de películas a las que recurrir para levantar el ánimo. Entre los clásicos de Hollywood, uno de los títulos más terapéuticos es *Qué bello es vivir*. Dirigida por Frank Capra. El desesperado protagonista que encarna James Stewart descubre, con la ayuda de un ángel, cómo habría sido la vida de sus seres queridos y amigos sin su existencia.

282
CONGENIAR

Hay personas con las que conectamos de manera rápida. Son aquellas que a su vez también congenian con nosotros, relaciones que duran en el tiempo de manera armoniosa.

Un signo de que hemos encontrado un vínculo de esta calidad es que podemos tratarnos de manera familiar, como si no hiciera falta explicar nada.

Son personas que nos parecen generosas y amables, al igual que nosotros les parecemos a ellas. Todo fluye y es fácil porque no hay dependencia mutua.

Existe una magia especial entre quienes congenian, ya que se sienten siempre cerca, aunque vivan lejos, y pueden pasar mucho tiempo sin verse, años incluso, y tener la impresión de que se encontraron ayer.

Tal vez sea porque entienden la vida de la misma manera y comparten los mismos valores. Respetan el espacio del otro, hay admiración mutua y les gusta pasar tiempo juntos. Tan simple como eso.

Si algo se mantiene en el tiempo es porque se vibra en la misma frecuencia.

EL ARTE DE ESCRIBIR CARTAS

No hace tanto, unas cuantas décadas atrás, los amigos que vivían lejos se escribían cartas de forma periódica. Estas viajaban por el mundo y era una gran ilusión encontrar en el buzón un sobre lleno de confidencias y amistad.

Hoy las cartas han sido sustituidas por los menos románticos correos electrónicos, sin embargo puede ser un bonito medio para compartir por escrito lo que vamos viviendo.

¿Qué tal si pactas con tu mejor amigo mantener correspondencia periódica que luego podáis conservar como un tesoro?

283
LA SABIDURÍA DE SÉNECA

Séneca es uno de los pensadores que nos enseña a vivir más y mejor con menos. Como buen representante del estoicismo, nos invita a retar las comodidades y bienes materiales, así como a cultivar la virtud.

Estuve en el lugar donde este filósofo cordobés fue desterrado en Córcega. Una torre romana desde donde se divisa el mar. Allí Séneca vivió y escribió varios libros.

Mientras subía por la torre, me acordaba de la importancia de su filosofía, de obras tan bellas como *De la brevedad de la vida*, de la que comparto un fragmento sobre el valor del tiempo:

La vida que se nos dio no es breve, nosotros hacemos que lo sea; ya que no somos pobres, sino pródigos del tiempo; sucediendo lo que a las grandes y reales riquezas, que si llegan a manos de dueños poco cuerdos, se disipan en un instante; y al contrario, las cortas y limitadas, entrando en poder de próvidos administradores, crecen con el uso. Así nuestra edad tiene mucha latitud para los que usaren bien de ella.

--------- **¿POR QUÉ ME RESULTA DIFÍCIL?** ---------

Dos milenios nos separan de este pensador, pero sus visiones y consejos son absolutamente actuales, como este sobre las dificultades que encontramos en la vida:

No nos atrevemos a muchas cosas porque son difíciles, pero son difíciles porque no nos atrevemos a hacerlas.

284
EL REGALO DE LA ABUNDANCIA

Hay ocasiones en las que damos algo que después se nos devuelve multiplicado. Es el regalo de la abundancia entregada desde el amor y la consideración.

Y lo más bello y misterioso de esta alquimia es que muchas veces el retorno llega desde una fuente distinta, no de aquella circunstancia o persona a quien hemos favorecido. El universo reparte juego y premia a los jugadores generosos.

Como dice Alejandro Jodorowsky: «Lo que das, te lo das. Lo que no das, te lo quitas».

Sé generoso, también con lo que le pides a la vida. Expresa al mundo lo que necesitas, así será más fácil que llegue a ti. Eso sí, llegará de formas inesperadas y sorprendentes.

CONJUGA EN POSITIVO

Cuando quieras motivarte con pensamientos empoderadores, evita formular deseos con negaciones, ya que según aseguran los expertos en PNL (Programación Neurolingüística), la mente inconsciente solo entiende las afirmaciones. Por lo tanto, en lugar de repetirte *no cometeré más veces este error,* por ejemplo, deberías decir *a partir de ahora voy a...*

285
UNA FIESTA PARA LA GAVIOTA

C huang Zhou, un destacado pensador del taoísmo del que ya hemos hablado, solía contar esta historia:

Una gaviota llegó a un barrio de la capital de Lu, donde nunca habían visto un ave marina. Entusiasmado, el marqués de Lu quiso darle la bienvenida con una fiesta en el templo. Dispuso para la gaviota la mejor música, carnes y licores. Pero el ave se mostraba aturdida y triste, y no llegó a comer ni beber nada.
Tres días después murió.

El marqués de Lu había agasajado a la gaviota como a él le habría gustado ser agasajado, no como al ave le habría apetecido.

La moral de este relato es que los demás no tienen por qué regirse por nuestras preferencias y prioridades. Si queremos beneficiarlos, es necesario ponernos en su lugar y entender lo que pueden necesitar en cada momento sin dar nada por hecho.

NADIE ESTÁ EN EL LUGAR DE NADIE

Trasladado a nuestra vida cotidiana, un error que cometemos a menudo es pensar que el otro debería reaccionar como nosotros lo haríamos. Entonces se pronuncia la fatídica frase: *Yo en su lugar...*

Hay que partir de la base de que nadie está en el lugar de nadie, y que la fiesta del marqués es muy distinta de la que desearía la gaviota.

286
LITERATURA QUE CURA

Recuerdo, de niña, curiosear las bibliotecas de los *mayores* para intentar saber lo que leían. También pedía prestados libros a mis padres, sobre todo a mi madre.

Los de Oriana Fallaci solo me los dejaron leer cuando fui algo más adulta. Más allá de lo que relataba esta increíble periodista y corresponsal de guerra, me atraía la idea de la narrativa epistolar. Especialmente la de *Un hombre*.

Era una escritura a la que no estaba acostumbrada y me parecía fascinante. Su forma de dirigirse a sus protagonistas, a los que hablaba de manera sabia, conociendo sus *sentires* hasta hacerlos cómplices con el lector, me parecía y me sigue pareciendo todo un arte.

Desde entonces, en ocasiones escribo de manera íntima solo para mí, o incluso escribo secretamente a alguien con quien necesito conciliar un asunto pendiente. Me resulta muy reconfortante.

——— TRES SEMANAS DE ESCRITURA TERAPÉUTICA ———

En su libro *Escribir en 21 días*, la pionera de los talleres de escritura en español Silvia Adela Kohan propone el siguiente desafío:
- Escribe cada día en tu cuaderno durante 7 minutos exactos. Pon la alarma o el cronómetro para · marcar el fin de la sesión.
- Agotado el tiempo, para de escribir de inmediato, aunque tengas ganas de seguir.
- Al completar los veintiún días, lee seguido todo lo que has escrito. El resultado será revelador, ya que te darás cuenta de qué tema domina en este punto tu vida.

287

LA CASA DEL ALBAÑIL

Cuando queda poco para llegar al final de un proyecto, puede que te relajes o que creas incluso que ya lo has logrado.

Justo en ese momento es cuando debes poner más atención para que tu andadura llegue a buen puerto. No solo para culminarlo, sino también para hacerlo de manera excelente. Con la misma ilusión e ímpetu con la que empezaste.

Sobre esto, hay un cuento de un albañil al que, tras una vida de edificar cientos de casas, le llega el momento de la jubilación. No obstante, el dueño de la constructora le pide que haga una última casa como favor personal.

De mala gana, el albañil construye esa última obra de forma precipitada y sin el cariño habitual, con lo cual concluye una casa llena de taras. Al terminarla, el dueño le entrega las llaves y le dice que es un regalo para él, como premio por tantos años de trabajo.

Entonces, el albañil se da cuenta, lleno de tristeza, de que vivirá en la peor casa que ha construido en su vida.

TRES CLAVES DE LA EXCELENCIA

Esta historia nos da tres claves para realizar cualquier cosa con un espíritu de excelencia:

1. Imagina que lo que haces es para la persona que más quieres en el mundo.
2. Tómate el trabajo como un juego estimulante, como una competición para superarte a ti mismo.
3. Si lo que estás haciendo fuera tu legado al mundo, ¿qué impresión te gustaría dejar?

288

CONTAGIO EMOCIONAL

El experto en comunicación Ferran Ramon-Cortés nos advierte de que entre las personas con las que nos relacionamos se produce un contagio emocional. Por lo tanto, nuestro estado de ánimo tiene mucho que ver con la energía de quienes nos rodean, y a la inversa.

El autor reflexiona de este modo:

Tomar conciencia del contagio emocional puede dar un giro de ciento ochenta grados a nuestras relaciones y a nuestra vida. En primer lugar, porque podremos hasta cierto punto protegernos de los contagios nocivos de los otros, evitándolos o tomando distancia. Pero, sobre todo, porque tendremos la oportunidad de dejar de contagiar accidentalmente emociones negativas, y elegir de forma consciente y deliberada lo que queremos contagiar.

¿QUÉ EMOCIÓN VAS A CONTAGIAR?

En Japón, es usual pedir permiso antes de contar un problema o algún suceso desagradable, por miedo a perturbar la paz mental del otro. Sin llegar a ese nivel de cortesía y delicadeza, antes de descargar nuestra emoción sobre otro, podemos hacernos tres preguntas:

1. ¿Qué clase de emoción le llegará a través de mis palabras?
2. ¿Es realmente útil o necesario que lo haga?
3. ¿Me aportará esta persona una visión diferente a la que tengo o solo quiero quejarme?

289
PRUDENCIA

Como dice Baltasar Gracián en su libro *El arte de la prudencia*: «Actúa siempre como si te estuvieran observando». Yo añadiría: actúa siempre observándote a ti mismo.

Me parece valioso tener la prudencia de cuidar tus formas y tus actos en cada instante.

A quienes trabajamos de cara al público nos sucede, y más aún cuando estamos con un micrófono muchas horas delante de una pantalla. Sabemos que hay siempre alguien al otro lado.

Quizá la única forma de llevarlo con naturalidad es tener presente que eres parte de un entorno: que debes cuidar de manera generosa e inteligente.

También en nuestra vida privada, al actuar con conciencia de lo que hacemos, nos sentiremos en armonía con nuestros valores y principios.

MÍRATE DESDE FUERA

Los actores de teatro se miran en filmaciones tras los ensayos o representaciones para pulir aspectos de su trabajo. Tú puedes hacer lo mismo desde tu mente, cuando quieras revisar una escena de tu vida, aplicando un ejercicio de visualización:

1. Pon atención a lo que hiciste y dijiste en esa situación.

2. ¿Hay algo que habrías expresado o hecho de forma diferente?

3. ¿De qué otra manera podrías haber afrontado *la escena* para ser más prudente, comedido y considerado?

4. Toma notas para cuando en el teatro de tu vida se presente una situación parecida.

290
ENTRE LAS OLAS

Las mareas van y vienen. El océano puede ser bravo, pero después llega la calma.

Es bueno agradecer también todos los acontecimientos que nos hicieron desfallecer y quedarnos, cual Mafalda revuelta por una ola, en la orilla de la playa. Sin saber qué ha pasado y cómo esa ola nos llevó hasta allí.

Desorientados, miraremos al mar inmenso, abatidos y aún con el susto en el cuerpo.

Agradezco todas esas embestidas de la vida que me demostraron que puedo ponerme de pie, respirar, quitarme la arena del bañador para ir más ligera y volver a meter los pies en el agua poco a poco, guiñando un ojo al socorrista.

LA MONTAÑA RUSA DE LA VIDA

Entender que ni lo bueno ni lo malo permanece supone un bálsamo para la vida, que es como una montaña rusa con sus subidas y bajadas. Todo lo que podemos hacer es *Enjoy the ride* —disfrutar del viaje—, como cantaba Marlango.

Cada vez que te sientas sacudido por una ola, pregúntate: *¿Es esto provisional o ha llegado para quedarse?* Si es provisional, no desesperes y aprende de esta experiencia pasajera.

291
LA PRÁCTICA DE LA CONCENTRACIÓN

Se cuenta que una vez preguntaron a un maestro de meditación cómo, pese a tener tantas ocupaciones, lograba mantenerse concentrado. Su respuesta fue:

–Cuando estoy de pie, simplemente estoy de pie. Y cuando camino, entonces camino. Cuando estoy sentado, pues estoy sentado. Cuando como, solo como. Y cuando hablo, entonces hablo.

Uno de los discípulos que lo escuchaban le respondió:

–Pero eso también lo hacemos nosotros... Tiene que haber algo más.

–¡No lo hacéis! –replicó el maestro–. Cuando estáis sentados, ya os estáis poniendo de pie. Y cuando estáis de pie, ya empezáis a caminar. Y cuando camináis, entonces ya estáis pensando en la meta.

¿ERES CAPAZ DE HACER UNA SOLA COSA?

Los estudiantes de zen aprovechan cualquier actividad para practicar la atención plena. Puedes hacer como ellos, poniendo tus cinco sentidos...

- Al cocinar con el espíritu de una meditación.
- Al caminar por la calle, observando tu peso y el trabajo de cada uno de tus músculos.
- Al leer totalmente concentrado estas líneas.
- Al escuchar lo que alguien te está contando, sin interferencia mental de ningún tipo.

292
SIN LÍMITES

En la década de 1960, Maxwell Maltz se hizo famoso con su manual *Psicocibernética*, donde este cirujano plástico explicaba cómo curar las cicatrices internas, en lugar de las externas.

Una de sus máximas era: «Puede que vivamos en un mundo imperfecto, pero las fronteras no están selladas ni todas las puertas cerradas». Es decir, que las capacidades del ser humano van mucho más allá de sus creencias.

Maltz relacionaba la baja autoestima con la falta de objetivos:

> *La gente que dice que la vida no vale la pena está diciendo en realidad que no tiene metas personales que valgan la pena. Pon un objetivo en tu vida que sea digno de luchar por él. Mejor aún, implícate en un proyecto. Siempre tendrás algo ante ti por lo que esforzarte y tener esperanzas.*

LA VENTA MÁS IMPORTANTE DE TU VIDA

Según Maltz, es venderte tú a ti mismo. Y eso implica:

- Ser consciente del valor que tienes.
- Encontrar el sol que brilla dentro de ti y ofrecerlo al mundo.
- Hacerte amigo de ti mismo.
- Entender que no eres una obra acabada, sino un ser que siempre avanza.
- Cultivar una imagen amable de ti, es decir, digno de ser amado.

293

SIMPLEMENTE, PREGUNTA

D e repente, algo que ha sucedido te roba la tranquilidad y no puedes dejar de pensar en ello. Le das vueltas a lo que crees que se ha malinterpretado o que simplemente no entiendes con respecto a una relación, a una amistad o a una pareja. Y te haces preguntas como estas: *¿Se habrá ofendido? ¿Será que no quiere saber nada de mí? ¿Piensa que no merece la pena responder a mi mensaje? ¿Prefiere que no le escriba? ¿Estará demasiado ocupado y le molesto? ¿Será mejor si le llamo? ¿Hay algo que le ha molestado? ¿Esperaba algo distinto de mí?*

Y así hasta el infinito...

Si tantas dudas tienes y el asunto te quita el sueño, el remedio es fácil: ¡pregunta! Con amor, palabras precisas y en el momento adecuado. Acércate a la persona y demuéstrale que te importa mostrando tu deseo de aclarar el asunto.

Te sorprendería las veces que la otra parte también está atascada y no sabe cómo explicarte lo que le sucede. Puede ser por timidez o por no saber expresar lo que necesita.

Así que pregunta las veces que haga falta hasta entenderlo. Sentarás las bases de una comunicación equilibrada y satisfactoria para ambas partes.

PREGUNTAR ES LA LLAVE DEL PROGRESO

Un proverbio chino dice: «El que hace una pregunta parece tonto por cinco minutos, el que no la hace es tonto toda su vida». Sin duda, las personas que van ganando sabiduría son aquellas que se atreven a hacer muchas preguntas, aunque parezcan absurdas.

¿Te atreves a preguntar más para avanzar?

294

CORRE MÁS EL ÚLTIMO CORREDOR QUE EL PRIMER ESPECTADOR

Recuerdo la decepción que sentí al no poder acabar la maratón de Nueva York en el tiempo para el que yo había entrenado. Era solo una marca, pero llevaba cuatro meses preparándome y la lesión que arrastraba hacía tiempo me la jugó en los últimos diez kilómetros.

Llegué a meta muy dolorida y frustrada, sin ser consciente de lo que había logrado. No era el tiempo ni la distancia. Eran muchas horas de entrenamiento y un reto personal y emocional, que, en mi caso, estaba ligado a mi padre y a las carreras populares que corrí junto a él durante años.

Muchas cosas se unían en aquella llegada a Central Park. La medalla conmemorativa en mi pecho, un poncho metalizado que te ponen para protegerte del frío de noviembre y el abrazo de mi comadre Elena, que me acompañó todo el recorrido.

Entonces, alguien me dijo: *Corre más el último corredor que el primer espectador.* Nunca he olvidado esa frase. Ya no me importa aquella marca. Me queda lo vivido y logrado en ese momento.

Hubo más carreras después y habrá otros retos. A todos les pido que me permitan disfrutarlo y vivirlo con alegría, ese es el verdadero triunfo.

TERMINAR MERECE PREMIO

El solo hecho de acabar algo que te hayas propuesto, con independencia del resultado, es digno de celebración. Piensa, si no, en cuántas personas no acaban lo que empiezan o en quienes ni lo comienzan.

En tu próximo proyecto márcate esta meta: terminar lo empezado. Y dedícate una pequeña fiesta por ello.

295
LAS TRES FALTAS

C onfucio, uno de los grandes maestros de China, decía que los ministros de un príncipe virtuoso deben evitar tres faltas:

1. La *petulancia*, que es hablar cuando nadie te ha pedido tu opinión.
2. La *timidez*, consistente en no atreverte a expresar tu opinión cuando se te invita a hacerlo.
3. La *imprudencia* al hablar sin haber observado antes el estado de ánimo del otro.

Aunque no tengamos que reunirnos con ningún príncipe o princesa, estas claves siguen vigentes y son totalmente aplicables a cualquier interacción.

──────── TRES REMEDIOS PARA LAS TRES FALTAS ────────

1. ¿Te descubres a veces dando tu opinión cuando no te la han pedido? Guárdala para ti mismo, escríbela o pregunta al otro si está interesado en tu parecer.
2. ¿Eres tímido para expresarte en los momentos y situaciones en las que deberías hacerlo? Date cuenta de que es tan natural que tú te abras como lo hacen los otros. Abandona la pasividad y la discreción excesiva cuando te corresponda ser protagonista.
3. ¿Acostumbras a *soltar* lo primero que te viene en mente sin medir el efecto que tendrán tus palabras? Examina primero quién tienes delante y cómo se siente en ese momento.

296
GANANCIAS Y PÉRDIDAS

Quizá ahora te duela el alma por una ruptura amorosa o bien llores el adiós a un ser querido. La vida está llena de ganancias y pérdidas que hemos de saber encajar.

El duelo es necesario para integrar una ausencia y después poder avanzar con dicha y volver a sonreír.

Como dice Leonard Cohen en uno de sus poemas: «Recordarás el bien que me hiciste, el bien que te hice yo. Y de pie en algún lugar dominante, como una ventana o un risco, conocerás el pleno gozo».

¡Qué bella manera de describir cómo nos sentimos al completar un duelo de forma natural y saludable! Las emociones amargas dan paso a los recuerdos placenteros y a la gratitud por haber vivido todo eso.

Ahora que lo has comprendido e integrado, se trata de seguir viviendo.

RESPETA TU *TEMPO*

La duración de un duelo varía de una persona a otra. Hay quien aparentemente lo asimila y encaja todo con gran rapidez y quien precisa de más tiempo para hacerse a la nueva situación.

La clave de todo duelo es no acelerarlo para liberarte de él antes ni tampoco prolongarlo a través de la victimización.

Respetar tu *tempo* y seguir con tu vida armonizarán cualquier experiencia por la que estés pasando, más allá de su impacto emocional.

297
TODO CAMBIA

Una de las canciones que más me gustan de Mercedes Sosa es *Todo cambia*. Me sorprendo tarareándola muchas veces.

Cambia lo superficial.
Cambia también lo profundo.
Cambia el modo de pensar.
Cambia todo en este mundo.

Me gusta pensar que el mundo puede cambiar. Que a cada giro del planeta Tierra alrededor del Sol tenemos una nueva oportunidad para ser parte de ese cambio, de ese giro. Que de la luz pasamos a la sombra y, de ese modo, la mirada también cambia. Que nos movemos de un lado a otro para cambiar también de perspectiva.

Asimismo, las personas a nuestro alrededor evolucionan y nos regalan metamorfosis increíbles. Incluso en nosotros mismos, al observarlas desde el corazón.

La naturaleza nos muestra a cada microsegundo que somos capaces de mutar y adaptarnos.

Todo cambia. Ya lo decía la Sosa.

―――― **CAMBIOS INTERNOS, CAMBIOS EXTERNOS** ――――

Como vasos comunicantes, al cambiar interiormente también se mueve nuestro entorno. En el capítulo de las relaciones, eso se traduce en más entradas y salidas, ya que...

- A algunas personas no les gustará el cambio que se ha obrado en ti.
- Otras se adaptarán a tu nuevo yo, quizá porque también están cambiando.
- Nuevas personas llegarán a tu vida, ya que tu cambio genera nuevas afinidades.

298
LA SERIE FIBONACCI

Hay una sucesión de números que permite dibujar la llamada espiral áurea. Desde un punto de vista matemático, empieza con los números 0 y 1, y a partir de aquí cada número que sigue es la suma de los dos anteriores: 0-1-1-2-3-5-8-13-21...

Al aplicar estas medidas a un gráfico, veremos que la figura se expande como una caracola o una galaxia.

Cuando contemplo una de estas espirales áureas, siento que también yo me expando, que todos los seres humanos lo hacen como la serie Fibonacci, que parece expresar el secreto de la vida y de la belleza del universo.

La proporción áurea es la única que me reconcilia con los números. Porque la entiendo y me emociona, cual helecho fértil que soy.

Crear y seguir creando, expandirme con el mar y el viento, como una caracola. Tal vez esa sea nuestra misión primordial como seres humanos.

DESARROLLO ÁUREO

Si aplicamos la serie Fibonacci a nuestro crecimiento personal, siguiendo la lógica de que cada nuevo número es la suma de los dos anteriores, puedes preguntarte:
- ¿Cuáles han sido las últimas dos experiencias transcendentes que has vivido?

- ¿De qué manera la suma de estas dos experiencias te ha llevado adonde estás ahora?
Puedes seguir proyectando tu propia serie Fibonacci hacia el futuro, viendo cómo los hitos y experiencias pasadas nos facilitan cada vez una comprensión más amplia.

299
UNA NUEVA PERSPECTIVA

Aseguraba Kobe Bryant que el amor es un viaje en el que tendrás altibajos, decepciones, alegrías y, sobre todo, aprendizajes. Me parece una excelente definición.

Muchas veces, sin embargo, estas enseñanzas necesitan la perspectiva del tiempo para poderlas comprender.

Cuando te alejas de un lugar, de una persona, de un puesto de trabajo, de una situación, y la ves en la distancia, solo entonces empiezas a conocerla de verdad. Comprendes por fin lo que significaba para ti y, además, entiendes quién eras en aquel momento y lo que valorabas.

Ahora puedes ver algunas cosas de una forma muy diferente y apreciar otras que antes no veías.

───── **TUS DESCUBRIMIENTOS A *POSTERIORI*** ─────

Elabora una lista de revelaciones sobre personas, lugares y situaciones que solo has entendido tiempo después. Agradece la lección aprendida, aunque haya viajado en el tiempo y no te haya llegado hasta ahora.

300
LA DISCUSIÓN

Una vieja fábula oriental cuenta que dos hermanos, viendo que se aproximaba una bandada de gansos salvajes, se dispusieron a preparar sus arcos.

—Si abatimos uno de esos gansos —dijo, entusiasmado, uno de ellos—, lo cocinaremos bien adobado.

—Nada de eso —le corrigió el otro—, eso es adecuado para cocinar los gansos cazados en tierra, pero los abatidos mientras vuelan hay que asarlos.

Para dirimir la discusión, fueron a consultar al más anciano de la aldea.

—Sugiero cortar el ganso por la mitad —aconsejó este—, así cada uno podrá cocinarlo a su gusto.

Satisfechos con esta solución, los hermanos volvieron al campo con sus arcos, pero los gansos ya habían volado lejos.

PON PRIMERO LO PRIMERO

Esta fábula nos enseña que las decisiones siguen un orden de prioridades. Así como los cazadores deberían haber decidido cómo cocinar la pieza después de cobrarla, en cualquier proyecto que emprendas, pregúntate: *¿Qué es lo que debo hacer ahora?* El resto de las decisiones ya encontrarán su tiempo y lugar.

301
TE PREFIERO

Muchas relaciones –de pareja, entre amigos o incluso familiares– pueden llevarnos a sufrir por la necesidad de reconocimiento externo, de aceptación por parte del otro, como hemos visto ya en este libro.

La falsa creencia de que el *amor verdadero* está relacionado con una entrega incondicional nos puede hacer perder nuestro eje emocional.

Al respecto, hay una frase del psicólogo Walter Riso que nos invita a reflexionar sobre el tipo de relaciones que establecemos. En lugar de hacerlo desde el apego a la persona amada, si optamos por la libertad podemos decir: *No te necesito, te prefiero.*

La libre elección mutua da a su vez plenitud para crecer y avanzar sanamente en la vida, sin depender de nadie.

TRANSFORMA LAS FRASES DE DEPENDENCIA

Así como el *te prefiero* abre un espacio de relación desde la libertad, hay frases y tópicos de la cultura popular que tienen el efecto contrario.

Veamos cómo transformar dos de ellas a modo de ejemplo:

- *Sin ti no soy nada / Sin ti me moriría.* Carga en el otro la responsabilidad de tener una vida con sentido o, incluso, de la propia existencia. Mejor decir: *Contigo soy todo / Contigo tengo aún más ganas de vivir.*
- *Eres mi media naranja.* La frase viene de Platón, pero transmite la idea de que sin el otro no estamos completos. Mejor decir: *Somos dos naranjas enteras y complementarias.*

302
EL EFECTO PIGMALIÓN

Si quieres empoderar a quien tienes a tu lado, si deseas educar y fortalecer a alguien que lo necesita, alimenta su alma recordándole las cosas que hace bien, en lugar de criticarle o señalar sus debilidades.

Es lo que se conoce en psicología como *efecto Pigmalión*: las expectativas que depositamos sobre los otros influyen de manera crucial en su rendimiento.

Cuando tratas a alguien como si no tuviera valor, se comportará contigo como si efectivamente fuera así, mientras que si alabas sus fortalezas, la persona se sentirá reconocida y tratará de demostrar que está a la altura de tu mirada.

Si optas por esto último, el efecto Pigmalión positivo, lograrás llenar al otro de motivación y espíritu de superación, protegiéndolo del desánimo y reforzando su autoestima.

Resumiendo: si quieres empoderar a alguien, comunícale todo lo bueno que tiene y hace.

EL EFECTO PIGMALIÓN EN EL TRABAJO

Aplicado al mundo laboral, esta ley se suele enunciar así:

Trátame como un empleado de tercera y me comportaré como un empleado de tercera; trátame como un empleado de primera y me comportaré como un empleado de primera.

Para aplicar el efecto Pigmalión positivo, podemos recordarles a las personas que trabajan para nosotros —desde el tendero a la asesora bancaria— todo lo que nos gusta de ellas y mostrarles nuestra gratitud por su labor.

303
LA LOCURA ES MARAVILLA

Sabios como Erasmo de Rotterdam ya sugerían que hay que aplicar cierta dosis de locura a la vida, ya que sin ella no puede darse una completa felicidad.

A mí siempre me costó entenderlo, porque relacionaba el concepto de locura con algo negativo. Sin embargo, con el tiempo he encontrado la manera de darle una vuelta a esta visión. Me atraía saber lo que escondían los recovecos del sin sentido, de lo no planeado y de lo desconocido e imprevisible.

Sobre eso, el poeta William Blake decía: «La locura es maravilla sin término, intrincadas raíces enredan sus caminos. ¡Cuántos han caído allí!».

LA LOCURA LO CURA

Guillermo Borja, un singular y controvertido terapeuta mexicano cercano a la Gestalt, contaba en su libro *La locura lo cura* cómo rehabilitó a los psicóticos de un penal reconociendo y encontrando una utilidad para la *locura* de cada uno.

Aplicado a tu propia vida:
- ¿De qué *locura* que te caracteriza te sientes más orgulloso?
- ¿Cómo puedes compartir esa *locura* para ayudar a los demás a vivir de forma más ligera y saludable?

304
¿SUEÑO O REALIDAD?

En uno de los textos más sugerentes de la China clásica, el filósofo Chuang Zhou formulaba el siguiente dilema:

Una noche Chuang Zhou soñó que era una mariposa: una mariposa que revoloteaba, que iba de un lugar a otro, contenta consigo misma, ignorante por completo de ser Zhou. Despertose a deshora y vio, asombrado, que era Zhou. Mas, ¿Zhou había soñado que era una mariposa? ¿O era una mariposa la que estaba ahora soñando que era Zhou? Entre Zhou y la mariposa había sin duda una diferencia. A esto llaman «mutación de las cosas».

¿Quién no ha pensado alguna vez que todo lo que vivimos podría ser un sueño? ¿Y si lo que sucede al cerrar los ojos fuera la realidad?

TU DIARIO DE SUEÑOS

Más allá de las dudas, nuestro mundo onírico tiene importantes mensajes que darnos, ya que nace directamente de nuestro subconsciente. Para recordarlo mejor y no perdernos sus enseñanzas...

1. Ten en la mesita de noche un cuaderno y un bolígrafo a mano.
2. Nada más despertarte, antes de que se pierdan los últimos retazos del sueño, apunta lo que recuerdas.
3. Lee tu diario de sueños cada cierto tiempo para ver qué temas o visiones son recurrentes.

305
VIDA ANTES DE LA MUERTE

Saber que vamos a morir es un buen revulsivo para hacer aquello que nos apasiona, sin más tiempo que perder. Le damos valor a la vida, justamente, porque sabemos que es efímera.

En este sentido, Antonio Gala nos recordaba que «En tanto que haya muerte, habrá esperanza».

Esta reflexión está en sintonía con un cuento de Anthony de Mello, un jesuita nacido en la India que fue un gran divulgador del orientalismo y la espiritualidad.

Cuenta que un grupo de alumnos planteaban a su maestro preguntas sobre la vida más allá de la muerte. El sabio se limitaba a sonreír sin dar ninguna respuesta.

Cuando le preguntaron por qué se había mostrado tan evasivo, él replicó:

—¿No habéis observado que los que no saben qué hacer con esta vida son precisamente los que más desean otra vida que dure eternamente?

—Pero ¿hay vida después de la muerte o no la hay? —insistió un alumno.

—¿Hay vida antes de la muerte? ¡Esta es la verdadera cuestión! —respondió el maestro.

¿QUÉ TE DA VIDA?

Imagina que te has ido ya del mundo terrenal y que, desde el más allá, puedes revisar los mejores momentos de tu existencia.

- ¿Qué fue lo que te hizo sentir más vivo?
- ¿Cómo y con quién lo viviste?

- ¿De qué manera podrías haber vivido más momentos así?

Completado el ejercicio, viene la buena noticia: sigues aquí, ¡puedes hacer todo eso que te da vida antes de la muerte!

306
AUTOAMOR

Observo cada emoción que me embarga como un nuevo camino a descubrir, sin emitir juicios negativos. Intento ser amable conmigo misma, ya que muchas veces pienso que soy un error andante y me echo la culpa de todo.

En caso de duda, me aplico el *autoamor*, el concepto que también da título al libro publicado por mi querida Laura Chica.

Esta psicóloga, *coach* y especialista en desarrollo del talento lo definía así en una entrevista a la prensa:

> *El autoamor es el amor desde lo más profundo de uno mismo, al margen del entorno y de las circunstancias, y se encuentra en el corazón.* Autoamor *es cuidar lo que eres, proteger lo que eres, respetar los propios sentimientos, hacer cosas que te hacen sentir bien y dejar de hacer lo que te hace sentir mal.*

CÓMO DESARROLLAR EL AUTOAMOR

Laura Chica propone que sigamos un proceso de cinco pasos:

1. *Poner luz.* Para darte cuenta de cómo te juzgas, de lo que rechazas de ti mismo, cuando no te amas ni crees en ti.

2. *Observar.* Presta atención a tu comportamiento, ya que muchas de las cosas las haces en piloto automático, de forma inconsciente.

3. *Comprender.* Sin enjuiciarte, acepta que eres producto de tus experiencias y aprendizajes.

4. *Abrazar.* De manera simbólica, abraza todo lo que eres, con lo que te gusta y lo que no te gusta de ti.

5. *Amar.* En la fase final del proceso, estás ya preparado para amarte por quien eres. Estás ya en el autoamor.

307
UN EJERCICIO CONCEPTUAL

Cuando te encuentres en un laberinto mental por cualquier cuestión que te preocupe, te propongo que hagas el siguiente experimento:

1. Elige una imagen para meditar sobre ella de forma libre. Puedes obtenerla al azar abriendo un diccionario o elegir la primera idea que te pase por la cabeza.
2. ¿Qué emociones te provoca, aquí y ahora, esa imagen?
3. ¿Por qué esa imagen suscita en ti esta reacción emocional?
4. ¿Qué tiene que ver el conflicto que te inquieta con esa imagen?
5. ¿Puedes extraer de esa imagen nuevos caminos o soluciones para abordar lo que te está preocupando?

Esta clase de ejercicio creativo lo puedes realizar tanto en solitario como en pareja o en grupo y seguro que te aportará nuevas perspectivas sobre el asunto.

LLUVIA DE IDEAS COMPARTIDA

Hay un ejercicio de *brainstorming* para realizar entre dos o más personas que puede ayudarte a descubrir nuevas perspectivas para abordar cualquier cuestión:

1. En una hoja de papel, escribe las primeras palabras que se te ocurren en relación con el problema.
2. Pasa el papel a la persona de tu lado, quien, tras leerlo, en silencio añadirá sus propias ideas y conceptos.
3. Repetid el proceso, cambiando de turno varias veces, hasta que se llene el papel o se agoten las aportaciones.
4. Leed juntos ahora todas las notas y debatid sobre qué idea parece más útil.

308

DAR Y RECIBIR

Un relato tradicional zen cuenta que un hombre muy adinerado no soportaba gastar ni una moneda, con lo cual vivía una vida de constantes privaciones.

Al darse cuenta de ello, un maestro le mostró su puño cerrado y le comentó:

—Imagina que mi mano estuviera así siempre, desde que nací hasta el día de mi muerte. ¿Cómo llamarías a esto?

—Una deformación.

Acto seguido, el maestro le mostró su mano abierta y prosiguió:

—Supón ahora que esta mano estuviera así siempre, sin cambio alguno. ¿Cómo lo llamarías?

—Sería también una deformación.

—Entonces, ahora ya sabes todo lo que necesitas para llevar una vida feliz y equilibrada.

PRACTICA LA VÍA DE EN MEDIO

Este concepto descubierto por Siddhartha Gautama, antes incluso de haberse convertido en Buda, tiene muchas aplicaciones en la vida cotidiana. Veamos algunos ejemplos:

- Tras una temporada de ahorro, puedes darte un pequeño capricho para premiarte por tu esfuerzo.
- Si tienes trato con una persona algo *intensa* pero valiosa, no se trata de seguir su ritmo ni tampoco de evitarla. La vía del medio sería dosificar los encuentros, siguiendo la máxima anglosajona «*He/She is ok in small doses*».
- Busca el equilibrio entre el trabajo y el ocio, de manera que no seas demasiado ocioso ni un trabajópata.

309
PUEDES HACERLO

Recuerdo que un día, jugando con mis hijos, no acertaba a encajar una pieza del mecanismo de un juguete. Entonces, les dije *no puedo* con voz tímida y mostrando desasosiego por no conseguir dar con la solución.

En ese momento, mi hija mediana, siempre tan sabia, me respondió:

—Mamá, sí puedes, pero no sabes cómo.

Esa era una frase que yo le había repetido infinidad de veces y que ella, en ese momento, recuperaba para evitar mi frustración.

Estoy convencida de que es cierto. Que no sepas ahora cómo hacer aquello a lo que te enfrentas no significa que no puedas. Simplemente, no has encontrado aún la manera. Piénsalo.

CUANDO EL *NO PUEDO* VIENE DE FUERA

En su discurso más conocido, el presidente Barack Obama reflexionaba así sobre la imposibilidad que viene del entorno o de la sociedad:

Los cínicos nos han dicho toda la vida que no podemos hacer lo que deseamos. Nos piden que nos ajustemos a la realidad, que no nos abracemos a falsas esperanzas. Pero no hay nada falso sobre la esperanza. Cuando nos enfrentamos a retos aparentemente imposibles, cuando nos advierten que no estamos preparados para hacer esto o aquello, cuando nos dicen que ni siquiera merece la pena intentarlo porque no lo lograremos, entonces es cuando debemos responder: sí, podemos.

310
RESIGNIFICA TU PASADO

Te invito a hacer un viaje al pasado con un propósito concreto: encontrar aquellos acontecimientos que te bloquearon en su día, pero que hoy pueden tener una lectura muy distinta.

Al encontrarte con ellos, debes *resignificarlos* para entender lo que sucedió.

Ese *tú* era distinto a tu *yo* de ahora, que es más consciente y empoderado.

En un ejercicio de visualización, tu *yo* de ahora puede conversar con quien eras entonces, comprendiendo por qué lo viviste de ese modo y cómo lo harías hoy con todo lo que has aprendido en el camino.

Este ejercicio de búsqueda interior te permitirá interpretar los *fósiles* de tu pasado y luego donarlos al museo del recuerdo para que no pesen en tu día a día.

¿QUÉ HABRÍA PASADO SI...?

Todos hemos tenido alguna vez la fantasía de saber *qué habría pasado si...* hubiéramos actuado de otra forma en una u otra ocasión. La novela de Matt Haig *La biblioteca de medianoche* juega con esa idea. La protagonista tiene la posibilidad de experimentar todas sus vidas no vividas y comprobar qué habría sucedido.

Te propongo un ejercicio con esta misma idea:

1. Completa tres frases sobre tu pasado que empiecen por *¿Qué habría pasado si yo...?*
2. Usa tu imaginación para contestar a esas tres preguntas.
3. Da un paso adelante y plantea ahora una sola pregunta que vaya del presente al futuro: *¿Qué pasaría si...?*
4. Respóndela y plantéate la posibilidad de llevarlo a la práctica.

311
TÓMATELO CON FILOSOFÍA

Esto es lo que propuso Lou Marinoff, un profesor de Montreal que, a finales del siglo pasado, sorprendió con el libro *Más Platón, menos Prozac.*

Creador del asesoramiento filosófico como terapia, su tesis es que en muchas ocasiones se pueden evitar los fármacos y los largos tratamientos psicoanalíticos con ayuda de la filosofía.

Los grandes pensadores, desde la antigüedad, abordan muchos de los temas que nos angustian hoy. En sus palabras:

> *La única manera de obtener una solución real y duradera para un problema personal es abordarlo, resolverlo, aprender de él y aplicar lo que se aprenda en el futuro.*

Para ello nos resultará muy útil leer obras divulgativas sobre filosofía y, por qué no, hablar, filosofar con personas afines sobre ello.

En mi caso, yo he tenido la suerte de tratar con José Carlos Ruiz y David Pastor Vico, dos autores y divulgadores de la filosofía, andaluces los dos y profesores de esta materia, que me han ayudado mucho.

¿CUÁL ES TU FILOSOFÍA DE VIDA?

El objetivo último del asesoramiento filosófico es llegar a comprender cuál es nuestra filosofía de vida y cómo podemos corregirla cuando nos perjudica. Dice Lou Marinoff:

> Comprender nuestra propia filosofía puede ayudarnos a evitar, resolver o abordar muchos problemas. Nuestra filosofía también puede ser el origen de los problemas que padecemos, de modo que debemos evaluar las ideas que sostenemos para modelar un punto de vista que obre a nuestro favor, no en contra. Usted es capaz de cambiar sus creencias para resolver un problema.

312
LA VERDADERA BELLEZA

Si me visto y luzco prendas de una firma de deporte en concreto, ¿me hace eso ser mejor atleta? ¿Más sana? ¿Más deportista?

Si conduzco un coche lujoso, ¿me convierte eso en una persona importante o en un gran conductor?

Si escucho a músicos inspiradores, ¿me hace eso una persona más especial?

Si me pongo un reloj valioso, ¿mi tiempo también valdrá más?

Siempre se ha dicho que la mona se puede vestir de seda, pero mona se queda. Pero lo cierto es que no somos lo que llevamos puesto ni lo que compramos ni lo que queremos emular o imitar.

Somos lo que somos. Y no son las cosas bellas, sino nuestros hechos y actitudes los que embellecen nuestra vida.

CLAVES DEL MAGNETISMO PERSONAL

Más allá de lo que lleves puesto, incluso cuando solo vistas tu propia piel, estas son algunas características de las personas con magnetismo natural, por si quieres emularlas:

1. No tratan de impresionar a los demás a través de su ropa, ni tampoco presumen de sus logros. Su atractivo viene de su autenticidad y transparencia.
2. Nunca hablan de más. Por eso, cuando abren la boca todo el mundo las escucha.
3. Hacen sentir cómodos a los demás, porque no se ponen por encima ni por debajo. Simplemente inspiran confianza.

313
ALEGRARSE POR LOS DEMÁS

En otra reflexión de este libro vimos cómo Oscar Wilde consideraba que la amistad más valiosa es la de aquellos que se alegran por nuestros éxitos.

Esa es una virtud que tiene que ver con la generosidad del ser humano. Pero, además de que alegrándonos por ellos, nos granjeamos la estima de los otros, está ese gran beneficio en ello: gracias al contagio emocional, del que ya os he hablado, la felicidad del prójimo acaba siendo también tuya, con lo que te llena de energía.

Por este motivo, celebrar los éxitos de las personas que te rodean sienta muy bien y te contagia de cosas buenas. ¿Te apetece participar de esta felicidad ajena para llenarte el alma de ella y hacerla tuya?

¿ABUNDANCIA O CARENCIA?

Cada vez que sentimos envidia, rabia o celos, cultivamos energía de carencia. Ponemos el foco en aquello que nos falta. En cambio, cuando experimentamos sentimientos de alegría por otro, generosidad o altruismo, proyectamos en nosotros la idea de que el universo tiene suficiente para todos, también para nosotros. Cultivamos energía de abundancia.

¿Con qué clase de energía eliges conectar?

314

PARA RECARGAR EL ALMA

Cuando te sientas abatido, puedes calentar a un lado del campo, bailar fuera de la pista, descansar en una esquina de la verbena, caminar un rato por el arcén.

Apartarte un tiempo del conflicto o de lo que te pesa en un momento determinado, te ayudará a volver a la acción lleno de vitalidad.

Tras esta *parada técnica*, podrás situarte física, mental y emocionalmente donde debes estar, cuando lo creas conveniente y de la manera que elijas afrontarlo.

Mirar desde el patio de butacas la obra de tu propia vida, como un actor exigente que trata de mejorar lo que sucede en el escenario, es la mejor manera de introducir los cambios necesarios en ella.

Hazte un rato a un lado cuando la vida te supere, pero solo para regresar con más fuerza, habiendo escrito un nuevo guion para ser protagonista de tu vida y bailar bajo los focos a tu ritmo y con alegría.

UNAS VACACIONES DE UN MINUTO

Si te encuentras en tu lugar de trabajo, en una reunión familiar o en cualquier otro sitio del que no puedes evadirte fácilmente, puedes hacer este ejercicio para recargar las pilas:

1. Retírate un minuto a un espacio donde puedas estar solo, aunque sea un rincón de la oficina, o incluso el baño.
2. Cierra los ojos durante ese tiempo y trasládate mentalmente a tu lugar favorito del mundo (o a uno de ellos).
3. Visualiza cómo caminas lentamente por ese lugar o, simplemente, respiras delante de ese paisaje.
4. Cuando regreses a la actividad, siente que llevas contigo parte de esa belleza y placidez.

315
LO NORMAL ES EXTRAORDINARIO

P hil Bosmans, un escritor y religioso belga, se hizo famoso en su país durante los años setenta con un libro que se traduciría como *Querido humano, te quiero* y que vendió dos millones de ejemplares en Alemania.

Este texto es una celebración de las cosas que a menudo consideramos *normales*, pero que son sin duda extraordinarias:

Redescubre las cosas normales,
el canto sencillo de la amistad, las flores para un enfermo,
una puerta abierta, una mesa acogedora,
un apretón de manos, una sonrisa,
el silencio de una iglesia, el dibujo de un niño,
una flor que se abre, un pájaro que canta,
una hilera de álamos, un riachuelo, una montaña...
La vida se vuelve una fiesta cuando sabes disfrutar
de las cosas normales de cada día.

¿QUÉ ECHARÍAS DE MENOS?

Imagina que tienes que pasar una larga temporada en un hospital. ¿Qué cosas de tu día a día echarías de menos? Haz una lista con todas ellas porque son tus *normales extraordinarias*.

316
ELIJO VIVIR

Asumo que los sinsabores son parte de la existencia, se alternan con lo agradable igual que la noche y el día. Nada de esto me causará desesperanza si amo la vida.

Quiero vivir, recibir lo que me llega y, cuanto más disfrute y alegría traiga, tanto mejor.

Eso no significa que niegue los otros tonos de la existencia. Friedrich Nietzsche dijo: «El sufrimiento y el fracaso son la clave de la felicidad y son parte de la vida».

Por eso, incluso sabiendo que habrá momentos en los que tendré que sufrir, yo elijo vivir.

El mismo Nietzsche dijo que «lo que no nos mata, nos hace más fuertes», y puedes utilizar esa nueva fortaleza para vivir con más plenitud e intensidad.

PROYECTA LA FELICIDAD

Cuando pases por un momento de dificultad, puedes compensarlo proyectándote al estado contrario al que estás viviendo. Algunos ejemplos:

- Si por tu situación actual no puedes viajar, aprovecha para leer e informarte sobre los lugares que visitarás en el futuro.
- Si ahora no tienes pareja, es momento de analizar qué quieres en ese sentido y qué mejoras aplicarás cuando vuelvas a estar con alguien.
- Si tu salud te limita ahora mismo, mientras trabajas por recobrarla decide cómo querrás vivir cuando estés en mejores condiciones.

317
ESCUCHAR COMO UN AMIGO

En una conversación que tuve con mi admirado Ángel Martín sobre su libro *Por si las voces vuelven*, este actor, comunicador y guionista mencionó una frase que había leído en un libro. Era algo así: *Nadie debería saber lo que va a decir hasta que termina de escuchar.*

Me decía que esta reflexión había sido un importante aprendizaje para él.

Me encantó escuchárselo decir, porque es cierto que, muchas veces, mientras nuestro interlocutor habla estamos pensando en la réplica que le daremos en vez de poner atención en sus palabras y en la emoción que las acompaña, es decir, en lo que quiere compartir verdaderamente.

Decía Ed Cunningham que «los amigos son esa gente poco común que nos pregunta cómo estamos y se espera a escuchar la respuesta».

¿CÓMO ESTÁS?

Esta pregunta muchas veces se lanza como una fórmula vacía, un saludo neutro para el que no se espera respuesta concreta. Como mucho un *Ya ves...* o *Voy tirando* que no nos paramos a escuchar.

Para este ejercicio, te propongo que la próxima vez preguntes *¿cómo estás, de verdad?*, afines el oído y la mirada con total presencia, y te des tiempo para oír hasta el final lo que te cuentan.

318
DISTINTAS SENDAS

Un relato glosado por el autor de origen indio Idries Shah cuenta que un discípulo de Nasrudín le planteó la siguiente cuestión:

—Tú eres un gran místico. Sin duda sabrás por qué los hombres siguen sendas diferentes a lo largo de su vida, en vez de seguir un único camino.

—Eso es muy sencillo —contestó el sabio—. Si todo el mundo siguiera la misma senda, todos acabaríamos en el mismo lugar. El mundo perdería entonces el equilibrio, se inclinaría y nos caeríamos al océano.

Esta fábula sufí transmite la importancia de que cada persona elija su propio sendero, sin hacer caso de los caminos que hayan sido válidos para otros.

SERENDIPIAS

Aunque la geometría nos dice que la línea recta es la distancia más corta entre dos puntos, eso no significa que sea el camino más interesante, de hecho, a veces un rodeo nos lleva al verdadero tesoro.

Las serendipias, los descubrimientos valiosos que se hacen mientras se buscaba otra cosa —el descubrimiento de América es el ejemplo más típico—, son la prueba de que a veces hay que perderse para encontrar algo aún mejor.

¿Te atreverías a desviarte del camino recto para descubrir algo inesperado?

319

EL RUMBO DE TU VIDA

E n la película *Los puentes de Madison*, una de mis favoritas, se relata una historia de amor contenida y, a su vez, llena de pasión que pasa por diferentes estadios.

Inspiradora y conmovedora al mismo tiempo, con una Streep y un Eastwood sublimes en sus papeles.

Me parece que incita a una deliciosa reflexión sobre las preguntas que nos hacemos al encontrar a alguien que nos fascina y hasta qué punto estamos dispuestos a cambiar el rumbo de nuestra vida.

Sí es una gran verdad que nunca volveremos a ser los mismos tras una historia amorosa.

Una de las frases más optimistas y conmovedoras de esta película es: «El corazón humano tiene una forma de volver a hacerse grande incluso después de que se haya roto en un millón de pedazos».

SIGUE TU INSPIRACIÓN

El autor de la novela en la que se basa la película, Robert James Waller, escribió el primer manuscrito en solo once días. Se inspiró mientras fotografiaba los puentes que cruzan el Misisipi en el condado de Madison.

Este es un ejemplo de que debemos seguir nuestras grandes inspiraciones. Cuando una idea aparezca con fuerza en tu cabeza, reclamando tu atención, merece la pena que le dediques toda tu energía a cristalizarla.

320
TU ROL EN LA OBRA

La vida es a veces como una ópera, una obra de teatro o una película en la que interpretamos un determinado rol o papel.

Para tomar conciencia de ello, te puede resultar terapéutico apuntarte a un curso de teatro o participar directamente en un montaje *amateur*. Estar en el escenario te permitirá adoptar diferentes actitudes y personajes, comprobando cómo te sientes en cada uno.

Porque cuando asumimos un papel en el teatro, por ejemplo, salimos de lo que somos habitualmente, lo cual nos relaja de muchas tensiones. Al mismo tiempo, también transmitimos lo que llevamos dentro con mayor libertad, con la excusa de interpretar un papel ajeno a nosotros.

Es un proceso divertido, pero si crees que no es lo tuyo, al menos quédate con una pequeña enseñanza: podemos cambiar el rol o personaje que interpretamos en nuestra vida, darle matices al papel o incluso, por qué no, romper el guion y escribir el nuestro propio.

EL MÉTODO STANISLAVSKY

El célebre maestro ruso proponía, como fundamento de su sistema, que los actores *experimentaran* el personaje, en lugar de *interpretarlo*. Es decir, si encarnas el papel de un avaro, no se trata de imitar sus movimientos y actitudes, sino de sentir la avaricia dentro de ti, y actuar desde ese nuevo yo.

El método Stanislavsky te puede ser útil en la vida diaria para adoptar un nuevo rol que sea más conveniente para el reto que estás afrontando. Lo has de vivir desde dentro hacia fuera. ¿Qué papel te gustaría tener en el actual momento de tu existencia?

321
BAILAR CON LA VIDA

Puedes sacarle más partido a la vida si bailas con ella, dejándole que te lleve de la cintura sin oponer resistencia.

Me gusta comparar la existencia con la danza, y se me ocurren varios paralelismos entre las claves para ser un buen bailarín y la vida:

- *Controla tu posición.* La actitud corporal es lo que da majestuosidad a quien danza. Lo mismo sucede con lo que vives: todo depende de la postura que tomes ante las circunstancias.
- *Siente la música de la vida.* Solo si te dejas llevar por ella podrás fluir con los distintos ritmos y matices que te ofrece.
- *Trata de entender a tu pareja de baile.* Así os deslizaréis mejor por los escenarios del mundo. Acompaña y déjate llevar sin perder el paso.

LOS CINCO RITMOS

Entre las distintas escuelas de danza terapéutica o experiencial está la de Gabrielle Roth y sus cinco ritmos, que decía: «La energía se mueve en ondas. Las ondas se mueven en patrones. Los patrones se mueven en ritmos. Un ser humano es eso: energía, ondas, patrones y ritmos... un baile».

En las sesiones de esta disciplina, que está al alcance de cualquier persona, se trabajan estos aspectos:

- *Enraizamiento.* Ante todo, ser consciente de tu propio cuerpo.
- *Atención.* ¿Cómo sientes tu cuerpo? ¿De qué manera percibes el entorno?
- *Movimiento.* Expresa todo lo que eres, incluidas tus emociones y pensamientos.
- *Respiración.* Forma parte de tu movimiento, es el aliento de la vida.

322
EL CONCIERTO DE LA VACA

Un cuento de Oriente relata que un célebre músico decidió experimentar algo nuevo tocando una pieza clásica ante una vaca.

El animal siguió pastando, sin levantar una sola vez la cabeza para atender al concierto.

No es que la vaca no oiga mi música, es que mi música no le interesa, pensó el músico que, acto seguido, utilizó un instrumento de viento para imitar el zumbido de las moscas y luego el mugido de los terneros.

La vaca empezó a prestar gran atención al concierto, y se acercó incluso al instrumentista, balanceando la cola, para poder escucharlo mejor.

El músico entendió entonces que el nuevo repertorio le había interesado porque, este sí, tenía un significado para la vaca.

¿A QUIÉN LE INTERESA ESTO?

Esta es una pregunta que deberíamos hacernos antes de soltar un largo discurso a alguien. Para medir si es adecuado lo que quieres explicar a quien tienes delante, pregúntate:

1. ¿Esta persona comprende y tiene afinidad por el tema que quiero exponer?

2. ¿Dispone del tiempo necesario para lo que quiero contar?

3. ¿Viene libre de expectativas o nos hemos encontrado para hablar de otra cosa?

4. ¿Le resultará útil y valioso lo que quiero contarle?

323
TODO LO QUE ERES

E res mucho más de lo que imaginas. Más incluso de lo que has aspirado nunca a ser. El maestro espiritual Amit Ray dice al respecto:

No estás solo en las luchas de la vida. Todo el cosmos está contigo. Evoluciona a través de la forma en que enfrentas y superas los desafíos de la vida. Usa todo a tu favor.

Cuando te das cuenta de eso, te conviertes en esperanza para otros, no solo para ti. Puedes tender la mano a los demás, animar a quienes tienen dificultades en el camino, transmitir calma a quien tiene necesidad de ella.

Date la oportunidad de ser inspiración para otros y para ti mismo. Ofrece todo el amor que tienes, eres y mereces.

TRES CLAVES PARA EMPODERARTE

1. *Elimina las excusas y justificaciones.* Frases como *Es que soy así, Es la vida* o *Qué le vamos a hacer* te desempoderan y te llevan a un papel de víctima.
2. *Date cuenta de tu influencia en los demás.* Todo lo que haces y dices tiene su repercusión en tu entorno. Si prestas atención al *feedback*, tomarás conciencia de tu poder.
3. *Busca buenos compañeros de cordada.* Así como una expedición a una alta montaña fracasará si hay montañeros pesimistas o temerosos, busca un buen equipo para alcanzar tu cima personal.

324
PURA ENERGÍA

Decía Leonard Bernstein, tras haber visto actuar a Maria Callas, que ella era *pura electricidad.*

No es de extrañar. Su manera de cantar llegaba más allá porque la diva nacida en Nueva York tenía el don de hacer vibrar con su talento. Sobre el secreto de su arte, una vez confesó:

> *Yo pertenezco a los dadores. Quiero dar un poco de felicidad, incluso si no he tenido mucha para mí (...) Si alguien salió de una ópera sintiéndose más feliz y en paz, ya logré mi propósito.*

Las personas como Maria Callas tienen esa generosidad y logran hacer felices a los demás porque saben convertir la emoción en puente y punto de encuentro.

Quizá no llegues a todos, como la gran soprano, pero tienes la oportunidad de conectar con muchas personas y darles un buen chute de vida.

Cada día tenemos la oportunidad de dar el do de pecho para animar la existencia de los demás.

¿CUÁL ES TU CANCIÓN PARA EL MUNDO?

El premio Nobel indio Rabindranath Tagore decía que «El bosque sería muy triste si solo cantaran los pájaros que mejor lo hacen». A partir de esta idea te sugiero que te preguntes:

- ¿Cuál es la *canción* que puedes entregar en tu vida cotidiana para alegrar la vida de los demás?
- ¿Con qué medios y talentos cuentas para ello?
- ¿Quién necesita más, en este momento, tu aportación a la vida?

325
DIVINAS TONTERÍAS

En un documental sobre René Magritte, se cuenta que una vez invitó a su casa a un experto en arte. Hacía frío y el salón estaba calentado por un hogar de leña.

El pintor surrealista preguntó a su invitado si podría poner un leño al fuego. Justo cuando se giraba para hacerlo, Magritte le dio una patada en el trasero.

Desconcertado, el visitante se giró hacia el anfitrión, que siguió charlando con gran seriedad, como si nada hubiera sucedido. Pensando, quizá, que se había tratado de una alucinación, el otro volvió a la conversación sin más.

Sin llegar a estos extremos, quizá te guste a veces hacer alguna tontería para demostrarte que no te tomas la vida tan en serio.

Esas tonterías, a veces, son tus mejores momentos de conexión contigo mismo y puede que contagien a otros de ligereza o, al menos, de un divertido sentimiento de sorpresa.

UN POCO DE LIGEREZA

Se cuenta que, en un aeropuerto de Alabama, cuando un pasajero se disponía a embarcar su maleta, el empleado de la aerolínea le hizo una pregunta rutinaria:

—¿Alguien ha puesto algo sin su conocimiento en su equipaje?

A lo que el pasajero contestó:

—Si hubiera sido sin mi conocimiento, ¿cómo podría saberlo?

Esto provocó la risa del empleado.

Es un pequeño ejemplo de cómo un tono ligero, pero respetuoso, puede hacer más agradables y divertidas las tareas y conversaciones áridas.

326

LECCIONES DEL *KINDERGARTEN*

En 1986, Robert Fulghum tuvo un enorme éxito con *Todo lo que realmente necesito saber lo aprendí en el parvulario*, un libro encantador en el que este autor norteamericano recupera las enseñanzas del jardín de infancia para el buen vivir de los adultos:

1. Compártelo todo.
2. Juega limpio.
3. No pegues a los demás.
4. Devuelve las cosas donde las encontraste.
5. Limpia lo que hayas ensuciado.
6. No cojas lo que no es tuyo.
7. Di que lo sientes cuando hayas hecho daño a alguien.
8. Lávate las manos antes de comer.

Sobre el valor de recuperar estas sencillas lecciones –con un nuevo sentido– en la edad adulta, Fulghum señala: «Que seas inteligente no significa que no seas estúpido».

CON TU MIRADA DE AHORA

Como ejercicio para esta reflexión, te propongo que leas cada una de las ocho reglas de parvulario y las interpretes para tu día a día. A excepción de la octava, que es literal —aunque muy útil en época de pandemia—, todas las otras tienen un sentido más amplio en la madurez. ¿Cómo se traduce cada regla a tu vida actual?

327
TU PROPIA *MATRIX*

Uno de los momentos icónicos de la película *Matrix* es la elección que tiene que hacer el protagonista entre la píldora roja y la azul. La primera permite conocer una verdad que puede hacer tambalear su mundo, la segunda lo mantiene en la ignorancia.

¿Cuál de las dos elegirías si pudieras decidir?

¿Optarías por la verdad, por incómoda que fuera, o preferirías no saber?

Me parece interesante esta reflexión, porque muchas veces en nuestras vidas podemos elegir entre esas dos posibilidades.

A veces la vida nos manda señales que equivalen a la píldora roja, para que nos atrevamos a indagar en la verdad sobre nosotros mismos o nuestro entorno. Podemos asumir el reto o tomar la azul y pasar de largo por el aprendizaje.

CUANDO ES MEJOR NO SABER

Hay situaciones concretas, sin embargo, en las que no tiene ninguna utilidad querer saber, como...
- Lo que otras personas puedan haber dicho u opinado sobre ti.

- Los rumores sobre terceros acerca de asuntos que no te incumben.
- Informaciones negativas, en general, que no tienen una utilidad clara.

328
TU AUTOBIOGRAFÍA

En esta reflexión te propongo un juego de imaginación. Si leyeras un ejemplar único de tu autobiografía, escrita con toda clase de detalles, ¿qué te faltaría por escribir?

Quizá sea un buen momento para redactar ese capítulo que se refiere a lo que aún, a día de hoy, no has vivido y darle una nueva dirección y sentido a la obra de tu vida.

Puedes diseñar el siguiente capítulo y algunos más, si te atreves. Llena las páginas del relato de tu vida con historias que merezcan la pena ser contadas.

Una vez completado el ejercicio, piensa en los cambios concretos que deberías introducir en tu rutina para que tu futuro tome el rumbo que dicta tu imaginación.

Todos los grandes logros tienen su germen en la fantasía, por lo tanto, ¡atrévete a repensar tu vida!

CUENTA TU VIDA EN SIETE PALABRAS

Silvia Adela Kohan, a quien nos referimos en un ejercicio anterior, recomienda en su manual *Escribe tu vida* utilizar la autobiografía como herramienta para conocerte mejor y clarificar cómo te gustaría vivir.

Si no te sientes aún preparado para escribir un texto largo, este ejercicio preliminar de la autora te puede servir:

1. Resume tu vida en siete palabras. Tómate unos minutos para elegirlas bien.
2. ¿Qué mensaje vital puedes deducir de cada término?
3. Por último, ¿qué tienen en común todas estas palabras? Quizá te ayuden a encontrar el argumento principal de tu historia.

329
TÚ

La ortografía es importante, y sus reglas me sirven como excusa para recordarte algo.

Date cuenta de que la palabra *tú* va con tilde para darle la singularidad que merece todo sujeto, que es único e irrepetible.

Tú eres la clave de todo. De ti parte todo y todo vuelve a ti, como un universo que se expande y se comprime en una larga respiración.

Tú haces que el significado de la vida tenga el acento, la tilde y la importancia que merece.

Tú eres tu fuerza.

¿Cuál es la persona más importante de tu vida? ¿Quién ostenta el poder, la magia, la capacidad de transformación? ¿Cuál es el sujeto de tus grandes aventuras?

Tú.

CUANDO EL LIBRO TE HABLA A TI

No son muchos los libros que utilizan la segunda persona de singular para dirigirse al lector, y uno de ellos es el *Diario de invierno* de Paul Auster, en el que encontramos pasajes como este:

Piensas que nunca te va a pasar, imposible que te suceda a ti, que eres la única persona del mundo a quien jamás ocurrirán esas cosas, y entonces, una por una, empiezan a pasarte todas, igual que le suceden a cualquier otro.

¿Cómo continuarías este hilo de pensamiento?

330
CREATIVIDAD PURA

En la década de 1960, cuando la psicología transpersonal y el orientalismo eran casi desconocidos en España, existió un divulgador pionero: Antonio Blay Fontcuberta.

Autor de obras monumentales como *La personalidad creadora*, esta es su visión de nuestra esencia:

> *El ser humano, en efecto, es naturalmente creador, del mismo modo que lo es en grado sumo la Vida de la cual él es una elevada expresión. La creatividad, pues, no la hemos de ver exclusivamente en aquellos grandes artistas cuyas obras admira la humanidad a través de los siglos, ni tampoco en esos hombres geniales en el terreno de los descubrimientos científicos, de las realizaciones tecnológicas o de las innovaciones comerciales. La capacidad creadora se manifiesta en toda acción que el hombre ejecuta con la plenitud de todo su ser, con la sinceridad, espontaneidad y totalidad de un alma despierta y sencilla.*

¿Eres consciente de tu poder creativo? ¿Qué relevancia le das en tu vida diaria?

UN CONSEJO DE ANTONIO BLAY

Decía este psicólogo nacido en Barcelona: «Voy a intentar llevarme bien conmigo; los demás también saldrán ganando».

Y ahora te pregunto: ¿De qué manera puedes llevarte bien contigo para mejorar tu vida y la de los demás?

331
LÁGRIMAS EN LA LLUVIA

Hay una película en especial que me hizo amar el cine: *Blade Runner*. En ella hay una secuencia inolvidable: el replicante Roy Batty, magistralmente interpretado por Rutger Hauer, tiene un monólogo final sublime.

Al parecer, este parlamento tan emotivo no estaba de este modo en el guion adaptado a partir de la novela *¿Sueñan los androides con ovejas eléctricas?*, de Philip K. Dick.

Fue el propio Hauer quien, la noche antes del rodaje, reescribió ese monólogo en el guion para tener una despedida del personaje como a él le parecía que merecía, antes de morir.

Te aconsejo que revises esta película. Es una de las secuencias más bellas de la historia del cine, sumada a la música del gran Vangelis. Los efectos de luz y la lluvia hacen el resto.

Al igual que eliges cómo quieres vivir, me gusta pensar que podemos elegir cómo despedirnos de este mundo, como el personaje de *Blade Runner*.

LA DESPEDIDA DE ROY BATTY

Antes de su final, mientras cae sobre él una lluvia torrencial, el replicante le dice lo que sigue al protagonista:

Yo he visto cosas que vosotros no creeríais. Atacar naves en llamas más allá de Orión. He visto rayos-C brillar en la oscuridad cerca de la Puerta de Tannhäuser. Todos esos momentos se perderán en el tiempo, como lágrimas en la lluvia. Es hora de morir.

332
HO'OPONOPONO

Cuando tengas la impresión de que no has obrado del todo bien, que quizá has hecho daño a alguien sin darte cuenta o que has estropeado algo, tienes a tu alcance una forma de remediarlo.

Es importante hacerlo, porque cuando no hacemos bien las cosas, nosotros también nos sentimos mal.

Hay una técnica sanadora preciosa de origen hawaiano que se denomina Ho'oponopono. Esta palabra tan larga y compleja se traduce en el idioma local como *higiene mental* y tiene como base un mantra u oración que se ha popularizado en los últimos tiempos:

Gracias, perdón, lo siento, te amo.

Aunque no seamos del todo conscientes de cuál es el conflicto, al repetir estas palabras cada vez que sintamos que hay un desequilibrio en nuestra vida, según la sabiduría del Ho'oponopono, devolvemos la armonía a nuestro ser.

Te invito a que indagues en torno a este ritual sanador que acerca corazones y alivia el alma cuando nos sentimos tristes por nuestra actitud.

LA CULPA PARALIZA

Decía el filósofo y orientalista Alan Watts que «Una manera de no hacer nada acerca de una situación es sentirse culpable», ya que la mayoría de las personas no toman medidas prácticas para devolver el equilibrio a su alma.

La sabiduría ancestral hawaiana nos propone este punto de partida para sanar: *Gracias, perdón, lo siento, te amo.*

Este mantra, junto a la decisión de no repetir viejos errores, ayuda a disolver la culpa.

333
VIAJAR DESDE EL SILLÓN

C orren tantas imágenes de lugares exóticos y paraísos vacacionales por las redes, que las personas que se quedan en casa pueden sentir que se están perdiendo algo.

Contra esta idea, George Sand, que además de pareja de Chopin, era una extraordinaria escritora y viajera, confesaba al respecto:

> *Mis viajes más bellos, los más dulces, los he hecho al calor del hogar, con los codos reposando en los brazos desgastados del sillón de mi abuela. ¿Por qué viajar si no se está obligado a ello? (...) No se trata tanto de viajar como de partir; ¿quién de nosotros no tiene algún dolor que distraer o algún yugo que sacudir?*

Partir es aquí una palabra interesante, porque implica abandonar un lugar –físico o mental– para dirigirnos a otro.

¿Adónde necesita viajar tu alma en este momento?

VIAJAR CON LA IMAGINACIÓN

Cuenta la leyenda que Jules Verne, siendo un niño, se fugó de su casa e intentó enrolarse como grumete en un barco que zarparía hacia la India. Sin embargo, su padre lo encontró a tiempo, frustrando el viaje. A partir de entonces, Jules decidió que viajaría con la imaginación.

Quizá nació aquí el maestro de las novelas de aventuras.

Mientras llega tu próximo viaje, te aconsejo que ejercites tu imaginación para trasladarte a lugares y momentos que enriquezcan tu rutina.

334

MALABARISTA DE LA VIDA

Has intentado alguna vez hacer malabarismos con bolas en el aire? Si tu respuesta es negativa, te diré que seguramente lo has hecho muchas veces en tu vida, aunque sea de otra forma.

¿No te has sentido a veces un verdadero equilibrista, tratando de conciliar tantas cosas en tu jornada?

Somos malabaristas de la vida, manteniendo viva la llama de muchos aspectos de nuestro día a día. Me encanta mirarlo así, aunque a veces necesitamos rebajar la carga que asumimos.

¿Cuántas bolas puedes manejar al mismo tiempo? ¿Te gustaría quitar alguna y observar mejor lo que baila en el aire?

Más allá de tu capacidad para gestionar tantas cosas, busca un equilibrio que te aporte la serenidad que necesitas.

NO EXISTE EL *MULTITASKING*

Observaciones llevadas a cabo en laboratorio han demostrado que los seres humanos, por lo general, no simultanean tareas, sino que cambian de una a otra con tanta velocidad que pueden pensar que las hacen al mismo tiempo.

Ya que salir y entrar constantemente de una actividad supone un desgaste energético, es esencial concentrar nuestra atención en labores importantes y, aunque queramos hacer muchas cosas, proceder por orden: una después de otra.

335
EL VALOR DE LA INTEGRIDAD

La integridad es uno de los aspectos que más me resuenan cuando pienso en la selección de valores que son fundamentales para mí.

Es curioso todo lo que engloba el concepto de integridad. Muchas personas definen la integridad como la capacidad de proceder *correctamente* respecto a lo que nos rodea, a nuestro entorno personal, siempre en coherencia con lo que somos. Pero ¿qué es *correctamente*?

Para responder, yo diría que es actuar con lealtad hacia nosotros mismos y nuestros principios. Solo así podemos ser íntegros en nuestra totalidad. Me parece un valor esencial a trabajar, porque engloba la posibilidad de ahondar en ideas como la coherencia y el respeto hacia nuestras prioridades y las ajenas.

EL GRADO MÁS ALTO DE INTEGRIDAD

Según Stephen Covey, autor que hemos mencionado anteriormente, «uno de los modos más importantes de poner de manifiesto la integridad consiste en ser leales con quienes no están presentes».

Si no practicas aún este grado de integridad, prueba a incorporarlo a tu día a día. Te sentirás mucho mejor, en coherencia contigo mismo y los demás.

336
AIREAR LAS IDEAS

Se atribuye a Leonardo da Vinci la siguiente reflexión, que de hecho es un consejo práctico:

De vez en cuando sal a dar un paseo y relajarte un poco.
Seguro que cuando vuelvas a tu trabajo, tu juicio será más preciso, pues cuando permanecemos constantemente en la tarea perdemos perspectiva. Cuando tomas un poco de distancia, el trabajo parece menor y podemos ver más fácilmente si hay una falta de armonía o proporción.

Ciertamente, cuando nos sentimos bloqueados ante cualquier cuestión o problema, muchas veces lo que necesitamos es perspectiva. Alejarnos del asunto por unas horas, incluso por un día entero, puede ser mano de santo.

——— CONVIÉRTETE EN UN FILÓSOFO ANDANTE ———

Aristóteles fue el fundador de la escuela de los peripatéticos, que acostumbraban a filosofar en el curso de largos paseos. Además de ayudarte a airear las ideas, caminar tiene otros beneficios:

1. Para el cuerpo es uno de los deportes más saludables que existen.
2. Ayuda a conciliar el sueño.
3. Mejora la circulación sanguínea (también la de la cabeza, quizá por eso acuden mejores ideas).
4. Reduce el estrés y la ansiedad.
5. Eleva nuestro humor y nos da nuevas perspectivas.

337
CUERPO Y EMOCIONES

La ciencia ha demostrado ampliamente cómo nuestras emociones repercuten en nuestro cuerpo, y a la inversa. Por este motivo, cuanto más nos conocemos y aprendemos a gestionarlas mejor será nuestra salud y calidad de vida, así como la de las personas que nos rodean.

Sin embargo, no todo el mundo tiene facilidad para leer sus emociones. El doctor Bessel van der Kork explica en su clásico *El cuerpo lleva la cuenta* que muchas personas padecen alexitimia, que es la incapacidad de poner palabras a sus sentimientos. Pero, nuevamente, conectar con el cuerpo es la solución. En palabras de este autor: «las personas con alexitimia pueden mejorar si aprenden a reconocer la relación entre sus sensaciones físicas y sus emociones (...) Cuando tenemos una conexión cómoda con nuestras sensaciones interiores (...) sentimos que tenemos el control de nuestro cuerpo, de nuestros sentimientos y de nuestro yo».

Ojalá esto sea la base de la sociedad para conocernos y relacionarnos mejor. Sueño con ello.

TOMA CONTACTO CON TU CUERPO

Para hacerte amigo de tu vehículo para la vida, este ejercicio que propone Anna Sólyom en *Reconecta con tu cuerpo* te servirá para tener más conciencia de cómo te sientes:

1. Frótate las manos y, cuando las notes calientes, toca suavemente con ellas tu cara, tu cabeza, tu cuello, tus hombros, tus codos, tus antebrazos y tus manos entre sí.
2. Luego recorre con ellas tu tronco, tu espalda, tus caderas, tus glúteos, la parte de arriba de tus muslos.
3. Baja a continuación por ambas piernas, primero una luego la otra, contactando con tus muslos, rodillas, gemelos y pantorrilla, con los tobillos, con el pie, la planta del pie y sus dedos...
4. Durante esta toma de contacto con tu cuerpo, con una respiración lenta y serena, deja que el cuerpo te hable. ¿Qué te está diciendo?

338

UN JEFE IGUALITARIO

Denis Waitely, un orador motivacional de Estados Unidos, reflexiona así sobre el uso que hacemos de nuestro recurso más valioso:

El tiempo es un jefe que ofrece igualdad. Cada ser humano tiene exactamente el mismo número de horas y minutos cada día. Las personas ricas no pueden comprar más horas. Los científicos no pueden inventar nuevos minutos. Y no puedes guardar tiempo para gastarlo otro día. Aun así, el tiempo es increíblemente justo y misericordioso. No importa cuánto tiempo has perdido en el pasado, todavía tienes un mañana completo.

¿Cómo calificarías el uso que haces de tu tiempo? ¿Das valor a cada hora, minuto y segundo?

ALGO DE LO QUE SENTIRTE ORGULLOSO

En la gestión del tiempo libre tienes dos opciones: matar las horas con cualquier cosa o hacer algo de lo que luego puedas sentirte orgulloso. Cuando uno tiene una conversación nutritiva o lee sesenta páginas de un buen libro, por ejemplo, le queda la impresión de haber aprendido, de haber aprovechado el tiempo, todo lo contrario que cuando nos entregamos a actividades sin sustancia.

¿Con cuál de estas dos opciones decides llenar tu tiempo libre?

339
VIVIR CON LA AUSENCIA

Hay ausencias con las que convivimos hasta que nos acostumbramos a ellas. En el caso de nuestras madres, el dolor de su marcha es tan grande que, al menos en mi caso, lo encubrí durante demasiado tiempo.

Creo que no sané hasta el día que empecé a honrar su figura, su amor, su increíble capacidad de hacer cosas y su alegría incombustible.

Fue a partir de ese día cuando pude convivir con ella en su ausencia. El dolor se fue y la abundancia se multiplicó en todos los sentidos, porque al integrar al ser amado, aunque ya no esté, vuelven a nosotros los momentos vividos, las palabras compartidas, tantas emociones que nos han convertido en quienes somos.

De este modo, la ausencia se convierte en una presencia amorosa y constante.

UNA CAJA DE MEMORIA

Este es uno de los ejercicios que recomiendan los especialistas en duelo para integrar una ausencia y honrar al ser querido:
1. Elige una caja en la que guardar algunos objetos personales de la persona que ya no está.
2. Puedes incluir en ella fotografías y escritos de esta persona.
3. Si no estás preparado aún para sumergirte en estos recuerdos, mantenlos en la caja hasta que tu corazón te pida abrirla para revisar cada cosa con amor y una sana melancolía.

340

LAS MEJORES COSAS DE LA VIDA YA SON TUYAS

Dale Carnegie, a quien recurrimos al principio de este libro, insistía mucho en que el secreto de la riqueza está en apreciar lo que tienes. Lo explica así, de manera lúcida e inequívoca:

> *Si la gente que se preocupa por sus problemas pensara en las riquezas que poseen, dejarían de preocuparse.*
>
> *¿Venderías tus dos ojos por un millón de dólares... o tus dos piernas... o tus manos... o tus oídos?*
>
> *Aprecia lo que tienes, y te darás cuenta de que no lo venderías por todo el oro del mundo. Las mejores cosas de la vida ya son tuyas, si puedes apreciarte a ti mismo.*

Tal como reza el título de la novela de Raphaëlle Giordano, *Tu segunda vida empieza cuando descubres que solo tienes una.* ¿Y si empiezas a vivir esa nueva existencia desde la abundancia y la gratitud?

HAZ INVENTARIO

¿Qué tal si haces un inventario de todas las cosas que tienes y que no venderías por nada? Tendrás más de un motivo para sentirte rico y agradecido. Te propongo que hagas este ejercicio cada vez que te sientas desanimado.

341
AYUDARNOS NOS FORTALECE

Una de las fábulas más bellas y motivadoras que existen es la que sigue:

«Un país fue invadido por el ejército enemigo, que avanzaba causando gran mortandad. Cuando un cojo explicó a un ciego lo que estaba sucediendo, el ciego cargó al cojo en sus espaldas y pudieron huir juntos».

Aprovechando lo mejor que tenía cada uno lograron salvarse.

Todos somos como estos dos personajes, ya que tenemos la capacidad de darnos ayuda mutua. Ciertamente, a veces las prisas y la tensión diarias nos alejan de cooperar para crear el mundo que deseamos.

La clave para remediarlo es la serenidad. Cuanto más tranquilos estamos, mejor actuamos y más espacio damos a nuestra alma para expandirse y hacer el bien.

Somos seres amables por naturaleza. Solo se trata de priorizar lo verdaderamente importante para crear ese entorno de dicha que depende de nosotros.

DESCUBRE NUEVAS SINERGIAS

Como los protagonistas de la fábula, contempla a las personas más cercanas y plantéate en cada caso lo que sigue:

1. ¿De qué manera podríais colaborar para que salgáis los dos ganando?

2. ¿Qué puedes aportar a la otra persona?

3. ¿Qué te puede aportar ella o él a ti? ¿Qué fortaleza tiene que a ti te falta?

342
DEJA CAER LA CORAZA

Como en la novela de *El caballero de la armadura oxidada*, de Robert Fisher, la coraza que has creado durante años se desmorona cuando permites que la emoción te embargue. Lejos de avergonzarte de ello, te animo a que celebres cada pieza de hierro que cae y des paso a tu ligereza.

Quiero verte el alma, sentir el latir de tu corazón si pongo mi mano en tu pecho. Quiero mirarte a los ojos y notar que confías en mí, saber que a veces tienes miedo y escuchar tu carcajada abierta cuando te diviertes.

Para caminar a mi lado, te necesito ligero para ayudarme a que también yo me despoje de mi propia coraza para saltar hasta las estrellas por la noche.

DEL MIEDO AL AMOR

Dice Robert Fisher en su novela, «Cuando hemos elegido vivir en el miedo en lugar de en el amor, reforzamos constantemente la armadura con angustias, aburrimiento y sospecha».

¿Percibes tu realidad desde el miedo o desde el amor?

A medida que viajes del primero al segundo, te irás desprendiendo de partes de tu coraza.

343
RECARGA TU MOTIVACIÓN

No debería haber nada capaz de amargarte la existencia, nada que pueda apagar tu luz ni tu entusiasmo.

A veces hay apagones, cierto, pero tienes en tu corazón una poderosa linterna para seguir iluminando tu camino. Si se cierra una puerta y hay que renunciar al plan A, ten el plan B bien armado.

En mi caso, mi secreto para recargar las pilas de la motivación es respirar hondo, buscar la calma, ordenar las ideas, ponerme unas zapatillas de deporte y salir a correr con una *playlist* de canciones estimulantes de los ochenta. Y, por supuesto, buenos amigos a mano y una lista de nuevos logros y retos por cumplir.

Tú puedes elegir tu propia fórmula, quizá un lugar en el mapa al que escapar. O cualquier otro recurso que te suba la energía para afrontar el chaparrón.

DOS INSPIRACIONES DE MURAKAMI

En su libro *De qué hablo cuando hablo de correr*, el más famoso escritor japonés de la actualidad y gran aficionado al *running* nos hace dos reflexiones muy útiles:

1. «En la autopista de la vida no es posible circular siempre por el carril de adelantamiento». Hay momentos en los que basta con seguir en marcha y está contraindicado correr o arriesgar.

2. «Tengo la impresión de que, caminando de manzana en manzana, podría llegar hasta el infinito». Un pensamiento muy *kaizen* sobre el poder que tiene cada paso que damos en la misma dirección.

344
ELEVA EL NIVEL

Muchas personas ya conoceréis a Tony Robbins por sus libros o por sus cursos, otras quizá lo hayáis descubierto en el documental de Netflix *No soy tu gurú*, donde asistimos a un encuentro con este gigante del *coaching*.

Una de sus consignas es: «Si haces lo que siempre has hecho, obtendrás lo que siempre has obtenido».

Para salir de esa trampa, su consejo es elevar el nivel:

> *Cuando desees sinceramente hacer un cambio, lo primero que tienes que hacer es elevar tu nivel de exigencia. Cuando la gente me pregunta qué cambió mi vida hace ocho años, les digo que lo más importante fue cambiar lo que exigía de mí mismo. Escribí todas las cosas que no aceptaría más en mi vida, todas las cosas que ya no toleraría, y todas las cosas a las que yo aspiraba.*

--- **PERMITIDO MIRAR ATRÁS** ---

Tony Robbins cuenta que, al desplazarse en su helicóptero de una ciudad a otra, pasó casualmente por un edificio en el que había trabajado de conserje una década atrás. Recordó entonces que en aquella época vivía atenazado por el miedo y la mentalidad de carencia. Me parece un ejercicio interesante que puedes aplicar tú también:

¿Cómo te ves cuando miras atrás?

¿Qué carencias y limitaciones tenías que ahora has superado?

Y, más importante todavía, ¿cómo te ves cuando miras hacia adelante?

345

LO QUE NO QUIERES SER

Cuando oigo decir que *todo es para bien*, pienso que en algunas ocasiones lo bueno es haber pasado por la experiencia de lo que no quieres ser.

Fuiste eso, pero ahora ya no.

En ocasiones, haber sido lo que no deseamos nos hace ser conscientes de ello para no serlo nunca más. Este es un ejercicio que hay que repetir tantas veces como haga falta en la vida.

Bienvenido al mundo de los pequeños sabios que sonríen cuando despiertan al mundo sencillo de la aceptación y la consciencia.

Quizá en el pasado fuiste algo de lo que no te sientes orgulloso, pero ahora que ya sabes lo que no quieres ser, el camino que no quieres tomar nunca más, ahí empieza la autopista hacia lo que sí quieres ser.

TUS MEJORES INVERSIONES

1. ¿Qué es lo que más detestas de tu yo del pasado? Pues no lo olvides y haz justamente lo contrario.

2. ¿Qué papel no te gusta haber adoptado? Elige un papel totalmente distinto.

3. ¿Qué es lo que lamentas haber hecho? No lo hagas nunca más, has pasado ya al otro lado.

346
CUESTIÓN DE ACTITUD

Mi querido Victor Küppers siempre nos recuerda la importancia de la actitud que ponemos en todo lo que hacemos en la vida.

De hecho, este conferenciante y escritor tiene una fórmula para medir el valor de una persona:

$$V = (C + H) \times A$$

La fórmula puede explicarse así: el valor es igual a la suma del conocimiento y las habilidades, multiplicada por la actitud.

Como él dice, una buena actitud es lo que multiplica nuestro valor.

¿Cuál es tu actitud ante la vida?

Tu forma de ser es lo que te abre posibilidades y hace de ti una persona sin límites. Más allá de tus conocimientos y habilidades, la actitud te ayudará a ser una persona querida y apreciada.

EL EFECTO BOMBILLA

Küppers afirma que «las personas somos como bombillas, porque todos transmitimos sensaciones y captamos las sensaciones que transmiten los demás. Sin embargo, aunque todos transmitimos, no todos transmitimos lo mismo».

Mientras que hay personas que emiten un poderoso resplandor, otras parecen ir fundidas por la vida. ¿Qué es lo que diferencia unas de otras?

La actitud.

¿Tu actitud es brillar o aceptas ser una bombilla fundida?

347
UN MISTERIOSO MONTAÑERO

Nadie sabe quién es Harold V. Melchert, pero una reflexión que se le atribuye es inmensamente popular en el mundo del montañismo, especialmente en los países anglosajones. Dice así:

Vive cada día tu vida como si fueras a escalar una montaña. Una mirada ocasional hacia la cumbre mantiene la mente objetiva, pero muchas escenas hermosas son para verlas desde cada nuevo punto de vista. Sube lentamente, de manera constante, disfrutando de cada momento a cada paso; y la vista de la cumbre servirá como el mejor clímax para el viaje.

Me parece una buena alegoría sobre el camino de la vida. Mirar la cumbre que te has propuesto te dará ánimo para seguir en el camino y que no decaigan las fuerzas.

Este mismo autor misterioso afirma: «Lo único que no puedes reciclar es el tiempo perdido».

SUBIR Y BAJAR LA MONTAÑA

El psicólogo Joan Garriga, autor de libros como *Bailando juntos* o *Decir sí a la vida*, compara la existencia con una expedición a la montaña:

1. En la primera parte de nuestra vida subimos hacia la cima. Es el momento de ganar cosas: logros, experiencia, amigos, amores, posesiones, dinero, méritos...
2. Una vez en la cima, en el ecuador de la existencia, vemos el mundo y decimos: *aquí estoy y esto es lo que he logrado.*
3. A partir de aquí hay que bajar la montaña. En esta fase no se trata ya de adquirir, de cargar con más cosas, sino de saber liberarse de ellas para caminar más ligero. Vamos soltando todo lo que no necesitamos hasta que, al final de la bajada, nos desprendemos de la propia vida.

348
NEGOCIA CON TU MENTE

No pretendas entenderlo todo. No permitas que lo racional acapare todo tu espacio existencial. Negocia con tu mente. Está bien que seas amigo de tu proceder más mental y lógico, pero a veces conviene dejarlo ir para aprender otras formas de moverte por la vida.

Para escapar del pensamiento vertical —en oposición al lateral de los creativos—, deberás observarte y ser consciente del papel que está desempeñando este pensamiento en tu toma de decisiones, observar tu mente. ¿Eres consciente de ello?

Como dice Jay Shetty en su libro *Piensa como un monje*:

> *Visualizar la mente como un ente separado nos ayuda a trabajar en nuestra relación con ella. Podemos pensar en nuestra interacción con la mente cómo hacer un amigo o negociar la paz con un enemigo.*

PON TUS RELACIONES EN TU SITIO

Al separarnos de la mente, observamos procesos que de hecho no tienen nada de racional ni de conveniente, sobre todo en lo que respecta a las relaciones que establecemos. En uno de los pasajes más brillantes de su libro, Jay Shetty afirma:

Lo que sucede muchas veces es que ignoramos a los que nos apoyan, apoyamos a los que nos ignoran. Amamos a los que nos lastiman y lastimamos a los que nos aman.

Te sugiero que medites sobre esta reflexión para asegurarte de que no incurres en uno de estos cuatro errores.

349
A TU MANERA

Llegados a este punto, ya sabes que eres único e irrepetible. Cuando te hicieron, se rompió el molde. Solo tú puedes hacer las cosas *a tu manera*. Nadie más las podría hacer igual.

Recordemos el tema icónico de Frank Sinatra, fruto de una adaptación de Paul Anka de una canción francesa anterior. Traducido, viene a decir:

> *¿Qué es un hombre, aquello que tiene?*
> *Si no es él mismo, entonces no tiene nada.*
> *Debe decir las cosas que realmente siente*
> *y no las palabras de alguien que se arrodilla.*
> *Mi historia muestra que encajé los golpes,*
> *y lo hice a mi manera.*

También tú haces y dices las cosas a tu manera, tienes tu propio camino, tu propia visión del mundo. Tienes una autenticidad que no se puede adquirir en ningún sitio. Viene de fábrica.

PEQUEÑO TEST DEL CAMINO

1. Si volvieras a nacer, ¿qué cosas volverías a hacer exactamente igual?
2. ¿Qué errores no volverías a cometer?
3. ¿Qué te atreverías a hacer que no hiciste en su momento?
4. ¿Cómo definirías, en pocas palabras, tu manera de vivir?

350
RECUPERAR LA ESPERANZA

Jordan Peterson, autor de *12 reglas para vivir*, habla, entre otras muchas cosas, de la importancia de mantener la mirada en ese anhelo que va más allá de un primitivo instinto de supervivencia. En sus palabras:

> *Una gran parte de la felicidad está compuesta de esperanza, por muy profundo que fuera el submundo en el que dicha esperanza se fraguó.*

Sin embargo, si queremos materializarla, la esperanza no debe ser un mero deseo de que cambien las tornas. Hay que acompañarla de acción comprometida y de verdad, como precisa el mismo Peterson:

> *El enfoque más audaz posible de la vida y diría que el enfoque más significativo es decir la verdad y dejar que pase lo que pase. Es una aventura.*

ESPERANZA Y AUTOCUIDADO

Cuando las cosas se ponen difíciles, es el momento en el que hay que cultivar más la esperanza, lo cual pasa por no abandonar el autocuidado, que es lo primero que pierden quienes tiran la toalla. Eso implica...

1. No relajar el aseo y tu aspecto físico.
2. Hacer ejercicio para tonificar el cuerpo y la mente.
3. Alimentarte de forma saludable, sin tirar de comida rápida.
4. Seguir frecuentando las buenas relaciones, aunque te sientas tentado a aislarte.
5. Emprender nuevos proyectos, por muy negro que lo veas ahora.

351

MIRAR HACIA DENTRO

Siempre que te sientas perdido, mira hacia dentro para aprender, para entender qué te está sucediendo y despertar la consciencia. Recuerda que lo de fuera es solo un reflejo de ti. Así de increíble es tu grandeza.

Para recobrar la paz y encontrar las respuestas que necesitas, el viaje es desde dentro hacia fuera. Descubrirás que todo lo que miras tiene tu esencia. Por lo tanto, cualquier cambio que quieras encontrar en el mundo tendrás que aplicarlo primero dentro de ti mismo.

Darte cuenta de esto marcará un antes y un después en tu vida.

Ya lo decía Carl Jung: «Aquel que mira fuera, sueña. Quien mira en el interior, despierta».

UN POCO DE INTROSPECCIÓN

El médico y psicólogo Wilhelm Wundt recomendaba a sus pacientes, ya a finales del siglo XIX, que analizaran sus pensamientos a través de la introspección. La técnica es sencilla:

1. Date una pausa de al menos diez minutos para parar y examinar qué te pasa por dentro.
2. Analiza qué suceso o idea está en el origen de lo que estás sintiendo.
3. Ser consciente de ello te ayudará a detener la mayoría de tus pensamientos mecánicos, con lo que aclararás tu mente.

352
UN CURSO DE MILAGROS

Gozo y me pierdo en los párrafos de *Un curso de milagros*, una experiencia a la que muchas personas dedican un año de forma disciplinada, ya que es un libro extenso y complejo, a la vez que transformador.

Yo disfruto interpretando de manera distinta alguno de sus pasajes cada vez que los releo. Me gustaría compartir contigo este pequeño fragmento:

> *Has concebido una diminuta brecha entre las ilusiones y la verdad para que sea un lugar donde reside tu seguridad y donde lo que has hecho mantiene celosamente oculto a tu ser.*

¿No es apasionante cuando un texto te da una bofetada de amor y te ayuda a ver la realidad de otro modo?

——— UNA ALTERNATIVA PARA PRINCIPIANTES ———

Si has intentado alguna vez empezar a leer *Un curso de milagros* y te resulta demasiado difícil, tienes una alternativa que muchos entendidos consideran una lectura preliminar mucho más sencilla. Se trata de *La desaparición del universo*, de Gary R. Renard, donde se resumen de manera amena muchos puntos del mencionado libro.

353
SOBRIEDAD

Una de las virtudes que más persigo es la sobriedad, ya que, como decía José Alberto Mujica, denominado «el presidente más pobre del mundo» y a quien me encanta escuchar...

Inventamos una montaña de consumo superfluo, y hay que tirar y vivir comprando y tirando. Y lo que estamos gastando es tiempo de vida, porque cuando yo compro algo, o tú, no lo compras con plata, lo compras con el tiempo de vida que tuviste que gastar para tener esa plata. Pero con esta diferencia: la única cosa que no se puede comprar es la vida. La vida se gasta. Y es miserable gastar la vida para perder libertad.

Yo añadiría también que no solo gastamos tiempo en lo material, sino también en experiencias y relaciones.

Así que vuelvo al concepto elemental para mí en todo esto: la sobriedad que lleva a la sencillez y a la vida en libertad.

MINIMALISMO RADICAL

Si alguna vez vas a Creta, en una colina cerca de la capital encontrarás la tumba de Nikos Kazantzakis, el autor de *Alexis Zorbas*. Sobre una humilde lápida se lee:

> *No espero nada,*
> *no temo nada,*
> *soy libre.*

La expectativa de que las cosas sean de determinado modo, y el temor a que sucedan cosas desagradables son otras fuentes de desgaste mental que nos hacen perder el tiempo.

¿Hasta qué punto estás libre de ambas?

354

KIKUBARI

Hay una frase que he ido diciendo a mis hijos a medida que crecen: *No estamos solos en el mundo.*

Poco a poco son conscientes de que forman parte de una gran familia con sus hermanos y sus distintas circunstancias.

Es hermoso ver cómo comienzan a conjugar su vida en plural y hacen sus aportaciones al núcleo familiar. En casa, siempre intentamos poner atención a lo que el otro necesita. Unas veces sale mejor que otras, pero siempre lo intentamos.

Creo que se parece a lo que en Japón denominan *kikubari*: la capacidad de tener en cuenta a las personas que te rodean, estando atentos a sus distintas sensibilidades.

SABER LEER EL AIRE

Un aspecto fascinante de las relaciones japonesas es lo que se conoce como *kuki yomenai*, que se traduce literalmente como *saber leer el aire*. Se refiere a comprender lo que quiere decir el otro, aunque no pronuncie una sola palabra. ¿Cómo se consigue esto?

- Prestando atención a la postura del cuerpo. El lenguaje no verbal también comunica el estado de ánimo. Unos hombros caídos, por ejemplo, indican desánimo.
- La expresión de la cara es, sin duda, una gran fuente de información que nos da pistas sobre lo que pasa por dentro.
- Observando otras señales, como un repentino silencio de alguien que normalmente es hablador. Todo eso te ayudará a *leer el aire*.

355
EMOCIONES QUE DESPIERTAN

A lo largo de la vida, el corazón se te quebrará más de una vez a causa de emociones que ni imaginabas. Experimentarás entonces también la grandeza de sentir, incluso por eventos poco agradables o afortunados.

Te sentirás abatido por desencuentros o malentendidos, o por tus propias dudas y miedos.

No eres de piedra. ¡Ni pretendas serlo!

Aprende de todo lo que estás sintiendo, cualquiera que sea tu dolor. ¡Bendita emoción, que te hace saber que estás vivo! Sobre esto, el gran Jim Morrison decía:

> *El dolor tiene el propósito de despertarnos (...) Nuestra fuerza se siente en la experiencia del dolor. Todo depende de cómo lo llevamos. Eso es lo que importa. El dolor es un sentimiento, y tus sentimientos son una parte de ti. Tu propia realidad. Si te avergüenzas de ellos y los escondes, estás dejando que la sociedad destruya tu realidad. Debes defender tu derecho a sentir dolor.*

DOLOR Y CREATIVIDAD

Dado que las emociones relacionadas con la tristeza y el dolor nos permiten profundizar en nuestro interior, te aconsejo que aproveches estos momentos para canalizar tu creatividad a través del medio que te sea más natural: escribir, dibujar, cantar...

Trata de plasmar lo que estás viviendo y conviértelo en tu obra de arte.

356
NEXO

Hay algo que me encanta hacer: juntar a personas que conozco y que creo que se van a llevar bien. Crear vínculos que lleven a proyectos conjuntos y que pueden derivar en una buena amistad o acompañamiento.

Con este fin reúno en casa a personas que creo que pueden aportarse mutuamente y si, además, tenemos algo que celebrar, todavía mejor.

Quizá no se vuelvan a ver, pero ese evento dejará huella al compartir otras percepciones, otras maneras de entender el mundo. Merece la pena poner todo el cariño y atención en esta clase de encuentros para que sean dignos de ser recordados.

NETWORKING

Los principales autores de libros sobre el éxito coinciden en que el *networking* es un ingrediente principal de cualquier logro. Para aplicarlo a tu vida cotidiana:

- Trata de *hacer red* con personas que comparten contenidos de valor.
- Abre la puerta a nuevas incorporaciones en tu círculo de amigos. Nunca se sabe quién puede aportarte aquello que necesitarás en tu próximo proyecto.
- Practica la generosidad con criterio. El flujo de dar y recibir forma parte de la rueda del éxito.

357
FLORECER

Siembro bien para que florezca en mí la mejor versión de lo que puedo dar. Cuido mi tierra y mi alimentación, el ambiente en el que crezco y las circunstancias que hacen que me convierta en una flor bella.

Cuido de mí para ser algo que merezca la pena, por mí y por los demás.

Recordemos el fragmento de *El principito* en el que charla con el zorro, que le dice:

> *Eres responsable de tu rosa (...) Eres responsable para siempre de lo que has domesticado.*

¿Cuál es la rosa que cuidas en tu vida y qué flores esperas que dé?

CUIDA DE TU JARDÍN INTERIOR

Si ves tu interior como un jardín en el que crece lo que has plantado —el zorro diría *domesticado*—, puedes embellecerlo al cultivar...

- Buenas lecturas, que nutran tu alma y enriquezcan tu conversación.
- Películas y documentales sobre temas que abran tu perspectiva sobre la vida.
- Conversaciones que vayan más allá de lo rutinario.
- Exposiciones o conferencias que aporten nuevas miradas sobre el mundo.
- Baños de naturaleza para recuperar tu conexión más íntima con lo que eres.

358
NUNCA EL TIEMPO ES PERDIDO

Empleamos buena parte del tiempo de nuestra vida en tratar de entender el mundo, lo que incluye tanto a los demás como a nosotros mismos.

Somos curiosos por naturaleza y, si se trata de emociones, aún más, porque al explorarlas el corazón late más rápido y nos sentimos más vivos.

Ya lo decía Manolo García: «Nunca el tiempo es perdido, es solo un recodo más en nuestra ilusión, ávida de cariño».

Cuando vivimos a flor de piel, el tiempo se mueve tan despacio que a veces sentimos que se detiene en un instante de eternidad.

Nunca el tiempo es perdido cuando nos dedicamos a conocer las profundidades del corazón.

CHRONOS Y KAIRÓS

Los antiguos griegos distinguían entre dos clases de tiempo:
- *Chronos.* Se refiere al tiempo lineal, el que podemos medir de forma precisa con un reloj.
- *Kairós.* Es el tiempo de calidad que no se puede medir. Dependiendo de la experiencia, se comprime o se estira, y un minuto puede contener una vida entera. En la teología cristiana a veces se le llama *el tiempo de Dios.*

¿Qué clase de momentos o actividades te permiten vivir ese tiempo divino?

359
EL AIRE QUE RESPIRAS

Cuando quieras volver a ti, quédate en el *aquí y ahora*, respira. Y no solo para anclarte en el presente o relajarte, sino también para llenarte de vida.

¿Sabías que, según estudios recientes, la esperanza de vida depende más de la capacidad pulmonar que de los genes, la alimentación o el ejercicio?

Una persona que respira bien, expandiendo sus pulmones, tiene muchas más posibilidades de tener una vida longeva y saludable.

Con todo, la mayoría de los seres humanos respiramos mal, de manera acelerada y sin consciencia de ello. Y esto el cerebro lo lee y lo interpreta como: *Me ahogo. No me llega el aire.*

La buena noticia es que a respirar se aprende.

Cuando nos acostumbramos a hacerlo de manera adecuada, poniendo la atención en ello, nuestro cuerpo se oxigena y podemos pensar, sentir y vivir mejor.

BOX BREATHING

Esta técnica de respiración, que se utiliza entre otras cosas para dominar la ansiedad, evita que hiperventiles, algo que a veces hacemos de forma inconsciente y que puede llevar a un ataque de pánico.

Llamada también 4-4-4, es una técnica muy sencilla:

1. Inspira, lenta y suavemente, durante 4 segundos.
2. Contén la respiración 4 segundos.
3. Suelta el aire, lenta y suavemente, durante 4 segundos.

Al repetir este proceso diez o doce veces sentirás cómo la tensión afloja y te sentirás mucho mejor.

360
CIELO E INFIERNO

Omar Khayyam, un matemático, astrónomo y poeta persa, tiene inspiraciones breves y reveladoras como esta:

Más allá de la Tierra, más allá del infinito,
intentaba ver el cielo y el infierno.
Y una voz solemne me dijo:
«El cielo y el infierno están en ti».

Esta visión de un autor que vivió hace un milenio coincide con la de muchos teólogos modernos, que consideran el cielo y el infierno de las sagradas escrituras no como lugares reales, sino como estados interiores.

Si, como dice Khayyam, el cielo y el infierno están dentro de cada uno, tenemos libre albedrío para elegir en cuál de ambos mundos mentales queremos habitar.

¿QUÉ TE LLEVA AL CIELO Y AL INFIERNO?

Examina cómo cambia tu panorama mental según diferentes acciones y actitudes. Por ejemplo, cuando te enzarzas en una discusión que no lleva a ningún sitio, porque ninguna de las partes se va a mover de su posición, ¿cómo te sientes *durante* y *después*?

Si te sientes irritado y luego exhausto, puedes evitar ese infierno no entrando en lo que lo provoca.

Pon atención, también, a lo que te hace sentir calma y placidez, de modo que puedas entrar a menudo en ese paraíso mental.

361
REALIDAD Y PROGRESO

En su biografía –fantástica, por cierto–, Michelle Obama se pregunta, haciendo balance al final de su carrera junto a su marido, en qué momento cambió su vida. Cuáles fueron los instantes clave en los que su vida dio un giro.

En *Mi historia* repasa mentalmente su juventud con Barack, el día de su primer beso, sus inicios en la política...

Al leer sus vivencias, te das cuenta de que el destino es fruto de muchas pequeñas decisiones que nos han llevado adonde estamos ahora, desde la imaginación a los hechos.

Michelle Obama lo explica así: «Sabía que era posible vivir en dos planos a la vez, tener los pies plantados en la realidad, pero con la mirada puesta en el progreso».

HAZLO REALIDAD

Decía Jules Verne que «todo lo que una persona puede imaginar, otros pueden hacerlo realidad».

Si asumimos que quien imagina y quien hace es una misma persona —tú—, pregúntate:

1. ¿Cuál es tu principal sueño ahora mismo? ¿Qué es lo que estimula más tu imaginación?
2. ¿Qué debes empezar a hacer para convertirlo en realidad?
   Ponte a ello cuanto antes y el progreso llegará.

362
COMO UN ESTANQUE EN CALMA

uando buscas respuestas, cuando aspiras a la verdad, debes esperar en calma para, desde ella, encontrar lo que anhelas. Una actitud inquieta, en cambio, te llevará a la precipitación, con lo que solo lograrás confundirte más.

Solo puedes ver el fondo del estanque si sus aguas están en calma. Cuando dejas de removerlas, se vuelven cristalinas y transparentes. Así funciona también la mente.

El pacifista indio Prem Rawat lo explica así en su libro *Escúchate*:

Acalla la mente, acalla los sentidos y acalla también el cuerpo. Luego, cuando todo esté en calma, no hagas nada. En ese estado la verdad se te revelará.

UNA BREVE MEDITACIÓN

Dice Prem Rawat:

Mira a tu alrededor, mira dentro de ti.
Deja que brote tu sonrisa, tu risa, tu agradecimiento.
La plenitud es una realidad, no un sueño.

Sentado en un lugar tranquilo puedes repetirte estas palabras cada vez que te sientas nervioso, triste o alterado, y llevarlo a la práctica:

1. Mira a tu alrededor, poniendo atención en la belleza que te rodea.
2. Mira a continuación dentro de ti. Date cuenta de todo lo bello que contienes.
3. Sonríe y siéntete agradecido por estar vivo.
4. Descubre que la plenitud es algo que ya tienes.

363
EL AUTOBÚS SALE CADA DÍA

Al ser preguntado sobre si uno puede siempre cambiar su vida, mi admirado Morgan Freeman dio una respuesta que me gusta por su sencillez y claridad: «El autobús sale cada día».

Es una bonita forma de decir que podemos tomar ese autobús y aprovechar la oportunidad que se presenta ante nosotros diariamente. Solo hay que prepararse y aguardar en la parada. Estar atento a cuando llega.

Esta es una imagen que, si has visto *Ghost World*, interpretada por Thora Birch y una jovencísima Scarlett Johansson, no habrás pasado por alto.

En la película hay un anciano que espera el autobús en una parada que ha sido anulada. Nadie sabe qué hace ahí y algunos se ríen de él, pero el autobús que espera acaba pasando.

¿PERDER EL TREN?

Del autobús pasamos al ferrocarril, ya que existe el *síndrome de perder el tren* cuando creemos que una situación es irreversible.

A quienes creen que es demasiado tarde para empezar de nuevo o encontrar nuevas soluciones, les recomiendo que piensen en los *late bloomers*. Son aquellas personas que *florecen tarde*, pero con gran belleza, como Kimani Maruge, el escolar más viejo del mundo. Con ochenta y cuatro años decidió que quería aprender a leer y escribir, con lo que cursó la primaria en una clase llena de niños.

Mientras sigamos vivos, siempre habrá un autobús o un tren que pueda llevarnos a otra parte. ¿Cuál estás esperando tú?

364
EL CAMINO MENOS TRANSITADO

Uno de los poemas más bellos e inspiradores del siglo XX fue escrito por Robert Frost y nos hace reflexionar sobre las elecciones que nos plantea la vida.

Te comparto el primer y último párrafo:

> *Dos caminos se abrían en un bosque amarillo,*
> *y triste por no poder caminar por los dos,*
> *y por ser un viajero tan solo, un largo rato*
> *me detuve, y puse la vista en uno de ellos*
> *hasta donde al torcer se perdía en la maleza.*
> *(...)*
> *Seguramente esto lo diré entre suspiros*
> *en algún momento dentro de años y años,*
> *dos caminos se abrían en un bosque, elegí...*
> *elegí el menos transitado de ambos,*
> *Y eso supuso toda la diferencia.*

EL VALOR DE SALIR DE LA BANDADA

En sintonía con el poema de Frost, en 1970 Richard Bach escribió *Juan Salvador Gaviota*, una fábula sobre la libertad personal que cosechó una inmensa popularidad. Para escapar de la vida rutinaria de sus compañeras, la gaviota protagonista decide abandonar la bandada para vivir a su aire. Eso le plantea no pocos peligros y desafíos, pero también le aporta grandes aprendizajes.

- ¿En qué momentos de tu vida decidiste tomar el camino menos transitado?
- ¿Qué miedos y dudas te asaltaron al principio?
- ¿Cuáles fueron tus aprendizajes?
- ¿En qué clase de camino te encuentras ahora?

365

TU *IKIGAI*

Dicen que la clave para alcanzar la plenitud es tener un propósito claro en la vida. A esto los japoneses lo llaman *ikigai*.

Mi querido Francesc Miralles lo explica así junto a Héctor García en su best seller *Ikigai: los secretos de Japón para una vida larga y feliz*:

> *Según los japoneses, todo el mundo tiene un* ikigai, *lo que un filósofo francés traduciría como* raison d'être. *Algunos lo han encontrado y son conscientes de su* ikigai, *otros lo llevan dentro pero todavía lo están buscando.*

El *ikigai* es la razón por la que te levantas cada mañana, el propósito en el que empleas horas y esfuerzo sin que te cueste, lo que hace que tu curiosidad y creatividad se multipliquen.

Tu propósito vital da un sentido a tu existencia y puede ser incluso un modo de vida.

Iki significa *vida* en japonés y, curiosamente, *gai* se traduce en euskera como *motivo* o *tema*.

¿Cuál es tu *gai* principal?

UNA PREGUNTA FUNDAMENTAL

Durante la pandemia, mucha gente se la planteó, siendo el origen de muchos cambios. De hecho, es una pregunta que vuelve de forma recurrente cada vez que sentimos que no estamos siendo fieles a nosotros mismos, y nos dirige de nuevo hacia nuestro *ikigai*:

¿Cómo quiero vivir el resto de mi vida?

366
EL FIN ES EL PRINCIPIO

Una de las frases más celebradas de Lao-Tsé reza: «Aquello que para la oruga es el fin del mundo, para nosotros es una mariposa».

Estás a punto de terminar este libro, en el que hemos compartido cientos de ideas, lecturas, historias, ejercicios e inspiraciones. Te doy las gracias por haber caminado conmigo hasta aquí.

Los africanos dicen que, si quieres ir rápido, vayas solo, pero que si quieres llegar lejos, vayas acompañado. Hemos andado mucho juntos y espero que haya sido, también para ti, un agradable viaje lleno de descubrimientos.

A lo largo de estas páginas la oruga ya se ha convertido en una mariposa a punto de levantar su vuelo. Y, al igual que le sucede a ella, esto no es el final, sino el principio.

Cuando cierres este libro, al que espero que vuelvas como se visita a un buen amigo, abrirás tu nueva vida.

¡Gracias por existir!

EL PRIMER CAPÍTULO DE TU NUEVA HISTORIA

Si tu vida fuera una historia por estrenar que, dejando atrás el pasado, empieza después de esta página, ¿cuál sería su inicio?

¿De qué manera va a comenzar el primer capítulo de tu nueva vida?

EPÍLOGO

de Francesc Miralles

Este libro se empezó a fraguar en un restaurante tailandés de Barcelona. Allí la autora nos confirmó su decisión de emprender este bello y ambicioso proyecto: escribir una inspiración para cada día del año.

He tenido el honor de hacer de *sherpa* literario de mi amiga Anne, que va a iluminar decenas de miles de vidas, como ya lo hace a través de las redes y de los medios de comunicación. La etiqueta de *sherpa* me la puso la doctora en física cuántica Sonia Fernández-Vidal, quien, tras acabar de escribir *La puerta de los tres cerrojos*, me dijo: «Al igual que el *sherpa* acompaña al alpinista a la cumbre, gracias a ti he coronado la cima de mi primer libro».

En el caso de *La vida empieza cada día*, ha sido una larga travesía llena de descubrimientos y compañeros de viaje inesperados. Una vez en marcha, Anne empezó a escribir sin cesar desde muchos puntos del planeta. Sus capítulos me llegaban a través del teléfono desde Madrid, Euskadi, Francia, Nueva York... A su vez, yo los recibía y ordenaba estando en el Pacífico, en el Amazonas o incluso en los glaciares de Islandia.

Poco a poco la criatura iba creciendo. Al revisar estas páginas llenas de perlas, yo le iba diciendo a Anne: *Está saliendo un librazo*. Podía sentir su sonrisa al otro lado mientras, página a página, seguía compartiendo experiencias, pasajes y visiones para este almanaque inspirador.

Además de su larga experiencia profesional y vital, de formarse ampliamente en temas de crecimiento personal, durante los últimos años Anne ha entrevistado a muchísimos autores. Ha conversado a fondo con toda clase de personalidades expertas en ciencia, espiritualidad, medicina, *coaching*, psicología..., y muchas de ellas han dejado su huella en estas inspiraciones.

Como primer lector de esta obra, tras veinticinco años dedicado a estos temas, la autora no dejaba de sorprenderme con nuevas referencias, teorías e incluso libros que yo no conocía. De hecho, estas páginas son un valioso ejercicio de generosidad por su parte, ya que pone en nuestras manos lo bueno y mejor que ella ha descubierto para cultivar el arte de vivir. Recuerdo que un amigo editor siempre me decía: «Cada vez que descubro un tesoro, corro a llamar a mis amigos». Y eso es lo que ha hecho Anne Igartiburu con cada página de este libro.

En 1996, dos autores norteamericanos escribieron *Sopa de pollo para el alma*, una nutritiva recopilación de relatos para calentar el corazón. Casi tres décadas más tarde, la autora de esta obra ha ido incluso un poco más allá, ya que junto a sus reflexiones y aprendizajes ha compartido ejercicios personales, recetas para la vida, preguntas para hacernos despertar.

No me cabe duda de que este libro es y será una poderosa fuente de inspiración para muchísima gente, comenzando por mí mismo.

Si algunos de los tesoros que contiene te han tocado el corazón, querida lectora, querido lector, no te los guardes solo para ti. Llama a tus amigos. Comparte este libro con otras personas a las que pueda hacer más sabias y felices en esta aventura compartida que llamamos Vida.

Te deseo un muy feliz viaje.

FRANCESC MIRALLES

Anne Igartiburu, comunicadora desde hace más de 25 años, es una de las presentadoras de televisión más queridas y reconocidas de nuestro país, con más de 7.000 directos a sus espaldas. Durante los últimos años ha desempeñado una bonita labor de divulgación en el ámbito del bienestar emocional, una de sus grandes pasiones y en la que se ha formado con algunos de los mejores profesionales en este campo. Sus encuentros en directo a través de diferentes canales de difusión, como son Instagram, YouTube y su pódcast *Mi Latido de Más*, le han otorgado el reconocimiento de su comunidad de seguidores y de los profesionales con los que comparte charlas sobre psicología, psiquiatría, neurociencia o filosofía, con el objetivo claro de hacer llegar las diferentes maneras de autoconocimiento y la coherencia vital. Eterna aprendiz, Anne busca, indaga y comparte los aprendizajes desde la curiosidad y el agradecimiento, aplicando sus dotes de cercanía y escucha presente.

Este libro
se terminó de imprimir
en el mes de febrero de 2023